The Geomorphology of the Great Barrier Reef:

Quaternary Development of Coral Reefs

The Geomorphology of the Great Barrier Reef:
Quaternary Development of Coral Reefs

DAVID HOPLEY

Associate Professor,
Department of Geography,
James Cook University of North Queensland
Townsville,
Australia

1807 1982
175 YEARS OF PUBLISHING

A WILEY-INTERSCIENCE PUBLICATION

JOHN WILEY & SONS

New York • Chichester • Brisbane • Toronto • Singapore

Library of Congress Cataloging in Publication Data:

Hopley, David.
  The geomorphology of the Great Barrier Reef.

  "A Wiley-Interscience publication."
  Bibliography: p.
  Includes index.
  1. Geomorphology—Queensland—Great Barrier
Reef. 2. Coral reefs and islands. 3. Geology,
Stratigraphic—Quaternary. I. Title.

GB441.H66   551.4′ 24′ 09943   81-16336
ISBN 0-471-04562-4   AACR2

Printed in the United States of America

10 9 8 7 6 5 4 3 2 1

To Lilla and Susan

Preface

It is twelve years since the publication of W. G. H. Maxwell's *Atlas of the Great Barrier Reef* and in this intervening period the amount of field research on coral reefs, as opposed to armchair hypothesizing, has increased enormously. The great expansion of radiometric dating has given us the framework of a real time scale for the evolution of coral reefs while the introduction of new technology has allowed estimates of the rates of past and current processes to be made. Any comprehensive statements on coral reefs made more than ten years ago are inevitably outmoded but although this volume is critical of some of these older statements and puts forward contrary views, it acknowledges the inspirational value and foundations laid by works such as those of Steers, Fairbridge, and Maxwell. Attempts have been made within this work to include literature published up to the end of 1980, but with the rapid increase in knowledge, particularly with the current expansion of research on the Great Barrier Reef, it is not possible to make this a final statement on the way modern coral reefs have evolved. Rather, it is intended as an account of current geomorphological views. As a university teacher and supervisor of postgraduate students, I have found it increasingly difficult to guide students through the mass of literature that has been appearing on reef evolution and processes. The major aim of this book is to summarize current ideas and data and to indicate where contrary views exist so that this book may act as a convenient point of embarkation for those engaging in reef research in the field of geoscience.

The scope of coral reef research is such that even partial understanding of the system requires a multidisciplinary approach. This is clearly seen from an examination of the proceedings of the four International Coral Reef Symposia held over the last twelve years. Such an approach has been attempted here from the viewpoint of a geographically trained geomorphologist. This provides a unity of approach that should compensate for some inevitable decrease in breadth. The book is the result of fifteen years of research on the coastline, islands, and reefs of north Queensland. My initial interest in coastal geomorphology and sea-level change was stimulated by the variety of features and the contradictory nature of evidence particularly on near-shore islands and fringing reefs. Thus, my ideas were first developed based on evidence from the mainland to the Great Barrier Reef areas, which highlighted the contrasts between the two environments. At a later stage a geographical approach to the Great Barrier Reef highlighted the spatial variations that exist, and an examination of their distribution patterns provided insight into the factors that have influenced the evolution of the Reef.

The book has a fivefold division. The first chapters examine the philosophical and physical environments in which current research workers on the Great Barrier Reef are working, indicating the way ideas have evolved and summarizing current knowledge on the environmental parameters that currently determine reef development. Chapters 3, 4, and 5 examine the major processes that operate on all reefs and, although differentiating between biological, physical, and chemical action, stress the strong interrelationships that exist between these sets of processes. Longer term geomorphological evolution is examined in the next three chapters, where Quaternary environmental fluctuations and their effects on coral reef development are assessed. The resulting morphology of modern reefs and the spatial variations within and between reefs are the subject of the following four chapters. The final chapter briefly examines the variation on a world scale of the most important influences on coral reef development and compares the morphology of the Great Barrier Reef with that of other reef systems.

Although the views expressed in the following pages are my own, I must acknowledge with sincere thanks the very many people and organizations that have helped at various stages of the research, writing, and compilation. Funds for original research have come mainly from the Australian Research Grants Committee, from James Cook University of North Queensland, and more recently from the Australian Marine Sciences and Technologies Advisory Committee—Funding Advisory Panel. Fieldwork, however, has involved many helpers and in particular I would like to thank my postgraduate students, especially Nick Harvey, Peter Isdale, Debbie Kuchler, and Ann Smith, whose work is incorporated in this volume. In addition the field and technical assistance given by Clive Grant, Trevor Shearn, Frazer Muir, and Doug Backshall, and the help of the master and crew of the research vessel *James Kirby* including David Duncan, John Barnett, and Bob Moss is gratefully acknowledged. Work carried out in Barbados on the exposed Pleistocene reefs was greatly facilitated by Dr. Finn Sander of the Bellairs Research Institute of McGill University. Discussion of various aspects of reef research with colleagues from other institutions has greatly widened my own experience. Particular thanks go to fellow participators on the 1973 Royal Society–Universities of Queensland expedition to the northern Great Barrier Reef led by Dr. David Stoddart, and to Dr. Peter Davies of the Bureau of Mineral Resources, Canberra.

Maps and diagrams have been drawn in the Cartographic Center, Department of Geography, James Cook University of North Queensland, where the help of Trevor Shearn, Bill Spiers, and Johnny Ngai is gratefully acknowledged. Where diagrams from published sources or photographs other than those of the author have been used, this is acknowledged in the caption. Manuscript typing was greatly aided by Mrs. Pat Goodall and Miss Pam Pemble. The photography in the book is by the author, except where otherwise specified, with the help of the Photographic Department at James Cook University and in particular its former head, Mr. H. L. J. Lamont.

Many others, too numerous to name, have helped, particularly in providing copies of publications and in general encouragement. However, especial thanks go to my wife Lilla, not only for patiently enduring the long periods during which I have been engaged in research or writing, but also for materially assisting in the field and in typing the draft and final copy of the manuscript. Without her help and encouragement the lengthy preparation of this book would have been even longer.

DAVID HOPLEY

Townsville, Australia
January 1982

Contents

Variations in Pleistocene Cooling, 386
Variations in the Holocene Transgression, 387
Variations in the Present Environment, 391
Discussion and Conclusions, 395

The Geomorphology of
the Great Barrier Reef:
Quaternary Development
of Coral Reefs

1

Development of Coral Reef Theory and the Great Barrier Reef

The first contact of science with the Great Barrier Reef of Australia was far from auspicious. H.M.S. *Endeavour*, under the command of Capt. James Cook and carrying a party of scientists led by Joseph Banks, sailed 1400 km inside the Great Barrier Reef northward up the Queensland coast. Having spotted reefal shoals only on the previous day, at about 11 PM on 11 June 1770, they struck hard upon what is now known as Endeavour Reef. Joseph Banks' own comments on the event are typical of the attitude of scientists of the day towards coral reefs:

> We were little less than certain that we were upon sunken coral rocks, the most dreadful of all others on account of their sharp points and grinding quality which cut through a ships bottom almost immediately.

Later, having beached and repaired the *Endeavour* at the present site of Cooktown on the mainland and prior to sailing, Cook, Banks, and others ascended a hill to view the reefs through which they were to sail:

> . . . . the prospect was indeed melancholy: the sea everywhere full of innumerable shoals, some above and some underwater. . . .

> *Beaglehole, 1962, Vol. 2*

Coral reefs were regarded first and foremost as navigational hazards. Indeed, it had been only 43 years previously that Andre de Peysonnel (1727) had indicated to the scientific world that coral polyps were animal, not plant, organisms, a fact that took the Royal Society of London a further 24 years to accept.

It is significant that it was the Royal Society that sponsored the voyage of the *Endeavour* to witness the passage of Venus across the sun from the southern hemisphere in 1769 as predicted by Halley in 1721, an event important for observation in relation to calculations then being conducted on the distance of the earth from the sun. Some 158 years later, in 1928, and again in 1973 the

Royal Society was to sponsor two major scientific expeditions to the Great Barrier Reef, the findings of which were to provide major advances in understanding of the reefs of the world's greatest carbonate province. Banks, who was to become president of the Royal Society for 41 years, although showing the seaman's dread of coral reefs, also recognized them as significant areas for research. After passing through the outer barrier into deep water on 14 August he commented:

> A Reef such as one as I now speak of is a thing scarcely known in Europe or indeed anywhere but in these seas: it is a wall of Coral rock rising almost perpendicularly out of the unfathomable ocean, always overflown at high water commonly 7 or 8 feet and generally bare at low water; the large waves of the vast ocean meeting with so sudden a resistance make here a most terrible surf Breaking mountain high, especialy when, as in our case, the general trade wind blows directly upon it.

and later still, on 17 August, the *Endeavour* having been forced to take shelter once more inside Great Barrier Reef waters:

> We had in the way of curiosity much better success, meeting with many curios fish and mollusca besides Corals of many species, all alive among which was the *Tubipora musica.* I have often lamented that we had not time to make proper observations upon this curios tribe of animals but we were so intirely taken up with the more conspicuous links of the chain of creation as fish, Plants, Birds etc. etc. that it was impossible.

in Beaglehole, 1962, Vol. 2

However, the Great Barrier Reef, 2300 km long and enclosing the world's largest carbonate province of about 230,000 km^2, was not destined to be in the forefront of research or even discussion. The attention of the scientific communities of both Old and New Worlds was drawn increasingly to the apparent simplicity and recurring pattern of the ringlike Pacific Ocean atolls by accounts from voyages of discovery and scientific collecting. Most significant were the voyages of the German botanist Adelbert von Chamisso (1781–1838) on the Russian ship *Rurik* under the command of Otto von Kotzebue, circumnavigating the globe between 1815 and 1818, and the two voyages of the French scientists J. R. Quoy (1790–1869) and J. P. Gaimard (1796–1858). Chamisso (1821) observed that corals grow towards the surface and appear to flourish best in the surf zone, which, on midoceanic prominences, will in time produce a ringlike form, with ever widening lagoon where, because of lack of food for corals, erosion may predominate. Quoy and Gaimard made two long voyages. The first, on the *Uranie* under Freycinet, left Toulouse in 1817 and, calling on the coast of Western Australia near Shark Bay in September, 1818, sailed around the northern and eastern coasts of Australia to Sydney. Although later wrecked on the Falklands and much of their scientific material lost, Quoy and Gaimard in 1825 published a paper that indicated that corals can only grow in shallow water and also suggested that volcanic foundations underlie many atolls, the original crater giving the annular form. Similar voyages of discovery by the British Navy were also concentrating on the Pacific. Frederick William

Beechey (1796–1856), captain of H.M.S. *Blossom* and later to become president of the Royal Geographic Society, undertook a three-year voyage between 1825 and 1828, mainly in the area of the Bering Straits but also within the Pacific, discovering several new atolls and reef-fringed islands, his reports being published in England during the progress of the voyage.

In the light of all this new data, Charles Lyell (1797–1875), in the second volume of his *Principles of Geology* (1832) devoted the entire final chapter to a summary of all that was known of coral reefs, giving strong support to the idea that atolls had grown on the rims of submerged volcanic craters. Important though this work was in its own right, its greater influence lay in the effect it had on Charles Darwin (1809–1882). Darwin's now famous voyage on the *Beagle* had already commenced, but a copy of Lyell's *Principles* was forwarded to him by his friend and correspondent Professor Henslow. As Stoddart (1966) has pointed out, Darwin was profoundly influenced by Lyell's work; its distinct components, uniformitarianism and actualism, are implicit in *On the Origin of Species*. Lyell's *Principles* appear to have reached Darwin at an extremely opportune time, while he was studying evidence for long-term intermittent uplift of the west coast of South America. Darwin was the first to think seriously about the anomalous thickness of reefs in relation to the depth at which reef-building organisms seemed to flourish. He reasoned that the three main types of reef—fringing, barrier, and atoll—were genetically related and controlled by slow subsidence (Darwin, 1838), and he indicates the way his ideas developed:

> No other work of mine was begun in so deductive a spirit as this, for the whole theory was thought out on the west coast of South America before I had seen a true coral reef. I had therefore only to verify and extend my views by a careful examination of living reefs. But it should be observed that I had during the two previous years been incessantly attending to the effects on the shores of South America of the intermittent elevation of the land, together with the denudation and deposition of sediment. This necessarily led me to reflect much on the effects of subsidence, and it was easy to replace in imagination the continued deposition of sediment by the upward growth of corals. To do this was to form my theory of the formation of barrier reefs and atolls.
>
> *in Judd, 1910*

On her homeward voyage the *Beagle* visited Tahiti, Australia, and some coral islands of the Indian Ocean, giving Darwin the opportunity of testing and verifying his conclusions. In England, Darwin described his new theory to Lyell, who received it enthusiastically, writing:

> I must give up my volcanic crater for ever, though it cost me pang at first, for it accounted for so much.
>
> *in Judd, 1910*

Lyell stimulated Whewell, President of the Geological Society, to invite Darwin to present his views formally, which he did on 31 May 1837 in a paper entitled "On Certain Areas of Elevation and Subsidence in the Pacific and Indian

Oceans as deduced from the Study of Coral Formations,'' an abstract of which appeared in the second volume of the Society's *Proceedings*. Delays from both ill health and other work prevented Darwin from finally completing his book *The Structure and Distribution of Coral Reefs* until May 1842.

The book was initially accepted enthusiastically by both geologists and zoologists and even attracted attention from the general public. It was, however, the starting point for over 100 years of scientific controversy. In succeeding years exponents of the subsidence theory presented evidence purporting to support Darwinian ideas, but even during Darwin's lifetime many alternative hypotheses were put forward, though Darwin himself remained convinced of his own ideas and, in a letter to Alexander Agassiz in 1881, stated:

> I wish some doubly rich millionaire would take it into his head to have borings made in some of the Pacific and Indian Ocean atolls and bring home cores for slicing from a depth of 500 or 600 feet.

Prophetic words indeed, for within 18 years such a boring was to be made at Funafuti and subsequent reef drilling has both resolved old problems and asked new questions about the structure and evolution of reefs.

In these hundred years of controversy the Great Barrier Reef has not figured prominently, and, in the application of hypotheses developed generally from atoll locations, it has often played the part of an irrelevant diversion. Stoddart (1969a) has pointed out that Darwin's theory was accepted or rejected through deductive argument, often based on field evidence of purely local significance. Ideas on the origin of atolls give little aid in explaining the origin of the shelf reefs that are built on submerged continental islands. Further, many of the hypotheses were overambitious in trying to explain all three basic questions about atolls with a single evolutionary sequence. These three interrelated problems were:

1   That reef building corals appear to grow only in shallow waters.
2   That many reefs rise from great depths.
3   That atolls had similar morphology, particularly in the nature of the lagoon, almost everywhere.

As so often happens in the development of science, more than one explanation is correct, and modified combinations of initially antithetic hypotheses may provide the simplest explanation. Thus the original subsidence theory may best provide the answer to the total development of a reef system, but in doing so the evolving reef itself will provide an antecedent platform for subsequent development over which the Quaternary sea level fluctuations will provide the fine detail. As Stoddart (1973a) and Steers and Stoddart (1977) noted, Daly's Glacial Control Theory was not the antithesis of subsidence theory, for Darwin's theory was one of reef structure whereas Daly's was one of reef surface morphology.

SUBSIDENCE THEORY: EXPONENTS AND
THE GREAT BARRIER REEF

Darwin's deductive model of atoll formation was, in his own mind, confirmed when, on 17 November 1835 he climbed the slopes behind Papeete in Tahiti and viewed the neighboring island of Moorea, with its central volcanic island encircled by lagoon and barrier reef. To transform such an island into an atoll required only the island to slowly subside, so that the coral reefs grew upwards, with fringing reefs first converted into barrier reefs and later into an atoll as the high island sank beneath the ocean level (Fig. 1.1). Thus the problem of coral foundations beyond the depth at which present corals live was

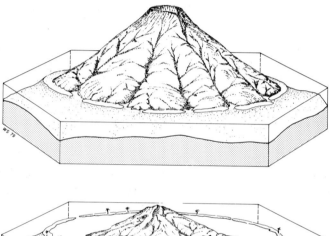

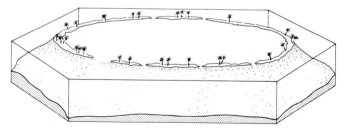

Figure 1.1 The classic subsidence model of Darwin (1842) as illustrated by Davis (1928). Slow subsidence of a volcanic island with fringing reefs produces first a barrier reef, then an atoll, as the volcanic core sinks beneath sea level.

overcome. Indeed, the Darwin theory required great thicknesses of shallow
water reef limestones beneath atolls.

Darwin's work was published at an opportune moment for James D. Dana,
the American naturalist, who was one of the scientists aboard six ships of the
United States Exploring Expedition to the Pacific Ocean. The cruise, which
lasted four years, commenced in 1838 and Dana was made aware of Darwin's
ideas by newspaper reports while the Expedition was in Sydney in 1839. Writing in 1872 Dana describes the influence of the newspaper report:

> The paragraph threw a flood of light over the subject, and called forth feelings of
> peculiar satisfaction, and of gratefulness to Mr. Darwin, which still come up
> afresh whenever the subject of coral islands is mentioned. The Gambier Islands in
> the Paumotus I have not seen; but on reaching the Feejees, six months later, in
> 1840, I found there similar facts on a still grander scale and of a more diversified
> character, so that I was afterward enabled to speak of his theory as established
> with more positiveness than he himself, in his philosophic caution, had been
> ready to adopt. His work on coral reefs appeared in 1842, when my report on the
> subject was already in manuscript. It showed that the conclusions on other points,
> which we had independently reached, were for the most part the same. The princi-
> pal points of difference relate to the reason for the absence of corals from some
> coasts, and the evidence therefrom as to changes of level, and the distribution of
> the oceanic regions of elevation and subsidence—topics which a wide range of
> travel over the Pacific brought directly and constantly to my attention.
>
> *Dana, 1872*

Dana produced a large number of publications and was the first to note the effect of cold currents in excluding reefs from the eastern sides of oceans (Dana,
1843). In all his work he strongly supports the Darwinian subsidence theory.
In 1859 Baron von Richthofen showed that thick masses of dolomitic limestone in the Tyrol could be interpreted as being of reefal origin formed during
long continued subsidence, a view supported by Mojsisovics in 1879 working
on the Italian side of the Alps (Judd, 1910). These observations were seen as
supporting Darwin's ideas.

Darwin did not have opportunity to view the Great Barrier Reef, because the
Beagle sailed around the southern shores of the Australian continent. Nevertheless, he was to relate his subsidence theory to this reef province, writing at
the start of Chapter 2 of his *Coral Reefs*:

> The term "barrier" has been generally applied to that vast reef which fronts the
> N.E. shore of Australia, and by most voyagers, likewise to that on the western
> coast of New Caledonia. At one time I thought it convenient thus to restrict the
> term, but as these reefs are similar in structure and position relative to the land, to
> those, which, like a wall with a deep moat within, encircle many smaller islands,
> I have classed them together.
>
> *Darwin, 1842, Chap. 2*

and later:

> If instead of the island in the diagram, the shore of a continent fringed by a reef had
> subsided, a great barrier reef, like that on the north-east coast of Australia, would

have necessarily have resulted; and it would have been separated from the main land by a deep-water channel, broad in proportion to the amount of subsidence, and to the lesser or greater inclination of the neighbouring coast-line.

Darwin, 1842, Chap. 5

Although Darwin could not directly relate his ideas to the Australian reef, he found an able exponent and illustrator of his theory in Professor J. B. Jukes who accompanied H.M.S. *Fly* on her surveying voyage between 1842 and 1846. At this time very little was known of Barrier Reef waters although Phillip Parker King on the *Mermaid* had examined and favored the route within the Great Barrier Reef, as opposed to the more open Coral Sea route, for vessels sailing northward to Torres Strait. However, numerous wrecks were occurring along both routes (Bateson, 1972) and the British Admiralty in 1841 decided to have the Great Barrier Reef explored with a view to charting a safe shipping channel. Capt. Francis Price Blackwood was selected to command H.M. Corvette *Fly* with her tender the cutter *Bramble* under Lt. Charles Jule. In a period of about three years Blackwood surveyed an area of 1500 km length and 250 km width, marking the outer line of the Great Barrier Reef from 16°40′S to 9°20′S, a distance of 1100 km. Even today the modern charts of the area acknowledge this initial survey of Blackwood (Ingleton, 1944).

Jukes, aboard the *Fly*, was the first scientific investigator of the Great Barrier Reef and his published account describes it:

> The Great Barrier Reefs are thus found to form a long, submarine buttress or curtain along the north-eastern coast of Australia, rising in general precipitously from a very great depth, but resting towards the north on the shoaler ground of Torres Strait, and towards the south on the bank stretching off from Sandy Cape. If it were to be laid dry, this great barrier would be found to have a considerable resemblance to gigantic and irregular fortification, a steep glacis crowned with a parapet wall and carried from one rising ground to another. The tower like bastions of projecting and detached reefs would increase this resemblance.

Jukes, 1847, p. 332

Although noting evidence of a small apparently recent elevation of the land along the Queensland coast, a feature later to provide so much controversy, he clearly supported Darwin in writing:

> After seeing much of the Great Barrier Reefs and reflecting much upon them, and trying if it were possible by any means to evade the conclusions to which Mr. Darwin has come, I cannot help adding that this hypothesis is perfectly satisfactory to my mind, and rises beyond a mere hypothesis into the true theory of coral reefs.

Jukes also produced an imaginary cross section of the Great Barrier Reef showing quite clearly that he conceived a very great thickness of reefal material over the continental shelf.

Further evidence was forthcoming from surveys of a similar nature to that of Jukes. The beginnings of a prosperous sugar industry were appearing along the Queensland coast, and ports were being developed under the guidance of Sir

George Bowen. In consequence further surveys by H.M.S. *Rattlesnake* (1846–1850), H.M.S. *Herald* (1859–1861), H.M.S. *Salamander* (1866–1868), and later in the century by both Royal Navy and colonial vessels, clearly charted an inner shipping channel. They delineated many of the massive outer reef areas but could not chart them in any detail, a situation that was not remedied for over 100 years, until aerial and satellite photographs were available. Several of these survey vessels carried scientific staff. The *Rattlesnake*, for example, had John Macgillivray and Leonard Huxley on board, while the *Salamander's* surgeon, Alexander Rattray, was an amateur geologist. The reports that they published (e.g. Macgillivray, 1852; Rattray, 1869) clearly presume a foundering of the Queensland continental shelf but while presenting new morphological details of the reefs, islands, and mainland, did little to advance the ideas of Darwin.

OPPONENTS AND ALTERNATIVES—ANTECEDENT PLATFORMS

The work on the Great Barrier Reef, producing superficial and circumstantial evidence for subsidence, was typical of much that was written about reefs worldwide between the first appearance of the subsidence theory and about 1865. It is not surprising therefore to find that over the last four decades of the nineteenth century and the first two decades of the twentieth century there developed a degree of opposition to subsidence (See Steers and Stoddart, 1977, for review), with alternative hypotheses being suggested, often by zoologists who, in the view of many Darwin supporters, did not fully appreciate the geological aspect of the question. The so-called Coral Reef Problem centered around the substrate from which the reefs grew, and, to a lesser extent, the ringlike morphology of atolls. However, many of the reef areas from which zoologists gained their evidence, such as Carl Semper (1863), working on the Palau Islands, and H. B. Guppy (1885, 1886, 1887, 1888, 1890), working in the Solomons, were located in the tectonically mobile regions of Southeast Asia and Melanesia. In these areas all Darwin's reef types were found in close juxtaposition, whereas adjacent mainland raised reefs showed apparently thin reefal deposits, apparently in contradiction to Darwin's subsidence theory.

Thus, largely ignoring the fact that Darwin's arguments related essentially to atolls of the deep ocean rather than the complex conditions of geologically young and tectonically active areas, a number of ideas for preexisting or antecedent platforms, of suitable depth for coral growth, were put forward. Rein (1870, 1881) after a visit to Bermuda in 1862–1863 suggested that organic deposits accumulated on stillstanding submarine summits provided the foundations for atolls. He was supported by Murray (1880, 1887–1889, 1889a,b) returning from the *Challenger* expedition with evidence for deep-sea organic deposition. Semper (1863, 1873) resurrected the idea of volcanic foundations, not for the morphology of atolls but by slow submarine eruption providing a rising mound to suitable depths for coral colonization. Guppy (1885, 1886, 1887, 1888, 1890) similarly suggested that reefs grew outwards on rising, not subsiding, foundations. Wharton, (1890, 1897) examining the depths of lagoon, floors, observed:

that there are a great many with a general depth of 30 to 40 fathoms and the question arises whether this may not be the general limit of the power of oceanic waves to cut down the mass acted upon when it is fairly friable.

Corals thus grow on the foundations made by submarine planation, a hypothesis developed further by Gardiner (1898a, 1902, 1903, 1903–1906, 1904) to explain in particular the morphology of the Maldive atolls. This too was a resurrection of an older hypothesis, developed initially in 1832 by Tyerman and Bennet, who stated that the steep coastal cliffs of Tahiti indicated that its barrier reefs were formed on the outer edges of wavecut platforms. Agassiz (1898, 1899) was an even stronger advocate for reefs being mere veneers over littoral platforms. Erosion was also advocated for the formation of atoll lagoons, generally by solution (Semper, Murray) though Agassiz (1899, pp. 135–139) suggested the processes were mechanical, producing "a modified gigantic pot-hole."

Several of these hypotheses have application only to open ocean atolls, and of the remainder, the only advocate to make a specific study of the Great Barrier Reef, was Alexander Agassiz. In 1896, by means of a specially chartered vessel, he made a reconnaissance survey as far north as Lizard Island at 14°40'S. He concluded (1898) that the Great Barrier Reef formed merely a thin veneer no more than "20 fathoms" in thickness over a continental platform that had been stationary since the Cretaceous. Reef blocks he regarded as undenuded residuals of former elevated coral reefs from which the present Great Barrier Reef is derived. Gardiner (1898b) in one of his earlier papers had made similar claims for reef veneers on wavecut platforms, stating that the theory of subsidence on the Great Barrier Reef is "absolutely excluded." Another supporter, at least initially, of Agassiz's model was the Australian geologist E. C. Andrews. Andrews was a student of Edgeworth David, Professor of Geology at Sydney University who, subsequent to Agassiz's visit in 1896, was involved in the drilling of a deep hole on Funafuti (see below) and who in 1898 nominated Andrews to lead an expedition to the reefs of Fiji and Tonga. The expedition was financed by Agassiz and Andrews came down firmly in favor of the Harvard professor's views (1900). He applied them subsequently to the Great Barrier Reef (Andrews, 1902), quoting widely from Agassiz's arguments against Darwin's and Jukes' ideas. However, shortly afterwards Andrews was envisaging coastal flexure with subsidence initiating the Great Barrier Reef (1900–1904a, pp. 214–215), a statement seized upon by W. M. Davis (1917, 1928) whom Andrews met in 1908 on a visit to the United States. In 1914 Andrews accompanied Davis on part of his tour of the reefs of the New Hebrides and New Caledonia and Davis appears to have been so convinced of Andrews' support for Darwin, that he wrote of Andrews' 1900 report of truncation at Mango in eastern Fiji:

> In view of Andrews' residence in Sydney N.S.W. and the publication of his report in Cambridge, Mass., the question may be raised whether the redrawing of his outlines there for reproduction in colour, did not give the submarine structures a greater definition than he intended.

Davis, 1928, p. 246

Nonetheless, Andrews appears to have had greater conviction of his earlier views than Davis imagined and in his final application to the coral reef problem in his presidential address to the Royal Society of New South Wales (Andrews, 1922) he restated his opinion, modified to some extent by the works of Vaughan and Daly, that the Great Barrier Reef grew on a foundation planed during the stormy periods of glacial low sea levels.

IN DEFENSE OF DARWIN

Darwin, before his death in 1882, had opportunity to hear many of these alternative hypotheses. His first responses came in the second and revised edition of *Coral Reefs*, published in 1874, where he admitted that special cases of rising banks, as Semper had suggested for the Palau Islands, may exist, but firmly maintained that such rare examples were insufficient to invalidate his general theory. Similary he accepted Murray's thesis, pointing out in a letter to Agassiz in 1881 that he had suggested himself that a bank at the proper depth would give rise to an atoll that could not be distinguished from one formed during subsidence. Three years after Darwin's death Dana (1885) published a powerful defense of subsidence in reply to an essay in favor of Murray's preexisting platforms by the distinguished Scottish geologist Geikie (1883). He restated his earlier supporting evidence of embayed shorelines of islands behind barrier reefs, evidence that W. M. Davis was to make so important.

It was true to say, however, that indisputable evidence of great subsidence of oceanic atolls was still needed, and the problem awaited the deep drilling that Darwin had advocated. An abortive attempt had been made by Belcher (1843) in the Tuamotus but the first organized effort to solve the problem came in 1896–1898 when the Royal Society organized the Funafuti Coral Reef Boring Expedition under the leadership of Professor T. Edgeworth David of Sydney University. David himself did not become involved in the coral reef controversy but one of his co-workers, Charles Hedley, who was sent out ahead of the expedition in 1896, was to become in 1925 the first scientific director of the Great Barrier Reef Investigation Committee and supervized the first deep bore into the Great Barrier Reef on Michaelmas Cay. There were thus strong Australian interests in solving the problem. In 1897 the bore reached 213 m and was extended down to 340 m the following year. Although the upper 194 m was in coral limestone and the rest in dolomite, which Judd (1904) and others regarded as being shallow water in origin throughout, it was also suggested that the lower section could be a forereef talus and hence inconclusive of subsidence.

However, Darwin was to find a champion of substance in no less a personality than W. M. Davis of whom H. C. Richards, the foundation Professor of Geology at Queensland University and a major force in the setting up of the Great Barrier Reef Committee, stated:

> W. M. Davis, in 1914, approached the Barrier Reef problem better equipped than any previous investigator, owing to his pre-eminence as a physiographer.
>
> *Richards, 1923, p. 1110*

It is appropriate that Davis became the major advocate of subsidence for, as Stoddart (1966) has pointed out, so much of Davis' work is inspired by the concept of evolution. Ironically, when Davis retired prematurely from Harvard in 1912 he succeeded by Daly, who was in the process of launching his Glacial Control hypothesis for reefs (Chorley, Beckinsale, and Dunn, 1973, Chap. 25). Davis' continued contact with his old department may well have stimulated his interest in reefs, for during the 15 years following his retirement he was primarily engaged on the coral reef problem, traveling across the Pacific and along the Queensland coast in 1914, examining the reefs of the Lesser Antilles in 1923, and prior to his major work of 1928 publishing 28 papers and a monograph (on the Lesser Antilles) in this time.

Largely by deductive argument in extending the various reef hypotheses available, Davis showed how subsidence was widely applicable, whereas alternative hypotheses were inadequate to explain all the facts. Davis described coral reefs as "inscrutable" (1928, p. 14) and largely ignored internal structure, instead concentrating on the subaerial forms and processes of the volcanic island around which the initial fringing and barrier reefs form. In particular he resurrected Dana's observations on the nature of a drowned, subaerially formed landscape of embayed shorelines behind barrier reefs (Davis, 1913) and suggested that the lack of wavecut cliffs indicated that a "maturely dissected" relief had formed since the barrier had come into being.

The general lack of large amounts of detritus in present lagoons may be explained only by subsidence during the production of this relief. In examining alternative hypotheses, Davis questioned both the facts and the reasoning presented. Against rising antecedent platforms he pointed out that where it has been possible to examine the contact between basement rocks and reefal material, there is a distinct unconformity, whereas arguments such as those of Murray, Semper, or Rein require conformable contacts. He dismissed solution as the process of lagoon excavation and was highly critical of Agassiz's mechanical excavation of such features. Indeed, he completely dismissed the Agassiz model (and similar ideas) of barrier reefs as mere veneers on wavecut platforms. Such a hypothesis, he argued, requires cliffed but nonembayed shorelines, whereas the field evidence is for embayed and noncliffed coasts, as would be produced by subsidence. In a sweeping statement against the alternatives Davis stated:

The theories vary greatly in their postulates and processes but in their presentation they all have two characteristics in common; namely defective deduction of consequences and hence a very incomplete confrontation of consequences with facts. Perhaps the chief reason for these deficiencies is that nearly all the inventors of these theories had been trained more in biological than in geological science. If they had heard of Dana's confirmation of Darwin's theory in the matter of the embayed shorelines of barrier-reef islands, they discredited it; if they had met the geological term, unconformity, they made no application of the principle it embodies. Some of them attributed overmuch work to marine abrasion, and none of them gave due attention to subaerial erosion. Their theories cannot be accepted because the consequences are strongly contradicted by the facts.

Davis, 1928, p. 88

Davis spent less than two weeks sailing up the Queensland coast and only one night on the Great Barrier Reef proper, at Green Island near Cairns, of which, with typical dismissal of fieldwork on reefs, as opposed to the examination of adjacent subaerial eroded landscapes, he stated:

> was an entertaining experience but, as might have been expected, entirely fruitless as far as the origin of the reef is concerned.

Davis, 1928, p. 347

Nonetheless, relying to a large extent on the physiographic works of Andrews (1902, 1903, 1900–1904a, 1900–1904b, 1910) and David (1911), he produced a coherent sequence for the development of the Queensland coast (Fig. 1.2) based on intermittent uplift of the east coast with synchronous downwarping of the adjacent shelf area upon which the Great Barrier Reef was established over a long period of geological time. The point of flexure was seen as migrating landward with time causing a progressive and embaying encroachment of

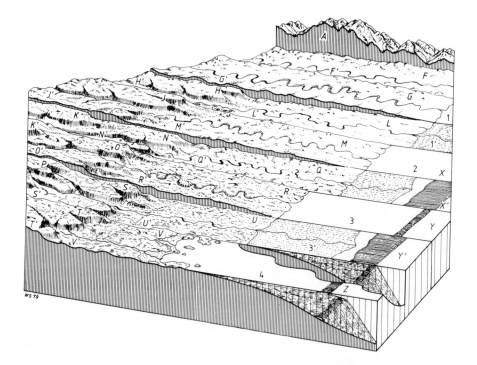

Figure 1.2 Davis' (1928) block diagram illustrating the development of the Queensland coast. Blocks 1, 1', 2, 3, and 3' show repeated patterns of continental uplift and shelf subsidence of a previously produced peneplain (F). Recent submergence due to gentle tilting is seen in Block 4. (Reprinted from W. M. Davis, *The Coral Reef Problem*, 1928 by courtesy of the American Geographical Society.)

the sea, as is displayed by the mainland and offshore islands, particularly the Whitsunday Group.

Two further points which Davis discussed were the contiguity of the reef-less New South Wales continental shelf with that of Queensland, and the encroachment of great sand masses from the south onto the southern end of the Great Barrier Reef province. The first was used as evidence by those who supported a preexisting platform beneath the Great Barrier Reef to support the idea that the reef cover over the Queensland shelf could have no great thickness. Davis, however, pointed to the cliffing on the N.S.W. coast and general absence of offshore islands there in contrast to the Queensland coast to suggest that the two areas had evolved in completely different ways: the Queensland offshore area as a subsiding reef plain, the N.S.W. area as a planated shelf that is "in general not well fitted for the upgrowth of reefs" (Davis, 1928, p. 358). While recognizing that the present southern limit of the Great Barrier Reef is largely temperature controlled, Davis further suggested that encroachment of large sand masses from the south, of which Fraser Island is the northernmost extension, may have shortened the length of the Reef and played a significant part in the development of that part of the Reef in the past. It is interesting to note that the difference in the N.S.W. and Queensland coasts, though partly explainable in terms of structure, is also due to contrasts in energy levels and processes operating as suggested by J. L. Davies (1972, 1977). The southern encroachment of sand, which Davis saw had a parallel on the Florida coast, is recognized, also by Davies (1972), as part of a major worldwide equatorward movement of coastal sediment at latitudes approximating the poleward limits of modern reef development.

THE EFFECTS OF QUATERNARY SEA LEVEL FLUCTUATIONS

The development of concepts on coral reefs during the nineteenth century parallel in a remarkably close way the development of ideas on glaciation (for discussion see Flint, 1971, Chap. 2). Indeed many scientists, with typical nineteenth-century naturalist width of interest, took part in the debates of both controversial issues. It was Lyell (1839) who first named the Pleistocene. Louis Agassiz, whose 1837 paper and 1840 book did so much to crystallize the ideas of his contemporaries on glaciation, was later to occupy the chair of zoology and geology at Harvard University and was father of one of the coral reef controversy's central figures, Alexander Agassiz. In America, Dana (1863, p. 541) was a major advocate of the glacial view. While the glacial theory was still in its infancy Charles McLaren (1842) perceived the role of glaciers in the hydrologic cycle and deduced that sea levels must have been lowered during glacial ages by as much as 350–400 feet. The term *eustatic* was introduced by Suess in 1888. By the first decades of the twentieth century there had slowly evolved, mainly from work undertaken in Europe, a standard glacio-eustatic theory of major sea level oscillations in the Quaternary (e.g. De Lamothe, 1911, 1918; Chaput, 1917, 1927; Depéret, 1918–1922).

T. Belt (1874), W. Upham (1878) and Albrecht Penck (1894) were among the first to see the significance of changing sea levels for coral reef development.

From what he considered to be a surprisingly uniform depth of atoll lagoons
and the embayed nature of continental coasts, Penck concluded that ocean
levels must have stood from 100–200 m below present for a considerable
period. Nonetheless he regarded the Great Barrier Reef of Australia as the
result of subsidence of the reef foundation (Penck, 1896). It was left to Reginald
Daly, also at Harvard University, to fully expound on the consequences of glacial episodes for coral reefs, both in terms of sea levels and of lowering of ocean
temperatures (Daly, 1910, 1915, 1916, 1917, 1919, 1934, 1948). His Glacial
Control Theory was based on the presumed uniformity of atoll lagoon depths
that could not be accounted for by aggradation over subsiding foundations.
Marine abrasion at the low sea level stand, aided by the lack of protection then
given by coral reefs that could not withstand the lowered temperatures, would
produce platforms truncating the older worn-down and deeply weathered volcanic islands to depths of between 30 and 40 fathoms (54–72 m) (Fig. 1.3). On
younger islands marginal platforms would be cut and from these benches and
platforms would rise the atolls and barrier reefs as the warming ocean rose during postglacial time. Lagoon depths would remain uniform, though some infilling could take place. Daly recognized that preglacial reefs would also be exposed at the low sea level stage but suggested that they too could be truncated,
especially as the fall in sea level would direct attack below the coral zone into
the talus sand and beaches that he presumed underlay the reefs. Erosion would
be carried out largely by undermining (Daly, 1915, p. 175). The Great Barrier
Reef was envisaged as developing in this way by Daly, although the shallowness of the southern part of the Reef was explained by:

> Recent rapid aggradation due to the local configuration of the coast and by a corre-
> sponding, special abundance of sand.

> *Daly, 1915, p. 196*

Shallow areas elsewhere were also explained:

> Large areas are comparatively shallow because of a specially rapid rate of organic
> deposition in Recent time, while the barrier has largely protected them against
> erosion by ocean currents.

> *Daly, 1915, p. 198*

While Daly's ideas can now be criticized (and were, by W. M. Davis in 1928)
in terms of the nature and rates of process, his time scale, his simplified pattern of glacio-eustatic changes, and even his factual information (see Stoddart,
1969a, p. 440) he found many able supporters, particularly T. W. Vaughan
(1914a, b, 1919, 1923). Vaughan's initial hypothesis for the Lesser Antilles
reefs was extended to cover all reefs:

> The data presented on the relations of the barrier reefs of Florida, Bahamas, Cuba
> and Australia showed that all of them stand on platforms submerged by rise of
> strandline, and that the platforms are independent of the limits of living reefs. It is
> evident that the reefs are superimposed on platforms formed by other than reef

agencies, and that reef building organisms grow only in those places on the platforms where conditions for their life are favourable.

Vaughan, 1914a, p. 42

Like Daly, Vaughan envisaged the platforms being formed during low sea level stands.

The importance of Daly's work lies not in the theory itself but in the attention he drew to the significance of sea level change on coral reef development. He even noted the existence in many parts of the Pacific of terraces of marine

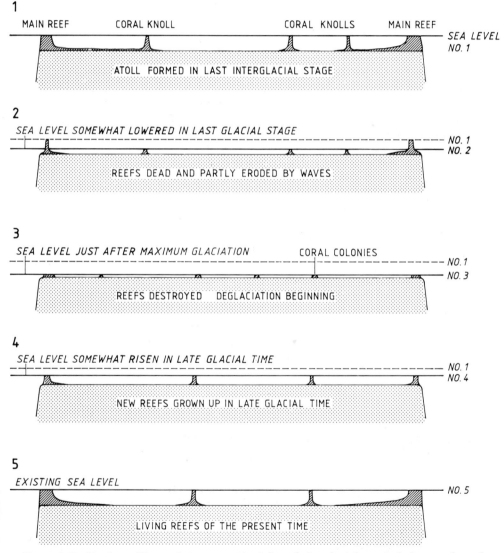

Figure 1.3 Sections illustrating some principles of the glacial control theory of coral reefs. (Reprinted from R. A. Daly, *The Changing World of the Ice Age*, 1934, Yale University Press.)

abrasion, elevated up to 6 m and assumed to be postglacial (Daly, 1925). This interpretation of a Holocene high, eustatic sea level and its effects on coral reefs was to become a central theme of reef research over the following decades. Steers, for example, allocated a number of morphological features on the low wooded islands of the Great Barrier Reef to this "Recent high stand" (Steers, 1929, 1937, 1938). Thus the concept of a fluctuating sea level became incorporated into the majority of subsequent coral reef hypotheses, a concept that had equal validity for both deep oceanic atolls and shelf reefs of marginal seas.

INTEGRATION OF CORAL REEF HYPOTHESES

Writing in 1948, the eminent New Zealand geomorphologist C. A. Cotton stated:

> The status of coral reef theories at present is that the "antecedent platform" theory and the two upgrowth theories—namely the century old Darwin subsidence theory, strongly maintained more recently by Davis (1928) and the Daly "glacial control" theory first formulated in 1910—are all accepted as working hypotheses, but that others which maintain fixity of sea level, such as the outgrowth theory of Murray, are ruled out by the general acceptance, of glacio-eustatism. Even these, and especially Murray's explanation of possible lateral growth of reef over a foundation of talus, are useful for the description of certain parts of reefs.

> *Cotton, 1948*

Thus deductive, a priori, models of coral reef development that have been constructed over the last 50 years have been largely integrations of former hypotheses.

Typical of these combined models is the theory of "glacially controlled subsidence" of Kuenen (1933, 1947), based largely on observations of the reefs of the southeast Asian archipelago. Kuenen envisaged volcanic foundations of Tertiary age, which, after an initial period of high turbidity which would inhibit coral colonization, would develop fringing reefs. Subsidence, in the manner of Darwin's hypothesis, would first form barrier and then atoll reefs, fringing reefs rapidly declining due to a high terrigenous sediment yield. While recognizing that, during periods of glacial low sea level, corals would be killed by low temperatures in marginal, high-latitude seas, allowing the formation of abrasion platforms and cliffs as Daly hypothesized, Kuenen considered that corals continued to thrive and to protect elevated reefs and barrier islands from severe wave attack in the low latitude coral seas. However, chemical marine solution in such areas was seen as an alternative process producing similar forms of hard, rocky reef flats at the height of the lowered sea level. With a postglacial rise in sea level, the corals already thriving as fringing reefs around the truncated surfaces would grow upwards immediately, mainly on the periphery of the platforms, the unsuitable substrate of the older lagoonal centers limiting growth there. The rapid rise in sea level was responsible for the passes developed in the new rims, there being insufficient time for them to be closed by coral growth before submergence had carried them beyond the depth limit of coral growth. Thus whereas subsidence was responsible for the foundational structure of reefs, especially atolls, the present morphology was due to glacial control.

The importance of a platform on which coral colonization could be initiated is implied in Kuenen's work and was emphasized by Hoffmeister and Ladd, who produced an antecedent platform theory maintaining that:

> any bench or bank—even one not "smooth"—that is located at a proper depth within the circumequatorial coral reef zone can be considered a potential coral reef foundation and that, if ecological conditions permit, a reef could grow up to the surface without any change in ocean level. This is a general principle that applies to coral reefs of all ages—preglacial, glacial and postglacial.
>
> *Hoffmeister and Ladd, 1944, p. 389*

These authors showed that extensive shoals are developed by a combination of submarine volcanic activity and marine erosion. Their theory differs from Murray's stillstand theory in not postulating any extensive lateral outgrowth of the reef over forereef talus and explains an atoll lagoon merely as an area formed by a ring reef of recent formation. In agreement with observed basal deposits of uplifted reefs they suggested that the initial veneer over the platform is a tuffaceous limestone, subsequently built up by foraminifera and algae into the zone of coral reef growth. While recognizing that sea level change may stimulate coral reef growth, they did not see it as essential.

Similarly, Stearns (1946) regarded an antecedent platform as essential for the formation of a reef. However, he introduced into the argument on coral reef formation an explanation for the widely reported variation in coral reefs east and west of the "Sial line" of the western Pacific. To the west of the line extensive Tertiary mountain building episodes produced related folded submarine ridges, which when shallow enough to provide foundations for reefs would develop atolls. Glacial lowering of sea levels brought further deeper ridges into depths possible for coral growth and atoll formation. Subsequent glacio-eustatic falls of sea level are envisaged as completely or partially truncating the reefs developed during rises, producing a variety of internal unconformities. To the east of the Sial line Stearns hypothesized the development of atolls with great limestone thickness on a subsiding volcanic basement during the Tertiary, in the manner of the classical subsidence theory. However, he believed that subsidence had ceased by the Quaternary and variations in sea level were again the major factor in producing atolls of complex structure with internal unconformities where the reef limestone is eroded on exposure during low sea levels.

Stearns made only a limited attempt to relate his theory to shelf reefs (1946, pp. 260–261), although the fact that many reefs rest on preexisting coral reef platforms that, in wet areas, had been subject to solution by rain water is applicable to all reef types. Indeed over the last few years the hypothesis of the development of reef complexes by slow subsidence but with periodic exposure during the Pleistocene, resulting in subaerial weathering when sea levels were significantly lowered, has become a central theme of coral reef debate. This idea, first fully envisaged by Tayama (1952, p. 170), developed earlier work of

Yabe (1942) and Asano (1942), both of whom suggested that reefs in the Pacific are growing on limestone solution forms. Umbgrove (1947) considered such an origin for reef features but rejected the idea.

However, the paper published in 1954 by F. Stearns MacNeil has become the most widely quoted source of the hypothesis of an inheritance from sub-aerial erosion forms for the shape of atolls. Interestingly, MacNeil notes that Hoffmeister and Ladd had previously concluded that the saucer shape of many uplifted Pacific limestone islands was due to solution, not to the fact that they were raised atolls, yet they did not develop the argument in their exposition on antecedent platforms. MacNeil's theory recognized the importance of organic growth during periods of submergence but placed at least equal importance on the role of solution in fashioning the lagoonal depressions and annular rims of atolls. Case-hardening and development of underground drainage systems were seen as important factors in the development of the subaerially exposed limestone surface (Fig. 1.4). MacNeil, in the introduction to his 1954 paper, stated:

> Though it is true that most authors have sought to explain barriers and atolls as the ultimate form of reefs, the inclusion of all reef hypotheses under one heading implies more conflict than really exists. Generally no distinction is made between theories dealing mainly with the foundation of reefs, and the shape of reefs. There is a general feeling among investigators at present that atolls are not always formed the same way, and therefore no one theory can explain atolls.

and later:

> It would seem that each atoll should be studied as an individual and it is not thought that the present hypothesis, believed to be true for the oceanic atolls of the mid Pacific, is necessarily true for the atolls (sic) of the Great Barrier Reef.
>
> *MacNeil, 1954, pp. 402–403*

It is possible here that MacNeil was too conservative in his application of his hypothesis for, more recently, Purdy (1974a, b) greatly extended the antecedent karst model to explain configuration of all reefs by means of preferential reef accretion on topographic highs in underlying subaerially weathered surfaces. His model, which has been applied to the Great Barrier Reef, and the general concept of karst erosion of early reef complexes is a central theme of this book.

However, MacNeil's statements implying that the coral reef problem has been largely a matter of confusing structure and surface morphology, and of assuming that all reefs have a similar evolution, is an illumination of the problem not previously considered. It is from about the time of his paper that general models of reef evolution have become unfashionable, a trend that is noticeable within geomorphology generally, as indicated by Higgins (1975). Higgins attributes this decline in landscape models to a change in the intellectual climate resulting from increasing quantification and interest in process, which in turn have suggested that complex landforms may be explained by more than one hypothesis. Empirical studies of forms and processes have shown that earlier general theories at best provide a standard for measurable deviations at specific locations or on local regional scales.

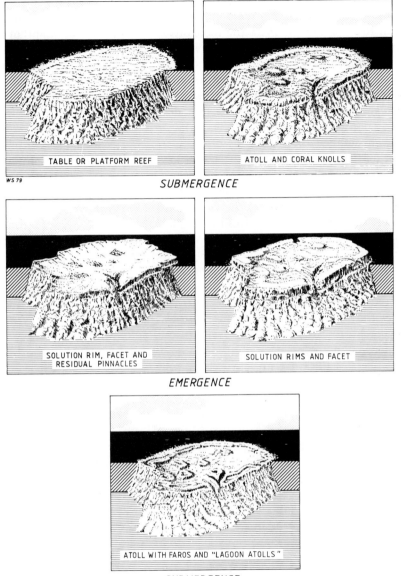

Figure 1.4 MacNeil's (1954) diagrams showing development of atolls and faros on sub-aerial erosion forms. (Reprinted from American Journal of Science, Vol. 252, 1954.)

DEVELOPMENT OF RESEARCH FACILITIES AND
EMPIRICAL STUDIES OF FORM AND PROCESS

While the Great Barrier Reef has never been the central theme or research area for the development of general coral reef theory, it has occupied a more central situation in detailed empirical studies of form and process. To a large extent this period of intensive study is linked with the recognition that many ancient reefs form excellent oil reservoir rocks. As early as 1911 Vaughan concluded that Palaeozoic reefs were formed under environmental conditions similar to today's, and in 1927 the recognition of the Permian Capitan limestone of west Texas and southeast New Mexico as a former reef tract, has greatly stimulated both directly and indirectly the study of coral reefs (see Ladd, 1961). In the Great Barrier Reef province it is notable that much of the geophysical work has been carried out by petroleum companies and of the six deep holes drilled into the Reef, the four deepest were drilled by petroleum companies (Hill, 1974).

However, detailed investigations of the Great Barrier Reef had commenced much earlier (Jones, 1974). In 1922, H. C. Richards, the foundation professor of Geology and Mineralogy at the University of Queensland, was invited by the Queensland Branch of the Royal Geographical Society of Australia to present an address on "The Problems of the Great Barrier Reef." He drew attention to areas where systematic research was needed, as the result of which Sir Matthew Nathan, then Governor of Queensland, supported an appeal to scientific societies, universities, museums, and some government departments from within and beyond Australia to nominate representatives to serve on a Great Barrier Reef Committee of the Branch. The Committee, set up in 1922, by 1924 had representatives from 34 institutions, with a further 22 members. Richards took over the chairmanship from Sir Matthew Nathan in the same year and, with increased funding, a full time scientific director was appointed. He was Charles Hedley, a zoologist, and although he died only two years later he and other members of the Committee travelled widely along the Queensland coast and on the Commonwealth steamer that serviced the many lighthouses on the reefs and islands. In addition three young Sydney University graduates, financed by Sydney University Research Scholarships, worked for two years on specific projects. Results were initially published in 1925 as the first volume of the *Transactions of the Royal Geographical Society (Queensland)*. Subsequently, after disagreement with the Society, the Great Barrier Reef Committee became a separate body, although it has retained the name Committee without a parent body.

One of the first achievements of the Committee was the drilling of a hole on Michaelmas Cay near Cairns in 1926 under the supervision of Charles Hedley, who 30 years earlier had been involved in the Funafuti boring. Although this bore was sunk to 600 feet (183 m) and 11 years later a second hole was sunk to 730 feet (223 m) on Heron Island at the southern end of the reef, neither did much to clarify the subsidence controversy, which was their intention. They did, however, provide much valuable information on the development of the reef. The cores have been reexamined several times and are still a useful source of data.

Another major aim of the Great Barrier Reef Committee was to set up a permanent research facility on one of the reef islands. Funds, however, were insufficient to do this and discussions were held with the British Association for the Advancement of Science to promote the mounting of an expedition based on an island for at least one full cycle of seasons. Thus in 1928–1929, with funds provided from the Commonwealth Government, the Great Barrier Reef Committee, the Royal Society (London), the British Association for the Advancement of Science, the Australian Association for the Advancement of Science, and the Zoological Society of London, a team of 23 scientists led by C. M. Yonge of the Marine Biological Station at Plymouth set up headquarters and laboratories on Low Isles near Port Douglas (Yonge, 1931a). The results of the Expedition, which appeared in publications of the British Museum of Natural History over several decades, provided a major basis for coral reef research worldwide.

Although mainly biological, the Yonge Expedition had a geographical section led by J. A. Steers of Cambridge University with Michael Spender and E. C. Marchant. The party worked for six weeks with the main expedition on Low Isles, but also made a reconnaissance along the Queensland coast between Whitsunday Island and the Flinders Islands (1350 km) visiting the mainland as well as many high islands and reef islands. In addition, Steers joined the Commonwealth lighthouse ship *Cape Leeuwin*, giving him the opportunity of visiting the Bunker–Capricorn Group of reefs, and Spender spent a further eight months on the Low Isles with the main party. Seven years later, in 1936, the Great Barrier Reef Committee invited Steers to return to Queensland, which he did with an assistant, F. E. Kemp, spending from May to August sailing along the Reef from Brisbane to Cape Direction and back to Bundaberg, a total of 4680 km. The publications from this geomorphological work (Steers, 1929, 1937, 1938; Spender, 1930) did much to highlight the value of reef islands for interpreting the evolution of reef systems. In particular the low, wooded islands (or island reefs, according to Spender) were established as a special type of reef island, that has since been identified elsewhere (Stoddart, 1965a). Their location was explained by Spender in terms of tectonic tilting, providing only the inner reefs with a suitably elevated reef flat for shingle rampart formation, whereas Steers explained the distribution of these low wooded islands in terms of wave exposure, the innermost reefs having sufficient exposure for steep seas to form shingle ramparts, the outer reefs being too exposed and thus swept clear of debris, and the intermediately located reefs being too protected by the continuous outer barrier.

Steers and Spender concentrated on describing the morphological features they saw, particularly on the low wooded islands where many of the cemented shingle platforms were interpreted as having formed from a relatively higher sea level, and where, on a number of islands, emerged reefs were recognized. Their work was carried out shortly after the publication of W. M. Davies' monograph and at the time when the results of the Michaelmas Cay bore were at hand. Steers in particular was interested in the question of reef evolution and was a strong supporter of subsidence. Extending the work of Andrews and incorporating the observations on the mainland and high islands published mainly in the Reports of the Great Barrier Reef Committee (e.g. Hedley, 1925a,b,c,d,e,f,g; Jardine, 1925a,b,c, 1928a, b; Stanley, 1928) he produced a model of development that relied heavily on downfaulting of the Queensland continental shelf, with reef development on topographic highs rising from the downfaulted Tertiary peneplain surface.

Spender made particular note of the variety of form of the Great Barrier Reefs, but his perspective of such variety was limited to surface observations and Admiralty bathymetric charts. Some aerial photography of individual reefs

had been taken as early as 1925 and in September 1928 the Royal Australian
Air Force made a vertical coverage of the Low Isles at a scale of 1:2500, which
was used extensively by the Yonge Expedition (Stephenson et al., 1931). In the
East Indies, Umbgrove (1928, 1929) was similarly discovering the usefulness of
aerial survey of reefs, a usefulness that was outlined by Steers (1945). However, only subsequent to World War II, and the widespread photography of
many Pacific Islands and reefs for military purposes, was reef photography
widely developed.

In 1945, R. W. Fairbridge and C. Teichert undertook an investigation for the
Royal Australian Air Force that involved photography of the northern Reef to
improve the accuracy of photo-interpretation of coral reefs. They concentrated
on the comprehensively mapped Low Isles and, subsequent to ground verifica-
tion, provided a new analysis of this reef (Fairbridge and Teichert, 1947; 1948;
Teichert and Fairbridge, 1950). These reconnaissance surveys prompted Fairbridge to review the whole question of coral reefs in Australia (1950, 1967). His
1950 paper, based on earlier work but incorporating the comprehensive view
obtained from the air, became the standard reference of the geomorphology of
the Great Barrier Reef. His interpretation of reef history is an integrated one,
his final conclusion stating:

> The Australian shelf reefs require the utilisation, at least of some parts, of a) the
> subsidence theory promulgated by Darwin, Dana, Davis, b) the antecedent plat-
> form theory as set forth by Wharton, Agassiz, Andrews, Vaughan, Hoffmeister and
> Ladd, and c) the glacial control theory of Penck, Daly and others.
>
> *Fairbridge, 1950, p. 394*

Thus Fairbridge reaffirms subsidence on the Queensland shelf, with faulting
playing a major part, and with the central area from Cairns to Townsville
showing greatest subsidence. He implies that most of the reefs postdate the
last low sea level, when coral growth at the southern limits of the reef was restricted. Foundations of reefs were on submerged fault scarps or ranges of
drowned hills, with major linear reef formations developing from fringing reefs
initiated at various stillstands in the postglacial transgression. Since modern
sea level was first achieved Fairbridge believed that the whole reef has experienced a eustatic lowering of sea level. However, he suggested that the present
shape of reefs is controlled principally by winds, waves, and currents.

Fairbridge's 1950 paper highlighted many research problems requiring investigation on the Great Barrier Reef, but there were few scientists in the 1950s
either equipped or financed to carry out such work. This resulted largely from
problems of working on the Great Barrier that still exist today. In addition to
the basic problem of working in an environment that is largely intertidal or
submarine, the distance offshore of the Reef from most centers of settlement
and the persistence of strong winds during much of the winter field season
have made scientific work of all kinds difficult and expensive. Islands situated
on the Reef have always been utilized as bases but the majority are situated
either at the southern end of the Reef (Bunker–Capricorn Group) or north of
Cairns, there being only one vegetated reef island, as opposed to high continental island, on the 1000 km of Great Barrier Reef between the Swains Reefs in

the south and Cairns. High islands have thus been used of necessity for research stations, although the best known was located by the Great Barrier Reef Committee in 1951 on the vegetated cay at Heron Island at the southern extremity of the Reef, and the Australian Museum and Sydney University have run a research station on One Tree Island (another cay of the same Bunker–Capricorn Group) since 1966 (Mather and Talbot, 1975). More recently the Australian Museum has set up a research station on Lizard Island, a high island on the northern Reef strategically located halfway between the mainland and the outer Reefs, and James Cook University of North Queensland in 1978 has initiated a research station at Orpheus Island, another high island in the Palm Group north of Townsville.

Not surprisingly the establishment of the research station at Heron Island concentrated further work on the southern end of the reef. In terms of understanding the processes and evolution of the Reef, however, the most significant work of the 1950s and 1960s was that of W. G. H. Maxwell and his graduate students, working on patterns of sedimentation. The results of this work are comprehensively seen in Maxwell's 1968 Atlas and in his later papers (e.g. Maxwell, 1973a, b). Although adding greatly to knowledge of the sedimentology of the Great Barrier Reef Province and its bathymetry and describing in greater detail than any previous author the variety and complexity of the reefs, (having available aerial photography of most the Province at a scale of approximately 1:63,360, which had been commenced by the Commonwealth Government in 1964), Maxwell relied heavily on circumstantial evidence for his geomorphological interpretation. This is particularly true of the reconstruction of submarine drainage systems, recent seismological work showing that where channels were incised into the continental shelf at low sea level stages, they have been completely infilled by more recent sedimentation (e.g., Orme and Flood, 1977). A further dilemma faced by Maxwell was the problem of Holocene sea levels, particularly as he suggested that the entire reef framework was built during the postglacial transgression (Maxwell, 1973a, p. 266). Submerged terraces and reef stratigraphy were correlated with stillstands in the Fairbridge (1960) sea level curve. By also referring to Shepard's (1964) and Curray's (1964) sea-level curves, Maxwell (1973a, Fig. 6) was clearly aware of the divergence of opinion on the nature of the postglacial transgression, but was unable at that time to resolve the problem in the context of the Great Barrier Reef.

Unfortunately Maxwell's work on sedimentology was not paralleled by other projects related to Great Barrier Reef evolution during the 1950s and 1960s. Major advance in knowledge of reef development came from elsewhere, particularly from oceanic atoll locations that were used as nuclear testing sites. United States Geological Survey work on Enewetak and Bikini atolls and related studies of other existing coral reefs and raised reefs in the Pacific (e.g. Midway and the Marianas) together with the great advances made in marine carbonate research in the Caribbean, have provided a baseline for coral reef studies throughout the world. Parallel work has been undertaken by the French, similarly stimulated by detailed investigation of the Muroroa atoll nuclear testing site but extending over much of the southwest Pacific largely under the auspices of the Office de la Recherche Scientifique et Technique

Outre-Mer (ORSTOM). Greater ease of travel over the last 20 years and the setting up of institutions in areas where coral reefs exist have generally helped to stimulate research into all aspects of coral reefs. So too has the development of new techniques (see, e.g., Stoddart and Johannes, 1978) including radiometric dating and improved methods of seismic survey and drilling that provide new insight into the coral reef structures which W. M. Davies had referred to as "inscrutable." Advances in the knowledge of and interest in coral reefs may be gauged from the Proceedings of the International Coral Reef Symposia held at four-year intervals (1969, Mandapam Camp, India; 1973 Great Barrier Reef Australia; 1977 Miami, United States; 1981, Manila, Philippines).

Thus it is not surprising to find that after a period of comparative neglect, the Great Barrier Reef is receiving renewed attention from researchers. A specific stimulus has been the 1973 Royal Society–Universities of Queensland (University of Queensland and James Cook University of North Queensland) Expedition to the northern Great Barrier Reef led by Dr. D. R. Stoddart, which has continued the long-standing relationship that the Royal Society of London and the University of Cambridge Department of Geography has had with the Australian reef. The main aim of the expedition was to elucidate the recent history of the reefs, especially in response to Holocene sea level change. Evidence was sought from shallow coring, geophysical surveys, studies of reef and interreef sediments, observations of modern reef communities and the analysis of the geology and geomorphology of reefs and islands (Stoddart et al., 1978a, b). Work immediately before and subsequent to the 1973 Expedition has continued similar investigations, but over a wider area of the reef. Of particular note is the work of P. J. Davies of the Bureau of Mineral Resources and his associates and G. R. Orme and colleagues of Queensland University on the southernmost reefs. The work of these and other researchers is combined in this book with that of the present author and his postgraduate students in analyzing the present morphology of the Great Barrier Reef.

BASIC PREMISES IN THE ORGANIZATION OF THIS BOOK

The advance of knowledge in the field of Quaternary geology and geomorphology, and specifically in the area of coral reef research as outlined above, provides a starting point for the present study. The premises upon which it is built and which are validated within the text are essentially those stated by Stoddart et al. (1978b) in the synthesis of the results of the 1973 Expedition, but include others that are also developed within this book. It is now widely accepted that:

1 The foundations of the Great Barrier Reef are at least Miocene in age, and suggest some continental shelf subsidence since initial foundation.

2 Extensive glacio-eustatic variations of sea level took place in the Quaternary. Sea level was last at or above its present position about 125,000 years ago and subsequently oscillated below its present position reaching a minimum level of about -130 m 18,000–20,000 years ago.

3 Once emerged by a negative movement of sea level, reefs are relatively persistent structures, subject to superficial modification but retaining their gross forms.

4 The melting of the continental ice sheets from about 18,000 yrs B.P. produced a transgression over a 10,000 yr period at an average rate of at least 10 m/1000 yrs.

5 The growth potential of reefs, dependent upon the rate of calcium carbonate production suggests that reefs could not keep pace with the major part of the transgression.

6 Partly because of "isostatic decantation" of water from areas rebounding after ice load has been removed and partly because of worldwide differential adjustments of the crust to the new water load, there has been a continuation of land-sea modification subsequent to the completion of major ice sheet melting by 7000 yrs B.P., resulting in differences in the Holocene sea level on both continental and local scales.

7 Complex organogenic structures of calcium carbonate, coral reefs are influenced by their environment both in an ecological sense and by physical and chemical postmortem modifications to the biogenic sediments.

In order to ascertain the variable importance and geographical variation of these factors on the development of the Great Barrier Reef, the following chapters will be developed from the observable environment and processes of the present to the reconstruction of the past evolution. Chapter 2 deals with the environment of the Great Barrier Reef province; Chapters 3, 4, and 5 with the biological, physical, and chemical processes; Chapters 6, 7, and 8 with the Reef's evolution in terms of antecedent platforms, sea-level changes, and reef responses; and Chapters 9 through 12 with the resultant morphology of the modern reefs. The final chapter compares the present morphology and evolution of the Great Barrier Reef to reef provinces elsewhere, noting the regional variations in reef geomorphology that exist within the intertropical zone.

In 1935, Hoffmeister and Ladd wrote:

Probably no single theory will explain all reefs. Certainly recognition of the complexity of the problem is essential to its solution. It does not belong within the realm of any one subject but requires the attention of scientists of many fields, each contributing his share.

In the following pages it is the interpretation of a geomorphologist that is given. The complexity of the problem is recognized, even within the single reef province of the Great Barrier Reef, but it is hoped that a geomorphological interpretation can give answers to at least some of the problems of this vast area of coral reefs.

2

Environmental Factors Affecting Reef Evolution in the Great Barrier Reef Region

From 9°15'S the Great Barrier Reef extends southwards off the coast of Queensland to Lady Elliot Island at 24°07'S, a latitudinal spread of 14°52'. The outer perimeter of the reef province is about 2300 km. The outer reef varies greatly in distance from the mainland coast, approaching within 23 km at 14°S to a maximum of 260 km at 21°S. The whole reef province incorporates an area of approximately 230,000 km² (Pickard, 1977) within which lie over 2500 reefs (Bennett, 1971) varying in size from small isolated pinnacles to massive reefs of up to 25 km long and 125 km² in area. Not surprisingly, great regional variation is found in such a large area. Contrasts exist in geological structure, bathymetry, and past and present geomorphological processes operating on the exposed shelf during periods of glacially lowered sea levels, which help to explain many of the major differences in reef morphology. In addition, the wide latitudinal spread of the Great Barrier Reef necessarily encompasses several climatic zones and many aspects of hydrology and oceanography have significant zonal and cross-shelf variations that will influence reef growth at the present time. This chapter describes the major features of the Great Barrier Reef province and examines the most important environmental factors involved in their gross evolution. The diversity of environments over this enormous area of reef growth provides an ideal field laboratory for examining the varying influences that have been identified worldwide as important in the development of reef morphology.

GEOLOGICAL EVOLUTION

The geological history and resulting structure (Fig. 2.1) of eastern Queensland and adjacent parts of the Coral Sea have determined both the location of coral reefs and their time of initiation. The Australian continent occupies a central position on the Indo-Australian plate and has been a remarkably stable area of continental crust since at least Paleozoic times. The western three-quarters of the continent has been rigid since the late Precambrian. However, the eastern

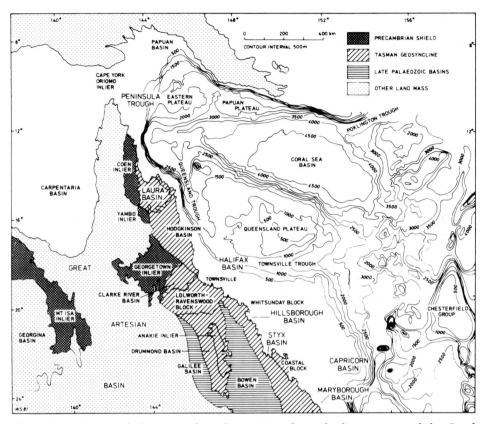

Figure 2.1 Structural elements of northeast Australia and adjacent parts of the Coral Sea.

part was more mobile in Paleozoic times and was the location of the Tasman Geosyncline, within which deposition was active until about 200 m.y. ago. These sediments were welded into northeastern Australia in two stages during tectonic movements and igneous intrusions of the Carboniferous–Early Permian and the early Triassic (Henderson and Stephenson, 1980; Benbow, 1980). The early Triassic landmass was possibly uplifted and remained emergent until partially inundated by the Aptian transgression of the Cretaceous in the Maryborough and Laura Basins (Smart and Senior, 1980).

Up to this stage Australia belonged to the massive Gondwanaland complex, the dismemberment of which commenced 150 m.y. ago (Veevers and McElhinny, 1976). By 53 m.y. ago at the end of the Paleocene, Australia separated from Antarctica and commenced moving northward at a rate of about 2 cm/yr (Carey, 1970). The Tasman Sea was brought into being when rift faulting along a north-south axis separated Australia from landmasses to the east and a little later the Coral Sea Basin was formed by similar rifting and sea floor spreading in the middle Eocene at a rate of about 5 cm/yr (Davies, 1975; Mutter, 1975). The great tensional forces resulting in this fracturing produced variable subsidence on the marginal Queensland and Marion Plateaus of the Coral Sea, and the sinking of the Queensland Plateau in particular had influence on the mainland shelf, with the Queensland Trough being formed by a tension fault system developing in the intermediate area (Davies, 1975).

Corals started growing on the Coral Sea Plateaus as they subsided beneath the sea as early as 60 m.y. ago. However, a widespread unconformity spanning late Eocene to mid-Oligocene times can be recognized on all plateaus. This is also recognized within the basins and has been attributed by Taylor and Falvey (1977) to the commencement of a significant equatorial circulation pattern in the developing Coral Sea Basin and its subsiding plateaus. Stabilization of this circulation by mid-Oligocene times permitted extensive coral reef development on residual basement highs of the marginal plateaus and eventually, by 18 m.y. ago on the subsiding Queensland continental shelf, although many areas of the shelf may not have subsided and obtained a reef cover until late Tertiary or even Quaternary times (Lloyd, 1977; Benbow, 1980). For example, Davies (1975) has suggested that the Bunker High at the southern end of the Great Barrier Reef may have remained above sea level until one million years ago.

At the same time as the Coral Sea Basin was opening, the easternmost areas of Queensland were subjected to uplift, and Cenozoic volcanic activity was widespread along and to the east of what is now the Main Divide (Stephenson et al., 1980). Accelerated erosion caused by this uplift has been largely controlled by the NNW–SSE structural and lithologic trends of the old Tasman geosyncline. These same structural trends extend beneath the surficial sediments and reefs of the continental shelf, which is composed of continental crust. The geology of the shelf is thus closely related to the onshore geology of Queensland (Lloyd, 1977). The transition from continental to oceanic crust takes place near the base of the continental slope in water depths of about 4.5 km (Taylor and Falvey, 1977). The shelf itself is complex and the Reef area is underlaid by seven basins and intervening highs that are either wholly or in part offshore. From north to south the basins are the Peninsula Trough (Jurassic to Recent), Laura Basin (Permian to Cretaceous), Halifax Basin (Cretaceous to Recent), Hillsborough Basin (Early to Middle Tertiary), Styx Basin (Cretaceous), Capricorn Basin (Cretaceous to Recent) and the Maryborough Basin (Jurassic to Tertiary). This structure has a marked influence on regional bathymetry and reef growth.

GEOMORPHOLOGY OF THE MAINLAND COAST

A brief review of the geomorphology of the mainland coast is of relevance to the Great Barrier Reef. As the contiguous region to the Reef Province it provides information on the geomorphic evolution, particularly in terms of sea levels, climate, and neotectonics, that is of direct relevance to reef evolution. Further, the mainland provides, through runoff, a source of sediments and freshwater, both of which may provide major restraints on reef growth and mineral nutrients that enter the biological food chain of the continental shelf.

Evolution of the Major Relief Features

The eastern coastal zone of northeastern Australia is backed by a nearly continuous main scarp varying in altitude up to 1611 m in Mount Bartle Frere near Innisfail, with numerous residual or fault-block coastal hills and ranges, the majority of which are aligned parallel to the regional NNW–SSE structural trend (Fig. 2.2). The coastline is generally parallel to this trend and, apart from comparatively short stretches such as near Cape Conway, south of Cairns, and around Cape Tribulation, is separated from the main escarpment by a coastal plain of mostly Quaternary sediments, varying in width up to 50 km. Where the coastline cuts across the regional structural trend, wider coastal plains are associated with embayed coastlines, as, for example, behind Princess Charlotte Bay, in the Townsville to Bowen area and around Broad Sound.

The origins of the eastern coastal escarpment and subparallel coastal ranges have been a matter of debate for at least 70 years. Hypotheses range from the disruption of a duricrusted Tertiary land surface of subdued relief by Cenozoic faulting (Taylor, 1911; de Keyser et al, 1965; Paine, 1972; Murray, 1975a, b), warping of this land surface along meridionally aligned flexure axes (Davis, 1917; Stephenson, 1970), to differential erosion of lithologic and structural units of the Tasman geosyncline (Marks, 1925; Bryan, 1925; Jardine, 1928a; King, 1962). It is probable that all three mechanisms are involved in the formation of the physiography of the coastal zone of eastern Queensland. Lithologic control of relief appears widespread with granites and volcanics generally forming the upland areas. However, elsewhere, for example in the Ingham area, de Keyser et al. (1965) have shown that physiographic units are independent of lithology. In the Proserpine region, on the margins of the Hillsborough Basin, fault lines clearly control the corridor systems (Clarke, et al., 1971).

The main earth movements, whether faulting or warping, have long been regarded as Plio-Pleistocene in age, part of the tectonic event that affected the whole of eastern Australia, and termed the Kosciusko Period by Andrews (1910). Ollier (1977, 1978) has reviewed more recent evidence of landscape evolution, including the isotopic dating of basalts extruded during the uplift period. This indicates that the uplift of the eastern highlands, and by analogy the subsidence of the continental shelf, commenced well before the Pliocene. Wellman (1974) considers that the movements may have commenced even in the Mesozoic and that the last major uplift took place in the Oligocene. However, there is some evidence to suggest that movements took place well into the Cenozoic and possibly into the Quaternary. Clarke, et al., (1971), for example, suggest that Quaternary adjustments have taken place along the faults of the Whitsunday area. Although regarded as aseismic, earthquakes have been recorded in the Tasman geosynclinal region (Doyle et al., 1968; Denham, 1976) and it is not unreasonable to assume that small movements may still be taking place. No earthquake greater than magnitude 6 on the Richter scale has been known to occur in eastern Australia but several medium-sized earthquakes have caused moderate damage including the 1918 disturbance with an epicenter probably on the continental shelf north of Hervey Bay (Hedley, 1925d) and the Gayndah (southeast Queensland) disturbance of 1935 (Denham, 1976).

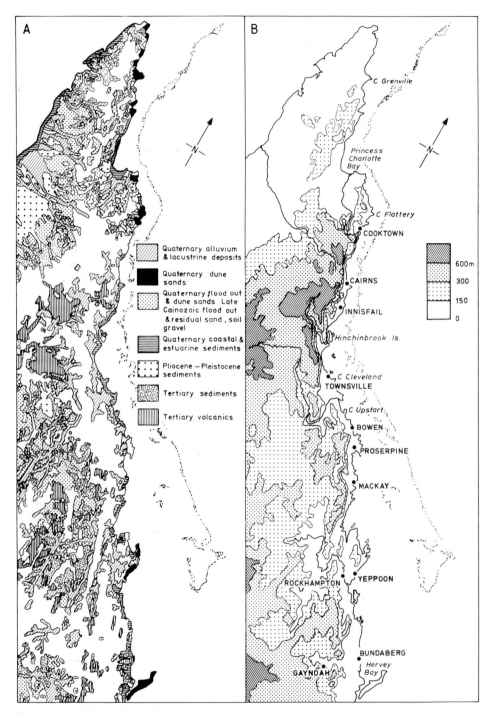

Figure 2.2 (*A*) Quaternary deposits. (*B*) Relief of the mainland opposite the Great Barrier Reef.

If volcanic activity is considered as synchronous with uplift (Wyatt and Webb, 1970; Ollier, 1977) then the evidence for earth movements extending into the Quaternary is even more convincing. Wellman and McDougall (1974) have shown that Cenozoic volcanic activity commenced about 70 million years ago in eastern Australia, continuing into the Quaternary with episodes in each volcanic region lasting about 5 million years. In North Queensland radiometric ages of basalts indicate major eruptions during the Pliocene and the youngest flows and pyroclastics are probably little more than 10,000 years old (Wyatt and Webb, 1970; Stephenson and Griffin, 1976; Stephenson et al., 1980). Eruptions have certainly taken place in the coastal zone during the evolution of the Great Barrier Reef. The Pleistocene pyroclastics of Maer and adjacent islands in Torres Strait contain occasional limestone fragments. An offshore volcanic center is also preserved at Stephens Island in the Barnard Group near Innisfail, and several scoria cones in the Cairns to Innisfail area and between Gayndah and Biggenden are almost certainly Quaternary in age. Not only do these volcanics suggest that earth movements have been active during even the latter phases of the evolution of the Great Barrier Reef, but there is a strong possibility that volcanics may be interbedded with reefal limestones in some areas.

Coastal Plain Deposits

The coastal plains and corridors of the Queensland coast are underlaid by unconsolidated deposits. Their total thicknesses are unknown over many parts of the coastal plain but the available information suggests that 30 m to over 150 m of sediment has accumulated in the major deltas. Most are assumed to be of Quaternary age. These deposits are the result of two contrasting processes: erosion of the main escarpment and coastal ranges in response to fluctuating climatic and eustatic conditions; and the pulsatory production of littoral, marine, and carbonate sediments on the continental shelf in response to the fluctuating sea levels. Terrigenous and carbonate sediments thus interdigitate over the inner shelf as a consequence of the marine transgressions and regressions of the Quaternary (Coventry et al., 1980).

By far the largest proportion of coast plain sediments is alluvial or colluvial in origin. In the Townsville area, where they have been studied in greatest detail (Hopley and Murtha, 1975) the surface deposits are considered to be no older than the last interglacial (c. 125,000 yrs B.P.) and it is likely that the underlying deposits are all of Quaternary age. They overlie a bedrock surface eroded during periods of low sea level. An older alluvial unit is the major component of the plain and consists predominantly of gently sloping alluvial fans and plains with some infilled stream channels; the sediments are often more than 40 m thick. Riverine silcrete (Grant and Aitchison, 1970) is associated with many of the older-stream channel deposits; at a number of localities it dips beneath Holocene beach ridges and outcrops on the lower beach. Hopley and Murtha (1975) provided a tentative chronology for these coastal plain deposits, which correlated with Kershaw's (1978) paleoclimatic reconstruction from the Atherton Tableland 250 km to the north. The pattern is one of fan accumulation and increased drainage density during more arid phases and severe weathering and fine-grained fluvial deposition in wetter times. The latest dry phase appears to have coincided with the maximum of the last glaciation.

The deposits of the Townsville area are typical of the coastal plains elsewhere in northeastern Australia (see, e.g., Hopley, 1972). In the Cairns area Bird (1970a, b) has described piedmont deposits trimmed by the sea at the foot of the Macalister Range and colluvial deposits passing beneath the Barron River delta to which he assigned a late Pleistocene age. In the Shoalwater Bay area Galloway (1972) reported deposition of similar extensive gravelly fans over the coastal plain during the late Cenozoic and suggested they extended down below present sea level. However, in this area the basal deposits, which are cemented and ferruginized, have been assigned an upper Tertiary age, mainly on the basis of their weathering crusts (Kirkegaarde et al., 1970; Malone et al., 1969; Burgis, 1974). In only one area of the coastal plains of the northeastern seaboard does it appear possible that a fuller record of the Quaternary, and possibly even the Tertiary-Quaternary boundary, is preserved at or close to the present surface. This is on the extensive depositional plains along the Normanby River within the Laura Basin where a much larger sequence of fans and alluvial deposits has been recognized (de Keyser and Lucas, 1968).

Along the river valleys incised into the main escarpment, major terrace sequences have developed but none have been studied in detail. Although minor terraces on the lower reaches of many streams may be the result of eustatic changes of sea level, the majority appear related to climatic change and its associated sediment yield and hydrological variations. Tectonism may also have contributed to the development of some of the sequences by minor uplift of the land.

A tropical climate with intense seasonal rainfall and a deeply weathered, uplifted hinterland is ideally suited to produce large fluvial sediment yields. Not surprisingly, therefore, the major rivers are associated with extensive deltaic or estuarine infill deposits. The Burdekin, draining 129,000 km^2, enters the sea across Australia's largest cuspate delta. Deltaic deposits are generally more than 70 m deep and reach a maximum depth of more than 150 m (Hopley, 1970a). The Fitzroy River, draining 140,000 km^2, has an estuarine infill 3-18 km wide and at least 45 m thick (Reid, 1946), while the deltaic deposits of the Pioneer River at Mackay are up to 30 m thick (Jensen et al., 1963), the Herbert at Ingham 93 m thick, and the Barron at Cairns at least 40 m thick (Bird, 1970a). Clearly the major rivers have been introducing massive amounts of sediment to the coast and shelf during the Quaternary.

Depositional shorelines dominate the coast of northeastern Australia. A narrow fringe of beach ridges, consisting of quartz sands, up to 5 m high occurs along all coastlines exposed to the prevailing southeasterly or easterly winds (Fig. 2.3). The ridges are usually less than 400 m wide except close to river mouths where wider ridge sequences may be found. The majority of beach-ridge systems overlie older Pleistocene coastal plain sediments and are of Holocene age. The earliest of the Holocene ridges appear to have been deposited between 5000 and 6000 yrs B.P., the time at which modern sea level was first achieved in the Holocene in this area (Coventry et al., 1980). Inner barriers of presumed Pleistocene age are much less continuous than elsewhere in eastern Australia. However small remnants of such shorelines do exist along

Figure 2.3 Upstart Bay is typical of much of the coastline opposite the Great Barrier Reef. An inner barrier of late Pleistocene age (foreground) is separated from the sea by salt pan, mangroves, and Holocene sand ridges.

the entire coastline. Most are low sandy ridges with podzol soil profiles, and although only background radiocarbon dates have been obtained from them, their height just above modern sea level is strongly suggestive of a last interglacial age (Coventry et al., 1980). Multiple barriers such as those described from southern Australia (e.g. Cook et al., 1977) are not found along the northeastern coast of Australia except behind Cowley Beach near Innisfail, where at least three systems appear to have survived.

Large dunes tend to be the exception rather than the rule on the coast of tropical Queensland south of Cooktown. Beach ridges, with or without small eolian cappings, are the dominant barrier forms on lowland coasts except towards the northern ends of arcuate bays where there is greater exposure to prevailing southeasterly winds (Bird and Hopley, 1969) (Fig. 2.4). This lack of dune development is the combined result of the reduced incidence of sand-moving winds in comparison with temperate coasts (Jennings, 1965) and, perhaps more importantly, the lack of an abundant sand supply away from river mouths. The large dunefields that occur north of Cooktown on Cape York Peninsula owe their formation to an unusually abundant sand supply provided by Mesozoic sandstones, which outcrop widely in the area (Bird, 1965). These dunefields, which cover an area of 700 km^2 at Cape Flattery and 400 km^2 at Cape Grenville, consist largely of elongate parabolic dunes up to 5 km

Figure 2.4 Massive sand dunes on the northern end of Hinchinbrook Island. Dunes of this size are generally rare. Recent work (Australian Institute of Marine Science, 1979) suggests that Holocene dunes have formed over a large Pleistocene sand body.

in length and over 100 m in height. Many of the dunes are stabilized beneath heath, scrub, or vine forest (Story, 1970; Pedley and Isbell, 1971), but up to 15% of the Cape Flattery dunefield consists of active dunes and a further 10% comprises swamps and lakes enclosed between the trailing arms of the dunes (Galloway, 1970b). Several generations of dunes are evident but their evolutionary history is not clear (Pye in Coventry et al., 1980).

On sheltered coastlines, particularly on the lee of headlands, fine-grained deposition dominates, coasts are fringed by mangroves, and chenier plains have been deposited during the Holocene (Fig. 2.5). They are particularly prominent around Princess Charlotte Bay, where the chenier plain is 25 km wide (Galloway, 1970b) and around Shoalwater Bay and Broad Sound, where the chenier plain is up to 20 km wide (Cook and Polach, 1973; Burgis, 1974; Cook and Mayo, 1977). Typically the plains consist of narrow chenier ridges of sands, fine gravels, and shell grit up to 2 m above the surrounding plain, which consists of grassland (mainly *Sporobulus virginicus*) towards the land and bare salt pan to seawards. Stratigraphy in the Broad Sound area (Burgis, 1974) shows about 3 m of Holocene sediments, the basal deposits being shallow-water marine muds, overlain by intertidal muds and sands, mangrove deposits, and finally high-tidal muds, which postdate the deposition of the cheniers. The deposits represent coastal progradation from the maximum of the Holocene transgression about 5000 years ago. The oldest chenier ridges in the area are more than 5000 years (Cook and Polach, 1973). According to Cook and Polach they formed during periods of low sediment supply leading to erosion of mangrove deposits and development of a ridge from the coarser lag materials. However, cheniers are also developed during low-frequency, high-energy events such as tropical cyclones (Hopley, 1974a).

Figure 2.5 Along coastline sheltered from the southeast, mangroves occur on the open coast with narrow 2–3 m high cheniers with intervening bare salt pan landward, Bowling Green Bay.

REGIONAL BATHYMETRY AND STRUCTURE OF THE CONTINENTAL SHELF

The most detailed discussion of the bathymetry of the Great Barrier Reef is that of Maxwell (1968) with further detail available only for the southernmost part of the region (Marshall, 1977). Bathymetric detail is important as an indicator of areas of potential reef growth at the present time, given the limiting depth factor (see Chapter 3), and as a basis for the reconstruction of shoreline location and paleogeography during the low sea level phases of the Quaternary. Major features of bathymetry and reef distribution are shown in Figure 2.6. The major feature is the contrast between the narrow, comparatively shallow northern shelf bordered by a sharp drop-off at the shelf edge, and the wider and deeper southern shelf with less steep margins and with reefal growth limited to the outer third of the shelf. For convenience the shelf may be divided into six regions.

Torres Strait to Cape Weymouth

The northernmost reefs of the Great Barrier Reef are located within sight of the coast of Papua–New Guinea. Massive amounts of freshwater flow and sediments from the Fly River are probably the cause of the lack of reefs in the Gulf of Papua (Winterer, 1970), which provides a break between the Great Barrier Reef and the contiguous reef system of Papua–New Guinea. Tanner (1969), however, suggested that tectonic subsidence was the cause, although any sub-

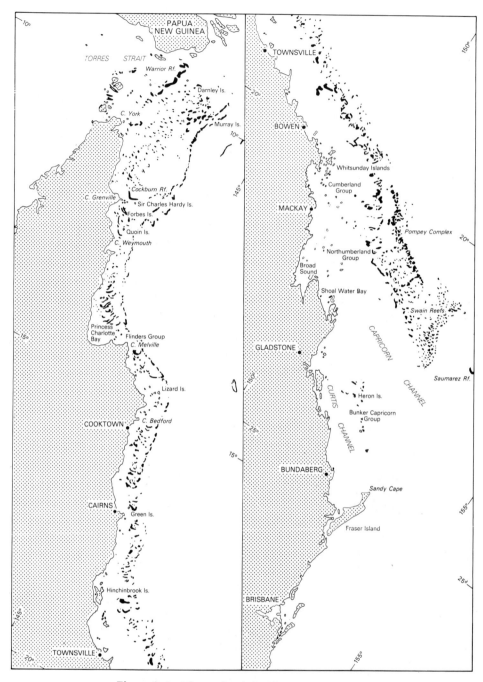

Figure 2.6 The reefs of the Great Barrier Reef.

sidence may be, in part, the result of isostatic loading by the huge sediment mass of the Fly River.

The far northern section of the Great Barrier Reef south to Cape Grenville at 11°57′S belongs to the widened continental shelf region of the Gulf of Papua. Opposite Cape Weymouth the outer edge of the shelf lies 50 km from the mainland but widens further north to over 150 km. Shelf depths are generally shallow, exceeding 50 m only near the shelf edge in deeper channels. The bathymetry and geomorphology of the area has been described by Jennings (1972a), who recognized a series of north to south zones (Fig. 2.7).

Figure 2.7 ERTS satellite photograph (MSS band 4) of the Torres Strait area. North of Cape York the high islands and massive reefs restrict tidal movement, the effects of which are clearly seen in reef orientation and sediment movement. The Warrior Reefs clearly separate this region from the region of smaller reefs to the east although the uncharted area in the upper right of the image shows a further zone of large irregular and lagoonal reefs separated by narrow channels. (NASA–ERTS)

The westernmost zone is the Torres Strait, which is extremely shallow, generally no more than 6–9 m deep, and contains the large continental islands of the Strait with massive east- to west-oriented reefs lying between them. The intervening narrow passes, 2–3 km wide, are rarely more than 12 m deep and are areas of strong tidal scour. The eastern edge of this zone is marked by a terrace break down to a 12–15 m level. Only small and isolated reefs are developed on this 12–15 m feature and continental rocks, mainly ignimbrites (Jones and Jones, 1956), are limited to small outcrops. However, to the east is a line of large reefs, including the Warrior Reefs, that appear to continue the line of the mainland of Cape York. Narrow channels up to 4.5 km wide and 27 m deep cut through the reefs and lead down to the next zone further east. This zone forms another terracelike feature between 20 and 30 m in depth, and extending southwards from the Bligh Entrance to form the inner shelf area as far south as Cape Weymouth. It contains a number of small oval reefs, many of which are island-capped. Recent satellite imagery shows the outer shelf to be occupied by a zone of complex and massive submerged reefs up to 60 km wide (Fig. 2.8). Only around Cape Grenville, on the western margins of the reef complex and around the high islands such as Quoin, Forbes, Sir Charles Hardy, and the Cockburns do the reefs reach modern sea level. Elsewhere depths average about 10 m. Towards its northern limit, in waters somewhat deeper than 35 m is a group of Pleistocene volcanic islands with fringing reefs, including the Murray Islands (an old crater rim being retained in Maer Island), Darnley and Stephens Islands, and the small outcrops of Black Rocks and Bramble Cay. A line of small broken reefs (deltaic reefs of Maxwell, 1970) occupy the outer edge of the shelf and form an effective barrier that is continued further south by the distinctive ribbon reefs. The continental slope drops away sharply to depths exceeding 600 m within 12 km. Small detached reefs rise from this slope within 25 km of the main barrier but are separated from it by water depths in excess of 250 m.

Bathymetry and reef distribution in the Torres Strait region is strongly controlled by structure. The outermost reefs have developed over a northern extension of the peninsula's structural high, of which the granites of the Cockburn Islands and Sir Charles Hardy Islands form the northernmost surface outcrop, and along the line of which in the north there has been Cenozoic volcanic activity. The 20 to 30 m open shelf to the east overlies the Peninsula Trough, with sedimentary rocks of probable Cretaceous age outcropping on a number of islands (Jones and Jones, 1956). The westernmost divisions, with continental islands, lie along the structural high of the Cape York–Oriomo Ridge.

Cape Weymouth to Cape Bedford

This area of the Great Barrier Reef is characterized by a narrow shelf generally no more than 50 km wide, and shallow bathymetry with depths in excess of 50 m being found only in the narrow channels between reefs on the outer shelf edge. Zonation across this part of the continental shelf has been described by Fairbridge (1950, 1967) and details of the area around Princess Charlotte Bay, where the shelf widens to 75 km, described by Frankel (1974). The inner shelf has a gentle slope seawards from the more steeply sloping Near Shore Zone of Maxwell (1968), in which sand movement is actively taking place, and which is characterized by shoals and sand ridges. Beyond it the inner-channel floor is

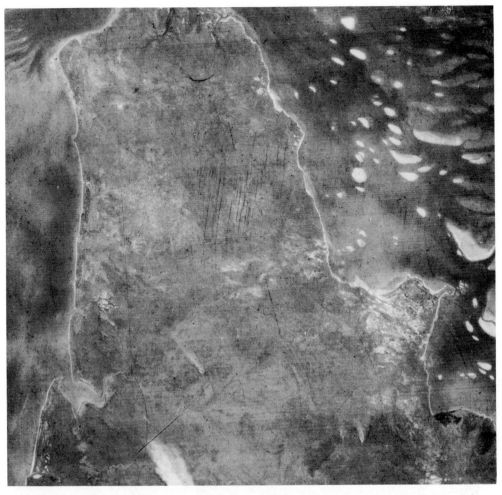

Figure 2.8 ERTS satellite photograph (MSS Band 4) of northern Cape York. Note the massive sand-dune complex near Cape Grenville and in areas further north and the sand banks related to tidal currents through Torres Strait (top left). Inner reefs are clearly seen but complex patterns of submerged reefs and intervening channels are just discernible (top right). (NASA–ERTS)

relatively featureless, ranging in depth from about 12 m near the mainland to 35 m near the large midshelf reefs. This inner channel is not entirely reefless and small ovoid reefs up to 4 km in diameter rise from it. Many are capped by distinctive low wooded islands (see Chap. 11). To the east the shelf deepens to 30 to 40 m, but many large reefs rise from these depths. In the Princess Charlotte Bay area they include some of the largest reefs of the whole Great Barrier Reef province. These reefs extend to within 20 km of the mainland. Beyond them the shelf maintains a depth of about 40 m, but is relatively reefless. However, occupying much of the outer shelf and marked by a sharp rise on both western and eastern sides, is an area of reefal shoal with depths within the range 20–25 m. This zone may be relatively continuous, broken only by larger channels of about 40 m depth that lead to main passes between the ribbon reefs. On some of these shoals a few irregular reef patches reach the surface. However, near Cape Melville, crescent-shaped reefs rise from the inner rim of the shoal (Fig. 2.9).

The shelf edge is occupied by a continuous line of linear or ribbon reefs. These reefs, up to 28 km long, are separated by narrow passes, most of which are less than 1 km in width. The majority of reefs are between 400 and 600 m wide. The back-reef area consists of a steeply inclined detrital sand ramp sloping into water depths of about 14 m, from which rise isolated massive coral colonies. The continental slope off this part of the reef drops away very sharply from depths less than 50 m to greater than 500 m within a few hundred meters

Figure 2.9 ERTS satellite photograph (MSS Band 5) Princess Charlotte Bay to Cape Bedford. The outer ribbon reefs are clearly discernible as are also the Howick and Turtle Groups of reefs. Lizard Island can be seen midshelf on the right of the photograph. On the mainland the major dune complex of Cape Flattery is seen lower right. The salt pan, mangrove, and chenier coastline of Princess Charlotte Bay is also clearly seen. (NASA–ERTS)

horizontal distance. Depths of at least 1000 m are found within a kilometer of the shelf edge.

High continental islands are few in this area of the Reef. The northern section of the shelf between Cape Weymouth and Princess Charlotte Bay is structurally part of the Mesozoic Laura basin and the Flinders Group of islands and the nearby outcrop on Clack Reef are composed of Lower Cretaceous sandstone, indicative of their position on the eastern margin of the basin. South of Cape Melville the shelf is essentially pre-Mesozoic basement composed of steeply folded and partly metamorphozed Paleozoic rocks, into which Permian granites, which form a few high islands, have been intruded.

Cape Bedford to Hinchinbrook Island

South of Cape Bedford the bathymetry of the continental shelf becomes simpler, due in part to the lack of large submerged reefal shoals. This is a critical area for understanding the geomorphology of the Great Barrier Reef, for it marks the southernmost extension of both the low wooded island reefs of the inner shelf and the ribbon reefs of the outer shelf, although submerged counterparts of these latter reefs extend as far south as latitude 17°20'S. The inner shelf extends from the active near-shore zone to the 36 m isobath, a line that coincides with the start of reef development on the shelf. On average, this lies 25 km from the mainland but comes within 11 km off Cape Grafton. This inner shelf is comparatively featureless, except for a number of high continental islands.

Coral reefs occupy the outer 50% of the continental shelf and although not large are closely and evenly spaced over the shelf. Between the reefs the shelf slopes evenly from 36 m to about 60 m on the outer shelf, the continental slope dropping away sharply from this depth into the Queensland Trough to 200 m within 1 km and over 1000 m within 10 km. Reefs reaching to the present sea surface extend out to the 60 m isobath, but beyond this are a number of submerged shoals close to the shelf edge, with a linear morphology parallel to the shelf edge, and which closely resemble the ribbon reefs of further north.

Hinchinbrook Island to the Whitsunday Islands

From Hinchinbrook Island to the Whitsunday Islands the shelf trends northwest to southeast obliquely across the regional structure. It remains parallel to the mainland coast, which also changes its orientation, but widens to between 90 and 125 km. Continental islands, composed mainly of Paleozoic granites and acid volcanic rocks, rise steeply from the surrounding sea floor, but the inner shelf is featureless. Apart from island fringing reefs, this inner shelf lacks reef development. Even beyond the 45 m isobath 50–80 km from the mainland, which marks the inner limit of reef development, coral reefs that occupy only the outer 30% of the shelf are generally smaller and more widely spaced than on any other major section of the Great Barrier Reef (Sugden, 1972; Hopley, 1978a). The shelf remains gently sloping to the 40 m isobath where it steepens slightly to 70 m at the shelf edge, the outermost reefs rising from close to the shelf edge. The continental slope here is much gentler than further north, depths of 200 m only being achieved within 3 km of the initial breakaway. Depths exceed 1000 m beyond 40 km of the shelf edge, the continental slope levelling off beyond this onto the Queensland Plateau.

Whitsunday Islands to Swain Reefs

From opposite the Whitsunday Islands southward the continental shelf widens considerably from 120 km to 290 km at the southern end of the Swain Reefs, the result of the shelf margin maintaining a northwest to southeast alignment, while the mainland trends north-northwest to south-southeast. The mainland coastline is more embayed and irregular than further north and has strong structural control, particularly in the Whitsunday area, where complex horst-graben structures exist in Paleozoic and Mesozoic rocks adjacent to the Tertiary Hillsborough Basin, and on the Broad Sound and Shoalwater Bay areas, where fault blocks of Paleozoic rocks are also clearly defined. The uplifted blocks that form the peninsulas are continued seaward parallel to the coastal trend by the numerous continental islands of the Cumberland and Northumberland Groups.

Because of the abundance of islands and the high tidal range, the near-shore zone is highly complex and active. Maxwell (1968) has noted that the area is characterized by long, narrow sand ridges parallel to the direction of tidal currents and extending out to the 18 m isobath. However, beyond and between the high islands the inner shelf slopes steadily down to the 50 m isobath 85–140 km from the mainland. Beyond this line, and occupying the outer 30% of the shelf, are the coral reefs of the southern Great Barrier Reef, which, from just north of the Whitsunday Passage to the southern Pompey Complex, are the largest and most intricate of the whole province. Shelf depths between the reefs are generally between 50 and 65 m. However, greater depths are recorded in the narrow channels that cut through the larger reef complexes, especially the hard-line Pompey Complex where depths in excess of 90 m occur at channel junctions. The outer reefs of this complex are up to 200 km from the mainland coast but are set back from the shelf edge (Fig. 2.10). Between the main complex and the shelf edge are numerous small submerged reefs and reefal shoals. A prominent line of reefs normal to the shelf edge, the Pompey T-line, forms the southern margin of this large reef zone. Beyond this the Swain Reefs form a region of smaller patch reefs rising from depths of about 40 m.

The Swain Reefs and the Pompey Complex to the north are situated on the Swain High and are separated from the mainland by the topographic Capricorn Channel and the structural Capricorn Basin (Marshall, 1977). The outer shelf slope, which is locally steep, commences at about 60 m off the northern part of this region and from 50 m off the Swain Reef, but descends to depths of only 300–400 m onto the Marion Plateau from which the Saumarez Reefs rise. The Capricorn Channel forms a broad embayment to the south and southwest of the Swain Reefs and has very shallow gradients forming broad, flat plains with areas of large fossil sand waves (Marshall, 1977). Beyond the 600 m line the gradient increases and the sea floor descends gently into the northwestern Tasman Basin.

The Southern Great Barrier Reef—Bunker–Capricorn Groups

To the south of the Capricorn Channel the continental shelf narrows to less than 100 km. The inner 50 km of the shelf forms the Curtis Channel between the mainland and the Bunker–Capricorn Group. The sea floor is smoothly sloping with an average depth of 30 m. The continental slope commences at

Figure 2.10 ERTS satellite photograph (MSS Band 4) of Pompey Reef Complex. These massive reefs are characterized by complex lagoons and intricate interreef channel systems. (NASA–ERTS)

depths between 60 and 80 m and extends to a depth of 300 m, becoming steeper to the south.

In the north the Curtis Channel is narrowed by an east to west series of reefs extending 28 km west of Heron Island. These are considered to have been built on a structural high branching from the major Bunker high, trending northwest to southeast and separating the Maryborough and Capricorn Basins (Marshall, 1977). The reefs occupying the highs rise from water depths between 55 and 60 m and, in the Capricorn and Bunker Groups, all reach modern sea level. However, to the north is a series of shallow shoals described by Maiklem (1968a). Most, even the deepest at 42 m, have recognizable forereef and lagoonal morphological features and are thought to be drowned reef structures.

Outside the Bunker–Capricorn Group the shelf is a further 12–19 km wide, its edge being situated at about the 64 m isobath in the north and 78 m in the south. Marshall (1977) has recognized two significant terrace levels in this area, at depths of 57 and 64 m. Off Fraser Island these terraces also possess banks that have been interpreted by Marshall as drowned reefal shoals. Further east, at depths between 96 and 103 m, is yet a further series of apparently drowned Pleistocene reefs on the continental slope.

The northern end of Fraser Island is only 21 km from the shelf edge. The great sand volume that constitutes this island reflects a strong south-to-north littoral drift, which is continued north of Sandy Cape for a further 30 km as Breaksea Spit. This dangerous shoal area consists of dead coral and sandbanks, including a series of asymmetric sand waves that are moving sediment eastward along the inner side of the spit, and extends to the edge of the continental shelf. Sand buildup on the edge of the shelf and on the upper continental slope is periodically removed by storm waves into a series of canyon heads, which may be still actively downcutting (Krause, 1967; Marshall, 1977). Continual transport of sediment to the shelf edge and eventually down into the Tasman abyssal plain effectively cuts off any movement of sediment northward.

Discussion

A number of important features of the Great Barrier Reef emerge from this regional description of bathymetry:

1 There is a general deepening of the continental shelf from north to south. During Pleistocene low sea level periods the northern shelf would thus have been exposed for the longest time, while the southern shelf margins would have been transgressed by the relatively higher sea levels of interstadial periods, a factor that is expanded in Chapter 6.

2 The width of the continental shelf also widens from north to south and the zone of reef development diverges from the mainland coast. Northern reefs are thus more prone to mainland influences in the form of terrigenous sediments and runoff.

3 The continental slope is generally steeper and extends to greater depths in the north compared to the south. At the lowest levels of the sea during the Pleistocene this would have meant that the depth zone suitable for coral growth on the outer shelf margin in the north would have been very narrow, and biogenic sediments produced by the reefal structures would have been rapidly transported downslope to great depths. Based on bathymetry alone, the southern shelf would have provided a greater area for coral growth even at the lowest of Pleistocene sea levels.

This review has not examined the minute details of shelf bathymetry, or attempted to identify submerged shoreline features or drainage lines as, for example, Fairbridge (1950, 1967) and Maxwell (1968, 1973a) have done. Both these authors recognized older strandlines that they considered to have had a strong influence on subsequent reef development. However, as discussed in Chapter 6, variations of several meters are recognized along the Queensland coast in the heights of both last interglacial (c. 125,000 yrs B.P.) and mid-Holocene (c. 5000 yrs B.P.) shorelines where topographic features are visible and known in detail. Over most of the Great Barrier Reef province, soundings are at least hundreds of meters apart or limited to widely spaced echo-sounding traverses. Interpretation of closely spaced shorelines of late Pleistocene age is also made difficult by the amount of Holocene sedimentation, which over parts of the shelf is in the order of several meters, as shown by recent continuous seismic profiling. Bottom contours may thus not represent the Pleistocene or early Holocene features that are now buried beneath later sediments. A further factor is the short time available for formation of these shorelines, in some cases only a few hundred years. Current knowledge of rates of process suggest that there is insufficient time for erosion of the shoreline features indicated by Maxwell, even in unconsolidated deposits, while the intricate and indented nature of the shorelines as mapped (Maxwell, 1968, Fig. 22*a–e*) is such that they are unlikely to be depositional. Present depositional shorelines along the Queensland coast are straight or zeta-curved in plan. It is considered that only in the southernmost area of the reef, particularly around the Bunker–Capricorn Group is sufficient detail of shelf bathymetry and structure known to enable identification of continuous strandlines. Elsewhere detail is limited to specific sites or lines of transect and correlation between these is not tenable at the present time.

Similar arguments can be made against reconstruction of low sea-level river courses across the shelf during low sea-level periods such as that of Maxwell (1968, 1973a). Continuous seismic profiles show that such channels do exist, but that the depth of Holocene or late Pleistocene infill is sufficient to mask their former location (see Chap. 7). Further bathymetric detail and knowledge of the sediment cover over the shelf from continuous seismic profiling is required before accurate mapping of either submerged shorelines or drainage lines is possible.

CLIMATE AND WEATHER

Atmospheric climate, often through the intermediary medium of the ocean, ultimately controls the energetics of the Great Barrier Reef region. It is not possible, however, to refer to a single climate of the Great Barrier Reef for, with such a wide latitudinal spread, several climatic zones are included along the Queensland coast. The most persistent feature is the dominance of the southeast trade winds along the entire length of the Reef. Strong seasonality of climate is also experienced, even on the wettest coast south of Cairns, where a summer rainfall maximum, though not as pronounced as in the areas to north and south, is still experienced. Cooler winter temperatures produce a thermal seasonality towards the southern limits of the Great Barrier Reef. Tropical cyclones may be experienced in any part of the province and form a most important influence on reef morphology.

Weather Dynamics

A winter dry season is a major feature of the climate, which is dominated by anticyclones crossing the continent at about 30°S with a prevalent high-pressure ridge along the Queensland coast. Subsidence is the dominant vertical motion but orographic rainfall may result from the lifting of the prevailing southeasterlies, particularly over the higher ranges south of Cairns that lie normal to this air stream. Upper air disturbances and transient cold fronts pushed up from the south are responsible for winter rainfall at the southern end of the Great Barrier Reef (Stewart, 1973). At the surface in summer, low pressure predominates, although a weak ridge along the coast is still a frequent feature of the charts. The surface flow is damper and moister than in winter and convectional activity increases. From December to March a most important synoptic feature is the Intertropical Convergence Zone (ITCZ). The southward movement of the ITCZ is associated with the large scale convergence of very moist air masses from the southeast and northwest. The heaviest rain occurs along and equatorward of the ITCZ. Surface disturbances associated with the ITCZ include tropical cyclones that are prolific rain producers.

Solar Radiation, Temperatures and Evaporation

Incoming solar radiation levels over the Great Barrier Reef are high for an oceanic area, the average daily amount exceeding 500 mW/hr/cm^{-2}, with a strong seasonal pattern (Bureau of Meteorology, 1975). Maximum radiation is received towards the end of the year when average daily rates exceed 650 mW/hr/cm^{-2} along all except the southernmost Great Barrier Reef. Variations in cloudiness play an important part in influencing the changes in solar radiation, which is a compromise between the sun's angle and the cloud cover. The persistence of cloud over the orographic coast around Innisfail reduces the amount of radiation received. However, elsewhere, the figures for Townsville indicate the nature of the sunshine record over the Reef. Over an 18-year period the annual average of overcast conditions was only 9.9 days while mean daily hours of sunshine vary from 6.7 hours in February to 9.5 hours in October (Oliver, 1978b).

The hottest month over the southern half of the reef tends to be January, but, because of cloud cover, December may be the hottest over the northern half. Average maximum January temperatures (Fig. 2.11A) over the southern reef are less than 30°C but are between 30° and 33°C further north. The summer temperature gradient is thus azonal and the extreme high temperatures found inland do not occur on the coast. As indicated in Fig. 2.11A most coastal locations have recorded extreme temperatures in excess of 40°C. Exceptions are the tip of Cape York and stations situated on promontories extending out into Barrier Reef waters (Cape Capricorn, Bustard Head, Cape Moreton) where extreme temperatures are between 35° and 39°C. Only one offshore island station, Lady Elliot Island, has records available and here the extreme is a modest 32.2°C. At Willis Island, situated 420 km out in the Coral Sea, the maximum is also relatively low at 34.4°C (Bureau of Meteorology, 1969). It is unlikely therefore that temperatures ever exceed 38°C over the waters of the outer reefs.

In contrast to the summer thermal gradient, that for winter is clearly zonal. Mean maximum temperatures range from about 21°C at the southern end of the reef to 30°C off Cape York. However, in terms of biological controls, mini-

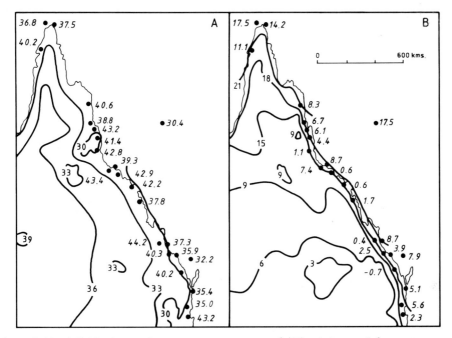

Figure 2.11 (A) Maximum January temperatures and (B) minimum July temperatures (°C). Absolute maxima and minima for coastal stations are also shown.

mum temperatures are probably more significant. Average minimum isotherms in July (Fig. 2.11B) while zonal over most of Australia, tend to be parallel to the coast of Queensland. These temperatures range from 12°C off Fraser Island to just over 21°C at Cape York. Extreme minima are much lower. Frosts are common on the highlands even as far north as the Atherton Tableland, where Herberton has recorded a minimum of −5°C (Oliver, 1978a). Even in the coastal plains only a few kilometers from the sea as far north as Townsville ground temperatures may fall below zero. A grass temperature of −4.9°C has been recorded at Brisbane (Gentilli, 1971). Extreme minima are indicated in Figure 2.11B. Again the ameliorating influence of the sea may be seen. While temperatures below freezing have been recorded at coastal stations as far north as Mackay, stations on promontories have extreme minima 4–6°C higher than adjacent inland areas. This influence is illustrated by the Bundaberg area at the southern limit of the reef. Extreme minima at Bundaberg, 12 km from the sea, Bustard Head on the coast and Lady Elliot Island 83 km off the coast are −0.7°, 3.9°, and 7.9°C respectively. Occasional incursion of cold air producing extremely low temperatures is limited to south of Cairns. Extreme minima rise rapidly north of Cairns (6.1°C) to Thursday Island (17.5°C).

Evaporation, as a result of the thermal regime, has important influences on salinity levels of the sea surface. Standard evaporation pan measurement at Townsville exceed mean rainfall totals in all months except January, February, and March. Maximum rates are recorded between October and December when monthly totals exceed 200 mm along the entire Reef. Average annual totals vary from about 2000 mm at the southern limit in the Bunker–Capricorn Group to in excess of 2500 mm in the northern Reef.

Rainfall

The relief along the coast of Queensland exerts a strong influence on the incidence of rainfall (Fig. 2.12). Isohyets largely parallel the coastline, indicating the general importation of moisture from the east; the highest totals in excess

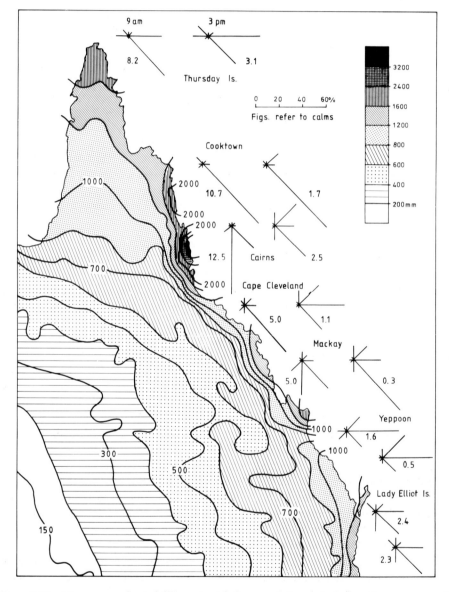

Figure 2.12 Mean annual rainfall (mm) with 9 AM and 3 PM wind roses for some coastal stations.

of 4000 mm occurring along the highest ranges in the Innisfail area. To the north, annual rainfall totals of between 1250 and 1750 mm are recorded over most of Cape York Peninsula. To the south, rainfall totals decline rapidly south of Ingham to a minimum coastal figure of 840 mm south of the Burdekin delta, coinciding with the length of coastline that trends parallel to the main southeasterly air flow. Mean annual rainfall totals again increase south of Bowen, where the coastline once more trends across this air flow, reaching as high as 2100 mm in the Eungella Ranges behind Mackay and 1600 mm near Cape Clinton. Further south a low rainfall belt is found around Rockhampton, with totals as low as 850 mm on the coast at Cape Capricorn, but generally rainfall totals along the coastline adjacent to the southern Great Barrier Reef are between 1000 and 1200 mm annually. From the limited data available, rainfall totals in the Great Barrier Reef should not vary by more than 15% in comparison to the adjacent mainland areas (Pickard, 1977).

The average proportion of the total yearly rainfall contributed in the period December to March declines from over 80% in the north to 60% at the Tropic, where ITCZ influences are relatively weaker (Stewart, 1973). The orographic influence on the coast around Innisfail, leads to summer period rainfall contributing only 60% to the annual total here. In addition to its seasonality, the rainfall pattern of northeastern Australia has great variability. The variability index (v) on the coast is less than 40% only on the northern part of Cape York Peninsula, along the wettest part of the coast near Innisfail, and to the south of Mackay, although nowhere does it drop below 35%. On the dry coast between Townsville and Bowen the variability index rises as high as 57%. The result is seen in both years with significantly below average rainfall and intense rainfall periods resulting in flooding. For example, Townsville, which has a yearly mean of 1129 mm has had annual totals varying from only 268 mm to as high as 2688 mm in the period 1871–1976 (Oliver, 1978b). Concentration of rainfall results in high-intensity figures. Probability figures for recurrence intervals of 10 and 100 years for maximum one-hour rainfall exceed 80 and 125 mm respectively along the entire coastline, while the maximum six-hour rainfall for the same recurrence intervals are generally in excess of 125 and 200 mm (Geographic Section, Dept. of National Development, 1965b, 1970). Indications of both variability and intensity of rainfall along the Queensland coast are given by some of the more extreme records, including a yearly total of 8026 mm (1950) at Tully, of 2159 mm in 120 hours at Kuranda near Cairns (1911), of 878 mm in 24 hours at Finch Hatton near Mackay (20 February 1958), and 305 mm in two hours at Ross River near Townsville (3 March 1946). Such rapid inputs of fresh water into Great Barrier Reef waters, particularly if coinciding with low spring tides, may have severe effects on reef organisms.

Winds

Although wind records are available for 24 coastal stations along the eastern coast of Queensland, many are influenced by local topographic features or by the diurnal land and sea breezes that appear to affect only the waters of the inner 10–20 km of the continental shelf, waters however, that are generally devoid of reefs. Nonetheless, the regional pattern (Fig. 2.12) is for winds from the southeast or east to dominate along the coast for almost the entire year. As the sea breeze is of greater significance than the land breeze (Oliver, 1978b) the 9 AM readings probably relate more closely to the regional wind pattern.

In order to evaluate the variation in wind patterns both latitudinally along the reef and throughout the year, four stations were chosen where local topographic or sea breeze effects appeared minimal. Proportional graphs for these stations are shown in Fig. 2.13. At the southern end of the reef, Lady Elliot Island has the most variable pattern, winds dominating from directions between east and south with southeasterlies tending to dominate in the early part of the year (January–May) rather than in winter when they have a more southerly component. At Cape Cleveland, making allowance for the sea breeze effect, winds are dominantly southeasterly throughout the year, with a more northerly component commencing in about September and extending into the summer. This pattern is seen even more strongly at Cooktown, where, from November to March, southeasterlies may be temporarily replaced by a northeasterly airflow. Even in the Torres Strait at Thursday Island winds are predominantly southeasterly, although the so-called northwest monsoon of northern Australia is in evidence from December to March.

Wind speeds are generally lighter in summer than in winter particularly on the northern reef where calms are clearly associated with the months November to March. Modal wind speeds over the whole reef are in the range 11–20 km/hr with a tendency to freshen during the afternoon, particularly in inshore waters. The winter wind speeds also tend to be higher than in summer, with commonly wind speeds of 31–40 km/hr being associated with high pressure ridges extending up the Queensland coast from anticyclones in southern Australia or the Tasman Sea. Away from the coast, wind speeds in excess of 41 km/hr have a reducing frequency towards the northern end of the Reef. This is in agreement with Jennings (1965), who mapped the frequency of gale force winds by 2° squares off the Australian coast. He showed that gale force winds occcurred 0.4–0.8% of the time off southern Queensland but reduced to 0.1% of the time over the northern Great Barrier Reef. Nonetheless, over 10% of winds at Thursday Island have velocities 41 km/hr or greater.

Tropical Cyclones

The wind speeds quoted above take little account of the occasional bursts of high energy that reef waters receive from the passage of tropical cyclones. These are extremely important events for reef morphology, for wind speeds may exceed 150 km/hr, passing through important process thresholds not normally experienced. Important rises in sea level, as storm surges, may also accompany the cyclone. On average three cyclones per year are experienced off the Queensland coast. Lourensz (1977) has shown that the most important months for cyclones are January to March, although cyclones frequently occur in December and April and occasionally at other times of the year.

The majority of cyclones affecting the Great Barrier Reef area originate in the Coral Sea and move in a generally southerly direction with a tendency for the majority not to landfall on the Queensland coast but continue southward into the Tasman Sea as rain depressions. A number of cyclones also develop in

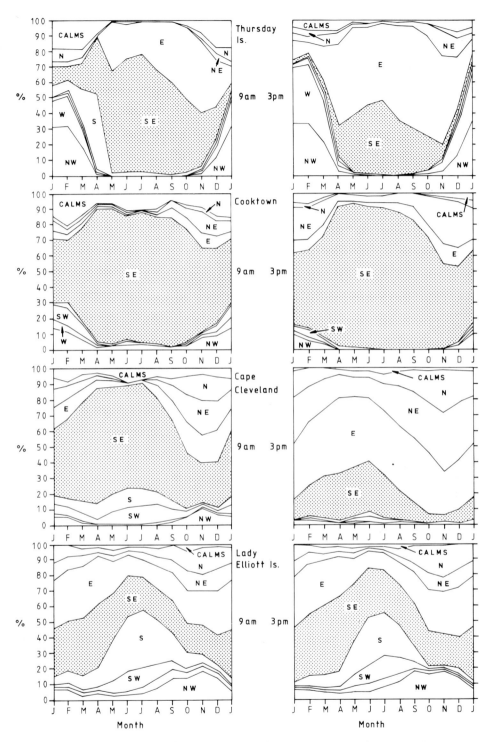

Figure 2.13 Yearly pattern of wind direction changes at 9 AM and 3 PM at Thursday Island, Cooktown, Cape Cleveland, and Lady Elliot Island. Proportion of southeasterly winds is shaded.

the Gulf of Carpentaria and either move southward as rain depressions or across Cape York, regenerating in the Coral Sea. The southern Great Barrier Reef is the most prone to cyclones (Fig. 2.14) with up to 20 per decade. Not only is there a greater frequency of cyclonic activity on the southern half of the reef, but cyclones in this area tend to be more intense. However, even the northernmost sector of the Great Barrier Reef, where fewer cyclones are experienced, may experience intense storms. Indeed, the officially recognized all-time lowest recorded pressure for the entire Australian region is 914 mb for a cyclone that crossed the coast at Bathurst Bay in March 1899 (Whittingham, 1958). Any part of Great Barrier Reef waters may be affected by storms with central presssures of less than 950 mb and wind speeds in excess of 150 km/hr.

Although cyclone tracks are very unpredictable, there is a tendency for a high proportion of cyclones affecting Great Barrier Reef waters to either move southward parallel to the coast or to cross the coast from an easterly to north-easterly direction at speeds varying from 8 to 24 km/hr. Circulation in these southern hemisphere storms is clockwise with maximum velocity winds in a band around the left forward quadrant of the eye (Oliver, 1973). This results in the strongest winds most commonly coming from a southeasterly to north-

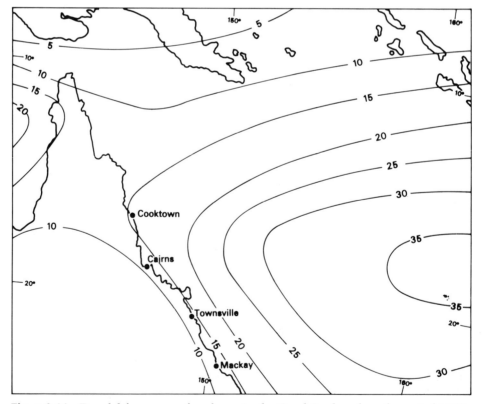

Figure 2.14   Decadal frequency of cyclones in the Coral Sea based on the period 1959–1975. (From Lourensz, 1977, reproduced by courtesy of the Bureau of Meteorology.)

easterly direction, i.e. coinciding with the predominant wind direction. However, even in other quadrants of the cyclone, wind speeds may be much higher than those normally encountered in reef waters, particularly from the more unusual western quarter, and considerable damage to coral reefs may occur on sides not normally experiencing high energy conditions (Hopley, 1974a). More unusual cyclone paths may also result in the highest wind speeds coming from quarters not normally associated with high energy conditions.

HYDROLOGY AND SEDIMENT YIELD FROM THE MAINLAND

The importance on Great Barrier Reef waters of the hydrological influence of the mainland and larger continental islands is indicated by the conclusions of Pickard (1977) who stated:

> river runoff does introduce a component of freshwater to the lagoon which is quantitatively comparable to the rainfall component. In the main, it will be contributed in phase with the rainfall but, being introduced at specific points along the coast, it could have greater effect in reducing salinity locally.

Unfortunately detailed runoff measurements are available for only about 75% of the total drainage area from Cape York to 25°30'S, and much of that which is monitored is in the low rainfall area (less than 50 mm/yr runoff), that does not contribute greatly to the total. Many of the smaller catchments of the high rainfall area are not metered and it is estimated that only a third of the total runoff is measured (Australian Water Resources Council, 1971).

The pattern of average annual runoff (Fig. 2.15) closely follows that of annual rainfall but, because of soil storages, evaporation, and vegetation uses, the differences between high and low rainfall areas and high and low seasons is even more pronounced. The largest volumes of runoff to streams is on the wet coast around Innisfail, where runoff exceeds 1500 mm generally and locally exceeds 2500 mm. Gilmour (1977) indicates an average annual runoff of 2616 mm for a small rain forest catchment near Babinda over a six-year period, where the mean annual rainfall total for the same period was 4,037 mm (i.e. 65% runoff). However elsewhere, particularly in the western headwaters of the Burdekin and Fitzroy systems, the runoff figures fall below 25 mm (c. 10% runoff), although no part of the coastal zone has less than 50 mm/yr. Most importantly, much of this runoff is channelled to specific outlets in the coast due to the nature of river-basin development. The Fitzroy River, entering the sea at the southern end of the Great Barrier Reef, and the Burdekin, emptying its waters into the central area of the Reef, are Australia's second and third largest river basins (140,054 and 129,694 km^2, respectively). Together these two systems contribute 64% of the coastal-zone area that drains into the waters of the Great Barrier Reef. In addition to the surface flow into the Queensland shelf waters, major rivers also contribute significant amounts in underground water. The Burdekin, for example, provides in excess of 250,000 megaliters per annum from underground resources for irrigation purposes (Burdekin Project Committee, 1977).

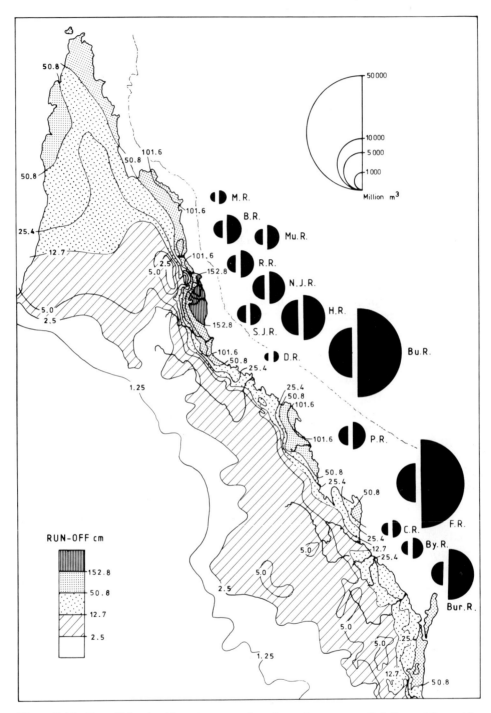

Figure 2.15 Runoff (cm) with mean annual and maximum recorded flows of specific rivers. Rivers from north to south are: M.R.—Mossman River; Ba.R.—Barron River; R.R.—Russell River; N.J.R.—North Johnstone River; S.J.R.—South Johnstone River; H.R.—Herbert River; Bu.R.—Burdekin River; D.R.—Don River; P.R.—Pioneer River; F.R.—Fitzroy River; C.R.—Calliope River; By.R.—Boyne River; Bur.R.—Burnett River.

There is a strong seasonality of flow along the entire coastline, even in the wetter rainforested area about Innisfail. Runoff parallels the seasonal rainfall pattern with peak flows occurring in the summer months, January to March, and occasionally extending into April. The Burdekin River typifies the concentrated discharge in the summer months, 90% of its flow occurring in the period January to April, and only between 1 and 2% in the driest months. Indeed it is not unusual for the Burdekin to cease flowing altogether. Smaller streams on the drier coast may cease flowing every year. The Haughton River, draining 1890 km^2, between 1927 and 1970 maintained a flow of 12 months or longer on only six occasions (Bonell, 1978). On the wetter coast it is much rarer for streams to cease flowing, but there still remains a high degree of seasonality in the flow pattern. Of even greater importance for the waters of the Great Barrier Reef is the very great variability of rainfall that occasionally results in massive flooding. Figure 2.15 shows the maximum annual flow compared to the mean annual flow for major streams along the coastline. Although flow records are limited for Cape York streams the ratio of maximum to mean flow appears to lie between 2 and 3. On the wetter coast between Cooktown and Cardwell the ratio falls to between 1.3 and 2.2, but then rises southwards to between 3.0 and 4.6 between Townsville and Mackay, and between 3.5 and 6.0 from Mackay to the southern end of the Reef. Pickard (1977) suggested that if the river component of fresh water delivered to the shelf waters were uniformly spread over the lagoon, the thickness would vary from about 0.15 to 2.55 m (compared to rainfall depths of 0.90 to 4.00 m). Combined, these amounts, if uniformly spread through a column of water 35 m deep (the depth of the lagoon), would reduce salinities by between 1‰ and 5.5‰. Temporal and spatial variations in both rainfall and runoff mean that locally, particularly close to river mouths and for short periods, salinities may be so drastically reduced that marine life will be severely affected and large areas of reefs may be destroyed (see Chapter 12).

The nature of rainfall distribution and intensity, combined with considerable basin relief along the Queensland coast, produce high rates of denudation (Douglas, in Coventry et al., 1980). However, considerable geographical variation may exist. Maximum sediment yield may be expected in the drier areas where vegetation cover is less dense and ground flora less continuous, thus allowing maximum effectiveness of the mechanical action of raindrops on the soil surface. Sediment yield may be expected to be less at higher rainfall totals as vegetation gives a greater protection to the ground surface, particularly inside the rainforest just beyond the savannah boundary. However, as this boundary occurs at about 1500 mm annual precipitation, and maximum precipitation totals exceed 4000 mm in the Innisfail area, there may be another peak in sediment yield in the higher rainfall areas. Maung Maung Aye (1976) found that in north Queensland many basin properties related to erosion rates, such as stream numbers, densities, and lengths, suggested minimal denudation rates at about 2500–3000 mm annual rainfall.

Actual sediment yield data is available for undisturbed catchments only in the wetter coastal area (Douglas, 1967a,b, 1968, 1969, 1973). In the rain-forested catchments 40% of the variability in total load, both clastic and dissolved, removed from north Queensland catchments can be explained in terms of mean annual precipitation (Douglas, 1973). Total estimated denudation rates varied with one exception from 6.74 to 44.6 m³/km²/yr, with the highest amounts removed being from basins with greater runoff (270.55 m³/km²/yr for Behana Creek), even though concentrations of both solute and suspended sediment were lower in these catchments (Douglas, 1973). Although rainfall in these catchments is more evenly spread than elsewhere in coastal Queensland, over 50% of the suspended sediment loads of streams is carried in less than seven days per year. After one heavy storm, Babinda Creek had a discharge of 1.5 m³/km²/sec with instantaneous rates of removal of dissolved and suspended matter of 600.5 and 1,448.4 m³/km²/yr. Such sediment yields appear associated with intense cyclonic rains and damage to the vegetation canopy.

No comparable figures are available for undisturbed catchments in the drier areas of the Queensland coast. Under drier eucalypt woodland the destruction of rock fragments is less complete and storm rains are able to carry more coarse debris to stream channels than those under rainforest. The westward flowing Wild River, under similar conditions, has a measured denudation rate of 24.4 m³/km²/yr (Douglas, 1973). However, this catchment is much disturbed by mining, and although Douglas' conclusions suggest that degree of disturbance of the basins is subsidiary as a factor to rainfall totals, Gilmour (1977) has shown that even in rainforested catchments logging temporarily accelerates erosion rates two- to three-fold and clearing can produce a tenfold increase in sediment yield.

Belperio (1977) estimated the present sediment yield of the Burdekin to the coast as 3.47 million tonnes/yr for wash load, and 0.47 for bed load and suspended load, giving an annual total of 3.94 million tonnes/yr (which, converted, give figures of approximately 9.9, 1.3, and 11.25 m³/km²/yr respectively). In the Nogoa catchment of the Fitzroy system Skinner et al. (1972) suggest that the annual soil loss is in the order of 14.2 million tonnes (approximately 315 m³/km²/yr) in an area extensively disturbed by man. However, as no catchment along the Queensland coast south of Cooktown can be shown to be completely undisturbed, the figure of Bird (1973) of 1.69 m³/km²/yr for long-term yield of sand-sized material from the Barron River basin, based on sediment volume in the river delta, may be taken as typical for the latter part of the Holocene for rainforest catchments.

OCEANOGRAPHY

The waters of the Queensland continental shelf that wash around, over, and through the Great Barrier Reef derive their characteristics from both the land to the west and the deeper waters of the Coral Sea to the east. Important ecological controls are provided by these waters on the biology of the reefs, both directly by way of temperature and salinity characteristics and provision of mineral nutrients, and indirectly through such things as distributions of plankton (including the larval stage of the corals by currents), response to variable tidal ranges, and through the effects of wave-energy conditions.

Waters of the Coral Sea

Waters of the Coral Sea are characterized by an upper mixed layer, in which seasonal variations in temperature and salinity can be recognized, overlying "Subtropical Lower" water between 50 and 150 m and "Antarctic Intermediate" water with a core depth between 700 and 1000 m (Pickard et al., 1977). The mixed surface waters have a maximum depth approaching 150 m close to the Great Barrier Reef but are shallowest along a line southeast from the Gulf of Papua. Summer temperature ranges are between 26° and 29°C and winter 21° and 26°C. Away from the land the isotherms are zonal but closer to the Great Barrier Reef, during winter months, the isotherms trend equatorward. Salinity levels range between 34.0 and 35.7‰ but may be as low as 32.0‰ at the end of the wet season in the northwest Coral Sea due to both the very high runoff from the Fly River of New Guinea and the inflow of low salinity Arafura Sea water through Torres Strait. Pickard et al., (1977) suggest that the major features of the circulation of the Coral Sea are an inflow towards the west north of about 15°S (the South Equatorial Current), outflow to the east between 15° and 17°S (South Tropical Counter Current) and inflow to the west south of 20°S at all levels. There is outflow much of the year northwestward into the Solomon Sea and southward all year across 30°S to the East Australian Current. Some inflow through Torres Strait occurs during the two or three summer months, with westerly outflow for the rest of the year. Flow budgets suggest that the waters of the upper 1000 m of the Western Coral Sea are replaced in between 6 and 12 months.

Waters of the Continental Shelf

The waters of the Great Barrier Reef are well mixed with vertical variations mainly in salinity associated with rainfall and runoff near the coast (Pickard, 1977). Thus 60% of temperature variations between the surface and 28 m depth at Low Isles were less than 0.2°C (Orr, 1933). Figure 2.16 shows seasonal variations in surface water temperatures in the northern central and southern sectors of the Great Barrier Reef, unfortunately based largely on nearshore stations. Greater contrasts occur in winter when southern reef waters experience temperatures below 21°C while northern waters remain close to 25°C. Maximum temperatures occur in January in the north and central shelf where they exceed 29°C, and February to March in the south, where maximum temperatures are about 28°C.

Variations in salinity are seasonal rather than geographical, reflecting rainfall and runoff occurrences and evaporation (Fig. 2.17). Least variation is seen in the southern Great Barrier Reef where salinities exceed 35‰ throughout the year with variations generally less than 0.5‰. The northern zone shows maximum salinities of about 36‰ between October and December reducing to 34‰ at the end of the wet season in April or May. Greatest variation occurs on the central reef in the area of maximum rainfall and runoff. Here salinities approach 35.5‰ towards the end of the dry season but may be reduced to less than 32.0‰ during February. Characteristically, salinities increase towards

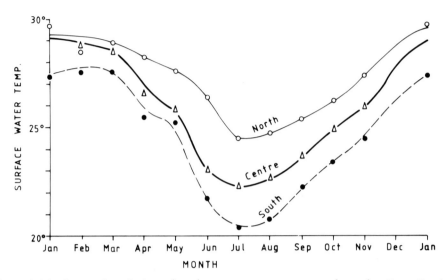

Figure 2.16 Seasonal variation of surface water temperatures along the Great Barrier Reef inshore stations, from Pickard (1977).

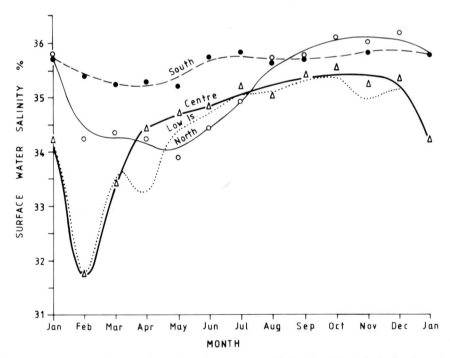

Figure 2.17 Seasonal variation of surface water salinity for 1° wide latitude strips. North zone (11–12°), central (16–17°) and south (22–23°). (From Pickard 1977.)

the outer reefs during summer, but decrease towards the shelf edge in winter (Pickard, 1977, Table 4).

Water transparency within the Great Barrier Reefs is largely a function of the nature of bottom sediments. Where these are fine-grained, as close inshore, higher wind speeds reduce Secchi disk measurements to less than 3 m (Hedley, 1925f; Orr, 1933; Pickard, 1977). Around the outer reefs where coarser carbonate sediments occur, Secchi disk depths of between 11 and 30 m have been recorded. Outside the outer reefs, values range between 14 and 40 m.

Generally small variations in amounts of dissolved oxygen with time or depth have been recorded in Great Barrier Reef waters (Orr, 1933), which are generally undersaturated. Orr considered that there was a significant oxygen demand by the particulate material and as this was continually mixed throughout the column, the demand showed little or no variation with depth most of the time. Only in calm periods was a greater reduction in oxygen content in deeper water compared to surface waters possible. Large variations, however, may take place over shallow reef flats especially between diurnal and nocturnal conditions (Kinsey and Kinsey, 1967).

Currents inside the Great Barrier Reef are a combination of wind- and tide-generated movements. Except in restricted channels the wind component dominates, producing currents to the north or northwest over most of the reef with speeds of between 0.25 and 0.6 m/sec. The reversing tidal currents (see below) are superimposed on this basic pattern.

Waters of the Inshore Areas

Waters near the mainland shore or high continental islands show the greatest influence of the adjacent land. Local conditions, particularly in proximity to major river mouths, are especially important and seasonal variations at any one site may be quite distinctive. Figures for Cleveland Bay (Grigg, 1972; Kenny, 1974; Archibald and Kenny, 1974), into which the Ross River drains near Townsville, illustrate this seasonality. Salinities are highest during winter and range from 34.6 to 35.4‰ in inshore waters rising in excess of 36.0‰ at the end of the dry season and reaching maxima in excess of 40‰ within the Ross estuary on neap tides when circulation is restricted. In summer, good mixing reduces salinities at all levels, with figures below 20‰ occurring close to river mouths and less than 25‰ over much of Cleveland Bay within 10 km of the mainland. Good mixing also produces uniform temperatures with depth in the bay. In winter, temperatures as low as 22°C are recorded, the lowest record just off the coast being 19°C. Summer temperatures are up to 5°C higher, with a maximum of 30°C being recorded in surface waters between the mainland and Magnetic Island 5 km offshore. Clearly it is the reduction in and great range of salinity and input of sediment from the land that may be detrimental to some marine life. Influx of low-temperature water into the nearshore zone during winter, as occurred in Florida waters in 1977 (e.g. Marszalek et al., 1977) does not occur in Queensland. This is precluded by the predominantly summer rainfall pattern and the lack of major cold air-mass influx over the continent due to the insulatory effects of the Southern Ocean. Even in

Moreton Bay at 27°30′S winter temperatures do not appear to fall below 15°C (Hedley, 1925g).

Mineral Nutrients and Upwelling

The supply of mineral nutrients at the base of the trophic structure is low in tropical waters. For example, Orr (1933) noted in his analysis of water samples from the vicinity of Low Isles on the 1929 Royal Society Expedition that, although both phosphate and nitrate were present throughout the year, the quantities were generally small, less than 30% of those found in temperate waters. Orr showed this was typical of tropical seas in general. He considered that photosynthesis should remove this small quantity of phosphate from the upper well-illuminated layers, with regeneration by decomposition and animal metabolism producing a phosphate-rich bottom layer. However, he noted that constant mixing of the sea in Great Barrier Reef waters did not allow an accumulation of regenerated phosphate at depth, and also prevented the complete removal of it from the photosynthetic zone. Even in calm weather, when mixing was incomplete, phosphate values did not rise in deep water. As a result, plant growth is possible throughout the year, though limited in quantity.

Atkins (1926) had shown that in deeper waters of the Pacific complete utilization of the phosphate takes place down to at least 50 m and that below this depth there is a considerable amount of phosphate. However, beyond the Great Barrier Reef, Orr (1933) considered that winter cooling of water was never sufficient to mix it at depths of more than 50 m, so that mineral nutrients cannot be reintroduced from the deeper layers to the photosynthetic zone by normal seasonal mixing. Because of this he introduced the idea of upwelling as a possible factor in the nutrient supply of the Great Barrier Reef. This was restricted to between 50 and 100 m and was wind-induced, bringing phosphate-enriched waters into the photosynthetic zone and giving rise to an increase in phytoplankton.

Brandon (1973) suggested that if contrary currents occur within (towards the northwest) and outside (southerly) the Great Barrier Reef, shearing of these currents could cause upwelling. Alternatively, if a southerly current is adjacent to the outer Barrier then Coriolis deflection of this current in the southern hemisphere would be to the left, away from the reefs, again resulting in upwelling adjacent to the reefs. Brandon presented evidence for such upwelling, including the uplift of phosphate. This is largely by some small-scale cellular motion in the upper few hundred meters whereby the waters rise along the continental margin, spread out, and sink again. The probability of contact with living reefs he considered to be fairly good. However, Godfrey (1973a,b) calculated a high value for upwelling of about 10 m a day, but noted that the upwelled water was not high in nutrient content, typical values for P-PO_4 being 0.1, 0.15, 0.3, and 1.0 μg atom/l at 100 m intervals between the surface and 400 m.

Tides

The twice daily tidal exchange involves up to 15% of the total volume of water, approximately 30,000 km^3, contained within the Great Barrier Reef

(Davis, 1978) and produces a significant degree of flushing and mixing of shelf waters. A remarkable feature of the Great Barrier Reef area is the great geographical variation in tidal range (Fig. 2.18). The tidal behaviour of the region is controlled by two amphidromic points, one near New Zealand, the other in the northern Coral Sea. Together they converge on the Great Barrier Reef to produce a maximum range greater than 10 m in the Broad Sound area. As the great tidal range is produced in part by amplification on the shallow continental shelf, the range reduces rapidly away from land, as well as to north and south of Broad Sound. As the inner reefs of the Great Barrier Reef lie 110 km offshore from the Broad Sound area, tidal range on these reefs is approximately 5.8 m, but probably little more than 4.0 m on the outer Pompey Complex reefs. The range on the inner reefs exceeds 5.0 m as far north as Redbill Reef off Mackay. The rapid reduction in tidal range to the south means that tides of the Bunker–Capricorn Group of reefs are less than 3.0 m. The mean high water

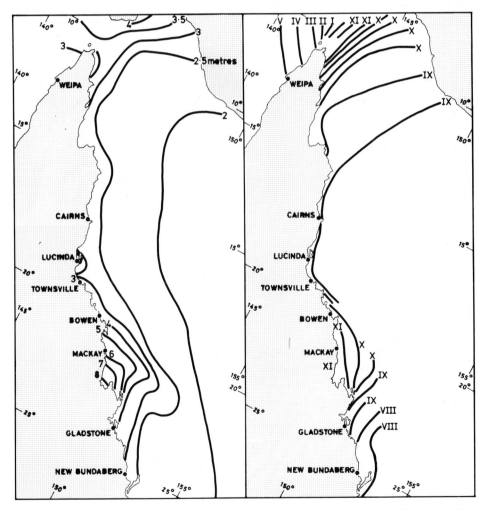

Figure 2.18 Tidal range and cotidal lines for the Great Barrier Reef area. (Based on data from Queensland Beach Protection Authority.)

springs (MHWS) at Lady Elliot Island are 2.2 m. To the north the tidal range also reduces, to less than 3.5 m north of Bowen and less than 3.0 m around Cairns. There is only a small degree of amplification over the continental shelf, and tides on the outer reef north of Townsville are generally less than 0.3 m lower than on the adjacent mainland. North of Cape Grenville the tidal range again increases as the tidal stream of the northwest Coral Sea is constricted between the Australian mainland and New Guinea in the Gulf of Papua. The maximum range in Torres Strait is 3.6 m.

The tides of the region have been analyzed by Easton (1970). They are essentially semidiurnal but to the north of Mackay, solar influence on tides is proportionately greater and neap to spring variations increase. Near the equinoxes on the northern Reef, only one tidal cycle is registered in a day. At spring tides adjacent high tides may differ by up to 1.0 m. Although the spring-tide range is greater at the equinoxes than at the solstices, extremely low spring tides occur during the night in summer (January and February) and during daytime in winter (June and July). Wide expanses of living corals are exposed at these times. Widespread mortality of corals and other living organisms appears to take place more readily during the summer low tides when they coincide with heavy rainfall and low surface salinities than in winter due to exposure to solar radiation.

At the southern end of the Great Barrier Reef the tides have less of a solar influence and show only a slight diurnal inequality. As on the northern reef, the spring-tide range is greatest at the equinoxes. Extreme low tides are not normally experienced during summer months, but occur at both nighttime and daytime between August and October.

Tides of the Torres Strait area are unique. As the Arafura Sea to the northwest of the Gulf of Carpentaria belongs to a diurnal tidal system controlled by amphidromic points in the Gulf of Carpentaria and the Indian Ocean, the tides of the western Torres Strait are frequently not in phase with those of the Coral Sea. Large differences in tide height may thus develop on opposite sides of the Strait and lead to strong tidal currents in excess of 3 m/sec.

The other major area of strong tidal currents is in the southern Pompey and Swain Reefs complex. Here the large tidal range on the adjacent coast demands on oscillation of a massive amount of water twice daily. Although most of this travels through the Capricorn Channel, tidal currents in excess of 4 m/sec have been recorded in the narrow passages between reefs of the Pompey Complex. Elsewhere, tidal currents are much less and rarely exceed 1.5 m/sec, even on spring tides in narrow channels between ribbon reefs north of Cairns. Away from constrictions the speed is about 0.5 m/sec in the southern reef waters and 0.25 m/sec in the north. Over most of the Great Barrier Reef the flood tide sets to the north and the ebb to the south.

Storm Surges Associated with Tropical Cyclones

The major departures from predicted tidal levels occur during the passage of tropical cyclones with the development of a storm surge. As this temporary rise in sea level is associated with high energy conditions, storm surges may be important influences on the development of coral reef morphology. A rapid rise in sea level of several meters may take place in a matter of an hour or two; the total height and extent of the surge are determined by such meteorological factors as the intensity of the storm and its speed and direction of movement, by local coastline configuration, and, most importantly, by offshore morphology in the area of landfall (Connor et al., 1957; Dunn and Miller, 1960; Jelesnianski, 1967; Nickerson, 1971; Hopley, 1974c). In response to the pattern of winds around the eye of the cyclone, in the southern hemisphere the maximum surge is found to the left of the eye, looking in the direction of storm movement, while the offshore winds to the right of the eye may produce a lowering of water levels.

Numerous storm surges of 3 m or more have been recorded around the Australian coast, and especially in Great Barrier Reef waters (Nelson, 1975; Silvester and Mitchell, 1977; Hopley and Harvey, 1979). In terms of the surge level above the predicted water level, the most important variable along the Queensland coast is the depth of the offshore shelf. Cyclone parameters, including frequency and severity, south of Princess Charlotte Bay are not considered to be of critical importance for surge probabilities over periods greater than 100 years. To the north of Princess Charlotte Bay, fewer and less intense cyclones may be experienced.

Tidal range is an important factor in determining the height to which unusual water levels occur. Where a high tidal range exists (over 6 m), the time that water levels are within a meter of MHWS will be very restricted, thus reducing the probability of a surge coinciding with a high tidal level. Further, the difference between neap and spring tides may be great and even if a surge were to coincide with a high neap tide, the absolute water level may not exceed MHWS. In contrast, an area of low tidal range has a much greater risk. Even the lowest spring tides may be only a meter or so below the highest astronomical tidal (HAT) level and the difference between HAT and MHWS may be negligible. For example, the difference between MHWS and HAT at Brisbane is only 0.5 m and the difference between LAT and HAT only 2.6 m. Thus a 3.0 m surge at any time could produce a total water level in excess of that normally predicted.

The 100- and 1000-year probabilities of surges and absolute water levels (surge combined with tide) are given for specific locations along the Queensland coast in Table 2.1. They suggest that the largest surges are likely to occur

Table 2.1 Probabilities for 10,100 and 1,000 year surge heights (m) and for heights of water levels above HAT based on 100 km of coastline centered on specific stations opposite the Great Barrier Reef (from Hopley and Harvey, 1979)

	Surge			Total Water Level About HAT		
Station	10	100	1000	10	100	1000
Thursday Island	1.25	2.50	3.70	—	0.95	2.15
Cairns	1.03	1.78	2.55	—	0.63	1.40
Townsville	1.45	3.25	4.90	0.32	1.93	3.25
Mackay	1.40	2.40	3.40	—	0.88	1.80
Gladstone	1.30	2.50	3.78	—	0.35	1.50

on the coast around Townsville, where moderately wide shelves and moderate tidal ranges exist, but decrease to the south due to increasing tidal range and to the north because of the narrowing of the shelf. However, these figures, which are supported by historic records of surges along the Queensland coast, are for mainland stations where amplification due to shoaling is greatest. Although figures of similar or only slightly reduced magnitude may be expected on high islands within 15 km of the mainland on the Great Barrier Reef south of Cairns (e.g. Palm and Whitsunday Islands) and on the reefs within a similar distance of the mainland to the north, especially on the low wooded island reefs, the surge figures on the outer reefs will be much less. On the outermost reefs surge figures may not greatly exceed the deep-water surge height. Although no surges have been measured on the outer reefs, development of computer simulated models (e.g. Stark, 1978) suggest that surge levels even of a 500-year return period will not exceed 1.5 m on the Great Barrier Reef proper.

Wave Climates of Great Barrier Reef Waters

Superimposed on cyclonic surges are wind waves of a magnitude far greater than normally experienced. For example in 1969 during Cyclone Camille in the Gulf of Mexico, significant wave heights of 14 m were recorded (Stark, 1978). Although wave-rider bouys have been installed at eleven coastal sites along the eastern coast of Queensland (eight of which were operating in 1978), analysis of records is limited (MacDonald, 1978). Empirical methods (Spillane and Dexter, 1976) suggest that in the central Coral Sea outside the Great Barrier Reef wave heights of up to 10 m may be experienced as the result of cyclones of 30 km diameter, which have a return period of 100 years (Dexter and Watson, 1976). Wave heights are reduced to about 7 m in the Gulf of Papua and are estimated at between 7 and 8 m inside the Great Barrier Reef, where fetch distances are reduced by the reefs. These figures closely approximate those of Stark (1978), who calculated maximum significant wave heights near Townsville of approximately 9, 7, and 4.5 m for cyclonic waves produced by tropical cyclones with central pressures of 930, 960, and 990 mb respectively.

The significance of these figures is seen in comparison to the wave heights normally encountered in Coral Sea waters. Based on observations from oceanographic cruise data Morgan (1973) produced histograms of annual mean sea states for various regions around the Australian continent. Modal wave height in regions adjacent to the Reef is only 0.1–0.5 m.

Analysis of wave heights for coastal stations in Queensland is limited to three stations, the Gold Coast, Yeppoon on the central coast, and Cairns (Fig. 2.19). The Gold Coast, at latitude $29°00'S$ lies south of the Reef but its wave climate may be similar to that of outermost reefs of the southern Great Barrier Reef. The records (Delft Hydraulics Laboratory, 1970) show that a significant wave height of 1.15 m may be exceeded 50% of the time; 2.19 m, 5%; 2.74, 1%; 3.38 m, 0.1%; and 3.99 m, 0.01%. Figures for H_{max} are almost twice those for H_{sig} with maximum wave heights of over 8 m recorded in the period August 1968 to December 1969. A high proportion of the waves recorded are long period swells.

In contrast even on the southern extremity of the Reef, offshore waves on

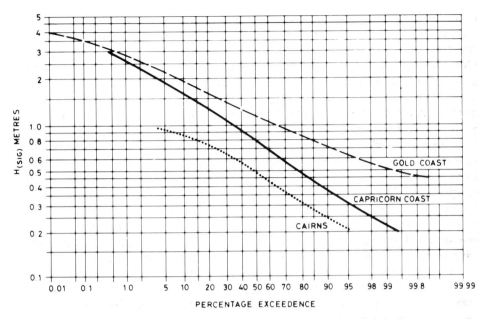

Figure 2.19 Percentage of time exceedence of wave heights (H_{sig}) for all wave periods at the Gold Coast (Delft Hydraulics Laboratory, 1970), Yeppoon (Beach Protection Authority, 1979) and Cairns (Beach Protection Authority, 1978).

the Capricorn Coast are predominantly locally generated southeast sea waves of relatively high steepness (Beach Protection Authority, 1979). Southeast to east swell has access to the coast but is generally altered by refraction and diffraction so that it is dominant only 27% of the time. Southeast waves occur about 60% of the time. The wave height (H_{sig}) exceeded 50% of the time is 0.8 m, but the average for southeast waves is about 1.0 m. Cyclonic waves typically reach 3–4 m in height and are considered by the Beach Protection Authority (1979) to exceed 5 m for a duration of 12 hours with an average return period of 50 to 100 years.

Figures for Cairns, from a site in 18 m of water inside the Great Barrier Reef, are both shorter and much lower, clearly showing the filtering effects of the Reef. Between May 1975 and September 1978 the wave heights occurring most commonly were in the range 0.2–0.6 m and the wave height exceeded 50% of the time only 0.5 m (Beach Protection Authority, 1978). Cyclone wave heights are restricted by the short generation fetch, and the highest significant wave height recorded was only 1.91 m, with a maximum wave height of 3.21 m during Cyclone Keith in January 1977.

AN ASSESSMENT OF EVOLUTIONARY AND ENVIRONMENTAL INFLUENCES ON THE GREAT BARRIER REEF

Northward movement of the Indo-Australian plate probably brought the proto-Australian continent into reef building waters by at least the early Tertiary.

Basins and highs, some of which have certainly been active during the Cenozoic reef-building period, have produced a variable basement for reef foundations and great variation exists in the age of oldest reef structures. As indicated by Lloyd (1973), major breaks in sedimentation took place during the Tertiary in at least parts of the Great Barrier Reef. Similar unconformities beneath Pacific atolls have been equated with exposure due to a major eustatic lowering of sea level with the formation of the Antarctic and Greenland ice caps (see, e.g., Savin, 1977; Adey and Burke, 1977). For a long period earlier reefal areas would have been exposed and subjected to subaerial weathering. Only with slow shelf subsidence were these areas once more submerged; in the meantime a mature karst topography may have developed that has subsequently influenced the morphology of Quaternary reefs along the lines suggested by Purdy (1974a,b). Younger reefal areas may not have experienced this long period of exposure and their opportunity for subaerial weathering was limited to the shorter glacial low sea-level phases of the Quaternary, which, as suggested in Chapter 7, may have been insufficient for the development of major karst features.

As the result of structural contrasts, bathymetry in the Great Barrier Reef is variable. Thus it is probable that the response of reefs to the Quaternary fluctuations of sea level, especially the interstadial high levels, has varied on different parts of the shelf. Reef growth during all but the major interglacial high sea-level periods was possible only in areas of deeper shelf; the shoulder of the continental shelf, where steep slopes at depths normally assumed to have been achieved during full glacials, would have restricted horizontal extension of reefs (see Chap. 6).

The physiography, geology, and weathering history of the mainland provides an environment adjacent to the Great Barrier Reef which, given suitable hydrological conditions, is capable of producing significant yields of terrigenous sediments. The thickness of coastal deposits of Quaternary, even Holocene, age is sufficient to indicate this potential, which may have been greater than at present during drier periods of the late Quaternary (see Chap. 6). Rivers flowing to the transposed littoral at the edge of the continental shelf during low sea-level periods would have carried significant amounts of terrigenous sediments, the presence of which in interreef areas is clearly seen in continuous seismic profiles that are discussed in Chapter 7. Although the outer shelf is characterized by almost pure carbonate sediments at the present time (Maxwell, 1968, 1973b), it is probable that the outer shelf is by no means a pure carbonate province. This is probably true of most shelf-reef areas of the world, and is a major contrast when compared to the Quaternary caps of deep oceanic atolls.

The climatic, hydrological, and oceanographic environment of the Great Barrier Reef displays great variability. Although normal conditions are generally conducive to reef growth, extreme events of low frequency may create disruptive stresses in the reef environment. A strong continental influence is seen in climatic factors, but these are rapidly modified away from the coastline, and at the southern end of the Reef there is a distinct contrast between the thermal regions of the mainland and the Great Barrier Reef. Further north the proximity of the Reef to the mainland results in the continental influences, particularly runoff and sediment yield, being of greater importance, at least to the development of inner shelf reefs.

Clearly measurements made at the present time, of both runoff and sediment yield of rivers draining into the waters of the Great Barrier Reef, are affected by modification of the natural environment by man. It is probable that today's figures are higher than under the largely unmodified conditions of the Holocene, when the present character of the Great Barrier Reef was being moulded. Nonetheless, it is clear that considerable amounts of terrigenous sediments and of fresh water are carried into Great Barrier Reef waters from the land and that the close proximity of reefs to the wetter coast between Cardwell and Cooktown make this part of the Great Barrier Reef more susceptible to land influences than elsewhere. Concentrations of fresh water runoff and of sediment yield close to the mouths of major rivers is important only south of Townsville, where the reef diverges considerably from the coast. The influence of terrigeneous influences may thus be less at the southern end of the reef than further north. However, as Fairbridge (1967) noted, the provision of an inorganic nutrient supply to the waters of the Great Barrier Reef from chemically weathered igneous rocks of eastern Queensland may be a critical factor when, in tropical waters, the supply of mineral salts away from areas of upwelling is normally low.

In general, wave-energy conditions are only moderate on the Great Barrier Reef, with greatest persistency of the southeast trades occurring in the central region where reef growth in response to a unidirectional wave influence is most strongly developed. Because of the normally moderate energy levels, features of reef zonation that are related to wave activity may not be as strikingly developed on the Great Barrier Reef as on open ocean atolls, where wave-energy levels are far higher (see Chaps. 10 and 13). However, the ultimate source of energy for all biological, physical, and chemical processes is solar radiation and on the Great Barrier Reef the recorded levels are among the highest for any coastal location in the world. Although the trophic structure that finally converts these radiation levels into reef growth is long and complex, it is clear that its basic input on the Great Barrier Reef is as high if not higher than on most other reef systems.

3

Biological Processes

Coral reefs, visible from several thousand kilometres from outer space, form the largest biologically constructed features on earth. Although anthozoan corals of the class Scleractinia (Vaughan and Wells, 1943) through their hermatypic or reef-building members are a major contributor to the construction of the reefs, other organisms, most notably the encrusting coralline algae, are important either in adding to the reef structure by contributing carbonate sediments, which may in turn be incorporated into the reef rock, or in stabilizing the structure by processes of biological or biochemical cementation. However, biological activity is not confined to purely constructional activities. Modern reefs represent a net result of constructional and degradational processes that together produce a continuous state of flux of reef carbonates and nutrients essential for both the biological maintenance of the ecosystem and for the long-term stability of the reef structure.

Close symbiotic relationships exist in many parts of this complex ecosystem and are so important to the total structure that it is thought that they explain why reef communities are so productive biologically although they are surrounded by waters very low in plant nutrients (Sachet, 1974). High productivity was first demonstrated by Sargent and Austin (1954) and Odum and Odum (1955) at Enewetak, where the estimated productivity of 83,000 kg/ha/yr was twelve times the existing biomass. Very high rates of photosynthetic carbon fixation, nitrogen fixation, and limestone deposition leading to the reef ecosystem probably supporting a larger number of animal and plant species than any other system, provides the key to this prodigious productivity (Goreau et al., 1979). Stoddart's (1969a) suggestion that bacteria and fungi play a major part as decomposers in such rapid recycling has been confirmed by the studies of Di Salvo (1973), Sorokin (1973, 1974) and in the review of Taylor (1977). The end result is that on coral reefs the rate of organic production is sufficient or more than sufficient to meet the internal needs of the reef community, thus indicating that reefs are autotrophic.

Geomorphologically, the biological aspects that have importance are those that affect the nature and net rate of calcium-carbonate production. Three biological processes form the basis of this chapter, namely construction, maintenance, and destruction of the reef framework.

BIOLOGICAL CONSTRUCTION

Processes of biological construction include the laying down of the basic reef structure carried out largely by corals and coralline algae, and the production of carbonate sediments that in either unconsolidated or cemented form provide significant contribution to the reef bulk.

Corals

Corals have been an extremely successful life form, the modern scleractinian corals succeeding the rugose corals in Middle Triassic times (Wells, 1956). From the original primitive shallow-water forms of the Triassic, the Scleractinia were essentially modernized by the start of the Cenozoic (Fig. 3.1). Difficulties of coral taxonomy have been discussed by Veron and Pichon (1976), who point out that in spite of the rigid appearance of the calcareous skeletons the Scleractinia are highly plastic organisms with a considerable range of variations in their skeletal characteristics. Species numbers from various parts of the world are thus estimates only. Essentially the division is between the western Atlantic and the Indo-Pacific area. Caribbean reef fauna was originally thought to consist of about 20 genera and 36 species (Wells, 1956), although more recent studies have indicated the presence of 62 species in Jamaica alone (Goreau and Wells, 1967), of which 48 from 25 genera are hermatypic. Glynn (1974) suggested that the entire western Atlantic fauna may consist of as many as 70 species of scleractinians. In contrast the Indo-Pacific area has a much richer fauna, Wells (1956) suggesting that the total number of species within the entire area is not less than 500 representing about 80 genera. On the Great Barrier Reef at least 350 species representing about 60 genera have been recognized (Wells, 1955a). In addition to the scleractinian corals, minor contributions are made to reef frameworks by other anthozoans such as the stoloniferan *Tubipora* and the coenothecalian *Heliopora* (Bayer, 1956) and also the hydrozoan *Millepora* (Boschma, 1956).

The Scleractinia are distinguished by a calcareous external skeleton consisting of radial partitions or septa, situated between the mesenteries and secreted by the ectodermal body layer within upward infoldings of the basal part of the polyp wall, with external sheeting and variously developed supporting structures (Fig. 3.2) (Wells, 1956). The expanded polyp consists of a smooth cylindrical column terminated above by the horizontal oral disc and surrounding tentacles. Body layers are composed of three distinct layers of tissue; ectoderm, mesogloea, and endoderm. The endoderm of most reef corals contains large numbers of symbiotic, unicellular, yellow-brown, dinoflagellate algae termed zooxanthellae, which are of great importance in the intense calcium metabolism of the corals. The skeleton or corallum deposited by the polyp and which contributes to the reef framework consists of a thin basal plate from which rise radiating vertical partitions, the septa. The polyps occupy the calices at the upper end of each corallum (Wells, 1956). Although there are many species of solitary corals that contribute to the sediments of

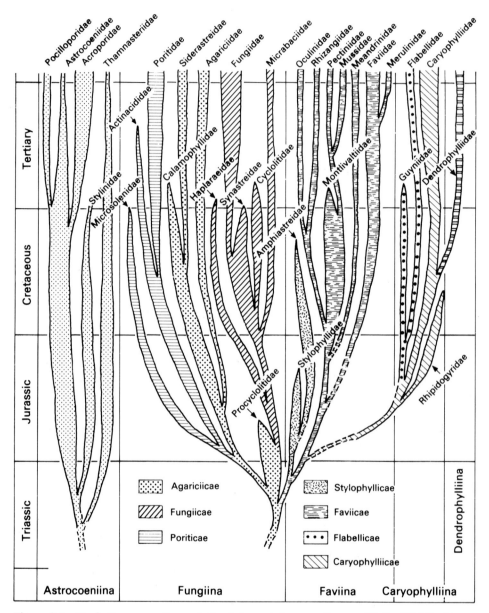

Figure 3.1 Evolutionary pattern of the Scleractinia according to Wells (1956). (From *Treatise on Invertebrate Paleontology*, courtesy of The Geological Society of America and University of Kansas.)

coral reefs, the fungids being the most common, the majority of reef-building corals are colonial.

Some corals have a continuous breeding season but with others a lunar periodicity has been noted. The larvae or planulae are 1 to 3 mm in length and may exist as free-floating plankton for periods up to months (Wells, 1956; Connel, 1973). However, the majority settle within days on suitable substrate and

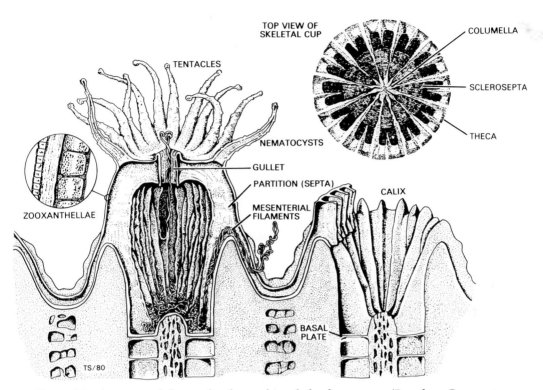

Figure 3.2 Anatomy of the coral polyp and its skeletal structure. (Based on Goreau et al., 1979.)

initiate a new colony, which expands asexually by various processes of budding for up to ten years before reaching sexual maturity. Coral polyps are carnivorous suspension feeders, their tentacles, laden with nematocysts, trapping zooplankton and transporting food to the mouth. Supplementary nutrition may come from carbohydrates and amino acids in crystalloidal solution in their environment (Muscatine, 1973).

The symbiotic relationship with the zooxanthallae is most important. These small plants contribute up to half the bulk of the tissue (Muscatine and Cernichiari, 1969) and, largely through the work of Yonge (Yonge, 1930, 1931b, 1944, 1968, Yonge and Nicholls, 1931a, b) and Kawaguti (1944, 1953) a threefold role is recognized. They are:

1 Important primary producers of oxygen and especially carbon during daylight hours in the process of photosynthesis.

2 Nutrient conservators, satisfying their own phosphorus requirements from the host metabolic waste, which they thus assist in removing.

3 Direct promotors of inorganic growth of coral skeletons. During daylight the algae produce more oxygen than can be used by polyp respiration and some of the carbon dioxide produced by the respiratory process is refixed by the algae into new organic matter. As photosynthesis takes up C-12 slightly faster than C-13, the organic matter synthesized by the zooxanthellae has a

relative preponderance of C-12, and a pool of carbon compounds enriched in C-13 is left behind and it is from these that the calcium carbonate skeleton is built (Goreau et al; 1979). Thus corals may grow 2 to 14 times more quickly in light as opposed to darkness, and twice as fast on a sunny as opposed to cloudy day (Goreau, 1959, 1961a; Goreau and Goreau, 1959, 1960a,b; Goreau et al., 1979; Buddemeier and Kinzie, 1976).

Many of the ecologic controls on coral growth are imposed by the symbiotic algae.

The skeletons secreted by the scleractinian corals are all aragonitic as also are those of the hydrozoan *Millepora*, although most other octocorals are composed of magnesian calcite. Barnes (1970) has shown that the coral skeleton is built of crystals arranged in three-dimensional fans, crystals growing outwards from individual centers of calcification. The polyp brings about skeletal growth by creating a cavity between skeleton and tissue in which a supersaturated solution of calcium carbonate is generated. As zooxanthellae aid the calcification by removing carbon dioxide, light increases the supersaturation of this solution, resulting in more rapid spreading of the crystal fans during daylight hours. This produces the diurnal growth bands in coral skeletons originally described by Wells (1963, 1969).

Unfortunately these daily growth patterns are too easily suppressed or duplicated by environmental conditions to provide detailed data on growth rates. However, Jell (1974) provided SEM evidence of internal skeletal patterns, including the possible grouping of daily structures into tidal cycles. Greatest advances in knowledge on the rates at which corals grow has come with the utilization of X-radiographic techniques (Buddemeier, 1978). This technique has shown that annual pairs of high and low-density bands normal to the axis of growth are laid down in corals (Knutson et al., 1972; Knutson and Buddemeier, 1973; Buddemeier, 1974; Moore and Krishnaswami, 1974; Macintyre and Smith, 1974; Noshkin et al., 1975; Buddemeier and Kinzie, 1976). The results either in linear growth-rate data or mass deposition rates (g $CaCO_3/cm^2/yr$) have outdated most other methods of direct measurement, calcification flux, and radiometric dating (see Buddemeier and Kinzie, 1976 for discussion) and, in addition, provide data on the mode of colonial growth. However, results published to date are ambiguous, for while density couplets making up annual bands are ubiquitously found, there is variation in the time of the laying down of each density layer. In general the low-density bands contain considerably more incremental growth than the high-density bands and thus would suggest that the season of their deposition is optimal for coral growth at that location. The problem has been highlighted in Table 3.1. It can be seen that the low-density bands vary in their season of deposition in different parts of the world. Controlling variables range from water temperature to light levels controlled by cloudiness.

It is reasonable to assume that the high-density band represents the season of stress or at least of nonoptimal growth for the corals. At locations towards the poleward margins of coral growth it may be expected that cool, winter water temperatures may provide inhibiting conditions, although Dodge (1978) suggests that, at Bermuda, growth is positively related to nutrient supply,

Table 3.1 Season of High- and Low-Density Bands in Corals Reported in the Literature

	Location	Hemisphere	Period of Low Density (Optimal Growth)	Suggested Control	Reference
1	Enewetak	N	Summer	Temperature, cloudiness	Knutson and Buddemeier, 1973.
2	Enewetak	N	Jan.–July	Light, cloudiness	Buddemeier, Maragos, and Knutson, 1974
3	Hawaii and Line Island	N	Dry season	Rainfall, light intensity	Buddemeier, 1974
4	Hawaii	N	May–Oct.	Water temperature	Buddemeier and Kinzie, 1975
5	Panama	N	Jan.–Mar.	Cold, upwelling water	Macintyre and Smith, 1974
6	Florida	N	Oct.–June	Seawater temperature	Hudson et al., 1976
7	Florida	N	Summer		Kissling, 1977
8	Great Barrier Reef	S	Winter		Isdale, 1977
9	Barbados	N	Spring–Summer	Light intensity, turbulence	Stearn et al., 1977
10	Indo-Pacific and Caribbean		Period of lower sea-water temperature	Seawater temperature	Weber et al., 1975
11	Jamaica	N	Dec.–July	Seawater temperature	Dodge, 1978
12	Bermuda	N	Spring–Summer	Upwelling	Dodge, 1978
13	Barbados	N	Spring–Summer	Seawater temperature	Dodge, 1978

which is greater in colder years through increased upwelling. Elsewhere, at least for near-surface corals, high summer temperatures may be the inhibiting factors while in other locations lower light intensities, lower salinities, and high turbidity resulting from cloudiness and tropical wet seasons (normally summer) may be the controlling variables. All these factors have been shown to have direct influence on rates of coral growth (Buddemeier and Kinzie, 1976).

In spite of these problems real figures are now available for rates of coral growth. Although Barnes (1973) suggested growth rate should decline with age, results to date indicate that young corals calcify most rapidly for a few years, but thereafter growth rates remain relatively steady, even for intervals of up to hundreds of years (Buddemeier and Kinzie), 1976). However, great variations in rates are noted even in apparently small uniform environments. Twenty-eight colonies of *Porites lobata* from a 15 m diameter area of reef flat on Fairey Reef, on the Great Barrier Reef north of Bowen, showed no common trends of growth rate apart from a decrease with increasing age (Isdale, 1977). In general results show that widest variations in growth rates occur on reef flats or in shallow water, where environmental fluctuations are greatest and tend to decrease with depth. However, growth rates as well as variation also rapidly decrease with depth. At a depth of 30 m *Montastrea annularis* has a growth rate only 10% of that at its optimum depth, (Baker and Weber, 1975) while for *Porites lutea* the figure is 40%. Results of Isdale (1978) for Wheeler Reef near Townsville suggest that whereas growth rates of *Porites lobata* vary considerably (5–8.9 mm/yr) over this one reef, maximum rates are generally found where populations are greatest i.e. there is a suggestion that, as may be expected, individual species have greatest population numbers in areas where optimum conditions for maximum calcification rates for that species occur.

Ranges of annual linear radial growth rates reported are between 4 and 20 mm/yr for massive species, 10–12 mm/yr being about the average; and about 100 mm/yr extension for branching species such as *Acropora*, though rates in excess of 200 mm/yr have been reported (Buddemeier and Kinzie, 1976). Some of the variations reported are related to the different growth forms of corals. This was shown by Maragos (1972) who converted the growth rate of five contrasting species of Hawaiian corals to uniform calcification rates. When expressed as changes in solid radius the results fall within the range 5–15 mm/yr, very similar to that recorded for hemispherical colonies.

On the Great Barrier Reef a review of growth rates of *Porites* using X-radiographic techniques has been made by Isdale (1977, 1978, in preparation). Major geographic variations are found in reef-flat corals, with corals from below approximately 5 m showing more uniform growth patterns. Although some variation is seen with latitude, greatest differences occur across the shelf (Table 3.2). *Porites* sp. from inshore fringing reefs have fastest mean annual growth rates and greatest year-to-year variation, whereas outer reef corals grow at more uniform rates, but with mean annual growth rates only two-thirds of those of inner reefs. Midshelf reefs have intermediate growth rates and variabilities.

With increasing depths, not only do growth rates decrease but colonial form also changes. Species with a wide depth range tend to be more flattened

Table 3.2 Cross-shelf variation in mean annual growth rates of Porites sp. heads from leeward sites on reefs near Townsville[a]

	Mean Annual Growth Rate (mm/yr)	Coefficient of Variation	n
Inshore fringing reefs (Magnetic, Palms, Holbourne)	10.8	4.56	39
Midshelf Wheeler Reef	9.15	3.70	52
Outer shelf Viper Reef	6.61	2.33	38

[a]From Isdale (in preparation).

becoming platelike or encrusting in contrast to their hemispherical shallow water form. For example, *Montastrea annularis* in Belize with a depth range down to 80 m is hemispherical down to 5 m, peaked or columnar at depths of 5–25 m, and platelike below that depth, maximum annual skeletal growth increment decreasing from 11 to 3 mm/yr over the same depth (Graus and Macintyre, 1976). Barnes (1973) in a theoretical consideration of the growth patterns shows that decreased light is the major determinant of the changing form with depth. He suggests that the various colonial types are produced by changing differentials between increase in tissue mass and increase in skeletal mass, which are accommodated through the effect on the division of polyps by a change in geometry of growth. Close interrelationships between ambient light and the skeletal morphogenesis of *Montastrea annularis* were also confirmed by computer-simulation studies by Graus and Macintyre (1976).

Although the recognition of the importance of organisms other than corals as both constructional and destructional agents on reefs has reduced the apparent primacy of corals as determinants of reef growth, they remain the major framework builders. Nonetheless, even the most massive corals may be removed from the site of growth by severe storms (e.g. Maragos *et al*, 1973) and it is difficult to assess the proportion of the reef structure that is derived from in situ corals. It is important to recognize that of the detrital material contributing to reef structure, coral fragments are major components.

Coralline Algae

Crustose coralline algae have an evolutionary development almost as long as that of the Scleractinia, members of the three major subfamilies (Melobesioideae, Lithophylloideae, and Mastophoroideae) dating back to the Middle or Upper Mesozoic (Fig. 3.3) and similar forms date back to the Ordovician. Unfortunately far less is known about these reef frame builders than the corals, with much confusion resulting from the consistent use of Lithothamnion as a generic term for all crustose corallines (Adey and Macintyre, 1973). Although considered as shallow-water tropical organisms, some species and genera extend into polar regions. They also have a considerable depth range, from the intertidal zone to the lower limit of the photic zone. Dominant com-

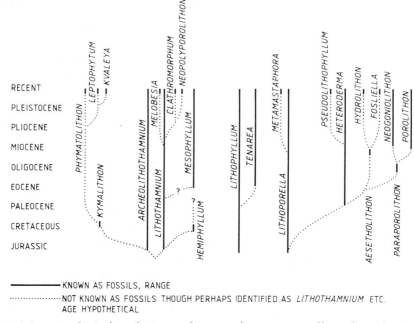

Figure 3.3 Hypothetical evolutionary history of crustose coralline algae. (From Adey and Macintyre, 1973, reproduced by permission of The Geological Society of America.)

ponents belong to the genera *Neogoniolithon, Porolithon,* and *Lithophyllum,* the Melobesioideae being weakly represented by *Mesophyllum* and *Archeolithothamnion* with *Lithothamnium* relatively unimportant. Paucity of knowledge of the crustose coralline algae of the Great Barrier Reef is indicated by Cribb (1973). However, although collections are incomplete, what data are available (Table 3.3) suggest that a rich algal flora exists throughout Barrier Reef waters.

The coralline algae consist of vegetative tissue (thalli) and reproductive structures (conceptacles). They are characteristically red or purplish due to the presence in the chloroplasts of special pigments besides chlorophyll. This gives them the ability to utilize the blue end of the spectrum, and in contrast

Table 3.3   Number of Algal Species Recorded from Great Barrier Reef Sites

Sites	Chloro-phyta	Phaeo-phyta	Rhodo-phyta	Cyano-phyta	Reference
Thursday Island	19	10	43	1	Cribb, 1961
Lizard Island	39	8	29	3	Price et al., 1976
Brampton Island	21	17	40	7	May, 1951
Swain Reefs	21	6	10	1	Saenger, 1979
Heron Island	28	16	35	19	Cribb, 1966
Masthead Island	26	7	19	9	Cribb, 1975

to the green algae can extend into much greater depths, living corallines being dredged from as deep as 300 m in tropical waters, (Fritsch, 1935; Johnson, 1961). Coralline algae are usually magnesian calcite although the order Nemalionales are aragonitic (Milliman, 1974). There are few physiological or biochemical studies on the mechanisms for calcium-carbonate precipitation but processes include cell-surface deposition resulting from CO_2 extraction from water during photosynthesis and intracellular metabolic processes (see Littler, 1976 for review).

In general the environmental factors influencing the coralline algae are similar to those for the Scleractinia. Light is the primary factor controlling depth distribution and most genera have characteristic ranges of occurrence.

Temperature is also a control as most of the genera found on coral reefs (*Porolithon, Neogoniolithon, Hydrolithon, Lithoporella,* and *Archeolitho-thamnium*) have approximately the same latitudinal distribution as the corals. They also require normal, open-oceanic salinity levels, between 25‰ and 35‰, most species being unable to tolerate low salinities. Grazing activities of animals may restrict growth, but Adey and Macintyre (1973) considered that most grazing is beneficial in that competitors, especially the fleshy algae, are limited. They also consider that space competition with corals, millepores, and sponges has had the effect of evolving faster growth rates by tropical crustose corallines.

Major factors affecting the nature of coralline algae are substrate and wave action. In terms of bottom types there are two major, though intergrading, groupings: those encrusting the reef substrate, and those encrusting unstable substrate or themselves forming part of the mobile sediment as rhodoliths. In many locations the rhodoliths depend upon a supply of material eroded from a stable encrusted substrate, but once developed it is possible a rhodolith bottom can support itself by fragmentation and growth (Adey and McKibbin, 1970). Rhodoliths have not been widely described on the Great Barrier Reef although Davis (in press) has noted that the leeward margin of One Tree Reef is covered by coralline concretions up to 10 cm in diameter. Each concretion is comprised of a nucleus of branching corallines, the encrusting external surface being formed of the fused ends of branches. Figure 3.4 idealizes the occurrence of various coralline morphological habitat types as a function of wave exposure, depth, and turbidity. Most rapid growth occurs in the upper layers (Adey and Vassar, 1975), rhodoliths from depths greater than 50 m (even with living crusts) having relict skeletal material, radiocarbon ages indicating a late Pleistocene origin for many (Adey and Macintyre, 1973). Actual recorded growth rates in tropical waters are an order of magnitude greater than in cooler waters. In St. Croix, experiments indicated mean marginal extension rates of 13.2 mm/yr with increases in thickness of 0.8 mm/yr within the upper 6 m of water depth (Adey and Vassar, 1975). Even shaded, or partially shaded, locations show rapid development of crusts, although here they have a leafy or imbricating habit that represents lower production of calcium-carbonate. Nonetheless, the figures given by Adey and Vassar suggest that in an open reef structure, as for example produced by *Acropora* sp. coralline algae, with the help of rubble, will quickly infill and strengthen the structures built by corals. Comparable data are not available for the Great Barrier Reef but Price (1975),

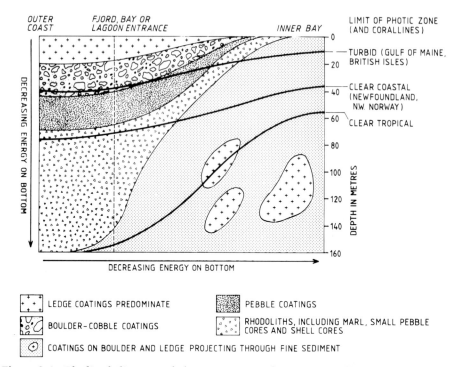

OUTER COAST — FJORD, BAY OR LAGOON ENTRANCE — INNER BAY

LIMIT OF PHOTIC ZONE (AND CORALLINES)

TURBID (GULF OF MAINE, BRITISH ISLES)

CLEAR COASTAL (NEWFOUNDLAND, NW. NORWAY)

CLEAR TROPICAL

DECREASING ENERGY ON BOTTOM

DEPTH IN METRES

DECREASING ENERGY ON BOTTOM

LEDGE COATINGS PREDOMINATE

PEBBLE COATINGS

BOULDER-COBBLE COATINGS

RHODOLITHS, INCLUDING MARL, SMALL PEBBLE CORES AND SHELL CORES

COATINGS ON BOULDER AND LEDGE PROJECTING THROUGH FINE SEDIMENT

Figure 3.4 Idealized diagram of the occurrence of various coralline morphological—habitat types as a function of wave exposure, depth, and turbidity. (From Adey and Macintyre, 1973.) Reproduced by permission of The Geological Society of America.

recording the progression of algal cover on deliberately killed *Acropora* branches on Lodestone Reef off Townsville, showed that by 77 weeks after death, 40.6% cover of crustose corallines had been achieved, with a rapid replacement of turf-forming algae occurring after about a year.

Bryozoans

Although not major framework constructors, bryozoans occupy an important position in reef building, as they are among the first organisms to attach themselves to coral substrates, even settling between living polyps, attaching themselves to the coral colony by a mucopolysaccharide adhesive (Soule and Soule, 1974). They reinforce the reef mass by encrusting the undersides of coral heads and ledges and partly filling cavities deep within the reef (Cuffey, 1972, 1974). They are not normally a major contributor to sediments in reefal areas nor do they bind unstable bottoms, but their cryptic habit allows them to consolidate frail coral foundations in areas where algae usually do not live or calcify only slowly. Bryozoan colonies are mainly low-magnesian calcite but mineralogy is highly variable, many species within the suborder Ascophora having mixed mineralogies. Aragonite may be precipitated in transverse fibrous ultrastructures of the superficial skeleton during the adult stages. Although of greater importance to reefs in the past, it is difficult to quantitatively assess the modern importance of bryozoans. Maxwell (1968) indicated they are most important on sheltered reefal shoals and in forereef areas below the breaker zone, a conclusion also reached by Schopf (1974) on the reefs of St. Croix. Ross (1974) found that shallow water species were widely dispersed on reefs off Townsville, on both windward and leeward sides. Certainly the Great Barrier Reef has as rich a fauna as anywhere in the world. Whereas 29 species are recorded at St. Croix (Schopf, 1974), 42 in the Bahamas (Cuffey and Fonda, 1977), and 200 in Hawaii (Soule and Soule, 1974), over 200 species representing 51 genera were found on only 13 reefs off Townsville on the Great Barrier Reef (Ross, 1974), although the available literature gives the impression of a poor fauna (Ryland, 1974).

Other Animal Producers of Calcium Carbonate

Apart from the corals and bryozoans, most other reef animals contribute materials to the reef sediments, rather than directly to the reef structure. The nature of these skeletal components has been summarized by Milliman (1974) and the sedimentary characteristics by Orme (1977a). They include:

1 **Molluscs** Molluscs range from the slow growing and relatively unimportant sediment producers such as chitons to the rapid calcium carbonate producers such as the clams, *Tridacna gigas* (also with zooxanthellae incorporated within their mantle tissues) having a recorded deposition rate of 23 g/100 cm^2/yr (Bonham, 1965). The majority of mollusc shells contain three or more layers, an outer chitinous periostracum and two or more calcareous inner layers containing up to 9% organic matter, the organic matrix between crystalline layers giving the shell increased flexibility under environmental stress (Wainwright, 1969). The majority of shells are aragonitic but some common reef species, such as *Crassostrea* secrete calcitic shells. Shell deposition is periodic with annual growth rings clearly identifiable (Buddemeier, 1978). In general the gastropods precipitate their shells most rapidly, although on coral reefs the pelecypods particularly the clams are probably the most rapid producers. Of the clams *Tridacna gigas* growing to over a meter in diameter is the largest and most spectacular with populations on some northern reef tops such as Michaelmas Reef being approximately 1/100 m^2. Rates of production for molluscs are generally not available. However, Hamner and Jones (1976) examined the very common, small, burrowing clam *Tridacna crocea* and suggested that while these molluscs are major eroders of reef-flat materials, they have a calcium carbonate increase in the shell of 60 g/m^2/yr. Assuming a stable population structure with annual mortality equal to annual estimated growth, they suggested that total sediment production is 200 g/m^2/yr, with as much as 4,500 g/m^2/yr in areas of dense populations.

2 **Foraminifera** Foraminifera are major producers of calcium carbonate and, because of the unicellular algal symbionts, are, like corals and clams, significant primary producers (Sournia, 1976). Chave et al. (1972) calculated a total annual potential productivity on coral reefs for foraminifera to be about 10^7 tests/m^2 representing 10^{4}g/m^2/yr of CaCO$_3$ with actual figures from coral mounds of 10^5 tests and 10^2 g/m^2/yr. Muller

(1974) calculated the production of 1.8×10^8 tests/m²/yr and 5×10^2 g/m²/yr of $CaCO_3$ for *Amphistegina madagascariensis* on reefs of Oahu, Hawaii, with growth rates of 7 microns per day. Estimates of the growth rate of *Marginopora vertebralis* are even more rapid (Ross, 1972). Maximum rate of increase in shell diameter is as much as 0.4 mm per week for individuals less than 3 mm in diameter and 0.14 mm per week for larger individuals. Figures indicating rates of similar magnitude are reported for *Marginopora* and *Calcarina* from the Great Barrier Reef area (Smith, 1977). Quite clearly the rapid production rates and high population densities on parts of reef flats, suggest that foraminifera play a very important role in carbonate production and it is not surprising to find some cay beaches made up almost entirely of these tests. Calcareous foraminifera can be separated into two broad groups on the basis of wall structure (Wood, 1949). Many of the prominent Caribbean reef forms are porcellaneous whereas hyaline foraminifera are the most common on Indo-Pacific reef flats (Milliman, 1974). Tests are mainly high-magnesian calcite and calcification occurs on organic templates (Towe and Cifelli, 1967). It is probable that the symbiotic algae aid in calcification in a similar manner to that in corals.

3 **Sponges** Sponges of the phylum Porifera are generally more important in degradation of reef materials. However, the sclerosponges can precipitate massive skeletons (mainly aragonite) and they can be potentially important elements in the formation and consolidation of the basal framework (Hartman and Goreau, 1970; Milliman, 1974).

4 **Echinoderms** All five major groups of the echinoderms are common on coral reefs. These are the echinoids (sea urchins), asteroids (starfish), ophiuroids (brittle stars), holothurians (sea cucumbers) and crinoids (sea lilies). While some of these organisms are most important in reef degradation, some skeletal parts, including echinoid plates and spines and crinoid stems, can be locally important components of reef sediments, especially lagoonal sands.

Other animal producers of calcium carbonate are relatively unimportant in the reef ecosystem. Brachiopods may have high populations in cryptic situations (Jackson et al., 1971; Logan, 1977) and may contribute directly to the sediment infilling crevices within the reef. Polychaetes are mainly reef degraders, although Vittor and Johnson [1977] suggested that there are contrasting populations and activities in reefs that are actively growing compared to decaying reefs. The deposition of calcareous tubes, particularly by the serpulids, at least produces a turnover of calcium carbonate within the system. Arthropods, especially barnacles have a high turnover rate and, with the carapaces of crabs and lobsters, contribute to reef sediments. With many of these organisms there is a fine dividing line between reef construction and reef degradation for, while contributing to reef sediments, the activities of many help to weaken the main structure of the reef produced by corals and coralline algae. For example Hunter (1977) estimated that the echinoid *Diadema antillarum* was the major producer of sediment on some Barbados reefs, producing approximately 97t/ha/yr, although a large proportion is fine enough to be easily removed from the reef.

Other Plant Producers of Calcium Carbonate

Algae other than the encrusting corallines play important energetic roles in the reef ecosystem (Marsh, 1976). Although the brown alga *Padina* is common on reef flats and has a partly calcified body composed of surficial bands of aragonite, it is only a minor carbonate contributor. In contrast the Chlorophyta, the green algae, particularly the Codiaceans, are major contributors to reef sediments. Disjoint aragonite needles up to 5 microns in length are released by many Codiaceans such as *Penicillus*, *Rhipocephalus*, and *Udotea* to the aragonite muds of shallow back reef and bank sediments (Lowenstam and Epstein, 1957; Stockman et al., 1967). However, the most important calcifier is *Halimeda*, composed of disjunct calcified segments of fused aragonite needles. In life the segments are joined by narrow uncalcified nodal regions but on death these decompose, releasing the separate plates that form distinctive sediments. *Halimeda* grows in a wide variety of reef environments (Hillis-Collinvaux, 1977). It can be extremely prolific with cover up to 90% (Hillis-Collinvaux, 1974). On the Great Barrier Reef various species of *Halimeda* grow in situations from reef flat to depths of 75 m. Some of the most prolific beds are found on old submerged reef surfaces at depths of about 30 m (see Chapter 7). Although Goreau (1961b) suggested that carbonate precipitation was directly related to photosynthesis, subsequent studies have found that *Halimeda* can produce carbonate at almost the same rate in darkness as in light (Stark et al., 1969). The specific mechanism of calcification is not known but it is possible that precipitation is a physiochemical process during photosynthesis (Milliman, 1974). Growth can be extremely rapid. Hillis-Collinvaux (1974) showed that areas of dense stands have productivity rates of 4 $gC/m^2/$ day gross and 2.3 $gC/m^2/$day net that compare favourably with most other productive parts of the reef system. Chave et al. (1972) estimated potential yields of 10^4 $g/CaCO_3/m^2/yr$.

Together the reef fauna and flora build up the reef structure, and from figures quoted the rates of calcification are rapid, not surprisingly in tropical surface waters supersaturated in calcium carbonate. Most important in terms of both primary productivity and the process of calcification are the symbiotic zooxanthellae. Sournia (1976) considers them to be the major primary producers of the reef system, acting with the corals on reef margins and lagoon coral heads, with clams on reef flats, and with foraminifera in lagoon sands. The scleractinian corals build a loose, open structure, infilled and consolidated particularly on windward margins by encrusting coralline algae, and in inner cavities by bryozoans. Sediment from these, and all other calcium-carbonate secreting organisms, further consolidates the reef structure, though with some alteration and loss from the total system.

ENVIRONMENTAL CONTROLS ON REEF GROWTH

Although some of the factors affecting the growth and viability of individual reef organisms have been discussed already, because of the interconnectivity within the ecosystem and the many essential symbiotic relationships, it is possible to consider environmental factors that control reef growth as a whole. Wells (1956), Stoddart (1969a), Milliman (1974) and Buddemeier and Kinzie (1976) have discussed the most important environmental controls, which include:

Temperature

Of the major reef builders, the corals appear to be the most sensitive to temperature, although some genera of coralline algae are restricted to warmer waters and others have their growth rates cut by an order of magnitude outside the tropics. As early as 1843 Dana suggested a temperature control on reef development, pointing out the restriction on reef growth brought about by cool currents on the eastern sides of oceans. Vaughan (1919) suggested a lower limit of 18°C for the annual minimum water temperature as a controlling parameter, with optimum conditions in the range 25° to 29°C. However, more recent work has indicated that corals can grow in water temperatures much lower than this. Macintyre and Pilkey (1969), for example, reported *Solenastrea* growing in water temperatures falling as low as 9°C in North Carolina. Rather than there being an absolute temperature limit for growth it would appear that corals initially lose their ability to capture food with decreasing temperature (Mayer, 1915; Edmondson, 1929) and then lose their ability to reproduce (Edmondson, 1946). The fauna becomes depauperate, as ideally illustrated by the Great Barrier Reef and waters to the south (Table 3.4), growth rates decline to a point where degradation is more rapid than construction, and individual colonies rather than complex reefs are the only forms present. The minimum temperature of 18°C would appear to be more related to the limit of reef growth than coral growth. Some research (e.g. Ma, 1959) has suggested a positive correlation between coral growth and temperature. However, this appears to be correct only up to the optimum temperature range of about 26°–28°C and it is possible that corals are adaptive enough to be able to adjust to relatively small temperature changes within a few weeks (Buddemeier and Kinzie, 1976). There are also maximum temperatures beyond which corals and other reef organisms cannot survive. This is generally regarded to be about 36°C but temperatures of 37.8°C have been recorded on the

Table 3.4 Decrease of Coral Genera with Latitude, Great Barrier Reef[a]

Latitude, Location	Number of Genera
9–17°S	60–59
17–20°30′ S	59–53
20°30′ –23°30′ S	53–35
23°30′ –24°30′ S	35–25
24°30′ –27°30′ S	25–12
20°30′ –34°S	12–2
Sydney (34°S)	7
Tasmania (41°S)	1

[a]From Wells (1955a) and Veron (1974).

reef flat of Low Isles (Orr and Moorhouse, 1933) while a temperature of 56°C has been reported in shallow waters in the Maldives (Gardiner, 1903). Excessive temperatures such as this are definitely lethal to corals and their associates and the depauperate fauna of reef flats is partly a reflection of occasional high temperatures. As Buddemeier and Kinzie (1976) have noted, there is probably no simple temperature control in terms of averages. Extremes and the frequency of their occurrence are probably most important. In this respect open-ocean atolls experience limited absolute air and water temperature ranges while shelf reefs adjacent to major continental masses experience greater extremes and average temperature may have less significance.

Salinity

Salinity affects both the major reef structure builders, corals and coralline algae, which have salinity requirements ideally about 36‰ or about the level of open ocean and with a normal tolerance range between 30‰ and 40‰. The importance of this factor is seen in the fact that it accounts for 36% of the environmental control of growth of *Montipora verrucosa* in Hawaii (Maragos, 1972). Lower salinity levels can be produced by heavy rainfall or runoff and, although corals may survive for short periods, the lowering of a freshwater lens over a reef flat on a low tide may cause widespread death (see Chapter 12). Higher salinities may be caused by excessive evaporation and again widespread mortality can result. However, Kinsman (1964) has reported large colonies of *Porites*, probably the most tolerant of all coral species, growing in salinities as high as 48‰.

Water Turbulence

Corals and coralline algae thrive best in areas of high water turbulence. As these are the upper few meters of the water over reefs, other factors related to shallow depth, such as high light intensity may be concomitant influences. Turbulent water movement has always been considered important in providing fresh supplies of nutrients and in providing a circulation that, particularly at night when photosynthesis ceases, supplements the oxygen supply. However, as oxygen levels in even sheltered locations on a reef rarely fall below 18% saturation it would appear that water movement is more important in the removal of biogenous carbon dioxide (Wells, 1956). Milliman (1974) considered that high turbulence also prevents siltation while Stoddart (1969a) suggested that water turbulence and wave energy are important controls of zonation. The success of the coralline algae in the highly turbulent reef crest zone is the result of the inability of competitors, such as the fleshy algae, and of grazers to exist in such a high-energy environment (Adey and Burke, 1976; Adey, 1978a).

Depth and Light

The early controversies over the development of coral reefs were largely the result of the recognition that reef organisms have a limiting depth at which they can grow successfully. Wells (1956) suggested that 90 m is the limit for hermatypic corals but their calcification rates are so reduced at depths far shallower than this that it is likely that rates of degradation exceed rates of growth and major reef building is limited to the upper 40 m. Milliman (1974) suggested that even the change in form of corals to more flattened or foliose forms not only reflects reduced rates of skeletal deposition, but renders them more susceptible to bioerosion. The major control determined by depth operates through the reduction in light intensity, so important for the processes of photosynthesis in all the algae, and, indirectly by way of the symbiotic zooxanthellae, for calcification in corals, clams, foraminifera, and other organisms containing these minute algae. Wells (1957) has shown that the number of coral species declines rapidly with a depth below about 20 m. (Although Milliman, 1974, suggests that in the Red Sea this figure should be 30–40 m, clarity of water may be a factor here). Oxygen levels and temperature show no significant variation in the upper 50 m and species numbers appear to have a closer correlation to illumination and radiant energy (Fig. 3.5). Buddemeier and Kinzie (1976) showed that coral growth rates as indicated by density bands certainly reflect the degree of illumination and Adey and Macintyre (1973) showed that the light factor is most critical for growth of crustose corallines. However, Buddemeier and Kinzie (1976) suggested that the exact relationships between coral growth and light and depth are poorly understood, probably because of the existence of nonlinear thresholds that modify any monotone relationship between light and growth. Nonetheless, there is little doubt that light enhances calcification and there are several studies showing profiles of growth rates as a function of depth/illumination (Buddemeier, et al., 1974; Baker and Weber, 1975). In general, results show that below about 25% of the surface illumination growth rates and species numbers decrease rapidly. Obviously water clarity plays a part, as does the angle of incidence of the sun. Wells (1957) suggested that of equal importance is the length of the "effective day" at various depths, which diminishes exponentially the total amount of radiant energy receivable each day at increasing depth, quoting the example of Funchal where the "day" is 11 hours at 20 m and only 15 minutes at 40 m. Illumination factors also vary with seasonal conditions. For example, Storr (1964) showed that in the Bahamas the light at 15 m was 2.7% of that at the surface in summer but only 1.5% in winter.

There are also upper limits to the biological construction of coral reefs. Corals and most other reef organisms may withstand a few hours of emersion at most, and biological construction in open water in a mesotidal area is limited to between MLWS and MLWN although this may be raised by natural moating (see Chap. 4). Some variation exists due to tidal range, the time of extreme low spring tides, and periods of high temperature and rainfall. Below the zone of emersion there may also be some photo-inhibition of calcification, where light is in excess of the needs of near-surface corals (Buddemeier and Kinzie, 1976). Most corals would thus appear to have an optimum light requirement and thus depth, producing maximum growth rates, for example, at 10 m for *Montastrea annularis* (Barnes and Taylor, 1973; Baker and Weber, 1975) or 2 m for *Montipora verrucosa* (Maragos, 1972; Jokiel et al., 1974). Similarly Spencer-Davies (1977) has shown that carbon autotrophy is possible only in shallow waters, the depth for *M. annularis* being c. 2 m and for *M. cavernosa* 13 m. He has suggested that at greater depths, particularly below 40 m, it is probable that only 50% of the carbon requirements can be met by photosynthesis of the zooxan-

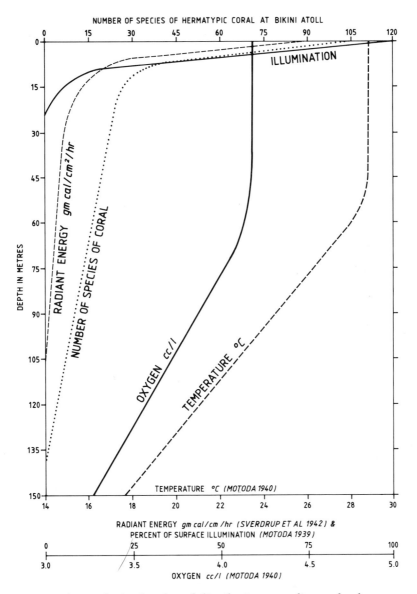

Figure 3.5 Graphic analysis of reef-coral distribution according to depth, oxygen, temperature, illumination, and radiant energy. (From Wells, 1957, reproduced by permission of The Geological Society of America.)

thellae and that at these depths corals will have to depend on other methods of feeding, the end result being reduced growth rates.

Turbidity and Substrate

Turbidity is a further factor that affects illumination, and effective depth is greatly reduced in waters receiving sediment laden runoff or where rough seas stir up a muddy sea floor. Coral growth rates have been inversely correlated with the amount of resuspended sediment (Dodge et al., 1974; Aller and

Dodge, 1974), and it is likely that most organisms requiring light will be affected. Heavy siltation has long been stressed as a cause of coral mortality (Wood-Jones, 1910) although the cilary action of some corals such as *Porites* combined with polyp inflation allows self-removal of sediment from polyps and short periods of burial can be withstood (Vaughan, 1919). Fungiid species in particular are efficient at sediment removal, and distribution of species over a reef is related to varying abilities to overcome local sedimentary stress (Schuhmacher, 1977). Motoda (1939) indicated that silt prevents the successful settlement of planulae, though Umbgrove (1928) has shown that corals may grow in muddy surroundings, particularly if there are occasional shells or other hard fragments for planulae settlement. Most observations on the effects of siltation have been related to corals. However, other reef organisms are affected. Bakus (1968) suggested that siltation patterns control the distribution of sponges and ascidians in the lagoon of Fanning atoll.

It is difficult to separately consider many of these environmental parameters. Illumination, for example is a function of depth, turbidity, and angle of incidence of the sun's rays. Water turbulence, oxygen levels, and turbidity are similarly connected. However, in terms of reef growth, as opposed to the maintenance of biological activity, the original observations of Quoy and Gaimard (1825) on a depth limit to coral growth, are probably still the most important. Reef growth is limited to the upper levels of the ocean and in clear oceanic waters the potential for deposition of calcium carbonate to exceed removal is probably limited to the upper 40 m.

PROCESSES OF REEF MAINTENANCE

Processes of reef maintenance are those that allow for the stabilization of the products of biological and chemical construction or retard the removal of sediment from the reef structure. To a large extent the complex trophic structure of the reef ensures that the original primary production is utilized in the most economic and profitable way for the total reef. However, it is possible to recognize specific reef maintenance mechanisms:

Protective Coating

Some organisms can give a protective coating to the reef structure. The encrusting algae are an obvious example. Although dead coral and coral fragments may initially be subjected to bioerosion, with boring algae being among the initial colonizers, within a year such surfaces may be covered by a coralline crust (Dahl, 1974; Price, 1975). Similarly, some of the sclerosponges may give protection to coral surfaces, particularly on the underside where encrusting algae are not as prolific. Goreau and Hartman (1966) describe the protection from the effects of boring sponges given by *Mycale laevis* on the lower surface of massive corals. Barnacles, such as *Tetraclita squamosa* and rock oysters (*Crassostrea amasa*) similarly give protection to specific parts of the intertidal zone.

Baffles and Binders

The growth form of many reef organisms is an effective agent of dissipation of wave and current energy. In addition the roots of many plants help to bind the sediment, hence making it more difficult to move (Gebelein, 1969; Neumann, et al., 1970). Scoffin (1970) has discussed many of the mechanisms of trapping and binding of reef-flat sediments by marine vegetation in Bimini lagoon, Bahamas. He observed the effects of the plants under both natural and laboratory conditions and concluded that the density of plant growth is crucial to the reduction of current strength at the plant-water interface. The most effective baffles were the roots of the mangrove *Rhizophora* and dense *Thalassia* blades, especially those with dense epiphytic algae. These plants had the ability to reduce the velocity of water from speeds of about 30 cm/sec to zero at the sediment-water interface. The subsurface roots of *Rhizophora* and *Thalassia* help to bind the sediment efficiently enough to produce accumulation rates higher than in adjacent bare areas. Scoffin concluded that growth of macroscopic green algae is insufficiently dense and the holdfasts too weak to appreciably affect the accumulation of sediment, although a degree of stabilization is provided to the substrate. Algal mats trap sediment chiefly by adhesion of grains to the sticky filaments and their ability to resist erosion by unidirectional currents varies considerably depending on mat type, smoothness, and continuity of cover. This enhanced deposition may be sufficient to form laminated stromatolites. Although extensive stromatolites have not been recorded from the Great Barrier Reef they are common in other reefal areas. Stabilization of sediments is not limited to fine-grained material. The pale green alga *Caulerpa racemosa* can be observed forming a fixing mat to coral shingle and rubble on many Great Barrier Reef flats (Fig. 3.6). It is probable that this initial stabilization allows time for subsequent chemical or biochemical cementation. Similar stabilization of subaerial sand cay deposits is caused by terrestrial vegetation.

Another form of baffle on a completely different scale is provided by the spur and groove system developed on a reef front. Although the origin of these fea-

Figure 3.6 A combination of the alga *Caulerpa racemosa* and small anemones binding a reef flat *Acropora* shingle, Pandora Reef.

tures is controversial (see Chapters 4, 7, and 10), it would appear that at least in some cases they are initiated as growth forms modified so that the coral branches can accommodate the forward thrust of impinging waves (Shinn, 1963; Roberts, 1974; Roberts et al., 1977). As with many other reef process-response systems, there would appear to be more than one advantage to the corals in this highly turbulent zone because well-developed spur and groove systems, besides being effective wave-energy dissipators, provide more biomass per unit area of reef margin and thus make full use of the highly favorable environment.

Cementation

Mechanisms of carbonate cementation are a topic of great debate. It is likely that many processes are operating, some of which include at least a contribution from biological or biochemical agents. The general processes of cementation are discussed in Chapter 5. However, it is worth noting that intertidal cementation has been attributed to the decay of organic matter trapped in beach sands (Field, 1920; Daly, 1920, 1924), to microbial action (Nesteroff, 1954; Guilcher, 1961; Puri and Collier, 1967), and to direct biological cementation, usually by algae (Kaye, 1959; Cloud, 1959; Nelson and Rodgers, 1969). Similarly, at least some shallow-water submarine cementation may involve some form of organic complexing (Milliman, 1974).

Sediment Moving and Mixing

In contrast to the inhibition of sediment movement provided by some biologic mechanisms, a large number of reef animals are involved in the movement and mixing of the skeletal debris which forms the reef sediment. This in turn allows organic matter trapped within the carbonate sediment to reenter the food chain. Holothurians are very effective sediment mixers; lagoon sands passing through the gut of the animal undergo a reduction in size (Emery, 1962). The general effect of this and other organisms is to create great bioturbation of areas of sediment deposition such as lagoons, and many attempts to estimate rates of sediment accumulation by radiometric dating have been foiled by this factor.

PROCESSES OF BIOEROSION

Primary constructional processes develop a reef network containing many cavities (Zankl and Schroeder, 1972). These are infilled by secondary frame builders and by sediments, but at the same time destruction of the reef structure is initiated and proceeds simultaneously with the secondary frame construction. In some cases the destruction results in the production of material fine enough to be swept from the reef, but with many of these erosional processes there is merely a transfer of calcium carbonate and a change in the development and structure of the reef frame. A variety of intraskeletal, interskeletal, and boring cavities are produced that are filled with reef-derived sediment, some of which is the result of the degradation of the primary structures. The sediment is lithified internally and cements may fill or line other cavities, so that the second-

ary reef framework itself may be subjected to renewed boring and cavity formation. In time the original framework and structure may be entirely replaced
(Zankl and Schroeder, 1972).

A very high proportion of reef degradation is carried out by organisms, although it is sometimes difficult to differentiate between the truly lithophagic
organisms and those which merely occupy the spaces created by others
(McLean, 1972). The importance of bioerosion on coral reefs has long been recognized. Gardiner (1903) was one of the first to raise the question of the importance of organisms in the destruction of coral reefs and Otter (1937) made a
study of the rock-destroying organisms at Low Isles on the 1928–29 Royal Society Expedition to the Great Barrier Reef. Subsequently a wide range of studies,
some involving quantification of the rates of rock destruction, have been
made. It is possible to classify the organisms in terms of the nature of their attack on the reef substrate into grazers, browsers, and burrowers and borers.

Rock-Grazing Organisms

Organisms that graze on reef rock surfaces in search of epilithic or endolithic
blue green algae include gastropods, echinoids, and fish. Weakening of the
rock surfaces by the algae aids in the erosion process and McLean (1967a)
noted that the depth to which the algae penetrate forms on important control
on erosional rates. In the development of an optimal feeding strategy, different
grazers scrape to different depths (Paine and Vadas, 1969; Taylor, 1971), thus
ensuring maximum removal of substrate. Many grazers also engage in boring
activities and it is difficult to separate the two bioerosional mechanisms. However, McLean (1967a, b; 1974) has estimated rates of erosion indirectly from
the dry weight of fecal pellets. Annual erosion rates of beach rock for individual organisms included 0.4–1.3 cm^3 for gastropods (*Littorina, Nodolittorina,
Nerita* and *Cittarium* sp.), 2–5 cm^3 for the limpets *Acmaea* and *Fissurella*,
8–13 cm^3 for chitons, and 14 cm^3 for the sea urchin *Echinometra lucunter* on
Barbados. At Heron Island on the Great Barrier Reef, McLean (1974) estimated
rates of removal of up to 18 cm^3 for the chiton *Acanthozostera gemmata*,
which excavated a homesite of 55 cm^3 in less than five years (Fig. 3.7). Notably,

Figure 3.7 The chiton *Acanthozostera gemmata* boring into beach rock, Heron Island.

the material that is excreted is in the size range of 0.027–0.044 mm, which is easily removed from the reef. The rapid erosion produced by chitons is due to their hard denticle cappings, which have a hardness of 6 on the Moh scale (Lowenstam, 1962) compared to a hardness of about 4 for calcite.

Grazing fish, especially parrot and surgeon fish, also removed much rock material as they graze on algal-covered reef surfaces. Surface abrasions caused by such grazing have been described on the beach rock at Heron Island by Stephenson and Searles (1960) and Stephenson (1961), who estimated an annual rate of erosion by this method of 0.5 mm/yr. In Barbados, Hunter (1977) estimated a sediment production of between 1 and 2 tonnes/hectate/year by grazing fish. Also in Barbados, Frydal and Stearn (1978) recorded erosion rates of 40–168 g/m^2/yr by parrot fish. Cloud (1959) estimated that fish consume 4–6 m^3/ha/yr of sand and gravel over reef flats in the Marianas while Bardach (1961) calculated that Bermuda reef fish transport about 2.3 ton/ha/yr of sediment.

Rock-Browsing Organisms

Rock-browsing organisms such as holothurians and browsing herbivorous gastropods may be important dissolvers of reef sediments that pass through their gut. Emery et al. (1954) and Emery (1962) found that acid pH's (6.9) in the intestinal fluid of holothurians was sufficient to remove finer sediments. Large amounts of sand are moved, amounts being between 16 and 40 kg/yr for each individual, with a total of 100,000 tonnes of sand per year passing through holothurians on Rangalap Atoll (Bonham and Held, 1963). Burrowing worms and crustaceans can also ingest and defecate enormous amounts of sediment, but erosive or corrosive activities are disputed (See Milliman, 1974, p. 261).

Burrowing and Boring Organisms

While browsing and grazing animals attack rock surfaces and sediments, a large range of burrowers and borers attack the internal reef structure for purposes of food and protection (Yonge, 1963a, b; Clapp and Kenk, 1963; Alexandersson, 1972). Although their cavities may be infilled later, carbonate rock materials may be severely reduced in strength (Trudgill, 1976a, for example, reports up to 30% of volume of fabric bored in intertidal areas of Aldabra.) and whole coral colonies may break off under their own weight after internal weakening (Goreau and Hartman, 1963). Both plants and animals are involved in the boring processes and resulting cavities range from only a few microns to centimeters in diameter.

The smallest cavities are formed by fungi and bacteria. Bacteria apparently play an important initial role in the breakdown of coral heads (Di Salvo, 1969, 1973). Fungi are also important in further degradation of carbonate debris. Rooney and Perkins (1972), for example, report that on Arlington Reef near Cairns on the Great Barrier Reef, fungi are the first organisms to attack fresh debris. Borings only 1–4 μ in diameter result from this attack. Cavities only slightly larger (5–15 μ) are produced by microscopic, filamentous blue-green algae (Golubic, 1969). Duerdon (1902) was one of the first researchers to recognize the significant part they play in direct reef disintegration as well as the result of grazing upon them. Odum and Odum (1955) suggested that these algae made up 70% of the biomass of coral skeletons in the upper few millimeters. The boring process is largely biochemical, the result of acid radicals excreted by the algae. Even encrusting algae may have a small bioerosion role. Ranson (1955) reported that *Porolithon onkodes* dissolves the structure over which it develops. A great range of algae are involved in the boring process. On the Great Barrier Reef, on high supratidal shingle banks, *Anacystis montana* and *Scytonema hofmanni* produce a typical gray-black color and, through time, a deeply etched surface. Undersides of the shingle pieces frequently show green coloration from the filamentous *Pseudonidoclonium submarinum*. Lower down, within the intertidal zone, *Entophysalis deusta* is the major disintegrator, especially on beach rock. This species also extends onto the reef flat where, with *Ostreobium reinekei* and *Acetubularia moebii*, most coral and coralline algal surfaces are attacked. Rates are difficult to assess as final disintegration of algal-weakened structures is produced by other organisms or processes.

Deeper on the reef and in cryptic situations, a high proportion of the boring is carried out by sponges, especially the Clionidae family and Siphonodictyon of the Adociidae family. These can excavate at depths below 70 m. Many borings are in the outer few centimeters of the substrate, but whole coral heads may become infested (Fig. 3.8). The process is a biochemical reaction to the secretion released by amoebocytelike cells in the cytoplasm (Cobb, 1969; Pomponi, 1977). The sponge excavates the more porous corallites, cutting back the septa to the septathecal wall and sending out (20μ) filaments to invade adjacent corallites (Ward and Risk, 1977; Risk and MacGeachy, 1978). Moore and Shedd (1977) suggested that clionid bioerosion rates are tied directly to the availability through time of substrate and may approach 7 kg/m^2/yr. Boring rates of sponges are reported within the range 0.1 to 1.4 cm/yr (Neumann, 1966; Bromley, 1978). On Barbados, 90% of reef borings in coral heads is reportedly carried out by sponges, with infestation up to 23% of the volume of *Montastrea annularis* colonies (MacGeachy, 1977). Total sediment production here is estimated at between 5 and 10 t/ha/yr (Hunter, 1977). Particles produced by *Cliona* sp. are in the range 15–100 μ and are easily removed from the reef (Futterer, 1974; Ward and Risk, 1977).

Figure 3.8 *Cliona* sp. in dead *Acropora formosa* clast which has been extensively etched by filamentous algae. (Photo, M. J. Risk.)

The rapid boring rates of sponges may be matched by some molluscs. Hamner and Jones (1976) reported that the small burrowing clam, *Tridacna crocea* (Fig. 3.9) produces 200 g/m²/yr of sediment on fringing reefs of the Palm Islands on the Great Barrier Reef, with a net erosion rate of 140 g/m²/yr, rates that are similar to those for *Cliona*. The boring mechanism of this, and many other bivalves, is purely mechanical, abrasion of the substrate being caused by movement of the retractor and abductor muscles. In contrast, boring gastropods, such as *Acmaea* accomplish primary penetration by chemicals secreted by the accessary boring organism, a small portion of the weakened substrate being subsequently scraped away by the radula and swallowed (Carriker, 1961, 1969). A combination of chemical action and rasping is also employed by the most important boring Mytilids, which also precipitate carbonate linings to their cavity walls. Lined borings of *Lithophaga* sp. are the most common. Trudgill (1976a) gave rates of over 9 mm/yr for *Lithophaga* boring on Aldabra while, on the Great Barrier Reef, Otter (1937) gave figures of 1.5 cm/yr for boring extension and 0.4 cm/yr for widening of cavities during the first three years of development (Fig. 3.10).

Boring worms, both Sipunculids and Polychaetes, are also important carbonate degraders (Fig. 3.11), producing tubes up to 0.5 mm in diameter, which Newell (1956) estimated caused up to 20% of the porosity of intertidal rocks of Raroia. The action is again initially chemical, the result of a secretion by the epidermal glands that weakens the substrate, subsequent removal being facili-

Figure 3.9 A small burrowing clam, *Tridacna crocea*, firmly embedded in the top of a reef flat microatoll.

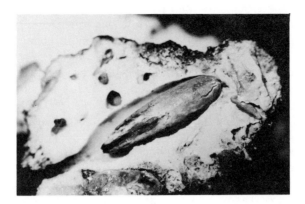

Figure 3.10 *Lithophaga* boring into reef rock. A small, partially infilled cavity can be seen just below the larger example.

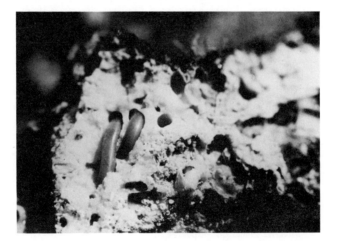

Figure 3.11 A wide variety of worms and polychaetes bore into old coral heads and cemented reef rock.

tated by the papillae and outer setae (Rice, 1969; Haigler, 1969). Of the polychaetes, the most important degraders are from the family Eunicidae (Vittor and Johnson, 1977).

Although echinoids are major grazers, they also bore into the reef for protection. Otter (1932) suggested that the borings are made by the rotary action of spines and teeth. Rates of erosion on reefs with large echinoid populations can be very high, though it is difficult to separate grazing and boring activities. On Barbados for example, *Diadema antillarum* produces 97 t/ha/yr/year of sediment, 65% of which is so fine it is winnowed out and is lost from the reef (Hunter, 1977). Also on Barbados, Stearn and Scoffin (1977) estimated that the same species of sea urchin is responsible for a loss of 163 t/yr from a reef area of only 10,800 m². Obviously their figures are related as much to the grazing as to the boring activities of *Diadema*. However, on Aldabra, Trudgill (1976a) measured boring rates for *Echinometra* of 4.93 cm/yr, faster than for any other intertidal organism he studied.

In general, crustaceans are not major burrowers except for some barnacles, such as *Lithotrya*. This has a measured burrowing rate of 8.44 mm/yr on Aldabra (Trudgill, 1976a). Ahr and Stanton (1973) suggested that *Lithotrya* produces bimodal sediment by its activities: large debris that is loosened from the substrate and a calcilutite that is easily moved to deeper water. It would appear that the larvae excavate by chemical action while adults enlarge the cavity by the action of their chitinous teeth (Tomlinson, 1969).

The bioerosion of coral reefs is so great that Stearn and Scoffin (1977) suggested that some Barbados reefs may at present have a negative carbonate budget. The cumulative effect of bioerosional activities is to weaken the reef framework, particularly as many bioeroders settle on and initially penetrate the circumference of the base of coral heads (Risk and MacGeachy, 1978). Overall rates may be rapid enough to reduce a 1 m-high head of coral to sediments in 150 years of less, giving average overall rates of removal of 0.67 cm/yr (Hudson, 1977). In the Caribbean the most important agents are the sponges and spionid polychaetes, which may rework up to 70% of the primary skeletal framework (Hein and Risk, 1975). Risk and MacGeachy (1978) have suggested that a succession of bioeroders may take place with one group of organisms preparing the substrate for the next group. Bacteria, fungi, and algae may invade coral skeletons within a few days, sponges within weeks, and spionid polychaetes shortly afterwards. Due to their inability to settle on live coral tissue, sipunculids and bivalves are relatively late arrivals. Not all reefs may be under the same extent of attack as those of the Caribbean. McLean (1974), for example, has suggested that there is a poorer bioerosional fauna on the Great Barrier Reef than on Caribbean Reefs, because of the larger tidal range. This tidal range also has the effect of giving a vertical zonation to the bioerosional agents. Grazers tend to be found high in the intertidal range while borers and burrowers are located in a lower tidal position. Risk (personal communication) has noted that boring sponge papillae are not as obvious on the Great Barrier Reef as in the Caribbean but sipunculids and bivalves are more numerous. As much of the material produced by bioerosion is fine enough to be removed from the reef, bioeroders are influential parts of the total reef carbonate budget and help to determine the net rate at which a reef may develop.

CATASTROPHIC DESTRUCTION OF CORAL REEFS

For most of the time, on most reefs, bioerosion is a parallel and continuing process operating with reef construction. At times, however, external influences may bring about catastrophic mortality to reef corals and other organisms. Subsequent recovery of major reef-framework builders may be slow and, for a period at least, the reef degraders dominate. Endean (1976) has reviewed the various factors involved in reef destruction and regeneration. He notes that:

> because of their great species diversity and concomitant trophic complexity, . . .
> mature coral reef communities possess a multiplicity of homeostatic mechanisms

that enable them to resist normal perturbations, particularly those relating to biological factors.

Localized destruction of part of a coral reef community may thus be incorporated in the natural development, both biological and geological, of the reef.

Catastrophic events are ones that are widely spaced in time and that cross thresholds not normally experienced. The rate of recovery of the reef community and the nature of the "secondary succession" through which it passes before stability is established or reestablished is important. Six types of catastrophic destruction may be experienced by coral reefs:

Mechanical Destruction

Purely mechanical breaking of corals and other reef organisms may take place as the result of heavy seas generated by tropical storms, tsunamis, or as the result of earth movements. Tropical cyclone damage has received the greatest study, particularly in Belize where Stoddart (1962b, 1963, 1965c, 1969b, 1971, 1974) has followed the effects and recovery of reefs from the catastrophic damage caused by Hurricane Hattie in 1961. Selective damage to fragile branching corals takes place over a relatively wide area affected by a tropical storm, but closer to the storm center more extensive damage takes place to greater depths, and recovery may take longer than 25 years. During Cyclone Althea near Townsville in 1971, severe damage occurred on a number of reefs (Pearson, 1975). A colony of *Leptoria* 3.3 × 2.7 × 2.1 m was cast up on the reef flat 200 m from the reef edge and smooth heads of *Porites* 2–4 m in diameter were overturned in water depths of 5–10 m. *Acropora* was damaged to depths of 20 m. Much new sediment is provided to the reef as the result of cyclone activity and many new surfaces are laid open to bioerosional processes. However, Pearson also notes that many broken corals continued to grow, with branches of *Acropora* fusing together to form a "secondary" reef framework.

The effects of tsunami waves on coral reefs are probably similar to those of tropical storms. Although reefs greatly reduce the tsunami at the coastline (Tracey et al., 1964; Shepard and Wanless, 1971) large reef blocks can be plucked from the reef front and thrown landwards (Shepard and Wanless, 1971, Fig. 15.55). Umbgrove (1947) reports that large reef blocks were thrown onto reef flats by the 1883 Krakatoa and other tsunamis in a similar way to those cast up by cyclones.

Although many reef areas are located in highly seismic regions, with severe earthquakes having a frequency of occurrence greater than that of tropical storms, there are few accounts of the effects on coral structures. Stoddart (1972a) has described the effects of an earthquake of force 7.1 on the Richter scale at Madang in New Guinea in 1970. Structural damage varied greatly with species and growth form; massive corals (*Porites, Goniopora, Lobophyllia*) disintegrating in situ or being uprooted and sliding or rolling downslope. Vasiform foliaceous corals (*Turbinaria, Echinopora, Echinophyllia, Pectinia, Mycedium*) were particularly fragmented because of their resistance to water movement. Branching *Acropora* colonies were snapped off, but, as with cyclone damage, these corals continued to live. Stoddart reported great variation in the degree of damage over short distances, so that no species was entirely removed from the reef. He considers that this is likely to lead to more rapid recovery than in areas affected by severe storms. It is possible that frequent destruction of corals may favor rapidly growing branching species that are easily destroyed but regenerate more rapidly. Reef fabrics in highly seismic areas may thus lack the interlocking frameworks of robust, ramose, and massive corals found in more stable areas. Eight months after the Madang earthquake the secondary succession of reef-degrading organisms including filamentous algae was commencing the bioerosional phase of degradation prior to recovery.

Exposure

Upper limits of coral growth are set by normal tidal exposure. Infrequently very low spring tides may coincide with heatwave conditions or with heavy rainfall, both of which may cause widespread coral mortality. Similarly during a tropical cyclone, the "negative" surge that may occur in the right forward sector of a southern hemisphere storm, can reduce water levels and expose corals to the associated heavy rainfall. Other unusual or infrequent variations of sea level can also result in death of reef organisms, particularly in areas of low or insignificant tidal range. For example, Yamaguchi (1975) described the mass mortality of reef animals at Guam when episodic anomalies in large-scale oceanographic conditions, reinforced by local wind stress, reduced monthly mean sea level by as much as 44.2 cm below MSL during 1972. Reef-flat communities, especially on windward reefs, were decimated and nearly all macroscopic organisms within the inner reef flat of Pago Bay were killed. Recovery three years later was small, particularly of corals, echinoderms, and some gastropods. Permanent exposure of reefs can take place by tectonic uplift in some highly seismic areas. Stoddart (1969c) considers this a factor in recently dead reefs in the Solomon Islands, where Grover (1965) has given an account of the emergence of reef flats and mangroves during an earthquake in 1961. Relative movements of 1–1.25 m have been described as the result of earthquakes and Stoddart (1969c) considers that movements of less than 0.5 m are sufficient to cause death of reef-flat corals. Exposure of reef-flat corals maintained behind shingle ramparts, which form effective dams for maintaining water levels on the low tide, may take place as the result of tropical cyclones. Breaching of the shingle ramparts causes a fall in water level exposing at least the tops of lagoon corals, as occurred on Holbourne Island near Bowen in 1918 (Hopley and Isdale, 1977). These changes are discussed further in Chapter 4.

Temperature and Salinity Variations

The narrow temperature and salinity limits within which corals grow makes them susceptible to any abnormal change in these parameters, particularly close to the extremes of their distribution. Fringing reefs are more susceptible than open ocean reefs, as reduced salinity is intensified by runoff and lowered temperature may also be associated with flow of cool waters from a cooled continental landmass. Reef organisms are particularly susceptible to these factors during low tides. Examples of extensive death of corals on the Great Barrier Reef and adjacent islands are discussed in Chapter 12. Increased salinity may also kill reef animals and plants. However, sudden salinity increases of a catastrophic nature are not frequent and are associated with highly unusual events.

An example is provided by Salvat et al. (1977) at Taiaro Atoll in the Tuamotus. Slight uplift about 1000 yrs B.P. isolated the lagoon from the open ocean by closing all but one of the "hoa" (lagoon exits). Complete isolation was caused during the nineteenth century as the result of the blocking of the remaining exit by a boulder rampart deposited during high seas. Corals were initially killed by the uplift, but subsequently hypersaline conditions (about 43‰) have developed and only *Porites lobata* survives, compared to about 14 species prior to the lagoon being closed. Other fauna have been similarly restricted.

Sedimentation

Sudden increases in sedimentation rates may blanket corals with sand or finer size material and, if this is not removed within a few days, may cause widespread mortality. Again, fringing reefs receiving runoff from the mainland are particularly susceptible. Coral growth is normally restricted close to river mouths. However, change in the location of a river mouth may cause sudden increases of sedimentation on previously thriving coral reefs. Bird (1971b) attributed the decline of reefs at Yule Point to changes in the location of the mouth of the Mowbray River near Port Douglas. Movement of sediment during tropical cyclones also causes burial of corals. Moorehouse (1936) described shingle ramparts moving over living reef flat corals during the 1934 cyclone at Low Isles. Pearson (1975) reported that several meters of sand were moved on reefs off Townsville down to depths of 10 m during Cyclone Althea in 1971. On Wheeler Reef a small unvegetated sand cay was completely destroyed, its sand being distributed over the adjacent reef flat, where it smothered several hectares of corals (Hopley, 1974a). Although the sand has since been removed and the cay reconstituted, this area of reef flat remains dead.

Biological Causes of Mortality

Beyond the normal levels of predation and bioerosion, there may be times when the ecological balance of a coral reef system is upset by unusual or infrequent population explosions. Baas-Becking (1951) described coral deaths as the result of masses of the planktonic alga *Trichodesmium* being washed onto a reef. Large slicks of these algae are commonly found in Great Barrier Reef waters but no damage to reefs has been reported and it is likely that other more unusual circumstances have to combine with the slicks to cause widespread mortality. Of greater significance in recent years have been the population explosions of the crown-of-thorns starfish *Acanthaster planci* in many areas of the Indo-Pacific (see Vol. 1, Proceedings of the Second International Coral Reef Symposium, Brisbane, 1974 and Vol. 1, Proceedings of the Third International Coral Reef Symposium, Miami, 1977). Some researchers (Chesher, 1969; Endean, 1973, 1974; Endean and Chesher, 1973; Randall, 1972) consider that the population explosions are abnormal events caused by human activities (pollution or overcollection of predators, such as the giant triton *Charonia tritonis*), but others (Newman, 1970; Dana, 1970) suggest that such population explosions have occurred previously. On the Great Barrier Reef, Frankel (1975, 1977) has suggested that previous population explosions have occurred at 250–300 year intervals. Normally *A. planci* has a population density of about $6/km^2$ (Endean, 1974) on reefs, but on infested reefs whole areas may be covered by the starfish, which feed on the coral polyps, leaving dead colonies that undergo subsequent degradation. Many reefs of the Great Barrier Reef have been reported as infested (Fig. 3.12) but it must be stressed that while locally damage may be very severe, in any one area there may be reefs relatively unaffected, and even on infested reefs parts may remain free of the aggregations.

Human Activities

Human activities may deliberately or indeliberately cause the death of reef organisms. Endean (1976) listed dredging and mining, land clearance, blasting and nuclear-weapon testing, sewerage pollution, thermal pollution from power stations, desalination effluents, oil pollution, chemical pollution, and collection of elements of reef biota as human activities that have demonstrably destroyed coral reefs. An excellent example of man's impact on the reef system is Kanehoe Bay in Hawaii (Banner, 1974). Dredging destroyed small areas of reef during and prior to World War II, but a postwar population increase of 8% per annum in the catchments flowing into the bay has led to clearing and extensive urbanization. This in turn has affected the hydrology of the area, with rapid runoff and erosion. In May 1965 alone, quickflow from between 460 and 830 mm of rainfall delivered fresh water to the bay equivalent to 16% of its capacity, producing mortality of corals to a depth of 1.5 m near streams and 0.3 m over the whole bay. Flow of over 4 million gallons per day of sewerage into Kanehoe Bay has produced intense eutrophication, with a 70% increase in zooplankton and large increases in benthic detrital and filter feeders. Corals previously killed have been replaced by algae, especially *Dyctosphaeria cavernosa*. The overall result has been the destruction of over 70% of the former 96.6 km of growing reef front within the lagoon of the bay, 29.3% being removed by dredging, 23.5% killed by overgrowth of algae, 8.5% by the direct effects of sewerage, and 9.8% by fresh water and sediment.

Reports on the nature and rates of recovery from these various catastrophic events is remarkably similar in all cases except where extensive siltation has taken place or where eutrophication of reef waters has led to an artificially stimulated ecoystem, as in Kanehoe Bay. There it is estimated that even under the control introduced into the environment in 1977, recovery will take many years (S. V. Smith, 1977). Elsewhere, partial recovery has taken place within as short a period as three years, and full recovery may have taken place within 20 years. For example, Pearson (1974, 1975) reported about 90% coral cover on John Brewer Reef near Townsville within four years of devastation by *A. planci* and even more extensive recovery has taken place on reefs near Innisfail, devastated during the mid-1960s. These figures are similar to those quoted by Endean (1976) for recovery of corals at Heron Island in 1967 following cyclone damage. Prior to the cyclone coral cover was 57%. After complete denudation, within three and a half years there was a 10% cover and a 20% cover within four and a half years. However, Stoddart (1974) suggested that recovery may take up to 50 years on reef areas severely damaged by cyclones. Grigg and Maragos (1974) showed that it takes 20 years for recovery of reefs damaged by lava flows in Hawaii, although sheltered areas may take up to 50 years.

In the intervening years the reef substrate and devastated corals undergo a series of changes, which again tend to be similar irrespective of the nature of

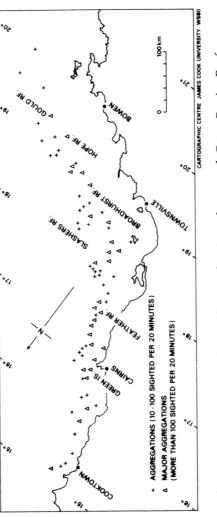

Figure 3.12 Aggregations of *Acanthaster planci* on the central Great Barrier Reef reported between about 1960 and 1975.

the catastrophe. Initial colonization of coral skeletons takes place within a few weeks and is by filamentous algae. These are followed by turf-forming algae that in turn attract invertebrate grazers and browsers. Subsequently within about a year the dead corals may be colonized by crustose corallines, although degradational organisms such as sipunculids and siliceous sponges may also move into the area at about this stage (Price, 1975). Depending on the local environment there may be a period of green algal growth (*Padina* or *Halimeda*) or, especially in silted areas, an increase in the numbers of soft corals, the extensive presence of which will slow down the rate of hard coral recolonization (Garrett, 1975). The first hard corals to recover are either the fastest growing, such as *Acropora*, or the most hardy, such as *Porites*, some colonies of which may survive the catastrophic event.

THE PRODUCT OF BIOLOGICAL PROCESSES

Scoffin and Garrett (1974) recognized five reef-forming processes, primary framework construction, boring, secondary framework construction, burial, and cementation, all of which involve biological processes. Zankl and Multer (1977) suggested that these processes result in a highly porous framework, but with the initial primary framework with pore spaces from 1 micron to 1 meter in diameter being replaced by destructive framework porosities with pore sizes ranging from a micron to a centimeter. Primary porosity is reduced continuously by organic encrustation, internal sedimentation, and cementation to produce the typical creamy reef rock that underlies most reefs. An increasing micritization caused by both chemical and biological activities obliterates sedimentary and biological structures. In turn these changes enhance microbiological activity and produce a chemically active environment that further favors the formation of a dense reef rock from the original primary framework. Cloud (1959) neatly summarized the geological and geomorphological significance of biological processes when he stated:

> Geologically the reef complex is an aggregate of calcium carbonate-secreting and frame-building organisms, associated biota and mainly biogenic sediments. Ecologically it is an essentially steady-state oasis of organic productivity featured by high population density, intense calcium metabolism, and complex nutrient chains, generally surrounded by waters of relatively low mineral nutrient and plankton content. Any reef complex at any given time is the resultant of its nutrient chains and their disintegration products (and of the past history of the reef).

In the following chapters the chemical and physical processes that act in harness with the biological processes are examined, while the processes operating over a geological time scale are discussed in the next section.

4

Physical Processes
on Coral Reefs

In contrast to the biological and chemical processes operating on coral reefs, physical processes have received little attention. Roberts (1974) considered this to be the result of the rigor of the reef environment, which makes measurement of these processes extremely difficult, and was able to quote only a handful of references that treated reefs in the context of energy fields to which they respond. These included the work of Munk and Sargent (1948, 1954), who examined the function of spur and groove systems as breakwaters against high wave-energy conditions, and the associated study of von Arx (1948, 1954), who researched lagoon circulation and exchange systems between lagoon and open ocean waters. Storr (1964) measured wave-induced circulation across a shallow reef in the Bahamas and other estimates of wave energy along reef coastlines were made by Walsh et al. (1962). However, the relationships between wave energy and variations in reef composition and structure were not incorporated in these studies and it is only in the last few years that the work of Roberts and his associates has indicated the importance of the physical feedback relationship that exists on coral reefs. Reef morphology and composition are at least partially dependant on the combinations, intensities, and spatial-temporal variations of physical processes while simultaneously the rates of these processes are distinctly influenced by reef morphology and its associated bottom roughness (Roberts et al., 1975, 1977).

The coral reef geomorphological system differs from most terrestrial geomorphological systems where the driving forces of physical processes are derived from a downslope gravitational component combined with atmospheric components deriving their energy from solar radiation and expressed in the hydrologic cycle. Such forces operate only on the small reef islands where the opportunity for potential energy is limited by the small elevation and where running water is in any case limited by very high percolation rates. In the submarine environment the gravitational force is important, but reduced by the water-pressure force or buoyancy (Kornicker and Squires, 1962). Instead, the driving force is provided by the atmospheric system transferring energy to the water surface as wind waves both within the local reef environment and more distantly (whence energy is transported to the reef system by swell waves) and by the gravitational forces of the sun and moon,

101

which are expressed in turbulent friction of tidal motion, particularly in shallow marginal seas. This chapter examines the ways in which this energy is expended on the reef in terms of waves, tides, and currents together with the resultant patterns of sedimentation that arise from the combination of the biological and physical processes.

WAVES ON CORAL REEFS

The influence of wave approach on coral reef morphology has long been recognized (Verstappen, 1968), reefs frequently being "streamlined" in their planimetric shape into the prevailing winds of the area in which they occur. Windward edges where waves break are straighter and more continuous (termed "hard-line" on the Great Barrier Reef) than the more broken leeward side, where the reef front may break into isolated patches. Although many coral reef regions are situated within the trade-wind belt, where vigorous wind speeds within the range 15–25 kn are experienced for most of the year, the wave energy contained within waves generated locally, even over fetches of several hundred kilometers, may be equalled by the energy imported into the region by swell waves generated in the high latitude storm belt (Davies, 1972). Within the Pacific the majority of swell waves are derived from the wide expanse of ocean in the southern hemisphere that lies within the high latitude storm belt. Swell is essentially southerly and in the northern Pacific this may result in an even distribution of wave energy from north and south, southern swells being matched by northern wind waves driven by the northeast trades. However, on the Great Barrier Reef swell and wind waves normally approach from the southeast, giving the majority of reefs distinct windward and leeward sides, although some variation may be produced by interference to wave trains by reefs that lie upwind.

In general, deep-water approaches very close to the shelf reefs of the Great Barrier Reef so that frictional interference to waves is minimal to within a few hundred meters of the reefs. In this way, and also in the fact that shallow water extends over the reef top for much of the tidal cycle, coral reefs differ in their effect on waves from continental islands of similar shape and size. Wave refraction around reefs can be seen quite clearly from the air, convergence producing a concentration of energy on the windward reef front, but much lower energy levels on the leeward side where wave fronts may have been reoriented by 180°. Wave convergence on a point towards the leeward side of the reef has long been considered the cause of sediment movement towards this point and eventual formation of a cay (see Stoddart and Steers, 1977, p. 94).

However, because of the shallow cover of water over reef flats and lagoons, coral reefs are not a solid barrier to waves and some energy is transmitted over the reef crest and onto the reef top. Movement of waves beyond the reef front is dependant to a large extent on the depth of water and an important factor is thus wave setup. Munk and Sargent (1954) noted that higher water levels on the reef flat of Bikini Atoll were due solely to waves breaking on the reef. In an examination of wave setup on coral reefs, Tait (1972) found that momentum-flux considerations gave reasonably good predictions of the amount of wave-induced setup. It is possible that water levels on the outer edge of sea-level reefs can be raised as much as 20% of the incident wave height above the mean water level just seaward of the reef, with significant effect on water circulation and sediment movement.

In a theoretical consideration of wave-energy transmission at the reef edge, Dexter (1973) suggested that the removal of energy from the incident wave at the reef edge is manifested by the breaking of this wave with a certain wave height transmitted reefward in shallow water and another wave reflected seaward. In order to determine the resulting wave height over the reef he assumed that the reformed wave would take the form of a solitary wave. Dexter also stated that during propagation of the solitary wave through the shallow water loss of energy will occur due to viscous shear within the boundary layer beneath the wave. This will be indicated by loss of wave height, which over a smooth bottom such as a sanded reef flat will occur only slowly. Dexter illustrated this with an example of cyclonic waves at Hixon's Cay in the Coral Sea. With a significant wave height of 7.62 m in open water, wave setup at the reef edge would be 1.21 m. Transmitted waves would have a height of 1.77 m and over 365 m of reef flat with a 2.4 m water depth would show little or no alteration before breaking on the cay.

Unfortunately no measurements of waves have been made in a systemmatic way over any of the reefs off the Queensland coast. However, work on Grand Cayman Island in the Caribbean supports the theoretical work of Dexter (Roberts, 1974; Roberts et al., 1975, 1977; Suhayda and Roberts, 1977). Although these are fringing reefs the wave climate of the area is similar to that of the outer Great Barrier Reefs, and as most wave attenuation takes place over the reef front, the observations made on Grand Cayman in a general sense may be applicable to the Great Barrier Reef. Certainly the forereef morphology of terrace levels and spur and groove systems can be seen on many Australian reefs. Roberts (1974) made calculations of wave power around Grand Cayman. His results clearly show the great difference between windward and leeward reef situations in a trade wind environment. Wave-power levels for the sheltered coast were about 80 times less than those on the open coast. Yearly mean wave power for 2 km long sample coastal sectors at 10 m depth was 4.33×10^9 ergs/sec on the open coast, compared to 0.08×10^9 ergs/sec on the sheltered side of the island, and at the shore the comparable figures were 3.48×10^9 and 0.04×10^9 ergs/sec.

The observed metamorphosis of waves on the reef edge is very similar to the predictions made by Dexter. Between the deep water and the shallow (8 m) forereef terrace, a distance of about 400 m, a general decrease in energy density of about 45% and a height reduction of about 20% was observed, although the general shape of the wave spectrum and the modal frequency remain the same. These changes are due to a number of processes including shoaling, refraction, reflection and scattering, and frictional attenuation. Roberts et al., (1975, 1977) could not quantify the individual processes but suggested that with a bottom roughness of about 2 m the bottom friction coefficient and wave scattering would be about ten times that on a sandy shelf of similar width. Wave reflection is also considered important, the reflection coefficient on the shallow terrace alone being about 10%, with refraction and shoaling possibly producing a reduction in wave height of the same magnitude. However, the variability in reef morphology also produces great variability in the rate of wave processes. Roberts et al. (1975, 1977) considered that the reef fronts are molded into natural breakwaters consisting of long ridges and channels (spur and groove systems) that efficiently dissipate the energy of incoming waves.

Observations have also been made on the formation of the transmitted waves beyond the reef crest in Barbados by Roberts et al (1975). As predicted by Dexter, there is a substantial loss of wave energy and a significant change in the wave-spectrum shape. The estimated energy loss calculated from the change in wave height for average trade-wind conditions (wind speeds of 6 m/sec) was about 75%. Breaking flattened the spectrum peak and transferred energy to low frequency, the exact amount depending on the depth of water over the reef crest and the input wave conditions. Although not directly comparable, figures for Redbill Reef on the Great Barrier Reef (Table 4.1) give similar results. Wave measurements were made (Hopley, in press) on the reef flat near the cay on this reef (see Fig. 9.7) and deep-water waves calculated from Bretschneider (1966). Energy loss varies from 60% for small waves travelling over 1100 m of smooth, sanded reef flat from the north, to over 90% for larger waves passing over more than 2 km of reef flat, much of which has a relief of up to 1 m, to south and southeast.

Over the reef flat and in the lee of the reef it is possible that the corals themselves contribute to the decline in wave height in a way not previously considered. Hicks et al (1974) observed surprisingly small wind stress over a fringing reef. Deacon (1979) suggested that this was the result of the mucus released by the corals on the windward reef edge. The mucus contains much cetyl palmitate, which on hydrolysis yields powerful surfactants of a type found in natural sea slicks. These are sufficient to modify the state of the sea surface under wind speeds of at least 20 kn.

WAVE AND TIDAL CURRENTS

Water movement around and within reef systems is produced by tidal ebb and flood, by wind stress on the ocean surface on a regional scale, and by wave action locally on the reef itself. Wave setup alone will tend to generate currents

Table 4.1 Wave Data, Redbill Reef 1975

Conditions	N Wind 6 kn	S Wind 16 kn	SE Wind 10 kn
Calculated deep-water wave height (m)	0.46	1.28	0.76
Measured reef-flat wave height (m)	0.29	0.41	0.33
Calculated energy loss (percent)	60	91	91
Distance over reef flat traveled from reef edge (m)	1100	2100	2500

moving water across the reef crest onto the reef flat or lagoon. Von Arx (1948) indicated that the setup due to normal trade-wind generated waves of about 2.1 m created currents that accounted for a third the lagoon volume in water added each day. Extremely large storm waves of 10 m or more can produce a setup of up to 2 m and, as Tait (1972) states, this is greater than the tidal range of many midoceanic and Caribbean reefs. However, on the Great Barrier Reef, where tidal ranges everywhere exceed 2.5 m and in places exceed 5 m, it is likely that currents produced by wave setup will rarely dominate over the tidal ebb and flow. Even at Grand Cayman, where the tidal range is only 30 cm, on the deeper forereef terrace a marked periodicity occurs in diurnal current speeds that is close to the tidal frequency (Roberts, et al., 1975, 1977). However, in this microtidal environment the ebb and flow is sufficiently strong to reverse the direction of the current only on the highest spring tides.

Vertical contrasts in current activity on the reef front have been clearly demonstrated by Roberts, et al. (1975, 1977) on Grand Cayman. On the shallow 8 m terrace, current speeds were rarely in excess of 15 cm/sec and usually less than 7.5 cm/sec. Bimodal distributions in current recordings and variations in direction suggested that both wave- and tide-induced water movements were operating here. In contrast, on the deeper, 20 m terrace, currents were more unidirectional and speeds generally greater than 15 cm/sec and as high as 30 cm/sec were recorded. Clearly a 60–70% reduction in current speed is indicated from the deep to the shallow shelf, produced by large vertical and lateral frictional forces induced by extreme values of roughness. Reef-crest currents may also be unidirectional. Results from Great Corn Island, Nicaragua, showed that a current operating in surges of 50–80 cm/sec for durations of a few seconds in response to wave action, continually moves water into the lagoon. At low tide, wave breaking is more complete on the reef crest and a greater amount of wave energy is utilized in driving the current over the crest and into the back reef region (Suhayda and Roberts, 1977). Once in the lagoon water is moved essentially by tidal currents with marked reversals in direction with tidal ebb and flow. Water movement out of the lagoon is through major gaps in the reef front rather than in the channels of the reef front spur and groove system. Roberts et al. (1977) showed by dye experiments that water movement is upgroove with high levels of turbulence.

Little information is available to confirm similar movements of water on reefs of the Great Barrier Reef. Wave action is strongest on the southeastern sides of reefs and wave-induced currents over reef crests are probably reinforced by the tidal ebb current, which generally sets to the north over much of the Great Barrier Reef. Flood-tide currents in the reverse direction may be considered to dampen or even reverse the wave currents during the rising tide. However, this is not suggested by the results of research on surface-water flow at Lizard Island (LIMER, 1976) where, under conditions of southeasterly winds of 12–15 kn, water movement is over the reef rim and into the lagoon at all stages of the tide but most strongly on the flood tide. Only in the lagoon exit is there an apparent reversal of currents with the tide. Similarly, on Three Isles, a low wooded island south of Lizard Island (see Chapter 11), experiments with Woodhead seabed drifters (Phillips, 1970) over two tidal cycles in 15 kn winds showed a net current movement from south to north across the reef flat.

Observations of individual drifters on both flood and ebb tides showed that this was the constant direction of movement at all times. These two examples are from areas where the tidal range is only 2.3 m. However, observations on Red-bill Reef opposite Mackay are more in keeping with the suggested model. This reef, which is completely surrounded by a high algal rim, experiences a 4.8 m tidal range. Within the lagoon and over the reef flat current velocities of be-tween 10 and 20 cm/sec from the northeast were recorded on the ebb tide, and velocities generally below 15 cm/sec from the south were recorded on the flood under light wind conditions (Hopley, in press). However, as the tide drops towards the level of the rim, velocities of up to 1.1 m/sec are recorded on the ebbing tide out through low points within the impounding rim and velocities of up to 32 cm/sec for short periods in the opposite direction on the flooding tide.

Even less information is available from the Great Barrier Reef on the behaviour of regional currents around the reefs. Although a thin layer of water overlies a reef at high tide, the steep rise of most reefs from the continental shelf in the Great Barrier Reef province suggests that current flow will be similar to that observed around oceanic islands (e.g. Knox, 1974), which can be simulated by relatively simple hydrodynamic models. Observations suggest that flow tends to stagnate upstream of the obstruction with acceleration along the flanks. Using basic hydrodynamic equations Murray et al. (1977) have modelled the current field around a cylindrical obstruction that simulates an island or reef. For the example where symmetry exists across the flow axis, stagnation zones of weak currents are formed on the nose of the obstruction and directly behind it while zones of very strong currents (jets or rips) form on the flanks. As a number of studies had indicated net circulations around islands, Murray et al. also produced a model with asymmetry across the flow axis. In this case the two stagnation zones migrate and coalesce to form a zone of weak currents around the northern end of the circular obstruction, and a belt of extremely high speeds is concentrated on the southwestern corner. These calculations were for far-field current speeds of 20 cm/sec, which are similar to regional currents reported in Great Barrier Reef waters, and it seems likely that the current pattern around many reefs will be similar to that described. In areas where reefs are closely spaced, interference between reefs will complicate the patterns.

REEF RESPONSE TO WAVE AND CURRENT PATTERNS

The combined effects of waves and currents may be expected to produce responses in the physical and biological characteristics of reef crest and forereef slope. Roberts et al. (1975, 1977) reduced the physical influences to a single force F calculation based on the common quadratic stress law

$$F = \frac{1}{2} \rho A C_d u^2$$

where ρ = the density of seawater
A = the exposed cross-sectional area (taken as 1 cm^2 on a vertical plane)
C_d = the drag coefficient (taken as 1.95)
u = velocity in cm/sec

The result, for representative total current velocities of 50 cm/sec and wave-force calculation for typical Grand Cayman trade-wind generated waves (T = 6 sec, H = 75 cm) are shown in Figure 4.1. A most interesting result of these calculations is the fact that at the shelf edge current-induced forces are approximately equal to wave-induced forces at a depth of about 3 m near the reef crest. However, there is a great difference between the rapidly fluctuating energy levels of the wave zone and the more steady forces associated with the current zone. Crossing of the wave and current profiles (Fig. 4.1) delineates the separation of the shallow wave-dominated portion of the shelf from the deeper current-dominated zones. In Grand Cayman, sediments in abundance have accumulated at this point forming a midshelf reservoir. Further, at this point the coral community changes from a shallow wave-resistant *Acropora palmata* dominated assemblage to a deeper group characterized by the more intricately branching *A. cervicornis.*

Two factors contribute to a less clear-cut division on reef fronts of the Great Barrier Reef. First, the greater tidal range on the Great Barrier Reef produces a current-force pattern quite different to that in the Caribbean. Observations by divers suggest that maximum tidal-current velocities occur on the upper 4 m of the reef front and gradually decline with depth (e.g. Wallace, 1975). Thus the combined force distribution would tend to show a simple peak in the upper forereef area, declining steadily with depth. The second factor is the greater diversity of species on Great Barrier Reef reef fronts, Wallace (1978) for example describing 40 species of *Acropora* in the central region, most of which can occur on reef fronts. Nonetheless, distinctive growth-form variations can be recognized. Wallace (1978) notes that all species that extend down the reef slopes exhibit a gradual flattening out of shape with depth, but this is due, at least in part, to reduction in radiant energy and illumination. However, the

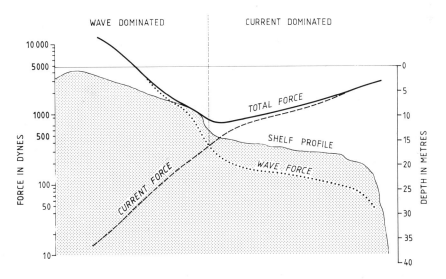

Figure 4.1 Distribution of wave and current forces across a forereef shelf calculated for a vertical surface oriented directly into the flow. (From Roberts et al., 1977, reproduced by permission of the Third International Reef Symposium Committee.)

greatest variety in colony shape seems to occur in areas with good water cover and reasonable water circulation. Such areas on reef fronts would appear to coincide with the depth at which normal wave and tide forces are much reduced, a depth which is about 8–10 m on the central Great Barrier Reef province, where all species and colony shapes of *Acropora* except species exclusive to the reef flat occur together. From a physical viewpoint this is the most benign area for coral growth and coincides with high levels of radiant energy and illumination. At greater depths these factors become more dominant. The possible lack of an intermediate area of minimal total force on the Great Barrier Reef also removes the possibility of a zone in which sediment may lodge. Small sediment accumulations can be seen on many reef slopes, even on windward edges but their location below the upper high-energy zone appears to be topographically controlled rather than influenced solely by energy conditions.

The results of energy measurements in the Caribbean also confirmed that reef morphology responds to the synoptic distribution of wave power. In Grand Cayman well-structured reefs occur along the intermediate to high-energy sectors of the coast (Roberts, 1974, Roberts et al., 1975). Here reef fronts are steep, have well-developed spur and groove systems and are oriented into the dominant wave approach direction. In contrast, low-energy sectors show less steeply sloping profiles and extensive sediment accumulations. Patch reefs may flourish on the leeward side but apparently energy levels are too low to promote amalgamation of these features into a thriving reef front.

The presence of sediment slopes on lee sides of reefs also reflects the pattern of regional water movement around the reefs. Murray et al. (1977) in their study of currents in the Caribbean, show that extensive areas of sediment accumulation occur to the lee of their high-speed current zones. As the carrying capacity of currents in the accelerated flow zone are decreased towards the lee side of island or reef, sediments are deposited and gradually moved shoreward or reefward. The shifting of these sediments restricts suitable substrate areas for coral colonization and subsequent reef growth. Where shallow reefs occur, they are generally patchlike, and frequent breaks in the reef trend allow for the movement of sediment. Although the original observations were made on fringing reefs of the Caribbean, the contrast between the higher energy hard-line reef, which is oriented to the southeast on the Great Barrier Reef, and lee-side patch reef development on the northwest sides is a similar response. The greatest contrast is seen on the ribbon reefs of the northern province where the hard-line eastern reef margin is frequently separated from the irregular lee side with detrital slopes and patch-reef development by only 400 m or so of reef flat (Fig. 4.2), but morphological contrasts between windward and leeward margins are seen on all reefs (see Chap. 10). The contrasting energy conditions as the result of wave refraction on One Tree Reef have been described by Davies, et al. (1976). Windward margins are characterized by perpendicular wave approach and the sediment forms are the result of swash action. Intermediate margins are influenced largely by longshore movements. In the low-energy leeward zone is a small shadow zone of minimal sediment import, but also a larger area where standing waves develop between the interference of the opposing wave fronts refracted around each side of the reef. These produce parallel, alternating very low- and high-energy zones producing alter-

Figure 4.2 Bowl Reef near Townsville. Hard-line windward reef contrasts with irregular leeward development. This young linear reef shows a reef top characterized mainly by aligned coral heads with only small areas of developing algal pavement (more even tone). A back-reef sand slope with isolated coral colonies is clearly seen.

nating rubble banks, deeper coral-rich areas and sand sheets indicative of standing-wave effects (Davies et al., 1976, Fig. 8).

PROCESSES OF TIDAL MOATING AND MICROATOLL FORMATION

Under normal unmodified tidal oscillation it has been stated in Chapter 3 that corals will grow to a level between MLWS and MLWN before being limited by emersion. In some circumstances, however, water may be held back at low water and not drain to the same level as in the open ocean. Moating may occur at any intertidal level and some lower-level moated pools may come into being only on the lowest spring tides. Smaller moated pools form in depressions within the reef flat or, on continental islands, within crevices in shore platforms. Much larger portions of reef flat are moated by a variety of damming agents. Most commonly these are rubble banks or ramparts of coral shingle deposited by storm waves around the reef-flat margins (Fig. 11.8). Although small gaps may occur in the dam, flow of water off the reef flat is retarded and the subsequent lowering of the water level on the reef flat may be very slow. Under such circumstances the water level on the reef flat may be at least 0.5 m higher than the open sea at MLWS. It is a situation that is very common on the low wooded island reefs of the northern Great Barrier Reef (see Chap. 11). Given sufficient time the efficiency of the dam may be enhanced by basal cementation of the shingle banks and/or filling of interstitial spaces by compaction and finer sediments. Water levels then drop to the level of the dam and show no further fall on the low tide. This too is seen on many low wooded island reefs with levels as high as MHWN being maintained. In the higher tidal-range area of the central Great Barrier Reef, high algal rims commonly form dams around pools varying in size from a few m² to several km². Typical is Redbill Reef (Figs. 4.3, and 8.8), which is completely encircled by a massive algal rim, terraced on its seaward side. MLWS here is 0.5 m and MHWS 4.8 m but the algal rim, which rises to over 2.6 m, maintains low-water levels within 1.6 cm of 2.6 m for up to 5 hours on each low tide. This is only 8 cm below MSL and on spring tides, up to 2.3 m above the adjacent open-water level as can be seen from the tidal record for the impounded lagoon (Fig. 4.4). Ludington (1979) has described similar moating within the reef crest of One Tree Reef where lagoon water levels are maintained near MSL for five to six hours of each tide. On the majority of lagoonal reefs the water is impounded to some extent but normally the level of the rim is much lower and less effective than the massive and relatively impervious algal rims of the central province. A more unusual form of moat on the Great Barrier Reef is formed by emerged platform rocks and associated emerged corals on the low wooded islands. Nymph Island and Turtle II Island near Lizard Island are examples. Both are low wooded islands containing large central lagoons with narrow exits, through which water drains at low tide, but not below the sill level that in both examples is between MHWN and MHWS.

Figure 4.3 The massive dam formed by the algal rim on Redbill Reef. Small terraces and algal rimmed pools occur on the seaward side of the feature.

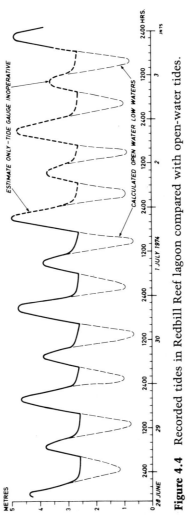

Figure 4.4 Recorded tides in Redbill Reef lagoon compared with open-water tides.

The most important aspect of moating is that behind the dam the tide consistently falls to the same level on every tide, unlike in the open-water situation where variations between spring and neap tides may produce low-water levels more than 2 m apart on the central Great Barrier Reef. The upper level of coral growth is thus firmly fixed and the result is the typical microatoll form (Fig. 4.5). In their simplest form microatolls are flattened disk-shaped coral colonies consisting of living vertical sides and dead centers often covered by crustose coralline algae. The majority are formed by the massive rounded corals such as *Porites* or *Goniopora* but Wells (1957) has described large, less compact microatolls formed by branching corals such as *Acropora palifera*. On the Great Barrier Reef branching corals such as *Porites andrewsi*, and *Helipora coerulae* also adopt the microatoll morphology. Agassiz (1895) was apparently the first to compare the morphology to "miniature atolls," although the specific term microatoll is attributable to Wood-Jones (1910).

Microatolls develop from evenly growing hemispherical coral colonies whose upward growth is interrupted by a specific level of subaerial exposure (Scoffin and Stoddart, 1978; Stoddart and Scoffin, 1979). Upward growth is limited to no more than 5 cm above moated tide levels, a height at which complete dessication of the upward part of the colony is prevented by the lapping of small waves, protective mucous coatings and by capillary action. The surface of a classical microatoll assumes a slightly raised rim above a flat or dished

Figure 4.5 A variety of microatolls, some coalescing into more complex forms, reaching moat level with the centre dying and colonized by algae. There is sufficient wave activity to maintain the uppermost living level a few centimeters above water level. The example comes from the Turtle Islands.

center that many believe to be an erosional feature (e.g. Fairbridge, 1968). As the microatoll develops, the leading edge of the rim grows outwards while the trailing edge dies. Undercutting of the inner edge may result from both solution and bioerosion, aided by filamentous algae and bacteria. After the erosional phase, an algal succession may take place and protective calcareous algae prevent further rapid attack, allowing a subhorizontal inner surface to form while the original width of the rim is maintained (Fig. 4.6).

This hypothesis assumes that the moated water level is constant throughout the life of the microatoll. Where this is not so, distinctive variations in surface morphology occur. A rise in the moated level will cause the living rim to grow upwards, producing, in time, a distinctive ring with deeper

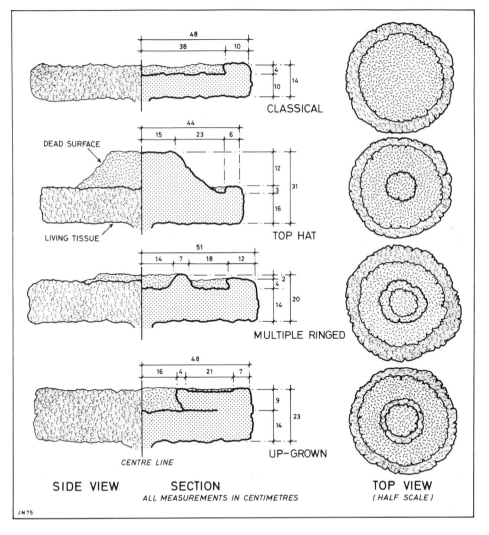

Figure 4.6 The various forms of microatoll formed by stable, falling, or rising moat levels. Dimensions are of field examples.

inner pool. If the raised level is sufficiently high the inner pool may provide a suitable environment with sufficient circulation and depth to allow the inner side of the rim to grow inwards (Fig. 4.6). A lowering of moated water level will cause the reverse effect and, providing that the new level provides a pool of depth greater than a minimum threshold value, a new lower surface will develop in the microatoll producing a ''top hat'' morphology (Fig. 4.6). A sudden drop in level may be due to breaching of a former shingle barrier during a tropical cyclone. A gradual lowering of level may be the result of a slower widening or deepening of trickle zones in the ramparts. A sudden rise may be a response to a new moating rampart system being thrown up during a cyclonic storm, while a slower rise may be associated with upgrading algal rims, or slow cementation of the shingle ramparts. Significantly, microatolls displaying rapid changes of level are associated with moated conditions provided by shingle ramparts. Such changes are not seen in pools dammed by the more massive algal rims. Similar modification to microatoll forms takes place when it is the microatoll itself that is moved, rather than the moat level. On many reef flats microatolls disturbed by cyclonic seas may be seen with new horizontal rims growing at an angle to the older central tilted disc (Fig. 4.7).

Where the date of disturbance of either microatoll or moat level is known and can be identified with a specific cyclonic event, rates of growth of reef-flat corals subsequent to that event can be calculated. An example is seen on the fringing reef of Holbourne Island near Bowen (Hopley and Isdale, 1977) where a cyclone in 1918 breached a former rampart dam, lowering moated water levels over most of the reef flat by nearly 40 cm. This has left a series of the pre-1918

Figure 4.7 A *Porites* microatoll that has been tilted during a cyclone, with renewed growth at an angle to the original. Nymph Island, with high platform of rampart rock in background.

microatolls completely emerged and these were mistaken by Marshall et al. (1925) as part of a "raised" reef. However, radiocarbon assay (GaK-5217) of the center of a *Goniastrea* colony from this raised reef produced a date of 60 yrs ± 70 B.P. Further, at the base of some, new surfaces have grown at the new lowered level (Fig. 4.8). Measurements of these new rims of the modified top-hat form of microatoll and of the smaller colonies that had grown completely since the attainment of the new water levels in 1918 suggested that radial growth rate of these microatolls was between 0.32 and 0.59 cm/yr (Hopley and Isdale, 1977).

Not all moats contain microatolls. Some, because of their small size, are rapidly heated on the low tide to temperatures that at times may be lethal to corals. Others may be so high that their waters are not sufficiently renewed or provided with enough circulation for coral growth. The pools behind the raised platforms on low wooded islands do not contain living corals for this reason. However, small living corals have been noted close to MHWN behind cemented rampart dams on the Turtle Islands, and at the same level within pools impounded in a mid-Holocene beach conglomerate on the windward side of Stone Island near Bowen. It is more usual to find microatolls extending only up to MSL and quite frequently below this level. Nevertheless there is a distinct variation between the upper limit of growth and that of their open-water counterparts. Given sufficient stability of moat levels, the reef flat may be considerably elevated above the level suggested by open-water coral growth

Figure 4.8 "Top-hat" style microatolls, Holbourne Island. The fall in moat level was the result of rampart breaching during the 1918 cyclone. Failure to recognize this led to the forms being regarded as "raised" reef. Growth rates can be calculated from the size of rims and new colonies growing to the post-1918 water level.

by coalescence of microatoll forms into a reef flat pavement (Fig. 4.9). Microatolls also produce problems when used in interpretation of past sea levels (see Chapter 6).

Moating also has important influences on sedimentation. Ludington (1979) has shown that on One Tree Reef, at high tide, water movement over the reef is determined by the normal southeasterly waves and swell. However, development of wind-stress currents at low tide is inhibited by the short fetch over the lagoon and the numerous patch reefs. Wind stress may induce short-period waves of up to 0.3–1.0 m height that may agitate sediments of the lagoon into suspension, but calculations by Davies, Radke, and Robinson (1976, Fig. 9) indicated that transportation by wind-induced wave motion is unlikely to occur. In the absence of significant tidal currents and with swash from the reef margins reaching only the lagoon edge, the major sedimentary process in moated lagoons is settling of sediment during the period of isolation, of material brought into lagoonal margins during high tide by the swash and transmitted waves of the reef edge. Lagoons are thus important sediment sinks in the reef.

MOVEMENT OF SEDIMENTS ON REEFS

A large amount of research has been carried out on reef sediments as indicated in recent reviews (Milliman, 1974; Orme, 1977a), and much of the geological

Figure 4.9 Elevation of reef flat level by microatoll growth behind shingle ramparts, Three Isles.

literature on the Great Barrier Reef, particularly the work of Maxwell (1968, 1973b) is concerned with sediment distribution and characteristics. Work on the mechanics of sediment movement, however, is less well developed and, as Orme (1977a) has indicated, there is doubt about the validity of the application of many terrigenous sedimentary criteria to biogenic reef carbonates. He suggests that important differences are:

1　Carbonate sediment particles exhibit great ranges in bulk densities and morphologies especially at larger sizes.

2　The net distance of transport may be short in contrast to terrigenous sediments, which may travel great distances from their provenance to their depositional site.

3　Significant additions to carbonate sediments may be made by post mortem contributions of skeletal material in situ or while the sediment is in process of transport which will alter the textural characteristics expected from the energy conditions at a particular site.

4　Because of these factors currents of removal may be more important in biogenic carbonate deposits than currents of delivery.

The distribution of sediments over the total continental shelf indicates an interdigitation of terrigenous and biogenic sediments produced not only by present sedimentary processes but also by fluctuations of sedimentary zones over the shelf during Pleistocene sea-level variations. The sediments of the reefs, however, are almost exclusively biogenic carbonates. Even on fringing reefs (see Chap. 12) a sharp line of demarcation exists between terrigenous and biogenic sediments. On the outer reefs, the only noncarbonate sediments that are introduced into the system are pumice fragments floated into the Great Barrier Reef area probably from the Solomon Sea area, occasional terrigenous material floated out to the reefs in the roots of trees during floods, and even more occasional rock fragments originating as ballast in ships' holds deliberately jettisoned or resulting from shipwreck. Rutzler and Macintyre (1978) indicated that very fine siliceous sponge spicules may also be incorporated into coral reef sediments. Generally these noncarbonate sediments are of local importance only and have no significant influence on the behaviour of the reef sediments as a whole.

The type and texture of the sediment grains thus reflect the basic ecological zonation, as well as energy levels and water circulation. Sediment sizes range from large boulders of reef rock weighing many tons, through shingle produced by the fragmentation of corals and encrusting algae, to sand-size and finer materials formed from particular organic matter and mechanical disintegration. Finest materials may originate as fecal material produced by sediment-ingesting and lithophagic organisms. The characteristics of the sediment components depend to a large extent on the character of the contributing organisms and in particular on the microarchitecture of their skeletons. Thus while the initial sediment formed by a storm consists of reef blocks, whole coral skeletons, and fragmented sticks of *Acropora* shingle, the next stage of mechanical breakdown may be largely controlled by the microarchitecture of the fabric. Orme (1977a) suggested that after the branching coral *Acropora cer-*

viconis has broken down into a gravel-size sediment determined by the size of the original segments of the coral, it next breaks down into a 2ϕ grit, determined by the approximate size of component crystal packets. Similarly, *Halimeda* contributes initially to the 0ϕ sand-sized section of the sediment and next breaks down to a 10ϕ dust, derived largely from the aragonite microcrystals of the skeleton (Folk and Robles, 1964). The result is a distinct sinusoidal curve of the grain-size distribution determined by the Sorby Principle, based on the breakdown of carbonate skeletons and their microstructure (Folk, 1962; Folk and Robles, 1964).

The action of waves and currents in sediment formation is threefold. First the sediments are dislodged from the reef structure by fracturing, particularly during storms, or are formed by detachment of whole reef organisms from the substrate. Second, the sediments are selectively transported and, third, they are worn by corrasion during transportation. A lack of durability is a feature of reef sediments. Stoddart (1969a) for example suggests that four to five times the amount of sediment is produced as is incorporated into the reef structure. The overall result of these processes is that a wide range of grain sizes, shapes, and components may occur in any reef area. Three types of sediments can be identified:

1 Immature sediments, the size, shape, and sorting of which are more dependent on the skeletal characteristics of the building organisms than on hydrodynamics. These are essentially death assemblages (Stoddart, 1969a, p. 447).

2 Mature sediments that have been transported from their area of provenance to a part of the reef where they are more or less in equilibrium with the prevailing dynamic conditions.

3 Lag deposits incapable of being transported from their area of deposition by prevailing dynamic conditions and from which finer debris has been winnowed. These are formed by large organisms living and dying in parts of the reef with relatively low energy conditions or by large debris thrown up by very occasional cyclonic storms.

Initial detachment of smaller organisms can take place at any time, especially under postmortem conditions when attaching tissue is weakened. Dislodgement of larger materials is more dependent on occasional storm conditions. Major deposition of shingle and boulder ramparts on reefs is related to these storm events. As there is a tendency for the upper 3–4 m of the reef front to consist of wave-resistant forms and for much of the storm debris to consist of broken *Acropora* sticks, a great deal of the material appears to come from a depth of 10–12 m, below the depth of normal wave activity, where fast growing, fragile forms of *Acropora* are most common. Hernandez-Avila et al. (1977) found that rampart rubble on Grand Cayman originated from these depths about 300 m from shore and Pearson (1975) described the fragmentation of *Acropora* beds at depths of up to 20 m on Wheeler Reef near Townsville as the result of Cyclone Althea in 1971. The components of the boulder ramparts on Grand Cayman are typically up to 1.0 m in diameter and are thrown up to 4.5 m above sea level. The most common constituent is *Acropora palmata* fragments (Rigby and Roberts, 1976). Field experiments by Hernandez-Avila et al. (1977) showed that for a mean diameter of 13 cm, forces of 23 to 35 kg were required to break *A. palmata* stems weakened by bioerosion. Forces of up to 60 kg were required to break healthy stems while outer parts of colony branches broke at forces as low as 6 kg. The forces required were well within the range produced by a design hurricane producing deep-water wave heights of 9.1 m and much less intense storms could break colony branches.

Movement of sediment particles under both storm and normal wave conditions depends on fundamental hydrodynamics, as discussed by Orme (1977a). The basic relationships between roughness velocity, threshold velocity of entrainment, and settling velocity are the basic determinants of sediment movement and deposition (Inman, 1949; Orme, 1977a).

However, sediment behavior depends to a large extent on shape and density. Plates and irregular angular fragments offer much greater resistance than rods and spheres. Orme (1977a) suggested that calcite (sp gr 2.72) and aragonite (sp gr 2.95) will behave similarly to quartz (sp gr 2.65) at grain sizes smaller than 0.125 mm (3ϕ), but at coarser grades, as Maiklem (1968b) has shown, shape and microstructure become increasingly important. A direct path of settling is taken by spheres (such as some foraminifera) and small blocks (corals and coralline algal fragments). Larger blocks and plates (such as *Halimeda* fragments and the large foraminifera *Marginopora*) tend to oscillate in their fall. The bulk density of bioclastic materials is also of great importance, as shown by Jell et al. (1965) and Braithwaite (1973). Because of microstructural variations, great contrasts exist in different materials and at larger sizes bulk density is of greater importance than shape. Although similar in shape, differences in bulk density cause *Marginopora* plates to settle more slowly than *Halimeda* flakes. Thus, bioclastic grains with a wide range of shapes and bulk densities create a more complex relationship between grain size and ease of transport than do terrigenous sediments. Nonetheless it is possible in some situations to recognize distinctive sediment populations. For example, Flood and Orme (1977) on the Great Barrier Reef, and Clack and Mountjoy (1977) in Carriacou, recognize lognormal grain-size populations, the mixing patterns of which suggest that they represent lag, rolling, saltation, or suspended-sediment populations. However, although mature and immature sediments exist on reefs, a wide distribution of sediment sizes may not necessarily indicate that a large portion of the sediment is out of equilibrium with prevailing hydrodynamic conditions.

THE EPISODIC NATURE OF SEDIMENT TRANSPORT ON REEFS

Long-term changes in sedimentation patterns have been shown to occur in relation to the development of the reefs themselves (Flood and Orme, 1977) and these will be discussed in Chapter 11. However, on a shorter time scale of perhaps a hundred years or so, particularly in areas affected by tropical cyclones, an episodic sedimentation model probably applies. It results from the contrasting conditions that exist during short-lived but extremely high-energy cyclonic events with recurrence intervals of 10–20 years compared to the prevailing conditions existing for most of the remaining time. The cyclonic event produces a new input of sediment into the reef system. Much of this comes from the reef front, where corals are fragmented by wave action at depths greater than normal. Finer sediments may be immediately moved to the center of the reef but coarser debris is deposited close to the reef crest, where initial wave breaking takes place. Subsequently this new wave of sediment is worked through the reef system. The finer debris, initially deposited widely over the reef top, is moved to reef-flat areas where it is in equilibrium with normal hydrodynamic conditions. Obviously changing weather and tidal conditions will vary the equilibrium criteria, and reef sediments, even mature suites, may be constantly moved. Coarser debris will remain as lag deposits on the reef margin, although all but the larger reef blocks may undergo some occasional transport or reorientation. Erosional processes can cause breakdown of the individual clasts to sizes determined by the microarchitecture of the skeleton, which can then be transported to join the mature sediment groups. At all stages and in all locations, further skeletal debris in either complete form (e.g. foraminifera or molluscs) or fragmented (*Halimeda* flakes) is added to the maturing sediment body. Given cyclone frequencies normally encountered on the Great Barrier Reef it is highly unlikely that complete reworking of the sediment input of a single cyclone will have taken place prior to the next cyclonic event. However it would appear that within 10 years or so there is sufficient regrowth of reef front *Acropora* beds to provide the necessary sediment for the next wave of sediment input during the succeeding cyclone. Considerable sediment loss may also take place both during the cyclonic event and in prevailing weather conditions. Sediment "sinks" are provided by deeper lagoons, "storages" by sand and shingle cays, and losses from the reef top take place down lee-side sediment chutes or to the lee-side detrital slope (see Chap. 10).

This idealized sediment sequence is supported by observations on reef sediments. Clack and Mountjoy (1977), for example, noted that at Carriacou, under "normal" weather conditions, waves are capable of transporting coarse sand at depths of 3.6 m, and they identify various sediment populations separated by different modes of transport under these conditions. During storms grain sizes up to -1.15ϕ are transported from the reef, new sediments are introduced into the system, and old sediments redistributed. An even more distinctive example from the Great Barrier Reef is the effect of Cyclone David (January, 1976) on the sediment distribution patterns of Heron Reef (Flood and Jell, 1977). Very coarse sand was added to the outer reef-top sediments and very fine sand ($<3\phi$) was removed from the reef top to interreef areas. The windward side of the reef, which also experienced the full force of the cyclone, showed the greatest changes. Considerable quantities of coarse sand, gravel, and boulder-sized skeletal fragments as well as complete coral heads were carried from the reef slope to the reef crest. By comparing the cyclone deposits with the more mature sediments that existed on this reef flat prior to the cyclone, it is evident that, given time, the maturing of the sediments will produce greater sorting, and with the breakdown of skeletal fragments an increase in the finer tail of the sediment, thus replacing the fines lost during the cyclone. Longer term changes between 1961 and 1975 on the western end of Heron Reef (Jell and Flood, 1978, Fig. 19) are not great, as might be expected, since both periods of survey occur several years after cyclonic events (the 1955 cyclone prior to the 1961 survey and the 1972 Cyclone Emily prior to the 1975 survey).

Periodicity in sediment movement also occurs in the short term. At one extreme are reef flats that dry for up to 3 hours on each low tide and sediment movement is halted for the period of drying. Moated reef flats also show distinct periods of low activity in sediment movement, coinciding with the low tide, when only small waves can develop within the fetch of the moat or lagoon. Experiments with a turbidity (Alpha) meter on a number of reef flats have illustrated this episodic nature of sediment movement. Forty-eight hours of records from Wheeler Reef (Fig. 4.10) can be divided into three phases. During the first 24 hours, wave activity was so minimal that only on the low tide was there any sediment movement. Then followed an 8 hour storm with wind speeds up to 55 kn. Seas were greatly disturbed and maximum sediment movement coincided with the highest water level during the period; that is, the correlation between water height and sediment movement was positive in contrast to the previous negative relationship. During the final phase of light northerly winds a low southeasterly swell was continuing to run as the result of the previous night's storm. Two peaks of sediment transport can be identified, one at water depths of about 1.9 m when the swell waves were breaking on the reef edge and reforming, the other on the high tide when the larger swell was not breaking on the reef but passing directly over the reef top. Similar sets of readings from other reefs also suggest that the time of maximum sediment movement varies according to tide height, wave height, and location on the reef flat. Under "normal" winter conditions of southeasterly winds of approximately 20 kn the period of maximum turbidity on reef flats close to coral cays occurred when tidal levels were either flooding to or ebbing from a high water position, with waves breaking close to the cay.

As maximum sediment movement takes place just seaward of the wave breakpoint (King, 1972, p. 239) the point of breaking of the transmited wave on the reef flat becomes a critical factor in determining sediment mobility. Under the 20-kt southeasterly conditions experienced on the Great Barrier Reef, with deep-water wave heights of about 2.0 m, at high water waves break directly on the cay beach, but at lower tidal levels the point of breaking is more distant from the cay. Maximum sediment movement thus occurs in a zone on the reef flat that oscillates about the cay according to tide height and height of the reformed waves crossing the reef flat. As waves move into shallow water towards their breakpoint, there is an increasing discrepency between the forward orbital motion under wave crests and the slower return flow beneath troughs. The forward movement is short in duration but high in velocity and may lead to the selective movement of coarser sediments in the direction of wave propagation, that is, towards the cay, while finer materials that may also be moved by the slower return currents, will readily move almost an equal distance in both directions. For movement of sediment of any particular size, the forward orbital velocity must exceed the required entrainment velocity. Bottom velocity has been shown to be a function of wave height and water depth (Inman and Nasu, 1956), and thus on a reef flat will vary at different

stages of the tide, hence producing the noted periodicity in sediment movement.

RESULTING SEDIMENT FORMS

The theoretical considerations and field observations discussed, suggest that waves breaking on a coral reef may have two areas of rapidly reduced transporting energy. Initially more than half the wave energy may be lost on the windward reef edge, where coarser debris in the form of amorphous rubble, boulder ramparts, or shingle tongues is deposited. The loss of wave energy over the reef flat is slow and it is only towards the lee of the reef, especially on sanded reef flats where frictional attenuation is least, that further deposition of fine gravel and sand-size sediments may take place. Once concentration of detrital material has occurred, breaking of the reconstituted wave over the shoal will tend to move coarser sediments towards the shoal, and lead eventually to a distinct cay form. Steep slopes are to be expected on depositional features of coral reefs. Windward deposits are of boulder or shingle size, whereas even leeside sand cays are formed of coarse to medium sands. Under standard beach processes (see, e.g., Komar, 1976, Chap. 11) the beach slope will result from the generally weaker backwash compared to swash in the breaking wave due to friction and percolation. This energy loss is greatest in coarse sediments and results in sediment being moved onshore until the slope is built up to an extent that gravity aids the return offshore movement. This equilibrium slope depends largely on loss due to percolation and as this is largest in coarser and less well-sorted sediments, at times sediments may be deposited close to their maximum angle of rest.

Large variations in energy conditions of both a temporal and spatial nature occur over coral reefs and these, combined with the biogenic origin of the sediments, produce a complex reef-sediment system that is not fully understood. Features of zonation of reef sediments are described in Chapter 10, but it must be remembered that sediments are constantly moving and changing in response to the prevailing wave conditions. Coral cays, which form the most obvious storage within the sediment system, are themselves dynamic, as indicated in Chapter 11 and most important interchanges take place between the cay and adjacent reef flat.

5

Chemical Processes

As has been suggested in Chapter 3, the utilization of acid secretions and other chemical agents by organisms and the provision of chemically active environments, particularly by microbiological activity, mean that the dividing lines between biological, biochemical and physicochemical processes in the reef environment are extremely fine. This chapter examines the processes of cementation, solution, and recrystallization in the shallow marine, intertidal, and subaerial environments of coral reefs. It is important to remember, however, that these processes and environments rather than forming discrete process units are part of a general continuum that, in a wide sense, produces the diagenesis of the biologically formed calcium carbonate into the reef rock forming the internal reef structure. As many excellent works are available on carbonate solution, precipitation, or recrystallization (including the processes involved in the development of subaerial karst) this chapter merely points out some of the more important processes for coral-reef development (see, e.g., Chilingar et al., 1967; Bricker, 1971; Bathurst, 1971; Jennings, 1971; Sweeting, 1972; Matthews, 1974; Milliman, 1974).

Many of the problems associated with chemical processes in this environment result from calcium carbonate not behaving as a simple salt in which the equilibrium concentration of both anion and cation is simply the square root of the solubility product. In the calcium carbonate system much of the CO_3 entering solution from the solid phase is removed by other reactions allowing Ca^{++} concentrations higher than the square root of the solubility product (Matthews, 1974). Further, the various crystalline forms of calcium carbonate each behave in an independent manner. The most common phases in reef rocks are aragonite, high-Mg calcite, and low-Mg calcite and each of these phases has its own solubility.

The K_{sp} of skeletal aragonite is about twice that of low-Mg calcite and the K_{sp} of skeletal high-Mg calcite is as much as ten times that of low-Mg calcite (Chave et al. 1962). Matthews (1974) has shown the significance of these variations in an environment such as a coral reef that contains at least two solid phases such as aragonite and low-Mg calcite, as the water in such a system simply cannot be at equilibrium with the rock. If the water is near saturation with respect to aragonite, it will be supersaturated with calcite and should precipitate calcite. Conversely, if the water is near saturation with respect to calcite, it should still be capable of dissolving more aragonite. Equilibrium is unlikely to be achieved without completely dissipating one of the solid phases, although a steady state may exist in which mineral matter is being removed from aragonite crystals and precipitated onto calcite crystals.

Thus calcium carbonate can dissolve in environments that are undersaturated with respect to one or more of the carbonate polymorphs. The actual processes involved are a series of reversible reactions and ionic dissociations involving calcium carbonate, water, and carbon dioxide, each governed by different equilibria (Bögli, 1960; Roques, 1964, 1969; Thrailkill, 1968). Calcite is not greatly soluble in pure water, the amount at saturation varying from 13 mg/l at 16°C to 15 mg/l at 25°C. Aragonite is about 26% more soluble but is slower in attaining equilibrium. The speed of the reaction is greater at higher temperatures and in agitated waters, with crystal size, morphology, and strain being important parameters of the limestone (Matthews, 1974). Far greater reactions take place when carbonic acid is introduced into the system. The total amount of calcium carbonate that can be dissolved at saturation equilibrium per unit volume of water is a direct function of the partial pressure of CO_2 in the air (PCO_2) and an inverse function of the water temperature because of the latter's control of dissolved CO_2 saturation equilibrium (see, e.g., Jennings, 1971). The temperature effect is modest with about a threefold range compared to the PCO_2 effect with a hundredfold range (Ek, 1969).

Chemical reactions within the subaerial environment are important to the development of coral reefs, for although this may form a restricted area now, during much of the Pleistocene significant proportions of reefs were exposed. Great concentrations of biogenic CO_2 were probably derived from vegetation, and the open nature of the reef framework on exposure allowed water to seep underground. While such water may have reached saturation level with respect to $CaCO_3$ on the surface, underground it is cooled and dissolves further CO_2, becoming aggressive again, a process termed "cooling corrosion" by Bögli (1964). Even more important may be "mixing corrosion." This results from the relationship between PCO_2 and $CaCO_3$ saturation equilibrium being exponential. Thus the mixing of two saturated bodies of water with different calcium bicarbonate concentrations produces water that is undersaturated. This mixing is most effective in reviving aggressiveness when a large body of water saturated in response to low PCO_2 mixes with a small body of water saturated at high PCO_2, as for example with the mixing of vadose seepage and vadose streamflow (Jennings, 1971). Precipitation of calcium carbonate in the subaerial environment may be brought about by evaporation, especially where underground waters seep out on cliff faces of emerged reef terraces, producing tufa curtains. However, the various reactions of the CO_2–H_2O–$CaCO_3$ system are all reversible without the need for evaporation. Thus precipitation may result from water that has acquired a high carbonate content in respect to high PCO_2 while passing through tight rock fissures without air, resuming contact with air as it passes into more open cavities or caves. The water will diffuse the CO_2 back into the air, causing supersaturation and deposition of calcite. Jennings (1971) considered this to be a major process in caves and quoted the work of Holland et al. (1964), who showed that cave waters depositing calcite continued to maintain their magnesium concentration, which would not be the case if evaporation was the cause of precipitation. Similarly, in the groundwater of the emerged reefs of southern Barbados there is a concentration of strontium and magnesium as most of the aragonite and high-Mg calcite dissolved by vadose seepage is reprecipitated as low-Mg calcite (Harris and Matthews, 1968; Harris, 1971).

The meeting of subaerial and marine carbonate systems as may occur within the shallow waters of the reef ecosystem is one of extreme complexity. It is important to remember that the surface of most tropical waters is supersaturated with respect to calcium carbonate and thus many of the shallow-water processes occur either in microenvironments where diurnal-nocturnal fluctuations occur, or beneath the sediment-water interface.

THE SHALLOW MARINE ENVIRONMENT

At great oceanic depth both aragonite and the various calcite phases tend to dissolve. However, at the depths at which shelf reefs normally grow, waters are usually supersaturated with respect to calcium carbonate, although dissolution can take place in restricted environments and changes may take place in the various carbonate minerals. Supersaturation apparently results from a combination of the CO_2 cycle associated with respiration and photosynthesis, the increased solubility of very small particles and the role of organic matter as a fouling substance inhibiting the growth of new precipitate on existing large crystals (Schmalz, 1967; Chave and Schmalz, 1966; Suess, 1969). As already indicated, the abundant microscopic life in the sediment of the shallow carbonate environment is also responsible for alterations to seawater chemistry, which can induce major solution and precipitation processes. Particularly in restricted environments decaying organic material can lower pH values sufficiently for solution to take place. Alteration of organic material after burial may also produce conditions suitable for solution, although the process appears to be significant only in the long term (Milliman, 1974, p. 266).

More important is the recrystallization of carbonates, of which there has been great discussion in recent years. The rate of change depends upon the ambient environment and in shallower water aragonite and magnesian calcite remain fairly stable relative to calcite, but in the deep oceans inversion can occur more rapidly. According to Milliman (1974) the most plausible sequence of stability is:

$$\text{very high magnesian calcite } (\leq 12 \text{ mole } \%) < \text{aragonite}$$
$$< \text{magnesian calcite } (\leq 12 \text{ mole } \%) < \text{calcite.}$$

Matthews (1974) considered that much of the change is due to the basic thermodynamic instability of the initial building blocks of several common grain types. Chave and Schmalz (1966) have suggested that the very small particles $(0.1 \mu$ in width) of which some organisms are formed are significantly more soluble than larger crystals of the same mineral phase. Most important of all, however, is the fact that, as Winland (1969) has suggested, aragonite or high-Mg calcite containing approximately 10 mole% $MgCO_3$ is significantly more stable in warm, shallow seawater than high-Mg calcite containing 15 mole% or greater $MgCO_3$. Such high-Mg calcite is common in modern reef constituents. The phenomenon has been explained by the work of Gebelein and Hoffman (1971), which suggests that organic matter associated with algae results in a local chemical environment that contains considerably more magnesium than does nearby sea water. Thus a calcite grown at equilibrium with these waters contains more $MgCO_3$ than a calcite grown at equilibrium with seawater. On death, and with removal of organic tissue, such high-Mg calcite is at disequilibrium with the normal marine seawater.

Matthews (1974) considered that as pore fluid can hold a very small amount of dissolved calcium carbonate, for volumetrically significant reactions to take place, time and some combination of a pump that exchanges the pore fluid continuously are needed. He suggested a number of transfer mechanisms including:

1 Tidal processes near reef margins that may allow suspension of sediments and renewal of pore fluids with each cycle.

2 Tidal processes in buried sediments that set up a head of water through the sediments due to lag effects within the reef.

3 Large waves that may provide a similar pumping action as the result of the short term hydrostatic head formed with each breaking wave.

4 Possible continental origin of pore fluid in subtidal rocks. Freshwater may flush through sediments considerable distances offshore (e.g., 50 km offshore according to Mannheim, 1967).

5 Intrasediment sources of CO_2 due to an interface within the subtidal environment with high partial pressure of CO_2 on one side and low partial pressure on the other. At depth within the sediment, pore fluid is relatively static and in the absence of photosynthesis high partial pressures of CO_2 may be maintained by any CO_2-producing reactions. As the pore fluid is likely to be more acidic than the seawater above, precipitation may occur near the sediment-water interface.

The net result of these transfers in many examples is submarine cementation. Although such a process has been recognized only recently there are many examples quoted in the literature (see, e.g., Bricker, 1971, pp. 47–118; Friedman et al., 1974). In general deep-sea cements are magnesian calcite or calcite while shallow-water cements are aragonitic. Many of these examples described produce only minor amounts of submarine cement but some appear to be of major importance in Holocene reefs (see, e.g., Shinn, 1969; Land and Goreau, 1970; Goreau and Land, 1974; Macintyre, 1977).

Some precipitation from seawater may result in unconsolidated sediments. Precipitation of aragonite needle lime muds has been a subject of controversy. Cloud (1962) summarized the arguments for direct physicochemical precipitation in a situation such as that which exists over the Bahama Banks. Upwelling water, as it rises from the Straits of Florida, warms, loses some CO_2, and undergoes a slight salinity increase as the result of evaporation. These trends are increased as the water moves across the shallow banks with sluggish circulation and increased evaporation. Salinity increases rapidly but calcium does not increase as rapidly as it would if it were maintaining constant relations with chloride. Cloud (1962) maintained that most of the $CaCO_3$ withdrawal is a matter of chemical precipitation. Similar precipitation may be expected elsewhere in tropical waters where upwelling occurs adjacent to shallow reef waters.

A related topic in similar environments is the formation of ooids. This too is a controversial subject as ooids are claimed to form by both inorganic and organic processes (Berner, 1971a; Mitterer, 1971, 1972). In a review of ooid formation Davies et al. (1978) differentiated between ooids formed in quiet and agitated water conditions. Quiet water types were shown to exhibit a radial orientation of crystals and to form in seawater containing humic acids, whereas those formed under agitated conditions showed a tangential orientation and required no organic intervention. Ooids have not been widely reported from the Great Barrier Reef area. However, Davies and Martin (1976) described an active ooid forming area at Lizard Island and Marshall and Davies (1975) report ooids from an area of 340 km^2 on the floor of the Capricorn Channel in water depths of 100–120m. The ooids are believed to be early Holocene and are composed of high-Mg calcite around foraminifera nuclei. Diagenetic alteration of the ooids has led to a secondary radial fabric on the primary concentric and radial ones, and later, by the progressive obliteration of these three fabrics, by the growth of an equigranular mosaic, producing a structureless ooid. The ooids comprise only about 10% of the sediments of the area in which they are found.

THE INTERTIDAL ENVIRONMENT

Although comparatively small, the zone between tidal extremes on most tropical coastal landforms, including coral reefs, is the most enigmatic. On the one hand, there is the paradox of supersaturation of surface waters with respect to calcium carbonate, with the apparently anomalous ubiquity of landforms such as deep notches and coastal lapiés that are morphologically characteristic of solution processes (Revelle and Emery, 1957). On the other hand, there is the apparently more easily explained occurrence of intertidal cementation forms for which there is a great amount of literature containing contrasting explanations for the phenomenon.

Although some intertidal chemical erosion has been explained in terms of growth of salt crystals during evaporation of sea spray or interstitial waters (e.g., Guilcher and Pont, 1957; Wellman and Wilson, 1965), it is now generally accepted that diurnal variations in pH may be sufficient in microenvironments to allow solution to take place. At night plants and animals consume oxygen, producing an increase in the CO_2 content of the water and decrease in pH. This is generally a small decrease of about 0.15 units but locally may be as great as two units (Schmalz and Swanson, 1969). Revelle and Emery (1957) showed that supersaturation of calcium carbonate in intertidal basin and reef waters can range from 175 to 800% and in such environments it is unlikely that diurnal variations can be sufficient to produce significant solution. They suggested three possibilities for solution:

1 Within interstitial water of algal mats.

2 In the films of water left on pool walls by the receding tide.

3 By much of the calcium being complexed or hydrated, the time involved in the formation and dissociation of complexes containing calcium being long relative to the time required to precipitate free calcium ions or to obtain them from solution of calcium carbonate. If this is so then solution can occur when the carbonate concentration and/or temperature are rapidly decreased even though the product of the concentrations of total calcium and carbonate remains above the equilibrium saturation value.

Most attempts to show variations in pH in the intertidal environment have been in small enclosed pools (Emery, 1946; Revelle and Emery, 1957; Kaye, 1959; Emery, 1962; Schmalz and Swanson, 1969). Trudgill (1976a), however, showed that undersaturation, to the extent that up to 7% (± 3%) more calcium carbonate could be dissolved, can take place in open water on Aldabra Atoll between 2030 hours and 0500 hours. However, Trudgill (1976a) has confirmed that in comparison to biological erosion in the intertidal zone, solution is insignificant. Of water sampled from various locations (Table 5.1) only that near mangroves was not saturated or supersaturated with respect to calcium carbonate. However, all waters were undersaturated with respect to magnesium, suggesting that magnesium may be selectively dissolved in many waters that will not be aggressive to calcite. The process appears to proceed by solution

Table 5.1 Saturation Status with Respect to Calcium Carbonate and Magnesium for Aldabra Atoll Waters[a]

Sampling Station	Calcium Carbonate		Magnesium	
	Natural $CaCO_3$ Content (mg/l)	% Saturation	$MgCo_3$ (mg/l)	% Saturation
1 Ocean water	875	105.5	5697	100.8
2 Inshore oceanic water	910	100.0	4908	94.8
	945	105.7	5196	102.1
	875	105.7	5680	96.5
3 Mangroves: peaty	825	75.8	5121	81.0
lagoon water (NW)	840	92.2	4946	97.0
4 Mangroves: peaty	815	n.a.	4314	84.0
lagoon water (SE)				
5 Lagoon: milky water	875	105.7	4080	93.8
6. East channel: tidal	840	113.7	5030	99.7
complex water	950	102.6	4790	84.0
7 West channel: tidal	875	116.6	5327	102.6
complex water	1000	107.5	5825	100.8
	825	n.a.	5212	81.0

[a]From Trudgill (1976a).

disintegration, which implies that wave action is as important as solution in removing grains. The production of fretted forms, Trudgill suggested, is facilitated by lithological inhomogeneity of the rocks, calcarenite matrix being eroded rapidly and leaving resistant biogenic fragments upstanding (Fig. 5.1).

In contrast, cementation in the intertidal and immediately supratidal zone is extremely common. Although the term "beach rock" is used to cover many of the resulting limestones there would appear to be a variety of mechanisms involved in the cementation process and contrasting morphologies, structures, and cements occur in these intertidal rocks. Reviews of descriptions and hypotheses of formation of beach rock may be found in Guilcher (1961), Kaye (1959), Bathurst (1971) and Milliman (1974).

In a broad sense, beach rock is a littoral sediment ranging in size from fine sand to boulders cemented in situ beneath a cover of unconsolidated sediments and exposed by migration or erosion of the overlying cover (Fig. 5.2). The materials cemented are usually identical in terms of size, sorting, and constituents to adjacent uncemented sediments, and the cemented material may retain the sedimentary structures such as the steep dip commonly found in tropical carbonate beaches. In coarser sediments no distinctive structures may be present and the resulting beach conglomerate is also structureless. The

Figure 5.1 Intertidal notch and visor cut into emerged reefal limestone on Sabari Island, Louisiade Archipelago, New Guinea. Although the floor of the notch has a protective cover of coralline algae, intense biological erosion in this zone, rather than wave action or solution, are responsible for this feature.

Figure 5.2 A coarse beach conglomerate, Holbourne Island, made up of *Acropora* clasts and head corals firmly bonded in a mainly aragonite cement.

shape of the cemented zone varies. In freshly exposed beach rocks there may be a frontal ramp or nose apparently formed beneath the sloping beach. This rises onto a surface that is horizontal or only slightly fretted, following the strike ridges of the cemented internal structures. This gives the impression of a truncated surface and explains why many early reports on beach rock regarded it as erosional in origin (Fig. 5.3). The thickness of the cemented strata varies with tidal range. The upper level approximates MHWS but may extend a little higher in areas subjected to strong swash. The lower level of cementation is flat and reported as being about MLWS (Kuenen, 1933). In microtidal areas or tideless

Figure 5.3 Typical exposure of beach rock on Two Isles cay made up of sand-sized material, consisting of a smooth, sloping outer surface and pitted but horizontal upper surface.

seas the beach rock may be very thin, reflecting the seasonal fluctuation of MSL but in areas of high tidal range such as along the Great Barrier Reef the cemented strata may reach over 3 m in thickness.

Beach rocks extend further polewards than do coral reefs but are especially well developed where coral reefs flourish (Russell, 1959, 1962, 1963, 1967; Russell and Macintyre, 1965). Although predominantly noncarbonate sediments can be lithified, beach rocks appear to form more rapidly in a high-carbonate environment. Thus along the North Queensland coast between Mackay and Cairns there are less than ten exposures of modern/late Holocene (less than 2500 yrs B.P.) beach rock, developed in mainland beaches where the carbonate content is usually less than 10%. However, nearly all continental islands with fringing reefs, and vegetated reef islands along the same stretch of coast, display outcrops of beach rock. The question of vegetation on reef islands has been raised by Steers (1929), who suggested that vegetation or acids derived from decaying organic matter may be involved in the precipitation of beach rock cements. However, he also notes that the stabilizing influence of vegetation may be more important for although beach rock can form very rapidly, the precipitation of the cement requires at least temporary stability of the sediments. These conditions may be provided by algal mats (see, e.g., Davies and Kinsey, 1973) but the relative stability of vegetated cays is unquestionable. Significantly, beach rock is usually absent from highly mobile beach areas, such as the spits that commonly occur on the ends of cays (see Chap. 11). The speed of formation is testified by the presence of human artifacts in the rock including soft-drink cans and bottles, World War II debris, and even human skeletons (e.g., Emery et al., 1954; Russell, 1959; Frankel, 1968). Daly (1924) reported cementation occurring on Tortugas in two years. Exposures over boat ramps on Magnetic Island near Townsville have formed within six months.

Russell (1959, 1962) reported beach rock cemented by iron or other cements besides calcium carbonate but it is doubtful if these are "true" beach rocks, in which the cement is undoubtedly calcium carbonate. There is much debate, however, over the form of the cement. Various claims have been made for calcite cements (e.g., Russell, 1959, 1962; Emery and Cox, 1956; Kaye, 1959), aragonite (Daly, 1924, Ginsburg, 1953; Illing, 1954), or magnesium calcite (Taft and Harbaugh, 1964; Ebanks, 1975). Ranson (1955) suggested that the cement may change with time from aragonite to calcite to amorphous $CaCO_3$. Similarly, Taylor and Illing (1971) have suggested that magnesium calcite might represent an alteration product of aragonite while Stoddart and Cann (1965) have suggested a two-stage cementation process involving initial bonding by aragonite and void-filling with calcite. These latter authors emphasized the importance of identifying the cement, as calcite is the form normally precipitated from freshwater and aragonite from solutions of high ionic strength such as seawater, with direct implications for the cementation process.

Numerous explanations have been put forward for intertidal cementation, but they fall into three broad processes:

1   Organic

2   Inorganic from freshwater
3   Inorganic from seawater

Microbial action (e.g., Nesteroff, 1954; Guilcher, 1961; Puri and Collier, 1967) decay of organic matter (e.g., Field, 1920; Daly, 1920, 1924) or the activity of algae (e.g., Cloud, 1959; Maxwell, 1962) have been the most frequent processes quoted. Milliman (1974), however, has dismissed organic mechanisms, quoting examples of the low amount of organic matter normally found in sands and pointing out that whereas algae are common on the surfaces of beach rock, they are normally absent from the interior. Davies and Kinsey (1973) came to similar conclusions in their examination of the Heron Island beach rock.

   Inorganic precipitation from groundwater has been proposed most extensively by Russell (1959, 1962, 1963, 1967) and his co-workers (Jones, 1961; Deboo, 1962). They suggested that cementation takes place along the water table, beach sands above that level being typically polished as percolating sea water is supersaturated with $CaCO_3$ and nonagressive. In contrast, beneath the water table circulating freshwater dissolves beach sands that are pitted and unpolished. At the water table, sand grains are coated with calcite, which coalesces to form the initial bonding. At a later stage the rocks are filled by a mottled brown cement of uncertain origin. Although it is notable that Russell's calcite cements were all reported from high islands with significant groundwater, his hypothesis has come under considerable criticism. Milliman (1974) questioned Russell's identification of cement and points out that many of the outcrops examined in the eastern United States are actually outcrops of the Pleistocene Anastasia and Pamlico formations. Stoddart and Cann (1965) were critical of a groundwater hypothesis on climatic grounds, that is, beach rock occurs on coral cays in excessively arid areas without groundwater, such as the Red Sea, and on physiographic grounds, that is, beach rock is found on islands too small to support a permanent water table.

   With more detailed studies of the cement of beach rock, particularly the use of SEM techniques, an aragonite cement, precipitated from seawater, is receiving increasing acceptance as the primary cement. This is usually acicular or fibrous although cryptocrystalline and drusy aragonite has been recognized (Milliman, 1974). Magnesium calcite may be present as semiopaque cryptocrystalline cement consisting of small (4–8 μ) rhombohedra. Most workers favour precipitation from seawater, lithification either occurring at depth after percolation or seawater evaporation and heating at the surface. However, any reversal of the $CaCO_3–H_2O–CO_2$ process system can result in precipitation. For example, Hanor (1978) has proposed that much of the cement is precipitated as the result of loss of CO_2 from carbonate-saturated beach groundwaters. His mass-transport calculations support the proposal that vertical fluid dispersion in the phreatic zones resulting from tidal oscillation of the water table is sufficient to induce degassing of CO_2 from a seaward-flowing groundwater. According to Hanor, loss of CO_2 is further enhanced by tidal pumping of the gas phase in the vadose zone across the sediment-atmosphere interface. As sediment porosity is lowered by precipitation of cement, the ability of the groundwater system to de-gas and form new cements is reduced. Thus, as Matthews (1971) suggested, for cementation to take place all that is required is that the waters have sufficient residence time in the landward areas to acquire a high PCO_2 and dissolved $CaCO_3$ and sufficient residence time in the fore-beach areas that de-gassing can take place before the water is discharged into the sea. Hanor (1978) considered this the normal situation in tropical climates where seasonal rainfall results in episodic variations in groundwater discharge. Precipitation is less likely in areas where high groundwater discharge results in low residence time and less likelihood of de-gassing forebeach sediments. The less frequent occurrence of beach rock on the wetter coast and islands between Ingham and Cairns along the Great Barrier Reef has been noted previously (Hopley, 1973) and may be so explained. Hanor further suggested that greater oscillation of the water table in areas of higher tidal range could greatly increase the dispersive transport of CO_2 and result in de-gassing and supersaturation of groundwaters. Distribution of massive beach rocks along the Great Barrier Reef, particularly on offshore islands where the seasonal variations in groundwater flow will not be masked by a more general groundwater flow as on the mainland, would appear to fit the model proposed by Hanor. The model does not require a permanent freshwater lens as the groundwater involved in the de-gassing and precipitation may be brackish or saline. The major requirement is an overall annual seaward flow of groundwater. In highly arid regions, where landward flow and deep refluxing of seawater occurs, the de-gassing hypothesis may not be applicable. However, indirect biological precipitation may be possible in anerobic environments where bacterial processes can consume CO_2 (Berner, 1971a,b; Morita, 1976) and calcium carbonate can be precipitated out of seawater by evaporation. Mixing of water types appears to be incidental to precipitation, but may influence cement chemistry and morphology. Hanor's (1978) experiments produced a low-Mg calcite cement, but clearly in other circumstances aragonite or high-Mg calcite may be precipitated.

The variety of cements, and by implication processes or environments of precipitation, in intertidal and immediately supratidal deposits of coral reefs, is illustrated by the northern Great Barrier Reef (Scoffin and McLean, 1978). Beach rocks normally have a fringe of acicular aragonite crystals, although some examples from windward cays that have formed close to mangroves display a micritic cement or a mixture of micrite and aragonite. Similarly the rampart rocks (Fig. 5.4) of the windward side of some reefs (see Chap. 11) are cemented by a white to rusty-brown micrite containing 68 to 95% high-Mg calcite (14% $MgCO_3$) and from 0 to 25% aragonite. Clay minerals make up 5–8% of the matrix (mainly kaolinite with some illite and montmorillonite). Cemented boulder tracts show the same variation in cements with micritic calcite cements to windward, fibrous aragonite to leeward. These results suggest that at least two environments of precipitation were involved. Beaches on leeward sand cays are kept free from fines, being washed by open-shelf seawater throughout the tidal cycle. Ramparts and windward boulder tracts in contrast are not cleared of trapped fines and are immersed in open-shelf water only at high tide and ponded reef-flat water, which seeps through the rampart at low tide. This reef-flat water may have been concentrated by evaporation at low tide, diluted by freshwater after heavy rain or influenced by passage through

Figure 5.4 Broken slab of rampart rock from Three Isles, composed largely of *Acropora* sticks in a white to rusty brown micritic cement.

mangroves. The occurrence of solution fabrics in rampart rocks and their absence from leeward beach rocks suggests conflicting compositions of interstitial waters. Beach-rock waters may be permanently saturated or supersaturated although rampart-rock waters may be undersaturated at times. A similar contrast between aragonitic cements associated with open-ocean beach rocks and high-Mg calcite on beaches of leeward lagoons with mangroves has been reported from Ambergris Cay, Belize by Ebanks (1975). Other cements recognized on northern Great Barrier Reef reefs were organic cements in reef rocks and phosphatic cements in cay sandstones caused by the downward percolation of guano (Fig. 5.5). The cemented sands contained 23% P_2O_5, mainly hydroxyapatite, as coatings that bring about centripetal replacement of the grains to phosphates (Scoffin and McLean, 1978).

THE SUPRATIDAL VADOSE AND PHREATIC ENVIRONMENTS

The vadose and phreatic environments for convenience are referred to as supratidal. However, the freshwater Ghyben-Herzberg lens, beneath reef islands in particular, can extend below present sea level, where it can respond to tidal fluctuations (e.g., see Buddemeier and Holladay, 1977) and even action of waves, particularly during major storms as shown by Ward et al. (1965). These environments in modern shelf reefs and atolls are very limited, the freshwater or brackish lens on Enewetak having a maximum thickness of about 10 m (Buddemeier and Holladay, 1977). However, due to sea-level changes (see Chap. 6), most reef complexes have been exposed by at least several tens of meters for over 50% of their history, allowing meteoric waters to filter through the coral caps. The internal structures of the reefs thus retain the effects of subaerial diagenetic environments. Analogous situations are found at the present time in reef systems that have been tectonically uplifted.

The vadose environment (Fig. 5.6) lies above the water table and its most important attribute is the presence of percolating freshwater. As aragonite and high-Mg calcite, of which most reef organisms consist, are unstable in the

Figure 5.5   Cay sandstone, Raine Island. Carbonate sands in a phosphatic cement laid down at a distinctive water-table horizon.

freshwater environment the major process is one of solution and reprecipitation as stable phase low-Mg calcite leading to removal in particular of magnesium and strontium in the groundwater (Matthews, 1974). In this environment the pump that maintains the constant renewal of pore waters and, by implication, the chemical processes they carry out, is provided by the gravitational movement of the vadose waters, although in the upper few meters this may be retarded by evaporation and by transpiration by plants. It is in this environment that development of PCO_2 may greatly exceed atmospheric PCO_2. However, the limited volume of vadose pore gas, according to Matthews, provides an important limitation on the amount of extra solution that can take place. He also suggested that the pattern of rainfall in some tropical areas may seasonally reduce the amount of water occupying vadose pore space. This allows a better communication between vadose pore gases and larger gas reservoirs, such as the atmosphere, the lower PCO_2 leading to significant precipitation of calcite.

The Upper Vadose Zone

The upper part of the vadose zone is in contact with waters in which the PCO_2 is close to that of the atmosphere and which quickly become saturated and precipitate calcite. This may be as horizontal stringers, along rootlets, or under certain circumstances as thicker crusts or caliche (Fig. 5.7). These crusts, which appear to be an early form of calcrete (for discussion see Goudie, 1973), if not subsequently removed by erosion retain their structures for long periods. The significance and nature of caliche has been realized largely from work carried out in Barbados (James, 1972a,b; Harrison, 1974, 1977a,b; Harrison and Steinen, 1978) although similar crusts have been described over Pleistocene reefal deposits from the Bahamas (Newell and Rigby, 1957; Korniker, 1958, Supko, et al., 1970), Puerto Rico (Kaye, 1959), Florida (Multer and Hoffmeister, 1968) and the Yucatan Peninsula, Mexico (Ward, 1970). The great horizontal variability found in these crusts is one of their diagnostic features

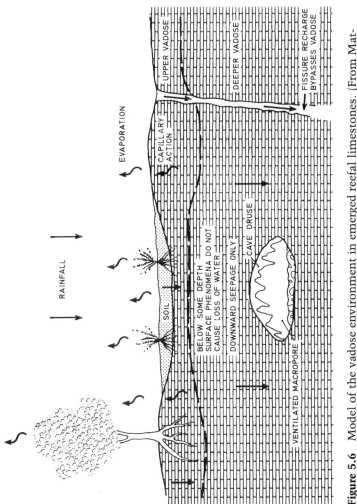

Figure 5.6 Model of the vadose environment in emerged reefal limestones. (From Matthews, 1974, reproduced by permission of the Society of Economic Paleontologists and Mineralogists.)

Figure 5.7 A brecciated caliche profile with numerous brown micritic stringers developed on Pleistocene reef limestones c.84,000 yrs B.P. on Barbados.

not found in the deeper vadose environment. Their importance on the Great Barrier Reef lies in their providing a strong seismic reflector surface at the top of the pre-Holocene reefal materials (see Chap. 7).

The caliche horizon is usually found in the upper few meters of the profile as a distinctive brown crust frequently underlain by other crusts and stringers, which locally may cut through original components such as massive corals, completely destroying the original structure. Individual crusts are separated by chalky white to brown carbonate and the whole profile tends to parallel the modern-day topographic surface. Although profiles may vary the upper crust is typically 0.5–6.0 cm in thickness, fractured and brecciated, and displaying rootlet tubes 1–3 mm in diameter. It may be underlain by up to 18 other crusts 0.5–3.0 cm thick, the deeper ones tending to be softer and more widely spaced. The intervening chalky areas contain corals and other recognizable organisms and also concentrically laminated nodules not found elsewhere in the profile. Porosity within the caliche profile varies from 4 to 20% and is generally 25–75% less than within the underlying strata (Harrison, 1977a). Caliche may form very quickly, as, on the coast in Barbados, it has developed on penecontemporaneous storm deposits. The most uniform caliche horizons are developed over homogeneous substrata such as backreef or lagoonal sands and are much more variable over heterogeneous sediments such as the coralgal forereef, except where the open framework has been plugged by marine sediments or soil.

Two processes are involved in the development of the caliche: alteration of the original reef limestone that is brecciated, partially dissolved, and recrystallized to microspar; and precipitation of new carbonate in the form of crusts and nodules as calcite, less than 4% mole $MgCO_3$ (James, 1972a). Up to 80%

of secondary components are comprised of 1–3 μ equicrystalline brown micrite, sometimes aggregated into ovoid pelletoids 0.03–0.5 mm diameter. In void spaces there may be precipitated a mesh of acicular randomly oriented calcite needles or flower calcite spar comprising bunches of crystals 10–20 μ long. On average about 12% of the profile on Barbados is new cement (Harrison, 1977a).

The climatic environment for the development of caliche is subhumid, with a distinct dry season giving a period of soil-moisture deficiency. On the higher interior areas of Barbados, where limestones are Plio-Pleistocene and annual rainfall totals exceed 1750 mm, caliche profiles are lacking or insignificant and solutional landforms dominate the surface, but along the north and south coastal regions where rainfall totals are 1100–1250 mm per annum well-developed profiles occur (Harrison, 1977a). Overlying soils contain volcanic ash from the Lesser Antilles 160 km to the east and, where montmorillonite has developed, caliche development appears to be particularly favored, since deeper diagenesis is inhibited by retarded infiltration. Although Harrison has developed a temporal model of caliche development (Fig. 5.8), time as an influence on thickness of the profile appears to be overridden by other factors. James (1972a) showed that deepest profiles, 0.5–3.0 m, were developed in the 83,000 yrs B.P. reef terrace, the 104,000 yrs B.P. terrace having 0.1–1.0 m deep profiles. The youngest exposed terrace (c. 60,000 yrs B.P.) has well-developed crusts 0.5–1.0 m deep but the base is a single, thin crust directly over original aragonite and high-Mg calcite mineralogy. On the older limestones profiles are rarely deeper than 0.5 m and are frequently less than 10 cm thick. Maximum thicknesses are achieved adjacent to the coast and James (1972a) sugggests that an external source of calcium carbonate in the form of sea spray may be an important addition to the caliche profile (Fig. 5.9). On higher terraces erosion has removed original caliche profiles and tectonic uplift has isolated reef terraces from the sea. However, caliche can be preserved in buried profiles on Barbados, and here and in other reef complexes provides a diagnostic indication of subaerial exposure (Harrison, 1977b).

The Deeper Vadose Zone

Within the deeper vadose zone the processes operating are essentially ones of recrystallization, with concommitant changes in porosity and permeability. The factors involved reflect the interplay between a number of kinetic steps operating at different rates and including the solution of aragonite, the nucleation of calcite, the growth of calcite, and the availability and movement of meteoric waters (James et al., 1977). Great variations in the degree and rate of alteration may take place regionally, with climatic factors, and locally, dependent on the nature of original fabrics. For example, in Barbados the regional pattern is the result of a combination of age of the numerous emerged reef terraces combined with the rate of meteoric water percolation (Matthews, 1968; Winland, 1971; James, 1974; Harrison, 1975). On the more arid south coast (mean annual precipitation 1100 mm) high-Mg calcite and aragonite are present in sediments as old as 300,000 years, whereas on the wetter, central west coast (mean annual precipitation 1700 mm) high-Mg calcite may be absent from even the 83,000 year terrace, and no aragonite is found in reefs older than

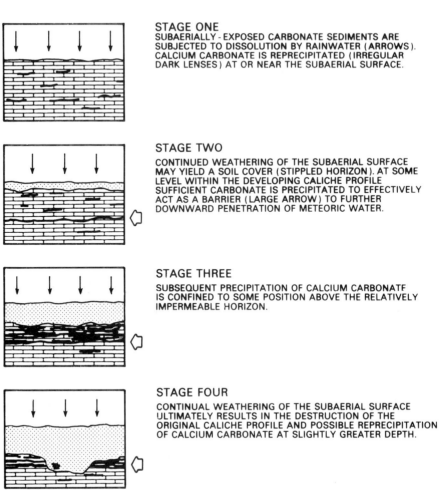

STAGE ONE
SUBAERIALLY - EXPOSED CARBONATE SEDIMENTS ARE
SUBJECTED TO DISSOLUTION BY RAINWATER (ARROWS).
CALCIUM CARBONATE IS REPRECIPITATED (IRREGULAR
DARK LENSES) AT OR NEAR THE SUBAERIAL SURFACE.

STAGE TWO
CONTINUED WEATHERING OF THE SUBAERIAL SURFACE
MAY YIELD A SOIL COVER (STIPPLED HORIZON). AT SOME
LEVEL WITHIN THE DEVELOPING CALICHE PROFILE
SUFFICIENT CARBONATE IS PRECIPITATED TO EFFECTIVELY
ACT AS A BARRIER (LARGE ARROW) TO FURTHER
DOWNWARD PENETRATION OF METEORIC WATER.

STAGE THREE
SUBSEQUENT PRECIPITATION OF CALCIUM CARBONATE
IS CONFINED TO SOME POSITION ABOVE THE RELATIVELY
IMPERMEABLE HORIZON.

STAGE FOUR
CONTINUAL WEATHERING OF THE SUBAERIAL SURFACE
ULTIMATELY RESULTS IN THE DESTRUCTION OF THE
ORIGINAL CALICHE PROFILE AND POSSIBLE REPRECIPITATION
OF CALCIUM CARBONATE AT SLIGHTLY GREATER DEPTH.

Figure 5.8 A temporal model of caliche development. (From Harrison, 1977a, reproduced by permission of the Canadian Society of Petroleum Geologists.)

200,000 years. Even portions of the 125,000-years-old last interglacial terrace
may be completely recrystallized. Differential preservation of original fabrics
is widely seen. The high-Mg calcite of coralline algae and foraminifera is more
soluble than the aragonite of corals and molluscs and this differentiation frequently leads to a rapid replacement of the original high-Mg calcite with low-
Mg calcite structures with preservation of structural detail, whereas aragonitic
structures such as corals undergo slow solution leaving secondary voids (Fig.
5.10). Similarly, detrital sands and muds quickly recrystallize whereas the corals they envelope alter more slowly. The rapid alteration of high-Mg calcite
takes place in an environment in which there is supersaturation with respect
to calcite and in which calcite nuclei are present whereas the aragonitic environments may be saturated with respect to aragonite but this is not sufficient to drive rapid local precipitation of low-Mg calcite (Matthews, 1968,
1974).

If no mineralogic inhomogeneity is present in the reef limestone, then selective solution may take place along burrows, as for example, within the calcisilt-

Figure 5.9 Extremely resistant caliche in cliff profile, northeast coast of Barbados. The density and resistance of the crust may result from the addition of calcium carbonate from sea spray.

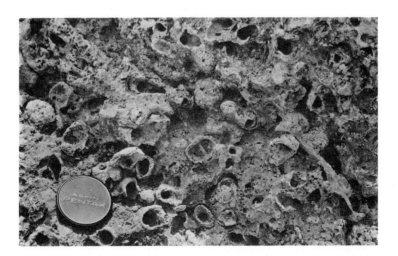

Figure 5.10 Leached *Acropora cervicornis*, Pleistocene reef tract of Barbados. Low Mg-calcite molds result from the more rapid replacement of encrusting coralline algae.

141

stones of lagoonal sediments. Alternatively, in the absence of macroscopic in-homogeneities, secondary porosity may be distributed throughout the rock in the form of molds selective of the original sand-sized particles, which can reduce the rock to a chalky consistency (Matthews, 1974).

The calcitization of corals may operate at two scales (Matthews, 1968; Pingitore, 1970; James, 1974). If meteoric waters move slowly through the fabric then a very fine-scale, concomitant, solution-precipitation process results in preservation of detailed structures. More rapid movement of meteoric waters may lead to total leaching and destruction with the later precipitation of a sparry calcite in the resulting moldic void. James (1974) has noted that the dissolution process frequently commences from the center and proceeds out-wards, especially around the trabecula, which may be preserved as a clear spar-filled canal. However, if the coral is covered in high-Mg calcite (e.g., coralline algae) then the dissolution may start adjacent to the high-Mg calcite. James also noted that different coral species have different rates of alteration, on Bar-bados the most resistant being the massive *Montastrea annularis* and *Diploria* sp., and the least resistant, the delicate *Acropora cervicornis*. These rates ap-pear to be related to the ratio of surface area to volume.

During the process of replacement the calcite-aragonite front may be clearly delineated as a sharp but irregular boundary moving across the coral with time. At the front itself the aragonite may be a soft, powdery chalk. As a result of the changes within the corals there is a decrease in total porosity due to the precip-itation of sparry calcite cement in preexisting voids, but permeability may in-crease due to loss of organic matter and formation of fewer but larger and better sorted pores (Pittman, 1974; James, 1974). Porosity changes also take place in the grainstones (Harrison, 1975). Where these are mainly aragonite or high-Mg calcite, the porosity is predominantly interparticle of a primary depositional nature. In the drier areas of Barbados 30% of this primary porosity may be re-tained even in 100,000-year-old sediments. However, with the precipitation from descending meteoric waters of sparry calcite at grain contacts or as dis-continuous rims around grains, there may be reduction of porosity by up to 12%. By the time 100% calcite has been achieved, the pore fabric is predomi-nantly secondary with moldic pores and irregular-solution vugs accounting for 80% or more of total porosity and interparticulate voids filled with sparry ce-ment (Harrison, 1975). However, total porosity remains at 15–30%. Thus, after the earliest changes there may be no increase or decrease in total porosity as, once initiated, the driving force of a mineralogic solubility contrast will have gone. On coastal sections there may be further decrease in porosity as the limestones that are equilibrated with fresh water and cemented by calcite are washed by sea spray from which a high-Mg cement may be precipitated. In the recrystallization of both grainstones and corals some initial reduction in po-rosity may be directly due to a theoretical increase in volume of about 8% dur-ing the transition from aragonite to calcite due to the less dense crystal struc-ture (Harrison, 1975).

The Phreatic Zone

The phreatic zone, beneath the permanent water table, is the least known pro-cess area within the limestone. The work of Jacobson and Hill (1980) on the uplifted atoll of Niue has shown that the Ghyben-Herzberg theory is not applicable to fissured and porous limestone. The thickness of the freshwater layer ranges from 40–80 m in the island center to 50–70 m beneath the former atoll rim and 0 at the coast. This is due to permeable recrystallized limestone underlying the rim of the island in comparison to the lagoonal sediments of the center. Although initially the coralgal reef margin may be more open and the groundwater pattern may be closer to the classical Ghyben-Herzberg lens, initial diagenetic changes may rapidly produce a pattern in emerged Pleistocene shelf reefs more analogous to that found on Niue. The phreatic lens requires sufficient rainfall and sufficient catchment area, which, if not available, may lead to only a brackish lens as developed on Enewetak (Schmalz, 1971, Buddemeier and Holladay, 1977) and probably most other modern reefs. During emergence associated with eustatically lowered sea levels the phreatic lens was far more extensive, particularly on reefs of 100 km^2 or more as occur on parts of the Great Barrier Reef.

All pore spaces within the phreatic zone are occupied by waters that may have flowed directly from the surface via fissures and sinks, without prolonged contact with the rock in the vadose zone. Alternatively the water may be derived by more lateral flow that, in tectonically emerged reef islands (Barbados, Guam) and possibly in eustatically emerged reefs of the Pleistocene, will have passed through terrain almost exclusively low-Mg calcite. Matthews (1974) considered that such waters will be chemically far simpler than those of the vadose zone, which frequently build up minor element concentrations that inhibit recrystallization to low-Mg calcite. Work carried out on this largely unknown phreatic environment (Harris and Matthews, 1968; Land, 1970; Matthews, 1971; Harris, 1971; Steinen, 1974) suggests that processes here are rapid with early and extensive mineral stabilization, dissolution, and cementation taking place. In Barbados, zones within the present phreatic lens or demonstrably within such a lens in the past are exclusively recrystallized to low-Mg calcite. Thus, mineralogically stable zones may develop, interdigitated with less stable zones of the vadose environment above and the seawater environment below. Matthews (1974) suggested that a period of about 5000 years stability of the phreatic zone may be sufficient for complete alteration. However such a period of sea-level stability, and hence by implication phreatic lens stability, has occurred within the latter part of the Quaternary possibly only at interglacial and interstadial periods. With rapid rises and falls of sea level the narrow phreatic zone may pass too rapidly through the limestone column for complete alteration to take place.

At its lower and outer margin the phreatic lens is in contact with seawater and a zone of mixing occurs, promoted by the oscillatory movement of the interface in response to sea-level fluctuations produced by tides and waves and by fluctuations in recharge (Ward et al., 1965). The mixing zone is one of complexity within which local water chemistry may lead to either supersaturation or undersaturation with respect to calcium carbonate (Runnells, 1969). Not surprisingly, therefore, both cementation (Schmalz, 1971) and solution (Harris, 1969, 1971) have been claimed for this zone. Matthews (1974) regarded it as a chemically active zone because of the pumping action provided by both the flow of fresh water and the replacement of seawater that is caught up in the flow along the mixing boundary.

THE RESULTANT REEF FABRIC

It has been shown that even within single reef columns the presence of contrasting chemical environments may produce sequences of horizons with differing degrees and types of cemented and diagenetically altered reef rock. Most reef complexes are of such an age, however, that with changing sea levels and climate (Chap. 6), these contrasting process horizons have been shifted vertically through the column by over 100 m even during the last 125,000 years. During the Quaternary there has been a continual repetition of reef buildup within the marine environment, then, with fall of sea level and subsequent emergence of the reef, the development of a vadose zone, and, if conditions of rainfall and catchment are suitable, a phreatic zone. Simultaneously the shallow marine environment is moved to the lower part of the reef column, while subaerial weathering processes alter the exposed reef surface. Subsequently a new transgression will submerge the reef complex, phreatic and vadose zones again moving up the column until they are replaced completely by the saltwater marine environment. Complete submergence may lead to the growth of a new coral cap, the aragonitic and high-Mg calcite fabric of which will contrast with the varying degrees of alteration seen in the underlying reef. Renewed emergence will again result in alteration of the reef fabric, the new cap going through its first cycle, the older material its second.

The product is a reef rock with distinct but discontinuous layering superimposed on the growth patterns of the original reef. It is composed of well-cemented subaerial exposure surfaces, chalky materials with well-developed secondary porosities formed within the vadose zone, or fully recrystallized reef rock developed within the phreatic lens. The subaerial exposure surfaces may be particularly prominent in the column, contrasting sharply with the less well cemented and frequently less altered material immediately above. The degree of contrast in these breaks, which have been termed "solution unconformities" by Schlanger (1963), may decrease with depth and age. Most Tertiary and lower Pleistocene reef materials whether exposed in emerged reef terraces, as for example on Guam (Tracey et al., 1964), or penetrated by drilling as on Bikini, Enewetak, or Midway atolls (Ladd et al., 1953; Emery et al., 1954; Ladd and Schlanger, 1960; Schlanger, 1963; Ladd et al., 1970; Tracey and Ladd, 1974; Ristvet et al., 1974, 1975; Couch et al., 1975), show signs of "multiple diagenesis" and are all well-cemented and mineralogically stable. As on Barbados, only reefal materials younger than about 200,000–300,000 years retain aragonitic or high-Mg calcite constituents.

Last interglacial materials of about 125,000 yrs B.P. show the greatest variations in alteration, with climatic setting and nature of the materials being the most important factors. For example, on the moist coast of Ambergris Cay, Belize (mean annual rainfall 1500 mm), Tebbutt (1975) has described reef rock similar to that on the wetter parts of Barbados. Aragonite persists in corals, molluscs, Halimeda, tunicate spicules, pellets, and ooliths and even high-Mg calcite is retained in encrusting algae and foraminifera. However, finer mudstones are completely calcitic and, locally, laminated crusts of caliche may be present. In selective dissolution, corals, especially *Montastrea* and *Diploria*, may be completely etched out. Within the vadose zone, replacement of aragonitic shells by advancing "fronts" of coarsely crystalline calcite spar is evident in large gastropods, the replacement being affected by solution and nearly simultaneous precipitation on a minute scale, as on Barbados. In contrast the degree of alteration in reefs located in more arid areas is significantly less, confirming the pattern in relation to climate determined in Barbados. The youngest of three Pleistocene reef terraces on La Blanquilla Island, Venezuela, is probably last interglacial (Schubert, 1977) and by analogy the older two of at least 200,000 yrs B.P. The island is situated in the arid belt of the northern South American coast (mean annual rainfall about 500 mm). Corals within the lower terrace remain aragonitic although sometimes chalky as the result of early diagenesis as described by James (1974). Subtle coarsening of aragonite fibres is also observable. However, the presence of low-Mg calcite is rare. In Terrace 2, alteration is more obvious, low-Mg calcite common and the trabeculae of corals thickened and replaced by sparry calcite. Nonetheless considerable amounts of aragonite remain. Only in Terrace 3 are corals completely altered although even here some coarse aragonite remains (Schubert, 1977).

Holocene reefal materials show least alteration, even when emerged for several thousand years. Nonetheless, as has been shown, processes of cementation may be very active within the marine environment. Boucher (1977) working on the upper 1.5 m of modern reef framework on Barbados showed that diagenetic modification below the reef surface included micritization of skeletal material (12% of total volume), deposition of internal sediments (10%), and precipitation of calcite (5%) and aragonite (3%) cements. As there was little difference between the near surface and 1-m deep parts of the framework, Boucher concluded that much of the early diagenesis takes place very quickly. However, much of the change is probably related to organic activity, Boucher (1977) considering that micritization is due primarily to algal and fungal boring. Slower changes probably take place at depth, particularly when the development of detrital reef islands permits the establishment of a low salinity lens. Buddemeier and Holladay (1977) suggested from work on Enewetak atoll that tidal pumping of saline water up natural "wells" formed by reef cavities can lead to mixing with the fresh high-alkalinity water at the surface of the water table. This may account for the widespread occurrence of a weakly to moderately cemented hard layer in the vicinity of the current water table.

Australian reefs have experienced diagenetic changes similar to those described elsewhere although the amount of data available is limited. Until recently the most comprehensive description of the reef materials came from the Heron Island borehole drilled in 1934 (Richards and Hill, 1942). This passed through a sequence of calcareous sands, in situ reef rock, foraminiferal and quartz sands, and lime muds. The nature of lithification and recrystallization was described by Maxwell (1962). Richards and Hill (1942) and Maxwell (1973a) regarded the whole sequence as Holocene, hence explaining Maxwell's apparent surprise (1962, p. 226) that "depth of burial would appear to be a subordinate factor in the process of recrystallization." He also considered the two anomolous features of the sequence to be the high-Mg carbonate content and high aragonite content of the upper strata and the appearance of aragonite again below 147.8 m together with a high-Mg carbonate content and small degree of recrystallization of the matrix. Subsequently Lloyd (1968) has shown the up-

Table 5.2 Heron Island Borehole Log[a]

	Depth (m)	Lithology	Diagenesis and Comment	MgCO$_3$	Unconformities (m)[b]
1	0–5.2	Unconsolidated sands	Cay sands, aragonite, and high-Mg calcite.		
2	5.2–33.2	Coralgal limestone, creamy, white	Progressive recrystallization of matrix with depth. To 18.2 m the corals aragonitic with progressive alteration to calcite to 30.5 m where corals are 100% calcite.	Between 6.7 and 5.3% to 15.2 m with abrupt decline to 2.1–1.1% below this.	20
3	33.2–88.1	Coralgal limestone	Calcite the dominant mineral. Faint traces of aragonite in intervals of 39.6–43.0 m and 55.8–64.9 m. Progressive increase of quartz from 0.1 to 3.9% at 88.1 m.	Between 1.3 and 1.5% to 55.8 m but declines abruptly below this to generally below 0.8%	36
4	88.1–93.9	Quartzose sand and sandstone	Fine-grained and moderately sorted. Contains foraminifera and is set in a calcite cement with low (less than 0.8%) MgCO$_3$ content.	Extremely low	
5	93.9–105.8	Coralgal limestone	Well-recrystallized and much secondary calcite in solution cavities.	Extremely low	96
6	105.8–147.8	Foraminiferal limestone	Creamy white to gray in color and with abundant *Orbitolites*. Quartz up to about 4% throughout and, locally, algal material and *Halimeda* abun-	Content from 105.8 to 117.6 m is very low (0.6%), from 117.6 to 135.6 m being slightly higher (1.1%), and	140

	Depth (m)	Lithology	Description	Porosity
7	147.8–154.2	Algal-foraminiferal limestone	dant. Although traces of aragonite remain in shell fragments, between 111.6 and 117.6 m calcite is the dominant mineral.	Up to 7.6% and averaging 5.2% between 148.7 and 154.2 m.
8	154.2–200.2	Quartzose sands with hard bands	Coarse texture and locally, high secondary porosity. Aragonite remains in shell fragments and foraminifera and algae appear to have retained their original calcitic structure.	Up to 16.1%, being highest in the foraminiferal limestone.
9	200.2–205.1	Quartzose-foraminiferal sands		
10	205.1–212.1	Foraminiferal limestone	Shallow water deposits with strong terrestrial influence. Foraminifera recrystallized and solution voids with secondary calcite. Some rare aragonite.	
11	212.1–214.6	Quartzose-foraminiferal sands		
12	214.6–223.1	Quartzose sands with hard bands		

[a]From Maxwell (1962) and Davies (1974).
[b]From Davies (1974).

147

per 133 m to be Quaternary in age, and Palmieri (1971) has recognized a Pliocene sequence down to 197 m. Davies (1974) thus reexamined the core and recognized four zones within the Holocene-Pleistocene section. (Table 5.2). He tentatively concluded that the levels at 20, 36, 96, and 140 m represented solution unconformities as described by Schlanger (1963) from the mid-Pacific atolls. Each level has formed a subaerial surface beneath which vadose and phreatic zones have occurred during low Pleistocene sea levels, the lowermost zones having experienced more exposure sequences. It is interesting to contemplate the reason for the occurrence of aragonite and high-Mg calcite below 147.8 m. Although alteration has obviously taken place in this deeper core it is possible that, even accounting for some shelf subsidence during the Quaternary, this zone has remained within the saltwater environment since deposition. The level is close to estimates for the maximum lowering of sea level during the last glaciation (see, e.g., Chappell, 1974a) and although Veeh and Veevers (1970) suggested a lowering to -175 m, the duration of sea level below 150 m could have been only very brief (see Chap. 6).

Comparison with other boreholes in the Capricorn area was not possible because of poor recovery in the upper 150 m (Davies, 1974). More detailed information on the northern Great Barrier Reef is available, however, as a result of the drilling carried out on the 1973 Royal Society–Universities of Queensland Expedition (Thom et al., 1978). Two holes were drilled, one on Stapleton Island to 14.6 m, the other on Bewick Island to 30 m. The Stapleton core (Fig. 5.11) passed through 14.5 m of Holocene detrital and marginal reef deposits from which the aragonite, high-Mg calcite content, and C^{14} dates indicated a Holocene age. This overlay a biomicrite with a calcite mineralogy that was considered to be the upper part of the Pleistocene (Thom et al., 1978).

The deeper Bewick core provided more information on upper-reef structure and diagenesis (Fig. 5.12). Diagenesis consists of a simple acicular aragonite cement in the highest unit to aggrading, neomorphic mosaics in the lowest, with complete conversion from aragonite to calcite in molluscs and corals. Thom et al., (1978) recognized eight lithologic units comprising five time units. At the top of each time unit the degree of alteration and iron-staining was sufficient to suggest that each represented a major solution unconformity developed as a reef cap was added during the prior marine transgression. As the lowest of these units is only 30 m below the present surface, all have been within a vadose or phreatic environment for a considerable period at least once. The difference in alteration between time units B and E is therefore not great, although development of secondary cavities with micritic or calcilutite fillings is apparently greater in the lower units. The quartz content also increases with depth. Mechanical wear and rounding in some grains indicate a terrigenous origin but authigenic growth of quartz is suggested by delicately spired boundaries and calcite intrusions (Thom et al., 1978).

The only other site for which information is currently available on the nature of diagenesis in subaerially exposed Pleistocene reef materials, is Hayman Island in the Whitsunday area (Hopley et al., 1978). The fringing reef on the southern side of this high island is 700 m wide and six cores were obtained to a maximum depth of 45 m (Fig. 12.6). Radiometric dating indicated that a Holocene reef cap 15–20 m thick overlies an older weathered reef unit. In the

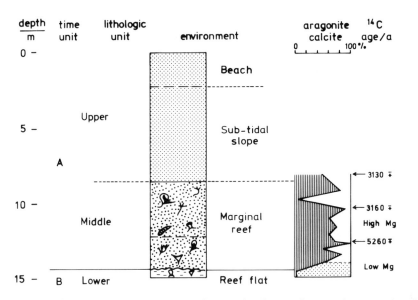

Figure 5.11 Stratigraphic units of the Stapleton Island core. (From Thom et al., 1978, reproduced by permission of the Royal Society.)

Holocene cap all coral samples were highly aragonitic (91–100%) whereas in the lower unit corals are calcitic and recrystallization is apparent even in hand specimens. Strontium values closely follow the pattern for aragonite, generally being in excess of 5000 ppm in the upper section and less than 2600 ppm in the lower. Magnesium values fluctuate from 600 to 3200 ppm throughout the core. Exact identification of the solution unconformity was not possible as materials were bagged in intervals ranging from 0.5 to 3.0 m. In one core (R1) the unconformity lies within the depth range 19–22 m. Geochemical analysis of three samples from this level indicates that nature of the boundary. One sample is 99% aragonitic and is clearly from above the unconformity, whereas another from below the unconformity is 99% calcite. A further hand-picked sample gave a bulk analysis of 87% calcite, 13% aragonite, and produced a radiocarbon date of 39,000 yrs or greater. SEM examination of the crystalline structure of this specimen showed that part of the original coral was recrystallized and part was not. This was confirmed by XRD and AA analysis of the two parts: one was 99% calcite (6000 ppm strontium, 800 ppm magnesium) the other 99% aragonite (700 ppm Sr, 2300 ppm Mg).

These results illustrate how variations in the nature and degree of alteration in the materials immediately underlying the Holocene reef cap may occur, although at depth, and presumably with greater age, the reef-rock fabric is similar at all sites. Factors that may be involved in the variability of the uppermost Pleistocene fabric are the nature of the original materials, age, and the climates experienced since deposition. Fine-grained, less permeable, lagoonal sediments may have reacted differently to more open coralgal framework and great variations may be present in the original mineralogy of the sediments and allochems. Although the reefal materials underlying the Holocene reef cap are Pleistocene, there is no reason why they should all have the same age. A last

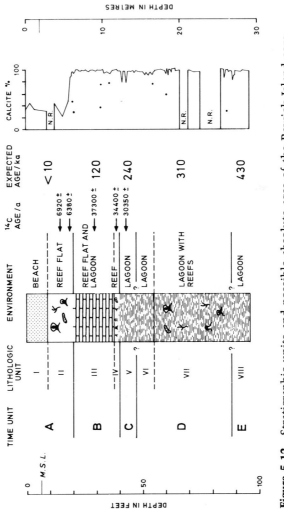

Figure 5.12 Stratigraphic units and possible absolute ages of the Bewick Island core. (From Thom et al., 1978, reproduced by permission of the Royal Society.)

interglacial age may be presumed (c. 125,000 yrs B.P.) but coral veneers may have been added to reef structures in intervening interstadial high sea level periods of the last glacial (see Chap. 6). Alternatively, younger Pleistocene reef veneers may have been eroded from the main structure during the last glacial and the materials of the surface that presently underlies the Holocene may considerably predate the last interglacial. At the present time on the Great Barrier Reef, regional variations in climate exist, particularly in terms of rainfall. Similar variations probably occurred during the Pleistocene, providing contrasting vadose and phreatic environments in different parts of the Reef. The importance of such climatic contrasts has been illustrated already from Barbados.

A most important aspect of diagenesis is the change it brings about in the mechanical properties of the rock. The response of the reef structures to subaerial geomorphic processes when emerged depends to a large extent on their permeability and mechanical strength. The original reef material similar to the modern Holocene reef caps is highly porous, poorly consolidated, only partially cemented, and mechanically weak. Such limestones may collapse into incipient caves and significant underground solution features are unable to develop (Jennings, 1971). In contrast, Jennings suggested that the fewer the intergranular voids, the more cemented and compacted the limestone, the more important become its planes of weakness, which promote permeability through their solutional enlargement. On such materials major karst features can develop that may have great influence on the development of modern reef morphology. This subject provides the central theme of Chapter 7.

6

The Influence of
Quaternary Climatic and
Sea Level Fluctuations

Since the papers of Reginald Daly in the early part of this century, climatic and sea level changes during the Quaternary have been recognized as having marked effect on coral reefs. Corals have a poleward distribution limited by critical water temperatures; as seen in Chapter 3, there is an upper limit to growth, not much above MLWS, of corals and related reef organisms and, largely through the diminution of illumination, a lower limit to coral growth. In Chapter 3 it was suggested that water temperatures of about 18°C and depths of about 20 m may be close to the limits of modern coral reef growth although individual corals may extend into cooler and deeper waters. However, fluctuations of both sea level and climate have been the characteristic feature of the Quaternary and it may be expected that in the past the low-latitude belt straddling the equator in which reefs are found has been much narrower during full glacial periods, and possibly more extensive during interglacials warmer than the Holocene. Similarly the 20-m-deep surface zone, in which carbonate accretion exceeds removal, has migrated vertically by over 100 m as growth of temperate ice sheets abstracted water from the oceans. On a greater time scale the implications of plate tectonics and continental drift also have to be acknowledged, but as these processes are likely to have had less influence on present than past reef morphology, it is the changing environmental conditions of the Quaternary and especially since the last interglacial upon which this chapter concentrates.

CLIMATIC CHANGE

It is generally acknowledged that since at least 37 m.y. ago there has been a general worldwide cooling of temperature upon which extreme fluctuations have been superimposed (see; e.g., Frakes, 1978). Glaciers in Antarctica reached the sea by 26 m.y. ago and it is clear that climatic fluctuations and accompanying changes in sea level were taking place during the period of establishment of the proto-Great Barrier Reef. Countering the general cooling was Australia's drift northward, which probably allowed continued coral growth at least on the northern Queensland shelf (Tanner, 1969), but periodic exposure of the protoreefs during low sea-level periods must have taken place, setting a pattern that has been repeated throughout the Quaternary. Although only the southeastern corner of the Australian continent and the highest mountains of New Guinea were glaciated, sufficient information is now at hand to indicate that Quaternary climatic changes in Australasia were as rapid and profound as they were in the middle latitudes of the better known northern hemisphere (Galloway and Kemp, 1977; Bowler et al., 1976; Walker, 1978). The nature and mechanisms of the changes of the various climates found in the Australian continent have been complex; however, changes of climate in the southern hemisphere appear to have been synchronous with those of the better documented northern hemisphere (Shackleton, 1978). In Australia, and particularly in the northern part of the continent, details of changes are known only since the last interglacial, a period of about 125,000 years. This is the period during which the present morphology of the Great Barrier Reef evolved and the nature and degree of change recorded during this period is likely to have been similar during earlier glacial-interglacial cycles.

Palynological work carried out in Australia and adjacent Papua New Guinea has indicated that during much of the last glacial eastern Australia was significantly drier than present and from about 40,000–15,000 yrs B.P. mean annual temperatures were lowered by between 6° and 10°C (Bowler et al., 1976). Although the cooling was a feature of worldwide climates, the drop in effective precipitation was a characteristic largely brought about by local conditions, particularly in North Queensland. Recent attempts to reconstruct the climatic features of the last glacial (Webster and Streten, 1978; Oliver, 1980) have stressed the important geographical changes brought about by the lowering of sea level. At present the frequency and distribution of tropical cyclones play an important role in determining rainfall patterns in eastern Queensland. A significant number of cyclones and smaller rain-producing tropical disturbances that affect eastern Queensland today originate in the eastern Arafura Sea and the Gulf of Carpentaria, moving either southward in western Queensland or across Cape York and regenerating in the Coral Sea. The shallowness of both these shelf areas means that they would have formed low-lying coastal plains for the larger part of the last 125,000 years. Tropical cyclogenesis would thus have been greatly reduced by this factor alone. In addition, generally cooler water temperatures may have reduced the number of disturbances developing in the Coral Sea, although probably not to the same extent as in northern waters off Western Australia (Webster and Streten, 1978). However, the reduced precipitation from expansion of the land area was probably superimposed on less active monsoonal influences (Oliver, 1980). Van Andel et al. (1967) have suggested that the equatorial rain belt was compressed and showed less seasonal movement from the equator in glacial times. Thus the pulsating movement of the ITC down the Queensland coast in summer (see Chap. 2) was probably restricted. The overall effect was one of much reduced rainfall. Webster and Streten (1978) estimate that at the full glacial stage coastal northern Australia may have experienced rainfall totals approximately half those of the present time.

The full glacial stage, however, probably constituted less than 25% of the time span since the last interglacial. Sea level records discussed below suggest that for much of the time climates intermediate between full glacial and interglacial existed. Fortunately the palynological work of Kershaw (1970, 1971, 1975a,b, 1976, 1978, 1980) on the Atherton Tableland provides a continuous record of vegetation and, by implication, climatic change for the whole of the last 120,000 years. Young volcanic crater lakes situated in rainforest but close to the rainforest-sclerophyll boundary at about the 1300 mm isohyet, have provided a sensitive record to changes in both rainfall and temperature. The most complete record comes from Lynch's Crater (Fig. 6.1). The presence of complex vine forest similar to that existing today suggests that conditions of the last interglacial were not far removed from those of the Holocene. Prior to this the latter part of the penultimate glacial period is marked by a complex notophyll vine forest with *Araucaria*, probably indicating rainfall totals a little more than half those of today. Similar rainfall reductions are clearly indicated by the vegetation changes during the last glacial. From c. 116,000–86,000 yrs B.P. the complex vine forest became simpler, although the complex form returned for a short period between 86,000 and 79,000 yrs B.P. Thus drastic changes in climate are not indicated in the early part of the last glacial. The first major change occurs between 79,000 and 63,000 yrs B.P. with the occurrence of a low araucarian vine forest suggesting rainfall totals of 1,000–1,200 mm, less than half those of today. A more complex araucarian vegetation returned 63,000–50,000 yrs B.P. with a subsequent low araucarian vine forest through to about 38,000 yrs B.P. Between 38,000 and 26,000 yrs B.P. a sclerophyll woodland dominated by *Eucalyptus* and *Casuarina* became established, although Kershaw considers that this is as much an expression of increased use of fire with the arrival of man in North Queensland as of the reduced rainfall totals. Drier conditions existed throughout the full glacial stage, and even during the early part of the postglacial. A simple subtropical notophyll vine forest, indicating increased rainfall, but also temperatures about 3°C cooler than present, moved into the Atherton Tableland from shortly after 10,000 yrs B.P., coinciding with about the time the shallow shelves of northern Australia, particularly the Gulf of Carpentaria, were being flooded. Higher rainfalls and temperatures are indicated by the complexity of the rainforest during mid-Holocene times, a feature noted from other areas of tropical Australia at about this time (e.g. Stocker, 1971). Kershaw (1978, 1980) showed that a close correlation existed between the rainfall interpretation from the Atherton Tableland records and the oxygen isotope and temperature curves from deep-sea cores (Hays et al., 1976). He also confirms the estimate of Webster and Streten (1978) of at least a 50% lowering of precipitation during the full glacial.

The Atherton Tableland record provides limited information on temperatures. At the start of the Holocene temperatures may have been 3°C below present, suggesting that at the full glacial, about 18,000 yrs B.P., they may have been even cooler. Nix and Kalma (1972) suggested that temperatures in northern Australia were depressed by as much as 5°C at the full glacial and evidence from New Guinea suggests temperatures were reduced by up to 11°C in the mountains (Walker, 1978). In contrast, CLIMAP (1976) and Shackleton (1978) indicated that surface temperatures in the Coral Sea were reduced by a mere

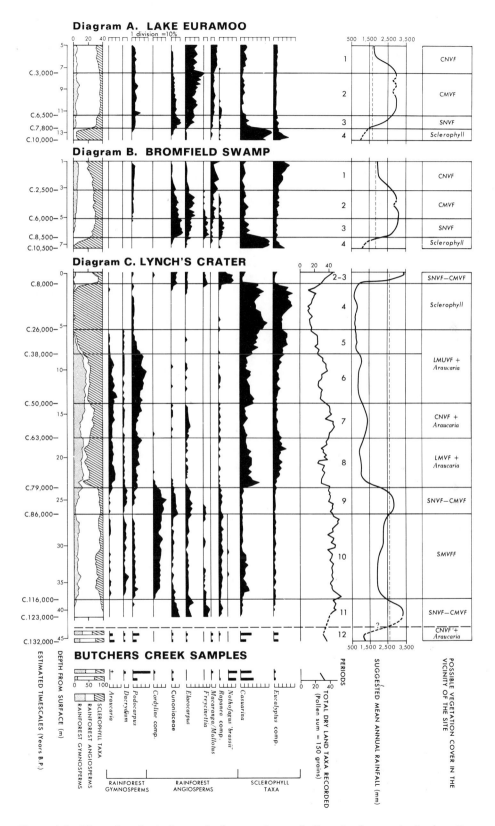

Figure 6.1 The palynological record of vegetation and climatic changes in the late Quaternary from the Atherton Tableland. (From Kershaw, 1980.)

2°C. This apparent anomaly has been noted by Webster and Streten (1978) who suggested that cold air incursions from higher latitudes (for which some analogies exist today) were sufficiently frequent to maintain a New Guinea snowline well below the freezing level of the ancient ambient tropical atmosphere. Vegetation responses to such incursions are also likely.

These climatic changes have been of great importance to the evolution of the Great Barrier Reef. Winter water temperatures at the southern end of the Reef are about 21°C. Although reefs extend into cooler waters it is probable that the southern limits of the Great Barrier Reef are controlled by water temperatures in exceptionally cool years. As Webster and Streten (1978) suggested that cold air incursions were more frequent in full glacial times, it is likely that shelf water temperatures of at least 21°C marked the southern extremity of shelf reef growth during Pleistocene glacials. If the 2°C lowering of Coral Sea temperatures in winter was also applicable to shelf waters, the southern limit of coral growth 18,000 years ago may have been at about latitude 20°30′S, that is, between Bowen and Mackay, or at the northern end of the Pompey Reef Complex. However, during much of the last glacial, the southern limit of reef growth may have been further south. Nonetheless, in the vicinity of the Bunker–Capricorn Group, reef growth may have been restricted to only the warmest interstadials. A further factor that may have decreased shelf water temperatures and inhibited reef growth on the southern reef would have been the increased influence of the cooler continental climate, which would have extended closer to the marginal shelf reefs with exposure of the inner shelf during lower sea-level periods.

Definitive data on the climate along the Great Barrier Reef during the last interglacial are lacking although the position of sea level at that time would suggest that conditions were similar to those of today. Indeed, there have been some suggestions that seawater temperatures may have been higher than today (Shackleton and Opdyke, 1973). If so, then it may be expected that reef growth would have extended further south. Marshall and Thom (1976) dated last interglacial corals from Newcastle (13°45′S) and Evans Head (28°04′S) on the New South Wales coast, which suggested to Galloway and Kemp (1977) "rather warm seas during interglacials." However, corals though not developing into reefal structures, are found further south than these sites today (Table 3.4), although the variety of species described by Marshall and Thom would suggest warmer waters than present. Examination of other fringing reefs also leads to the conclusion that fringing reefs may have been more flourishing in the last interglacial (see Chap. 12).

A southern extension of the shelf reefs of the Great Barrier Reef during the last interglacial has not been conclusively demonstrated. The problem lies in part with the southern limit of the Reef coinciding with the spilling of sand across the continental shelf from Fraser Island and Breaksea Spit, at the end of its northern migration up the coast (see Chap. 2). Thus it is difficult to separate the effects of sedimentation and temperature in determining details of present and past reef growth. Close to and to the south of the Bunker–Capricorn Group are numerous submerged reefal shoals. Some irregular shelf-edge topography attributed to reef growth at very low sea-level stages by Conolly (1969) has been shown by Marshall (1971) to be outcrops of Pliocene age. However coralline material from other shoals together with a morphology of annular rims and central depressions clearly suggest a reefal origin (Marshall, 1977). These shoals occur in four areas:

1 To the north of the Bunker–Capricorn Group along an east-west axis, rising from depths of 55–60 m to within depths of 8–42 m of the surface.
2 Within the Capricorn Channel from depths of 74–103 m and relief of up to 25 m.
3 East of the Bunker–Capricorn Group as small reefal shoals to depths of 18 m.
4 Opposite Fraser Island rising from depths of 57–77 m. The largest, Gardner Bank, rises to a depth of at least 24 m.

Marshall (1977) suggested that the shoals off Fraser Island developed from banks of sand moved across the shelf at low sea level stages and subsequently colonized by corals during the "late Quaternary." He suggested that adverse conditions such as a rapid rise in sea level (see also Jell and Flood, 1978, p. 15) or cool currents may have inhibited reef growth and they were gradually submerged. However, Marshall describes terracing of Gardner Bank at depths of 52 m and 31 m, which indicated to him that: "Gardner Bank was exposed during a series of low sea-level fluctuations during the late Quaternary" (Marshall, 1977, p. 20). Similarly, he suggests that other shelf-edge irregularities east of the Bunker–Capricorn Group "are formed of small coral formations which may be remnants of older coral reefs that were subaerially eroded during late Quaternary low sea level stands," (p. 15).

Although it is quite probable that submerged reefal shoals further north, where water temperatures during the last glacial were not lowered sufficiently to prevent coral growth, were overwhelmed by rapid sea-level rises during the Holocene transgression, this is considered unlikely for the shoals at the southern end of the Great Barrier Reef. Kershaw suggested that temperatures on the Atherton Tableland were 3°C lower than present until almost 6000 yrs B.P. and as these reefs are in the vicinity of the present temperature control of reef growth, it is unlikely that corals became established during early postglacial times. An earlier warm phase equivalent to the Allerød of Europe has not been recognized in Australia (Bowler et al., 1976). By the mid-Holocene when temperatures may have been 1°C warmer than today (Kershaw, 1975a), modern sea level had been achieved and depth would have been the factor limiting development of deeper shoals.

It is therefore suggested that the reefal shoals extending to 26°S on the continental shelf predate the last glacial maximum. If last interglacial in age, then their present depth may be explained by erosion during subaerial exposure and/or marginal shelf subsidence. Alternatively thay may have developed during an early interstadial, although their distribution suggests that shelf waters at their time of growth were marginally higher than present.

In addition to the importance of truncation of the poleward extension of coral reefs during the late Quaternary, climates of the period are also important to reef development as they determined the nature and rates of process that operated on the pre-Holocene reef structures exposed by glacially lowered sea levels. Douglas (1980) has suggested that along the moister north Queensland coast, climatic change would not have greatly altered fluvial processes in comparison to today. The critical aspect for coral reef evolution is the rate and nature of erosion on the limestone terrain of the exposed coral reefs. The evidence from the Atherton Tableland suggests that temperatures, although depressed, would remain "tropical" at the level of the emerged shelf throughout the last glacial cycle. More important is the pattern of rainfall change.

Presuming that reef tops were constructed to at least the level of present sea level during the last interglacial, then their early phase of subaerial weathering would have taken place in a climate of relative humidity. Two types of karst landscape develop in the tropics. Williams (1978) has indicated that in areas where the excess of precipitation over evapotranspiration exceeds 800 mm, surface solution will produce a polygonal karst of enclosed depressions, whereas in areas of less than 800 mm excess, a more arid landscape of flat-floored box valleys and pediments would develop. Considering the lower rates of evaporation with slightly lower temperatures, it is suggested that along the more humid parts of the Queensland coast during the last glacial the tendency would have been for polygonal karst to develop only between the last interglacial and 79,000 yrs B.P. and subsequently the more arid type of landscape would have evolved. On drier coastal sections, particularly those where orographic uplift is limited, the subhumid karst landscape may have developed over a longer period. Whether or not there was sufficient time for significant alteration of the original growth structure of the older reefs by erosion is a matter of debate that is taken up in Chapter 7.

QUATERNARY SEA LEVEL CHANGES

The response of coral reefs to sea level change is both direct and immediate, as indicated by the suites of coral terraces on rapidly uplifting coasts such as the Ryukyus, Barbados, or New Guinea (Fig. 6.2). Here, relatively minor regressions and transgressions are separated by the mechanism of emergence of the substrate upon which the reefs are established. Dating of the terraces is accomplished by radiocarbon and uranium-series methods, and although each has its limitations (for discussion see Thom, 1973; Chappell et al., 1974; Veeh and Green, 1977) there have accumulated over the last decade sufficient data to allow the compilation of a detailed chronology of late Pleistocene sea level changes. Prior to the last interglacial the degree of error associated both with the dating methods and the assumed rates of uplift by which tectonic factors are extracted from eustatic changes, has meant that the chronology is by no means certain.

The major feature that has emerged from these studies is the inadequacy of classical systems of dividing the Quaternary based on North European, Alpine, or North American glacial stratigraphy. In 1969 Guilcher provided an excellent review of the state of knowledge of Quaternary shorelines and even then it was clear that the concept of steadily lowering sea levels from the end of the Tertiary upon which up to four major Quaternary fluctuations were superimposed (e.g. Fairbridge, 1960, 1961) did not agree with the increasing amount of evi-

Figure 6.2 The back of the 83,000-year reef terrace with sea stack displaying notch and visor cut into older Pleistocene reef limestones, northeast coast of Barbados.

dence that was emerging. He thus restricted detailed discussion to the penultimate interglacial and later, and highlighted in particular the problems that have been central to subsequent Quaternary shoreline research and that are vital to the understanding of the present morphology of coral reefs. These are:

1 The height and length of time of the last interglacial sea level.
2 The nature of interstadial sea levels during the last glacial.
3 The degree of emergence achieved during the maximum glacial stage.
4 The nature of the postglacial transgression.
   These themes are central to the remainder of this chapter.

Evidence from solution unconformities both on the Great Barrier Reef and elsewhere (Chap. 5) suggest that the history of reefs prior to the last interglacial was one of periodic emergence and submergence. It is probable that this pattern was extremely complex. Ice-core and oxygen-isotope analysis of deep-ocean cores (Frakes, 1978) indicate that severe glaciation and probable sea level lowering had taken place in the Antarctic by 26 m.y. ago. By 5.5–3 m.y. ago the Ross Ice Shelf had expanded to the edge of the continental shelf. Although some glacier retreat took place 4.25–3.95 m.y. ago, subsequent cooling led into a period of short-term fluctuations that between 3.35 and 0.7 m.y. ago had periodicities of about 170,000 years, and later about 110,000 years. Clearly, throughout the history of the Great Barrier Reef, even without the relative changes produced by slow but steady shelf subsidence, sea level fluctuations of a glacio-eustatic origin have periodically emerged and submerged the shelf reefs. In a review of Pleistocene chronology in Europe, Kukla (1977) suggested that there had been at least 17 glacial-interglacial cycles during the last 1.7 million years. In South Australia slow uplift in the southeastern part of the state has resulted in the preservation of a 100-km-wide strip of littoral sediments, which record at least 20 major high sea level stands during the past 690,000 years (Cook et al., 1977).

It is very probable that prior to the last interglacial coral reefs had grown up to and possibly higher than the level of modern sea level, and had developed a morphology not significantly different than that of present reefs. The lack of agreement on elevations of these earlier transgressions is not surprising. With acceptance of a dynamic earth model of modern plate tectonics, as Walcott (1972) has pointed out, the concept of coastal stability has only relative meaning and the possibility of minor vertical movements of the crust even at locations far removed from plate boundaries cannot be excluded. Indeed, sea-floor spreading and changing morphology of the ocean basins will have a eustatic effect even at the scale of a single glacial-interglacial cycle. Bloom (1971) suggested that the spreading of the ocean basins since the last interglacial alone could produce almost 8 m of sea level lowering. In view of the discrepancies in data on Holocene shorelines discussed below, correlation of heights of shorelines hundreds of thousands of years old should neither be attempted nor expected.

The Last Interglacial (Sangamon) Sea Level and Coral Reefs

The last interglacial is important for reef evolution as it is the last period before the Holocene that sea level reached or exceeded its present position. The majority of extensive outcrops of emerged reefs are of last interglacial age and, as many come from relatively stable areas and have heights and radiometric dates that are closely comparable, it is now accepted that sea level about 125,000 years ago was a few meters above present. The period over which the radiometric dates stretch and their grouping into two sets has suggested that transgression maxima may have occurred 130,000–140,000 yrs B.P. and 118,000–125,000 yrs B.P. Such evidence has come from widely separated areas such as Jamaica (Moore and Somayajulu, 1974), New Guinea (Bloom et al., 1974; Chappell, 1974b), eastern Australia (Marshall and Thom, 1976) and Timor (Chappell and Veeh, 1978). For example, in Timor, transgressions at about 135,000 yrs B.P. and between 118,000 and 125,000 yrs B.P. to levels between 5 and 8 m above present were separated by a regression of between 7 and 15 m. The elevation of the transgressions of between 5 and 8 m is similarly reported from areas where evidence for only a single interglacial is retained, including Western Australia (Szabo, 1979), the Tuamotus and Seychelles (Veeh, 1966), the Yucatan Peninsula (Szabo et al., 1978), Hawaii (Ku et al., 1974) and Aldabra (Thomson and Walton, 1972).

In eastern Australia it is now accepted that the inner sand barrier that occurs along much of the coastline is last interglacial in age (e.g. Thom, 1978). The uranium series dates from Newcastle and Evans Head reported by Marshall and Thom (1976) indicated the two stages of the interglacial high sea level and locate its position as +5 m relative to modern sea level. On the Queensland coast opposite the Great Barrier Reef the inner barrier is more fragmentary and has not been firmly dated. However, radiocarbon dates of 14,680 ± 310 for pedogenic carbonate nodules in an inner barrier-beach ridge near Townsville (Hopley and Murtha, 1975); radiocarbon dates between 25,150 and 28,980 yrs B.P. for calcarenites and coquina from the Burdekin Delta (Hopley, 1970a); radiocarbon dates of 20,200 ± 600 yrs B.P. for coralline beach rock on Camp Island (Hopley, 1971a); and dates of 15,640 ± 490 yrs B.P. for calcarenite on Cockermouth Island (Hopley, 1975) are all considered minimal due to contamination of organic material of an age beyond the range of radiocarbon dating. A last interglacial age is most likely for these deposits, the sea level indicated, of between 2.4 and 4.5 m, being at the lower end of the range reported from relatively stable areas elsewhere.

With the possible exception of the Torres Strait region (A. Barham, personal communication), no Pleistocene reef outcrops on the Great Barrier Reef, and evidence presented in Chapter 7 indicates that pre-Holocene reefal material generally lies between 3 and 20 m beneath modern reefs. Arguments are presented in this following chapter to suggest that this is the result of a combination of minor subsidence of the shelf and erosion. However, the extensive development of last interglacial reefs elsewhere is indicative of the degree of reef growth that was possible. Szabo (1979) concluded that the last interglacial was an exceptional event in that sea level was above present and, presumably, also above earlier high sea levels of the middle Pleistocene. It was also of considerable time span and in view of the amount of reef development that has been possible during the shorter and incomplete Holocene "interglacial" (see Chaps. 8 and 9) it seems possible that a large mass of limestone was laid down on the Great Barrier Reef. The limestone formed the basic fabric of the topographic features, which were subsequently subjected to subaerial exposure and weathering of the last glacial, and the emerged island cores around which fringing reefs of interstadial age were attached.

Interstadial and Stadial Sea Levels of the Last Glacial Period (Wisconsin)

Although sea level remained below present, after it regressed from the interglacial high about 118,000 years ago, for the full period of the last glacial, the rapid tectonic uplift of areas such as Barbados and the Huon Peninsula of New Guinea (Veeh and Green, 1977, Table 1) has meant that some of the reefs, deposited during interstadial transgressions and as much as 40 m below present sea level, have been uplifted many meters above modern sea level (Fig. 6.2). Based on presumptions of a last interglacial sea level of about +6 m 120,000 years ago and steady rates of uplift, it has been possible to reconstruct the fluctuations of sea level throughout much of the c. 110,000-year period between the last interglacial and the Holocene transgression. The remarkable degree of correlation achieved in the results from such widely separated areas as the Huon Peninsula and Barbados vindicates the assumptions made in the reasoning. No sea level higher than the present was achieved at any stage between 118,000 yrs B.P. and the Holocene, as had previously been argued (e.g. Milliman and Emery, 1968). The clustering of radiocarbon dates around 35,000 yrs B.P. related to a sea level at least as high as present, is the result of organic material of last interglacial age requiring only 1–5% of modern carbon to produce a finite date within the range 36,000 to 24,000 yrs B.P. (Mörner, 1971a; Thom, 1973; Chappell et al., 1974).

The pattern of sea level oscillation through the last 125,000 years is shown in Figure 6.3. It is constructed around the curve based on Huon Peninsula data (Bloom et al., 1974), but an envelope of error could be added by incorporating the results from Barbados (Mesolella, 1968; Broeker et al., 1968; Mesolella et al., 1969; James et al., 1971; Steinen et al., 1973; Taylor, 1974; and Fairbanks and Matthews, 1978), Ryukyu Islands (Konishi et al., 1970, 1974) and East Timor (Chappell and Veeh, 1978). At least five transgressions are recognized. The earliest is at c. 105,000 yrs B.P. Estimates based on uplift rates indicate levels of about – 14 m. The 84,000 yrs B.P. interstadial is assigned a height of c. – 20 m by Bloom et al. (1974) from Huon data and – 13- – 16 m by Broeker et al. (1968) and Mesellola et al. (1969) from Barbados data. Fairly close agreement occurs in data from different areas for the c. 60,000 yrs B.P. interstadial. Figures of – 20 m are suggested by the terraces on Huon Peninsula (Bloom et al., 1974) and the Ryukyus (Konishi et al., 1970, 1974) and a figure of – 18 m from Barbados (Taylor, 1974). Later interstadial high sea levels are lower than those recorded in the early part of the last glacial. This is indicative of the general cooling and ice expansion taking place toward the maximum of the glaciation about 18,000 yrs B.P. The transgression about 40,000 yrs B.P. was complex and possibly involved two stands at about – 20 and – 40 m (Bloom et al., 1974), only the lower level being recorded in the Ryukyus (Konishi et al., 1970, 1974) and neither presently outcropping above sea level on the more slowly rising Barbados. A final transgression to about – 40 m may have taken place at c. 29,000 yrs B.P. according to the Huon record. Although some further research

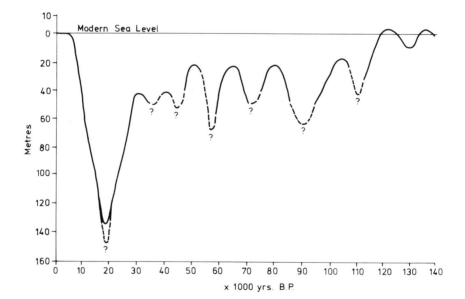

Figure 6.3 Pattern of sea-level changes over the last 140,000 years. (Based on Bloom et al., 1974, and others.)

is still required to fix more definitely the level of some of these interstadial sea levels, the close correlation between sea level and temperature (0^{18}) indicates the degree of confidence with which the general pattern can be accepted.

The level of the ocean during the glacial advances that intervened between the interstadials cannot be determined easily from the reef terrace data. On the basis of the level of a subaerial weathering crust at the unconformity between the 125,000 and overlying 105,000 coral terrace on Barbados, Steinen et al. (1973) calculated that the intervening regression reached -71 ± 11 m relative to present sea level. However, such a regression should correlate with a major glacial advance and there is no record of a glaciation or a lowering of ocean temperatures of this magnitude so soon after the last interglacial. Unfortunately, other direct evidence of the height of stadial sea levels other than at the maximum regression is lacking. Suggestions of major regression of the same magnitude of that of 18,000 yrs B.P. in the early part of the last glacial (e.g. Guilcher, 1969) cannot be substantiated. Based on estimations from paleotemperatures and ice volumes, and presuming that rates of regression and transgression were no greater during the early stadial-interstadial phases of the last glacial compared to the changes around the maximum glaciation period, the sea levels prior to 18,000 yrs B.P. probably did not fall below -60 m.

There is a considerable weight of evidence to suggest that the maximum extension of ice sheets and minimum sea level during the last glaciation occurred about 18,000 years ago. Sea level appears to have fallen rapidly from the 29,000 year interstadial to below -100 m. The exact amount of lowering is uncertain and due to variable hydro-isostatic response, which is discussed further in the next section, may have been of a different magnitude and peaked at different times in various parts of the world. Great difficulties are involved in estimating the volume of water locked in the ice sheets at the full glacial stage (Bloom, 1971). Further problems arise from survival of evidence on the continental shelves of the world which may predate the last glacial period. Thus, although dredges and cores from the world's shelves regularly encounter shallow water and lagoonal deposits to depths of 80–100 m, evidence from greater depths is less widespread and dates are more controversial. This does not preclude a regression of greater than 100 m, for the time available for such a low sea level is short, probably less than 2500 years, and the time for accumulation of datable evidence is thus limited. Also, as Chappell (1974a) has commented, the pinpointing of paleosea levels is difficult during a period when rates of sea level change ranged up to 10 m/1000 yr. Chappell's (1974a) estimate of 130–135 m of sea level lowering at the glacial maximum, acknowledging the various uncertainities, appears to be the most acceptable compromise. However, taking into account global elastic and relaxation effects on a broad scale and differential shelf flexures on a more local scale due to hydro-isostatic loading, Chappell estimates that a lowering of -160 m may be expected off the broad northern Australian continental shelves. This is in accord with the small amount of dated evidence available. Veeh and Veevers (1970) dated coral off the edge of a terrace at -160 m at 17,000 yrs B.P. by Th-230/U-234, and this age is supported by a radiocarbon age of 14,000 yrs B.P. for beach rock on a second smaller terrace at -150 m. Similarly, Jongsma (1970) reported a radiocarbon age of 18,700 yrs B.P. for material at -150 m. Dates in the same age range from terraces or dredge samples at about −130 m have also been recorded on the Sahul Shelf (Van Andel and Veevers, 1967) and northern New South Wales (Phipps, 1970).

Coral Reef Response to Sea Level Change During the Last Glacial Period

The pattern of sea-level changes that took place over the 110,000 years prior to the Holocene oscillated the 20 m layer of water within which coral growth is at its maximum through a vertical range of up to 150 m. Utilizing the sea-level curve of Figure 6.3 it is possible to estimate the total time within which each depth zone at 10 m intervals related to modern sea level, has been in the photic zone within 20 m of the paleosea level (Fig. 6.4). A number of assumptions on stadial sea levels are made in these calculations, and no allowance is made for tectonic or hydro-isostatic deformation of the continental shelves, but the general pattern is considered to be valid. Prior to the mid-Holocene, late Pleistocene reef growth above −18 m was limited to the last interglacial. Growth at depths below 70 m was probably limited to the maximum regression around 18,000 yrs B.P. and for any particular depth was possibly less than 4000 years. In contrast, for all depths between 20 and 60 m, more than 35,000 years of reef growth has been possible, although not continuously. Emergence of reefs between −20 and −40 m took place at regular intervals as did submergence of deeper levels of −40 to −60 m and periods of continuous growth were prob-

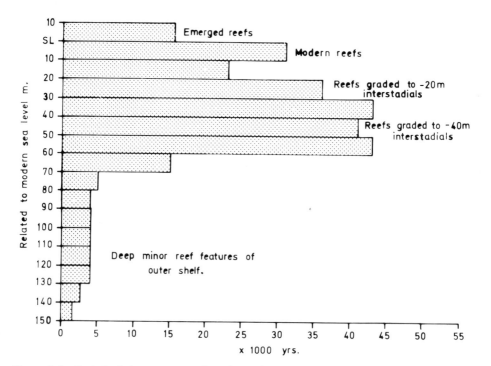

Figure 6.4 Period of time spent within the reef-building zone of the upper 20 m of the sea for depths to 150 m at 10 m intervals during the last 140,000 years. (Based on Fig. 6.3.)

ably limited to about 5000 years each. Based on even the modest amounts of reef accretion that have taken place during the Holocene, it seems probable that significant amount of reefal material could have been added to the exposed last interglacial reefs as fringing reefs, and, on suitable substrates, as discrete reefs on the outer continental shelf. That such accretion was possible is confirmed by the raised reef terraces that are found around tectonically rising areas. On Barbados, the 60,000 year terrace varies in width between 3 and 30 m (James et al., 1971), while the 84,000 and 105,000 year reefs are up to 1 km wide (James, 1972b). However, greatest widths are associated with reefs that have thinly veneered preexisting reefs or platforms. For example the 60,000-year-old terrace overlies a shore platform and has a thickness of only 4 m (James et al., 1971). On steeper coasts, such as parts of the Huon Peninsula, the terraces are only a few tens of meters wide, but still form distinctive topographic features (Chappell, 1974b).

Separation of these terrace sequences at such rising locations as Huon and Barbados has been caused by uplift. On stable shelves, or shelves that are slowly subsiding, as is contemplated for the Great Barrier Reef, the various terraces related to the 60,000, 84,000, and 105,000 year transgressions are probably not discrete but overlap each other and form a distinctive morphological feature. Similarly, transgressions to about -40 m in the time interval 30,000 to 40,000 years may have seen the addition of reefal material to structures at about this depth that could have been initiated at earlier regressive periods. Because of uncertainities resulting from both growth rates of such features and subsequent hydro-isostatic displacement, widespread correlation of exact levels should not be expected. The complexity of the problem is indicated by comparing the depth of reported terrace levels on the Great Barrier Reef area (e.g. Maxwell, 1968, 1973a; Marshall, 1977; Orme et al., 1978a). Consistency is almost entirely lacking. However, the majority of features lie within the depth range of 18–67 m, that is, the postulated range of sea-level oscillation between about 118,000 and 29,000 yrs B.P. As no stillstand of more than 5000 years is indicated during this period, the maximum width of intertidal erosional platforms that could be cut into carbonate substrate, based on Trudgill's (1976a) figures (see Chap. 7) is 35 m and probably much less. It is thus postulated that the majority of "terrace" levels recognized on the Great Barrier Reef area, particularly around the margins of the reefs and on the continental slope, are reefal growth features. Although they may be related to specific sea-level events, there is every possibility that not all reefs of any particular period were able to grow to their maximum elevation (i.e. MLWS). Thus it is not surprising to find a great spread of depths for reported "terrace" levels.

The number of reported terraces is greatest in the -18 to -25 m range, which corresponds to the postulated maximum level of interstadial reef growth, a level that was achieved at least three times. Maxwell (1968, 1973a), Davies et al. (1976), Marshall (1977), Jell and Flood (1978) and Orme et al. (1978a) all report significant features to this depth. In addition, there are reefal shoals far more extensive than modern reefs, from which the modern reefs rise. For example, Davies et al. (1976) reported a platform at -25 m from which One Tree Reef rises, while Maxwell and Swinchatt (1970) suggested that the Arlington Reef complex near Cairns rises from a 29 m platform and nearby Green Island from a platform of 18 m. Although absolute dating of these terrace features is required, it seems probable that many evolved as fringing reefs around emerged reef islands of the last interglacial and older age during interstadial transgressions of the last glacial period (Fig. 8.11).

The extent to which interstadial age reef could be added to the older reefal structures during the last 120,000 years depends to a large extent on bathymetry, as well as the temperature factor already discussed. Figure 6.4 suggests that several transgressions to about – 20 m occurred and that at least one and possibly two other transgressions reached c. – 40 m. Maximum lowering of sea level was at least – 135 m. The effect this would have on the continental shelf of Queensland is seen in Figure 6.5, which is based on modern bathymetry. Insufficient data are available to reconstruct the geographic detail of each transgressive-regressive phase, but the thickness of shelf sediments and nature of the underlying surface as indicated by seismic survey (see Chap. 7) suggest that the gross pattern is correct.

At c. – 20 m transgressive peaks, the majority of reefs would have emerged as limestone islands, not much larger than the modern reefs, although larger shoal areas, possibly the developing fringing reefs, would have surrounded many. The mainland coastline would have been moved eastward by up to 25 km opposite low-lying coastal plains, but by less than 1 km adjacent to major headlands. At the southern end of the Great Barrier Reef, the Fraser Island sand mass would have extended almost to the edge of the continental shelf. Many of the high continental islands would have remained as islands, but enlarging as island groups coalesced into single land masses. Greatest changes would have been to the north of Cairns on the shallow northern shelf. Between Cairns and Lizard Island, an inner channel would have been flooded by a – 20 m transgression, but it would have had limited access to the sea by way of the main channel to the south and the deeper passes within the limestone island barrier to the east. Innermost reefs would have been exposed completely and, between Lizard Island and Cape Melville and in smaller areas north of Princess Charlotte Bay, the coastal plain would have been extended to the midshelf reefs. Torres Strait would have been closed and it is in the Gulf of Papua that the greatest extension of land took place, with limestone cliffs facing the coastline along the eastern edge of the Warrior Reefs. Providing that water temperatures were sufficiently high, coral growth would have been possible around all reefs and the majority of continental islands as far north as latitude 18°S. However, the migration of terrigenous influences eastward may have affected the growth of fringing reefs around some of the closer continental islands. North of 18°S reef growth was possibly limited to only the outer reefs as restricted circulation and low-energy conditions behind the island barrier of the outer reefs would not have provided an environment conducive to coral growth. Further, each transgression to – 20 m took place after a regression that had exposed the deeper shelf area. Deposition of terrigenous sediments and development of a regolith over this area would have resulted in highly turbid waters during initial stages of a transgression. On open high-energy coasts this period may have been relatively short, but in the very sheltered conditions that would have existed on the midshelf area of the northern Great Barrier Reef, turbid conditions may have been a permanent feature of each transgression to – 20 m. Deterio-

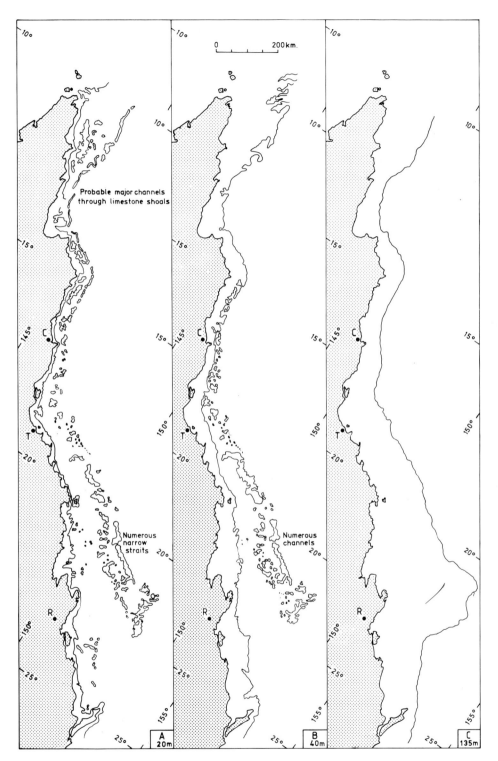

Within the figure:
Probable major channels
through limestone shoals

Numerous
narrow
straits

Numerous
channels

0   200km.

A
20m

B
40m

C
135m

Figure 6.5 Emergence of the continental shelf of Queensland at − 20, − 40, and − 135 m low sea-level stages.

rating water quality associated with shelf flooding is believed to be the cause of the demise of several Caribbean reefs during the early part of the Holocene transgression (Adey, 1978a).

In many ways the shallow northern shelf at − 20 m transgressions would have resembled southern Florida, where today the discontinuous island barrier formed by the Pleistocene Key Largo reef separates an outer reef tract from a series of shallow bays and sounds (Ginsburg, 1956, 1972; Marszalek et al., 1977). The exchange of water between Florida Bay and the Atlantic is limited by the islands and within the bay shallow-water depths with large mud banks further restrict water movement. Seasonal fluctuations in salinity between 10 and 40‰ occur, far greater than in the adjacent open ocean.

> The rapidity of change from one major environment to the other depends on the extent of the barrier between them. Where there are channels through the Pleistocene limestone islands, . . . the nearshore reef-tract environment extends tongue-like into Florida Bay, and the change to restricted conditions is gradual. Where the barrier is more complete, as along Key Largo, the change in conditions is more rapid but there is still a transition zone paralleling the islands because the extremely porous limestone permits some tidal exchange between Bay and reef tract.
>
> *Ginsburg, 1956, p. 2396*

It is considered that such a description could apply to much of the northern Great Barrier Reef shelf at 105,000, 84,000, and 60,000 yrs B.P. If the analogy were extended to the biology, then the shallow shelf between the extended mainland and the outer limestone islands would have had a very restricted flora and fauna at these times, with reef forms extending only along major tidal channels into the shallow bay environment. It is interesting to note that *Halimeda* occurs up to 8 km into Florida Bay. Large banks of *Halimeda* sediments on the northern Great Barrier Reef shelf, which are probably younger than the last interglacial but older than the Holocene transgression, occur in the area behind the present outer barrier (Fig. 7.16). Cross bedding has been identified in the banks that are apparently not of coralline material. The banks have a depth of 20–40 m and it is possible they accumulated as mud or sand banks in shoal water less than 20 m and sometimes as little as 5 m deep during one or more of the interstadial transgressions, similar to the modern banks within Florida Bay.

At a − 40 m sea level stage a far greater proportion of the shelf would have been exposed, including the whole of the northern shelf south of latitude 16°30'S. A cliffed limestone coastline would have existed continuously along the outside of the protoribbon reefs interrupted only at the major passes by estuarine embayments. From 16°30'S to 18°S some midshelf reefs would have been completely exposed and the outer reefs would have formed a dense pattern of limestone islands although water depths and circulation were probably sufficient to allow coral growth. Further south still, all reefal areas would have been exposed as islands, some of large proportions on the outer shelf edge. Relatively shallow water of less than 18 m depth around most may have allowed rapid extension of fringing reefs built to this level. The Capricorn Group of reefs would have been incorporated within the mainland, but the Bunker Group would have remained as a series of near-shore islands. Extension of the drainage system from the mainland across the exposed shelf took place but channels were not deeply incised.

At the lowest sea-level stage 18,000 years ago, the whole of the Queensland shelf apart from the upper continental slope would have been emerged. Reef development would have been limited to a very narrow fringe with only the detached reefs of the far north forming offshore islands. The position of this shoreline would have been only a few kilometers east of the − 40 m strandline and incision of streams on the outer edge of the shelf would have taken place. However, the short duration of the lowest sea level probably did not allow incision to extend right across the shelf, particularly the wider central section. Seismic and echo-sounding survey of various sections of shelf (see Chap. 7) show that inner-shelf channels though terraced are generally incised less than 15 m below the present surface and are infilled, but channels on the outer shelf are simpler and may be incised up to 25 m and have not been back-filled subsequently (Orme et al., 1978a; Searle et al., 1980; Searle and Harvey, in press).

Examination of the approximate position of interstadial shorelines thus suggests that reef growth during the whole of the last glacial period was very limited on the northern Great Barrier Reef where even during interstadial high sea levels, it occurred only on the outer shelf. Further south, on the central and southern sections, the deeper shelf would have allowed considerable additions to be made in the form of fringing reefs to the older Pleistocene cores. Whether or not coral growth would have been possible on the southern extremity of the Great Barrier Reef at all, interstadial high sea levels would depend on the extent of lowered water temperatures. If only 2°C lowering took place at the maximum glacial, then it seems probable that growth was possible during most interstadial phases. It seems equally probable, however, that growth was restricted or even halted as far north as the northern Pompey Complex about 18,000 years ago. Recolonization of reefal shoals during the Holocene transgression may thus have been slower on the southernmost Reef.

THE HOLOCENE TRANSGRESSION

It is generally acknowledge that recovery of world temperatures, ablation of ice sheets, and rise in sea level from the glacial maximum was rapid after about 14,000 yrs B.P. when about 88% of the total glaciated area was still ice covered. By 10,000 yrs B.P., 50% of the ice had gone. Final melting is estimated at about 6500 yrs B.P., (Bloom, 1971), yet from many parts of the world there is evidence of sea level rising right up to the present day, while others appear to have achieved modern sea level far earlier. This is the dilemma of the Holocene sea level problem that, from the publication of the first extensively based radiometrically dated sea-level curve by Fairbridge in 1960, has been a central issue for workers on Quaternary sea levels. (See, e.g., Guilcher, 1969; Mörner, 1971b,c; and Curray and Shepard, 1972, for discussion on a world scale and Hails, 1965; Thom et al., 1969, 1972; Gill and Hopley, 1972; and Thom and Chappell, 1975, for discussion of Australia.) The problem is not simply one of when modern sea level was first achieved, but includes whether or not the transgression involved minor regressive phases, and most controversially, whether or not modern sea level was exceeded at some time during the mid-Holocene. These issues are vital to the understanding of modern reef morphology.

Reasons for the controversial discrepancies with special reference to the Great Barrier Reef have been discussed by Hopley (1974b, 1975, 1978b). Problems are associated with accurate height measurement and interpretation of paleo–sea levels from particular types of data. Major errors may result from the radiometric dating technique (Thom, 1973; Chappell et al., 1974; Veeh and Green, 1977). Even allowing for variations produced by waves and tides, the present ocean surface is nonhorizontal, varying with temperature and salinity (Fairbridge, 1966), centrifugal and Coriolis forces operating in currents (Hamon, 1958), and even in response to changes in the geoid (Mörner, 1976).

Inevitably movements of the land were quoted as major reasons for sea level discrepancies in early discussions of the problem. Close to plate boundaries tectonic dislocation of shorelines can be clearly demonstrated and Davies (1972) has suggested that vertical movements of small amplitude but long period may take place along coasts in central plate locations. However, in recent years there has been an increasing awareness of the sensitivity of the earth's crust to loading and unloading. Movements of hundreds of meters have long been recognized in association with the waxing and waning of Pleistocene ice sheets. Response of the oceans and continental shelves to the fluctuating glacio-eustatic sea levels of the Quaternary has only recently received adequate attention, although Daly (1925) speculated on the idea. More recently Bloom (1967) showed that response to loads as little as the 10–12 bars produced by glacio-eustatic sea level variation could take place and that the amount of postglacial submergence of a coast will be in part a function of the isostatic depression of the sea floor, variation being produced by the morphology of the continental shelf. Subsequently the concept of hydro-isostasy has been further developed by Walcott (1972), Mörner (1972), Chappell (1974a) and Clark et al. (1978), and today this mechanism is recognized as a major factor in producing regional variation in Holocene, and possibly earlier, shorelines.

Walcott (1972) showed how relative sea level at great distances from the glaciated regions was affected by the meltwater loading of the ocean floor, the continents rising slightly relative to the ocean floor. Chappell's (1974a) work concentrated in particular on the critical hinge zone between oceans and continents. He suggested an average depression of ocean basins of about 8 m and mean upward movement of continents of about 16 m relative to the center of the earth in the last 7000 years. Deflection in the ocean margin hinge zone was shown to vary with continental shelf geometry and rigidity of the underlying lithosphere. In particular he suggested that for broad "box section" shelves such as occur in parts of the Great Barrier Reef, the deflection is great. Depth variations of the shorelines of the last glacial maximum (e.g. North America, 90–130 m, compared to Australia, 130–170 m) were explained by Chappell in terms of combined elastic and relaxation isostasy, terms that he considered went a long way towards explaining differences in Holocene eustatic records. A more sophisticated spherical viscoelastic earth model was used by Clark et al. (1978), which they considered explains a large proportion of the observed variance in the global sea level record. They suggest that six zones can be recognized with distinctive Holocene sea level signatures (Fig. 13.4). Their results reinforce the earlier work in emphasizing that variations should be most rapid across the continental margins of the world, although their model assumed the oceans to have vertical sides. They showed that continental margins as little as 100 km apart can have different relative sea level curves.

The macroregional variation in Holocene sea levels predicted by these models has great significance for explaining differences in age and morphology of coral reefs around the world, and is taken up as a major theme in Chapter 13. That smaller scale variations can be expected along, and more especially normal to, the continental shelves of the world is equally of relevance in explaining differences in morphology within single reef provinces. There are few areas in the world where there are better opportunities for studying such variations, and where the differences in relative sea levels can have such great significance, than on the Great Barrier Reef.

Holocene Sea Level Models and Actual Evidence in the Great Barrier Reef Region

Australia lies in Zone V of the sea level regions designated by Clark et al. (1978), where emergence took place as soon as the ocean volume ceased to increase. The predicted amount of emergence is about 1.5–2.0 m, with the highest level being the 5,000 yrs B.P. shoreline. On continental margins, such as along the Queensland coast, sea level curves are predicted to have even greater emergence because continental tilting is superimposed on the general emergence. More recently Clark (personal communication, 1979) has produced calculations of the height of the 5,000 yrs B.P. shoreline along a transect normal to the east Australian coastline at 30°S. Continental emergence of between 5 and 6 m is contrasted with emergence of less than 1 m within 100 km offshore from the coast, about 3 m of emergence being predicted at the coastline itself.

Chappell's model has been applied directly to the Great Barrier Reef (Thom and Chappell, 1978). Shelf width and depth were seen as the major controls of regional variation of Holocene sea levels. On the narrow northern shelf maximum predicted emergence is of the order of only 0.5–1.0 m on the inner shelf and neglible on the outer margin. Further south, as the shelf widens, the differential increases with inner shelf emergence being up to 1.5 m and outer shelf subsidence exceeding 1 m. A greater degree of submergence on the outer shelf would occur assuming an oceanic lithosphere beneath the shelf.

Although variations exist in the different models, there is a common suggestion of emergence on the inner shelf during the last 6000 years and stability or submergence on the shelf margin, which would result in modern sea level apparently being achieved at a later date on the outer shelf. Differences in shoreline elevations should occur both along the coast and normal to the shelf edge. Significantly much of the early literature on the Great Barrier Reef described features that were attributed to Recent emergence of about 3 m (see Fairbridge, 1950 for review; Hopley, 1974b, 1975, 1978b for discussion). Further, Spender (1930, p. 284) noted that there was an increase in height of reef tops from the outer barrier north of Cairns in towards the low wooded island reefs and, from the degree of island development that also increases across the shelf, hinted that there is a difference in age of reefs across the shelf. He suggested that while emergence is indicated by features of the inner shelf "the amount of emergence decreases from the coast towards the Pacific" (p. 287).

Unfortunately many of the early studies of sea-level variations in the Great Barrier Reef area were of a reconnaissance level only and frequently evidence was misinterpreted or relationships between the level of occurrence of paleo-features and of their modern equivalent were not established. In particular, cemented shingle ramparts and beach rocks were wrongly identified as erosional in origin and their upper levels equated not with the uppermost modern level of cementation but with low tide or reef flat levels (see, e.g. Steers, 1929, 1937, 1938). Reefs built up to former moated water levels were identified as eustatically emerged features. An excellent example is the description of Marshall et al. (1925) of the dead microatolls on Holbourne Island (Fig. 4.8), which have since been shown to have grown to a water level moated behind shingle ramparts that were removed in a cyclone in 1918 (Hopley and Isdale, 1977). Problems are associated with each kind of evidence utilized to reconstruct former land-sea relationships and because of this it is necessary to discuss and evaluate each type of evidence individually, especially as many of the older reports have been quoted recently without further corroboration (e.g. Fairbridge, 1950, 1967; Maxwell, 1968).

Depositional Materials

Many early reports describe "raised beaches" more than 5 m above present beach levels (e.g. King, 1827; Jukes, 1847; Jack and Etheridge, 1892). Three types of deposits form these unconsolidated supratidal features and each occurs at a wide range of heights (Fig. 6.6). Sand beach ridges occur on many islands both continental and reefal and frequently coalesce into subhorizontal sand terraces. Heights range from only a meter or two above MHWS to as much as 8 m. Sometimes a series of sand terraces or ridges are found decreasing

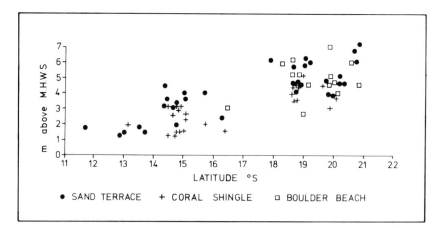

Figure 6.6 Surveyed heights of boulder beaches, shingle ridges, and sand terraces on inner-shelf locations along the Queensland coastline.

in height from the oldest ones at the rear of the sequence towards the modern beach. For example on Penrith Island, sand terraces occur at 7.2, 6.1, 4.5, 3.8, and 2.6 m above MHWS. On many reef islands an outer sand terrace (1–2 m above MHWS) with minimal soil development surrounds a higher core (3–4 m) with organic staining to 1 m or more (see for example McLean et al., 1978; Stoddart et al., 1978a). Dune cappings to the ridges of more than 0.5 m are found only on a few southeasterly oriented beaches and in general the composition of the ridges is coarse, poorly sorted sand. Distinctive pumice layers are common, with pumice pebbles up to 0.3 m in diameter occasionally found, strongly suggesting a wave-deposited origin. However, the frequency of tropical cyclones and accompanying storm surges in Great Barrier Reef waters makes the task of differentiating between deposits laid down when sea levels were relatively high, as opposed to during storms, extremely difficult.

Coral shingle ridges have a similar wide range of heights, with measured values up to 5.2 m above MHWS. Again, the elevation and descending suites of shingle ridges are suggestive of regressive sea levels and there can be little doubt of the wave-deposited nature of these materials. However, massive amounts of fresh shingle are only produced during cyclones (Chap. 10) and radiocarbon ages of 1,125 ± 75 yrs B.P. for a *Tridacna* valve at an elevation of 4.4 m on Holbourne Island, 820 ± 75 yrs B.P. for similar material on a 3.7 m ridge on East Armit Island (both near Bowen) and ages younger than 1550 years for ridges on northern reef islands (McLean et al., 1978) clearly cannot be associated with sea levels significantly different from present.

Boulder beaches (Fig. 6.7) are even more a product of the occasional high-energy storm. Although the boulders are derived from the regolith of the lower slopes of the continental islands, analysis indicates distinctive downdrift in-

Figure 6.7 Boulder beach rising to a maximum elevation of 5.2 m above MHWS on Curacoa Island, Palm Group. See also Fig. 12.9. Radiocarbon ages in excess of 5000 years have been obtained for biogenic material incorporated in this boulder beach.

creases in degree of roundness and decreases in size (Table 6.1). Individual boulders can be up to 1 m in diameter and heights of the ridges rise to 7.0 m. Biogenic material with radiocarbon ages in excess of 5000 yrs B.P. (see Chap. 12) suggest that higher sea levels could be involved in the emplacement of these beaches, but the size of the material is such that cyclonic events are also required.

The majority of early researchers who originally described these high depositional features were from stormy temperate latitudes and, although storm beaches many meters above MHWS are accepted as being modern within these researchers' home areas (e.g. Chesil Beach, England), the normally low energy levels of seas within the Great Barrier Reef were obviously responsible for the all too ready acceptance of higher sea levels in the geologically recent past. However, the high incidence of tropical cyclones and storm surges in the reef severely reduces the value of depositional features as evidence for former sea levels.

Shore Platforms

A number of processes are responsible for cutting platforms or terraces in the intertidal or immediately supratidal zone. Researchers experienced in temperate landforms are accustomed to wave abrasion platforms sloping gently up from low tide level. In the tropics, lower energy levels and a general lack of abrasive tools frequently leads to the formation of a high-tide platform in the area of alternate wetting and drying or along the line of freshwater seepage from fractured or weathered cliff faces. Alternatively, deep weathering down to a level of constantly wet rock near the top of the intertidal zone may lead to platform formation with subsequent removal of the regolith by even small waves (Bird and Hopley, 1969; Hopley and Hamilton, 1973). The product is a platform at or near high watermark, generally horizontal but with an uneven surface. A notch may be present at the rear of the platform but its elevation varies with lithology, structure, and exposure. In areas of high tidal range these features may appear to be "emerged," particularly to a person more familiar

Table 6.1   Rattlesnake Island Boulder Beaches—Reduction in Size and Increase in Roundness in Downdrift Direction (Moving from East to West Along Shore).

Station[a]		Mean Size (Phi Units)	Mean Cailleux Index of Roundness
East	1	− 8.77	297
	2	− 8.54	164
	3	− 8.84	144
	4	− 7.82	331
	5	− 7.32	413
	6	− 6.12	647
	7	− 5.69	611
West	8	− 5.54	755

[a]Stations are 50 m apart at midbeach level. A number of gullies are introducing new coarse sediments into the beach zone between Stations 1 and 3.

with wave-abrasion platforms (see, e.g., Stanley's 1928 description of platforms in the Whitsunday Passage area). The height variability of shore platforms and general lack of datable materials that can be used to provide absolute ages makes them unsuitable as primary evidence for former sea levels in the Great Barrier Reef area. Occasionally, beach conglomerates are cemented to the platforms, but there is no way of indicating if they are contemporaneous with the platforms, or subsequent to them. Undoubtedly notches of different elevations and ages exist along the mainland and high islands, but only careful survey and statistical analysis can separate them successfully (e.g. Driscoll and Hopley, 1967).

Mangrove Peats

Mangroves have a distinctive zone of growth from just below MLWS to just above MHWS. Individual species have narrower zones of occurrence, and identification of roots or stumps in situ may make possible the determination of the height of former growth to less than 1 m even on mesotidal coasts. Roots, stumps, or the peat itself provides material suitable for radiocarbon dating. A major problem may be compaction (Bloom, 1964; Gill and Lang, 1977) but this will be minimal in thin peat beds overlying, for example, deltaic sands (e.g. Hopley, 1970a) or can be overcome by sampling the basal peat layer from different positions on a sloping substrate, as suggested for saltmarsh peats by Bloom (1964). In areas with tidal ranges of less than 3 m, as occurs along much of the coastline within the Great Barrier Reef, mangrove peats may fix former sea levels to within ± 1 m.

Beach Rock and Other Cemented Materials

Processes of cementation were discussed in Chapter 5. Although submarine cementation does occur, and supratidal lithification by carbonate or phosphatic cements as dune calcarenite or cay sandstone is relatively common, beach rock *sensu stricto* is an intertidal feature that may be differentiated from other materials. The problem of using beach rock as a paleosea level indicator has been discussed by Scoffin (1977), Scoffin and McLean (1978), and McLean et al. (1978). The upper level of cementation is possibly as high as the absolute tide level but in most samples considered as "modern," the upper level does not exceed MHWS by more than a few centimeters. An aragonite or high-Mg calcite cement is suggestive of a marine origin but the morphology of outcrops in Queensland is the most convincing evidence of a relationship with sea level (Hopley, 1980). The upper surface is so horizontal that a relationship with a water table is most probable. In small cays and high island spits of coarse coralline debris, the area is too small for significant water-table gradients to develop while the materials are too coarse to allow significant upward migration of carbonate-rich groundwaters by capillary action. The upper level is thus related to the most commonly achieved high level of the sea, the MHWS.

Dating of beach rock may provide some problems. Constituent shells or corals may be considerably older than their date of deposition, although if the original beach were a storm deposit there is a good chance that the biogenic materials were living immediately prior to their transport shoreward. The cement, on the other hand, will produce a date that is minimal, as the cementation process or exchange of cement may continue until the rock is finally emerged above tidal level. Thus, on Herald Island near Townsville (Fig. 6.8), where a cliff of emerged beach rock rises to 4.9 m above MHWS, *Trochus* sp. from near the top of the cemented layer gave a radiocarbon age of 4280 ± 100 yrs B.P. whereas whole beach rock including up to 50% cement from near the basal layer produced a date of only 3540 ± 90 yrs B.P. (Hopley, 1971a).

On the low wooded islands of the northern Great Barrier Reef cemented shingle ramparts, termed rampart rocks (Scoffin and McLean, 1978) appear to be closely related to beach rocks. Although internal structure and cement may be different, the level of cementation is also intertidal. On the basis of height relationships with modern equivalents, McLean et al. (1978) have suggested that a series of "upper platforms" of rampart rocks on the northern Great Barrier Reef with altitudes up to 3.8 m (in an area where MHWS is 2.3 m) were built to a sea level about 1 m higher than present (Fig. 6.9). Morphological relationships with other features support such an interpretation.

Beach rocks and rampart rocks are thus good indicators of paleosea levels provided that they are carefully identified and, where possible, related to parallel morphological features such as emerged reefs. As many of these outcrops are found emerging from beneath sand terraces or coral shingle ridges, there is a strong suggestion that if the cemented materials are related to higher relative sea levels, then so too are the purely depositional features. However, it is still probable that emplacement of the deposits took place during cyclones, when storm-surge levels where superimposed on any postulated higher sea level.

Figure 6.8 Emerged beach rock rising to 4.9 m above MHWS on Herald Island near Townsville.

Figure 6.9 Upper and lower platforms of rampart rocks on Three Isles. The upper platform has an elevation of 0.7 m above MHWS and the lower platform 0.3 m below MHWS.

Corals

Although open-water corals grow to about MLWS, in moated situations they may be found at levels up to MHWN (Chap. 4). Such examples are unusual and very restricted and large fields of moated microatolls do not normally grow to levels in excess of MLWN (see, e.g., Scoffin and Stoddart, 1978, Stoddart and Scoffin, 1979). Thus a relative degree of accuracy can be given to paleosea levels from microatolls (Fig. 12.8). However, greater problems exist with open-water corals. Although a maximum level of growth may be established, the actual sea level at the time of growth of particular corals may be significantly higher. No single species has a narrow enough range of growth to provide sufficient control. This problem is particularly important for dating and interpretation of reef cores. Identification of in situ corals may be assumed from the attitude of corallites and growth bands, but in terms of paleosea levels all that can be said is that at times of growth MLWS was at or higher than the level from which the dated coral came. The problem is less acute for emerged corals. Most of those identified along the Great Barrier Reef have been in microatoll form, and open water corals, where identified, have been related to either nearby microatolls or emerged beach rocks. Exposures at Rattlesnake Island near Townsville illustrate these relationships. An emerged reef consists purely of open-water corals (mainly *Acroporids*) that rise to 1.6 m, almost exactly MSL, thus suggesting an emergence of 1.4 m in comparison with modern MLWS. Higher on the reef about 20 m landwards, a field of microatolls (mainly

Favids and *Goniastrea*) rise to 1.86 m, suggesting a minimum emergence of 0.66 m compared to modern MLWN. A radiometric date from a microatoll of 5,530 ± 130 yrs B.P. indicates the age of this reef and the paleosea level. It is overlain by two suites of beach rock, a higher level rising to 3.78 m above MHWS and a lower level to 0.96 m above MHWS, unconformably lain against the higher level. An age of 3,240 ± 100 yrs B.P. for whole beach rock from the upper level is probably a minimal age for a paleosea level of about +3.7 m. A lower sea level about 0.9 m higher than present is obviously younger. Similar sequences have been described on other high islands (Hopley, 1971a, 1975) and further examples are given in Chapter 12.

Holocene Sea Levels on the Inner Shelf

Reconstruction of former sea levels by latitude on the inner shelf of eastern Queensland has been made in Figure 6.10. It is based on evidence from the mainland and from continental islands generally within 25 km of the mainland. On the northern shelf evidence from low wooded islands has been incorporated. Continental island and mainland sites have advantages over reef locations as "antecedent platforms," since all elevations are available for reef growth and it is likely that horizontal reef flat development was possible immediately sea level became relatively stable. Such sites may thus retain evidence of the earliest time that modern sea level was achieved. In contrast, reef sites, where prior reef platforms are below present sea level, depend not only on the rise of sea level but also on the ability of corals to maintain an upward growth equal to that rise in order to produce evidence of sea levels at any specific time. These problems are discussed in the next section and attempts to resolve them are made in Chapter 8. In the following discussion levels of evidence are related to their modern equivalents, that is, open-water corals are compared to a modern level of MLWS, microatolls to MLWN, beach rocks and rampart rocks to MHWS, and mangrove peats to MSL. No account is taken initially of possible changes to tidal range.

Hydro-isostatic models suggest that the inner shelf should retain the earliest evidence of the achievement of modern sea level and possibly indicate sea levels higher than present. Figure 6.10 confirms these suggestions, but shows that the pattern is anything but uniform along the Queensland coast. Details of the reconstruction are given in Hopley (1974b, 1978b). The record is in general agreement with the sea level curve of Thom and Chappell (1975) in that modern sea level appears to have been achieved prior to 6000 yrs B.P. along the entire coastline. However, although the shoreline at the southern end of the Reef in the area of the Whitsunday Islands, between Hinchinbrook Island and Cairns and north of Princess Charlotte Bay, show that sea level varied little from its present position over the last 6000 years, varying degrees of emergence are indicated in the intervening areas. North of Cairns the amount of emergence is little more than a meter (see Bird, 1971a,b; McLean et al., 1978). On the eastern side of Broad Sound it is as much as 6 m (Cook and Mayo, 1977). However, the largest stretch of coastline displaying evidence of emergence is between Bowen and Hinchinbrook Island. Significantly, shorelines of three separate ages can be recognized in this area:

1   A largely terrigenous beach deposit of reworked regolith formed during the exposure of the last glacial period, marking the first time Holocene sea levels were achieved. Innermost reef flats also appear to have developed from about this time. Boulder beaches and reefs have been dated between 6000 and 5000 yrs B.P. and show a maximum emergence of no more than 2 m.

2   A highest level rising to a maximum of 4.9 m with radiocarbon ages straddling 4500 yrs B.P. Most of the evidence comes in the form of emerged beach rock, although emerged mangrove peat in the Burdekin Delta also indicates about 3 m of emergence at 3870 ± 50 yrs B.P. (Paine et al., 1966).

3   A regression shoreline somewhat lower with dates of about 3500 yrs B.P. or younger.

The level of the maximum transgression varies in this region being of the order of 3.7–3.9 m in the Bowen area, 3.0 m in the Burdekin Delta, 4.9 m at Herald Island near Townsville and 3.0–3.7 m in the Palm Islands. Material dated at younger than 2500 yrs B.P. in the whole of this area appears to relate to modern sea level.

The major features of the pattern of Holocene shorelines along the Queensland coast are the relatively large proportion of the coastline where emerged features are found, and the sharp dislocations in heights of shorelines at at least three locations. Emergence is expected from the calculations of hydro-isostatic warping, but the amount particularly in the Townsville area and east of Broad Sound is greater than has been predicted. Hopley (1974b) noted the correlation between the sea level evidence and the structure of the coastal area, regions of emergence corresponding to structural highs, and regions with no emergence with basins or depressions. Tectonic dislocation is also suggested by the differences in elevation of shorelines on either side of Broad Sound, at the northern end of the Whitsunday Passage and just north of the Palm Islands. In at least the first two instances fault zones along which Tertiary and probably Quaternary movement has taken place are well documented, and there are a number of major faults trending seawards on the mainland near the Palm Group. It is possible therefore that at least part of the variation is a product of tectonic movement along old, established structural weaknesses. However, it is also probable that the stresses produced beneath the inner shelf by hydro-isostatic movements may be released most readily along the same preexisting fault systems. Glacio-isostatic adjustments have been shown to act in this way. For example, Sissons (1972) has described small dislocations in glacio-isostatically warped shorelines where they cross older fault lines in eastern Scotland, and Mörner (1978) has described the reactivation of old fault lines in Fennoscandia at the time of maximum rate of glacio-isostatic uplift. That the major deformation of Holocene shorelines is isostatic rather than tectonic is strongly suggested by the relatively undeformed nature of Pleistocene, presumably last interglacial, shorelines. Although absolute dating of these features in Queensland is lacking, if they are last interglacial then the movements that have deformed shorelines over the last 6000 years are simply a recovery under water loading towards the position of 125,000 years ago. It has already been noted that along the Queensland coastline the level of this Pleistocene shoreline is slightly lower than the reported level of the last interglacial sea

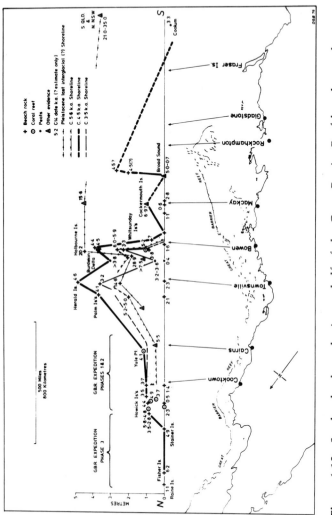

Figure 6.10 Sea levels along the inner shelf of the Great Barrier Reef based on published radiocarbon ages (see Hopley 1974b, 1978b). (From Hopley, 1978b reproduced by permission of the Royal Society.)

level elsewhere. This suggests that some further recovery is necessary, and it is pertinent to note that while most of the world's tide gauges have been recording contemporary rise of sea level, gauges at Townsville and Mackay showed 4.9 and 0.16 mm of fall in sea level in the decade 1950–1959 (Colquhoun, 1979).

Relationships between shorelines and shelf morphology also suggest that the major movements are hydro-isostatic. Highest evidence is associated with the broader shelves and with shelves that trend east-west. High sea level evidence is not found on narrower shelves, particularly those which trend north-south (northern Cape York, Cape Tribulation area, Cairns to Hinchinbrook Island, and southern Queensland). Clearly the dislocations are influenced by a complex combination of geological structure, shelf morphology, and water loading during the Holocene transgression.

No account has been taken in this discussion of the possibility of changing tidal ranges or degrees of storminess during the Holocene that may have affected reefal deposits. If the tidal range had contracted in the Holocene, features related to HWM such as beach rocks and rampart rocks may have become emerged without any change in MSL but features related to LWM such as open-water corals and microatolls may reasonably be expected to show parallel submergence, as both MLWS and MLWN would now be higher. As emergence is indicated by deposits that are related to both high- and low-water stages of the tide, a change in the relative level of land and sea is strongly suggested. The possibility of changing tidal ranges due to the later upgrowth of outer reefs, especially in the northern region where the ribbon reefs form a very effective barrier to tidal movement, cannot be substantiated for it has been shown that the ribbon reefs grew up to modern sea level about the same time as the inner reefs (Hopley, 1977). However, on the mainland, local sedimentation has altered coastal and bottom geometries. For example, Cook and Mayo (1977) have shown that as Broad Sound has become increasingly V-shaped over the last 6000 years, there has been a gradual increase in tidal range.

If higher energy conditions existed in the past, then storm beaches may have been deposited far higher than is possible today. Neumann (1972) has suggested that as reef growth lags behind a rising sea level there will be a period immediately after sea level has stabilized but before reef crests reach the surface when wave activity will not be dampened or excluded by coral barriers. This "high energy window" will only be closed by growth of the reefs themselves. Although this does not appear to be the case of the northern reefs where both inner and ribbon reefs reached modern sea level very soon after it was first achieved, there is some evidence to suggest that on the coast between Cairns and Townsville the outer reefs are much younger than mid-Holocene (see below and Chap. 9). However, because there is the possibility of hydro-isostatic subsidence on this part of the outer shelf, there is the strong possibility that even though the outer reef tops apparently lagged behind the fringing reefs of the continental islands, during mid-Holocene times an effective barrier still existed. More pertinent may be the suggestion of Stoddart et al. (1978b) that as reef tops develop extensive depositional features, including ramparts and mangroves, internal baffles on energy levels of waves sweeping over reef tops are provided, resulting, for example, in storm deposits on leeward sand cays being thrown to lower levels. Thom and Chappell (1978) have also suggested that greater storminess during mid-Holocene times may have been a factor in explaining high-level features. However, both these factors affect only depositional evidence, and would have had little effect on either coral growth or cementation levels which depend on long-term tidal levels.

Thus it can be concluded that there is sufficient evidence to indicate that along a significant proportion of the inner shelf of Queensland relative emergence has taken place during the latter part of the Holocene. Indeed, the acceptance of variable degrees of emergence helps to explain the irregular elevations of sand terraces, coral shingle ridges, and boulder beaches (Fig. 6.6). Simple correlation (r) between their elevation and 1000-year-surge predictions, or local highest elevation of Holocene sea levels (from coral and cementation levels), produced nonconclusive results (Table 6.2) but calculation of multiple correlation coefficients (R) combining these two factors results in a much higher degree of explanation. These high-level deposits are thus the product of both higher Holocene sea levels and storm surges. The reef levels themselves, however, are the result of the local Holocene sea-level history. Where emergence is indicated dead, sanded, reef flats predominate and massive amounts of sediment are stored in beach ridges and spits in bayheads and on leesides of high islands, as, for example, on most continental islands between Bowen and the Palm Islands. In contrast narrow fringing reefs and minimal areas of Holocene unconsolidated deposits typify islands where little or no emergence is signified, such as the Cumberland Islands (Fig. 12.3). Here fringing reefs are generally extensive but narrow, and bayhead deposits are largely terrigenous rather than biogenic, as there have never been exposed reef flats to provide extensive amounts of coralline debris.

Holocene Sea Levels on the Outer Shelf—a Preliminary Examination

If variations in Holocene sea levels due to hydro-isostasy and local tectonism have affected the morphology of inner shelf reefs, mainly the fringing reefs and low wooded islands, then it may be expected that at least some of the variation in outer-shelf reef morphology may be explainable in similar terms. Unfortu-

Table 6.2 Relationship of heights of sand terraces, shingle ridges, and boulder beaches with surge water levels achieved above HAT at 1,000 year return periods and highest mid-Holocene sea level recorded within 10 km of specific sites.[a]

	n	Sand Terraces	Shingle Ridges	Boulder Beaches
(r) 1000 yr surge	37	0.6394	0.8351	0.4670
(r) mid-Holocene sea level	24	0.4644	0.7910	0.2590
(R) Surge and sea level	14	0.6394	0.8529	0.4677
Significant at 1%		Yes	Yes	No

[a]Note that the best explanation is achieved for shingle ridges. Results for sand terraces may be less clear because of variable dune cappings and for boulder beaches because of reworking of older Pleistocene deposits.

nately emergent platforms in the form of high islands or emerged Pleistocene reefs do not exist on the outer shelf and reef growth has taken place from pre-Holocene reefal foundations at variable depths below present sea level (see Chap. 7). An extensive dating program of shallow cores from the outer reefs has been undertaken by the author but because it is probable that the rise in sea level during the latter part of the Holocene transgression was more rapid than the rate of upward reef growth, radiocarbon dates from the near surface of the reefs can show only a minimal age for the attainment of modern sea level.

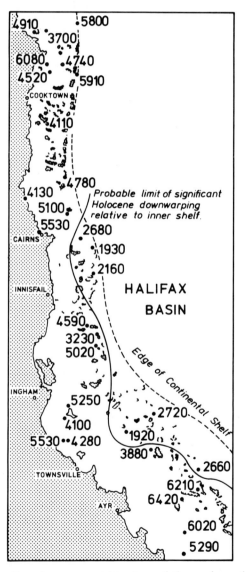

Figure 6.11 Oldest radiocarbon ages within 2 m of the surface of reefs on the central Great Barrier Reef and oldest ages relating to modern sea level or higher on the adjacent mainland.

Their ages are dependent on a combination of the depth of the antecedent reefal platforms from which the modern reefs are growing, and the maximum net rate of calcium carbonate production that will determine the upward growth rate of the reef. Only where this latter rate equals or exceeds the rate of sea level rise will the age of reef tops legitimately show the time that modern sea level was first reached.

Only after the resolution of these two influential factors in Chapters 7 and 8 can a realistic attempt be made to show that variations in Holocene sea levels have taken place right across the Queensland continental shelf. This is done at the end of Chapter 8. Part of the raw data from which the problem is resolved is shown in Figure 6.11, which plots the location of the oldest dates at each sample locality that can be related closely to modern sea level on the central Great Barrier Reef. On the mainland some of these dates refer to materials already described that relate to higher sea levels. On the outer reefs they refer to in situ coral or algal samples from cores taken within the upper 2 m of the modern reef flat, which on outer reefs is usually close to MLWS. Significant features of Figure 6.11 are:

1   Samples from as shallow as 15 cm on the outermost ribbon reefs north of 17°S are almost 6000 years old, suggesting that on this narrow shelf modern sea level was achieved at about the same time as on the inner shelf. However, there is no evidence of any emergence on these outer reefs, nor is there indication of any truncation of former evidence (see Chap. 8).

2   Between 16°30' and 19°00'S the oldest dates obtained for many reef tops are less than 3000 years old. Innermost reefs such as Wheeler may be slightly older but only in the area off Hinchinbrook Island (Taylor, Britomart, Barnett Patches) do the dates exceed 5000 yrs B.P. and only in this area has an outer shelf reef top been dated at greater than 3000 yrs B.P. (Moss Reef at 17°56'S). Within the upper 3 m ages as great as 7420 yrs B.P. have been obtained on Taylor Reef (17°48'S), but beneath the younger reefs elsewhere in this region no date older than 2720 yrs B.P. has been obtained, even at depths as great as 4 m.

3   South of 19°00'S ages as great as 5530 yrs B.P. have been recorded in the upper 12 cm of reef flat, 6420 yrs B.P. in the upper 60 cm, and 7160 yrs B.P. in the upper 3 m (Darley and Stanley Reefs).

4   Distinctive changes in reef morphology appear to take place within each of these age determined regions (see Chap. 9).

The full meaning of these observations can only be understood in relation to variations in the depth of the platform on which these reefs are growing, and their rate of upward growth. However, already there is a suggestion of a regional variation on the outer shelf that may be related to variations in Holocene sea levels. The next two chapters will show that such a suggestion has a reasonable basis.

7

The Foundations of Modern Reefs

The second half of the nineteenth century and early twentieth century was a period that saw the beginnings and early development of many fields of study now incorporated within geomorphology. Chapter 1 has already outlined the growth of coral reef studies. Over the same period investigations of the erosion of limestone terrains were expanding and developing discussions as heated as those over Darwin's coral reef subsidence theory (Jennings, 1971, Chap. 1). Simultaneously, ideas were evolving on changing sea levels and even after the significance of these for coral reefs was recognized by Belt, Upham, and Penck (see Chap. 1) and expanded into a detailed hypothesis by Daly, it is surprising that no link was made between the exposure of the limestone structures of reefs during low sea levels, and the development of solution-dominated karst landforms on this limestone. Complete planation of reefs to these low levels was presumed. The two areas of study remained discrete until the 1940s when the Japanese first recognized that karst features may explain part of the morphology of atolls (Yabe, 1942; Asano, 1942). These papers were not readily available to the English-speaking world even after their translation by Burke nine years later (Burke, 1951). Their development into a model involving incremental accretion of thin limestone sequences on intermittently emerged and karst eroded older reefs was also Japanese in origin (Tayama, 1952).

Islands of emerged coralline limestone in the western Pacific had been accepted as raised atolls on the basis of their central depression and surrounding reeflike rim. Hoffmeister and Ladd (1945), however, suggested that the morphology was due not to original growth form, but to solution subsequent to exposure. Similar raised rims around a central depression had been reported on flat-lying joint blocks of limestone by Smith and Albritton (1941) and were simulated in the laboratory by Hoffmeister and Ladd by placing a slab of Solenhofen limestone beneath a shower of dilute acid. The resulting annular form varied, as do the full-sized atolls, according to initial slope and Hoffmeister and Ladd suggested that further asymmetry may be produced by the effect of prevailing winds on runoff and solution. That similar solution forms may have developed on emerged reefs during Pleistocene low sea levels, was not discussed by Hoffmeister and Ladd (1945). The idea was considered briefly by Kuenen (1947) but dismissed on the grounds of the lack of exposure of Pleistocene reefs developed to interglacial sea levels higher than present within modern reef complexes and he returned to the hypothesis of general reduction of former reefs during low sea-level periods. However, unlike Daly, who supposed that reduction was carried out by mechanical wave abrasion, Kuenen proposed intertidal and subaerial solution as the main processes.

The link between the morphology developed by subaerial weathering during periods of exposure and the shape of modern atolls was finally made in 1954 by MacNeil. He seized upon the forms produced on limestone blocks in the laboratory by Hoffmeister and Ladd (1945) and developed the theme that:

> emerged limestone platforms will weather with the formation of marginal rims and central depressions and that emerged irregular limestone islands will have their topography accentuated by the initial stages of weathering.
>
> *MacNeil, 1954, p. 413*

He stated that the growth form of reefs can be accentuated by such processes, two major characteristics of emerged limestones and karst processes being:

1   The case hardening of upstanding exposed surfaces which will continue to stand in relief.
2   The gradual wasting away beneath a soil cover of flatter and low-lying surfaces.

Applied to atolls, MacNeil sought to show that features such as lagoons, reef rims, and even coral pinnacles reflected the underlying topography developed by karst processes (Fig. 1.4).

That similar subaerial erosion forms could determine the morphology of shelf reefs was acknowledged by MacNeil, who cited the shape of the islands of Muaras, Maratua, and Kakaban on the Borneo shelf as evidence. However, the alternative hypothesis of Fairbridge (1950), who explained the development of central lagoons of shelf reefs by growth of crescentic reef forms in response to prevailing winds (see Chap. 9), gained more following, especially by Maxwell (1968). As Purdy (1974a) has noted, MacNeil's ideas were not received with enthusiasm. In contrast, Purdy's model of a karst-determined morphology for modern reefs (Purdy, 1974a,b) has been adopted widely, including on the Great Barrier Reef (e.g., Davies et al., 1976; Davies and Kinsey, 1977; Davies et al., 1977a,b; Harvey, 1977a; Orme et al., 1978a). Of major importance is the departure from a preoccupation with deep oceanic atolls and the recognition of morphologic detail in shelf reefs that directly parallels that of atolls. In the manner of Hoffmeister and Ladd (1945), Purdy (1974a) used limestone blocks subjected to acid rains to produce experimental analogues of reeflike features. He further compared the morphology of subaerial karst, particularly of tropical regions, to that of reef morphology and provided convincing evidence from the Belize shelf barrier reef for Holocene reefs being merely veneers over older presumably Pleistocene surfaces. This chapter examines the karst-induced antecedent platform hypothesis as stated by Purdy and others, discussing features on the Great Barrier Reef that may be inherited from the former subaerially exposed surface that underlies the Holocene. While it is accepted that such sub-

aerially exposed surfaces exist beneath the modern reefs as solution unconformities (see Chap. 5), two areas that have been either ignored or received only
cursory attention are critically examined. These are the suitability of young
reefal limestones as a substrate for the development of significant karst landforms, and the rates and scales at which karst processes may operate.

THE KARST-INDUCED ANTECEDENT PLATFORM HYPOTHESIS

Karst signifies terrain with distinctive characteristics of relief and drainage arising
primarily from a higher degree of rock solubility in natural waters than is found
elsewhere.

Jennings, 1971, p. 1

The result of this solubility is an apparently disorganized relief in which valley
systems are often interrupted and where there are many kinds of closed depression. Karst landforms vary with factors such as type of limestone, available relief, and climate. Since the majority of coral reefs are situated within the
tropics, and climates even at the height of glacial periods probably remained
tropical or at least subtropical, then if karst landforms developed on emerged
reefs during the Pleistocene, features analogous to those of reef morphology
should be sought in tropical karst areas. Here chemical reactions proceed faster
than elsewhere because of higher temperatures, and high intensities and
amounts of rainfall result in prolonged and rapid solution. As Jennings (1971,
1972b) has indicated, rapid plant growth and decay and intense microbial activity with high soil PCO_2 make tropical water very aggressive. However, in a
recent review of the relationships of karst processes and landforms with
climate, Smith and Atkinson (1976) concluded that erosion rate depends largely
on runoff and comparatively little upon latitudinal climatic zones, and, from
data presently available, tropical areas show no tendency for higher runoff.
Nonetheless, as there is much reprecipitation of carbonate in this environment, net removal rates may conceal greater absolute solution and it is probable also that saturation equilibria rarely control process in the tropics (Jennings, 1971).

The result of these rapid processes is a greater variety of karst landforms in
the tropics than is found anywhere else (Verstappen, 1960, 1964; Jennings and
Bik, 1962). In the wetter tropics, three basic types may be recognized:

1   A doline karst consisting of numerous enclosed depressions developed on
    limestone plateaus and associated with marly limestone, interbedding with
    impervious rocks, mechanically weak limestones, long dry season, or
    closeness to sea level (Jennings, 1971, p. 187).

2   Cone karst, kegel karst, or polygonal karst consisting of hemispheroidal
    residual limestone hills typically 30–70 m high and with a density about
    $30/km^2$. The closed depressions between them are often star-shaped, the
    form of a centripetal drainage system that controls the development of the
    relief (Williams, 1971, 1972). The shapes that develop as a consequence of
    such activity depend very much on the mechanical competence and perme-

ability of the limestone being karstified. Massive crystalline rocks support steep slopes and towerlike cones while thinly bedded or chalky rocks yield rounded hemispheres (kugel karst), unless case hardened when the forms are steeper (Williams, 1978).

3 Tower karst or turm karst, consisting of residual hills with steep, even undercut lower slopes rising from swampy alluvial plains. The towers may surround flat-floored depressions and karst margin plains may frequently be associated with tower karst. Vertically walled linear depressions can dissect the hill masses.

Analogies of these landscapes have been recognized in coral reef morphology and incorporated into the model developed by Purdy (1974a). Drawing on the inspiration of MacNeil's (1954) paper he has noted the widespread occurrence of enclosed depressions of all scales. Intertidal pools as described by Emery (1946) have case-hardened rims. Central depressions may be seen on limestone blocks bounded by solution widened joints. Similar central depressions surrounded by case-hardened rims can be found on many limestone terrains, particularly tropical islands (Hoffmeister and Ladd, 1945; MacNeil, 1954; Ollier, 1975). What Purdy (1974a) terms solution rims are also found on either side of limestone hills in Okinawa (Flint et al., 1953). These simulate natural levees in form but are composed of limestone standing as much as 27 m above the surrounding terrain and 40 m above the adjacent stream levels. When combined with the similarity in form produced by laboratory experiments with limestone blocks and acid rains, there is a considerable amount of circumstantial evidence to suggest that the relief of modern reefs has been derived in a similar way.

It was the Belize shelf and barrier reef from which Purdy derived much of his evidence and subsequently used to illustrate his hypothesis. Great contrasts exist in the rainfall of Belize, although high temperatures prevail throughout. On the northern plain annual rainfall totals are generally lower than 1500 mm but reach 4500 mm adjacent to the Maya Mountains. A karst landscape adjacent to and dipping beneath the present shelf, together with subsurface information from seismic profiling and drilling, provided Purdy with an ideal field area to illustrate his hypothesis. The shallow northern shelf, with pre-Holocene recrystallized limestone outcropping on Ambergris Cay and on Blackadore Cay in the Shelf lagoon is characterized by broad, shallow depressions with a rectilinear pattern suggestive of joint or fault control. According to Purdy (1974a) the effect is that of a drowned, doline, gerichteter karst surface, buried by a maximum of only few meters of Holocene reef. The central shelf comprises an inner-shelf lagoon and outer barrier platform which, from seismic survey, appears to be a continuation southward of the Ambergris Cay outcrop and is interpreted by Purdy (1974a) as a solution rim. The deeper southern shelf has a morphology similar to that of the central shelf except that the barrier platform narrows southward, and the lagoon contains numerous carbonate shoals. Many of these have atoll-like rims and central lagoons (rhomboid shoals of Miller and Macintyre, 1977). They mimic the underlying pre-Holocene surface and were interpreted by Purdy as solutional in origin. The widening and deepening of the shelf lagoon and narrowing of the barrier platform was equated with the development of a karst marginal plain, especially as this change in morphology occurs adjacent to the noncarbonate Maya Mountains where rainfall and runoff increase dramatically. The adjacent mainland morphology with isolated remnants of tower karst would appear to be supporting evidence.

Purdy quoted further evidence from other areas, including the Great Barrier Reef, which will be discussed below. His final conclusions, developed into a model of reef development, are summarized in Figure 7.1. Atolls form from emerged limestone masses as rim-bound solution basins. If rainfall is high the rim may be breached and the central basin characterized by conical karst. If lower rainfalls exist during the period of emergence a doline-dominated landscape results within the annular rim. The development of a barrier reef is similar, and because of its significance for the evolution of the Great Barrier Reef, is worthy of greater attention. The major feature is the development of a karst marginal plain, the result of runoff over a subaerially exposed seaward-sloping contact between carbonate and noncarbonate rocks. With retreat of the limestone a plain covered by alluvium results, with increasing emphasis on lateral corrosion and development of tower karst. On the original surface, which is slowly consumed by the karst plain, cone karst and tropical polje occur. With inundation, the karst plain becomes a shelf lagoon, and the tower karst shelf reefs, the cone karst, and intricate relief of the outer platform develop into complex reef systems behind the outer barrier that marks the solution rim. Purdy further stated that with lesser amounts of rainfall, the relief of these features would be less and, "under temperate rainfall conditions," (sic) the relief would be dominated by dolines, presumably the saucerlike dolines similar to the northern part of the Belize shelf, of solutional origin rather than steep-sided collapse dolines, the result of underground solution.

A DISCUSSION OF THE HYPOTHESIS

There are three indisputable facts in the arguments postulated in favour of a karst antecedent platform hypothesis. These are:

1 Reefs have a complex morphology, are often saucer-shaped, and contain many enclosed depressions.
2 Karst landforms, especially in the tropics, have a similar morphology.
3 Pre-Holocene reefal limestones underlie the majority of modern reefs.

The major problem that arises from the hypothesis is to provide the link between karst processes and the morphology of the pre-Holocene surface, a problem that revolves around the questions of the suitability of young reef limestones to form karst landforms and the rates at which karst processes operate.

Relatively young reefal limestones that have undergone few diagenetic changes are highly porous, poorly consolidated, and mechanically weak. Such a material is not suited to the development of karst landforms (Jennings, 1971). In Barbados, Tricart (1968) has argued that high intergranular porosity

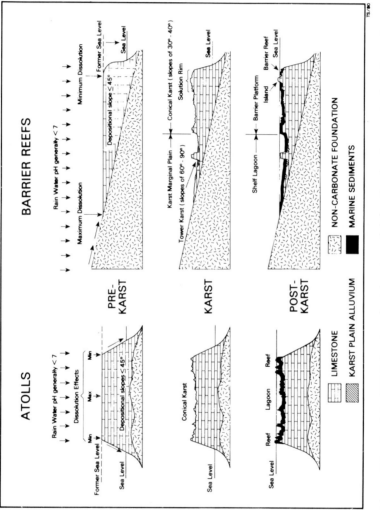

Figure 7.1 Purdy's (1974a) antecedent karst model for the development of atolls and barrier reefs. (Published with permission of the Society of Economic Paleontologists and Mineralogists.)

and lack of joint development is responsible for poor karst development through failure to canalize underground water, despite the solubility of the Quaternary reef limestones, heavy rainfall, and originally lush vegetation. Reef limestones of Quaternary age generally do not display significant jointing, and development of caves and subsequent collapse features may not be great. The majority of emerged reefs with solution rims and other features clearly of a karst origin that are cited by Purdy are Tertiary or, at youngest, early Quaternary in age. In contrast, outcropping of last interglacial reef limestones may display evidence of only surface solution, as for example, the phytokarst of Grand Cayman (Folk et al., 1973) or the champignon of Aldabra (Stoddart et al., 1971; Trudgill, 1976a,b, 1979).

Of possibly even greater significance is the rate at which karst solution processes operate. The amount of relief developed beneath modern reefs is suggestive of the removal of great amounts of limestone. This is particularly true of the development of karst marginal plains, cone karst, and residual tower karst. Purdy (1974a) was noncommittal on the age of the limestone in which these landforms had been etched (and hence on the amount of time available for their formation). His mainland karst analogy for shelf atolls in Belize is the Sierritas Hills, composed of upper Cretaceous limestone (Purdy, 1974a, Fig. 29 caption). The limestone beneath the modern reef was considered to be Pleistocene in age, based on the occurrence of aragonite beneath the solution unconformity. Rates of karst development, however, may be insufficient to produce the relief found on the pre-Holocene subreefal unconformities. Purdy recognized this difficulty, quoting the work of Land et al. (1967) on Bermuda which suggested that since the last interglacial, net reduction of the land surface would be of the order of only 1.25 m and even in an area of 5000 mm rainfall the figure would be increased to only 4.52 m, far less than the depth of most atoll lagoons and clearly insufficient to account for the relief in excess of 25 m developed on the Belize pre-Holocene reef limestones. More recent figures come from Aldabra atoll in the western Indian Ocean, where mean annual rainfall is about 670 mm (Trudgill, 1976b, 1979). Measurements provided average values of 0.26 mm/yr for vertical erosion, although rates varied with lithology, mineralogy, and soil cover (Table 7.1). Maximum rates of horizontal notch cutting within the intertidal zone were 4–7 mm/yr on exposed coasts, 1 mm/yr on protected coasts, and 2–3 mm/yr for the lagoon (Trudgill, 1976a).

Conservatively presuming an emergence of 100,000 years during the last glacial for reef caps, 26 m of erosion is possible on last interglacial reefs, and, as Trudgill (1976b) suggested, figures could be higher if annual rainfall were in excess of the modest total presently found on Aldabra. Important for the development of local relief on emerged reefs would be the facies control of weathering, as discussed by Bloom (1974). The highly permeable reef framework and coarse rubble facies would be more resistant to solution weathering as they would be highest above the water table, and rainwater would pass rapidly through the massive voids. Lagoon sand and mud facies, he suggested, would be more likely to form a karst plain with numerous sinks. Thus weathering would emphasize the constructional relief differences between reef and lagoon floor and with resubmergence during transgressive periods later reef facies would be underlain by ancient reef facies and lagoons underlain by ancient

no large karst depressions occur, only small features up to 3 m wide and 6 m deep. There is a general absence of surface drainage but a well-developed fresh-water lens underlies most islands and below the water table aggressive solution is taking place. A wide range of cave types is found, but most are small and, confirming Jennings' (1971) observations, Ollier noted that the rate of collapse in Trobriand caves is higher than in most karst areas. Major relief features on these young islands are almost exclusively the result of growth of coral reefs rather than karst erosion.

On Barbados, where mean annual rainfall totals of 1100 to 2100 mm are significantly higher than on Aldabra, control is given to estimates of rates of landscape development on reefal surfaces by intensive study and radiometric dating of the series of Quaternary reef terraces found here (Mesolella, 1967, 1968; Mesolella et al., 1970; Matthews, 1973; James, 1971; James et al., 1971; Bender, et al., 1972; Taylor, 1974). Although Tricart (1968) has noted a paucity of karst development on the terraces, both surface and subsurface karst features exist. Surface features of a scale likely to direct the pattern of reef growth if submergence were to occur are mapped in Figure 7.2 from the 1:10,000 Barbados map series (contour interval 20 ft). The older reef tracts show pronounced and widespread development of solution relief, which, in places, produces enclosed depressions in excess of 12 m in depth. Such relief is restricted almost exclusively to the upland plateau above the Second High Cliff of c. 480,000 yrs B.P. age. Below this, depressions are less than 6 m deep even on the wetter west-coast terraces and those on the 125,000 yrs B.P. and younger terraces are generally less than 1 m in depth (Fig. 7.3). Many of the depressions mapped on these youngest terraces from field examination appear to be old growth features developed in reef-crest situations rather than karst-eroded. Similarly, the large, shallow depressions shown on the southern part of the island adjacent to the Christchurch Ridge are probably lagoonal in origin, exposed about 200,000 yrs B.P. Notably the number and depth of depressions decreases in the lower rainfall areas on the northern and southern ends of the island. Small cave systems occur in the upper coral cap and the distribution of sink holes (Fig. 7.2) is suggestive of greater development of subterranean karst in the older limestones.

Important lessons can be learned from Barbados. As suggested by Bloom (1974) there is a strong control exerted on erosional landforms by the original reef facies. In particular enclosed depressions of a solutional origin have been eroded most easily in back-reef lagoonal sediments, more especially in those which are firmly lithified. However, Harrison (1974) noted that greatest karst relief is in general terms related to the well-lithified low-Mg limestones older than 480,000 years. Apart from the fluvially eroded gullies, surface alteration on the high-Mg calcite and aragonite surfaces of the younger limestones is largely limited to the formation of caliche. Even the uppermost facies of each terrace of 125,000 years age or younger, comprising a meter or so of beach calcarenites that have prograded over lagoon and reef facies during the final phases of emergence, remain as evidence of minimal erosion during the last 125,000 years (Fig. 7.4).

Thus there is inconclusive evidence for the erosion, during the last glacial alone, of a karst landscape of sufficient relief to provide the intricate substrate

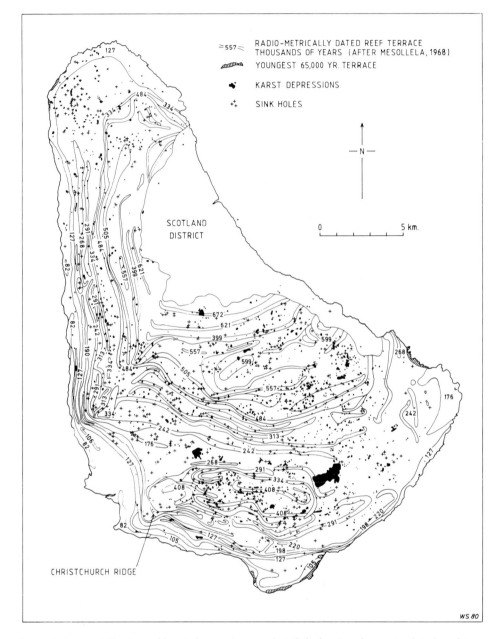

Figure 7.2 Distribution of karst depressions and sink holes in relation to dated reef terraces on Barbados. Terraces from Mesollela (1968), depressions from field mapping and Barbados 1 : 10,000 map sheets (Directorate of Colonial Surveys, 1956.)

upon which the antecedent karst hypothesis relies. Purdy (1974a) recognized this problem and suggested that the karst relief was a feature not just of the last glacial period but of all the major glacial periods of the Pleistocene:

> each of which undoubtedly resulted in subaerial exposure of shallow water carbonates and consequent formation of solutional topography. Consider also the fact

Figure 7.3 Sink hole developed below the Second High Cliff, Barbados of c.480,000 years age. Features of this size are not found on limestones of last interglacial age or younger.

> that succeeding stages of interglacial submergence favoured an enhanced rate of carbonate deposition on the residual prominences, as in the case of the Holocene sediments of British Honduras (Belize). The result is that the original karst relief is not only perpetuated but also exaggerated by differential rates of carbonate deposition.
>
> *Purdy, 1974a, p. 70*

When combined with Bloom's (1974) suggestion of facies control of solution, a perpetuation and accentuation of a karst topography throughout the Pleistocene is possible.

THE ANTECEDENT KARST HYPOTHESIS AND THE GREAT BARRIER REEF

The essence of the problem of reef morphology is the extent to which it is karst-induced as opposed to growth-determined. On the Great Barrier Reef, the ideas on reef development put forward by Fairbridge (1950, 1967) and Maxwell (1968, 1970) prior to the publication of Purdy's work definitely favored a growth-determined origin for modern reef morphology and this is reflected in the classifications of reefs that these two authors devised (see Chap. 9). Purdy (1974a) in contrast, considered the Great Barrier Reef to be "simply a large scale version of the British Honduras example" with all the attached implications for karst inheritance. He quoted as supporting evidence the anastomosing pattern of lagoonal reefs that he considered closely mimicked karst patterns, the numerous enclosed depressions of lagoons, and the reef patterns bordering channels that Maxwell (1970) had previously described as "deltaic reefs." The largely reefless inner continental shelf, particularly in the south,

Figure 7.4 Minimal erosion on beach calcarenites overlying the last interglacial coral reef on Barbados. The section is approximately 2 m high.

he compared with the Belize morphology and came to the conclusion that this too was a drowned karst marginal plain. He noted that both the shelf lagoon and the "barrier platform" increase in width to the south, where the "lagoon" is also deeper. As this is so analogous to the Belize barrier reef a similar explanation is provided, although a direct correlation with rainfall is not possible. Instead, the development of the karst marginal plain in the south is related to the concentrated runoff of the large Burdekin, Fitzroy, and Burnett River systems. An enclosed depression on the south-central shelf, which Maxwell (1968) regarded as structural, is thus explained as a karst feature. It is interesting to note that Sugden (1972) explained the paucity of reefs on the shelf opposite the Burdekin River in terms of erosion of reef foundations by runoff during low sea level periods. The massive Pompey Reef complex at the southern end of the Great Barrier Reef (Fig. 2.10) was interpreted by Purdy as a barrier platform forming a major drainage divide during low sea-level periods.

This interpretation is directly opposed to that of Maxwell, who rejected most of Purdy's suggestions (Maxwell, 1976). While accepting that subaerial exposure and sculpture must have taken place during the Quaternary, Maxwell considered that the only effect would be the localization of reef development, not a control of detailed reef morphology. He suggested that much faster growth rates of reefs in the western Pacific generally, as compared to the Caribbean, would mean that growth-induced influences dominate over morphological control by substrate. Although this latter presumption is challenged by data produced in Chapter 8, the dichotomy of views expressed by Purdy and Maxwell necessitates a critique of the types of morphological features attributed to karst control, particularly in the Great Barrier Reef region.

REEF FEATURES POSSIBLY ATTRIBUTABLE
TO ANTECEDENT KARST

On the Great Barrier Reef, Pleistocene limestone outcrops only in Torres Strait (Barham, personal communication) and on high continental islands of the inner shelf (Camp and Cockermouth Islands; see Chap. 12). However, information on the pre-Holocene surface is provided by a limited number of boreholes. In addition, in recent years considerable data has accumulated from continuous seismic profiling (CSP) over the continental shelf (Orme and Flood, 1977; Jell and Flood, 1978; Orme et al., 1978a,b; Searle et al., 1980; Nelson, 1980) and seismic refraction work on reef tops by Harvey and co-workers (Harvey, 1977a,b, 1978, 1980; Davies et al., 1977a,b; Harvey et al., 1978, 1979; Backshall et al., 1979).

At Stapleton Island the pre-Holocene surface was located by drilling at a depth of 14.6 m, and at Bewick 7 m below the cay surface or approximately 3 m below reef-flat level. Two cores from Britomart Reef just north of Townsville have yet to be dated but geochemical data suggests that the Holocene is about 20 m thick over this reef (E. R. Rhodes, personal communication). Similarly, geochemical analysis and preliminary dating of cores taken by the author on the central Reef indicate the unconformity at 18 m below Wheeler Reef, 20 m below a lagoon patch reef on Stanley Reef, at least 13 m below the reef margin of Darley Reef, 11 m to 14 m below Redbill Reef and 18 m to over 29.5 m below Gable Reef. Beneath the fringing reefs of Rattlesnake Island and Orpheus Island (fig. 12.7) the unconformity is at 12 m and 14 m respectively. On the fringing reef at Hayman Island a sequence of boreholes allow some interpretation of the trend of the pre-Holocene surface, which rises from about 20 m below MLWS beneath the present reef crest to 15 m below MLWS beneath the reef flat (Hopley et al., 1978). Recently, radiometric dating of the core at Heron Island has established the unconformity at about 18.5 m and at 10.0 m on One Tree Reef, where it is close to outcropping along the sides of the reef (Davies and Marshall, 1979, 1980). These results confirm that the immediate substrate of the modern reefs comprises carbonate rocks. They also confirm the pre-Holocene age of the materials underlying the Holocene veneer, for although no uranium-series dates accurately fixing the age of the unconformity are available, the radiocarbon dates from this material (Thom et al., 1978; Hopley et al., 1978) are either beyond the range of the method or so close to the maximum age possible that they should be considered as minimal only.

Seismic refraction survey has provided a more continuous picture of the pre-Holocene surface beneath the modern reefs (Harvey, 1977a,b, 1978, 1980; Davies et al., 1977a,b; Harvey et al., 1978, 1979; Backshall et al., 1979). Seismic velocities through the poorly consolidated and porous Holocene reef veneer are within the range 1200–1540 m/sec, close to the speed of sound through water and indicative of the open nature of young reefal material. In contrast the velocities recorded below the first major discontinuity range from 1910–3350 m/sec, the greater range probably reflecting the variable degree of diagenesis of the pre-Holocene surface and its morphological variability. The higher velocities suggest a denser, more consolidated, surface, as might be expected from a major solution disconformity upon which caliche may have de-

veloped. The minimum depth to the pre-Holocene on the reefs surveyed ranges
from 3 m below reef flat level on Bewick to 15.5 m on Wheeler Reef. Maximum depths recorded on single reefs ranged from 9.4 m (Nymph) to 24 m
(Wheeler). However, on lagoonal reefs the depths of lagoons is frequently
greater than the maximum depth to the pre-Holocene indicated by seismic survey on adjacent reef flats. In general the average depth to the pre-Holocene surface as indicated by seismic refraction survey is between 10–15 m with 5–10 m
relief developed or retained upon this surface (Fig. 7.5).

   As suggested in the previous chapter, the last interglacial sea level was probably a few meters above present and it is known that coral reefs grew to this
elevated level. On the mainland adjacent to the Great Barrier Reef the height of
presumably last interglacial shorelines has been shown to be only a little
below that quoted from other "stable" areas, that is, about 5 m above modern
sea level. The question is thus raised concerning the lower level of the pre-
Holocene surface beneath the Great Barrier Reefs. The two most likely explanations are substantial erosion of the older reef surfaces during subaerial ex-

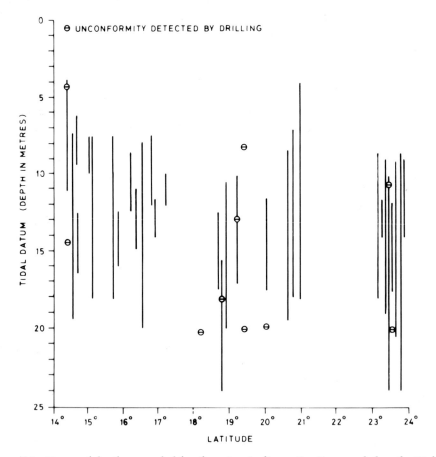

Figure 7.5 Range of depths recorded for the seismic discontinuity regarded as the Holocene-Pleistocene unconformity on the Great Barrier Reef, with depths of the uniformity
at specific drilling sites.

posure of the last glacial, or shelf subsidence. However, the lack of lowering of last interglacial reef terraces on Barbados and elsewhere, as described above, and the presence of last interglacial emerged reefs in stable areas of the Pacific, where rainfall totals are similar to those along much of the Great Barrier Reef, suggest caution in accepting a purely erosional lowering of earlier reef levels. Undoubtedly some erosion has occurred but the presence of a series of thin reef veneers superimposed over each other with clear solutional unconformities between, as shown by both the Bewick and Heron Island boreholes, could only have been developed during the general lowering of interglacial sea levels of the Quaternary if subsidence had been occurring on the continental shelf. The level of the unconformities beneath the Great Barrier Reefs is similar to that recorded on Pacific atolls (8–10 m at Enewetak, 31 m at Funafuti, 20 m at Midway, 6–11 m at Muroroa) where continuous subsidence to produce the great thickness of Cenozoic limestones is generally accepted, (see, e.g., Tracey and Ladd, 1974). Subsidence on the Great Barrier Reef shelf may not have been as great, but it is more probable than ubiquitous solutional lowering.

Clearly there exists beneath the reefs and shelf of the Great Barrier Reef a surface that has been exposed to subaerial processes and that is composed of largely carbonate rocks. The degree to which this surface is karstified and to which it controls detail in modern reef morphology has yet to be determined. Morphological features in modern reefs that are possibly controlled by antecedent karst are thus discussed in more detail.

Solution Rims

The development of solution rims is central to the antecedent karst hypothesis. Purdy (1974a) related rim development to rapid runoff adjacent to steep slopes. He acknowledged the effects of case hardening on exposed surfaces and accelerated solution beneath the soil cover of the central depression, as accentuating the initial rim feature once an initial saucer-shaped morphology has been developed. Examples of solution ramparts developing on emerged reef limestones are common (Hoffmeister and Ladd, 1945; Flint et al., 1953; MacNeil, 1954; Cloud et al., 1956). Tracey et al. (1964) have described a well-defined peripheral rampart on the limestone plateau of Guam up to 9 m high and 15 m wide and noted that near cliffs and steeply inclined surfaces

> a part of the water within the rocks evaporates, leading to precipitation of calcium carbonate. Secondary cementation occurs selectively on steep surfaces, which are in consequence less affected by solution than are the comparatively uncemented horizontal surfaces.
>
> *Tracey, et al., 1964, p. A62*

To this process James (1972a) added the effects of salt spray on the exposed reef margins, producing an external source of calcium carbonate for the development of caliche. Bloom (1974) emphasized facies control in the development of the rim, slower solution taking place on the more open framework of the emerged reef front.

Subsurface peripheral rims certainly exist on the Great Barrier Reef (Fig.

7.6). Near Lizard Island on the northern Reef, Orme et al. (1978b) have shown the pre-Holocene surface rising from a depth of about 45 m on the continental shelf towards Carter Reef, a shelf edge ribbon reef. Harvey (1977a) picked up apparently the same seismic discontinuity at a depth of almost 20 m at the rear of the reef, rising to about 9 m beneath the present reef crest. The similarity in depth recorded beneath Lark Pass Reef, another ribbon reef to the south, strongly suggests that the present ribbon reefs of the northern Great Barrier Reef have grown over former rimlike features. Lagoonal reefs with peripheral reef-flat rim appear to be perfect analogues of karst plateaux. This was suggested by Davies et al. (1976) and Davies and Kinsey (1977) for One Tree Reef (Fig. 8.4) in the Capricorn Group on purely morphological evidence, and later confirmed by seismic survey (Davies et al., 1977a,b; Harvey et al., 1978, 1979), which showed a discontinuity beneath the annular rim of the reef about 9 m shallower than in the lagoon. Similar results have been obtained for other reefs in the Bunker–Capricorn Group (Harvey et al., 1978, 1979) and on Redbill Reef (Fig. 9.7) and Cockatoo Reef (Fig. 7.7) further north (Backshall et al., 1979). In each case where sufficient data are available the presumed pre-Holocene unconformity forms a semicontinuous raised rim 6–12 m beneath the reef flat, which slopes down towards the lagoon to depths of at least 13–18 m.

A further feature of reef rims that Purdy (1974a, p. 67) attributed to karst control is the widening of peripheral reef flats at bends, angles, or corners of reefs, a feature previously noted on atolls by Wiens (1962). Parallel examples can be found on many of the reefs of Queensland. Widening of reef flats at dis-

Figure 7.6 Deep channel between Gould and Cobham Reefs with peripheral reef-flat rim analogous to the fluvial solution rims on Okinawa described by Flint et al. (1953).

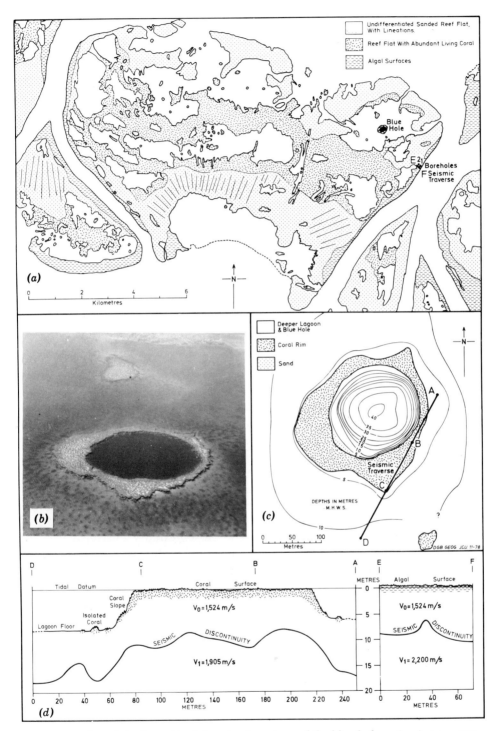

Figure 7.7 Plan of Cockatoo Reef showing locations of the blue hole, seismic traverses, and drill holes. Oblique aerial photograph of Cockatoo blue hole. Plan of blue hole drawn from closely spaced echo profiles and location of seismic section A–D. Seismic sections. (From Backshall et al., 1979.)

tinctive corners of midshelf reefs or at bulging "forelands" along the northern ribbon reefs is clearly the same feature as noted by Wiens on atolls. However, the control of reef-flat width may not be purely a function of pre-Holocene substrate as illustrated by One Tree Reef, where part of the widest reef flat has developed from a prograding sand wedge (Harvey et al., 1979). Leeward growth of reefs by sedimentation (Davies, 1977) has widened the leeward reef flat on One Tree Reef where seismic results indicate no wide pre-Holocene high. Results of drilling through 14.6 m of leeward reef detritus and marginal reef materials on Stapleton Island (Thom et al., 1978) suggest that similar leeward growth of reef flats largely uncontrolled by subsurface morphology has taken place here.

Undoubtedly there are many examples of high rims around the margins of pre-Holocene reefal platforms that have determined the pattern of modern reef growth. However, evidence that these rims are karst-induced, rather than the product of reef growth at an earlier period with minimal subsequent modification, is not unequivocal. As presented in the next chapter, patterns of reef productivity are such that maximum growth may be expected on reef margins, thus producing a rim effect without resort to solution.

Lagoons and Blue Holes

Lagoons are the antithesis of the solution rims. Harvey et al. (1978, 1979) clearly show that the pre-Holocene unconformity slopes down from the outer rim into saucerlike central depressions up to 10 m deeper than the highest part of the rims. This is most apparent beneath those reefs that have lagoons, for example One Tree and Fitzroy Reefs, but also occurs beneath reefs with continuous reef flat such as Wreck and Fairfax, suggesting that the lagoons of these reefs have been infilled. The subsurface information from these few examples (including Redbill Reef, Fig. 9.7) indicates such a strong control by the pre-Holocene on the modern reef morphology that it is tempting to extrapolate the results to all lagoon reefs of the Great Barrier Reef (Fig. 7.8). Circumstantial evidence is provided by the depth of some lagoons (in excess of 20 m) compared to the maximum depth of the seismic discontinuity measured beneath reef flats or rims anywhere on the Great Barrier Reef (rarely in excess of 15 m). Intricate lagoon patterns, particularly in the massive Pompey Reef complex, suggested to Purdy that a karst relief of many enclosed depressions was being mimicked by the present reefs. Preliminary seismic results from two of these reefs, Cockatoo (Fig. 7.7) and Molar (Fig. 7.9), would support the concept of substrate control. On Cockatoo Reef the seismic discontinuity occurs at depths of 16.5–18.0 m beneath lagoons, 9–11 m beneath coral rims of the central reef flat and 7–11 m beneath the algal rim of the outer perimeter of the reef (Backshall et al., 1979).

Again, these results suggest strong substrate control, but fail to confirm that the morphology of that substrate is karstic. However, more convincing evidence is forthcoming from the deep lagoonal features known as "blue holes." Examples of these circular steep-sided holes were described in the Bahamas by Northrop (1890) and Agassiz (1894), who firmly attributed them to terrestrial solution prior to subsidence. Subsequently these blue holes have been researched by Doran (1955), Newell and Rigby (1957), and Benjamin (1970) and

Figure 7.8 Showers Reef, Central Great Barrier Reef (19°30′S). Typical lagoonal reef with large isolated reef patches. The central lagoon has a maximum depth of about 10 m.

others have reported from Belize (Stoddart, 1962a), the Florida Straits (Jordan, 1954), and Clipperton Island in the Pacific (Sachet, 1962). Depths vary from less than 30 m to a maximum recorded depth at Lighthouse Reef, Belize, of 144 m (Stoddart, 1962a). A solution mechanism has been generally accepted for their origin but combined with glacio-eustatism rather than subsidence. Blue holes hold a central place in Purdy's (1974a) arguments for antecedent karst, their size indicating to him the potential for development of significant solution relief on pre-Holocene surfaces. Strong support has recently been provided by Dill (1977), who described associated cave systems and stalactites and stalagmites down to depths of 122 m in the Lighthouse Reef blue hole. The innermost layer of a stalactite from a depth of 50 m had a C-14 age of 10,200 years.

Deep blue holes are not common on the Great Barrier Reef. Aerial photographs suggest their occurrence on some of the larger reefs of Torres Strait but the best examples are found in the Pompey Reef complex, where three have been recognized. The two largest, on Cockatoo Reef (Fig. 7.7) and Molar Reef (Fig. 7.9) have been examined in detail (Backshall et al., 1979). Cockatoo Reef is large (13.6 × 8.7 km), with a complex series of lagoons about 10 m deep. The blue hole is situated in the large lagoon at the southeastern end of the reef. It has a rim of living coral 10–60 m wide and is nearly circular in plan with a length of 240 m and width of 205 m. Echo-sounding traverses show it to be bowl-shaped and slightly asymmetrical with the steepest side to the east,

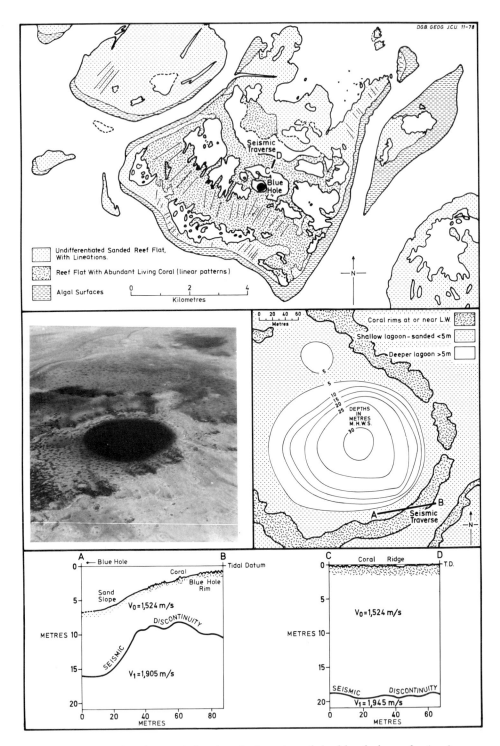

Figure 7.9 Plan of Molar Reef showing the location of the blue hole, and seismic sections. Oblique aerial photograph of Molar blue hole. Plan of blue hole drawn from closely spaced echo profiles. The position of seismic section A–B is marked. Seismic sections A–B and C–D. (From Backshall et al., 1979.)

204

where the upper slope is 60–70°. Elsewhere the upper slope is 45–50°. Maximum depth is just over 40 m. Coral veneers the upper slopes to a depth of 25 m where it forms a spur and chute morphology that leads to a series of coalescing sediment fans, and flat bottom with soft plastic sediment. A seismic discontinuity was recorded at a depth of 16.5–18.0 m below the adjacent lagoon, but rising to 9–11 m beneath the coral rim ringing the blue hole. The present surface is thus similar in gross morphology to the presumed pre-Holocene.

Molar Reef (7.75 × 7.4 km) is another large reef with complex lagoons having maximum depths of 7 m. The blue hole is near the center of the reef and has a living coral rim on the southern and eastern sides but a lip of shallow (5 m) lagoon to north and west (Fig. 7.9). It is larger than the blue hole on Cockatoo Reef with an east-west length of 295 m and a width of 260 m. It is also slightly asymmetric with the steeper side to the east. It has a similar bowl shape to the Cockatoo Reef hole, the shallow, concave floor commencing at a depth of 25 m and having a maximum depth of 32.5 m. The upper coral cover does not extend as deep in this blue hole and more rubble is present. Some coral is present on the floor of the hole, which is composed of mud and admixed sand. The seismic discontinuity is highest beneath the irregular coral rim (– 8.5 m) and deepest (– 16 m) beneath the sand slope bordering the inner margin.

In a careful analysis of the morphology of these blue holes, it was concluded that karst processes are the most likely for their origin (Backshall et al., 1979). Comparison with subaerially exposed karst (Backshall et al., Table 2) suggests that blue holes in general originate as either solution or collapse dolines. The Pompey Reefs blue holes appear to be collapse dolines for the following reasons:

1 Their isolation within the reef complex. Collapse dolines arise from large chambers and these are generally few in extensive systems of cave passages.
2 Their slopes are more likely due to collapse than solution.
3 Although roundness of structure is more easily seen as a solution doline in origin, circular structures of undoubted collapse origin do occur.

The evidence is not conclusive however, and it is possible that solution may have played a part in their formation. Indeed, the location of the Molar Reef hole suggests that the rim is based on a divide around a solution doline within which a smaller collapse doline has opened. In contrast, the rim around the Cockatoo Reef hole is strongly suggestive of an annular solution rampart around a collapse doline as has been described from the emerged reefs of Okinawa (Flint et al., 1953). The rise in the seismic discontinuity over the rim fits the interpretation of a solution rampart produced during past low sea levels.

The processes of subterranean solution to form a large cavern followed by collapse and subsequent subaerial solution and modification are unlikely to have occurred only over the short period of the last glacial low sea level. Certainly the depth of the holes, when compared to the depths of solution unconformities reported elsewhere on the Great Barrier Reef, indicates that cavern formation probably took place in limestones of far greater age than the last interglacial. This also overcomes the problem of mechanical strength of the roofs of developing caves, which is likely to be insufficient in last interglacial limestones. If the origin of the blue holes is much older than last interglacial, then more compact older reef limestones have been involved in their formation. Evidence for shallower lagoon features being of karst origin is much more circumstantial, but if such an origin is accepted then the data presented by Backshall et al. (1979, Table 2) suggests that shallow lagoonal patterns represent fields of solution dolines.

Positive Relief Features of Lagoons—Reef Patches and Ridges

Few lagoons of either atolls or shelf reefs are simple saucer-shaped depressions. In some cases the reef may be divided into numerous discrete lagoonal areas, as in the Pompey Complex (Figs. 7.7, 7.9). Even relatively simple lagoonal reefs have varying degrees of complexity produced by lagoon "bommies," growths of coral varying from isolated pinnacles to massive patches up to 50 m across. Maxwell (1968, Chap. 6) recognized two types of lagoonal reef patterns: a reticulate type characterized by anastomosing coral ridges (Fig. 7.10) and a dispersed type comprising discrete reefs with varying degrees of density of occurrence (Fig. 7.8).

Figure 7.10 Lagoon of One Tree Reef, with combination of reticulate and patch reefs.

By analogy with upstanding features produced by laboratory experiments on limestone blocks (in which an undersupply of acid rain results in the formation of residual solution prominences) and the irregular relief found at all scales in limestone terrain, Purdy (1974a) has suggested that coral pinnacles and lagoonal labrynths (reticulate reefs) are founded on karst topography of similar form. Drilling of a small lagoonal reef in Belize (Halley et al., 1977) has confirmed that it has developed over a Pleistocene high with about 8 m of relief. As the reef has grown at rates of about 1.6 m/1000 yrs in comparison to offreef sedimentation rates of only 0.4–0.5 m/1000 yrs, the morphology has been accentuated during the Holocene. Unfortunately, seismic results from the Great Barrier Reef are contradictory. Patch reefs in the lagoon at One Tree Reef have grown on prominences 6–9 m higher than general lagoon depths (Harvey et al., 1979). However, on Molar Reef a prominent ridge, which grows to a level slightly above MLWS and has a dense cover of *Pocillopora* sp., *Seriatopora* sp., and *Acropora humilis*, has not grown over a substrate high, for the seismic discontinuity marking the pre-Holocene level is at a depth of 20 m. Geochemical analysis of cores from Stanley Reef (19°18'S) locates the unconformity at 20 m, generally below the depth of the lagoon floor and far deeper than the depth of the seismic discontinuity on the reef rim, which is at only 8 m. This evidence would suggest that some patch reefs, at least, are unassociated with residual karst prominences and, even where positive features exist beneath lagoonal reefs, there is no evidence to suggest that they are not older growth features unrelated to karst erosion.

Reef Slope Features—Terraces and Spur and Groove Systems

Reef-slope terraces and spur and grooves figure prominently in the discussion over the determination of modern reef morphology by growth or by inheritance from earlier forms. The recognition of a prominent break of slope between 14.5–18.0 m in locations as widely spaced as the Marshall Islands (Tracey et al., 1948; Emery et al., 1954) and the Bahamas (Newell, et al., 1951) during the 1940s and 1950s led to the fallacy of a worldwide "10-fathom terrace" of eustatic origin. However, the problems of sea-level correlations, even in the latter part of the Holocene, suggest that worldwide correlations of older submerged features are unwise. Reef-front terraces do not form a major part of Purdy's arguments but he does suggest that terraces may result from differential solution (1974a, pp. 30–31) and that terrace levels may form prominent solution rims that can be the location of coral colonization after drowning. Stoddart (1969a) recognized the diversity of processes that may result in terrace forms and suggested that they could be either an erosion feature related to a lower sea level and forming a platform possibly equivalent to the level of the pre-Holocene surface (the Thurber discontinuity), or they could be an equilibrium feature related to the growth habits of the major reef-building corals and to wave action. Goreau and Land (1974) considered both explanations for prominent terraces in Jamaica and concluded that there at least the forereef morphology is determined by pre-Holocene bedrock morphology.

Marginal terraces similar to those on Pacific atolls have been recognized on the Great Barrier Reef. Maxwell (1968) claimed the most prominent is at a depth of 1.8–2.3 m with a width of up to 28 m, and deeper terraces occurring at 12.8–18.3 m. Jell and Flood (1978) recognized terraces at depths of 4–6, 9–15, and 22–24 m. On northern reefs windward terraces occur principally at depths of 3–5, 10–13, and rarely at 18 m (Scoffin et al., 1978). Deeper terraces on the continental shelf or reefs of the shelf edge are recognized by Maxwell (1968), Marshall (1977), and Orme et al. (1978a,b).

Although Maxwell (1973a) related many of these terraces to the Fairbridge (1961) sea level curve, he stated earlier that an alternative explanation may be one related to the growth habit of particular corals. Scoffin et al. (1978) supported an origin by erosion at former low sea levels for the terraces. Harvey (1978) showed that the prominent terrace developed at 19–22 m around Wheeler Reef (Fig. 9.8) is closely related to the major seismic discontinuity located beneath that reef, suggesting, in a similar manner to Stoddart (1969a), that the terrace is a thinly veneered expression of the edge of the pre-Holocene platform. Such an idea is implicit in Davies' work (e.g. Davies and Kinsey, 1977, Fig. 4; Davies, 1977; Davies et al., 1977a). However, an alternative explanation has been offered in Chapter 6: that the terraces represent growth of fringing reefs around the margins of the emerged platforms at times of interstadial high sea levels of the last glaciation.

Spur and groove systems (Fig. 7.11) have been described from nearly all reef areas and debate as to their origin as growth or erosion features predates even MacNeil's 1954 paper. It has been argued that the grooves are inherited from erosional features cut into the pre-Holocene reef foundations at low sea-level stages (e.g. Newell et al., 1951; Cloud, 1954, 1959; Emery et al., 1954; Newell, 1961; Kendall and Skipworth, 1969). Alternatively it has been suggested that the spur and grooves reflect reef growth in response to wave-power variation, the system providing a baffle that dissipates wave energy (e.g. Tracey et al., 1948; Munk and Sargent, 1954; Roberts, 1974). Observations of Friedman (1968) and Sneh and Friedman (1980) from the Red Sea, where the systems may be aligned at an angle 25° from normal to the reef front, apparently in response to wave refraction, lend further support to the growth hypothesis. Similarly, Shinn's (1963) excavations into spurs in Florida support a biological growth origin for the spurs, which were composed of *Acropora palmata* branches oriented in the direction of wave approach. These had coalesced into fingerlike projections. Moving sand in the grooves prevented coral attachment while periodic hurricane seas removed accumulating debris from the adjacent spurs.

Purdy (1974a, p. 65) acknowledged this evidence for a growth origin but maintained solution as a viable alternative. His major evidence was the solution furrows etched on experimental limestone blocks and *rillenkarren* and flared solution pits found on natural karst. The problem is one of scale. Although these experimental and small, natural features form analogs of spur and groove systems at the reduced scale of the limestone blocks or natural outcrops, grooves of a size similar to present reef-front features have not been reported from the margins of limestone plateaus or terraces.

The problem of origin of these features on the Great Barrier Reef is epitomized by the contrasting views of Maxwell and Davies and his co-workers. Maxwell (1968) was firmly in favor of a growth origin, stating:

The structure reflects the manner in which the reef expands, the spurs or ridges extending seaward so that maximum surface area can be exposed to the undepleted oceanic water.

Maxwell, 1968, p. 110

Alternatively, Davies et al. (1977b) suggest that:

Present day spur and groove structures have been localized to some degree by grooves in the limestone substrate.

Davies et al., 1977b, p. 72

Supporting evidence comes from the extension of grooves into iron-stained recrystallized limestone (Davies, 1977; Davies et al., 1977b). However, as the grooves are presently extending into the algal flat by formation of scour pools (Davies et al., 1977b) and Davies (1977) advocates growth of modern reefs only on the leeward sides, it is possible that erosion of the grooves is independent of and later than the processes of solution during Pleistocene reef exposure.

As Stoddart (1969a) has noted, the variety of forms and scales of spur and groove formations suggest different origins. Quite clearly some have originated as growth features, but the extension of some grooves into apparently pre-Holocene materials is just as clearly an indicator of an erosional origin. However, such evidence does not necessarily lend support to the concept of the grooves being karst solutional features. Subaerial solution remains only one of many possible origins for spur and grooves.

Interreef Channels and Marginal Rims

Features developed far more extensively on the Great Barrier Reef than in any other reef province are steep-sided, gently meandering interreef channels. They are most clearly seen in the hard-line Pompey Complex but extend northward from this area to Darley Reef at 19°12′ S. Similar channels are also found on the far northern reefs north of 13°30′ S. Again, diverse opinions have been expressed as to their origin as either growth-induced (Maxwell, 1970, 1976; Veron, 1978a,b), or influenced by a karstified substrate (Purdy, 1974a).

The channels of the Pompey Complex are by far the deepest. The one to the south of Cockatoo Reef (Fig. 7.7) has a maximum depth of 93 m and is close to this depth along its entire length. Soundings across the inner western sides of the hard-line Pompey Complex showed that the channels were incised into the shelf to a depth of 70 m at least 2 km distant from the reefs. They also extend eastward beyond the reefs, although their extent and ultimate terminus is not known. Veron (1978a) reported depths of 98–109 m in another Pompey Complex channel with the continental slope to seaward being "scored" to about twice-normal depth seaward of major channel openings. In plan, the channels are gently winding or meandering, are up to 1 km wide, and frequently show a simple pattern of apparent tributaries, sometimes at the northeastern end branching into apparent distributaries (Fig. 7.12). Such terms are used here in a purely descriptive sense without genetic implication. "Tributary" branches

Figure 7.11 Deep spur and grooves on the windward front of Hoskyns Reef, Bunker Group. Sand-floored groove cut in the front of the Belize barrier reef. (Photo, I. G. Macintyre.)

Figure 7.12 Complex interreef channels in the Pompey Reef complex with depths up to 100 m.

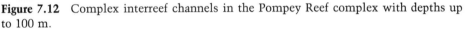

are generally longer than "distributaries." Common features are "blind" channels in which one or both ends of channels may be blocked either partially by submerged reefal shoals or completely, to the extent that algal-covered ridges surmount the blocking walls (Fig. 7.13). As the tidal range exceeds 4 m in this area tidal streams reach velocities exceeding 4 m/sec.

Further north the channel system is less distinct largely because the intervening reefs are not as large as the Pompeys, nor have they developed extensive reef flats (Fig. 7.6). The whole shelf is shallower but channels are up to 70 m in depth (Edgell, 1928a). Several generations of channels may be present. Between Darley and Dingo Reefs is a major channel 900 m wide and up to 55 m deep with relatively smooth sides and floor. A tributary channel (Fig. 7.13) that cuts through the Darley complex has a maximum depth of only 29 m and is choked and partially blocked by patch reefs. The tributary has a discordant junction with the main channel, its exit hanging some 20 m above the floor of the main channel.

The northernmost channels are more distinctive. They separate massive reef complexes (see Chap. 2) that have reef-flat development only on their western sides, the remainder of the reef sloping eastward to depths of about 18 m. The passages have a dendritic pattern coverging towards the east and are 30–50 m deep. Veron (1978a,b) described similar but smaller channel systems through shelf marginal reefs of the northernmost Great Barrier Reef, which he compared to the "deltaic" reefs of Maxwell (1970). The major channels are up to 700 m wide and 5.5 km long with depths between 18 and 35 m. Walls of the

Figure 7.13 Partially blocked channel on Darley Reef. The channel has a maximum depth of 30 m with numerous coral pinnacles. Beneath the reef rim to the left the Holocene-Pleistocene boundary has been detected by drilling at 13 m. The channel into which this leads is 55 m deep and largely clear of obstructions.

major channels are vertical to depths of between 12 and 19 m. The floors are smooth and hard with little rubble. A distinctive feature is a rim developed on the eastern side of the channels.

Discussion of the origin of these features once more highlights the contrasting views of Maxwell and Purdy. Maxwell (1970, 1976) suggested that there is a causal relationship between the channel systems, or associated "deltaic" reefs, and high-tidal ranges and current velocities. Tidal currents are seen as being responsible for localized deposition of debris, which forms elevations suitable for coral growth, a pattern developing that is analogous to tidal deltas. Once the pattern is initiated, scour in the tidal passages and adjoining back reef areas maintains the channel openings. Purdy, on the other hand, compared the channels to the steep-sided flat-floored drainways developed in karst terrain, equating the high marginal rims to the solution rim levees described in Okinawa by Flint et al. (1953). Parallel features were reproduced in model experiments (Purdy, 1974a, Fig. 20).

Certainly the evidence presently available supports Purdy rather than Maxwell. The channel systems are not restricted to the highest tidal areas but are found in the Bowen area and off Cape Grenville, where tidal ranges are less than 3 m. Even in the Pompeys the tidal range is far less than on the adjacent mainland. It is true, however, that current velocities within the channels are the highest recorded in the Great Barrier Reef and it seems probable that, once formed, the strong flow channelled through these features maintains their morphology. Seismic survey on the rims of channels beside Cockatoo Reef in the Pompeys and Darley Reef near Bowen indicated high pre-Holocene surfaces beneath each at -7 m and -12 m respectively and the patterns of coral growth alongside other channels are highly suggestive of the marginal rims described by Purdy. The depth of channels and size of associated reefs, when combined with evidence from the whole of the Great Barrier Reef of shallow pre-Holocene foundations also militates against a simple growth origin. Moreover, subsequent erosion as envisaged by both Maxwell (1970) and Veron (1978b) seems unlikely in view of known rates of abrasion and general lack of abrasive tools within the channels. Indeed the description by Veron (1978a) of pitted and grooved walls cut into hard limestone in the northern channels, is strongly suggestive of a little-modified, karstified surface with swamp slots (Wilford and Wall, 1965) or solution ripples (Wall and Wilford, 1966).

There seems little doubt therefore that the channels are the result of surface drainage during low sea level periods. Their pattern is identical to that developed in surface karst, particularly in subhumid or seasonally wet tropical climates (Jennings and Sweeting, 1963; Jennings, 1969; Williams, 1978). The box valleys of the Fitzroy Ranges of Western Australia are particularly reminiscent of the forms developed in the Great Barrier Reef (Fig. 7.14). The steep walls and flat floors of the valleys, from which rise isolated karst towers that are particularly similar to the channel features of the Great Barrier Reef. It is easy to imagine towers such as that shown by Sweeting (1972, Plate 54, p. 292) forming the foundation for Maxwell's plug-type reefs, particularly as growth after submergence would be strongly influenced by tidal currents to produce an elongated hydrodynamic form.

It is unlikely that these channels have been cut during the last low sea level

Figure 7.14 Windjana Gorge, Limestone Ranges of Western Australia, a karst morphology similar to that of the Pompey Reefs and intervening channels of the Great Barrier Reef. (Photo reproduced by courtesy of the Western Australia Department of Lands and Surveys.)

phase only. Their depth suggests that they, like other relief features of the pre-Holocene surface, have developed during successive periods of Pleistocene emergence. The partial or complete blocking of some channels may be more recent, resulting from changes in drainage patterns during the last glacial and subsequent blocking of parts of the channels by rock falls from the valley sides that have become the site for growth of coral during the Holocene (Fig. 7.13). Analogous rock falls partly blocking valleys are described from the Limestone Ranges of Western Australia (Jennings and Sweeting, 1963). The development of calcrete ridges up to 3 m high and 60 m across is also common on the pediments adjacent to the channel exits on the Limestone Ranges, explain the rims described by Veron (1978a) at the mouths of the channels on the far northern Reef. Thus the "deltaic" and "dissected" reefs of Veron (1978a) may be a reflection of only partial reef development on the pre-Holocene substrate in response to the hydrodynamic factors that Maxwell (1970) considered so important. In general, therefore, it is concluded that the interreef channels have been determined by erosion during periods of emergence, but are maintained during high sea-level periods by the strong currents that are directed into them during every tidal ebb and flow.

Karst Marginal Plains

Karst marginal plains are defined as bedrock plains with an alluvial veneer, with hums projecting through it, and with margins embayed by steepheads (Jennings, 1971). It is in the humid tropical karsts that the best examples of karst marginal plains are to be found, as climate and vegetation are favorable for lateral solution. Thus, conditions during regressive phases of the Pleistocene were probably ideal for the planation of the upstanding reef masses of the Great Barrier Reef. However, it is highly unlikely that the whole of the inner continental shelf, particularly at the southern end of the Reef, could have evolved from a marginal plain as Purdy (1974a) suggested. Such a contention can be rejected on two grounds. First, the scale of erosion required is so great that a time period far greater than the Quaternary would be needed to produce the current morphology. Second, the stratigraphic evidence of the Queensland shelf is indicative of slow subsidence, particularly of the outer margins where the present reefs are found. There is no evidence for the inner shelf ever having had a limestone cover. Although seismic traverses have indicated that many modern reefs are smaller than their precursors (Orme et al., 1978a) they also suggest that the terrigenous deposits of the coastal plain extend out over the continental shelf for some distance (Searle et al., 1980).

Seismic profiling suggests that a great deal of irregularity is present in erosion surfaces beneath the seabed and although clear signs of planation exist, the pre-Holocene morphologies are, at least in part, depositional in origin. Exposure of the shelf took place during the Pleistocene and the seismic work reported by Orme et al. (1978a,b) from the Cairns and Lizard Island areas, Searle et al. (1980, in prep.) from the Cairns to Bowen area, and by Jell and Flood (1978) and Searle et al. (1978) from the Capricorn–Bunker Group all show similar features. A smoothly sloping inner shelf with wedges of terrigenous sediments up to 20 m thick and 20 km wide is dissected by numerous small gullies that are extensions of the present stream courses of the coastal plain. Larger rivers are incised more deeply and may show terraced sides to their channels that are infilled by fine bedded sediments. In some instances the channels have not only been filled but now form slight prominences on the sea floor (Fig. 7.15). These infilled channels cross the central shelf where, in general, Holocene sediments are very sparse. In contrast, in the interreefal areas of the outer shelf Holocene sediments that are largely bioclastic sands derived directly from the reefs, may reach 14 m in thickness. Greater relief exists in the pre-Holocene surfaces of the outer shelf where not all channels have been infilled. The area of pre-Holocene reefal limestones appears to increase towards the north and only on the northernmost of the seismic surveys off Cape Grenville could the outer shelf be described as a limestone plain, although in the Cairns area in particular the distribution of modern reefs does not fully reflect the extent of older limestones. Although relief of scales up to about 5 m appears karstic, there is no evidence to distinguish between a growth or a karst erosion origin for the major relief features. It is unlikely, however, that the inner continental shelf has ever been a karst marginal plain.

Uncolonized Pre-Holocene Reefal Surfaces

In some locations in the Great Barrier Reef province are reefs that no longer have an extensive living coral veneer. Some, like the deep shelf-edge reefs near Cairns, and reefal shoals of the Capricorn–Bunker Group may be reefs of early Holocene age overtaken by the rapid rise in sea level. However, there are other

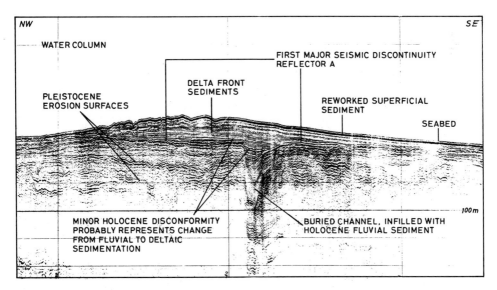

Figure 7.15 Infilled channel near Rib Reef off Townsville, probably the Pleistocene Herbert River. Seven meters of flat-bedded deltaic sediments overlay the channel, which is incised about 20 m into the Pleistocene surface and infilled with estuarine and fluvial sediments. (From Searle et al., in press, reproduced with permission of the Queensland Geological Survey.)

reefal banks that are almost certainly pre-Holocene and the surface relief of which give clear indications of the scale at which karst processes operated during the last glacial emergence.

The most continuous zone of reefal banks over which there is only a thin Holocene veneer is found in the lee of the ribbon reefs, occupying the outer 30% of parts of the northern shelf from Lizard Island northwards (Fig. 7.16). The exact distribution of these shoal areas is unknown but it shows up clearly on aerial photographs between Princess Charlotte Bay and Cape Grenville and has been identified by echo-sounding traverses in the Lizard Island area. On the western side the shoals rise sharply from water depths of about 60 m. To the east in places they appear to merge into parts of the platform from which the ribbon reefs rise. The surface, which lies in water depths of 20–40 m, consists of an irregular series of enclosed depressions quite unlike constructional reef morphology. Individual depressions can be up to 200 m in diameter but most are less than 100 m. The relief within them is about 12 m on the margins of the "platform" but less than 5 m near the center. Opposite Cape Grenville, on Great Detached Reef and near Lizard Island, a thick cover of *Halimeda* sediment covers the shoals.

The age of these reefal shoals is unknown. Seismic reflection profiles have been taken across them in the Lizard Island area (Orme et al. 1978b) and near Cape Grenville (Nelson, 1980). Near Lizard Island the major pre-Holocene reflector passes beneath the shoals. However, there is evidence of an erosion surface in the overlying deposits that are interpreted as *Halimeda* sands and that reach a thickness of 18 m. The section off Cape Grenville is similar, with the thickness of the layer on which the relief has formed varying from 1–8 m. The relief of the banks, particularly the patterns seen on aerial photographs, is so similar to that of undeniably karst-eroded surfaces such as on Aldabra (Stoddart et al., 1971; Braithwaite et al., 1973; Trudgill, 1979) that it is difficult to avoid a similar explanation on the Great Barrier Reef. It is highly unlikely that such features could have developed during any minor regression in the postglacial transgression. A possible explanation, as suggested in the previous chapter, is that the sediments above what may be the last interglacial surface accumulated as a shallow bank deposit during an early, last glacial, interstadial high sea level and have been subsequently exposed for most of the time. During the Holocene transgression the karstified surface has redeveloped a cover of *Halimeda* sediments. If such an explanation is accepted, then clearly the reefal surfaces of the Great Barrier Reef acquired mesoscale karst features during the last glacial period.

CONCLUSION

The increasing amount of data available on the structure of the Queensland reefs and adjacent continental shelf clearly show that an antecedent model of reef development is applicable to the Great Barrier Reef. This can be illustrated by individual landforms or, at a more general level, by classification of seismic-refraction results according to Holocene morphology (Fig. 7.17). The general saucer shape of the underlying pre-Holocene reefs controlling modern reef

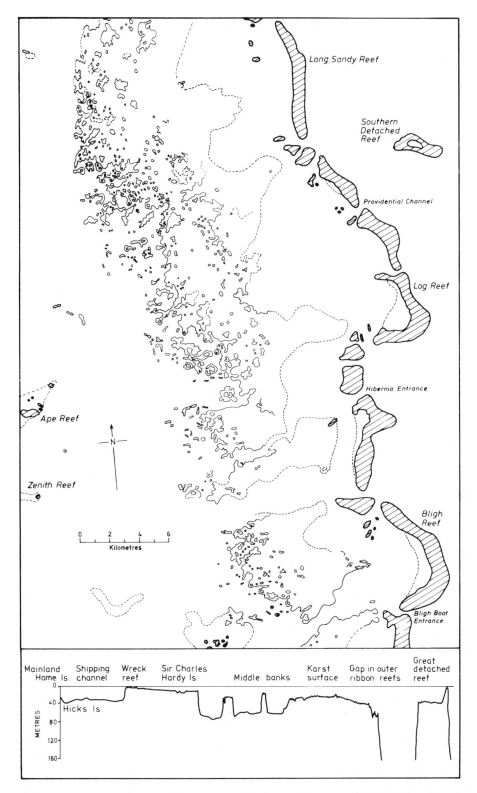

Figure 7.16 Distribution of karstic reefal banks on the outer shelf of the far northern Great Barrier Reef at about 12°45′S with profile from echo sounding from Cape Grenville to the Great Detached Reef.

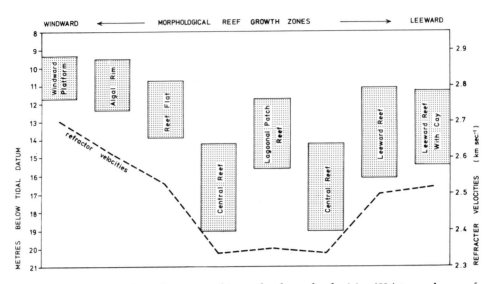

Figure 7.17 Relationship of average refractor depths and velocities (V_2) to modern reef morphological zones on the Great Barrier Reef. (From Harvey, 1980.)

morphology can be clearly seen. The physical properties of the pre-Holocene reefal materials show a similar arrangement in the pre-Holocene substrate, for the range of seismic velocities is highest beneath modern reef margins and lowest beneath lagoons. These results reflect a variation in degree of lithification, the greater competence of pre-Holocene reef margins possibly reflecting the greater degree of diagenesis in the prior coralgal reef framework in comparison to the lagoon sediments and open patch-reef framework of the old reef center.

Facies control of the processes operating during the long period of reef exposure as discussed by Bloom (1974) is indicated. Undoubtedly the Queensland shelf was exposed to subaerial processes during the last glacial low sea levels, and the morphology of surfaces uncolonized during the Holocene transgression indicates that small-scale karst landforms analogous to those developed on last interglacial reefs, and still exposed above sea level elsewhere in the world, were developed on the Great Barrier Reef. However, there is no evidence for larger karst features such as marginal plains or towers having evolved. Only the blue holes, and possibly the gorgelike interreefal channels, provide evidence of a major karst process, and both features are very localized on the Great Barrier Reef. As highly competent limestone is necessary for their formation, it is possible that the areas in which these features are found correspond to structural highs where early Quaternary or even Tertiary limestones may be much closer to the surface of the modern reefs than elsewhere.

However, an antecedent karst hypothesis cannot generally be sustained on the Great Barrier Reef. Certainly modern reef growth is restricted to topographic highs on the pre-Holocene surface (although not all these highs have been colonized by modern reef growth), but the location and morphology is in all probability the result of former reef growth at high sea-level phases in the past rather than solution during subaerial exposure. Relief features may have been enhanced over several glacial-interglacial cycles, as subaerial processes may be guided by contrasts in original reef facies. But more influential in providing the relief of both the pre-Holocene foundation and the Holocene morphology is the pattern of growth during submergence that will favor the colonization of prominences at the expense of depressions. The processes of reef growth are thus the subject of the next chapter.

8

Carbonate Budgets and Holocene Reef Growth

Coral reefs constitute a quantitatively significant global sink for calcium, conservatively estimated by Smith (1978) as equivalent to 50% of input into the world's oceans. Gross rates of calcium carbonate deposition for individual reef organisms have been quoted in Chapter 3, but these rates require modification to take account of bioerosion, dissolution, and physical loss of sediments from the reef before realistic figures of net productivity are determined for the total reef system. Quite clearly small-scale areal and larger regional variations exist in both productivity and loss, and similar scales of net productivity variation are to be expected. The importance of such calculations for the Great Barrier Reef stems from the data presented in the last two chapters. During the Holocene transgression, sea level rose from about − 135 m 18,000 years ago to close to its present position by 6000 yrs B.P., an average rate of rise of 11.25 mm/yr. However, reefs did not have to grow from the level of lowest sea levels, but have recolonized older reef remnants lying at depths generally between 10 and 20 m below present sea level. Although data on early Holocene levels are sparse from the Great Barrier Reef area, what little there is (e.g., Hopley et al., 1978; Davies and Marshall, 1979) suggests that sea level stood at about − 16 m 8500 yrs B.P. and that the rate of transgression lay within the envelope of sea-level rise published by Thom and Chappell (1975) based on data from elsewhere in eastern Australia. Vertical reef growth over the older reef tops thus commenced 9500 to 8000 yrs B.P. on the Great Barrier Reef, when sea-level rise was at a rate about 7 mm/yr. There are important questions that arise from these figures:

1 Are productivity rates for calcium carbonate sufficiently rapid to allow reef-top accretion to keep up with the rise in sea level?
2 Are there variations in productivity rates over reef tops that are likely to produce variation in the thickness and relief of the Holocene veneer?
3 What alterations in carbonate productivity rates have taken place since sea level became more or less stabilized 6000 yrs B.P. and since reefs grew up to sea level?
4 Can regional variations in vertical reef accretion be recognized?

Answers to these questions will add significantly to the explanation of modern reef morphology.

RATES OF CARBONATE DEPOSITION AND REEF GROWTH

Three approaches have been used to produce carbonate budgets for coral reefs. The first uses observations of rates of biological growth occurring at the present day. At their simplest, rates of coral growth have been extrapolated into rates of surface reef accretion. More recently, greater sophistication has been introduced to such an approach by taking account of the variety and density of reef organisms to produce figures of potential, gross, and net production. The second approach is to study modern calcium carbonate budgets either by monitoring CO_2 flux through the "organic" cycle by way of oxygen, there being an inverse relationship between O_2 and CO_2 flux, or by monitoring the reduction in the total alkalinity of the water taking into account the flushing rate of water through the reef system (Kinsey, 1978; Smith and Kinsey, 1978). A basic problem of both these approaches is that they are observing processes operating on reefs that, at least in the Great Barrier Reef area, have been at or close to a near-stable sea level for 6000 years. Growth patterns may have been very different during the period sea level was rising rapidly over reef tops and possibly reefs were lagging behind the rate of sea level rise. The third approach is to use the stratigraphic record, usually by the radiometric dating of reef cores, to produce an account of net accumulation rates. The problems associated with this method largely result from the fact that relatively few points over a reef can be measured, and from the frequent inability to recognize changing reef morphology that will affect productivity rates at specific locations as the reef grows upward. Nonetheless results from the three approaches show a remarkable degree of accord and in combination permit the development of theoretical models of reef development in the Holocene.

Deposition of calcium carbonate is mainly in the form of aragonite, except near the reef crest, where the crustose algae dominate and deposition is high-Mg calcite. Aragonite density is 2.89 gm/cc but rates of productivity, generally cited in kg/m^2/yr, need to take account of the natural porosity of reef rock even after compaction, before the figures can be converted into vertical reef growth rates. As densities vary, different modes of reef growth may result in different rates of upward growth. For example, a reef composed of loosely compacted *Acropora* sticks may have a porosity as high as 70% whereas hard algal pavement may have a porosity less than half this amount, with resulting upward growth rates significantly less than those for the *Acropora* reef, even though productivities may be identical. Porosities for various reef fabrics are shown in Table 8.1 and are generally in the range of 40–60%. Thus the common use of a 50% porosity figure to convert carbonate productivity to growth rate appears to be justified (e.g., Chave et al., 1972; Smith and Kinsey, 1976; Davies, 1977; Kinsey and Davies, 1979a).

Biological Measurements

Guppy (1889) was probably the first person to translate rates of growth of reef-top corals into rates of surface accretion. Taking into account the area of each

Table 8.1   Porosities in Great Barrier Reef Corals and Sediments

Location	Lithology	Porosity (%)	Reference
One Tree Reef	*Favites* sp.	55	Kinsey and Davies (1979a)
One Tree Reef	*Porites* sp.	60	Kinsey and Davies (1979a)
One Tree Reef	Incipient beach rock	45–49	Kinsey and Davies (1979a)
One Tree Reef	Partially cemented beach rock	30	Kinsey and Davies (1979a)
One Tree Reef	Medium sands	46–50	Kinsey and Davies (1979a)
One Tree Reef	Fine to medium sands	33–41	Kinsey and Davies (1979a)
Magnetic Island	Head corals	47–64	Smith (1972)
Hayman Island	Reef rock from cores	41–61	Smith (1972)
Keeper Reef	*Porites* sp.	41.5–46.0	Foster (1974)

kind of coral on the Cocos-Keeling atoll reef flat he estimated reef growth rates of generally less than 10 mm/yr. Vaughan (1919) extrapolated from growth rates of single species, suggesting that reefs of *Montastrea annularis* would grow upwards at 6–7 mm/yr and reefs of *Acropora cervicornis* at about 25 mm/yr. Mayer (1924) estimated deposition rates of 1.45 kg/m^2/yr, equivalent to 8 mm/yr upward growth on a Samoan reef flat. His productivity figure is remarkably similar to that of more recent calculations. Similar approaches are still being used to calculate reef growth rates, although at a more sophisticated level. For example Chave et al. (1972) estimated the potential growth rates of individual organisms, which they then converted into gross productivity based on organism distribution and density for typical reef habitats (Table 8.2). Estimated potential growth rates were well in excess of 10 kg/m^2/yr, equivalent to upward growth rates greater than 7 mm/yr. However, they suggested that gross production is rarely likely to exceed 7 mm/yr. As they considered that modern sea level was rising by 1 mm/yr, net production, or the amount of material retained by the reef system, is likely to produce upward growth of this amount only, equivalent to a productivity of 1 kg/m^2/yr. A similar approach has been made to organisms of an individual fringing reef on Barbados by Stearn and Scoffin (1977) and Stearn et al. (1977). Their productivity figures of 15 kg/m^2/yr for planimetric area or 9 kg/m^2/yr for reef area (taking into account the highly irregular surface) are comparable to those of Chave et al. (1972). However, their accompanying rates of bioerosion are 17.4 and 10.4 kg/m^2/yr respectively, due mainly to the grazing activity of the sea urchin *Diadema antillarum*. The budget synthesis (Scoffin et al., 1980) indicates a CaCO$_3$ production on the reef of $206 \pm 10 \times 10^6$ g/yr and a removal from the reef of $123 \pm 7 \times 10^6$ g/yr.

Measurements from the Geological Record

Published figures for growth rates from cores through Holocene reef caps dated by radiometric methods are summarized in Table 8.3. A great range of accretion rates is seen from less than 1 mm/yr to a maximum between 14 and 21

Table 8.2   Gross Carbonate Production for Coral Reef Environmental Components, for Environments and for Reef Types[a]

	Production ($g\ CaCO_3/m^2/yr$)
Components	
Sand flat with calcareous aglae	410
Coral mounds on sand	13,000
Algal ridge	9,000
Complete coral coverage	55,000
Environments	
Lagoon	5,000
Reef flat	3,000
Algal ridge	9,000
Upper slope	60,000
Lower slope	8,000
Reef types	
Circular atoll	7,000
Barrier reef	8,000
Fringing reef	10,000

[a]From Chave et al. (1972).

mm/yr achieved for short periods during the growth of a fringing reef in Panama (Macintyre and Glynn, 1976; Glynn and Macintyre, 1977). Highest rates are associated with the accumulation of high porosity *Acroporid* or *Pocilloporid* reefs, in which encrusting algae are rare. These are mainly fringing reefs in the Caribbean and eastern Pacific. Overall, fringing reefs are reported as having mean growth rates between 3.3 and 10 mm/yr. Atolls (Enewetak, Bikini, Muroroa) where a much lower porosity reef framework has accumulated, have reported mean growth rates of between 1.0 and 2.9 mm/yr. Shelf or barrier reefs have reported mean growth rates of between 1.1 and 5.0 mm/yr, apparently lying between the extremes of fringing and open-ocean atoll reefs. Few sites have sufficient bore holes to allow some comparison of growth rates at different locations on reefs. However Goreau and Land (1974) reported a growth rate of only 1.2 mm/yr on the front of a Jamaican fringing reef at a depth of 25 m, far slower than rates reported at shallower depth and beneath fringing reef flats. Coring on a patch reef on the Belize shelf produced comparable figures of 1.6 mm/yr accretion for the patch reef and only 0.4–0.5 mm/yr for the adjacent lagoon floor (Halley et al., 1977).

In an analysis of dated cores from the Great Barrier Reef, including from the Bunker–Capricorn Group, Davies and Marshall (1979) showed that, throughout the Holocene, rates have varied from as little as 0.2 mm/yr to as much as 6.0 mm/yr. Variations are due to differences in accretion rates in different parts of the reef and to three distinctive periods of growth being present. These consist of an early period of slow growth probably due to difficulties in

Table 8.3 Holocene Coral Reef Accretion Rates Based on Published Radiocarbon Dating of Reef Cores

Location	Mean growth rate or range of Rates (mm/yr)—Maximum Rate for Sections of Core in Brackets	Reference
1 Fringing Reefs		
Caribbean		
St. Croix	8–9 (15.0)	Adey (1975, 1978a)
Jamaica	1.2	Goreau and Land (1974), Land (1974)
Florida	10.0	Lighty (1977a)
Florida	0.38–4.85	Shinn et al. (1977)
Curacao	1–4	Focke (1978)
Panama	0.6–3.9 (10.8)	Macintyre and Glynn (1976)
Indo-Pacific		
Panama	1.3–4.2 (14–21)	Glynn and Macintyre (1977)
Oahu, Hawaii	3.3	Easton and Olsen (1976)
New Guinea	4.7 (8.0)	Chappell and Polach (1976)
Hayman Is., G.B.R.	1.2–5.0	Hopley et al. (1978)
Reunion	4.0 (10.2)	Montaggioni (1976)
2 Shelf, Bank, or Barrier Reefs		
Caribbean		
Alacran	2–12 (12.0)	Macintyre et al. (1977)
Belize	1.1–5.0 (7.8)	Purdy (1974a)
Belize	2.23	Miller and Macintyre (1977)
Dry Tortugas	1.91–4.47	Shinn et al. (1977)
Martinique	4.0	Adey et al. (1977a)
Indo-Pacific		
Great Barrier Reef	0.2–6.0	Davies and Marshall (1979)
3 Open Ocean Atolls		
Enewetak	1.8 (3.5)	Thurber et al. (1965)
Enewetak and Bikini	1–2	Tracey and Ladd (1974)
Muroroa	1.6–2.9	Lalou et al. (1966)

colonizing the Pleistocene surface, a period of accelerated growth when the reef was lagging behind the sea level rise, and a final period of decreasing growth as the reef approached the stabilized modern sea level (Fig. 8.1). This pattern is illustrated by the Hayman Island fringing reef (Hopley et al., 1978), which reached modern sea level between 5000 and 4000 yrs B.P. after growing from a pre-Holocene platform at a depth of -15 to -20 m and which was inundated about 9000 yrs B.P. (Fig. 12.6). Growth rates of 4 to 5 mm/yr are indicated (Fig. 8.1) on the reef crest but only 1.2 mm/yr on the reef front (core R5). However, the major divergence of growth rates on different parts of the reef took place after 5500 yrs B.P. when the reef was growing to within 8 m of modern sea level. The deceleration of upward growth is also illustrated by dated cores from a number of reef flats taken by the author (Fig. 8.2). The uppermost 3 m of a wide range of reefs have accreted at between 0.1 and 10.0 mm/yr. Although the reefs have reached sea levels at different times since about 6000 yrs B.P., a general pattern of upward growth of 3–6 mm/yr to within 1 m of sea level is seen, followed by a slower net rate of about 1 mm/yr in the accretion of the top meter.

A recent program of deeper coring from reefs in the Townsville area by the author has provided further examples of growth rates in the Holocene. The fringing reef on Orpheus Island (Fig. 12.7) has accreted at rates of 7.3 mm/yr during its mid-Holocene period of establishment (Hole 3), 7.1 mm/yr subsequently (Hole 2) but at only 2.6 mm/yr in the last 3000 yrs (Hole 1). These

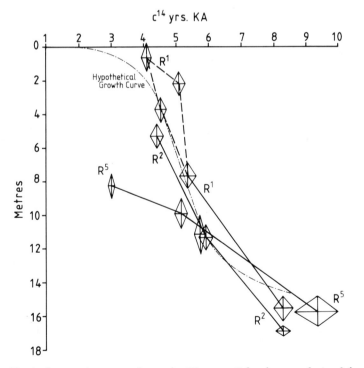

Figure 8.1 Vertical accretion rates from the Hayman Island cores derived from radiocarbon dating. The hypothetical growth curve of Davies and Marshall (1979) has been superimposed.

rates are high but are paralleled by the accretion of Rattlesnake Island fringing reef which accreted from 11.5 m at 7010 ± 180 yrs B.P. (GaK-9292) to 0.5 m depth by 5380 ± 120 yrs B.P. (GaK-9294) at an average rate of 6.7 mm/yr. An identical accretion rate of 6.7 mm/yr is also shown for mid-shelf Wheeler Reef (Fig. 9.8) where cores from the centre of the reef produced radiocarbon ages of 7110 ± 240 yrs B.P. (SUA-1536) from 18.5 m depth and 4550 ± 90 yrs B.P. (SUA-1528) from 1.35 m. A patch reef on Stanley Reef (Fig. 9.6) grew from 20.0 m at 7010 ± 100 yrs B.P. (SUA-1554) to 4.5 m depth by 3950 ± 90 yrs B.P. (SUA-1539) at a compatible rate of 5.1 mm/yr.

The data from Redbill Reef (Fig. 9.7) are sufficient to compare accretion rates in different parts of the reef. The windward algal rim has accreted at an average rate of 0.48 mm/yr over the last 4000 years, the leeward algal rim at 1.29 mm/yr, and the central reef flat at 0.33 mm/yr. This pattern is very similar to that shown by One Tree Reef (Fig. 8.4), although the actual rates from the deeper cores obtained from this reef are higher. The windward reef flat has accreted at rates of 3.2 mm/yr, the leeward rim by about 6 mm/1 yr, and the accreting sand wedge of the lagoon by only 1.7 mm/yr (Davies and Marshall, 1980). Rates of lagoon sediment accretion can also be estimated from Frankel's (1977, 1978) data for dated sediment cores. Although some distortion may be present because of bioturbation, his figures give a mean accumulation rate in the upper meter or so of 2.62 mm/yr with the range from 0.34–5.91 mm/yr. These figures of net accretion are at least in part due to transport of sediments from more productive zones to sediment sinks such as lagoons.

Carbonate Budgets from Water Studies

The major feature of results, summarized by Smith and Kinsey (1976), is the difference in productivity between windward areas of good water circulation, where mean figures of 4.0 ± 0.3 kg/m²/yr are recorded, and protected lagoon environments where mean productivity figures are as low as 0.8 kg/m²/yr. Research on the Great Barrier Reef has given further detail for the variation in productivity in individual reef zones (LIMER, 1976; Kinsey, 1977; Davies and Kinsey, 1977; Davies, 1977; Kinsey and Davies, 1979a; Davies and Marshall, 1979). Kinsey and Davies (1979a) have shown that the organic carbon cycle is in a position of equilibrium with little or no net gain of organic carbon in the reef systems. All the organic material created by photosynthesis is consumed by respiration and decomposition. The seaward perimeter zones were shown to be the sites of major activity with the outermost zones (outer slopes and algal crests) probably being net producers of organic matter, which is then fed back into the remainder of the system as suggested by Smith and Marsh (1973). In contrast, the inorganic carbon cycle shows that all reefs are notable accruers of calcium carbonate with gains in the range of 0.5–1.8 kg/m²/yr over the whole reef. Seaward margins are the main producers with 3.6–4.5 kg/m²/yr being recorded. The general distribution of net carbonate deposition follows the pattern of organic activity (Table 8.4), except that the algal pavement has as high a level of productivity as areas of heavy coral cover.

The major problem area of carbonate budget studies has been the seaward slope where rich coral cover, taking advantage of the extra area provided by

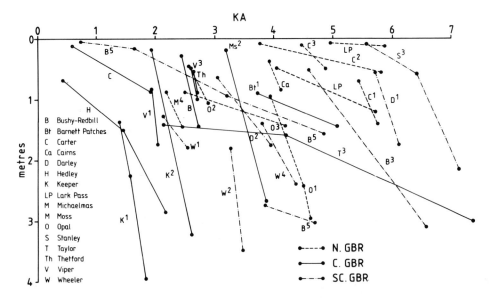

Figure 8.2 Vertical accretion rates from the upper 3 m of windward reef flats. Note the rapid deceleration of growth in the upper 2 m, similar to that suggested by Davies and Marshall (1979).

Table 8.4   Present Calcification Rates and Their Indications for Vertical Growth Potential for Various Zones of One Tree Reef[a]

Zone	Calcification Rates ($Kg\ CaCO_3/m^2/yr$)	Vertical Growth Potential (mm/yr)
Outer slope[b]	1.4	0.9
Algal crest	4.0	2.8
Reef flat coral zone	4.5	3.1
Sand flats	0.3	0.2
Reticulated lagoonal patch reefs	1.5	1.0
Deep lagoon	0.5	0.3
Integrated system	1.5	1.0

[a]From Kinsey and Davies (1979a).
[b]Outer slope figures from Enewetak from Smith and Harrison (1977).

spur and groove systems, has suggested optimum conditions for carbonate production. However measurements from the upper reef slope of Enewetak Atoll by Smith and Harrison (1977) have shown that there is an abrupt change from high rates of productivity on the reef flat to very slow rates on the slope. The potential productivity of both corals and crustose algae reduces with depth, with mean production figures of only 1.4 kg/m²/yr being achieved if production is not limited by daylight hours, or about half that figure if there is no nighttime production. Topographic irregularities and steep slopes increase the effective surface area by as much as 50%, so that actual planimetric area figures may be as high as 2 kg/m²/yr. Small areas of virtually total coral cover may produce at rates as high as 3–6 kg/m²/yr but are very restricted. Thus, CaCO₃ production on reef slopes is only about 50% of what it is on the adjacent reef top. Smith and Harrison (1977) consider that optimum environments are probably broad shoal areas a few meters deep, open to oceanic swell but sufficiently shallow to break the disruptive forces of the waves without restricting water movement or reducing light intensities. Such conditions are likely to have existed on reef tops during the Holocene transgression.

Using an average porosity figure of 50% these productivity figures can be translated into vertical growth rates (Table 8.4). Highest growth rates of about 3 mm/yr are possible on the windward rim while more modest figures of about 1 mm/yr occur on the reef slope and lagoons with coral and algal cover. Very slow rates of growth are recorded on sanded reef flats and deeper lagoons. Such upward growth was unrestricted during the Holocene transgression, as rates of sea level rise exceeded the probable rate of reef growth as long as the reef crest was not too deeply submerged. With stable sea levels, an upper limit to reef growth has been achieved and productivity, although probably only a little less than it was on the shallowly submerged reefal banks, has been channelled into horizontal reef development with the transport of CaCO₃ as sediment from one part of the reef to another.

The maximum accretion rate of 3 mm/yr is less than that established by other methods. Recently, however, Kinsey (1981) has suggested that the rate may be a mixture of two "modes" of growth found on reef flats: a calcification rate of 10 kg/m²/yr typical of narrow reef edge zones of moderate energy levels being mixed with a low activity "mode" producing only 0.5 kg/m²/yr. Mixtures of the two modes will give vertical accretion rates of up to 7 mm/yr, thus becoming compatible with rates quoted from the geological record.

IMPLICATIONS OF GROWTH RATES
FOR HOLOCENE REEF DEVELOPMENT

As the rate of rise of sea level at the height of the postglacial transgression was probably greater than the rate at which most reefs could grow upwards it is probable that three quite distinctive phases of reef development have occurred during the Holocene. Initially reef development was limited to a narrow fringe on the edge of the continental shelf and, although the first half of the transgression was rapid, the flooding of the shelf provided preexisting substrates in the form of pre-Holocene residual reefs. Thin veneers of coral would have been patchily attached to the older limestone, possible with many gaps when transgression rates were too rapid for continuous reef growth, as suggested by Davies and Kinsey (1977). From about 10,000 yrs B.P. it is possible that the rate of rise may have slowed to about 7 mm/yr. It is from about this time that the upper surfaces of the older reef remnants became submerged. The second phase of reef development during the first half of the Holocene comprised a period of steady sea level rise leaving behind the upper surface of most reefs. However, it is unlikely that the majority of reefs growing from platforms shallower than -25 m would ever have been in water depths greater than 10 m. According to the data of Smith and Kinsey (1976) and Smith and Harrison (1977) this would have meant that reef tops would have been within the zone of maximum vertical accretion until they caught up with the stable or only gently rising sea level of the last 6000 years. The actual time that individual reefs caught up with sea level would depend on three factors:

1 The depth of the platform from which they had to grow.
2 The actual rate of accretion achieved and the porosity of the material deposited.
3 The exact nature of sea levels during the last 6000 years.

The maximum rate of vertical growth would have occurred only on the reef rim, particularly on windward sides, thus increasing the dished shape of many of the antecedent platforms. As the reefs were below the level of most wave activity, little horizontal transport from this highly productive zone would have occurred. Kinsey and Davies (1979a) suggested that even most particulate material loosened by chemical bioerosion is likely to have remained virtually in situ. Actual rates of accretion across different reef zones may have varied compared to those of today (because of better water circulation in the back reef area of a submerged reef, rates of accretion may have been higher) but it is reasonable to assume that the general pattern was the same.

The third phase of reef development has taken place since the reefs reached sea level. This would have occurred initially in the most productive seaward rim zone which would become a primary source for sediment to be transported to lagoon and back reef areas. Such a situation has been modelled by Smith et al. (1978). The model (Fig. 8.3) presumes a circular atoll larger than most shelf lagoon reefs and a presently rising sea level of 1 mm/yr. The lagoon receives 65% of the total inorganic carbon fixed in the system. This gives a vertical infilling rate of 1.5 mm/yr. If a stable sea level is presumed or the lagoon were smaller, then the rate of deposition could be significantly higher. What this model suggests is that once a reef has grown up to a more or less stable sea level, the relief of rim and lagoon, inherited from an antecedent platform and accentuated during periods of rapid vertical growth, is slowly reduced. Given sufficient time the lagoon may be infilled completely, leaving only a wide sandy reef flat.

The intensive study of One Tree Reef in the Capricorn Group by Davies and his co-workers confirms the pattern of Holocene reef development suggested by Smith et al. (1978) and adds further detail. This reef is the most intensively studied of any part of the Great Barrier Reef and has had data collected relating to coral calcification (Kinsey, 1972, 1977; Kinsey and Domm, 1974; Kinsey and Davies, 1979b), geological development (Davies et al., 1976; Davies and Kinsey, 1977; Davies et al., 1977a,b; Harvey et al., 1978, 1979; Davies and Marshall, 1979, 1980), and Holocene growth through carbonate budgets (Davies, 1977; Kinsey and Davies, 1979a). The reef, which is triangular in shape and measuring 9 km along the longest southern margin (Fig. 8.4), has grown from an antecedent platform with a general depth of 20–25 m but a

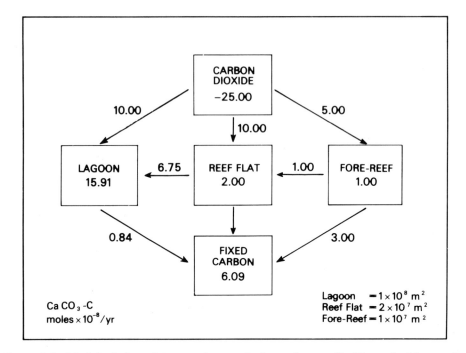

Figure 8.3 Model of the calcium carbonate budget of an atoll. (From Smith, et al., 1978.)

depth of only 10–14 m beneath the algal rim and up to 9 m deeper beneath the lagoon.

Based on present growth rates Kinsey and Davies (1979a) calculated that growth from the main platform, first inundated about 9000 yrs B.P., lagged behind the rise of sea level, being at a depth of about 10 m when modern sea level was first reached 6200 yrs B.P. and reaching sea level only 2000 years ago. In contrast they estimated that growth from the rim, inundated only by 7800 yrs B.P. was only 5 m deep at 6200 yrs B.P. and reached modern sea level by 4400 yrs B.P. Subsequently, production from the windward rim has been transferred leewards with the formation of lagoonward prograding sand sheets at rates of sediment accumulation of up to 2 kg/m²/yr (Table 8.5). This basic pattern has been confirmed by drilling (Davies and Marshall, 1980). The windward rim, consisting of head corals with a coralline algae–*Millepora*–vermetid assemblage that produces a massive framework, reached modern sea level just prior to 5000 yrs B.P., and subsequently the lagoon began to receive sediment. Originating as episodic storm deposits, the sand wedges built upwards at a rate of 1.7 mm/yr. Acceleration of growth of the leeward reef rim also occurred after the windward rim reached sea level. The upper framework here is similar to the windward side but with thinner algal crusts. The lower reef on the leeward side is dominated by branching corals. Both sand wedges and leeward reef flat reached sea level within the last millenium.

This model for development of a single reef in the Great Barrier Reef pro-

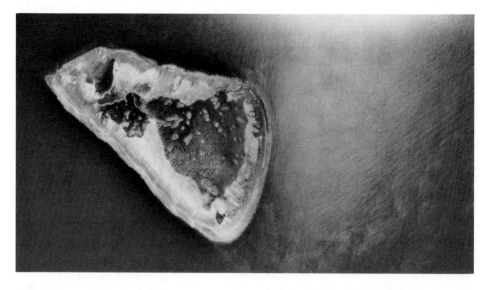

Figure 8.4 One Tree Reef, Capricorn Group. (Air photo Crown Copyright, reproduced by permission of the Director, Division of National Mapping, Dept of National Development and Energy, Canberra.)

Table 8.5   Calcium Carbonate Budget on One Tree Reef[a]

Sediment contributing zones	Area (km²)
Windward reef edge	0.413
Windward algal ridge	0.190
Windward reef flat	0.670
Leeward reef flat and front	0.850

Total excluding algal ridge = 1.933 million kg/yr
Total including algal ridge = 7.732 million kg/yr

Sediment receiving zones	Area (km²)
Lee edge	2.480
Southern sand sheet	0.822
Northern sand sheet	0.538
Lagoon	2.670

Overall growth = 1 kg/m²/yr
Growth of lee edge and sand sheets = 2 kg/m²/yr (equivalent to 6 m vertical growth in 4000 yrs)

[a]Contributing zones are assumed to calcify at a rate of 4 kg/m²/yr, from Kinsey and Davies (1979a).

vince is probably applicable to many other reefs, as there appears to be little variation in productivity with latitude (Smith and Kinsey, 1976). Minor variation may occur with differences in rates and times of change from essentially vertical growth to horizontal transportation depending on the rate of vertical growth (which in turn depends in part on the porosity of the reef fabric laid down) and morphology, depth of pre-Holocene platforms, and differences in sea-level curves. Dominant growth on all reefs probably is to leewards. Davies (1977) and Kinsey and Davies (1979a) suggested that windward sides of reefs may be eroding, implying that the windward reef front is probably composed of pre-Holocene materials and that features such as spurs and grooves are also of pre-Holocene age. This has been confirmed on One Tree Reef (Davies and Marshall, 1979). However, it was shown in Chapter 6 that during the late Quaternary, terraces at − 20 and − 40 m may have developed during interstadials and growth from these levels may add to the windward extension of reef flats. Presuming a sea level curve similar to that of Thom and Chappell (1975) and growth rates in this zone of 3 mm a year then, while growth from the − 10 m reef rim may have reached modern sea level by 4400 yrs B.P., that from a − 20 m level would have reached the same level by 2300 yrs B.P., and growth from − 40 m would still be at least 4 m below water at the present time. However, the deeper submergence of the reef growing from the − 40 m terrace is likely to have adversely affected productivity rates and seriously retarded upward growth. Significance of reef growth from earlier reef front terraces is discussed further in Chapters 9 and 10.

The figures produced by Kinsey and Davies (1979a) suggest that massive transport of sediments takes place on modern reef flats, to the extent that they question how coral reefs can exist at all. They consider that such a question emphasizes the critical role of encrusting calcareous algae as stabilizers. Calcification in the algal zone is considered by these authors to accrue in situ, accounting for the topographic prominence of algal flats.

A final most important point raised by the carbonate budget studies of Kinsey and Davies is the suggestion that subsequent to horizontal reef growth at modern sea level an equilibrium situation will arise when the amount of calcium carbonate precipitated on windward reef flats will exactly balance the amount lost. From their research on Lizard Island a reef flat of about 400 m width would provide such an equilibrium. A narrower flat would continue to grow to leeward as the capability for removal is greater than the amount of carbonate produced and new reef would be added on the leeward side. Widening of the reef flat beyond 400 m would result in production greater than could be lost, and it is suggested that the reef flat would become sanded, reducing its own productivity by natural negative feedback mechanisms. The equilibrium width allows continued productivity at 4 kg $CaCO_3/m^2/yr$ most of which is added to the back-reef detrital slope on linear (ribbon) reefs, or to the lagoon on reefs growing from more oval platforms. As Kinsey and Davies (1979a) figures were based on productivity-removal studies at Lizard Island, inside the Great Barrier Reef, rates of removal may be greater on the more exposed atolls and outer ribbon reefs, thus allowing a wider reef flat to develop before the equilibrium stage is reached, and hence explaining the occurrence of reef flats 1 km or more in width in some areas.

INDIRECT MEASUREMENTS OF REGIONAL ACCRETION RATES ON THE GREAT BARRIER REEF

The age of the reef top has been shown to be a function of the rate of upward growth of the reef and the depth of the platform from which it grows. If the date of the reef cap and the date of inundation of the antecedent platform as well as its depth are known, then a mean growth rate can be calculated. Unfortunately, as sea levels are likely to show local variation over the continental shelf in response to hydro-isostatic deformation (Chap. 6) no "standard" sea level curve can be applied to give the exact date of platform inundation. However, this problem can be overcome without recourse to expensive drilling and dating of the basal Holocene veneer by using differences in depths of platforms beneath various reefs and differences in the ages of the reef caps. This has been undertaken using the minimum recorded depth to the seismic velocity contrast (Fig. 6.11) and the maximum C-14 age of the reef cap (Table 9.2) above a level of − 1.5 m (Tidal Datum) on windward reef caps on 21 reefs between 14°30′ and 21°00′ S, with additional input derived from other sites such as Bewick (Thom et al., 1978) and Hayman Island (Hopley et al., 1978).

If all reefs sampled had grown upwards at the same rate, then a plot of oldest C-14 age from the reef cap against minimum recorded pre-Holocene platform depth should produce a straight line, the slope of which will be resolved by the actual upward growth rate. All data are plotted in this way on Figure 8.6. A general relationship is indicated that is statistically significant at the 1% level, and suggests a growth rate of 3.2 mm/yr. However, presuming that the original data are accurate, i.e., the age closely indicates the date of the reef reaching modern sea level and the seismic discontinuity is truly the depth of the pre-Holocene, then the spread of the data on either side of the regression line may be the result of either of the following:

1   Variations in reef growth rates on different parts of the Great Barrier Reef.
2   Variations in the sea level curves of different parts of the Great Barrier Reef.

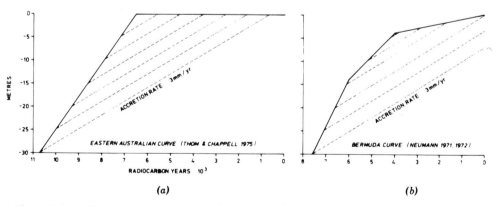

(a)   (b)

Figure 8.5   Relationship of reef growth at a postulated rate of 3 mm/yr and sea-level rise for two contrasting Holocene sea-level curves: (a) eastern Australia (From Thom and Chappell, 1975) and (b) Caribbean (From Neumann, 1971, 1972.)

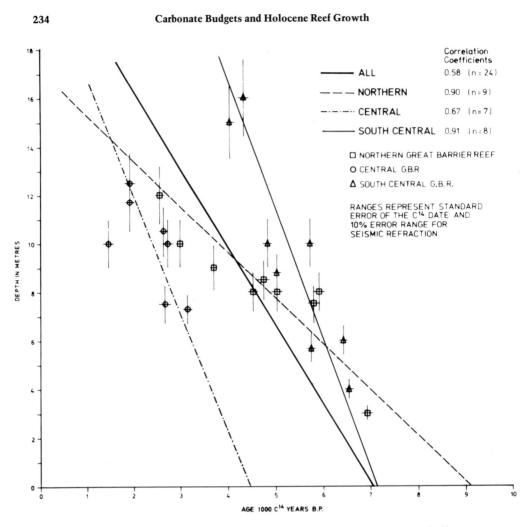

Figure 8.6 Plot of oldest radiocarbon age of windward reef cap against shallowest recorded depth to the pre-Holocene platform.

The effect of this latter factor can be seen in Figure 8.5, which shows the contrasting sea-level curves of Thom and Chappell (1975) from eastern Australia and of Neumann (1971, 1972) from Bermuda. Assuming a maximum vertical accretion rate of 3 mm/yr, then growth from any pre-Holocene platform inundated by the eastern Australian-type sea-level curve will take place at this maximum rate until the reef reaches modern sea level. However, slowly declining rates of sea-level rise shown by the Caribbean-type curve will have allowed any reef growing from a pre-Holocene platform shallower than − 30 m to catch up with the transgression, its subsequent upward growth not being the maximum 3 mm/yr but one determined by the actual rise of sea level.

For this reason, more meaningful results on accretion rates may be obtained by taking data from smaller areas within which variations in growth rates and in sea-level curves may have been minimal. For this reason a threefold regional division of the data is shown in Figure 8.6. The division is by no means arbitrary but is based on significant morphological differences in the reefs as well as in the data used in the analyses. The three regions (Fig. 6.11) and their major characteristic are:

1   The narrow shelf north of Cairns. Ages in excess of 5500 years have already been shown for reef caps in both inner and outer shelfs. Prominent features of the area are the presence of low wooded island reefs on the inner shelf and ribbon reefs on the outer shelf. Little living coral is found on reef tops except in moated positions, and most reef flats are rubbly with wide, thick algal pavements.

2   The broadening shelf south of Cairns to opposite Townsville but not including the innermost reefs from Taylor Reef south. Total area covered by reefs in this region is less than to both north and south, and reef flats form a significantly lower proportion of each reef platform. Moreover, reef tops are lower and covered by dense, living coral veneer. Whereas reefs to north and south reach or exceed the level of MLWS, these reefs generally do not exceed absolute low-tide level by more than 15 cm. No vegetated reef islands are found in this region and only three small unvegetated sand cays exist. Ages obtained for reef cap materials are all less than 2800 years, confirming Fairbridge's (1950, p. 364) suspicion that reefs between Cairns and Townsville are "more juvenile."

3   The south central area of the Great Barrier Reef including the inner reefs from Taylor Reef southward. This is the largest and most diffuse area, but general lack of data prevents further division. Features of this region are the presence of algal pavements, higher more rubbly reef tops, and ages for the reef cap generally in excess of 5000 years.

A further point of differentiation is the nature of the windward reef cap. This is generally a solid algal cemented fabric of low porosity (<45%) in the northern and southern areas, but more fragmented, containing much uncemented sand and shingle and of higher porosity (>60%) in the central region. This can be shown in Figure 8.7 where the proportion of unconsolidated sand and shingle found in the uppermost meter of all reef cores, averaged for each reef, is plotted against the oldest age obtained for each reef. A correlation coefficient (r) of 0.81 (n = 20) is highly significant at the 99% level. One way analysis of variance of data from the three regions shows that there is no statistically significant difference in the depth of the Pleistocene unconformity (although there is a tendency for the reefs in the central region to have deeper foundations, Fig. 7.5) but that the different ages displayed by the reefs are probably not from the same populations (statistically significant at the 99% confidence level).

Results of the plot of age versus platform depth for the northern region (Fig. 8.6) show a correlation coefficient (r) of 0.90 (n = 9), significant at the 99% level. The regression line is resolved by an upward growth rate of 1.9 mm/yr, less than that predicted by modern carbonate budget studies, but midway in the range of rates shown by the geological record for midoceanic atolls and at the lower end of the range of rates shown for shelf reefs (see Table 8.3). The Bewick core recovered too shallow a Holocene depth to provide significant accretion rates, but that on Stapleton Island, although through mainly leeside

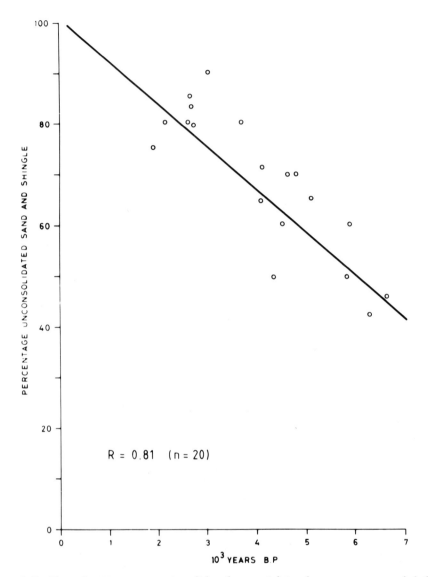

Figure 8.7 Plot of percentage unconsolidated material in the upper meter of drilled windward reef caps against oldest radiocarbon age for the reef cap.

detrital sediments, provided radiocarbon dates of 5,260 ± 130 yrs B.P. from a depth of 12.2 m and 3,130 ± 80 yrs B.P. from 7.9 m (Thom et al., 1978), giving a highly compatible rate of accretion of 2.0 mm/yr.

The plot of oldest radiocarbon data against depth of unconformity for samples from the south central Great Barrier Reef (Fig. 8.6) includes two points for Redbill Reef. This reef has been more intensively surveyed and differences in the depth of the pre-Holocene platform to windward, and partially to lee-ward, allow both sets of data to be used. Again the linearity of the plot is quite clear. The correlation coefficient is 0.91 (n = 8) and the regression line sug-gests an upward growth rate of 5.3 mm/yr. This is remarkably similar to the growth rates from dated cores from Hayman Island, Orpheus Island, Rattle-snake Island, Wheeler Reef and Stanley Reef quoted above.

The confirmation of results from northern and south central regions by borehole information reinforces the anomalous position of the central Reef region (Fig. 8.6). The regression line is based on a correlation coefficient of only 0.67 (n = 7). The suggested growth rate is 4.7 mm/yr, very similar to that of the area to the south. However, although the range of depths of pre-Holocene foundation from which the modern reefs are growing is no different from those of the northern and south-central regions, the ages of the reef tops are clustered far more closely than elsewhere and are significantly younger. No ages greater than 4000 years have been obtained within the upper 3 m from this area and only from Moss Reef, which is considered to be close to the margin of the region, has a radiocarbon age greater than 2720 yrs B.P. been obtained. The significance of this for interpretation of Holocene sea levels is discussed below.

These data suggest two important features for growth of reefs in the Great Barrier Reef province. First, there appears to be a considerable difference in growth rates (vertical accretion) of reefs in southern and northern shelf waters (5 and 2 mm/yr respectively). The reason for the difference in growth rate can only be surmised at the present time. Proximity of the reefs of the northern shelf to the mainland and terrigenous influences in the form of sediment and runoff may be a factor, especially as these reefs would have been very close to the mainland when their pre-Holocene platforms were first submerged. In contrast, on the wider and deeper southern shelf the reefs would have been almost the same distance from the mainland when their pre-Holocene platforms first became submerged. However, geological evidence from around the world suggests that fringing reefs with high terrigenous influence have the most rapid growth rates (see below). Thus the influential factor may not be distance from the mainland but distance from the truly oceanic waters on the outer shelf. None of the reefs sampled in the northern area was more than 40 km from the shelf edge and three (Carter, Lark Pass, and Opal) were situated in close proximity to the edge. In contrast the southern reefs sampled were all from inner shelf (Hayman) or midshelf (Taylor, Barnett, Wheeler, Stanley, Darley, and Redbill) locations, and only two (Barnett and Wheeler) are within 45 km of the shelf edge, the remainder being more than 100 km distance. However, the reason for proximity to the shelf edge being important in determining slower growth rates is not clear, although it is the pattern also shown by growth rates of corals at the present time (see Chap. 3). The small-scale upwelling of waters along the shelf edge discussed in Chapter 2 is most likely to affect the outermost reefs. Insight into the effect such waters may have on coral reef growth has recently been given by Kinsey and Davies (1979b). They showed that long term phosphate and nitrogen enrichment can cause more than 50% suppression of reef calcification and suggest that this effect, together with algal competition and the more usually accepted depression of temperature, is involved in reducing the growth rates of reefs adjacent to upwellings. They also suggested that more intense circulation and increased upwelling, particularly along the equatorial divergence, took place close to the glacial maximum so that the effect may have been more intense during the early part of the Holocene transgression. The relatively slow rates of growth shown by open ocean atolls (Table 8.3) may also be related to the same phenomenon.

IMPLICATIONS FOR SEA LEVEL VARIATION
ON THE OUTER SHELF

Retardation of growth rates cannot explain the nature of the results from the outer shelf between Cairns and Townsville. Indeed, a slow growth rate from platforms of variable depth should have resulted in a spreading of reef ages rather than their clustering. A possible explanation for the young reef-top ages and their apparent clustering is that each reef, growing from pre-Holocene platforms of varying depths at a growth rate of about 5 mm/yr, caught up with a rise in sea level that was considerably behind that indicated by Thom and Chappell (1975). Modern sea level in this region may have been achieved as late as 2500 yrs B.P., almost 4000 years later than on the adjacent mainland and on the shelf reefs to the north and south. The rise to modern sea level in this region is unknown. The oldest radiocarbon date obtained from the Reef here was from a depth of 2.75 m on Moss Reef, which gave an age of 3910 ± 120 yrs B.P. However, this reef has an age of 3230 ± 140 yrs B.P. for in situ coral only 25 cm below the reef flat and lies very close to what is considered to be the margin of this region of retarded sea level rise. Sea level envelopes may be constructed for different parts of the Great Barrier Reef, by using the growth rates indicated and extrapolating from the reef-top age and depth to the pre-Holocene platform, to calculate the age of the initial submergence of the platform. Thus an upward growth rate of 4.7 mm/yr would suggest that growth from the − 10 m level on Bowl and Viper Reefs did not commence until at least 4900 yrs B.P. and possibly even later on other reefs of this region.

In contrast on the Reef north of Cairns control to the transgression is given by the oldest radiocarbon date for in situ reef top materials on Low Wooded Island (6080 ± 90 yrs B.P.) and Fisher Island further north (6310 ± 90), indicating modern sea level had been achieved by this date (Polach et al., 1978) and the 6920 ± 130 yrs B.P. date from − 3 m on Bewick (Thom et al., 1978). Extrapolation from the reef top dates, growth rates, and platform depths produces an age of 8900 yrs B.P. for submergence of the − 12 m level, and 8300 yrs B.P. for submergence at − 10 m. Divergence of inner- and outer-shelf curves also takes place subsequent to 6000 yrs B.P. Inner shelf reefs indicate about 1.5 m of emergence about 3500 yrs B.P., while outer reefs show no emergent features. The possibility that emergent reef on the outer ribbon reefs has been eroded must be considered unlikely, not only because of the total lack of evidence over such a long and continuous stretch of reef, but also because the growth curves based on shallow cores (Fig. 8.2) suggests no such truncation. It has been previously noted that the reefs, as they approach within 1 m of sea level, show a rapid decline in upward growth. If the outer ribbons has been truncated by 1 m or more then the upper meter or so of present reef should not show this slowing down in growth rate. In fact this is not so and both Carter and Lark Pass Reefs appear to have grown to a sea level very close to that of present between 6000 and 5800 yrs B.P.

Very similar results are found for the inner reefs south of Taylor Reef and the southern central Great Barrier Reef. Using the oldest reef-top dates, the depth to the pre-Holocene unconformity and a growth rate of 5.3 mm/yr it would appear that the 6 m platform on Stanley Reef was inundated by c. 7500 yrs and the 10 m platform on Darley Reef by c. 7850 yrs. Results from other reefs widen the envelope of the transgression but control to the transgression estimate here is given by the date of 6210 ± 140 yrs B.P. for the reef cap on Darley Reef and the date of 9320 ± 730 yrs B.P. for the submergence of the − 15.7 m platform on Hayman. Further, the early approach to modern sea level is confirmed by two dates greater than 7000 years for materials in the upper 3.05m from reefs in this region; 7420 ± 190 yrs B.P. from 3.05 on Taylor Reef and 7160 ± 170 yrs B.P. from 2.2 m on Stanley Reef.

It is possible that emergence is indicated at Redbill Reef, although the high tidal range here (5 m) makes the evidence difficult to decipher. The reef is shown in Figure 9.7, and a section through the high (2.5 m) algal rim shown in Figure 8.8. Open water corals grow to MLWS on this reef (0.5 m) but moated corals behind the algal rim to 2.6 m. However, in situ corals occur beneath the rim at heights of 2.1 and 1.7 m, and these have been dated at 4570 ± 150 yrs B.P. and 3920 ± 150 yrs B.P. respectively. The corals are *Goniastrea* sp. and *Favia* sp., both found along the open water reef crest as well as in the lagoon. These corals were growing 1.2 to 1.6 m above the present level of open water coral growth about 4000 yrs B.P. As they occur close to the outer edge of the algal rim, if an algal rim existed at that time, it must have been extremely narrow or have been eroded subsequently. An equally plausible explanation is provided by a higher relative sea level of about 1.5 m 4000 yrs B.P. along a continuation of the line of the faulted eastern side of Broad Sound, a line that is continued also by the emerged evidence on the intermediate continental islands.

The data provided by the reefs, when combined with the results from the inner shelf (Fig. 6.10), make possible an approximation of the regional pattern of shelf warping (Fig. 8.9). Delineated are the areas of higher sea level evidence and the degree of emergence shown at 2 m intervals. All these are inner shelf areas and lie inside the line indicating modern sea level being achieved by 6000 yrs B.P. Small areas of the inner shelf north of Cairns show only minimal emergence (<2 m). The shelf between Cairns and Hinchinbrook Island shows no emergence at all. Maximum emergence is in the Townsville-Bowen area and east of Broad Sound. This latter area of Holocene emergence (see Chap. 6) extends out towards the Great Barrier Reefs to include Redbill Reef.

The area within which modern sea level was reached by 6000 yrs B.P. includes the whole of the outer shelf south to Opal Reef but probably little of the shelf between Cairns and Dunk Island. To the south this area extends out across the shelf to include the inner reefs from Taylor Reef southward, an extremely steep gradient of warping being indicated on the inner shelf in this area. Lack of dates older than 5000 yrs B.P. south of Hayman Island suggests that the outer limit of the area within the 6000 yrs B.P. isoline may curve towards the mainland in this area in the vicinity of the Hillsborough Basin. The oldest dates of 5450 ± 85 yrs B.P. from the western side of Broad Sound (Cook and Mayo, 1977) suggests that here too modern sea level may have been first achieved after 6000 yrs B.P.

An important feature of the data discussed in this section is the strong possibility of subsidence on the outer shelf of the central Reef region producing a depressed sea level curve in comparison to adjacent areas. This type of movement, producing lower reef heights on the outer shelf and younger reef forms,

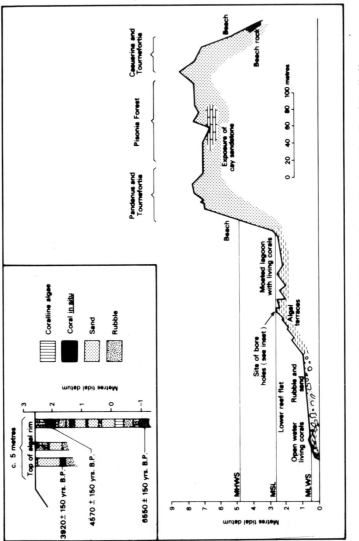

Figure 8.8 Surveyed sections through the algal rim and cay (Bushy Island) of Redbill Reef, suggesting the presence of an emerged mid-Holocene reef beneath the rim.

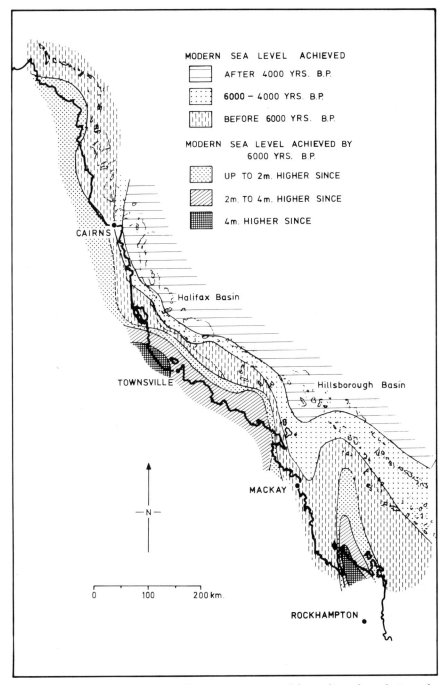

Figure 8.9 Regional pattern of shelf warping suggested by radiocarbon dating of subaerial deposits of inner shelf and reef caps of outer shelf.

has been suggested for the northern shelf by Spender (1930) who noted not only that an abrupt point of change along the Great Barrier Reef occurs off Cairns (p. 275) but also that outer reefs were significantly lower than inner-shelf reefs (p. 286). Even earlier, Hedley (1925i) had commented on the paucity of sand cays and nature of reef development at about 17° to 18°S suggesting that "this section of the Great Barrier Reef is recovering from a drowning movement" (p. 159). Fairbridge (1950) stated that the reefs south of Cairns "are more juvenile than those in the northern sectors" (p. 364). Reef morphology on the outer shelf consistent with subsidence between Cairns and Townsville is discussed in more detail in Chapter 9, but was noted as early as 1847 by Jukes. Paradice (1925) produced a map of the outer shelf between 17°00 and 17°20′ S (Fig. 9.9) showing a southern extension of ribbon reefs, but submerged to depths of at least 18 m, the "drowned outer barrier" of Fairbridge (1950, p. 367) who went on to comment that it "suggests very rapid subsidence locally" (p. 391). Such subsidence is predicted by models of hydro-isostasy, particularly in this area by Thom and Chappell (1978) as discussed in Chapter 6. They suggest that on the shelf edge north of Townsville depression of the order of 1 m based on a continental lithospheric model and 3 m based on an oceanic lithospheric model may have taken place since 6000 yrs B.P. Reef growth of 5 mm/yr would have resulted in reefs being able to make up 3 m of growth in only 600 years, but as the central region reefs lag behind their northern counterparts by up to 4000 years it is possible that downwarping as great as 20 m has occurred. This likely subsidence has produced the effect of a slowly rising sea level to about 2500 yrs B.P. with reefs catching up with the transgression and growing upwards with sea level rise. This may be due to more than hydro-isostasy. On the inner shelf it has been noted that the differential movements are closely linked with major structural features (see Chap. 6 and Hopley, 1974b). This is also probable on the outer shelf for it is exactly the portion of continental shelf in question that is impinged upon by the active Halifax Basin, forming part of the Townsville Trough (see Figs. 2.1 and 6.11). Subsidence in this area is possible throughout the Quaternary and earlier.

The effects of this warping over the shelf are seen in the differences not only in ages of reef tops, but also in their heights. General differences have been previously noted by Hedley (1925i), Edgell (1928a), Spender (1930) and Fairbridge (1950). This is seen even more clearly in Figure 8.10, which shows maximum height of in situ coral (including fossil corals of mid-Holocene age) across four transects normal to the trend of the shelf, together with the known maximum age of the reef cap. Inner-shelf reefs are clearly higher and, on the Townsville and Bowen transects, older. Maximum heights are found at the innermost sites of these southern transects but at almost a midshelf location on the two northern transects, although this may be an artifact of the limited data. The elevation of the 6000 yrs B.P. reef level on the inner shelf and its depression on the outer shelf except to the north of Cairns where its height is very close to modern sea level is clearly shown. This is a pattern very similar to that predicted by Thom and Chappell's (1978) hydro-isostatic calculations.

Although these figures for shelf warping are, at best, first approximations only, they do indicate that Holocene earth movements need acknowledgment in any attempt to explain the evolution of the Great Barrier Reef. Of equal importance are the variations in rates of vertical accretion that have occurred on

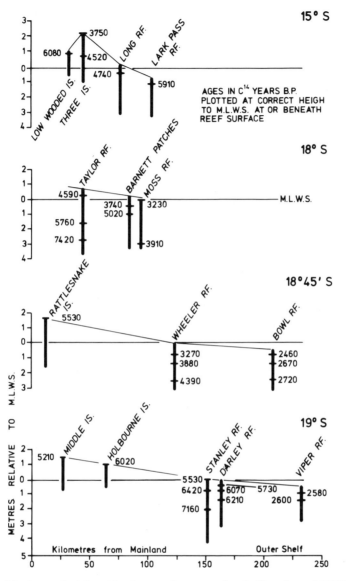

Figure 8.10 Maximum height of in situ corals across the shelf at about 15°00′, 18°00′, 18°45′ and 19°00′S, clearly showing decline in height to seaward. Radiocarbon ages of reef caps are shown where available.

the Great Barrier Reef. Both these factors have helped to produce the regional diversity of reef types and morphological zones that are the basis of the discussion in Chapters 9 and 10.

TOWARDS A MODEL OF LATE QUATERNARY EVOLUTION OF THE GREAT BARRIER REEFS

Chapters 6, 7, and 8 have presented the available data on the most important features of reef development during the late Quaternary. In spite of the enormous size of the Great Barrier Reef, great advances have been made in the last 10 years towards understanding the way in which the reefs have evolved, particularly when ideas from other corals reef areas are added to those developed solely on the Australian scene. An idealized evolution for a shelf reef over the last 125,000 years is seen in Figure 8.11. It comprises nine stages:

1   125,000 yrs B.P.   The development of coral reefs with morphology similar

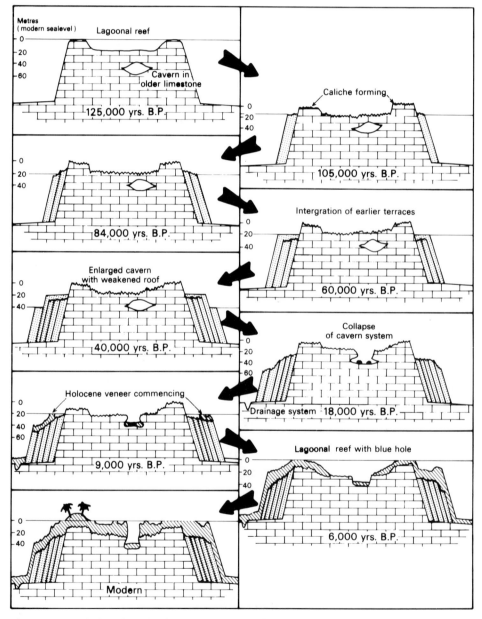

Figure 8.11   Idealized model for the evolution of a shelf reef from the last interglacial to the present.

to reefs of today took place over older coralline limestone foundations to a sea level about 5 m higher than today. These reefs in turn have formed the foundations for Holocene reefs and their upper surfaces are generally 10 m below modern sea level. This is the result of both erosion and shelf subsidence at a rate of about 0.12 m/1000 years. This rate is used as a basis for all further stages of reef development subsequent to 125,000 yrs B.P.

2 **105,000 yrs B.P.** After a lower sea level, which allowed the first weathering and diagenesis of the 125,000 yr reef, an interstadial transgression resulted in the formation of small fringing reefs to about − 14 m around the older reef core. At this stage the surface of the 125,000 yr reef had been lowered by about 2 m. Caliche developed over the surface of the outer rim but some solutional deepening of the old lagoon may have taken place.

3 **84,000 yrs B.P.** A lowering of sea level 105,000–84,000 yrs B.P. resulted in more weathering and alteration. The 125,000 year reef had been lowered by about 5 m, the 105,000 year terrace by 2.5 m. Sea level at 84,000 yrs B.P. was about − 20 m and new fringing reef that developed may have been less than 3 m lower than the outcropping 105,000 year reef.

4 **60,000 yrs B.P.** The recurrence of a − 20 m sea level during this interstadial transgression probably resulted in the integration of both earlier interstadial terraces into a single morphological feature. By this time, the 125,000 year reef had been lowered by almost 8 m, the 105,000 year terrace by 5 m (to − 20 m) and the 84,000 year terrace by 3 m. Thus a − 20 m sea level would have transgressed over both earlier terraces, adding a very thin veneer to them and building outward to produce what should have been a significant morphological feature.

5 **40,000 yrs B.P.** This complex interstadial period probably resulted in the extension of the c. − 20 m terrace as the sea probably reached this level for a short period. At the very least it may have provided a further veneer to the 60,000 terrace, which in the intervening period would have been lowered by about 2 m. In addition a further terrace at about − 40 m was probably added to the reef. By now the older 125,000 year reef was at a level of about − 5 m relative to present sea level. Minor karst landforms had possibly developed, reinforcing the original constructional morphology. The rise and fall of sea level had produced migration of the vadose and phreatic zones and alteration of at least the 125,000 year limestone was probably advanced.

6 **18,000 yrs B.P.** At this lowest sea-level stage the reef would have been completely emerged as a limestone hill on an extended coastal plain. A deep vadose zone existed allowing enlargement of any pre- 125,000 year cave systems on larger reefs. Without the support of water it is possible that a few older cave systems collapsed, producing the dolines that during the Holocene transgression were to become blue holes.

7 **9,000 yrs B.P.** By now the 125,000 year reef had been lowered to almost − 10 m relative to modern sea level, the compound terrace which had formed at − 20 m levels (the latest c. 40,000 yrs B.P.) to almost − 24 m and the − 40 m terrace to about − 44 m. Sea level at 9000 yrs B.P. was about − 20 m and had risen rapidly to this level. Minimal reef growth had possibly taken place on the deepest terrace but flooding of the compound terrace had commenced

and probably resulted in luxuriant reef growth. The oldest reef core remained as a low limestone island, but it too was to be submerged within 2000 years.

8 **6000 yrs** B.P. Modern sea level had been achieved, but the rate of transgression had left behind the upward growth of reefs. The reef crest was several meters below sea level, probably growing at the maximum possible rate with a further distinctive terrace about 15 m below it. Blue holes and solutionally deepened paleolagoons were submerged and being colonized by Holocene reef organisms.

9 **The present day** Over the last 6000 years reefs have reached modern sea level and vertical growth has been converted into lagoon filling and horizontal growth, particularly on the leeward side. Growth from the compound terrace has also reached sea level on most reefs, adding to the horizontal extent of reef flats. Where growth has been slower, Holocene construction from this terrace, and possibly from the deeper paleofringing reef, may be just reaching modern sea level, forming a distinctive line of outer reefs beyond the main reef front. Where extensive reef flats have formed, deposition of rubble on the reef margins and sand on the lee side has resulted in island formation. Locally, the moating of water levels behind shingle ramparts or algal rims has led to the deposition of a final, slightly higher veneer of coral laid down in microatoll form. Variation in the morphology and size of the older reef foundations, and in rates of accretion and sea level fluctuation during the Holocene, have produced the diversity of reef types found in the modern Great Barrier Reef.

9

Coral Reef Classification and Reef Types

Classification of landforms has been a central feature of traditional geomorphology, leading to genetic explanation and recognition of regional variation. It is surprising to find, therefore, that the extremely broad and simple classification of Darwin (1842) is still in common use for describing reef forms. Within each class of reef, fringing, barrier, or atoll, there is much morphological diversity. This is particularly true of the reefs of continental shelves that fall generally within the barrier reef division of Darwin, and nowhere is the diversity as great as in the Great Barrier Reef of Australia. Two significant attempts have been made to produce a genetic classification of these reefs. A simple classification by Fairbridge (1950, 1967) was elaborated and extended by Maxwell (1968). Although both classifications were based on a premise of a purely Holocene origin for the Great Barrier Reef, in broad outline, if not in detail, their progression of reef form with time is similar to that which is presented here based on criteria discussed in the three previous chapters. Variations in reef morphology are the result of factors such as the depth and morphology of the pre-Holocene foundation from which the reef is growing, the exact nature of the sea-level rise during the Holocene since the foundations were inundated, and the rate of production of calcium carbonate. Acknowledgment of these factors may allow recognition of regional variations in their distribution from the spatial patterns of reef forms displayed by the Great Barrier Reef.

THE CLASSIFICATIONS OF FAIRBRIDGE AND MAXWELL

The classifications of both Fairbridge (1950, 1967) and Maxwell (1968) are based on organic and sedimentary growth of reefs in response to prevailing wind and wave conditions during a single period of relatively stable eustatic sea level. This latter point is most important because both authors, either directly or by implication, presume that the reefs have developed exclusively during the Holocene and it is presumed that during each glacial low sea level stage preexisting reefs have been removed by erosion. Fairbridge (1950, p. 359) states:

In attempting to interpret these reef stages, it should be borne in mind that on the Queensland shelf area a relative degree of stability has persisted probably throughout the Recent epoch, at least during the last four thousand years. Furthermore, the sea level remained nearly constant, having dropped only 10 feet over this period. Accordingly the developments in surficial reef morphology during the last four thousand years cannot be related to major changes in level of land or sea. The evolution of reef morphology can thus be related to the molding action of the wind, waves and currents.

His classification envisages reefs developing downwind detrital horns, which on larger reefs at least will form open lagoons. With time, lagoons become enclosed and finally infilled by sedimentation and organic growth.

Similarly, the more elaborate classification of Maxwell is based around the premise that:

> organic reefs, once initiated, will expand in directions controlled by the hydrologic—bathymetric—biological balance.
>
> *Maxwell, 1968, p. 99*

Eustatic changes were seen as providing only modification to these basic controls. Maxwell considered the whole reef column to be Holocene in age, as is clearly seen from his attempt to relate stratigraphic breaks in the Heron Island core to fluctuations in the Fairbridge sea level curve (Maxwell, 1973a, p. 267). A higher Holocene sea level is recognized in producing the higher reef surfaces with heavy detrital blanket in the Inner Shelf and Near Shore Zones, features that Maxwell considered to have been eroded from more exposed outer reefs. The possibility of reef truncation on these reefs has already been dismissed (Chap. 8). The ultimate fate of the shelf reef is "resorbtion," an enigmatic term not fully explained by Maxwell but suggesting retarded reef growth or even:

> the extinction of reef organisms and the progressive resorbtion of the reef mass.
>
> *Maxwell, 1968, p. 107*

This has been interpreted by Bloom (1974) as "geochemical resorption" (sic) and apparently refers to the erosion by solution of the older reef mass. Such a process is also suggested as forming the shallow lagoons of platform reefs by "reef decay."

That once reefs have reached modern sea level, their growth is strongly influenced by winds, waves, and tides is not disputed, but to give these ambient environmental factors prime place in a genetic classification, as Fairbridge and Maxwell have done, too greatly subordinates the other factors of substrate control, sea level change, and growth-rate variation. In the previous chapters it was these influences that were shown to have greatest control over present reef morphology and it is these factors and their variations that need to be considered in any genetic classification. Growth from embryonic colonies to mature platform, ring, or mesh reefs requires more time than is available during the Holocene alone. Maxwell's (1976) claim that growth on the Great Barrier Reef is more rapid than elsewhere is not substantiated by the facts discussed in the previous chapter.

If Maxwell's scheme represents an evolutionary sequence then resorbed reefs should be the oldest reefs of the Great Barrier Reef province and small platform reefs and wall or cuspate reefs among the youngest. Radiocarbon dating of the upper reef cap as discussed in Chapter 8 indicates almost the reverse pattern. Resorbed reefs are young (see below) and are growing from deeper pre-Holocene platforms in areas where shelf subsidence is significant and/or in areas where reef accretion rates are low. In contrast some of the reef forms that should be youngest from Maxwell's interpretation have been at or close to modern sea level for more than 6000 years.

THE FRAMEWORK OF A GENETIC CLASSIFICATION

At the end of Chapter 8 an outline of the probable evolution of coral reefs over the last 120,000 years was given. Morphology of modern reefs is derived to a large extent from the morphology of their antecedents. The extent to which this antecedent morphology has been initially mimicked and later masked by Holocene growth is the basic framework for a classification of shelf reefs. Flood (1977a), Flood and Orme (1977), and Jell and Flood (1978) incorporated tectonic, isostatic, and biological growth as variables in an explanation of the succession of reef types (Fig. 9.1). The rise or fall of sea level relative to an upward-growing reef was seen as producing a succession of reef types that may be reversed by a change in direction of the rise or fall of relative sea level. Over most of the Great Barrier Reef the course of evolution during the Holocene has been one of drowning of pre-Holocene reefal platforms beneath a eustatic sea level rise aided locally by isostatic subsidence. Initially the reef morphology closely mimics that of the underlying platform with planar surfaces producing platforms reefs, antecedent platforms with shallow depressions producing lagoonal platform reefs, and broad surfaces with very deep, centrally located depressions producing closed ring reefs (all terms referring to morphological types of Maxwell). If the rate of vertical reef growth equals the rate of relative sea-level rise, the reef type will persist. If the reef growth is greater than this rise then the sequence through which the morphology progresses is $1 \rightarrow 2 \rightarrow 3 \rightarrow 4$, starting at whatever reef type was in existence when the reef first reached sea level. Where reef growth is overtaken by the relative sea level rise then the sequence may be reversed.

This simplistic model does much to explain the progression of morphology developed over antecedent platforms of moderate size and generally oval shape. Not only does it use the terms of Maxwell, but it also parallels the sequence suggested by that author for the development of closed ring and closed mesh reefs. Radiocarbon dating of reef tops of this type suggests that the sequence may be correct. However, a major criticism of the scheme of Flood and co-authors is the basic presumption that growth over a pre-Holocene surface after drowning is of the same magnitude over the whole platform, thus leading to a maintenance of form after drowning. Data presented in Chapter 8 indicated that initial growth can be expected on the windward reef margins and

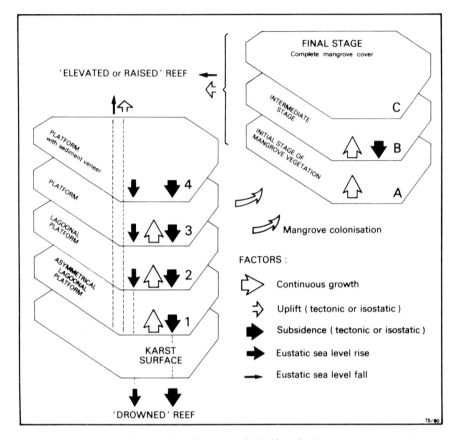

Figure 9.1 Framework for the classification of shelf reefs showing major evolutionary influences, from Flood (1977a). The scheme illustrates the development of successive reef types as a function of tectonic, isostatic, eustatic, and biological growth variables.

slower rates will operate elsewhere. Thus, in time, as a reef is drowned, whatever the initial morphology, a crescentic reef form will develop and after reaching a stable modern sea level, slowly change into an open ring, then closed-ring type as growth elsewhere around the margin reaches sea level. A related criticism of the scheme of Flood and his co-authors is that the ringlike morphology of modern reefs is not necessarily a pattern controlled entirely by the morphology of the pre-Holocene surface. Although this has been shown in Chapter 7 to be true in many examples, growth patterns may also produce similar morphology.

Degree of lagoon development is a major diagnostic feature in reef classification and to a large extent is related to size of the antecedent platform. The largest pre-Holocene reef platforms have been capable of developing complex relief consisting of multiple enclosed depressions while smaller platforms may develop simpler saucerlike morphology consisting of a single depression. Smallest reef platforms may not have any central depression. The question of origin of these depressions, whether growth-induced or the result of karst erosion is immaterial. To determine the size of reef platform required to produce single and multiple depressions, 150 reefs were randomly selected between latitudes 15°S and 24°S. None had reached a planar stage of development, that is, had extensive reef flats, but had considerable areas of reef top close to present sea level. Fifty had multiple lagoon cells, 50 had single lagoon cells and 50 had no lagoon. Results are seen in Table 9.1. The groups are clearly differentiated on a size basis, although some overlap between groupings occurs. As a general rule, however, the analysis suggests that multiple cells are developed on reef tops with widths greater than 3.25 km, single cells on reef widths between 1.75 and 3.25 km and no lagoons on reefs less than 1.75 km wide.

Discussion in the previous chapter suggested that development of Holocene reefs from antecedent platforms may involve several stages. Dependent upon a series of complex interrelated factors, present reefs may be at any stage in the sequence. Initial colonization of the antecedent surface after inundation may be slow. There follows a period of growth in which the relief of the antecedent surface is enhanced until the reef reaches sea level. If sea level is still rising then a proportion of the carbonate productivity will continue to be directed into upward reef growth the amount depending on the rate of sea-level rise. The residual amount will be transported leewards. As sea level stabilizes, the amount transported laterally, especially from the productive reef margins, will increase and from this stage onward, presuming sea level remains stable, the reef evolution processes are ones of lagoon infilling and obliteration of the inherited relief of the pre-Holocene substrate.

The stage of a modern reef is dependent on many factors. Of paramount importance is the depth of the antecedent surface. As the sea level rise during much of the Holocene transgression may have outstripped the capability of reefs for upward growth, the reefs growing from the shallowest platforms are most likely to have greatest lateral as opposed to vertical growth, which will mask the underlying morphology. Variation in carbonate productivity will also be a factor. In extreme cases Holocene growth may be nonexistant but at the other extreme may be measured in centimeters per year, based on the most rapid growth rates quoted for Caribbean fringing reefs. Again, the more productive reefs are most likely to have masked their pre-Holocene foundations. The final major factor is the variation that may have occurred in the relative sea-level curve. Where subsidence has taken place, growth from the antecedent platform may have been essentially vertical from the topographic highs on this platform, and even though this growth may have been most rapid on the windward margins, the gross morphology of the antecedent platform may have been retained. In contrast, only where modern sea level has been relatively stable

Table 9.1 Width of Reef Platforms without Lagoons, with Single Lagoons and Multiple Lagoons

	Sample Size	Mean Width (km)	σ	Minimum Width (km)	Maximum Width (km)
No lagoon	50	1.05	0.58	0.25	3.25
Single lagoon	50	2.53	0.73	1.25	4.25
Multiple lagoons	50	4.93	2.00	2.25	12.75

for over 5000 years, has there been opportunity for significant lateral growth on the reefs that have reached sea level, and on these the process of masking of pre-Holocene relief by lateral growth will have progressed significantly. Together these factors produce a continuum from no modification whatsoever of the relief of the antecedent platform where Holocene colonization has not taken place, through a stage where Holocene growth mimics the relief of the platform during upward growth, to a final stage where the preexisting relief is masked by Holocene growth, largely through lateral reef accretion including transport of sediments from the most productive windward margins.

It is not necessary for all reefs to go through all the stages as indicated. Acceleration of the earlier phases takes place if the antecedent platform is particularly shallow and enhancement of its relief is not possible. Similarly the later phases may be accelerated by a relative fall in sea level, exposing more reef flat and hastening the production of sediment for infilling of lagoons. However, much depends on reef size. As indicated in the previous chapter the most productive zones are on the reef margins (algal and living coral areas), which may be limited in the width which they can attain. Therefore, for any given depth of lagoon a major factor in the rate of infilling will be the ratio between productive reef margin and lagoon area. This ratio is smallest on the largest reefs, which may thus take the longest time to mask the initial relief forms and infill their lagoons.

A CLASSIFICATION OF HOLOCENE SHELF REEFS

Based on the criteria discussed above, a classification of Holocene shelf reefs is presented in Figure 9.2. It presumes that the majority of reefs are located over pre-Holocene reefal foundations at no great depth and is set in the eustatic history of the Holocene; that is, a period of transgression over these antecedent platforms.

Three phases of Holocene reef development are recognized in the classification. In the juvenile phases initial colonization takes place on the antecedent foundation and upward growth of the reef lags behind sea-level rise, enhancing the original relief of the foundation. In the mature phases reefs reach modern sea level and develop reef flats over the highs in the antecedent surface and especially around the reef margins. One or more lagoons typify this phase but in the later stages of maturity lateral transport of sediment from the productive margins leads to initial infilling of lagoons, masking of the inherited relief forms, and widening of reef flats. The senile phase is reached when lagoons are infilled completely and lateral movement of sediment from the windward margins is leading to progradation to leeward.

The basic classification is applicable to medium-size reefs growing from antecedent platforms with single depressions, which were indicated above as being generally within the diameter range of 1.75–3.25 km. Smaller reefs, where antecedent surfaces may lack a protolagoonal relief may develop along similar lines but because the width of reef flat initially developed around the reefal margins may occupy such a high proportion of the total reef area any lagoon that forms will be shallow and quickly filled and the mature phases will be

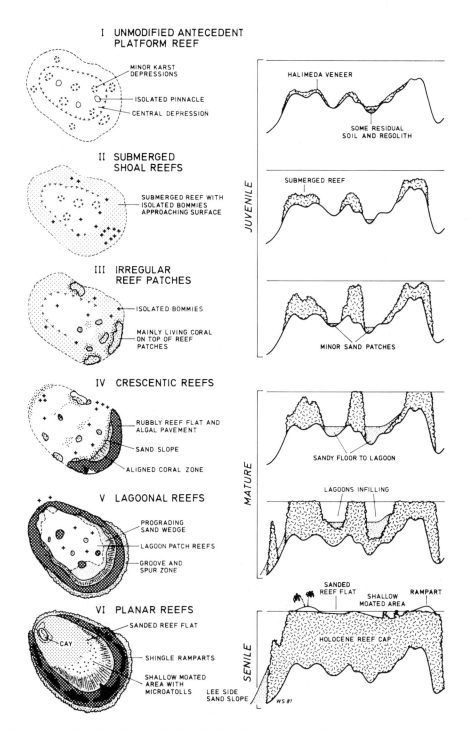

Figure 9.2 Classification of shelf reefs. It is based on a medium-sized antecedent platform. Larger reefs may develop more than one lagoonal cell whereas smallest reefs may not pass through a lagoonal phase.

either bypassed or be present for only a very short period. In contrast, the largest reefs will be at the mature stages for the longest period because of the low ratio of productive margin to lagoon area. These reefs may also differ from the basic classification during the mature phase by having more than one lagoon.

A major subgroup of reefs are ribbon reefs. They grow from linear foundations that are either discrete antecedent platforms or higher rims on much larger and usually deeper platforms. The basic feature is depth of water behind the narrow reef flat that develops from the foundations. Although sediment moves to leeward, accretion is very slow and widening of the reef flat is retarded. However, the three stages in the development of a ribbon reef can be equated with those in the basic classification (Fig. 9.2).

Juvenile

1 **Unmodified Antecedent Platform Reef** All reefs must go through this stage during their initial submergence. The relief is almost completely that of the antecedent platform and may include mesoscale karst features. Soil and regolith formed during subaerial exposure will be removed.

2 **Submerged Shoal Reefs** Enhancement of relief has commenced as the reef accretes vertically at its maximum rate, particularly around the windward margins of the platform.

3 **Irregular Reef Patches** It can be expected that the reef will reach modern sea level and commence the development of reef flat very irregularly. Even if growth were at the same rate over the whole reef shoal, irregularities in the initial platform surface would lead to a period of patchy reef development. Windward margins may have advantages in terms of growth rates (see Chap. 8) and the patches may develop here first. However, if significantly higher prominences occurred elsewhere on the antecedent platform then those areas may be the first to develop reef patches.

Mature

1 **Crescentic Reefs** Once at sea level the advantages for growth on the windward margins are fully realized and coalescence of initial reef patches in this area quickly takes place, forming the first hard-line margin to the reef. Lateral movement of sediment commences very quickly and progradation of a sand wedge into the central reef area is initiated. This central area becomes increasingly enclosed as the reef perimeter develops. In the lee of the crescentic hard-line reef, rates of upward growth may be accelerated as reef patches become dominated by branching corals and a more porous reef framework is laid down.

2 **Lagoonal Reefs** Closing of the reef flat around the marginal rim on the leeward side creates a lagoonal reef. Wave refraction around the hard-line reef margins produces extension of the prograding sand wedges into the lagoon but internal carbonate productivity of the enclosed area may now be decreased. Leeward accretion may commence as sediment is carried beyond the original margins of the antecedent platform, aided by scattered coral growth from these new foundations being provided by the sediment trains.

With increasing development of reef flat and sand wedges, segmentation of the original lagoons may take place during the latter stages of maturity.

Senile

1 **Planar Reefs** Final choking of lagoons takes place with complete sediment infill and coalescence of lagoonal patch reefs. Living coral veneers on the reef flat become restricted as a blanket of sediment covers the whole of the reef top. Intermittent and irregular phases of microatoll development may occur as moating of parts of the reef top takes place as a consequence of shingle rampart formation. The height of the reef flat may thus be elevated above the level at which open water corals grow. As most of the reef-top production of carbonate sediments is now removed to the leeward side of the reef, the senile reef form may continue to grow downwind, the exact pattern depending upon the local hydrological conditions.

EXAMPLES AND COMPLEXITIES

Juvenile Reefs

All reef types with a great range of dimensions occur in the Great Barrier Reef, clearly indicating the complexity and regional variations in the factors that influence Holocene reef development. The least known are the juvenile, unmodified antecedent platform reefs. The only areas where extensive banks are found with presumably karstic relief is on the northern Great Barrier Reef where they occur in water depths of 20–40 m and in places extend to the edge of the continental shelf, merging into the platform from which the ribbon reefs rise (see Chap. 7 and Fig. 7.16). It is possible that many other uncolonized surfaces exist at greater depths or in more turbid waters in the Great Barrier Reef province.

Reasons for a lack of Holocene growth can only be surmized. Fairbridge (1950, 1967) suggested that such reefless (i.e. without modern growth) areas in the northern Great Barrier Reef were at depths over which the rising postglacial sea transgressed very rapidly, not giving time for the establishment of reef colonies and being subsequently too deep for colonization by the major reef builders. However elsewhere on the Great Barrier Reef, Holocene reefs have developed from Pleistocene surfaces of about the same depth, and even a depth of 40 m should place these platforms within the zone in which some reef growth is presently possible.

Many submerged reef ridges and banks on which little growth is presently taking place have been described in the Caribbean (Macintyre, 1972). Both Pleistocene and early Holocene ages have been placed on these reefs but the lack of mid to late Holocene growth may throw some light on the lack of colonization on Great Barrier Reef banks. The explanation given by Lighty (1977a,b) and Lighty et al. (1978, 1979a,b) lays prime emphasis on the rapid increase in turbidity with transgression over the shelf behind the reefs established on the shelf edge in early Holocene times and reworking of soils and lagoon deposits. A subsidiary factor is temperature, as the presence of tropical bryozoans in the early Holocene reefs suggests warmer waters at this time. After transgression over the shelf, shallow waters would have been more susceptible to winter cooling. However, further south at St. Croix, the similar cessation of growth of an early Holocene reef at about the same time is unlikely to be associated with water temperatures, reinforcing the explanation of increased turbidity as waters first flooded the shallow shelf (Adey et al., 1977b). Adey (1978a) has stressed that inundation of surfaces of carbonate platforms during deglaciation results in deterioration of water quality, impeding growth of marginal reefs.

Most of the reefal platforms lacking Holocene growth in the Great Barrier Reef province occur north of latitude 15°00′S, exclusively within the area where continuous shelf-edge ribbon reefs are found. As in St. Croix, reduced water temperatures during the early Holocene when the platforms were first flooded is an unlikely cause for the lack of recolonization. High turbidity, however, is most probable. It has already been suggested (Chap. 6) that interstadial sea levels of the last glacial period produced shallow lagoonal conditions on and around these banks. Lagoonal sediments and soils produced when the banks were exposed would have provided adequate material for high turbidity levels during the early part of the Holocene transgression. In Chapter 7 it was shown that the ribbon reefs overlie a distinctive pre-Holocene shelf-edge rim rising to about − 10 m. This would have precluded any possibility of high energy conditions in the early Holocene, quickly removing the fines and, after a relatively short-lived period of turbidity, allowing recolonization of reef organisms. Instead, at the time when water depths should have been ideal for recolonization, a nearly continuous line of limestone islands would still have existed just seaward, maintaining shallow lagoonal conditions similar to those existing during interstadial high sea-level episodes. From the continuous seismic profiles reported by Orme et al. (1978 a,b), it would seem that a sediment cover still exists over these platforms (Chap. 7). Simultaneously, as the northern Great Barrier Reef shelf was first flooded in early Holocene times, there is the indication that rainfall in North Queensland was increasing (Chap. 6). High sediment yield and increased flow of fresh water from the mainland, after a period of relatively arid glacial conditions, would have added to the deterioration of water quality in the shelf area, conditions that may have improved only during the short period after the outer limestone island chain was submerged and before the ribbon reefs growing from them caught up with modern sea level. The present status and distribution of reefs in the northern Great Barrier Reef is discussed below, but the reestablishment of restricted circulation behind the outer barrier, especially on the narrow shelf north of Princess Charlotte Bay, may be responsible for the general paucity of Holocene reefal structures here.

Most pre-Holocene reefal platforms have been at least partially colonized by Holocene corals. Even the large karst banks of the northern Reef have isolated coral patches apparently established over substrate highs. Rapid transgression rates over the antecedent platforms combined with even a small delay in recolonization would have resulted in reef growth lagging behind sea level rise, although remaining within the most productive zone. According to Smith and Harrison (1977), the initial reef patches, a few meters below sea level, may have been in the optimum location for rapid calcification rates. Certainly the most common corals on submerged patches are the rapidly growing *Acropora* sp. Initially, therefore, the accretion rate may be relatively even over the whole of the antecedent platform, slightly slower rates in depressions being compensated for by deposition of materials from the highest pinnacles, which may reach the zone subjected to storm-wave turbulence. Subsequently, as parts of the reef reach sea level, protection is given to inner and leeside colonies, and most favored locations for growth will move to the reef margins. A large submerged bank between Centipede and Bowl Reefs off Townsville (Fig. 9.3) is typical of this early stage of development, although it is unclear why this reef should be only just now acquiring a living veneer of coral. The southern weather side of the shoal has numerous coral pinnacles rising to within 3 m of the surface. Lower coral growth occurs towards the leeward margin. However, in the center of the reef is a smoother surface apparently without living corals, which may represent uncolonized pre-Holocene platform. This may also outcrop on the lee side of the reef. In the reef center it is at a depth of between 16 and 18 m, separated from the area of living reef by steep 2–3 m slopes. Although the antecedent platform appears to be higher in the reef center, it is clear that present growth trends are likely to produce a lagoon form with growth most rapid on the windward side. Most large reefs have probably passed through this phase except where the pre-Holocene surface is extremely shallow. Where present reefs are still of a patchy nature then slow growth rates and/or deep pre-Holocene foundations are suggested. Local shelf subsidence giving the impression of a continuously rising Holocene sea-level curve, may aid in producing this type of reef.

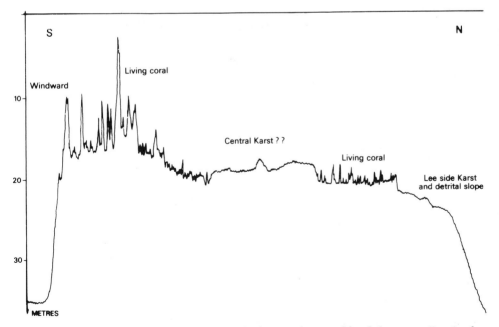

Figure 9.3 Echo-sounding profile across the large submerged bank between Centipede and Bowl Reefs off Townsville. Horizontal distance is approximately 2.5 km.

Smaller submerged reefs characteristically display a peripheral rim surrounding a central depression. An excellent example is Morinda Shoal (Fig. 9.4) (19°08′S) originally mapped in 1928 by Henderson (1931) who described it as follows:

> The shoal bears all the characteristics of a typical atoll formation; it is roughly circular in form, steep to the eastward and southward with a more gradual slope to the north-westward. The shortest soundings obtained are somewhat towards the edges of the shoal. The bottom appears to be entirely live coral with patches of coarse coral sand.

The shoal reaches within 7 m of the surface.

Like the larger karstic surfaces submerged beneath northern reef waters, reasons for the lack of growth or slow growth of these reefs are not known. It was suggested in Chapter 6 that at the southern extremity of the Reef the shoals may have been established at warmer periods in the Pleistocene but that at the time the postglacial transgression was passing over them, shelf waters were too cool for coral growth and the reefs are now too deep for significant growth. Similarly, Morinda Shoal is only 32 km offshore from the Burdekin delta and during major floods may be affected by the freshwater plume from the river (AIMS, 1979), resulting in retardation of growth rates. However,

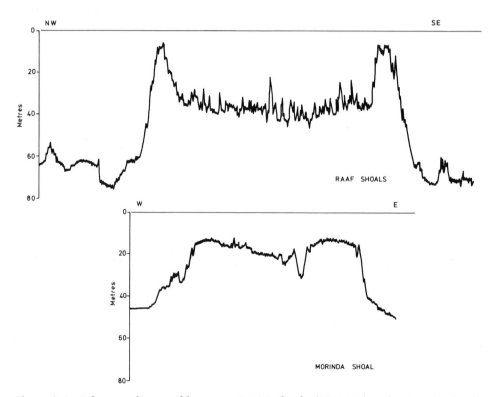

Figure 9.4 Echo-sounding profile across RAAF shoals (17°11′S) and Morinda shoal (19°09′S), submerged lagoonal reefs. Horizontal extent is approximately 3.5 km for RAAF shoals, and 3.0 km for Morinda shoal.

there are several examples of this type of submerged reef much more distant from the coast, between latitudes 19°00′ and 20°00′S within the main body of the Reef and growing adjacent to other reefs, which have grown up to modern sea level and developed wide reef flats. Another series is found at about 17°S close to the outer edge of the shelf but behind a distinctive linear shoal (Fig. 9.9). An example from this area is RAAF shoals (17°12′S) which around the rim rise to within 5.5 m of the surface from a depth of 55 m. A central lagoonal depression has a general depth of 30 m with isolated pinnacles rising to 18 m (Fig. 9.4). Neither local subsidence nor very localized retardation of growth rates can be envisaged for such reefs, which may thus be the result of deeper than average antecedent foundations. Seismic reflection traverses (Searle et al., 1980) suggest that the pre-Holocene platform adjacent to RAAF shoals is at a depth of 37 m, with 15 m of Holocene cover.

Irregular reef patches are identical in morphology to Maxwell's resorbed reefs. Hedley Reef near Innisfail (17°14′S) is characteristic. It rises from a platform depth of 20–25 m. Greatest reef-flat development has taken place at the southwestern end and particularly along a central ridge. Beneath this ridge a seismic discontinuity was detected at 10 m confirming that parts of the reef first reaching sea level are growing over substrate highs. However, C-14 ages (Table 9.2) of 420 ± 90 yrs B.P. from a depth of 0.75 m, 1460 ± 110 yrs B.P. from 1.30–1.75 m, and 2160 ± 130 yrs B.P. from 2.65–3.00 m confirm the relatively young age of the reef-flat development. The northern part of Hedley reef, growing from a deeper platform has numerous reef pinnacles enclosed within a more continuous marginal reef rim.

Table 9.2 Largely Unpublished Radiocarbon Ages for Reef-Cap Samples From the Great Barrier Reef Between 14°30′S and 20°45′S.[a]

Reef	Latitude S	Hole No	Depth (cm)	Material	Identification (All GaK −)	Age (C-14 yrs B.P.)
Carter	14°33′	1	70	Coralg.[b]	6477	5420 ± 130
Carter		1	140	Porites	6478	5750 ± 130
Carter		2	5	Porites	6479	3760 ± 100
Carter		2	55	Porites	6480	5800 ± 100
Carter		3	10	Acropora	6481	4480 ± 100
Carter		3	50	Porites	6482	4870 ± 120
Nymph	14°39′	1	40	Goniastrea	7666	2130 ± 100
Long	15°03′	2	5	Acropora	6483	4740 ± 120
Long		2	70	Goniopora	6484	4430 ± 120
Lark Pass	15°05′	1	14	Coralg.[b]	6683	5910 ± 110
Lark Pass		1	130	Acropora	6684	5720 ± 130
Lark Pass		2	8	Acropora	6681	4940 ± 140
Lark Pass		2	50	Coralg.[b]	6682	4040 ± 130
Three Isles	15°07′	3	25	Goniastrea	7667	4520 ± 110
Cairns	15°39′	1	50	Acropora	6685	3910 ± 110
Cairns		1	100	Leptoria	6686	4110 ± 130
East Hope	15°45′	3	20	Porites	6687	2570 ± 100
East Hope		3	150	Favites	6688	1540 ± 80

Table 9.2 (Continued)

Reef	Latitude S	Hole No	Depth (cm)	Material	Identification (All GaK –)	Age (C-14 yrs B.P.)
Opal	16°14′	1	100	Acropora	7668	3970 ± 100
Opal		1	247	Hydnophora	7669	4780 ± 120
Opal		1	300	Acropora	7670	4590 ± 130
Opal		2	45	Acropora	7671	2560 ± 110
Opal		2	110	Acropora	7672	2670 ± 90
Opal		3	100	Acropora	7673	2490 ± 110
Opal		3	150	Acropora	7674	4140 ± 130
Michaelmas	16°35′	1	110	Acropora	7675	5100 ± 130
Michaelmas		2	310	Porites	7676	2910 ± 150
Michaelmas		3	90	Plesiastrea	7677	3510 ± 130
Michaelmas		4	90	Acropora	7678	2180 ± 120
Michaelmas		4	150	Coralg.[b]	7679	2450 ± 120
Thetford	16°45′	1	60	Porites	7680	2600 ± 140
Thetford		1	110	Porites	7681	2680 ± 120
Channel	16°56′	1	30	Acropora	7682	560 ± 90
Channel		1	95	Acropora	7683	1930 ± 110
Channel		1	125	Acropora	7684	610 ± 80
Hedley	17°18′	1	75	Acropora	7685	420 ± 90
Hedley		1	175	Acropora	7686	1460 ± 110
Hedley		1	300	Platygyra	7687	2160 ± 130
Taylor	17°48′	1	60	Coral?[c]	8924	4590 ± 130
Taylor		1	240	Favid	8799	3220 ± 90
Taylor		2	240	Cyphastrea	8925	5760 ± 180
Taylor		2	350	Acropora	8800	3560 ± 120
Taylor		3	145	Coral?[c]	8926	2140 ± 110
Taylor		3	165	Acropora	8927	4180 ± 150
Taylor		3	305	Acropora	8936	7420 ± 190
Moss	17°56′	1	430	Acropora	8798	3030 ± 110
Moss		2	25	Acropora	8934	3230 ± 140
Moss		2	275	Porites	8935	3910 ± 180
Barnett Patches	18°04′	1	90	Coral?[c]	8932	3740 ± 140
Barnett Patches		1	150	Acropora	8933	5020 ± 160
Barnett Patches		2	370	Porites	8797	3820 ± 110
Bowl	18°28′	1	146	Acropora	7842	2720 ± 100
Bowl		2	86	Acropora	7843	2670 ± 100
Bowl		3	25	Pocillopora	7844	2460 ± 130
Bowl		3	90	Acropora	7845	2440 ± 100
Keeper	18°45′	1	137	Acropora	7273	1380 ± 90
Keeper		1	229	Coralg.[b]	7274	1570 ± 90
Keeper		1	400	Coralg.[b]	7276	1840 ± 80
Keeper		2	20	Acropora	7272	1920 ± 80
Keeper		2	327	Porites	7275	2610 ± 90
Keeper		2	427	Acropora	7277	1960 ± 120
Wheeler	18°46′	1	127	Lobophyllia	7833	2140 ± 110
Wheeler		1	152	Porites	7834	1860 ± 130
Wheeler		1	178	Cyphastrea	7835	2540 ± 130
Wheeler		1	254	Acropora	7836	2050 ± 110

Table 9.2 (Continued)

Reef	Latitude S	Hole No	Depth (cm)	Material	Identification (All GaK –)	Age (C-14 yrs B.P.)
Wheeler		2	180	Favia	7837	3270 ± 120
Wheeler		2	265	Leptoria	7838	3470 ± 110
Wheeler		3	86	Acropora	7839	3270 ± 100
Wheeler		4	140	Acropora	7840	3880 ± 120
Wheeler		4	241	Acropora	7841	4390 ± 100
Viper	18°50'	1	100	Acropora	7015	1930 ± 100
Viper		1	200	Coralg.[b]	7016	2020 ± 110
Viper		2	70	Acropora	7017	2060 ± 100
Viper		3	50	Favid	7018	2580 ± 100
Viper		3	100	Acropora	7019	2660 ± 90
Darley	19°12'	1	60	Acropora	7020	5730 ± 150
Darley		1	130	Acropora	7021	6210 ± 140
Darley		1	180	Favid	7022	6090 ± 130
Darley		2	70	Porites	7023	3040 ± 110
Darley		2	180	Acropora	7024	3940 ± 80
Darley		3	80	Acropora	7025	6070 ± 130
Stanley	19°16'	2	85	Coral?	8928	4920 ± 160
Stanley		2	150	Symphillia	8796	3280 ± 110
Stanley		3	12	Coral?[c]	8929	5530 ± 120
Stanley		3	62	Acropora	8931	6420 ± 160
Stanley		3	220	Acropora	8937	7160 ± 170
Stanley		4	105	Acropora	8930	5580 ± 130
Redbill	20°58'	1	100	Favia	7283	3920 ± 150
Redbill		3	55	Goniastrea	7280	4570 ± 150
Redbill		3	310	Acropora	7288	6550 ± 150
Redbill		4	115	Symphyllia	7284	1160 ± 100
Redbill		5	7	Goniastrea	7278	720 ± 100
Redbill		5	20	Leptoria	7279	1670 ± 100
Redbill		5	94	Favites	7282	3240 ± 120
Redbill		5	160	Coralg.[b]	7285	4830 ± 140
Redbill		6	61	Acropora	7281	690 ± 100
Redbill		7	280	Porites	7286	3820 ± 100
Redbill		7	305	Porites	7287	4640 ± 160
Molar	20°38'	1	75	Acropora	7268	1310 ± 100
Cockatoo	20°45'	1	22	Acropora	7270	4100 ± 100
Cockatoo		1	70	Acropora	7271	3480 ± 120
Cockatoo		2	17	Coralg.[b]	7269	30 ± 100

[a]For details of other dates quoted in the text see Maxwell (1969), Hopley (1971a, 1975), Hopley et al (1978) and Polach et al (1978).
[b]Coralline algae with corals.
[c]Coral unidentified.

Barnett Patches off Cardwell (18°4'S) is another example of irregular reef patches (Fig. 9.5). The patches cover an area of approximately 50 km² rising sharply from a general shelf depth of 65 m to a level of between 20 and 25 m, from which the irregular coral patches rise. This platform appears to be the antecedent surface from which the Holocene reefs are growing, as seismic survey on the largest of the patches indicated a sharp discontinuity at a depth of 7 m near the cay and 9 m near the southern reef edge. All the patches have a veneer of living corals, although the largest has a small unvegetated sand cay rising to about MHWS and adjacent to which the reef flat is generally sandy with little coral. Seismic survey clearly suggests that the present patches are growing

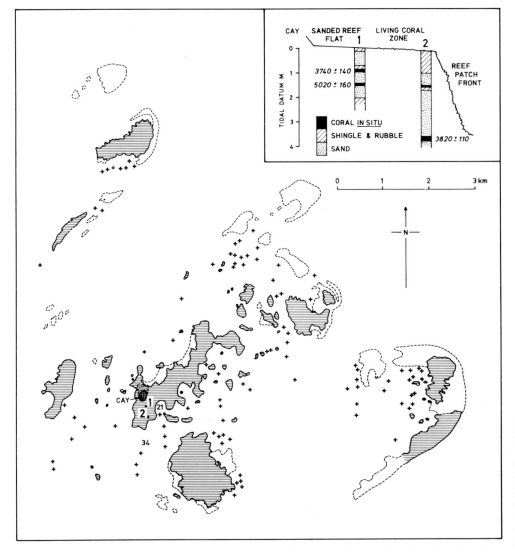

Figure 9.5 Barnett Patches (18°04'S), an example of irregular reef patches developed over a highly uneven antecedent surface.

over highs in the pre-Holocene substrate. Many of the embayments approximately 200 m in diameter, which are found around the margins of the patches, appear to have originated from depressions in the antecedent platform. Most have depths of 20–25 m and some, like the one immediately south of the cay have continuous rims. Patchiness of reef-flat development here is not due to the reef reaching modern sea level very recently. An age of less than 3740 yrs B.P. has been obtained for in situ coral from a depth of 82 cm and 5020 yrs for similar material at a depth of 1.38 m (Table 9.2). Apparently the patchy nature of the present reef is a reflection of an extremely irregular pre-Holocene foundation with present reef flat restricted to the highest areas of the antecedent foundations.

Mature Reefs

The importance of growth for the most exposed margins of reef platforms is clearly seen from the orientation of crescentic reefs. In most locations in the Great Barrier Reef this is towards the southeast or east, but where this side is given some lee by windward reefs then another side may be the first to develop a crescentic hardline. Thus north of 12°30′S many of the reefs of the central shelf are protected by the proximity of the outer ribbons and hard-line development is on the western sides of reefs overlooking the open inner shipping channel (e.g. Eel and Gallon Reefs) while many of the inner Pompey Reefs face towards the most open southwest. Crescentic-shaped reefs with isolated patches trailing from the lee-side arms are very common and were originally described by Paradice (1925). Extensive detrital slopes may be found in the lee of these reefs and on some there is development of algal pavement on the windward reef flat, upon which numerous reef blocks may rest. These features suggest that reef-top ages should be older than found on reef patches.

An example is Thetford Reef (16°49′S) near Cairns. A wide crescentic reef flat at the eastern end of the reef platform is covered by living corals clearly aligned normal to the refracted wave pattern. Deeper pools exist in the flat away from the windward margin that has only minimal algal pavement developed on its northeastern edge. Scattered irregular coral patches occur in the lee of the reef from water depths of up to 10 m. A more continuous submerged rim trails along the northern edge of the reef platform. Seismic survey determined the depth of the pre-Holocene at only 7.5 m beneath the southern reef margin. The reef flat however, is relatively young, radiocarbon ages of about 2600 yrs B.P. obtained in the upper 1.1 m of the reef cap (Table 9.2), that is, slightly older than on the nearby Hedley Reef, which is classified at the earlier patch stage.

With larger reefs the reef tops may be even older and exact morphology is very strongly controlled by the antecedent surface. This is illustrated by comparisons of Opal, Stanley, and Taylor Reefs (Fig. 9.6). Opal Reef (16°13′S) is the smallest. Major hard-line reef is developed towards the windward southeastern margin of the reefal platform. The windward side of the reef flat rises to just above MLWS and consists of a hard, algal cemented pavement with a partial rubble cover and a leeward zone of living corals at slightly greater depth (just below MLWS). The seismically determined depth of the pre-Holocene

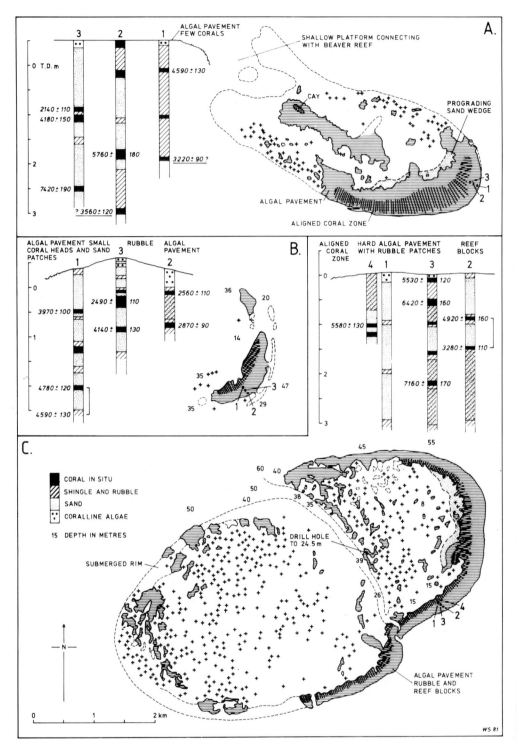

Figure 9.6 Examples of crescentic reefs with varying degrees of reef-flat development. (A) Opal Reef (16°13′S). (B) Stanley Reef (19°18′S). (C) Taylor Reef (17°50′S).

beneath the windward reef flat is relatively shallow at 8.5 m. Consequently reef-top ages are comparatively old, a maximum age of 4780 ± 120 yrs B.P. being obtained from a depth of 2.4 m beneath the leeward side of the algal pavement (Table 9.2). Most of the reef area has developed on a – 20 m substrate high, however, and it is from this, and from a – 28 m platform in the back-reef area that the leeward reef patches rise. Up to 22 m of Holocene reef has developed on the northern margin of the – 28 m platform (Searle et al., 1980).

Stanley Reef (19°18′S) is larger (about 12 km long). A 400-m-wide reef flat surrounds 45% of the reef and is continued as a submerged feature around a further 30% of the reef. Algal pavement is developed only on the windward side. Scattered reef patches are found throughout the lagoon, the major feature of which is a deep channel heading from a narrow blocked passage in the southern rim. General depth of the lagoon is 5–15 m while the channel reaches over 60 m near to its northern exit from the reef, and 39 m in the center of the reef. Both seismic refraction and continuous seismic profile (CSP) surveys have been carried out on this reef. CSP indicates the pre-Holocene reflector about 40 m beneath much of the channel, rising to 15 m beneath reef patches. Drilling of a patch reef adjacent to the channel established the unconformity at – 20 m. Seismic refraction showed the unconformity at only 6 m beneath the rim. Thus growth from the rim would have commenced late in the Holocene transgression, and reached modern sea level relatively early. This is confirmed by radiocarbon for ages of in situ corals from shallow-reef rim boreholes: 7160 yrs B.P. from 2.2 m and 6420 yrs B.P. from 0.6 m (Fig. 9.6; Table 9.2).

Taylor Reef (17°50′S) exhibits a crescentic windward margin enclosing a shallow (< 10 m) lagoonal area with numerous reef patches including a major area of shallow flat to leeward with a substantial unvegetated sand cay. Scalloped margins to this area of reef flat are suggestive of karst depressions while the general nature of the reef possibly indicates that the pre-Holocene platform is relatively shallow. Seismic survey determined its depth on the windward margin as only 5.7 m. Not surprisingly, therefore, reef-flat ages are old, a 7420 yr date coming from 3.05 m and 4590 yrs from 0.6 m (Fig. 9.6; Table 9.2).

These examples of crescentic reefs illustrate the importance of substrate control. Highest pre-Holocene foundations exist beneath the windward rims of each of these reefs, which retain their crescentic form because of the relative relief of the foundations. Thus while the windward rims have been at modern sea level for several thousands of years, there has still been insufficient time for complete outer rim development or lagoon infilling. Taylor Reef, where the foundation in the reef center is possibly shallowest, is most advanced in its development of reef flat. Stanley Reef clearly shows the importance of windward growth, illustrated by the contrast between windward reef flat and leeward submerged rim, although even here the initial contrast appears to have been brought about by differences in the height of the antecedent rim.

Given sufficient relief in the pre-Holocene foundations so that reef flat can develop around the leeward margins before the reef center becomes infilled, lagoonal reefs will evolve from the crescentic forms. Larger reefs of this type are usually more complex. The Pompey Reefs of the Great Barrier Reef are the epitome of this reef type (Fig. 7.12). Reef rims from 500 to 800 m wide with hard algal pavement enclose sandy lagoons with depths of between 5 and 20 m separated by meandering ridges rising to just above MLWS and with a dense cover of living corals mainly *Pocillopora* sp., *Seriatopora* sp. and *Acropora humilis*. The presence of blue holes and meandering drainage channels through these reefs strongly suggests a karst-influenced substrate control on modern reef development (see Chap. 7). Some reefs display a pattern of small karst-like depressions in the lagoon floor similar in dimensions to those in the karst platforms of the northern Great Barrier Reef. Cockatoo Reef (Fig. 7.7) and Molar Reef (Fig. 7.9) both containing blue holes and described in Chapter 7 are typical of the reefs of this type (Backshall et al., 1979). Where the pre-Holocene surface is shallow or lacks significant relief the multiple lagoonal stage may be short and nondistinctive. Taylor Reef, for example is unlikely to go through a distinctive multiple lagoonal stage and many of the large sanded reefs of the Princess Charlotte Bay area and Torres Strait, where the antecedent platform appears to be very shallow, have probably not passed through a multiple lagoonal stage.

Smaller reefs are simpler and initially may have only a single central lagoon, which in some examples may remain open to the sea on the leeward side. One Tree Reef (Fig. 8.4) is probably the most studied reef of this type on the Great Barrier Reef. As shown in Chapter 8 it displays strong substrate control. Over the shallow windward rim the reef has been at modern sea level for at least 5000 years (Davies and Marshall, 1979, 1980). Thus it is not surprising to find that prograding sand sheets have partially infilled the lagoon. Infilling of lagoons on their windward sides probably commences at the crescentic reef stage on most reefs.

Continual infilling of the central lagoon by prograding sand sheets aided by expansion of lagoonal reef patches, slowly reduces the size of the lagoon, even dividing it into smaller areas. Aligned coral colonies grow within the shallow waters of the infilling lagoon, particularly behind the windward margin of the reef. As the reef flat develops, detrital material not entrapped within the lagoon is carried towards the lee side and extensive areas of sanded reef flat may result. Cays can also form at this stage. Around the margins of the lagoon, algal pavements may be slowly raised as shingle fragments are cemented by the crustose corallines and further heightening of the rim may take place as rubble banks are thrown up during storms. Thus, at low tide, water may be impounded either locally or more generally over the reef flat, resulting in many of the corals assuming a microatoll form as they grow to the moated water level. This also has the result of slightly raising the level to which the reef grows from about MLWS to at least MLWN.

Redbill Reef (20°58′ S) off Mackay typifies this reef type (Figs. 9.7, 10.15). This pear-shaped reef is 4.5 km long and 3.2 km wide with a reef flat surrounded by a wide algal rim in which are located two lagoons that at low water have maximum depths of 10 m. Around much of the reef the lagoon and central reef flat is moated behind algal terraces (see Chap. 4). The pre-Holocene topography has clearly influenced the modern reef. The seismic unconformity is highest beneath the leeward algal rim at − 6 m and at − 10 m beneath the algal pavement to windward. The influence of this variation is clearly seen in the reef top ages (Table 9.2). Beneath the leeward rim radiocarbon dates of between 3920 and 6550 yrs B.P. have been obtained while to windward the dates range from 690–

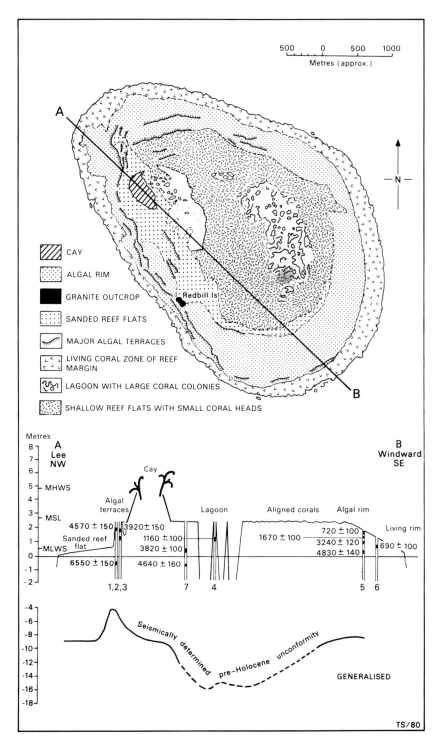

Figure 9.7 Redbill Reef, morphology and results of shallow drilling and seismic refraction survey (generalized). Recent deeper drilling has suggested that the pre-Holocene surface is highly variable in depth on this partially infilled lagoonal reef.

4830 yrs B.P. Beneath the central reef flat, where the seismic unconformity indicates that the pre-Holocene is deeper than − 18 m and there is the suggestion of a much larger lagoon in the past, much younger radiocarbon ages have been obtained. An age of 1160 ± 100 yrs B.P. was indicated from a depth of 1.15 m beneath a lagoonal patch reef. However, closer to the algal rim a date of 3820 ± 100 yrs for in situ *Porites* sp. from a depth of 2.8 m, and 4460 ± 160 yrs for similar material at a depth of 3.0 m, show that lagoonal infilling around the margins took place as the rim was developing. As indicated in Chapter 8, the corals beneath the algal rim may have grown to a relatively higher sea level (Fig. 8.8), the fall from which may have accelerated the lagoon infilling process. On Redbill Reef the former morphology perhaps 3000–4000 yrs B.P. was strongly controlled by the antecedent surface, but in the intervening period lateral movement of sediments from the margins has seen the reef move into a phase typified by masking of this antecedent morphology.

Senile Reefs

Given sufficient time all internal lagoons may be infilled leaving a largely sanded reef flat with low microatolls growing only in shallow depressions. Living coral is found elsewhere only around the reef margins, particularly on the lee side where reef extension may take place. It is possible for extensive sand cays to form and significant ramparts of shingle may build up on the windward margins, overlying older algal pavement and with tongues extending back from the margins as low ridges. However, this sheltered area may also become the site for colonization by mangroves and the reef assumes a low wooded island morphology (see Chap. 11). Sand chutes are commonly found towards the lee of the reef, directing a portion of the reef top sediment into deeper water (Fig. 11.3). Accumulation of talus slopes, partially stabilized by coral growth in the form of intricate banks of *Acropora* sp. or massive *Porites* colonies extend the reef area to leeward of the original pre-Holocene reefal bank.

It is probable that there has been insufficient time in the Holocene for this reef type to have developed over anything except shallow and/or smaller antecedent platforms. Some of the large reefs off Princess Charlotte Bay are of this type, as are the Warrior Reefs of Torres Strait (Fig. 2.7). Shallow substrate is quite probable in both areas. Stoddart et al. (1978b) have suggested that the reefs of Princess Charlotte Bay may be thin veneers on flat-lying Mesozoic sedimentary rocks of the adjacent Laura Basin. Similarly the reefs of Torres Strait from aerial photography appear to be little more than drowned karst plateaus presently at modern sea level with minimal Holocene growth. Sanded reef tops are interspersed with meandering channels reminiscent of mangrove creeks on the adjacent mainland. Indeed some reef tops maintain a mangrove cover and their creek drainage patterns may be older inherited features. Small karstlike depressions of dimensions similar to those described as drowned karst further south are also found. Most are only a few meters deep but some larger depressions on Wapa Reef in particular are deeper and may be small blue holes. Such an interpretation is supported by the recovery of recrystallized reef limestone from the surface of Sabai Island (Barham, personal communication).

Wheeler Reef (18°48′ S) characterizes a reef just reaching the planar stage (Harvey, 1978; Hopley, 1978c). The reef is only 1.25 km² and situated on a roughly circular bathymetric high, rising from a shelf depth of about 54 m (Figs. 9.8, 11.3). The reef flat is very close to tidal datum, rising to about 0.3 m around the cay a level approximately MLWS. Most of the reef flat consists of small coral colonies of great species variety, growing most densely around the rim and becoming more scattered towards the lee side where they are interspersed with a sandy reef-flat floor. Around the cay, which rises to about 3 m, the reef is completely sanded. On the lee side are scattered coral heads between which are distinctive sand chutes leading off the reef flat. Very small areas of algal pavement are found on the eastern side of the reef, which appears to be just reaching its final stage of consolidation as it is cut by a number of deep gutters and holes up to 3 m deep and as much as 50 m from the reef edge. A terrace between 19 and 22 m deep is found around much of the reef margin. A small amount of seismic survey over this reef suggests that this terrace is controlled by the pre-Holocene platform which is found at 15.5–24 m beneath the reef flat (Harvey, 1978). Although a dish shape is suggested for the antecedent platform the small size of the reef has never allowed a deep lagoon to form. Shallow drilling on the windward margin to depths of 3 m showed the reef top to consist of algal cemented shingle with some head corals in the upper meter and much shingle, rubble, and branching *Acropora* sp. at slightly greater depth. Radiocarbon dates (Table 9.2) of between 1860 and 4390 yrs B.P. were obtained from these cores.

Even greater ages have been obtained from the small planar reefs of the inner shelf north of Cairns. Many are low wooded island reefs with cays, shingle ramparts, platform rocks, and mangroves and may be considered as the final stage in the evolution of small planar reefs (see Chap. 11). Stainer Reef (13°57′ S) is typical of many of the inner reefs of the Princess Charlotte Bay area. It has a small lee side, vegetated cay, and nearly all the reef flat is sanded. In places brown algal mats give some stability to the sand surface. Fossil microatolls emerging only 5 cm above the sand to a level just below MLWN are found in a number of areas and probably underlie much of the reef flat sand. One sample, a *Favites abdita* head from near the cay, gave a radiocarbon age of 4980 ± 80 yrs B.P. (Polach et al., 1978). An even older age of 6310 ± 90 yrs B.P. (Polach et al., 1978) was obtained for a Tridacna valve taken from its growth position in an old microatoll protruding from beneath platform rock on Farmer–Fisher Reef (Piper Islands) at 12°15′ S. This is a low wooded island with a narrow cemented platform around the windward margins, seaward of which is a rubble zone, algal pavement, and narrow open-water coral fringe. Most of the leeward reef flat is sanded although dead microatolls protrude irregularly through the sand. In the lee of the platforms, low water levels are moated at depths of between 10 and 50 cm and only here on the reef flat is there an extensive area of living coral colonies, many in microatoll form, including the dominant *Heliopora* sp. Between the living coral zone and the sanded area, the shallow water of the reef flat maintains an extensive sward of *Thalassia*.

Ribbon Reefs

The origin of linear reefs can only be surmised. Fairbridge (1950, 1967) suggested that they represent the upgrowth of fringing reefs of former low sea-level shorelines and this is quite possible, though the shorelines are definitely

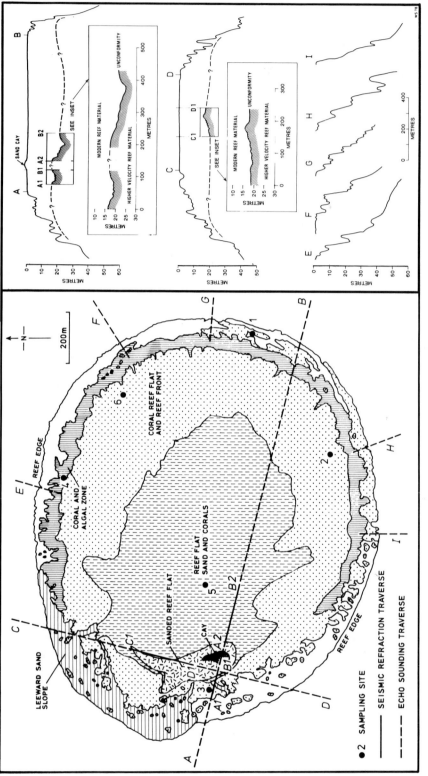

Figure 9.8 Wheeler Reef, morphology and internal structure as indicated by seismic survey, from Harvey (1978). Deeper drilling in the center and windward edge has confirmed the depth to pre-Holocene on this small planar reef.

older than the Holocene transgression. The ribbon reefs on the northern shelf are probably of this origin. The steepness of the continental slope and shallowness of the shelf determined that most low sea-level shorelines below – 50 m occurred within a very narrow belt. Structural control of subreefal prominences may be responsible for the linearity of some reefs, especially those running transverse to the shelf edge.

In spite of their distinctive shape, the development of ribbon reefs is probably similar to that of other reef types. Submerged linear reefs are common between Cairns and Townsville where narrow shoals parallel to the shelf edge have been noted by Paradice (1925) and Fairbridge (1950). The depth of the shoal is generally between 35 and 50 m and is very persistent, especially between the southern end of the recognized ribbon reefs in the Agincourt Complex (16°00′ S) to about 17°30′ S. This appears to be an ancient feature but from it rise shorter linear shoals upon which modern growth is taking place (Fig. 9.9). Of these Hervey Shoals (17°02′ S) is typical and provides a profile almost identical to that of the ribbon reefs further north except for the reef top, which consists of irregular coral pinnacles rising to a minimum depth of 7 m (Fig. 9.10). The shelf edge is only 4 km to the east of these shoals and the general depth of water from which they rise is 73 m. Continuous seismic reflection profiles indicate a major reflector about 5 m below this but is lost within the reef mass itself. However, the CSP survey clearly showed talus slopes behind the reef crest and also in the lee of the reef as a whole.

Another two profiles are shown off over the shelf edge at latitude 17°53′ S, near Moss Reef and a further two near Bowl Reef at latitude 18°25′ S (Fig. 9.10). In both areas the shoulder of the continental shelf is more extensive than Hervey Shoals, with relatively gentle slope down to 70–75 m before plunging to depths beyond 400 m. In such a situation low sea-level shorelines of different depths are likely to have been more widely separated and in each area parallel lines of submerged linear reefs are seen. Major platforms with a depth of 70 m provide the surface from which the larger reefs rise in both areas. Coincidence of levels of the submerged reefs at 13–14 m and 45 m is probably not significant as the higher reefs have a veneer of living coral and have obviously grown from a level below this. However these and other profiles along this part of the continental shelf suggest that a 70 m surface from which a number of uncharted submerged linear reefs rise is a fairly constant feature. Minor irregularities at greater depth on the continental shelf (for example at 110 m near Moss Reef and at 142, 159, 170, 179, and 214 m near Bowl Reef) may also be reefal, related to the lowest sea levels of the last or earlier glaciations.

Reefs such as Hervey Shoals are completely submerged but further growth will result in a phase when such reefs will have irregular pinnacles rising to the surface in a linear pattern. Wardle Reef (17°25′ S) provides one of the few examples in the Great Barrier Reef province of this phase of reef development, which is probably short lived. Some irregular reef patches reach sea level at the southern end of this reef, which extends northward for 5 km with only one major pass. Its morphology, with a well-developed lee-side sand slope from which rise scattered coral patches, is identical to that of the ribbon reefs to the north.

The mature reef form from linear foundations is the ribbon reef. The morphology of these reefs has been previously described (e.g., Spender, 1930; Fair-

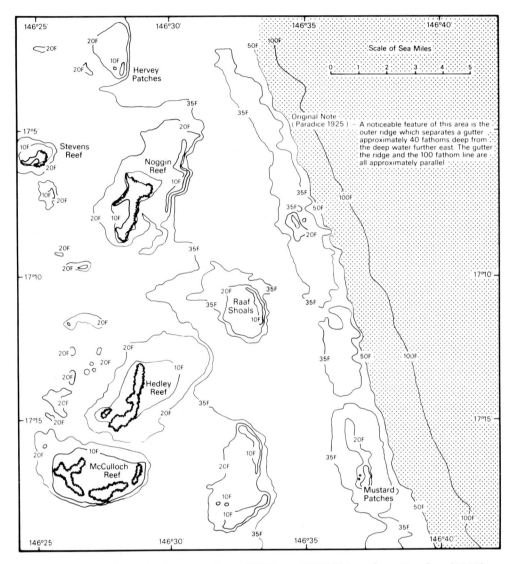

Figure 9.9 Shelf-edge bathymetry from 17°00 to 17°20'S based on Paradice (1925). (Reproduced with permission of the Great Barrier Reef Committee.)

bridge, 1950; Veron and Hudson, 1978). All rise steeply from at least 50 m depth, although some have secondary fronts with intervening gutter (see Chap. 10). The longest, Ribbon Reef, is over 35 km long, and Tijou Reef is 27.8 km long but on average the length of individual reefs is between 6 and 8 km, some being as short as 2.5 km. Widths are within the range 600–800 m, occasionally widening at sharp bends in the reef, where small lagoons may be found in the reef flat. Reef flats are strongly zoned, as shown in Chapter 10.

Some details are available on the age and structure of two northern ribbon reefs and for two reefs of similar morphology further south. Carter Reef (Harvey, 1977a; Hopley, 1977) has been previously discussed in Chapter 7. It

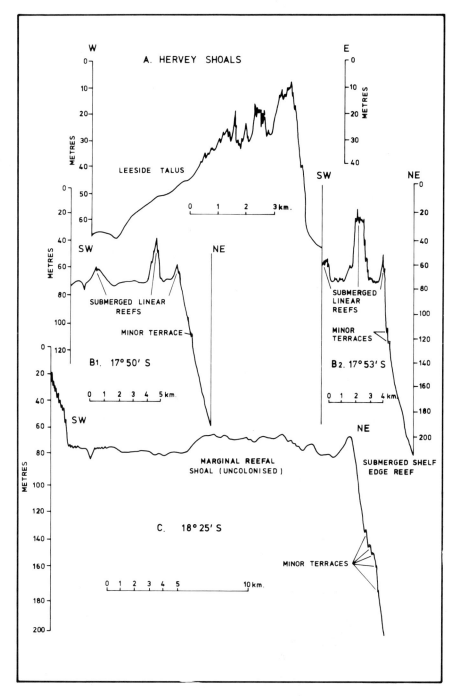

Figure 9.10 Echo-sounding profiles of linear submerged shelf-edge reefs: (A) Hervey Shoals, typical of the ribbonlike reefs of the shelf edge south of Cairns showing steep seaward slope, reef crest rising to 7 m of the surface, and back reef zone of coral pinnacles and detrital sand slope. (B) Two profiles at about 17°53′S. (C) Profile at 18°25′S near Bowl Reef.

appears to have formed over a pre-Holocene rim that rises to within 9 m of the surface near the reef crest and dips at least 20 m to leeward. Radiocarbon ages of between 3760 and 5800 yrs B.P. have been obtained from the upper 2 m of this reef (Fig. 9.11; Table 9.2). Lark Pass Reef (15°04′ S) is very similar. Here the seismic unconformity representing the pre-Holocene surface is only 9.5 m below the present reef top. Radiocarbon ages of between 4040 and 5910 yrs B.P. (Table 9.2) are similar to those of Carter Reef and suggest that many of the ribbon reefs have been at or close to modern sea level for at least 6000 years. Reef caps in both cases consist largely of rubble cemented by coralline algae with occasional small coral heads and flattened *Acropora* sp.

Moss (17°56′ S) and Bowl (18°30′ S, Fig. 4.2) Reefs differ from the northern ribbons only in that they are lower (reaching about tidal datum as opposed to MLWS for the northern reefs) and have a denser cover of living corals over the reef flat and much less algal pavement. The pre-Holocene surface was detected at 8–11m beneath Moss Reef and at 10 m beneath Bowl. Radiocarbon ages between 3030 and 3910 yrs B.P. from Moss and dates ranging from 2440 to 2720 yrs B.P. (Table 9.2) from Bowl suggest that both these reefs are much younger than their northern counterparts.

DISTRIBUTION OF REEF TYPES IN THE GREAT BARRIER REEF

The distribution of each reef type as defined has been plotted using available aerial photography in Figures 9.12 and 9.13. Photographic cover is complete as

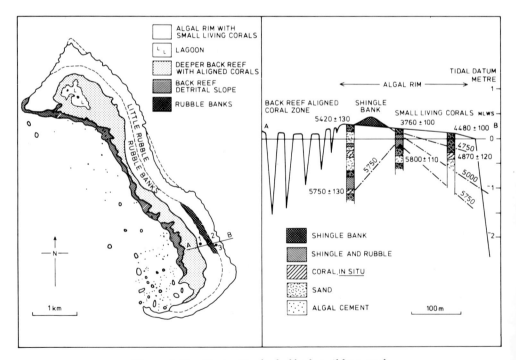

Figure 9.11   Carter Reef, shelf edge ribbon reef.

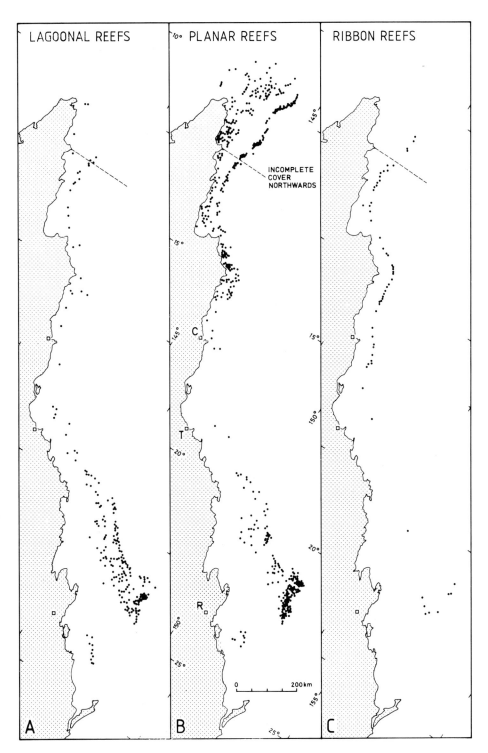

Figure 9.12 Distribution of submerged shoal, irregular reef patches, and crescentic reefs on the Great Barrier Reef. Air photograph cover is incomplete north of 12°S.

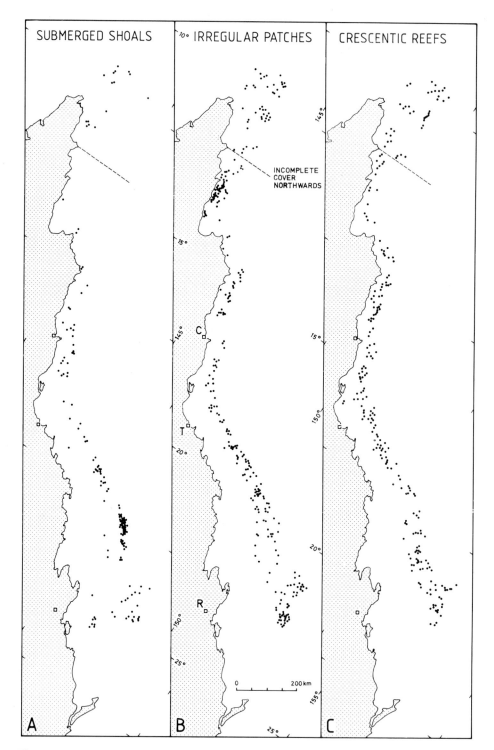

Figure 9.13 Distribution of lagoonal, planar, and ribbon reefs on the Great Barrier Reef. Air photograph cover is incomplete north of 12°S.

far north as Cape Grenville at 12°00′ S but only partial north of this latitude and distribution in the Torres Strait area is incomplete. Table 9.3 indicates the distribution of reefs by size classes (as determined by lagoon development discussed above) and Table 9.4 summarizes the number of reefs of each class by latitude at 30-minute intervals. South of latitude 11°00′ S a total of 1301 reefs were plotted. A further 400 are estimated between 9° and 11°S but this total is still below estimates made elsewhere. Bennett (1971), for example, suggested the total number is about 2500. Although the incomplete coverage by aerial photography contributes to these discrepancies, the lower estimate made here is due partly to reef patches growing from a single antecedent platform even where individually named, being recognized as a single reef. Further, large submerged platforms have not been included in the count (although an indication of their occurrence, major, minor, or absent, is indicated in Table 9.4). Nor is it possible to plot all submerged reefs. Only those that are close enough to the surface to show on aerial photographs are included.

The number of reefs and the shelf area covered by reefs is relatively constant as far south as 19°S. Maximum numbers of reefs occur between 19°00′ S and 22°30′ S and although this is partly an artifact of using latitudinal divisions and of the shelf trending away from a directly north to south alignment, widening

Table 9.3　Distribution of Reef Diameter Classes by Latitude, Great Barrier Reef

Diameter: Latitude	>3.25 km	1.75–3.25 km	<1.75 km	Ribbon	Total
12–12½°	5	15	24	7	51
12½–13°	1	12	26	8	47
13–13½°	4	10	30	5	49
13½–14°	11	12	17	4	44
14–14½°	7	17	10	5	39
14½–15°	0	10	30	7	47
15–15½°	2	14	21	6	43
15½–16°	3	13	8	3	27
16–16½°	6	6	10	3	25
16½–17°	3	7	10	1	21
17–17½°	7	10	3	5	25
17½–18°	8	8	4	1	21
18–18½°	7	14	4	0	25
18½–19°	8	22	10	1	41
19–19½°	15	45	11	0	71
19½–20°	26	26	23	0	75
20–20½°	24	15	34	0	73
20½–21°	36	38	30	1	105
21–21½°	55	93	84	3	235
21½–22°	14	69	56	2	141
22–22½°	0	24	40	3	67
22½–23°	0	3	2	0	5
23–23½°	0	10	4	0	14
23½–24°	0	9	1	0	10
Total	242	502	492		1301
Percent	18.6	38.6	37.8		

Table 9.4 Distribution of Reef Types by Latitude, Great Barrier Reef

Latitude	Juvenile		Mature			Senile		Ribbon	
	Unmodified	Submerged	Patch	Crescentric	Lagoonal	Planar	Subm.	Patch	Planar
12–12½	Major	0	11	4	5	24	0	0	7
12½–13	Major	0	15	2	5	17	0	0	8
13–13½	Major	2	25	2	1	14	0	0	5
13½–14	Minor	0	8	5	4	23	0	0	4
14–14½	Minor	1	3	11	2	17	0	0	5
14½–15	Minor	2	8	2	1	27	0	0	7
15–15½	Minor	2	6	9	4	16	0	0	6
15½–16		0	8	10	1	5	0	0	3
16–16½		6	6	7	1	2	2	0	1
16½–17		6	3	7	0	4	1	0	0
17–17½		4	6	9	1	0	5	0	0
17½–18		4	4	12	0	0	0	0	1
18–18½		2	10	11	2	0	0	0	0
18½–19		5	8	19	5	3	0	0	1
19–19½		14	32	19	6	0	0	0	0
19½–20	Minor	9	25	13	13	15	0	0	0
20–20½	Minor	20	13	11	21	8	0	0	0
20½–21		15	11	16	35	27	0	0	1
21–21½		5	26	39	86	76	0	1	2
21½–22		6	11	20	53	49	0	0	2
22–22½		10	21	4	12	17	0	1	2
22½–23		5	0	0	0	0	0	0	0
23–23½		4	0	0	4	6	0	0	0
23½–24		0	0	0	7	3	0	0	0
Total		122	260	232	269	353	8	2	55
Percent		9.9	21.0	18.8	21.8	28.5	12.3	3.1	84.6

of the continental shelf does occur and actual numbers of reefs per unit length of shelf increases significantly. Reefs of all sizes reach their maximum numbers here. Widening of the continental shelf towards Torres Strait accounts for increasing numbers of reefs in the far north, although the majority are of small size. Reefs with a width between 1.75 and 3.25 km are the modal reef size on the Great Barrier Reef. Large reefs have a major distribution only within Torres Strait and between 19° and 22°S. Not counting the ribbon reefs, 30.9% of reefs are classified as juvenile, 40.6% as mature, and 28.5% as senile.

Unmodified antecedent platforms appear limited to the northern Reef north of 15°S, where they lie in the lee of ribbon reefs and where Holocene growth is negligible, possibly as the result of high turbidity at the time of initial shelf flooding. There also appear to be similar but smaller shoals between 19°30′ S and 20°30′ S. Of the 122 submerged reefs detected almost 50% are located between 19° and 21°S. They are particularly common between the Pompey Reefs and the outer edge of the continental shelf. Irregular reef patches are found in all except the southernmost Great Barrier Reef but reach maximum numbers north of 13°30′ , particularly on the outer shelf opposite Torres Strait and between 19° and 20°S opposite Townsville. Small patches are also common in the southern Swain Reefs.

Mature crescentic reefs are found throughout the Reef province north of 22°30′ S. They reach maximum numbers on the Swain Reefs but make up the highest proportion of reefs on the shelf between 15°30′ S and 19°S. Lagoonal reefs are much more restricted. Small numbers are found north of 15°30′ S but they reach maximum concentration between 19°30′ S and 22°00′ S. They are very rare between 15°30′ S and 18°30′ S. Although the numbers are smaller, these reefs are the most common form in the Bunker–Capricorn Group. Senile planar-reef forms are the most common reef type. However, of the 353 reefs of this type recognized, 278 (79%) are less than 1.75 km in diameter. Planar reefs make up the highest proportion of reefs north of 15°30′ S and are also numerous south of 19°30′ S. They are rare or absent from the intervening area. The ribbon reefs have the most distinctive distribution of all reef types, all but nine occurring north of 16°30′ S, almost exclusively on the very edge of the steep continental shelf.

Distribution of the different reef types indicates that morphological variation is not random but occurs in distinct regional patterns. Stages in reef development may represent a progression from one or a combination of minimal growth rates, deep foundations, and shelf subsidence (juvenile reefs) to rapid growth rates, shallow foundations, and shelf stability (or even uplift), as displayed by senile reefs with intermediate mature reefs resulting from a central position in the continuum of these influential factors. It is not surprising to find that in areas where there is evidence for modern sea level being achieved as early as 6000 yrs B.P. mature or senile reef forms predominate. The ultimate planar reef form is particularly prominent in areas where a fall from a higher sea level may have accelerated the reef development process. This is seen on the inner shelf north of Cairns and may be involved in the high proportion of planar reefs found in the Bunker–Capricorn Group where slightly higher Holocene sea levels have been reported (e.g., Flood et al., 1979). The notable exception to the dominance of mature or senile reefs is the central Great Barrier Reef between 16° and 20°S. In the center of this area is the region discussed in the previous chapter, within which reef-top dates are younger than elsewhere. It seems highly probable that the extension of the Halifax Basin into this region has had a profound effect on reef development.

It was suggested in Chapters 6 and 8 that variations in Holocene sea levels as the result of hydro-isostatic loading or other tectonic factors had a cross-shelf variation. Locally this may be detected in the distribution of reef types. For example, if the low wooded islands (see Chap. 11) are the end product of planar-reef development, their inner-shelf location may be aided by local uplift in this area. Similarly there are many examples of submerged reefs that have an outer shelf edge location (e.g., outside the Pompey Reefs) and planar reefs with an inner-shelf location that may support a hypothesis for shelf-edge submergence and inner-shelf emergence. However, attempts to show a constant pattern of cross-shelf reef distribution with an applicability to the whole of the Great Barrier Reef failed to produce positive results. Probably the amount of movement involved particularly in the Holocene is insufficient to overcome the influences of larger scale latitudinal variations. The effect is seen not so much in gross morphology but in the distribution of smaller details, such as proportion of living coral on the reef flat, which may be high in areas of relative subsidence but low or absent in areas of stable or relatively falling Holocene sea levels.

Reef size appears to be a factor influential on the stage a particular reef has reached. Because the smallest reefs may never have had a significant central depression, and because they have the highest ratio of productive margin to internal area, they develop most quickly to the planar stage. Thus, of the smallest reefs (< 1.75 km diameter), 56% have reached the planar stage, while only 13% of medium size (1.75–3.25 km) have reached this stage, and 3% of larger reefs. As accumulation of such large amounts of calcium carbonate within the larger reefs can be assumed to have taken place over many glacial-interglacial cycles, their distribution may represent areas of relative stability or slow shelf subsidence. It is probable that there has been insufficient time of Holocene sea-level stability for large planar reefs to develop and this is supported by their distribution in the Great Barrier Reef. Only 8 large (< 3.25 km diameter) planar reefs occur south of 12°S, all but one within the Princess Charlotte Bay area, where shallow nonreefal foundations may be found. Other reefs of this type are found in the Torres Strait area where it has been suggested that Pleistocene foundations are very close to the modern reef-flat level.

The limited distribution of ribbon reefs coincides with the area in which the edge of the continental shelf slopes most steeply from relatively shallow depths of about 50 m, that is, providing conditions ideally suited to the narrow horizontal grouping of former low sea-level shorelines. While the two reefs of this type of the central area (Moss and Bowl) appear to be of a similar nature, the group of linear reefs further south, particularly around the margins of the Swain Reefs, are situated in locations that suggest an origin on the margin of larger platforms, over an antecedent rim.

Earlier phases of linear reef types are difficult to detect. Only three have been mapped, Wardle Reef, discussed above, and two examples around the margins of the Swains. Submerged linear reefs are most easily detected in the area immediately south of the ribbon reefs between 16°00′ and 19°00′ S although it is quite probable that they have wider distribution. Their presence between Cairns and Townsville coincides with the area where the edge of the continental shelf becomes progressively deeper towards the south, but still within the range reached by low glacial sea levels, and where the top of the continental slope is slightly less steep than further north. These factors appear responsible for the horizontal separation of low sea-level shorelines and the development of several lines of less well-developed linear reefs. However, distinction should be made between the origin of the shelf edge 35–50 m shoal with a width of about 2 km and the narrow linear reefs with some living coral that rise from it. Shelf subsidence may be responsible for the depression of the major shoal feature, which is analogous to that from which the ribbon reefs rise further north. In contrast, the smaller linear reefs rising from it appear younger, having living, or apparently recently living, coral veneers (as suggested by echo-sounding traverses) but appear to be retarded in their progress towards modern sea level. Searle et al. (1980) have suggested that small linear reefs were established on the seaward flanks of the major bank during the Holocene transgression, probably initially as fringing reefs. With the rise in sea level new reefs were established further shoreward and sediments from these caused deterioration of growth conditions over the reefs in deeper water to the east. Indeed CSP results show a number of reefs to have been buried beneath the sediment cones spreading from the younger reefs to the west. The end result has been the formation of fragmentary linear reefs in parallel sequences as seen in Figure 9.10.

THE REGIONS OF THE GREAT BARRIER REEF

In spite of its complexity the distribution of reef types does provide the basis for a regional division of the Great Barrier Reef province (Fig. 9.14). Major regions and their characteristics are:

Region 1: Torres Strait (Fig. 2.7). This area of large planar reefs rises from shallow water and probably from very shallow pre-Holocene foundations. The region is very sharply defined on its eastern side.

Region 2: Inner shelf Cape Grenville to Cape York extending northwards across the midshelf zone opposite Torres Strait (Fig. 2.8). Radiocarbon dates from the southern end of this region suggest that modern sea level had been achieved by 6000 yrs B.P. The region is dominated by medium-sized reefs of partially infilled lagoonal or planar type.

Region 3: Largely a shelf-edge zone from the Gulf of Papua almost to Cairns, but including the full shelf width around Cape Direction and near Cooktown (Fig. 2.9). This region has an outer fringe of ribbon reefs (Fig. 9.15) extending as far north as Cape Grenville, and the outer line then being maintained by small planar reefs. Radiocarbon dates from at least the southern half of this region suggest that modern sea level was achieved close to 6000 yrs B.P. even on the shelf edge. However, behind the ribbons, reefs are poorly developed with large karstic banks and many reefs in early stages of develop-

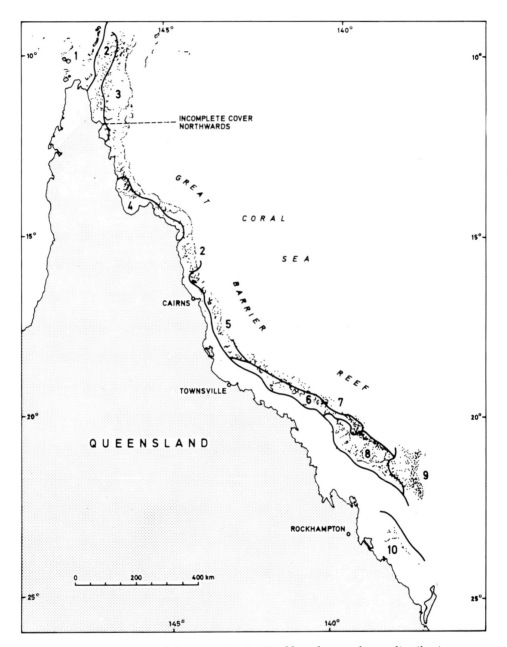

Figure 9.14   Regions of the Great Barrier Reef based on reef-type distributions.

ment probably the result of retarded growth rates, initially due to turbidity as the shallow shelf was submerged, and later due to restricted circulation and slow growth in the lee of the ribbons. Pre-Holocene platform depths in this area are not deep.

Region 4:   Inner shelf centered on Princess Charlotte Bay. This area has evidence not only of modern sea level being achieved early (6000 yrs B.P.) but of

Figure 9.15 Ribbon Reef (14°45′S) showing high-energy reef front, flat algal pavement, aligned coral zone, and back-reef detrital slope with isolated coral "bommies", mainly *Porites* sp.

relatively slightly high levels, which have aided in the production of planar reef tops. Shallow foundations of the reefs possibly including nonreefal platforms in Princess Charlotte Bay have also helped to produce senile reefs, including a large number of low wooded island reefs.

Region 5: Total shelf width, Cairns to Townsville. This area has been shown to have slightly deeper pre-Holocene foundations and a relatively late date (c. 2500 yrs B.P.) for the attainment of modern sea level, both factors possibly resulting from long-term subsidence. Consequently most reefs are juvenile or early mature, that is, the "resorbed" reefs of Maxwell. All reef tops are young (<2700 years) in this area.

Region 6: The major reef tract from Townsville to opposite the Whitsunday Islands (Fig. 9.16). At least in the northern part of this region modern sea level was achieved by 6000 yrs B.P. but it may have been progressively later towards the south and there is suggestion of some shelf subsidence opposite the Whitsunday Islands (Fig. 8.9), possibly in line with an extended Hillsborough Basin. Large and medium reefal platforms are present but mainly of a juvenile or early mature stage, suggesting relatively deep foundations away from the reef rims.

Region 7: Shelf margin of the central Great Barrier Reef (Figs. 2.10, 9.16). Probable subsidence and slow growth combine to give the shelf edge the extremely poor reef development. Submerged reefs and reef patches of

Figure 9.16 ERTS satellite photograph (MSS band 4) of the Whitsunday Passage and adjacent Great Barrier Reefs including Wallaby and Gould Reefs (top left), Hook and Hardy Reefs, and Stevens Reef (bottom right). Note the narrow interreef passages and tidal gyres in the turbid waters of the Whitsunday Islands. (NASA–ERTS.)

medium and small sizes are found here. They may be especially numerous in the uncharted area east of the Pompey Complex.

Region 8: The Pompey Complex (Fig. 2.10). Situated on a structural high this area has the bulk of the Great Barrier Reef's large reefs. Large reefs also dominate the western edge of the Pompey Group, the center of which has a large number of medium-sized reefs of all types. It is known that modern sea level was achieved by at least 4000 yrs B.P. in this area. Where surveyed, pre-Holocene antecedent platform depths are only moderate.

Region 9: Swain Reefs. South of the Pompey T-line large reefal platforms are entirely absent. Instead the Swain Reefs have great numbers of medium-size and small reefs of lagoonal or planar types.

Region 10: The Bunker–Capricorn Group. This distinctive reef province has mostly medium-sized reefs, of late stages of growth. Antecedent platform depths are not deep, sea level was achieved by at least 5000 yrs B.P. and was possibly higher than present. These factors, combined with Davies and Marshall's (1979) evidence of relatively rapid growth rates, appear responsible for the late stages of reef morphology. However, numerous submerged reefs are also found in this area, possibly a legacy of the marginal position of this area for coral growth, particularly early in the Holocene when deeper reefal platforms were first being submerged.

Although some control on the distribution of reef types is given by variation in Holocene sea levels, depths of antecedent platforms and variation in growth rates, it is suggested that the major control is that determined by structure. Sharp discontinuities in reef morphology, for example east of the Warrior line of reefs in Torres Strait and along the Pompey T-line are strongly suggestive of structural dislocations, whereas relative sea-level patterns (see Chap. 6) and reef distributions appear closely correlated with major structural features of the mainland. Neotectonic movements over the shelf during the Quaternary, when most of the modern reef morphology was evolving, have probably occurred and have had a profound influence on the nature of the Great Barrier Reef.

Details of reef morphology, particularly the degree of reef flat and lagoon development, may be a feature of Holocene growth, with influence from the underlying pre-Holocene surface, but the overall size and shape of the reefs may be much older features. Hedley and Taylor (1908), Fairbridge (1950, 1967), Maxwell (1968) and, more recently, Scoffin et al. (1978) have all noted the influence that the dominant southeasterlies have on reef orientation. Most of these authors suggested that the influence of wind and waves is through the movement of sediment from windward to leeward. However, Scoffin et al. (1978) also hypothesized that winds may influence the orientation of the reef foundation, for example in the building of longitudinal dunes that may subsequently become the loci for reef development. Certainly many of the pre-Holocene platforms from which the modern reefs grow appear to have similar orientations to modern reefs (predominantly southeast to northwest), a factor that has implications for the consistency of a southeasterly trade-wind dominance throughout reef-growing (high sea level) periods of the Quaternary.

The genetic classification of reefs of the Great Barrier Reef introduced in this chapter clearly emphasises the importance of Holocene reefal development. However, consideration of the nature of the reef foundations just as clearly indicates the importance of much earlier environmental factors, the full importance of which will become apparent only with more extensive drilling programs. Distribution of the different reef types, with their implications for foundation depth, growth history, and shelf stability suggest that such investigations may indicate distinctive geographical variations in these major factors influencing reef growth throughout the Great Barrier Reef region.

10

Intrareef
Morphology and Zonation

As a coral reef grows towards a stable or slowly rising sea level it transgresses from a deeper zone of relatively small environmental fluctuations and contrasts into the shallow area of diurnal and seasonal environmental fluctuations, which impose a series of horizontal variations on the reef. These contrasts are seen initially in terms of energy conditions, with energy gradients developing from the windward to leeward sides of the reef, gradients that in turn may affect the way the total reef morphology develops as seen in the previous chapter. Energy conditions in turn affect the sedimentary environments and physical processes operating on the reef, producing small but important variations in the heights of reef tops. Biological zonations result from these physical contrasts but both the morphology and ecology of the reef are not stable through time, as suggested by Pichon (1974) for the coral reefs of Tulear, Madagascar. Immature reefs on which the reef flat shows a continuous succession of coral reef communities from ocean to lagoon edge only slightly differentiated were seen as the forerunners for the major biotopes of mature reefs in which clear zonation could be seen. Similarly, a regressive evolution of coral reef benthic communities, in which algae become dominant, was seen as a later sequence that also resulted in less conspicuous zonation.

Morphological zonation and biological zonation have long been recognized over the Great Barrier Reef (see, e.g., Flinders, 1814, Vol. 2, p. 87; Agassiz, 1898; Hedley and Taylor, 1908; Stephenson et al., 1931; Manton, 1935) and, because a two-way interaction between physiography and biology operates on reefs, there is a close correspondence between the two approaches to spatial organization. However, differences do exist, and this chapter gives prominence to the physiographic rather than biological zonations recognized on reefs. Although this results from the nature of this book, on the Great Barrier Reef at least, and possibly on other Indo-Pacific reefs, the complexity of biology is such that the relatively simple biological zones recognized on Caribbean reefs (see Chap. 13) are far more difficult to define. Done (1977), Veron and Done (1979), and Done and Pichon (in press) have shown prevailing hydrodynamic conditions are prime influences on zonation, which, in the northern Great Barrier Reef is most clearly seen on the outer ribbon reefs. Lower energy gradients on midshelf and inner fringing reefs tend to diminish the distinction of zones.

Hydrodynamic regimes resulting from depth, position relative to the reef edge, and prevailing wave action produce a zonation that is expressed in growth form, encrusting and digitate forms dominating in high-energy locations, branching forms in moderate-energy areas, and massive forms where wave energy is low. Much greater variety probably exists in the biological zonation of the Great Barrier Reef than in morphological zonation because of the large latitudinal spread of the reef and great biogeographic contrasts zonally from mainland to reef (Endean et al., 1956a; Straughan, 1967). Details of the biological zonation may also change rapidly through time, though some differences noted may be the result of contrasting survey techniques which are used (see, e.g., Stephenson et al., 1958). Morphological zones may also change as the result of cyclones, freshwater flooding, or man's interference. This is amply illustrated by the photographic plates of Saville-Kent (1893), showing luxuriant coral growth on reefs that today have little living hard coral and are largely covered by rubble, sand, and soft corals. Nonetheless, the nature of the specific morphological zones, if not their faunistic and floristic components, is much more standardized. The listing of 125 morphological zones and features on Indo-Pacific Reefs by Battistini et al. (1975) is applicable to the Great Barrier Reef, although a more simplistic approach is used here. The major division is fivefold, consisting of reef front, the windward high energy margin up to the neap-low-tidal level, the reef flat consisting of the intertidal zones of the reef top, the lagoon zones permanently below water within the reef top, and the leeward margins. Features of reef islands are discussed in Chapter 11.

THE WINDWARD REEF FRONT

The windward reef front coinciding with hard-line reef development contains the highest energy zone of the reef in the upper 15 m or so of the reef slope. Average gradients are about 30° (Maxwell, 1968) but can vary locally from less than 10° to vertical or overhanging. The gradient may be an important indicator of the way the reef front has evolved in the Holocene. Davies (1977) and Davies and Kinsey (1977) have suggested that reef fronts may be eroding and evidence is quoted of pre-Holocene radiometric ages for materials taken from reef-front depths of 19.8 and 22.0 m on One Tree Reef (Davies and Marshall, 1979). However, this reef has pre-Holocene foundations at 18 m only a few meters from the windward reef edge (Harvey et al., 1978, 1979) and quite clearly the modern reef front is a reflection of the steepness of the margin of the pre-Holocene reefal platform. The present reef front is steep to a depth of 10 m and vertical to 25 m with only gorgonians growing on the steep cliff face, which is cut by caves and crevices (Davies et al., 1976). It is apparently little modified from its pre-Holocene condition. The main reef grows from the 25 m level, apparently a larger pre-Holocene reefal platform. In this morphological situation most erosional notches and fringing reef additions during the interstadial high sea levels of the last glacial were on the larger platform rather than the One Tree Reef front, the steepness of which would not encourage modification during the short stillstands that may have taken place at levels shallower than 20 m.

The factor of reef growth during interstadial high sea levels, as discussed in Chapters 6 and 8, is also important for the nature of modern reef fronts. If water temperatures were sufficiently lowered to prevent coral growth, modification by interstadial sea levels would be restricted to erosional notches and only narrow terrace features may be expected. In contrast, where coral growth was permitted, wider fringing reefs could have been added and modern reef fronts developed from wider, more complex, terrace sequences. Maxwell (1968) quoting evidence largely from the southernmost Reef states that terraces at about 4, 13, and 18 m are only 9–27 m wide. In contrast, much wider terrace features are found on reefs of the Central and Northern Great Barrier Reef and it is from these features up to 100 m wide that multiple reef fronts grow.

Steep reef fronts may thus be a reflection of both the Pleistocene reef-front morphology and the lack of major constructional modification since the last interglacial. In contrast more gently sloping reef fronts may have evolved from the inverse situation of less steep pre-Holocene foundations, which provided suitable substrate at suitable depth for constructional additions during the interstadial high sea level phases. On mature reefs of this type, considerable amounts of Holocene growth may have taken place during the postglacial transgression and Pleistocene reef may not be exposed at all in the windward face, or be exposed only at the base of the reef front (Fig. 10.1). This may be a major difference between southern and central reefs of the Great Barrier Reef. Further, the very shallow shelf depth on the northernmost reef probably determined that few interstadial additions were made to the reefs of this area and Pleistocene outcrops on steeper reef fronts inside the outer barrier could also occur. Certainly multiple reef fronts are most common in the central area of the Great Barrier Reef.

The general lack of coral cover described on the One Tree Reef front is not typical, although a coral cover greater than 50% is limited on most reefs to depths above 5 m. Below 15 m coral cover is much restricted though species diversity increases (see, e.g., Veron and Hudson, 1978) with no one species dominating. Branching *Acropora* sp. are the most common corals of the reef front (Fig. 10.2) with low-profile corymbose shapes within the wave-affected upper 5 m, arborescent forms below this, but gradual flattening with greater depth in response to the reduced light conditions, as the ratio of radial to axial corallite numbers decreases (Wallace, 1975, 1978). Actual species and species associations change with latitude, local energy conditions, and substrate slope. On the northern Reef *Acropora palifera* tends to dominate the upper slope, giving way to *Porites lichen* at depths to 30 m. At greater depths species diversity increases and no one species dominates (Veron and Hudson, 1978). Elsewhere, *Acropora* sp. dominate, *A. pulchra* being most common on the southern Reef (Maiklem, 1968a). On Redbill Reef, Wallace and Lovell (1977) have described contrasting assemblages on steep and gently sloping reef fronts, the gentler slopes having the greatest diversity. Clearly great variations in biological zonation occur on different parts of the Great Barrier Reef.

Sediments of reef fronts are poorly sorted and formed predominantly of coarse coral detritus, especially broken *Acropora* fragments (Jell and Flood, 1978). On the northern Reef, reef-front sediments are generally greater than

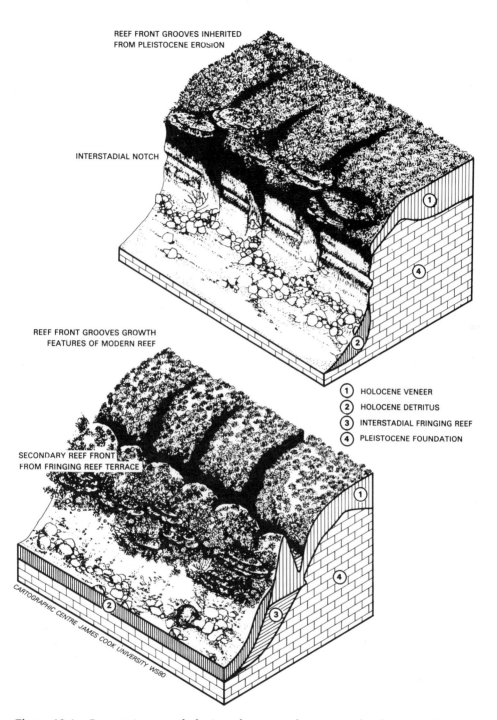

REEF FRONT GROOVES INHERITED
FROM PLEISTOCENE EROSION

INTERSTADIAL NOTCH

REEF FRONT GROOVES GROWTH
FEATURES OF MODERN REEF

SECONDARY REEF FRONT
FROM FRINGING REEF TERRACE

1 HOLOCENE VENEER
2 HOLOCENE DETRITUS
3 INTERSTADIAL FRINGING REEF
4 PLEISTOCENE FOUNDATION

CARTOGRAPHIC CENTRE JAMES COOK UNIVERSITY WS80

Figure 10.1 Contrasting morphologies of steep and more gently sloping reef fronts, which may reflect different histories during the last glacial period, together with contrasting amounts of Holocene construction.

Figure 10.2   Reef front of Wheeler Reef showing the dominance by *Acropora* sp; mainly corymbose forms on the crest, but arborescent and platelike within the deeper channel.

50% coarser than 1 ϕ and less than 10% finer than 4 ϕ. They contribute mainly coarse sand with gravel moderately to poorly sorted, strongly fine skewed, and with variable kurtosis (Flood et al., 1978). At the base of the reef slope whole heads of coral and broken reef blocks may form a scree slope of boulder-size sediments.

Specific features of the reef fronts include:

1 **Marginal Channels**   Many reefs have channels at the foot of the reef-front slope. Although not found on all reefs they are sufficiently common for them to be regarded as a distinctive zonal feature. On Keeper Reef near Townsville a channel surrounds the reef on all sides and is 2.8–5 m deep and 500–1,000 m wide. CSP survey over this feature suggests that it is cut into at least the first reflector beneath the present seabed and that the sediment infill is small (Searle et al., 1980). A channel at the base of Thetford Reef (16°45′S) is similar though shallower. Figure 10.3 shows that the present channel is clearly located over successively deeper features of similar location and magnitude. Smaller troughs, only a few meters wide and one or two meters deep were reported only on the windward margins of some of the northern reefs by Scoffin et al. (1978, p. 133). They were presumed to result from scour related to currents from the southeast as they disappear around the reef flanks. As this is part of the reef front receiving sediment, Scoffin et al. consider the trough-forming mechanisms to be still active. Although it is possible that some marginal channels resulted from

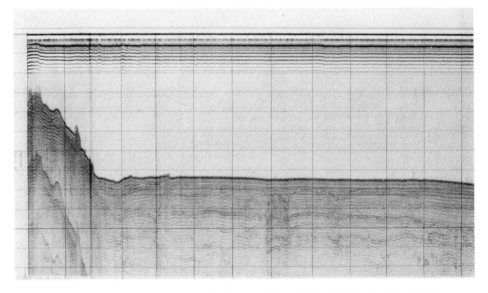

Figure 10.3 Continuous Seismic Reflection profile of Thetford Reef (16°45′S) showing a 3 m deep trough or marginal channel underlain by a buried moat at the base of the Holocene and other buried channels beneath that. Vertical scale of intervals of 10 msec or approximately 7.5 m, horizontal scale at 400 m intervals. (Published by permission of the Queensland Geological Survey.)

subaerial processes during low glacial sea levels, it seems most likely that they result from the failure of sediment shed from the reef to settle at the base of the reef where strong tidal scour takes place. The results from Thetford Reef indicate that similar conditions existed during reef constructional periods of the past.

2 **Terraces and Multiple Reef Fronts** Persistent breaks of slope have been noted around many reefs although interreefal consistency in depths is lacking. Several explanations for the features have been forwarded. (see Chaps. 7 and 8). They provide foundations for multiple reef front development (Fig. 10.4). A reef front growing from the deepest terrace levels, although flooded and presumably colonized first during the Holocene transgression, would have been left behind by the rising sea level. Reefs growing from the antecedent platform summit, would reach modern sea level first, followed progressively by reefs from deeper terraces. Fastest growth on the margins of each terrace produces an intervening moat that is slowly filled by internal growth and sediment from the windward reef wall. In time the secondary rim or rims will become part of the main reef structure, the former moat being entirely filled and overlain by algal pavement and rubble. On the double reef front of Moss Reef (17°56′S) the outer reefal wall is partly attached to the main reef by narrow bridges of algal-crusted reef top with corymbose *Acropora* spp. These separate long narrow gutters or moats 6 to 8 m deep with dense *Acropora* growth mainly on the seaward facing walls and Alcyonarions on the reef facing wall. Coarse rubble floors the gutters.

Figure 10.4 Double reef front on an unnamed reef near Townsville at 18°51'S, the outer front a complex feature just reaching modern sea level.

The outer reef is 1–2 m below the lowest tide levels. Its outer slope is about 35°–45° steepening to 45°–50° near its base at 27 m. Gutters 2–3 m wide and 6 m deep with a dendritic pattern cut the reef front. A rich coral cover is maintained on the upper 15 m dominated by *Acropora* spp. Large reef blocks occur at the base of the slope.

3 Spur and Groove Systems   The problematical nature of spur and groove systems was discussed in Chapter 7. On steep reefs, such as One Tree Reef where the pre-Holocene is exposed on the reef front, the grooves may be erosional and result from Pleistocene subaerial sculpture. Elsewhere, on more gently sloping reef fronts with thicker Holocene veneer, the grooves are probably growth features maintained by movement of water and sediment along the channels. Spur and groove systems are common on the Great Barrier Reefs. As elsewhere they are best developed on windward sides but can extend to the leeward. They are not always normal to the reef front but may form an angle apparently determined by the approach of refracted waves. Small variations in size and morphology occur. Veron and Hudson (1978) described deep spur and grooves penetrating the front of Tijou Reef, a northern ribbon reef, at an oblique angle. At their seaward end the grooves are up to 7 m deep and 10 m wide. The grooves may penetrate the reef front up to 80 m. Coral cover on the spurs is about 30% and dominated by *Acropora humilis* and *A. palifera*. Elsewhere the features are generally within this size range (Davies et al., 1976, 1977a; Jell and Flood, 1978).

THE OUTER REEF CREST

It is on the windward reef flat that annular zones are most strongly developed. Major differentiation is between the zones of the productive margin and the central reef flat, which is produced largely by lateral sediment movement. The morphological zones of the reef crest are discussed from outer edge inwards.

Outer Living Coral Zone

The outermost edge of the reef invariably consists of a zone of luxuriant coral growth (Fig. 10.5) the width of which varies largely with the stage reached in reef development (Chap. 9). On young reefs that have reached sea level relatively recently and on reefs in areas experiencing tectonic or hydro-isostatic submergence, this zone may dominate the reef top (Fig. 10.6). However, on the majority of reefs at later stages it forms a narrow edge 10–50 m wide from the top of the reef front to the level of MLWS. Most hard-line reef fronts are cut by numerous surge channels, often leading down to reef front grooves. Much of this zone may be the uppermost parts of the buttresses of spur and groove systems. The surge channels a meter or two deep may cut back into the reef front for up to 100 m, although 10–20 m is a more common distance. Former reef-front grooves may have been overgrown and leeward remnants occur as deeper holes in the living coral zone. Some may be connected subsurface with the reef front and act as blowholes at low stages of the tide.

A great variety of coral species is found in this zone with many of the same species of corals found on the upper part of the reef front dominating. These are mostly *Acropora* spp. but there is a distinct change in morphology from ramose

Figure 10.5 The outer edge of Michaelmas Reef (16°35′S) at absolute low tide level. Surge channels are separated by low ridges with rich cover of *Acropora* sp.

Figure 10.6 Channel Reef (16°56'S) with reef flat below MLWS level and covered with a veneer of living corals, mainly *Acropora* sp.

to densely branching and more flattened corymbose forms as they grow in higher energy conditions. Other branching corals are also found, particularly in the surge channels and trickle zones from the reef flat, including *Pocillopora verrucosa. P. damicornis,* and *Stylophora* whereas large head corals (*Porites* sp., *Goniastrea* sp., and *Favites* sp.) occur close to LWS, their uppermost surfaces often flattened into irregular microatoll forms (see Scoffin and Stoddart, 1978, p. 106). Alcyonarians may also be common on the shoulder of the reef and crustose coralline algae overgrow any dead coral colonies.

Sediments of the outer reef flat occur only in small pockets or pools where some protection is given from the pounding waves. Although most sediment zones do not correspond exactly to the morphological zones of reef flats due to variable transport and mixing (see Jell and Flood, 1978), the sediments of this zone are fairly distinctive, being locally derived and located here only for a short time before being transported further back from the reef front. The work of Maxwell (1973b), Maxwell et al. (1961, 1964), Orme et al. (1974), Orme (1977a), Jell and Flood (1978), Flood and Scoffin (1978), and Hopley (in press) from a variety of reef types suggests that sediments in this zone are composed largely of coral and coralline algal fragments locally derived, with additions of *Halimeda* fragments and benthonic foraminifera from the reef front. They are mainly coarse to medium sands, poorly sorted, negatively skewed, and with only moderate kurtosis values.

Algal Pavement

No other zone causes as much confusion as that which is dominated by the crustose coralline algae. To some extent this is the result of the influence of descriptions of the "Lithothamnium" rim or ridge on midoceanic atolls (e.g. Marshall, 1931), actually dominated by *Porolithon* species. On atolls the algal-dominated zone forms cuestalike ridges with steep seaward sloping faces and gentle leeward slopes on the windward sides of reefs and rising to 0.3–0.6 m above low tide (Stoddart, 1969a). No identical feature is found on the Great Barrier Reef and on most reefs a distinctive positive topographic feature is lacking, which Marshall (1931) attributed to lower energy levels.

Examination of contrasting zone situations on a number of reefs in the Great Barrier Reef suggest there are at least four contrasting morphologies.

1 On low, relatively young reef tops no distinctive zone is present, but an embryonic algal pavement may be indicated by the presence of pink algal crusts on the tops of some coral colonies and on detrital materials lodged on the reef top (Fig. 4.2). Small areas of *Acropora* shingle may be stabilized by the cementing activity of the thin and irregular algal crusts. Drilling into these reef-front areas shows that the underlying reef is largely unconsolidated with algal encrustations very much limited to the surface, and nowhere more than a few centimeters thick.

2 Typical of the ribbon reefs of the northern Great Barrier Reef (Fig. 9.15) are the low pavements described by Veron and Hudson (1978) and drilled and dated by Hopley (1977). Although this zone was termed the "reef crest" by Stephenson et al. (1931) it extends from the living coral zone at about MLWS between 100 and 150 m back to where it attains a maximum height possibly only 0.5 m higher and where it disappears beneath the rubble zone that forms the reef crest. The surface is a flat denuded limestone pavement with flattened encrusting algae irregularly distributed over it (Fig. 10.7). Hardly any sediment is present on this surface apart from small amounts of shingle-size debris in process of transport across the zone. Shallow depressions normal to the reef front sometimes occur and in these, very low small and flattened colonies of *Acropora* sp. and some head corals less than 10 cm in diameter may be present. Green filamentous algae and hydroids occur irregularly over the surface. Drilling into the pavements of Carter (Fig. 9.11) and Lark Press Reefs indicated that beneath the surface was at least 0.5 m of rubble, in situ *Acropora*, and small head corals completely infilled and firmly cemented by the encrusting algae. Radiocarbon ages of greater than 5000 yrs B.P. (Table 9.2) from this upper 0.5 m suggest great stability for the surface with minor abrasion from passing shingle balanced by slow coralgal growth. Similar surfaces overlying sediments much the same as those beneath the ribbon reefs also occur on some of the more exposed reefs of the middle shelf. Results of dating from Darley Reef (Fig. 10.16) and Stanley Reef (Fig. 9.6) suggest that these reefs too reached sea level about 6000 years ago and have old surfaces.

3 The commonest form of algal pavement found on the windward margins of inner reefs is an extremely smooth surface interrupted only by linear features a few centimeters high and a few meters apart. Stoddart et al. (1978b) suggested that these result from the erosional planing of reef flat structures. Occasionally, small 2–3 cm algal rims occur over the surface (Fig. 10.8). No corals occur on this surface, which varies from 10 to 100 m in width, has an average slope of about 1:80 (Stoddart et al., 1978b), and disappears towards

Figure 10.7 Reef surface, algal pavement zone of a ribbon reef.

Figure 10.8 Algal zone on the windward rim of East Hope reef showing shallow rimmed pools.

the inner reef beneath the rubble zone with which it may have a very sharp junction (Fig. 10.11). The surface is covered by a turf of fleshy algae similar to the algal surfaces of St. Croix (Adey and Burke, 1976). Although the crustose corallines are present, the substrate consists of sand and rubble, which is given a smooth compact surface by the sandbinding algae *Laurencia pannosa* and *L. obtusa* together with the yellow-brown zoanthids of the genus *Palythoa*. (Cribb, 1966) An algal fur mainly consisting of *Gelidiella bornetii* and *Herposyphonia tenella* gives the surface its turflike appearance. On Three Isles the substrate beneath the algal turf consists of about 10 cm of reef rubble, friably cemented by crustose corallines overlying what appears to be an open-water reef assemblage including *Acropora* sp., *Favites* sp., and *Cyphastrea* sp., the height of which is about 0.5 m higher than presently growing open-water corals. (Fig. 10.9). An age of 4520 ± 110 yrs B.P. is close to that for an emerged microatoll (3750 ± 110 yrs B.P.) as indicated by McLean et al. (1978). This algal pavement may thus have overgrown slightly emerged open-water reef, although drilling into other such pavements such as East Hope Reef (Fig. 10.8) indicates that this is not true of all examples.

4   Closest to the algal rims of the mid-Pacific atolls are the algal pavements of some of the southern reefs and of the very high tidal-range area of the central Great Barrier Reef. The rim on Redbill Reef (Fig. 4.3) causes the moating of the inner reef flat to almost mean sea level. On the windward side (Fig. 10.15) the pavement is similar to that on Three Isles, but much wider and thus reaching much greater elevation (about 2.0 m above MLWS). This too has a green algal turf cover but drilling (Fig. 9.7) indicated that crustose coralline algae form a cementing matrix between coral rubble and in situ

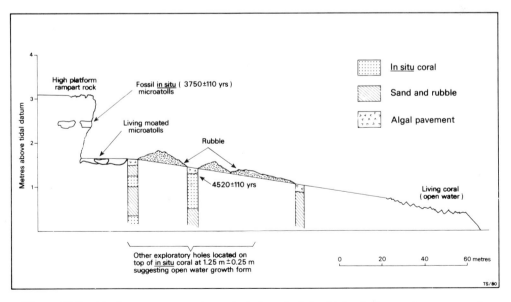

Figure 10.9 Algal pavement section to windward of the high platform of rampart rock on Three Isles.

coral for at least 1.6 m and that this type of pavement has been accumulating at a steady rate for at least 4830 years. On the eastern side of the reef the algal zone maintains a width of about 500 m and it is broken into low (c. 5 cm) terraces by small algal-rimmed pools (Fig. 4.3). In places the algal banks end abruptly on the reef flat side in a sharp break of about 0.5 m into the shallow moated lagoon of the reef flat. On the western side of the reef the terraces are even more striking, forming anastomosing ridges that together produce a series of steps across a zone varying from 50–200 m wide. Corals beneath this rim have been dated at 6,550 ± 150 yrs B.P. and rise to an elevation that may suggest a degree of emergence (Fig. 8.8). Although calcareous algae occur to depths of at least 3.1 m beneath the highest rim, they form a consistent matrix only in the upper 40 cm above the highest level of in situ corals. Davies (in press) described similar but lower stepped pavements on the southern Reef. He too has shown that the coralline crusts are thin, although thicker accumulations occur 4–8 m below the reef surface associated with *Millepora* sp.

On the Great Barrier Reef algal pavements are generally best developed on the windward fronts of the reefs but may extend around 70% of the perimeter. The small amount of evidence available to date suggests that great thicknesses of crustose coralline algae built upward from the level of open-water coral growth are rare. Where older reef does not provide the foundation, then rubble banks provide the bulk of the material, the algae providing only a small amount of cementing matrix. Notably radiocarbon ages of greater than 5000 years are associated with all reefs which possess wide, well-developed algal pavements that veneer the reef top after the development of other reef-flat features. Reef tops dated at younger than 3000 yrs B.P. have only patchy areas of algal pavement.

Sediment cover is very sparse in this zone although small amounts are caught in the algal turf and in the pools between steps where series of algal terraces have been built. It consists of moderately sorted medium to coarse sands, moderately skewed with a moderate to high kurtosis value. On Heron Island Maxwell (1973b) suggested that this is an algal-dominated facies, but greatest diversity of components was noted in this zone on Redbill Reef, the nature of the sediment depending to a large extent on the nature of the adjacent reef flat (Hopley, in press). Where a turf cover is present, Foraminifera frequently adhere to the algae including *Baculogypsina*, *Calcarina*, and *Marginopora*, the tests of which may locally dominate the sediment components.

Reef Blocks or Boulder Zone

Occasionally lying on the algal pavement or in the rubble zone up to 200 m from the reef front are large blocks of coral several meters in diameter (Fig. 10.10). Largest boulders on the Great Barrier Reef are about 4 m but elsewhere in the world they may reach 7 m in largest dimension (Stoddart, 1969a; Battistini et al., 1975, Fig. 50). Although the largest occur on the windward margins, they are generally isolated in such locations and topographically significant enough to appear on marine charts. However, towards the lee side of reefs, particularly on the northern side of many of the reefs north of Cairns, slightly smaller boulders with mean diameters of about 1 m occur as zones

Figure 10.10 Old bioeroded reef blocks firmly cemented to the reef flat, outer reefs near Cape Grenville. These features have previously been reported as emerged reef (see Fairbridge, 1950).

200–300 m in length and 20–50 m wide (Scoffin and McLean, 1978; Stoddart et al., 1978a). The term negro head or nigger head has been used for these features in the past since its use by Flinders (1814, Vol. 2, p. 88) but quite apart from its racial implications the term is confusing, for, as Spender (1930) noted, it is used to describe isolated, rounded, living coral colonies as well as the reef-top features. Their origin is as storm-tossed material, and although Kornicker and Squires (1962) indicated that, in water, large coral colonies may possess a degree of bouyancy, few cases have been cited of new blocks appearing after specific storms. An exception is a 3.3 × 2.7 × 2.1 m colony of *Leptoria* sp. cast up 200 m from the reef edge during Cyclone Althea in 1970 (Pearson, 1975).

Close examination of many of the blocks and boulders indicates that they are single coral colonies rather than consolidated reef rock. Seventy percent of those examined by Scoffin and McLean (1978) were *Porites* and only 5% consisted of more than a single coral colony. Many become firmly cemented to the reef substrate and this, with the retention of bioerosion structures in their original pattern, led Scoffin and McLean (1978) and Scoffin et al. (1978) to suggest that once in position the boulders do not move. However, Stephenson et al. (1958) thought it likely that on Low Isles many of the boulders noted on the 1928–29 Royal Society Expedition (Stephenson et al., 1931) had been eroded at their base and converted into reef-flat rubble and many of the boulders on the windward eastern and southern sides had disappeared altogether. Nonetheless there is sufficient evidence to suggest great ages for some reef blocks. On Ingram–Beanley Reef in the Howick Group a block of *Porites* 80 m from the reef front was dated at 640 ± 70 yrs B.P. and another 1.5 m high and 130 m from the reef edge at 4310 ± 100 yrs B.P. (Polach et al., 1978). Although the age of the coral may not necessarily indicate the time of deposition of the block, Scoffin et al. (1978) considered the data reliable enough to tentatively suggest they represented a reef-flat extension of 1.5 cm/yr. However, as happened during Cyclone Althea, the large reef block thrown 200 m from the reef front now stands further from the reef front than other blocks that were cemented to the reef flat and had experienced considerable bioerosion prior to Cyclone Althea. Stratigraphic evidence suggests a long period of stability for at least some blocks. Sherrard Island, a vegetated sand cay of the northern reef (12°59′S), for example, has transgressed over an older boulder tract that is now incorporated beneath the island beach, and at Howick Island a block of *Diploastrea* sp. dated at 2420 ± 70 yrs B.P. is incorporated in rampart rock (Polach et al., 1978).

The degree of bioerosion is also indicative of a long period of immobility. Many blocks are severely undercut with typical tropical intertidal notch and visor morphology. Being the highest point on reefs without islands, the surfaces of the blocks display the best intertidal zonation, with an upper zone of oysters (*Crassostrea amasa*), a zone dominated by the chiton *Acanthozostera gemmata*, and a basal zone in which the burrowing clam *Tridacna crocea* is most common (Stephenson et al., 1958). Internally the blocks are also severely eroded with filamentous algae near the surface and sipunculids and *Lithophaga* (Otter, 1937) deeper in the blocks.

Much confusion has existed over the origin of reef blocks. Fairbridge (1950, 1967) claimed there were two types: those thrown up by waves on the Great Barrier Reef, as originally suggested by Saville-Kent (1893), and those that were corroded remnants of higher reefs, as originally claimed by Agassiz (1898) and Maxwell (1968, p. 114). However, the examples of higher reef remnants near Raine Island quoted by Fairbridge (1950) were conclusively shown to be cemented reef blocks in 1973 (Fig. 10.10) and all blocks examined elsewhere are not in original growth position.

The boulder zone on the lee side of reefs may be the result of the growth structures normally found in these sheltered waters. Spender (1930) noted the common occurrence of mushroom-shaped coral colonies on the lee side of reefs and considered that this shape could be particularly prone to movement during cyclones. As Hopley (1974a) noted during Cyclone Althea, lee-side reefs of the Palm Group suffered far more damage than reefs oriented to the southeast or normal windward side, the more compact growth structures of which are better able to withstand cyclonic waves.

The Rubble Zone and Shingle Ramparts

Beyond the algal pavement, and often deposited over it on its inner side, is a morphologically diverse zone characterized by deposition of coarse material from the reef front. On many reefs this zone lacks recognizable organization and occurs as a low-angle ramp gently sloping upwards towards the reef interior, into a steeper, even abrupt, slope to the central reef flat (Fig. 10.11). Elsewhere the rubble is better sorted and forms single or multiple rampart systems (Fig. 11.18). These are best developed on the low wooded island reefs north of Cairns (Chap. 11) where their morphology and changes have been

Figure 10.11 Junction between the algal zone consisting of sand-binding algae and rubble zone, on Nymph Reef.

described by Steers (1929), Spender (1930), Moorhouse (1933, 1936), Fairbridge and Teichert (1947, 1948), and Stoddart et al. (1978a,b). Stoddart et al. (1978a, p. 49) described these features thus:

> Ramparts are asymmetric ridges of coral shingle with a steep inward face locally reaching 80° and a gentle seaward slope of less than 10°. Their outer margin is a feather edge of shingle on the reef flat and is often too indistinct to map; in plan it roughly parallels the edge of the reef. The inner edge is arcuate with occasional shingle tongues which on the windward side are at right angles to the reef edge but elsewhere are at an angle to it.

On some reefs a rampart may extend around almost the entire perimeter of the reef, on others it may be only 100 or 200 meters long, usually on the windward side. Individual ramparts are from 20 to 70 m in width, but accompanying shingle tongues can extend back across the reef as much as 340 m as on Houghton Reef (Stoddart et al., 1978a). They vary in height from 1 to over 3 m. Where multiple ramparts occur they form an overlapping sequence of shingle sheets. On Low Isles Fairbridge and Teichert (1947, 1948) described four separate systems, the youngest of which had formed since 1934.

The materials of the shingle ramparts and rubble zone are dominated by coral fragments and whole colonies, and originate from the reef front. In the ramparts especially, sticks of *Acropora* dominate the materials, varying in length up to at least 20 cm. However, as noted by McLean and Stoddart (1978), other branching forms such as *Porites*, *Seriatopora*, and *Pocillopora* are also common and many hemispherical corals may be present. They observed a similar number of coral genera in the windward shingle deposits of Bewick Reef as were then living on the reef edge down to depths of 12 m. In the less organized rubble-zone head corals are more obviously present. The materials in such areas are poorly sorted and little or no bedding is present. In contrast, shingles of the ramparts are better sorted and dip away from the reef edge at an angle similar to that of the steeper inner edge of the ridge. McLean and Stoddart (1978) commented that beneath the shingle there may be a basal layer of cobble-sized hemispherical and highly irregularly shaped corals, a feature noted elsewhere on the Great Barrier Reef and in storm deposits on reefs elsewhere in the world (e.g., McKee, 1959). Hedley (1925h) noted the interlocking nature of coral shingle and the tendency for individual fragments to be laid in the direction of the waves. Imbrication is a notable feature of most of these deposits and, on any particular part of the reef flat, there is a strong preferential orientation that is normal to the fronts of waves refracted over the reef top (Fig. 10.12). This is well illustrated by Pandora Reef (Figs. 10.13 and 11.2), where there is a strongly preferred orientation (Fig. 10.13), especially towards the southeast on the southern windward margins and towards the northeast on the northern edge of the reef, which becomes the weather side during some periods of summer. The shingle is also preferentially oriented on the southern face of the shingle ridge, but much less so on the northern side.

Spender (1930) interpreted ramparts as successive waves of shingle driven across the reef flat by normal wave action until it reached a limiting distance from the reef front determined by declining wave energy, at which time a new rampart started to form. However, there is sufficient evidence to suggest that initial formation of both ramparts and rubble zones takes place as episodic events associated with tropical cyclones. The most spectacular example of a new rampart is that on Funafuti, thrown up by Hurricane Bebe in 1972

Figure 10.12 Imbricated shingle, mainly *Acropora* clasts, oriented normal to refracted-wave fronts, Pandora Reef.

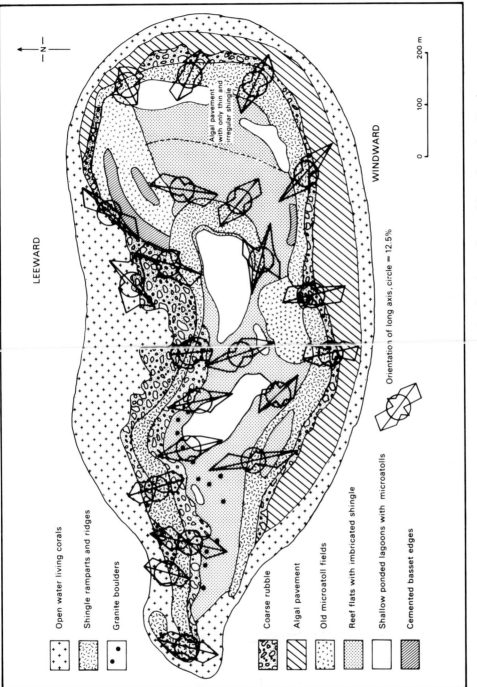

LEEWARD

WINDWARD

Open water living corals

Shingle ramparts and ridges

Granite boulders

Coarse rubble

Algal pavement

Old microatoll fields

Reef flats with imbricated shingle

Shallow ponded lagoons with microatolls

Cemented basset edges

Algal pavement with only thin and irregular shingle

Orientation of long axis, circle = 12.5%

N

0   100   200 m

Figure 10.13 Morphology and orientation roses for shingle on the reef flat of Pandora Reef.

(Maragos et al., 1973; Baines et al., 1974; Baines and McLean, 1976). On the southeastern side of this atoll, a ridge 19 km long, 30–40 m wide and up to 4 m high was formed during this single storm from material dredged from up to 20 m depth on the reef front. On more sheltered areas discontinuous low rubble tracts formed. On the Great Barrier Reef, a new rampart approximately 1.5 m high was formed during a cyclonic event in February 1931 (Moorhouse, 1933). Similarly modifications to existing ramparts particularly breaching and inward migration have been ascribed to cyclonic seas (Moorhouse, 1936; Gleghorn, 1947; Stoddart et al., 1978c). However, as Stoddart et al. (1978c) observed on Three Isles, there may be a continuing process of redistribution of shingle after the initial depositional event, which may be interrupted by later major storms that can locally strip the reef flat of its rubble layer. Under normal weather conditions since 1972, the Funafuti ridge has altered its original convex profile to a concave one, migrated 10–20 m shoreward and significantly reduced in height. In some areas it now remains only as a rubble zone and in its migration has left large coral heads as residual reef blocks (Baines and McLean, 1976). Such migration back from the reef front of cyclone-deposited ridges during "normal" weather conditions appears to be common (e.g., Stoddart, 1969b; Stoddart et al., 1978c). Much of the preferential orientation, imbrication, and compaction of shingle and rubble deposits may take place after the initial deposition.

Although postdepositional modification of shingle ramparts and rubble take place, stabilization can eventually result. This may be brought about biologically by the growth of sea grasses or algae, particularly *Caulerpa racemosa* (Fig. 3.6), but more permanently by cementation of the lower portion of the structures into rampart rock (see Chaps. 5 and 11). Removal of the overlying unconsolidated material can produce a relatively smooth horizontal platform of coral shingle in a finer matrix (the "honeycomb rock" of Stephenson et al., 1931), or where the steep dip away from the reef front is preserved, a jagged surface of strike ridges or basset edges (Figs. 6.9 and 10.14).

Apart from forming a very distinctive morphological area, the rubble zone has its own flora and fauna. The fabric itself is intensively attacked by bioeroding organisms, and older shingle in particular acquires a microphytokarstic architecture as the result of boring by filamentous algae (McLean and Stoddart, 1978). Destruction of larger fragments by the boring clam *Tridacna crocea* and by *Echinometra mathaei* is common, while an infauna of Lithophaga and Sipunculids is similar to that of the reef blocks. Stephenson et al. (1958) showed that subtle biological variations take place consequent upon the size and degree of consolidation of the rubble. Tufted algae, particularly *Gelidium*, are found amongst the rubble down to LWS. Other plants that provide baffles or directly stabilize the substrate are *Caulerpa racemosa*, the fan-shaped *Padina gymnospora*, the brown alga *Turbinaria ornata*, and various species of Halimeda, including *H. macroloba* and *H. cylindrica*. Beds of the small mussel *Modiolus agripeta* completely cover some hard rock surfaces.

Moats

As the shingle and rubble is piled up into a series of overlapping ridges, the intervening areas may retain water in long narrow pools or moats at low tide.

Figure 10.14 Cemented basset edges, windward margins of Low Isles, partially colonized by the mangrove *Avicennia marina*.

This is particularly so when cementation of the lower portion of ramparts reduces their porosity. As the ramparts migrate, the moats are to some extent ephemeral features. Moorhouse (1936) described the changes to rampart and moat systems at Low Isles, noting especially the effects that lowering water levels had on *Porites* microatolls. The moats provide ideal locations for the study of changes in microatoll form with variation in the moating level (see Chap. 4). On the Great Barrier Reef north of Cairns moat corals commonly grow to 0.9–1.0 m above tidal datum and exceptionally to 1.8 m (Stoddart et al., 1978a). Although up to 40 species of corals have been recorded from various moats, *Montipora*, *Goniastrea*, *Pocillopora*, and *Porites* are the most common (Bennett, 1973).

Some clams also occupy the moats, the most common being *Hippopus hippopus*, but very occasionally large giant clams, *Tridacna gigas*, are found, and these together with microatolls over 1 m in diameter suggest a degree of permanence for some moats. The moats act as sediment sinks for sand-sized material and in time may be considerably shallowed by this process, as has occurred on Low Isles. *Thalassia* may colonize the sandy moat floors.

THE INNER REEF FLAT

The radial zones of the inner reef flat are often less well defined than those towards the reef rim (Fig. 10.15). These are areas that receive sediment from the productive margins and individual zones tend to merge. Three types of reef

Figure 10.15 Windward margin of Redbill Reef showing outer living coral zone with buttresses, algal pavement with isolated reef blocks, aligned and nonaligned coral zones.

flat are recognized, each of which may retain up to 50 cm of water cover even on the lowest tides, due to the moating effects of rim deposits.

Aligned Coral Zone

Immediately behind the rim on many reefs is a zone of dense coral growth in which there is a linearity radiating out from the reef center. On ribbon reefs this is simply a zone of parallel coral colonies separated by sandy channels up to 2 m deep that are normal to the reef front (Fig. 9.15). On platform reefs the pattern appears to be determined by the refraction of waves around the reef margins and the aligned corals grow normal to the refracted wave fronts. Davies et al. (1976) on One Tree Reef and Orme et al. (1974) on Lady Musgrave Reef noted that the linearity of reef flat corals is identical to that of spur and groove systems of the adjacent reef front.

The detailed morphology of this zone depends on the depth of water over the reef flat at low tide and whether or not it is dammed, i.e., reaching the same moated level on each low tide. In deeper water, as occurs in this zone behind the northern ribbon reefs, the coral banks have irregular tops just above MLWS with much living coral over the surface, although dead patches with encrusting algae indicate the effects of emersion at the highest level of coral growth. Sides of the coral colonies are often overhanging, with *Acropora* sp. dominating. The corridors act as sediment chutes into the adjacent back reef detrital slope and tend to deepen towards the back reef area. Infilling by rubble is apparently taking place at the windward end. The floor of the corridor generally is coarse, moderately sorted sand of a wide range of organic debris.

In shallow reef-top locations individual coral colonies may make up the linear reefs although even here it is not uncommon for a variety of species to be combined in a single reef patch 1–2 m wide and 20 m or more long. The sand corridors perhaps 0.5 m deep are far more persistent and individual corridors can be traced right across the zone, which on some reefs is up to 1 km wide. Close examination of aerial photographs shows the elevated coral colonies to be wider, more densely spaced, and more continuous towards the windward margins, becoming narrower and discontinuous to leeward, where the alignment may be maintained only by rounded colonies that are arranged in line. Where the lagoon waters are moated, most of the corals have flat tops and grow in microatoll form, including many of the branching species. At least 55 species of coral were recorded by Wallace and Lovell (1977) in this zone on Redbill Reef. On many reefs, including Redbill, towards the windward margin of the zone, *Acropora cuneata* growing in low vertical plates perpendicular to the reef edge may be dominant. These and many of the other more delicate corals form a "crunchy" easily broken pavement along the aligned reef tops. On the northern Great Barrier Reef this zone may be host to numerous *Tridacna gigas*, locally reaching densities of $1/100$ m^2.

The cause of the linear pattern of coral growth in this zone has received surprisingly little attention, although most authors acknowledge that wave action is responsible (e.g., Maxwell, 1968, p. 115) and aligned coral zones are missing on many reefs that lie in the lee of other reefal banks (e.g., Wheeler Reef near Townsville, Fig. 11.3). In some cases, the corals may have grown initially on the hard substrate formed by long shingle tongues that extend into this zone from the reef front, as can be seen for some of the major linear features towards the windward side of Redbill Reef, but such a control seems unlikely for most aligned coral zones. Once formed, however, the pattern may be self-perpetuating as water movement across the reef flat is channelled into the intercoral grooves along which most sediment movement takes place.

Nonaligned Coral Zone

Behind the aligned coral zone, or on reef tops normally receiving lower wave energy, the reef flat may be formed from randomly scattered ovoid coral colonies with intervening sand patches (Fig. 10.15). In most other respects the morphology and ecology of this area is similar to that of the aligned coral zone. In particular the sediment characteristics appear very similar. The sand is made up of materials transported from the reef edge to which have been added local constituents. Results from a number of reefs (Heron, Lady Musgrave, Redbill, and the northern Great Barrier Reef) suggest that it is moderate to coarse, becoming finer and better sorted towards lagoons. There is also an increase in negative skewness away from the reef edge and the size distributions are platykurtic (Orme et al., 1974; Jell and Flood, 1978; Flood and Scoffin, 1978). Because of the mixture of translatory and local sediments there is a range of components, although there is a tendency for reef-flat sediments near the reef front to be dominated by a Foraminifera facies. This gradually changes through the aligned coral zone to a Halimeda facies, the decline in coralline algal and foraminifera components and increase in coral and Halimeda being characteristic of the change from higher energy reef front to lower energy reef flat.

Sanded Reef Flat

Towards the lee side of many reefs, around coral cays, especially more mobile nonvegetated cays, or over the bulk of the reef top of planar reefs, the reef flat forms a monotonous area of sand, interrupted only by occasional half-buried coral colonies, the tops of old microatolls or planed-down hemispherical coral heads protruding only a few centimeters through the sand. Where a shallow cover of water is maintained during low tide, swards of algae (*Padina, Dictyota, Hydroclathrus,* and *Sargassum* sp.) that may vary in their cover seasonally, occur together with sea grasses, most commonly *Thalassia hemprechii* with *Halophila* sp. and *Halodule* sp. (Cribb, 1966).

The sediments of the reef flat are the blanket sands of Flood and Scoffin (1978, p. 58) and are normally only a few centimeters thick. The grains are made up of corals, benthonic Foraminifera (many of which are attached to the soft plants of the reef flat), and calcareous algae. Where reef-flat vegetation is present it acts as a binding and baffling mechanism allowing the settling of silt and fine sand, resulting in a sediment with a wide range of sizes. However, in bare areas the sediments may be highly mobile (see Chap. 11) and shallow asymmetric ripples with well-sorted, well-rounded grains occur.

Although the larger plants are the only obvious life forms in this zone, there is a rich and varied fauna present (see for example Stephenson et al., 1958, Table 7; Gibbs, 1978, Table 3). Close examination of the reef flat reveals numerous burrows, faecal casts, and mounds produced by the infauna, indicating a high degree of biological mixing of the sediments.

LAGOONS

A large proportion of a reef-top surface can be occupied by one or more lagoons, within which the tidal waters may be moated to varying degrees at low tide by the surrounding rim and reef flat. This may be sufficient for a more or less static level to be maintained for several hours, as on Redbill Reef (Fig. 4.4) or One Tree Reef (Ludington, 1979). As indicated in previous chapters the lagoonal systems result from a combination of inheritance from the morphology of the underlying pre-Holocene platform and concentration of Holocene growth around the periphery. Maxwell (1968) differentiated between shallow lagoons resulting from "central decay" of platform reefs, and deeper lagoons formed by the enclosure of back reef floor by the growth of recurving linear reefs. While the latter may be accepted as the generalized model for all lagoon development as outlined in the previous chapter, central decay is highly dubious as a process. Depth of lagoon may be regarded as a function of the relief and depth of the antecedent platform together with the degree of endogenic and exogenic infilling that has occurred since the reef reached sea level. Lagoons form major sediment sinks in the reef and although endogenous growth may be slow and on the order of 0.5–1.5 kg of $CaCO_3/m^2/yr$ (Davies and Marshall, 1979) giving vertical accretion rates of only 0.3–1.0 mm/yr, import of sediment from the reefal margins can result in recorded lagoonal infill rates of up to 5.91 mm/yr (see Chap. 8; Frankel, 1977, 1978).

Although most lagoons are centrally situated in reefal platforms and are discrete from the outer reef zones, some lagoons occur within the rim zone.

Reef Rim Lagoons

Reef rim lagoons can occur within 100 m of the reef front (Fig. 7.8). Although some smaller shallower pools and elongate moatlike features may result from consolidation and growth of the reef front, others are more significant features. Some occur on the outer ribbon reefs where the reef-top width is greater than average. The best described example from such a locality is on Tijou Reef (Veron and Hudson, 1978). The lagoon, about 450 m wide, occurs behind the rubble zone and extends across to the aligned coral zone of the back reef area. It has a depth of 43 m. Its eastern wall is formed by a prograding sand and rubble slope and its western edge has a vertical wall to about 15 m, where it merges into a soft sandy floor. Lagoon reefs also rise vertically from the soft muddy sand of the lagoon floor.

Although no geomorphological work has been carried out on this feature the morphology suggests that this lagoon and its smaller counterpart just to the north (Veron and Hudson, 1978, Fig. 5) have formed from growth of a secondary front from a reef slope terrace (40 m depth) and is merely a wider example of the multiple reef-front gutters discussed above. However, an alternative though similar evolution is suggested by Darley Reef (Fig. 10.16). The wide algal pavement of this reef has numerous small pools up to 350 m long, most aligned centrally along the most consolidated part of the reef flat. Drilling and seismic survey in close proximity to some of these lagoons, about 3 m deep, indicated that this wide rim of the Darley Reef complex has grown from a similarly wide rim on the antecedent platform, apparently wide enough for it to have developed its own central, elongate depression. Holocene growth has reinforced the relief of the antecedent platform and a central lagoon has probably had greater extent in the past, as indicated by the age-growth lines. Where a lagoon is now lacking, central reef top ages are up to 3000 years younger than to either side.

Prograding Sand Sheets of Central Lagoons

Where rapid and prolonged infilling of a lagoon takes place from the windward margins, the windward side of the lagoon may not be a near vertical wall of coral as it is elsewhere, but have the form of a prograding subtidal sand sheet sloping down into the lagoon. The sand sheet on One Tree Reef (Davies et al., 1976) is particularly striking on the southern and eastern margins of the lagoon and is up to 500 m wide sloping from the intertidal reef flat to a depth of about 3 m (Fig. 8.4). The sand-engulfed outlines of previous lagoonal patch reefs are visible within the southern sand sheet. Elsewhere the sand sheets may be narrower and partially inundated patch reefs rise from them, their upper parts still maintaining a coral growth. The aligned coral zone of the windward reef flat appears to extend over earlier parts of prograding sand sheets on some reefs. Although gravel sized materials may be found at the top of the sand sheet,

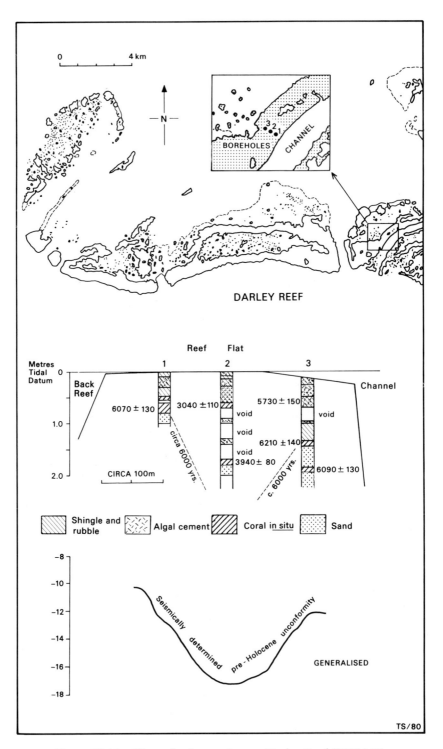

Figure 10.16 Channel edge section on Darley Reef (19°12′S).

most of the sediments are coarse to medium sands grading finer downslope towards the lagoon. Components derived from the windward rim are very similar to those in the aligned coral zone of the reef flat on the upper part of the sand sheet and the nonaligned coral zone deeper into the lagoon.

Leeward Lagoon Walls

On the lee side of lagoons, the northern and western sides on the Great Barrier Reef, no massive influx of sediments is taking place and a vertical or overhanging wall of coral may occur.

Lagoon Floor

The depth of lagoon floors at low water varies from a few meters to in excess of 40 m, although figures of 6–10 m appear to be the mode. Floors are irregular and almost exclusively sandy with a general pattern of finer sediments being found in deeper water. Thus muds are found as predominant constituents only in the deepest lagoons and blue holes. Most commonly the sediments are fine to medium sands that are moderately to poorly sorted. This is in part due to the admixture of transported fines and local coarse debris, which may produce a distinct bimodal distribution of sediment sizes, and to extreme bioturbation which mixes the layers deposited under contrasting energy regimes. The sands are generally negatively skewed and leptokurtic. Lagoon sediments in the Pompey Reefs (Backshall et al., 1979), Redbill Reef (Hopley, in press), Heron Island (Jell and Flood, 1978), One Tree Reef (Davies et al., 1976) and Lady Musgrave Reef (Orme et al., 1974) show a surprising degree of uniformity. In particular, they are dominated by coral fragments, with smaller amounts of *Halimeda*. Coralline algae and molluscs generally make up only a small proportion of the sediment compared to other reef zones whereas Foraminifera show greatest variation between locations. The depth of lagoon sediments is difficult to estimate. Frankel (1977, 1978) showed at least 1–2 m to be relatively common on lagoon floors. Harvey et al. (1979) indicated by seismic refraction that at One Tree Reef lagoonal sediments are 8–12 m thick. As is the case with atoll lagoons (Milliman, 1974, p. 181) the smaller lagoons receive proportionately greater quantities of peripheral reef flat sediments than do large lagoons, and there is the probability of a wide variation in lagoon-floor sediment thicknesses related to reef size.

Lagoonal Reefs

Few lagoons are completely reefless. Thickets of *Acropora* sp. occupy many deeper lagoon floors but typically lagoonal reefs grow up to the moated water level of the lagoon. Even where there is a continuous dam around the reef edge, the flow of water is often sufficiently retarded and lagoonal waters quiet enough for corals to grow to a more accordant level than around the reef margins.

Although further research is required on the nature and evolution of lagoonal reefs, (Figs. 7.8, 8.4) a tripartite division is suggested with three modes of formation:

1 Large patch reefs may form over prominences in the pre-Holocene substrate, as indicated in at least one such reef in One Tree lagoon (Harvey et

al., 1978, 1979). They are associated with deeper lagoons as such pre-Holocene prominences are associated with deeper and more irregular central pre-Holocene depressions

2 Small isolated reefs (Fig. 11.9) are usually found in shallower water and are considerably younger. They appear to develop within the lagoon without an antecedent foundation, although they may initially colonize coarser debris, which provides a more stable foundation than the sandy lagoon floor.

3 Reticulate reefs (Figs. 7.10, 8.4), forming a meshwork of anastomosing ridges, are generally found in shallower (< 8 m) lagoons. Their geographic distribution in the Great Barrier Reef appears random. The pattern is similar to the shallow karst pits and ridges of Pleistocene emerged reef surfaces and it is suggested that reticulate patterns may develop where the central area of the antecedent platform is not deeply buried beneath Holocene deposits. Such a hypothesis requires testing, as other factors related to lagoonal water circulation may be influential.

All types of lagoonal reefs have rich coral assemblages. Wallace and Lovell (1977) report at least 27 species from patch reefs of Redbill lagoon. The tops of lagoonal reefs are similar to the tops of microatolls and once at the highest level of growth the reefs expand radially outwards. The surfaces acquire a cover of both encrusting coralline and turf-forming algae. On some the central area is depressed relative to the rim to form a "miniatoll," which may contain a thin veneer of sand. Scoffin and Stoddart (1978, p. 114) have discussed the development of this type of feature. They suggested that once the patch reefs reach the surface, the central areas are choked with sand that cannot escape over the rim of living coral. The central areas then subside by a more rapid rate of bioerosion.

LEEWARD MARGINS

The leeward margins of reefs are morphologically analogous to the deeper lagoons, with prograding sand sheets and large patch reefs, usually within 1 km of the main part of the reef. On the northern ribbon reefs and many crescentic reefs the leeward sand slope is almost continuous (Figs. 4.2, 9.15), but on more ovoid reefs sand is directed off the reef top along more limited depressions or chutes between patch reefs that resemble a more open and irregular system of spurs and grooves, the sediments forming fans at the base of the chutes (Fig. 11.3).

Lee Side Detrital Slope

This is frequently close to the angle of rest of the materials being shed from the reef top. Commonly the slopes average 15°. Behind the ribbon reefs, depths of 30 m are achieved within 80 m of the top of the sand slope (Veron and Hudson, 1978). The sediments are generally fine to medium sands better sorted than on windward margins, which are made up largely of coral detritus and benthonic Foraminifera (Jell and Flood, 19778; Flood et al., 1978). Although these sand slopes are actively receiving sediment from the reef tops, scattered open colonies of fast growing *Acropora* sp. may be patchily developed. The slope may also contain occasional boulder-sized material.

DISCUSSION

All the zones described can be found on single reefs, but have varying widths and cover different proportions of the reef tops, entire zones being absent from some reefs. From the descriptions of Holocene reef evolution in Chapters 8 and 9 it may be concluded that as total reef morphology evolves, concommitant changes in reef-top zonation will also take place. Reef zones are thus dynamic features, with the greatest and most rapid changes taking place just after the reef first reaches modern sea level and as rapid upward growth changes to lateral reef-flat development. Completely sanded planar reefs may be the end stage, which subsequently show little change.

The shallow drilling program referred to elsewhere (Table 9.2), although concentrating on the windward margins, has resulted in cores up to 4 m long being obtained from all intertidal reef-flat zones (Figs. 9.6, 9.7, 9.11, 10.16). Identification and dating of materials indicates progressive evolution of reef-top zones is a valid concept, leading to the formation of a three-dimensional model of Holocene reef top structure (Fig. 10.17). Pichon (1974) considered the sequence to occur over periods of only "one or two centuries." However, results for the Great Barrier Reef suggest that the full sequence on some reefs may not have been completed over the 6000 years or more of relatively stable sea level.

Initially, as Pichon suggested, minimal variation may exist over the emerging reef top. While the reef is still submerged, the structure of the Holocene veneer is constructed mainly of corals of both branching and head morphology. Some internal pockets of sediment can form, although internal cavities may be relatively common. As the reef approaches modern sea level, the effect of waves is felt and sediment is transported to the lee side of emergent patches. Initial emergence thus produces a twofold division on the reef flat of a living coral zone and a lee-side sand slope. Both of these zones migrate leeward, the coral zone over the detrital slope and the detritus over the initial back reef zone of the protolagoon. Subsequently the reef-front living coral zone, which may also migrate to windward if the pre-Holocene frontal slope is not steep, provides material for detrital infill of the initially irregular reef-flat surface and the formation of a rubble zone. At this stage the windward reef flat may be occupied by crustose and turf-forming algae developing from irregular patches into clearly defined algal pavement. Once formed the algal pavement appears to accrete vertically very slowly, with net rates of about 0.1 mm/yr being indicated by all the reefs for which cores through this zone are available. As the rubble bank of the reef top provides both leeward protection and tongues of shingle for the location of some aligned coral growths normal to the reef front, the aligned coral zone becomes a noticeable feature of the reef top. Detrital material now moves steadily over the reef top, all except the largest reef blocks lodging beyond the windward margins. The algal zone migrates to leeward consolidating and capping the rubble zone at rates that may approach 1 cm/yr lateral extension. In turn the rubble zone is also extended to leeward, infilling

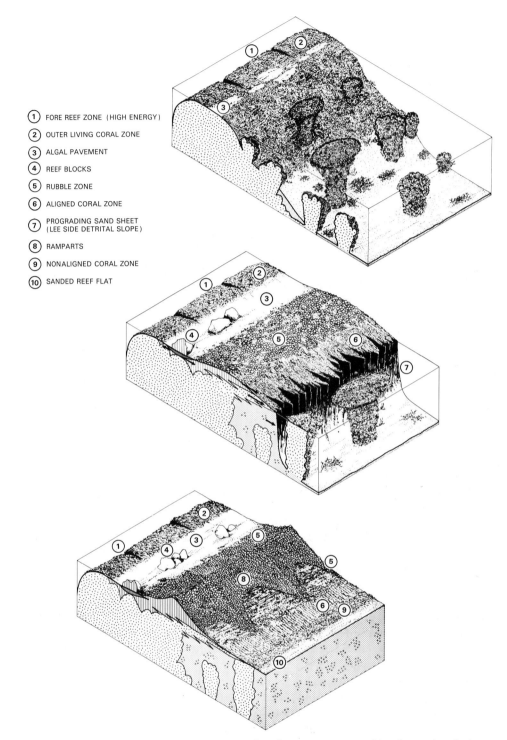

1. FORE REEF ZONE (HIGH ENERGY)
2. OUTER LIVING CORAL ZONE
3. ALGAL PAVEMENT
4. REEF BLOCKS
5. RUBBLE ZONE
6. ALIGNED CORAL ZONE
7. PROGRADING SAND SHEET
   (LEE SIDE DETRITAL SLOPE)
8. RAMPARTS
9. NONALIGNED CORAL ZONE
10. SANDED REEF FLAT

Figure 10.17 Model of the development of reef-top structure and its dynamic relationships. (*a*) Immature reef top with little zonation. (*b*) Mature reef top with well-defined zonation. (*c*) Regressive reef top with sediment cover.

the gutters of the aligned zone at rates that have been measured at between 0.2 and 0.4 mm/yr. Finer materials can be carried further into the lagoon, forming the prograding sand slope over which the aligned coral zone may migrate. However, as the reef flat extends further back from the reef edge the influence of translatory waves is reduced and further colonization of the sand slope may be as scattered, nonaligned heads. As the constructional morphology of constituents of each zone, especially the corals, appears to be controlled by wave intensity an equilibrium stage is likely to be reached in which no further leeward migration of a particular zone is possible. A regressive sequence may then take place, with the zones of sediment deposition enlarging and blanketing adjacent zones. Outer reef areas become rubble-covered and dominated by algae while the interior of the reef is converted entirely into sanded reef flat. Reef-top dates in excess of 5000 years have been obtained from reefs with such zones, indicating the considerable period of time required for the regressive sequence to commence.

Sediment zones, although less precisely defined than the morphological zones, change and migrate in a similar way. With lagoon filling and leeward migration of windward zones an initial differentiation between coarse rim deposits and fine lagoonal sediments is gradually lost. The pattern of change from a lagoonal reef to a planar reef has been modelled by Flood and Orme (1977) in which this trend can be seen with a change in the modal size of central reef deposits from finer than 3 ϕ to about 1 ϕ. However, the formation of ramparts (and, at a later stage, mangroves as a low wooded island reef develops) sees the superimposition of a further set of fine sediments in the lee of the ramparts and mangroves.

Zonation on the Great Barrier Reef may not be as marked as on some open-ocean atolls where much higher energy levels exist (see Chap. 13). Clearest morphological and biological zonations are associated with the reefs receiving highest wave energy, notably the Bunker–Capricorn Reefs in the south and the outer shelf reefs, especially the ribbon reefs, further north. Distortions of zonal patterns may be seen on inner shelf reefs where energy levels are lower, or wave patterns refracted by reefs which lie upwind.

Three factors may retard the regressive phases. If the internal lagoon is large and deep then it will act as a major sediment sink and sand-sized sediments in particular will continue to migrate over the various zones into the lagoon rather than lodging on the reef flat and blanketing the aligned and nonaligned coral zones. Only after the lagoon is infilled will the regressive phase become dominant. Rejuvenation of reef-top construction may also take place after effective moating has led to renewed upward growth of corals in microatoll form, requiring extra sediment infill to produce the sanded reef-flat stage. The final factor that may retard the erasing of distinctive zonation is a renewed period of relative sea-level rise. However, the reverse situation of a fall in relative sea level has the opposite effect, leading to emergence and acceleration of the production of sediment. As Maxwell (1968, p. 115) observed, on inner shelf reefs much of the zonation is masked by a heavy sediment cover. This is particularly true of the low wooded island reefs north of Cairns where McLean et al. (1978) suggested that reef-flat productivity reached its zenith during the period 5000–3000 yrs B.P., coinciding with the period of highest sea level and the initial regression from this level. The rates at which the various zones develop on a reef top probably vary with the nature and depth of the platform from which the Holocene reefs are growing; particularly, its relative relief, the exact nature of the local sea level curve in the last 6000 years, and local exposure to wave action. Such factors have considerable variability over the geographical extent of the Great Barrier Reef, accounting for the contrasting morphology of different reef tops.

11

Coral Cays and Low Wooded Islands of the Great Barrier Reef

Coral cays and related island features constructed from the biogenic materials of the reef are a distinctive morphological zone of some reef flats. A cay may form as soon as there is sufficient area on a reef flat, the number of cays found on relatively small reefs less than 1 km^2 suggesting that a large area is unnecessary. However, concentration of sediments into positive features rising above the general reef-flat level, though not necessarily above the highest tidal levels, does not take place on all reef flats and specific sets of circumstances are required. A supply of biogenic sediments is obvious, but again the majority of reef tops have partial veneers of sand and shingle and there are many reefs with large areas of sand or shingle that remain in sheets over the reef top without being concentrated into even ephemeral cays. The most influential factor is the pattern of sediment movement produced by waves and currents.

Two related features of wave passage over a reef control whether or not there is an area of concentrated deposition. The first is the convergence of waves. As previously noted, the depth of water just beyond the reef front means that waves do not fully refract and accommodate themselves to the reef front. Instead, away from the windward apex, they pass over the reef crest at a slight angle, leading to an asymmetrical location of the zone of wave convergence towards the leeward reef flat. This is indicated clearly by the pattern of the aligned coral zone on many reefs. However, the pattern is not centripetal on all reefs. Interference of wave patterns downwind by other reefs may mean that the waves breaking around a particular reef are already refracted and no clear focus point results from further refraction on the reef. Similarly, the shape of the reef is of utmost importance as this too will affect the exact pattern of refraction. Convergence of wave trains is most likely on circular or oval reefs. On ribbon reefs there is a tendency for waves to pass directly over the reef top without significant refraction. On crescentic reefs lying across the direction of dominant wave approach there is incomplete refraction over the reef and the point of convergence lies to leeward rather than on the reef top. On elongate reefs lying along the line of wave approach, refraction may produce

317

wave convergence from either side of the reef, not focused on a particular area but along the entire central zone.

The second important feature of the waves is their ability to transport sediment. As noted in Chapter 4, much wave energy is lost on the reef edge due to breaking and reflection but a transmitted wave reforms beyond the break point and moves over the reef flat where it is attenuated very slowly unless water depths are exceptionally shallow or the bottom very rough. Using the fluvial concept of competency, the ability of the waves to move sediment is very much reduced in the area of reformation at the reef margins, even during major storms. Thus there is a windward location for coarse sediment deposition that may lead to the formation of a shingle cay. This may be a linear feature paralleling the reef edge and producing rampart systems where waves tend to break normal to the reef front. At the apex of a reef, or in projecting ''foreland'' areas along a reef front there may be sufficient refraction to concentrate these coarser sediments in a specific area to form a more compact island morphology. This is seen, for example, on One Tree Reef (Fig. 8.4), where the windward shingle cay is located at the southeastern corner of the reef at the point where refracted waves from both the eastern and southern reef edges meet (Davies et al., 1976). On relatively small reefs the area in which shingle can be deposited may extend over most of the reef flat and, as on Lady Elliot Island, discussed below, the 0.54 km^2 shingle island is placed centrally on the 1.8 km^2 reef platform (Flood et al., 1979), although it is in fact no further back from the windward reef edge than is One Tree Island.

Beyond the reef rim the transmitted waves have competency most of the time to transport only sand-sized material. As these waves are attenuated slowly this material may be transported some considerable distance leeward. Deposition takes place where refracted waves converge, either along the center of the reef or in a nodal area towards the lee. However, on the very largest reefs the waves may loose competency to transport even sand-sized material and sediment may be spread more evenly over the reef top, the distance leeward that sediment is transported varying from day to day with the energy conditions of the waves breaking on the reef. Some of the large reefs in Princess Charlotte Bay that have very sanded reef tops may lack reef islands for this reason. Leeward sand cays thus form where there is a tendency for both a centripetal convergence of refracted waves and sufficient wave power to transport sand-sized sediments to this focal point.

CAY SEDIMENTS

Reef-sediment characteristics aid in this twofold division of sediment deposition on reef tops. The tendency for shingle and rubble to next break down into sand sizes of approximately 2 ϕ (Orme, 1977a) means that there is a distinctly bimodal distribution of sediment sizes that under the wave-energy conditions described results in a clear division of depositional environments. Nonetheless this basic division of reef islands into windward shingle cays and leeward sand cays is very much oversimplified.

Studies of Great Barrier Reef cay sediments (Maxwell et al., 1961, 1964;

McLean and Stoddart, 1978) suggest that for each cay type, either sand or shingle, there is a remarkable degree of uniformity in the nature of the sediments. The most comprehensive study is that of McLean and Stoddart (1978) on the northern Great Barrier Reef, which noted that whereas shingles, which are relatively homogeneous in composition (mainly *Acropora* clasts), show a great range of size and shape, sediments of sand cays show great uniformity, mainly in the range of medium to coarse sands that are well sorted.

The most common size range is $0-1.5 \phi$ and sorting is generally less than 1ϕ. Constituents are similar to those of the reef flat sediments. However, compared to the reef flat the cay sediments are generally better sorted, though of a similar mean size. The beaches of the sand cays are the coarsest sediments, particularly on the windward side. Winnowing by the wind moves finer sand to the cay interior or berm. McLean and Stoddart (1978) found the finest sediments to be associated with present and buried soils and suggested that this was due in part to the incorporation of fine organic matter.

Studies of cay sediments elsewhere on the Great Barrier Reef indicate that the findings on cays north of Cairns are generally applicable. Although sand-cay sediments occur within a narrow range, local differences can be noted. McLean and Stoddart suggest that small but distinct variations between cays are due to differences in proportions of constituent components (which may be related to the nature of the reef flat), differences in distances, modes, and rates of transport from source area to cay (dependent on the size of the reef and the location of the cay upon it), and variations in residence time since deposition. Thus on Redbill Reef (Fig. 9.7, 11.8) Bushy Island cay sediments are coarser and more strongly negatively skewed than those of northern sand cays and have a higher proportion of coralline algae in their components, the result of proximity to the massive algal ridges of the reef margin. These sediments are also coarsest on the windward southern and eastern beaches of the cay (Hopley, in press).

Some noncarbonate sediments are incorporated in coral cays. The most common are pumice fragments that are floated in from their source area in the Solomon Sea–New Hebrides area. Individual fragments up to 0.5 m in diameter have been found, but more commonly they range from about 1 to 5 cm in size. Pumice fragments form distinctive strata in cay sediments up to 30 cm in thickness. Occasionally continental rocks reach the Great Barrier Reef cays in the roots of floating trees.

CLASSIFICATION OF REEF ISLANDS

In a review of the literature on reef islands, Stoddart and Steers (1977) suggested that the cays and low wooded islands of the Great Barrier Reef display greater variety and more complex morphology than reef islands of any other coral reef region, a view that was supported by Stoddart et al. (1978a) after examination of the geomorphology of reef islands of the northern Great Barrier Reef. Forms vary from small ephemeral sand patches emerging only at low water to the complex low wooded islands consisting of leeward sand cay, windward shingle island with cemented rampart rocks and central mangrove swamp. A considerable literature exists on reef islands (see Stoddart and Steers, 1977) and on the Great Barrier Reef most of the purely geomorphological work carried out prior to 1970 was concentrated on the islands. The first extensive studies were those of Steers (1929, 1937, 1938) who recognized three types of island: sand cays, shingle cays, and low wooded islands. Fairbridge (1950, 1967) extended the classification of islands of the Great Barrier Reef in a scheme that uses vegetation as a basic criterion and again differentiates initially between leeward sand cay and windward shingle deposits. He also included the effects of sea-level change in the latter phases of the scheme.

Fairbridge's classification was designed specifically for the Great Barrier Reef, but there are difficulties in successfully applying it to all islands of the region. Location to windward or leeward on the reef flat, caliber of the materials, and presence or lack of vegetation are obvious criteria to use in a classification. However, in the division of island types used here (Table 11.1), the number of islands on reef tops, their degree of complexity, and the overall morphology in relation to the presence or absence of centripetal processes, are used as further factors. Examples are given in the following discussion but the cays of the Great Barrier Reef form a continuum from the sanded reef flat with low sand banks to the complex morphology of the low wooded islands.

Unvegetated Solitary Islands

Unvegetated cays are unstable and may migrate over several hundreds of meters of reef flat during periods of several years, changing shape and height as they move. Some may disappear completely. For example, Admiralty charts show a cay on Pixie Reef near Cairns. In 1928 this was reported as being about 45 m in diameter and in 1929 as having separated into two smaller cays about 65 m apart, whereas today there is no sign of even an ephemeral sand bank (Carter, 1973). Instability is an obvious reason for the lack of vegetation, although some larger cays have been stable enough for beach rock to form. Steers (1929,

Table 11.1   A Classification of Reef Islands of the Great Barrier Reef

A   Unvegetated Solitary Island

    1   Linear sand cays
    2   Linear shingle cays
    3   Compact sand cays
    4   Compact shingle cays

B   Vegetated Solitary Islands

    1   Sand cays
    2   Mixed sand and shingle cays
    3   Shingle cays
    4   Mangrove cays

C   Multiple Islands

D   Complex Low Wooded Islands

p. 249) found no example of a cay with beach rock and without vegetation, (although a number do exist) and suggested that vegetation may play a part in the formation of cemented beach deposits. Although this is highly debatable, both features tend to stabilize cays and it is possible that vegetation existed on the cay at the time of beach-rock formation. Stoddart et al. (1978a) noted that some of the larger islands which they classified as unvegetated possess vascular plants though only as scattered and ephemeral individuals. Spender (1930, p. 285) mentioned that Pickersgill Cay was reported as vegetated but in 1929 had no vascular plants, a situation which remains today. Similarly several of the islands visited by Steers (1929, 1938) including Sudbury, Mackay, and Arlington cays, which had some vegetation in the 1929–1930 period, are now completely bare (Stoddart et al., 1978a).

It is probable that windward shingle cays, which owe much of their development to cyclonic storms, may be more stable or move more slowly than sand cays. Greater stability of the unvegetated shingle cays is suggested by the common occurrence of cemented deposits such as basset edges or conglomerate with the coarser materials. However, examination of a number of stable shingle banks without vegetation suggests that they acquire a plant cover more slowly than sand cays. Their exposed location and open framework of coarse shingle that will not retain fresh water are probable factors in this slow colonization.

Unvegetated cays are divided into four categories based on shape and constituents

Linear Unvegetated Sand Cay

Linear sand cays form on large or medium-sized planar reefs either where the reef is long and narrow, producing a wave-refraction pattern dominated by opposing wave trains meeting along the entire length of the reef, or in areas where seasonally reversed wind conditions exist. This latter situation occurs more commonly on the northernmost Great Barrier Reef with the winter southeasterlies contrasting with the lighter winds that have a northerly component in summer; for example, the large planar reefs of Princess Charlotte Bay, which have seasonally migrating sand banks up to 1 m high. Centrally located linear sand banks occur on a number of reefs in the Lizard Island area, including Linnet and Martin Reefs, while on adjacent Eagle Reef a sand spit towards the leeward margins of the reef is an extension of the Eagle Cay. These linear sand cays, many no more then ephemeral sand banks, appear to be the least stable of all the coral cays of the Great Barrier Reef. Beach rock is found on only a few examples examined (Fig. 11.1).

Linear Unvegetated Shingle Cay

A shingle ridge parallel to the reef front is in reality a form of shingle rampart discussed in Chapter 10, while similar features normal to the reef front are analogous to the shingle tongues which commonly extend back over the reef flat from ramparts. Apart from the shingle components of the low wooded islands, unvegetated linear shingle ridges, although common, rarely rate the term cay. A rare example is on Pandora Reef, a small reef 1.2 km long lying east to west between the Palm Islands and the mainland (Figs. 10.13 and 11.2).

Figure 11.1 The beach rock remnants (1960 m^2) of Ellis Island, a linear, unvegetated sand cay.

Much of the reef flat is covered with shingle and rubble and it is exposed to the southeast. Low shingle ramparts occur towards the windward margin. A second shingle ridge is set further towards the lee of the reef flat, running along the length of the reef. Towards the west it is relatively low, rising to only 1.5 m above reef flat level (which is about 0.7 m tidal datum). However, at its eastern end the ridge heightens as it curves around a shallow pool and reaches a height of more than 3 m, remaining above all except the highest tides. Although the slope on the shingle has changed with time, the general location of this ridge has been stable over at least ten years of observation and suffered only minor modifications during Cyclone Althea, which passed very close to this reef in 1971 with wind speeds in excess of 100 kn. The pool, around which the shingle ridge curves contains numerous microatolls. Occasionally mangrove seedlings have lodged here but none have survived for more than a few months. Although comparatively stable in the short term, destruction of a previous shingle cay or major migration of the present cay has taken place in the past, as an extensive area of basset edges occurs on the reef flat northeast of the present cay, their alignment suggesting a hooked morphology to this earlier feature similar to the present cay.

Compact Unvegetated Sand Cay

Strong centripetal transport of sediment over even small reef tops can produce oval cays. However, all stages of formation from oval to linear are found on reefs and it is likely that the balance between wave factors, which determine the two extremes of morphology, forms a continuum rather than a discrete set

Figure 11.2 Oblique aerial photograph of Pandora Reef from the northwest showing central shingle ridge. Compare with Figure 10.13.

of circumstances. Moreover, changing wave regimes can rapidly alter the morphology of this type of cay, which may migrate and alter with daily weather changes. The ephemeral nature of these cays is well documented. Taylor (1924), for example, recorded about 90 m of migration on Beaver Cay in a two-week period.

Detailed study of the sand cay on Wheeler Reef indicates that this degree of mobility is not unusual (Hopley, 1978c). Wheeler Cay is situated on the western side of the reef (Fig. 9.8, 11.3) and, although the cay changes shape as well as location (Fig. 11.4, Table 11.2), is normally oval about 80 × 50 m in size. It lies on an area of sanded reef flat that rises from a height of about MLWS (0.3 m), an area that apparently defines the extent of cay migration (Fig. 11.3). This area has been extended eastward during 1975 as the result of cay migration burying and killing the living corals of the adjacent reef flat. Although normally oval the cay frequently develops a spit extending towards the north or northwest. Occasionally, with excessive elongation of the cay, two separate sand bodies are formed up to 100 m apart (as in April and October, 1976). During Cyclone Althea in December 1971, the cay was completely flattened and the sand spread over the sanded reef flat area but reformed within six months.

Over the eight-year period the cay has moved over approximately 11,000 m^2 of reef flat (Fig. 11.4). The highest point marks its approximate center of gravity and has moved as much as 13 m in a 24-hour period (19–20 November, 1976) in association with a three-hour storm (Fig. 4.10). However, even in light

Figure 11.3 Oblique aerial photograph of the cay on Wheeler Reef. The area of sanded reef flat over which the cay migrates is clearly seen as are also the sand chutes along which sediment leaves the reef flat.

southeasterly winds (10 kn) in June 1975 and light northerly winds in July 1975 (6 kn) the whole cay was moving up to 6 m in 24 hours. Predominant movement during periods of ground survey has been southerly but this is by no means constant. Although no observations have been made when strong southeasterly winds have been blowing (25 kn), cay movement is apparently northward and the shape becomes elongated. When moving rapidly the cay has a steep convex leading edge with slope angles up to 15°. The trailing edge is less steep, about 5°.

Stoddart et al. (1978a) distinguished three types of unvegetated sand cay:

1   Small ephemeral cays, which may be intertidal sandbores, like Wheeler, or may just be emergent at high tide.
2   Larger oval-shaped islands up to 300 m long and 100 m wide with areas of 1.0–1.4 ha. These commonly have depressions surrounded by pronounced swash ridges and steep beaches.
3   Cays with extensive relict beach rock. These have variable dimensions, up to 400 m long and the present form and size of the cay may differ from that outlined by the beach rock (Fig. 11.5).

Whatever their size, the lack of vegetation is a factor of both low height and instability. Even the larger cays of this type migrate and change. Comparison

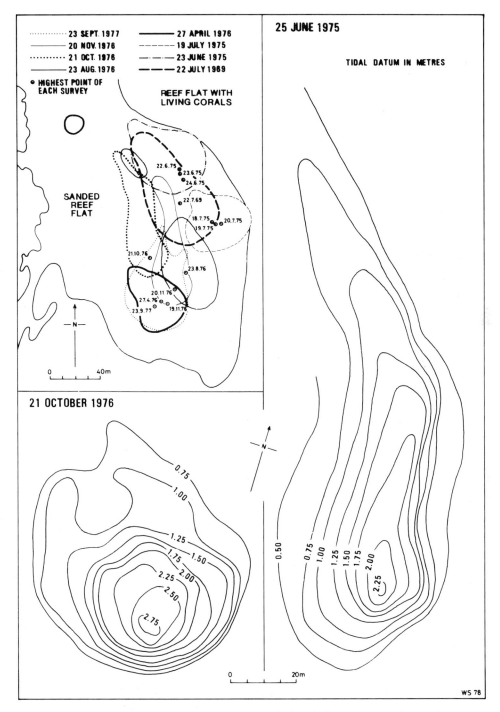

Figure 11.4 Changes in cay location and morphology on Wheeler Reef.

Table 11.2   Summary of Range of Wheeler Cay Dimensions June 1975–November 1976

	Mean	Maximum	Minimum	Standard Deviation
Length (m)	75.8	107	59	18.1
Width (m)	47.7	25	60	11.3
Area (m²)	2308	3120	1429	456
Volume (m³)	1791	2736	693	649
Height (m)	2.79	3.27	1.92	0.46
Distance moved in 24 hrs (m)	5	13	1	4.5
Area change in 24 hrs (m²)	± 221	+ 451	− 541	(n.b. + accretion, − erosion)
Volume change in 24 hrs (m³)	± 236	+ 373	− 397	(n.b. + accretion, − erosion)
Height change in 24 hrs (m)	± 0.09	± 0.07	− 0.17	(n.b. + accretion, − erosion)

of 1936 and 1973 surveys of six cays in the Cairns area showed that all had declined in area by up to 80% (Stoddart et al., 1978a). In spite of this degree of change and mobility, a surprisingly old radio-carbon age of 2330 ± 70 yrs B.P. was obtained for a bulk sample from the top of unvegetated Pickersgill Cay (Polach et al., 1978; McLean and Stoddart, 1978). McLean and Stoddart suggested that sand-cay deposits, if not their morphological entity, may be relatively stable.

Compact Unvegetated Shingle Cay

The majority of compact shingle cays are associated with small reefs and range from constantly moving shingle mounds to more complex structures consisting of a series of recurved shingle ridges, beach rock, and conglomerate. An example of the former is the shingle cay on MacGillivray Reef just east of Lizard Island (Fig. 11.6). Normally no more than 1.5 m high, this oval cay, approximately 40 × 30 m in size, is located on the lee side of this small (1.2 km) reef among a large number of reef blocks. It consists of a simple asymmetric dome of coral shingle and rubble with a trailing leeward spit of sand. Although constantly changing location, the cay remains within a restricted area of about 100 × 50 m on the reef top. Other shingle cays of more complex structure have greater stability and a large number have cemented deposits. The presence of beach rock and conglomerate paralleling the present cay outline is an indication of a degree of stability in larger unvegetated shingle cays. No radiocarbon ages are available from purely shingle islands of the northern Great Barrier Reef, but Maxwell (1969, 1973b) gives two dates for intertidal beach rock from separate shingle cays on Twin Cay Reef in the Swains Group. Two small cays exist on separate reef patches, each with coarse beach rock from which ages of 630 ± 90 yrs B.P. for the southern, and 1110 ± 80 yrs B.P. for the northern cay were obtained by Maxwell. These dates, like that for Pickersgill Reef, suggest a degree of permanence for nonvegetated cay deposits, and even for the shingle cays themselves.

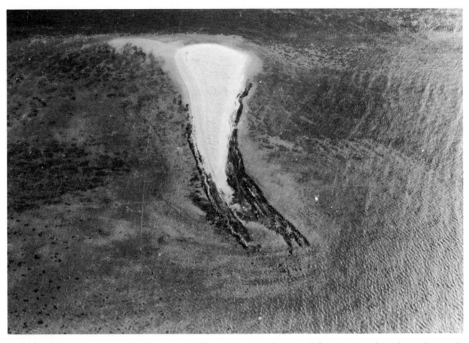

Figure 11.5 Waterwitch Cay, a small unvegetated cay with massive beach rock on the outer ribbon reefs.

Figure 11.6 Shingle cay formed amongst massive reef blocks on MacGillivray Reef near Lizard Island.

Vegetated Solitary Islands

Occasionally even unstable cays may acquire an ephemeral vegetation developing from drift seeds or seeds brought in by birds. However, only if there is a core area of the cay that does not alter over a period of several years can a true vegetation develop and even then single storms or a period of prolonged erosion can revert the cay to its original unvegetated condition. Birds are most important in the vegetation process, for not only do they bring in seeds to the cay, but in adding guano to the raw carbonate sands they transfer some of the high productivity of the surrounding reef waters to the terrestrial habitat. Even small sand patches exposed to low tide can attract hundreds of sea birds and the potential for colonization by vegetation is constantly present.

The first vegetation to become established probably arrives as drift seeds. Some of the common species are capable of germination after long periods at sea (up to 10% germination after 90 days) while some germinate underwater and the seedlings floated (Heatwole, 1975). Once some vegetation is established the cay attracts sea birds and other plants may be brought in as seeds, either adhering to the plumage or surviving the passage through the birds' digestive tracts. Heatwole (1975) noted that One Tree Island has a vascular flora of 19 species of which six have seeds with either hooks or sticky substances covering them. The seeds of *Pisonia grandis*, the most common of the forest trees on Great Barrier Reef cays, are particularly sticky and easily dispersed in this way. Proctor (1968) showed that some shore birds retain viable seeds in their digestive tract for up to 340 hours and are thus capable of transferring vegetation for several thousand kilometers.

The presence of initial vegetation also has other effects, which tend towards selfperpetuation of the cay. The roots help to bind the sand while the surface cover, particularly of ground creepers, may retard erosion when occasionally overtopped by waves. Moreover, the vegetation helps to trap sand blown from the beach slope, initiating dune development above the highest level of the waves. In turn, the greater stability provided to the cay allows beach rock to form, giving further protection to the sediment mass. The presence of a freshwater lens allows additional plant species to inhabit the island. Island size and plant species diversity are closely interrelated, with the smallest cays able to support only salt-tolerant strand plants; while greatest species diversity is associated with the largest islands, which are close to the mainland or other island groups (Whitehead and Jones, 1969).

Colonizing vegetation and the presence of birds allows some initial soil development. Fosberg (1954, 1975) has described the change in soils of coral islands from the initial biogenic carbonate fragments. The presence of trees such as *Pisonia grandis* and *Casuarina equisetifolia* allow the accumulation of acid, peatlike raw humus; and, under *Pisonia*, the addition of guano from fish-eating birds produces a horizon of phosphatic hardpan underlying the humus, an early phase of cay sandstone (Fig. 5.5). Initial pH is about 8.3, but with the addition of some humus this may be lowered to 7.5 or 7.0 and under *Pisonia* the pH may be lowered to 6.0 or 5.0. Nesting of turtles or burrowing by shearwaters (see Fosberg, 1961b) can constantly turn over the soil, sufficiently in some instances, as on Heron Island, to prevent the formation of phosphate rock.

Changes in the cay environment thus take place through time, some of which are induced by the initial colonizing vegetation, to produce a simple vegetational succession. Strand flora, which Whitehead and Jones (1969) suggested is the only vegetation normally found on cays smaller than 1.4 ha, is generally pantropical and only at later stages are there major divergences dependent on location and rainfall. The most common initial colonizers on cays of the Great Barrier Reef are *Ipomoea pes-caprae* and *Sesuvium portulacastrum*, both of which may be found on cays where the vegetation is ephemeral. With longer establishment a greater range of ground creepers, herbs, and grasses becomes established. Particularly common are *Thuarea involuta* and *Lepturus* on relatively high sites, with *Sporobolus virginicus* on open beach sites or lower depressions where spray or waves may occasionally bring in salt water. Swards of succulents including *Sesuvium* and *Portulaca* may form dense mats in such situations. Other creepers that join *Ipomoea* to produce a dense foredune cover include *Canavalia maritima* syn. *C. rosea*. Early colonizing shrubs found at the top of the beach are *Tournefortia argentea* and *Scaevola*, while behind the beach a shrub layer of *Euphorbia* spp. and *Abutilon* can start to give the island a bushy appearance. Woodland vegetation requires islands of sufficient stability and size although a strandline of *Casuarina equisetifolia* is common on both wooded and sparsely vegetated cays, and occasional coconuts can be found at the top of the beach on islands of almost any size. The most common woodland is formed of almost pure stands of *Pisonia grandis* growing to about 8 m with *Pandanus* and *Cordia subcordata* around the margins. On some wetter cays *Ficus* sp. may be common in the woodland.

These plants make up the vegetation of the majority of the sand cays of the Great Barrier Reef (see, e.g., Fosberg, 1961b; Fosberg and Thorn, 1961; Gillham, 1963; Heatwole, 1975; Stoddart et al., 1978a). Although local variations occur, ten to 20 plant species are normally recorded from well-established cays with low vegetation cover dominated by herbs and grasses, and up to 40 on cays with a denser vegetation (Stoddart et al., 1978a, Table 4). Changes in species numbers through time can take place on even well-vegetated cays. Heatwole (1975), for example, noted that three separate surveys of Heron Island in 1927 (MacGillivray and Rodway, 1931), 1958 (Gillham, 1963), and 1960 (Fosberg, 1961b) recorded 25, 35, and 40 species respectively, of which only 17 were common to all three.

Most of these observations on cay vegetation apply to sand cays or shingle islands that contain a proportion of sand. On most shingle cays soil development is limited to the accumulation of highly humic soils in interstices, crevices, and pockets in the shingle and in the cemented platform rocks that develop from the shingle deposits. Possibly for this reason the nature of vegetation succession is less clear. Stoddart et al. (1978a) have noted that even low ramparts may be colonized by a scrub of *Aegialitis annulata* and *Avicennia marina* (Fig. 10.14) whereas older shingle sheets characteristically carry succulent mats of *Sesuvium portulacastrum*, *Salicornia quinqueflora*, *Arthrocnemum* sp., and *Sueda australis*. High cemented platforms and beach rock on low wooded islands commonly carry a dense cover of *Pemphis acidula* and *Suriana maritima* forming a dense, evergreen microphyll scrub. Higher shingle ridges may acquire a cover of herbs and grasses similar to sand cays while the oldest of all, (radiocarbon dating suggests ages greater than 4000 years on the northern Great Barrier Reef, Polach et al., 1978) may carry a dense woodland.

Mangrove seedlings can appear ephemerally on the lee of any cay, but typically are associated with moats and lee-side situations of shingle ramparts and rampart rocks. Stoddart et al. (1978c) have described the mangroves of the low wooded islands. On the ramparts where higher energy conditions may still occasionally reach the mangroves, the trees are generally low and scrublike, dominated by *Aegialitis annulata* and *Avicennia marina*, with higher stands of *Osbornia octodonta* in more sheltered locations (Fig. 10.14). Within the lee of ramparts and platforms, more extensive mangroves can become established, with *Rhizophora stylosa* being the most prolific in area and growing to 20 m. Higher areas closer to the shingle ridges may be dominated by *Bruguiera gymnorrhyza* and *Ceriops tagal*.

The mangroves play a number of geomorphic roles. They add considerable noncarbonate organic matter to the reef top, which probably has an effect on the chemistry of reef-flat waters, with consequences for cementation processes in the adjacent coral shingle deposits (see Chap. 4). In addition they help provide the low-energy environment in which deposition of fine sediments can take place. Although their role in accelerating deposition is debatable (Spenceley, 1977) their rootlet system certainly helps to stabilize the underlying sediments.

Vegetated solitary cays of the Great Barrier Reef form a continuum from purely sand to purely shingle but for discussion it is convenient to have a fourfold division.

Vegetated Sand Cays

Vegetated sand cays of the Great Barrier Reef range in size from less than 1 ha to over 1 km^2 in area. For example, Kay Islet on the northern Reef (12°14'S) has an area of only 4300 m^2 of which only 285 m^2 is vegetated (Stoddart et al., 1978a) whereas North West Island in the Capricorn Group (Flood, 1977b) has an area of 1.16 km^2. Similarly their heights range from only a little above MHWS, making them liable to overtopping on king tides, to several meters above this level on older cays with dunes. Beach rock on the sand cays forms an integral part of island morphology. It plays a major role in the stabilization of the islands, although the occurrence of beach rock outlining the location of islands now completely disappeared (as at Sherrard Island, 12°59'S and Hoskyns Reef, 23°48'S) indicates that major storms can remove the uncemented deposits from within the beach-rock defences. Hopley and Mackay (1978) have shown that zones of erosional hollows are superimposed over the seaward dipping strata of the beach rock. Hollows tend to be more elongated and parallel to the beach in landward zones, where they exploit the bedding planes of the outcrop, but normal to the beach in seaward zones where exploitation of joint lines occurs. The cause of zonation would appear to lie in the way the beach rock is exposed. Episodic beach retreat associated with severe tropical cyclones produces an initial banding due to contrasts in case hardening, across which a zonation dependent on processes is superimposed.

Vegetated cays vary from elongate to oval, the more elongate islands resulting from two-directional wave convergence while the more equidimensional result from the centripetal sweep of waves. Least stable of all are the elongate islands lying transverse to the dominant wave direction. Examples include Eagle Cay (14°42′S) and Michaelmas Cay (16°36′S) (Fig. 11.7). Such islands have clearly developed from the unvegetated cays with central depressions. They have steep beaches with up to 4 m of dune capping above MHWS. An indication of the constant change that takes place around the margins of these islands is the small proportion of the cay that is vegetated, (26% of Michaelmas according to Stoddart et al., 1978a), the wide areas of beach rock exposed, for example 4630 m² compared to 8230 m² of vegetated area on Eagle Cay (Stoddart et al., 1978a, Table 4), and the nature of the vegetation, which is generally low, dominated by colonizing species, and lacking species variety. For example on Michaelmas, Stoddart et al. recorded only five species of vascular plants. Nonetheless, some degree of stability exists on these islands, as indicated by a radiocarbon age of 2960 ± 70 yrs B.P. for a bulk sand sample from the main sand ridge on Eagle Cay (McLean et al., 1978).

Oval islands come in a great range of sizes and shapes. Comparison of cay shape with the pattern of aligned corals on adjacent reef flats supports the suggestion that the stronger the centripetal action of the waves, the more equidimensional the cay. All oval islands show a similar gross morphology with the most mobile areas being small sand spits which form off the widest part of the beach on the two ends of the cays (Fig. 11.8). Beach rock is rarely found here.

Figure 11.7 Michaelmas Cay, site of the 1926 borehole. Vegetation consists of only five species of vascular plants. Beach rock outcrops on the southern side of the island, indicating a shift in position of the cay.

Figure 11.8 Bushy Island on Redbill Reef. The nearer part of the island is younger and dominated by *Tournefortia argentea* and *Pandanus*, with a strandline vegetation of *Casuarina* and ground cover of *Ipomoea* and *Canavalia*. *Pisonia grandis* covers most of the remainder of the island and overlies a phosphatic cay sandstone. Note the anastomosing pattern of algal ridges in the left foreground (See also Fig. 8.8.)

However, the larger sides of the islands are stable enough for beach rock to form within the beach, though subsequent erosion can expose massive beach rock on one or both sides up to 30 m in width. The internal morphology is more variable. Some apparently older islands have a central area rising to up to 5 m above MHWS and consisting of a series of low sand ridges with probable dune capping, although the material is a medium to coarse sand. McLean et al. (1978) have argued against a wholly dunal origin on the grounds of the presence of layers of drift pumice. On the northern Reef, McLean et al. (1978) recognized two distinct levels on cays of this type (including some cays of the low wooded islands), which they termed high terrace and low terrace. The high terrace generally has deeper soils, the depth of organic staining frequently exceeding 1 m, and surveyed heights range from 4.5 to 6.8 m above tidal datum (MHWS, 2.3 m). A dense broadleaf forest occupies the interior of many cays with a high terrace and, on some, where erosion has cut into the high terrace, horizontal beach rock is found in the area of erosion up to 1 m above the level of what is considered as contemporary beach rock (McLean et al., 1978, p. 179). In comparison, the low terrace has only incipient soil development and a more open scrub or herbaceous vegetation, frequently dominated by *Tournefortia argentia*, with a strandline fringe of *Casuarina* the only major trees present. Their heights range from 3.2 to 4.5 m above datum, while the tops of the modern beach range from 2.5 to 3.6 m. Beach rock adjacent to the low terrace is consistently lower and inclined towards the sea. Clearly, at least two periods of cay sediment accumulation are recorded. This was confirmed by radiocarbon dating of sediment samples. High-terrace samples ranged from 3020 ± 70 yrs B.P. to 4380 ± 80 yrs B.P., while low-terrace samples were from 2190 ± 70 to 3280 ± 80 yrs B.P. (McLean et al., 1978, Tables 3 and 4). Although overlapping, two periods of accumulation are confirmed. What is surprising is the relatively old and consistent set of ages for the younger terrace deposits. Although no dates are published for other vegetated sand cays of the Great Barrier Reef, descriptions of the islands of the Capricorn Group (Steers, 1937, 1938; Domm, 1971; Flood, 1977b) are very similar.

Although relatively stable, changes have been noted on vegetated sand cays. Flood (1977b) compared recent aerial surveys of the Capricorn and Bunker Groups with the maps of Steers. Of seven sand cays of the Capricorn Group for which comparison could be made, only one island (Wreck) had not changed, three (North West, Wilson, and Erskine) had grown in size, two (Heron and Masthead) had eroded, and the final cay (Tryon Island) had migrated to the northwest. Erosion of at least 6 m in two years was previously recorded on the western end of Masthead Island (Edgell, 1928b). Similar results were seen on northern Great Barrier Reef sand cays by Stoddart et al. (1978a). Of three islands for which comparisons could be made with Steers' (1929, 1938) surveys, two (Michelmas and Combe) had decreased in size and, especially, in area covered by vegetation, while the third (Stapleton Cay) increased in total area from 3.96 to 4.67 ha, and in vegetated area from 1.69 to 2.68 ha.

More detail of sequential changes is available for two islands, Heron and Green, the only two reef islands permanently occupied on the Great Barrier Reef. Heron Island (Fig. 11.9) is about 830 × 300 m and changes there have been documented by Flood (1974, 1977b) and Jell and Flood (1978). Major changes are associated with the spit at the western end of the island, although sand erosion on the northern and eastern beaches has exposed new beach rock since 1936. Greatest changes have been associated with tropical cyclones (Dinah in 1967, Emily in 1972, and David in 1976) but most of the erosion since about 1960 on the western spit is the result of man's activities. The initial blasting of a boat channel through the reef about 1945 and deepening in 1966 to form a harbor have provided the sediments that normally interchange between cay and reef flat (see below), with a routeway by which they may leave the reef top under the influence of accelerated ebbing tidal currents. Similarly the construction of a retaining wall on the northwestern end of the cay has enhanced the erosive capacity of waves from the northern quadrant. Although spoil from the harbor has been dredged and placed near the northwestern beach (20,000 m^3 in 1972), this sediment has subsequently migrated westward along the beach, and has again reentered the harbor. In all approximately 2900 m^2 have been lost from the western end of the cay between 1960 and 1972.

Green Island near Cairns is the site of a resort and changes have been documented by Kuchler (1978) for the period since 1936 from aerial photography and ground survey. Again, the greatest changes are associated with the western spit of the island (Figs. 11.10, 11.11). Overall, the vegetated area of the cay has varied from a minimum of 108,150 m^2 in 1945 to 116,798 m^2 in 1978. However, the location of the spit has changed from the northern

Figure 11.9   Heron Island, site of a scientific research station and tourist resort. Minor reorientation of the island in response to changing weather patterns has been aggravated by loss of sand via the artificial boat channel seen at top left. Cay vegetation is mainly *Pisonia grandis*. The reef flat has numerous scattered coral heads.

side in the 1940s, to the southwestern side of the island in the 1950s, and back to the northern side during the 1970s, a pattern determined largely by cyclone incidence in the area. Although the vegetated area has increased since 1945 and notwithstanding artificial replenishment, the total cay area and the volume of cay sand has probably reduced. Reasons can again be found in man's activities. Although the building and later destruction of a small groyne off the southwestern end of the island has aggravated the erosion problem on the adjacent beach, a major change has been the growth of sea-grass beds (*Thalassia, Halophilia, Halodule,* and *Symodocea*) and algal mats, which have increased in area from about 900 m^2 in 1945 to over 130,000 m^2 in 1978, most growth taking place between 1972 and 1978. This dense cover of sea grass is almost certainly a eutrophication response to the emptying of sewerage onto the reef flat, as the initial spread was from areas where the sewerage was known to extend. The baffle effect and binding action of the marine vegetation has trapped fine sediment that would otherwise be part of the normal reef flat-cay interchange system. Thus, even the pumping of 18,000 m^3 of fine sand from deeper water onto the eroding beach near the jetty by the Beach Protection Authority from 1974 to 1976 has merely retarded the loss of sand from the cay. Most of this finer sediment had moved to the northern side of the island by 1978 and much appears to have been lost to the marine grass beds adjacent to the northwestern beach.

Figure 11.10 Green Island near Cairns, the most visited reef island on the Great Barrier Reef. The cuspate spit formed during the 1970s is clearly seen to the left of the jetty. Major erosion is taking place just right of the jetty. The dark areas on the reef flat, lower left and off the left hand side of the cay, are sea-grass beds which have appeared almost entirely since 1945.

Many other changes have been brought about by human activities on the vegetated sand cays of the Great Barrier Reef. Introductions of exotic plants and animals, especially goats, have greatly altered the natural vegetation of many islands. Even more important from a geomorphological standpoint has been the removal of phosphatic cay deposits. Although the more accessible Bunker–Capricorn Group of islands, including the shingle cays, were exploited in the mid 1800s, probably the most devastated of all was Raine Island (11°36′ S) on the outer Reef, where mining took place between 1890 and 1892

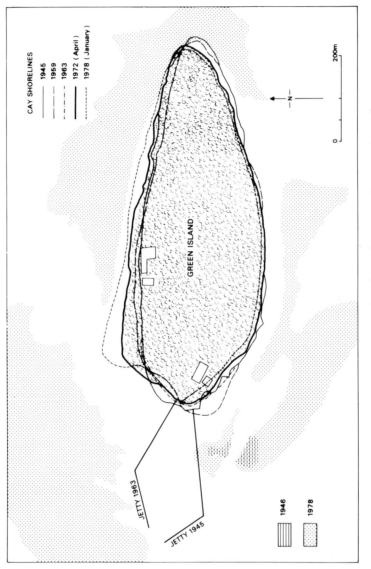

Figure 11.11 Green Island, showing major shoreline changes and expansion of sea-grass beds, from Kuchler (1978).

(Stoddart et al. in press). This small island, about 850 × 430 m, has been completely altered by the removal of the phosphate.

Vegetated Mixed Sand and Shingle Cays

Although Stoddart and Steers (1977 have suggested that the majority of atoll islands fall into this class, only a few occur on the Great Barrier Reef. Lady Musgrave Island (Fig. 11.12) at the southern extremity of the Reef has been described by Orme et al. (1974) and by Flood (1977b), following earlier surveys of Steers (1937, 1938). The present island beaches are mainly sandy, but much of the interior of the island is constructed of shingle ridges, the lower parts of which are cemented. This conglomerate outcrops on the southeastern corner of the island, and coarse beach rock occurs towards the northeastern end. The vegetation is less dense than on some of the nearby sand cays, but Steers (1938) noted that this is due in part to goats. It consists of *Pisonia* with *Tournefortia*, *Casuarina*, and *Pandanus*. It is probable that the *Pisonia* forest had greater extent in the past as guano, normally associated with *Pisonia* forest, has been taken from the island. Flood (1977b) notes only minor changes on the cay since 1936.

Mixed sand and shingle islands can form in several ways. The shingle can originate from specific storm events, sand being added during more normal weather. Alternatively the shingle may be supplied from the windward margin, sand coming from the lee side of the reef flat. This is most likely in areas experiencing a marked seasonal change in direction of dominant winds and the sparse data available suggest that some cays of the Torres Strait area

Figure 11.12 Lady Musgrave Island, a mixed sand-shingle cay. The northern reef edge is at the top of the photograph.

may be of this type. Declining sediment productivity and supply from the reef flat may also cause a change in caliber of the material supplied to a cay. This may result from changes in storminess, sea-level variations or changes in geometry of the reef top with time. Although solitary mixed sand and shingle islands are not common, some of the low wooded islands of the northern reef contain admixtures of these sediments and some may have evolved initially from this type of cay.

Vegetated Shingle Cays

Like their unvegetated counterparts, the vegetated shingle cays are located either on the windward margins of larger reefs, or centrally on the reef flat of exposed small reefs. The majority are of a compact morphology as linear shingle cays, are sufficently mobile to prevent the establishment of a permanent vegetation. Nonetheless, some shingle cays with plant cover appear to have developed from more stable areas of older rampart systems (like West Hope Island, Fig. 11.13), and the windward shingle components of the low wooded islands are most certainly of a linear form. Although less hospitable to rapid colonization by plants than sand cays because of the coarse nature of the sediments and their lack of water retention, once vegetation has gained a foothold, the greater stability of the shingle cay allows for a steady progression towards a climax vegetation, interrupted only by cyclone activity.

The shingle cays are formed from series of coral shingle ridges. The initial

Figure 11.13 West Hope Island, with many features of the windward section of a low wooded island. Coral shingle ridges rising to 3.3 m overlie cemented rampart rocks. A modern shingle rampart is seen on the reef edge.

focus for a developing shingle island may be a hammerhead spit or tongue of shingle in the rubble zone. This would appear to be the origin of One Tree Island (Fig. 11.14), one of the most exposed of all the shingle cays and consisting of extremely coarse rubble and shingle much of it in excess of 0.3 m in diameter. The island has formed over a low cemented conglomerate platform probably originating as a shingle tongue. It forms the foundation for a series of shingle ridges of crescentic shape with a central depression containing a pool of brackish water which is surrounded by a flat of conglomerate thickly carpeted by *Sesuvium* sp. The remainder of the island has a vegetation of scattered *Tournefortia argentea* and *Scaevola taccada* with several small groves of *Pisonia grandis* (Flood, 1977b). The island's stability is indicated by ages of about 4000 years for material from the cemented foundations (Davies and Marshall, 1979; Davies, personal communication).

Very similar ages come from Lady Elliot Island, the southernmost island of the Great Barrier Reef (Flood et al., 1979). This shingle cay occupies about 30% of the reef-top area and consists of a concentric arrangement of lithified beach ridges composed of coral shingle and *Tridacna* clam shells lithified in a phosphate cement (Fig. 11.15). The lithified beach ridges are in excess of 4 m high. Beach rock occurs around the eastern side of the island and eroded cay rock is exposed within the beach zone, suggesting at least some migration of the island. Radiocarbon ages obtained from *Tridacna* valves by Flood et al. (1979) ranged from 3635 ± 85 to 3195 ± 85 yrs B.P. Although closely spaced, the dates and concentric arrangement of the shingle ridges indicate the rapid growth of the island about 3000 yrs B.P. from a cay lying across the dominant

Figure 11.14 One Tree Island, a vegetated windward shingle cay.

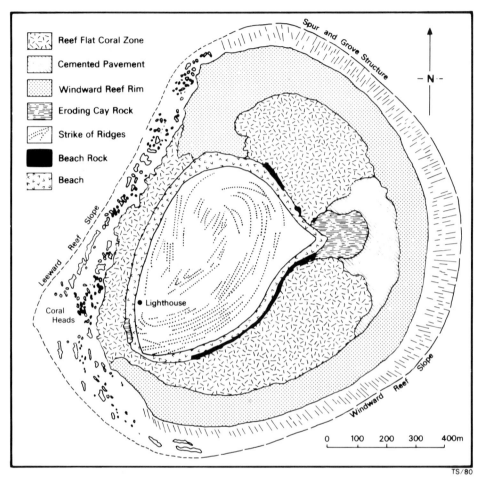

Figure 11.15 Lady Elliot Island. (From Flood et al., 1979, reproduced with permission of the Queensland Department of Mines.)

southeasterlies. Little of the original vegetation of this island remains, due to extensive phosphate mining between 1863 and 1873 (Flood et al., 1979).

Although recently formed shingle ridges are a brilliant white in color and may remain in this condition when occasionally moved by waves, shingle deposits of the island ridges rapidly acquire a dull, gray appearance as they are colonized by boring algae. As noted by McLean and Stoddart (1978) old surfaces may be extremely pitted and irregular, with clam valves being similarly weathered in the subaerial environment. Although the fresh shingle undergoes some abrasion, McLean and Stoddart showed that older blackened shingle sticks were only 51–67% of their original size. Calcite is also present in the clasts, indicating early diagenesis. The proportion is commonly in the range of 3 to 10% but values up to 52% were recorded by McLean and Stoddart. Internal boring also increases primary porosity by up to 20% in the clasts, though much of this is achieved on the reef flat rather than in island deposits.

Changes in shingle-island morphology are much smaller than those on vegetated sand cays. For example Flood (1977b) reported that the only change on One Tree Island between 1936 and 1973 was the addition of a small spit to the northern end of the western beach. Similarly changes induced by man are small on such islands as they do not form as attractive an environment. However, a number are used for the location of navigational beacons. On Lady Elliot Island (Flood et al., 1979), not only are there many pits and mounds from the days of guano extraction, but the island has been the site of a lighthouse since 1866 and of an airstrip since 1969.

Mangrove Islands

Stoddart and Steers (1977) noted that, in the Caribbean, islands formed by the colonization by mangroves of shoal areas without the shingle ramparts and rampart rocks of the low wooded islands are common. Without windward protection such islands can only form on high reef tops, in low energy conditions, and in areas of relatively low tidal range. The few examples on the Great Barrier Reef occupy a high proportion of the reef top and, in places, approach to within 100 m of the reef edge. Irregular sand ridges occur around the margins of the mangroves and remnants of older ridges can be seen within the swamps on aerial photographs but these are mostly on the leeward side. No studies of these islands have been made but aerial photographs indicate great uniformity of species, probably *Rhizophora*, with a dense cover except for some open patches in the center of the reef in which fallen trees can be seen. These result from cyclone damage to the canopy and resultant increase in salinity levels from greater isolation as described by Spenceley (1976).

Multiple Islands

Although it is possible for more than two discrete islands to exist on a single reef flat, as far as is known, no such situation occurs on the Great Barrier Reef. There are, however, a small number of examples of two vegetated islands on a reef, invariably a windward shingle cay and a leeward sand cay. For classification purpose it is presumed that both are vegetated. However, there several vegetated sand cays with unvegetated shingle ramparts. For example East Hope Cay (15°44′ S), which is heavily vegetated, is accompanied on the reef top by a small shingle bank rising 1.5 m above the reef flat on its windward margin. It has developed from a distinctive shingle tongue and cemented basset edges occur just seaward of the main bank. Dual islands with mangroves are not discussed here, but included in the complex island class.

Two examples in the Bunker Group illustrate the nature of these islands. The eastern cays of both Fairfax and Hoskyn Reef are composed of shingle ridges developed from shingle tongues on the windward reef edge (Figs. 7.11 and 11.16). Although more elongate, they are similar to One Tree cay with extensive cemented deposits and small groves of *Pisonia grandis* (Steers, 1937, 1938; Flood, 1977b). Eastern Fairfax Island has been much disturbed by phosphate mining and use as a bombing range. The western cays are mixed sand-shingle islands, Hoskyns being the more sandy. Their vegetation is similar to that of the larger sand cays of the Capricorn Group, such as Heron Island.

Figure 11.16 Fairfax Reef (Bunker Group) with windward shingle and leeward sand cays on a small partially infilled lagoonal reef.

There is no evidence to indicate the chronological development of these islands. Fairfax Reef is included in the parcel of radiocarbon dates for island rocks dating back about 4000 years published by Davies and Marshall (1979). There is little doubt that wave refraction around the shingle cays affects the leeward sand cay. On Fairfax Reef this appears to be breached regularly (Steers, 1937; Harvey et al., 1978) but the relationship is such as to suggest that the shingle cay is the older. If this is also true on Hoskyn Reef then the remains of an older cay, more centrally situated on the reef in the form of a remnant cay outline in beach rock (originally described by Steers, 1938), may represent the earliest island on this reef, unable to maintain its position once the shingle cay had formed and modified the wave refraction pattern of the reef top.

Complex Low Wooded Islands

On the inner reefs north of Cairns are a group of reef islands with a complexity unique to the Great Barrier Reef (Stoddart et al., 1978a). Described by many explorers and expeditions to the Great Barrier Reef they were termed "low wooded islands" by Steers (1929, p. 250–257). Although this name is now generally accepted, the islands occupy such a high proportion of their reef tops that Spender (1930) preferred the term "island reef," while Fairbridge and Teichert (1947) compromised with "low wooded island-reef." At their simplest, they consist of a windward shingle island and leeward sand cay, with intervening mangroves in the lee of the shingle. However, these islands display a complex range of features not associated with discrete sand or shingle cays and the presence of mangroves provides both an immediately recognizable unique feature and a unifying reef-top unit. As stated by Stoddart et al. (1978a), the low wooded islands are the most informative of all the Reef cays in terms of preserving information on reef-top development, and they have been the focus of much research since the 1896 voyage of Alexander Agassiz (e.g. both 1929 and 1973 Royal Society Expeditions concentrated their attentions on low wooded islands). The basic descriptions of Stoddart et al. (1978a), the discussion of the relationships of specific features to sea levels (McLean et al., 1978) and descriptions of changes at Low Isles and Three Isles by Stoddart et al. (1978c) provide a comprehensive survey of these islands.

Description of a low wooded island is essentially the description of an entire reef top as the islands may occupy up to 79.5% of the reef flat (Stoddart et al., 1978a, Table 6). More commonly it is between 25 and 50%, much depending on the area of mangroves, but the enclosed reef flat is so intimately related to the islands that any analysis needs to incorporate the whole rather than just the subaerial parts of the reef. Low Isles, although the most investigated, in many respects is not completely typical and Three Isles (Figs. 11.17, 11.18) provides a better type of example.

The outer reef flat has a zonation of an outer living coral zone, a boulder zone, an algal pavement (usually a gently sloping area, bare of rubble and covered by a turf of green and brown algae) and a rubble zone (Fig. 10.11). Rampart systems may extend around almost the entire reef perimeter, with long shingle tongues or hammerhead spits extending more than 100 m onto the reef flat. Where older rampart systems are eroded, basset edges indicate the former extent of the ridges (Fig. 10.14). Most low wooded islands have several shingle ramparts making up the outer part of the shingle island and occupied by a low mangrove scrub and swards of succulents (*Sesuvium*, *Salicornia*, *Suaeda*) particularly on the older cemented areas. Between the ramparts and the platforms are moats that retain their water at low tide and form the location for extensive microatoll growth.

The most stable part of the windward shingle islands is provided by conglomerate platforms of rampart rock. These are cemented shingles of older rampart systems with very horizontal surfaces. They are usually cliffed on the seaward margins where on some islands they can be seen to overlie older microatolls (Figs. 5.4 and 6.9). These have grown in former moats and subsequently been overridden by landward migrating shingle ramparts. Some are probable related to sea levels about 1 m higher than present (Fig. 10.9). Elsewhere the lowest platforms may disappear seawards beneath the reef-flat rubble without sharp break of slope or degenerate into basset edges. Most researchers have recognized two distinct levels of platforms on low wooded islands, although on some islands the distinction is not clear and the upper platform is not always present. Mean High Water Springs is about 2.3 m on the northern Reef and the mean level of the lower platform is exactly this, whereas the upper platform has a mean level of 2.9 and reaches as high as 3.5 m. At specific locations the two platforms are usually separated vertically by between 1.0 and 1.2 m. On Three Isles the lower platform has an elevation of 2.0 m (above tidal datum) and the upper platform 3.1 m. Both upper and lower

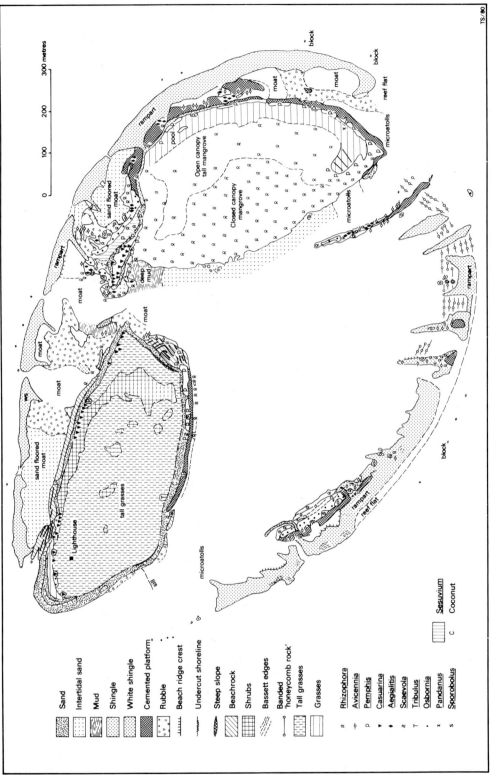

Figure 11.17 Geomorphology of Three Isles, low wooded island. (After Stoddart et al., 1978c.)

Sand

Intertidal sand

Mud

Shingle

White shingle

Cemented platform

Rubble

Beach ridge crest

Undercut shoreline

Steep slope

Beachrock

Shrubs

Bassett edges

Banded 'honeycomb rock'

Tall grasses

Grasses

R   Rhizophora

Avicennia

Pemphis

Casuarina

Aegialitis

Scaevola

Tribulus

Osbornia

Pandanus

Sporobolus

Sesuvium

C   Coconut

300 metres

0   100   200

rampart

pool

Open canopy tall mangrove

Closed canopy mangrove

microatolls

microatolls

block

moat

moat

reef flat

block

sand floored moat

deep mud

moat

moat

moat

ws

sand floored moat

tall grasses

Lighthouse

ill

microatolls

rampart

reef flat

block

rampart

TS/80

Figure 11.18 Three Isles from the east. Note the ramparts and shingle tongues extending over the reef flat. The major example in the foreground is cemented and has been colonized by mangroves.

platforms vary in width from less than 10 m to mean widths of 30 m and maximum width of almost 70 m. The majority of platforms are surmounted by a series of old shingle ridges that form the highest part of the shingle cay. Maximum elevation varies from 3.5 to 4.9 m.

In the lee of the shingle island and peripheral ramparts are mangrove swamps, the areas of which range to over 125 ha on Bewick Island, where they occupy up to 68% of the reef top (Stoddart et al., 1978a, Table 6). *Rhizophora stylosa* is the predominant mangrove, but Stoddart (1980) recorded 15 species from the low wooded islands. Although extending onto reef-flat sands on some islands the mangroves, where well established, have accumulated thick, black organic mud deposits up to 2 m deep. Exposed within the mangroves of a number of islands (Houghton, Low Isles, Two Isles, Leggatt, Hampton, Bewick) are fields of fossil microatolls reaching elevations of up to 1.35 m (compared to 1.2 for MLWN).

The leeward sand cays display a great range of size and morphology from ephemeral unvegetated sand patches (e.g., Lowrie, Binstead, Chapman) to massive vegetated cays approaching the dimensions of the Capricorn Group of islands. Most have woodland or scrub vegetations and the number of species of vascular plants is generally greater than that on solitary vegetated sand cays (Stoddart et al., 1978a). Two terrace levels are well displayed by the majority of the larger cays, with difference in soils, vegetation, and elevation as noted above. Beach rock is also widely distributed around the sand cays of low wooded islands, with exceptionally high levels ranging up to 2.7–3.0 m where the older terrace has been eroded to expose the outcrop.

The reef flat between the sand and shingle islands, where not occupied by mangroves, varies from shallow lagoons with scattered living coral heads to completely sanded ones. The majority are at least partially moated by peripheral ramparts and islands and microatoll forms are especially prevelent (Fig. 4.9). Sea-grass beds are common on a number of low wooded islands reef flats.

Stoddart et al. (1978a) recognized that the low wooded islands are heterogeneous, their diversity depending on more than just the extent of mangroves. They recognized three distinct types:

1   Mangroves of limited extent, sand cay separate. This is the most common type and typified by Three Isles (Fig. 11.17).
2   Mangroves extensive, joining the sand and shingle cays. Within the lee of extensive shingle islands and ramparts, the mangroves may occupy the whole of the reef top, surrounding the sand cay and joining it to the shingle cay. Nonetheless the sand cay may retain all the features of more discrete islands, including extensive beach rock. (Fig. 11.19).
3   Turtle-type islands (Fig. 11.20). Although having all the features of low wooded islands, the cays of the Turtle Group just north of Lookout Point lack a central reef-flat area, as noted first by Steers in 1929. Ramparts and associated rampart rocks are closely linked with the leeward cay, which is

Figure 11.19   Low Wooded Island. The entire central area of this reef top is occupied by mangroves. Shingle tongues extend from the active ramparts to a low platform of rampart rock. High platform outcrops around the tree-ringed pool in the foreground. An age of 6080 ± 80 yrs B.P. was obtained for a microatoll below the lower platform on the left-hand side (southern) of the photograph.

constructed largely of shingle ridges rather than sand, and mangroves are limited to the linear depressions between shingle ridges or between the platforms and main cay. All these islands are on very small reefs generally less than 60 ha in area and occupy a large proportion of the reef top. Larger ones, such as Turtle II, (Nymph may also be regarded as peripheral to this category) have large central lagoons lined with mangroves. Stoddart et al. noted that the shingle-cay areas display upper and lower terrace levels similar to sand cays elsewhere.

The major advance made by the 1973 Great Barrier Reef Expedition was to provide an age framework for the construction of the low wooded islands. The reports (Polach et al., 1978; McLean et al., 1978; Stoddart et al., 1978a,b) indicated that the reef tops on which the low wooded islands are situated were developing at modern sea level prior to 5000 yrs B.P. and in some examples (Fisher, Bewick, Houghton, Leggatt, Low Wooded) prior to 5800 years B.P. Emerged reef in the form of excessively high microatolls is associated with many low wooded islands and McLean et al. suggested that high cay terraces, high beach rock, and upper platforms with associated shingle ridges may all have been formed during a high sea-level stand about 1 m above present lasting until 3000 yrs B.P. Although each island type shows individual features, Turtle I is characteristic in its patterns of evolution (Fig. 11.20). Radiocarbon ages (Polach et al., 1978) show that a reef flat existed about 5000 years ago, an age of 4910 ± 90 yrs B.P. being obtained for coral shingle beneath mangrove deposits in the small depression enclosed by two shingle ridges. Overlying organic mud was dated as 1100 ± 80 yrs B.P. and 2210 ± 170 yrs B.P. A *Tridacna* shell from the upper platform gave an age of 4420 ± 90 yrs B.P. and similar material from the lower platform, 1430 ± 70 yrs B.P. Shingle samples from the islands ridges were dated between 3320 ± 80 yrs and 2480 ± 70 yrs B.P. (see Polach et al., 1978 for details).

While considerable stability is indicated by the dates obtained from low wooded islands through a long period of evolution that suggests that both shingle and sand cays may have developed simultaneously, continual modification has occurred. Most of the low-terrace sediment, ramparts, younger shingle ridges, and lower platforms have developed over the last 2500 years, especially over the last 1500 years. Short-term changes are continually taking place. Complete remapping of Low Isles and Three Isles in 1973 has allowed some estimation of the rates and nature of change over the 44-year period since Spender's original surveys (Stoddart et al., 1978c). As might be expected, few changes occurred in the cemented platforms, but many of the rampart systems have been eroded (producing gaps in moats and lowering water levels) or have been moved bodily forward. Near Third Island on Three Isles, the ramparts had moved 60–90 m. Mangroves on Low Isles had expanded 67% from 21.9 ha to 36.5 ha, with the open mangrove park of Spender (1930) becoming continuous mangrove woodland. In contrast, little or no change had taken place in the distribution of mangroves at Three Isles. Although the sand cays appear to receive considerable protection, the cay on Low Isles has moved between 30–40 m to the east. Changes on Three Isles cay have been more complex, with erosion and expansion of beach rock on the northern shore but significant aggradation

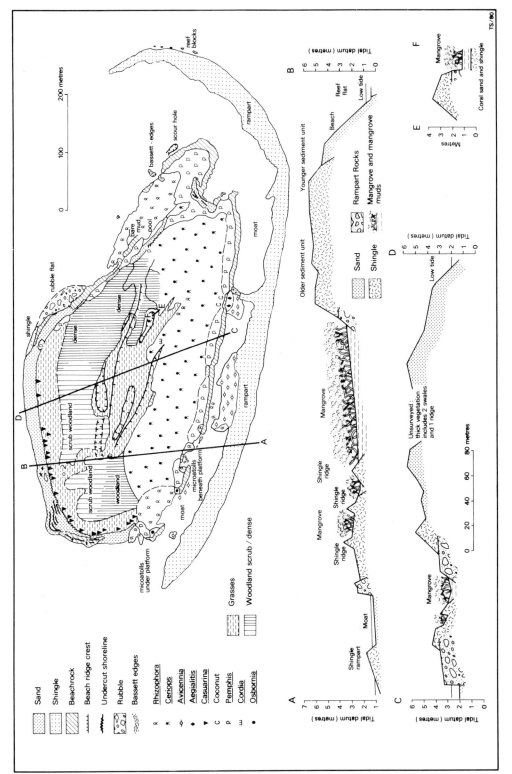

Figure 11.20 Geomorphology of Turtle Island from a survey in 1973 by D. R. Stoddart with profiles by the author.

at the western end of the island in the form of a low terrace 30–40 m wide and covered by pioneer vegetation.

THE CAY–REEF FLAT INTERRELATIONSHIP AND COMPARATIVE DYNAMICS OF DIFFERENT CAY TYPES

In the total reef system the reef island is a store in which reef sediments are locked for varying lengths of time. It is similar to a mainland beach and fore-dune area and, in an analogous way, the effects of high energy events on a cay are lessened by an exchange of sediment with the adjacent reef flat similar to the formation of the offshore bar of mainland beaches. The relationship between the cay beaches and adjacent reef flat has been demonstrated by a research program on an unvegetated cay (Wheeler Reef, Fig. 11.3) a simple vegetated cay (Bushy Island, Fig. 11.8), and a low wooded island cay (Three Isles, Fig. 11.18). Cay-beach changes were recorded using aluminum rods while reef-flat movement was monitored by a series of sediment traps (see Hopley, in press, for details of methodology).

On all three cays greatest changes took place around the previously mobile spits at the ends of the islands, and least on the beaches of longer sides, especially adjacent to or overlying beach rock. Maximum movement of reef-flat sands took place on the sandier areas of reef flat and least where living coral colonies were densest. However, the three cay types were clearly differentiated with by far the greatest changes on reef flat and cay taking place on Wheeler cay (Hopley, 1978c), the least on Three Isles. A feature common to all cays was a relationship between reef flat and the most active area of the cay beaches (the spits on Bushy Island and Three Isles), which clearly indicates that sand eroded from the cay is taken up by the adjacent reef flat and that buildup of beaches is from sand bodies of the reef flat. However, these movements may be superimposed on more general transport patterns. At Bushy Island, which was studied most intensively, the sediment circulation on the reef flat is clockwise around the cay at the southern end and anticlockwise at the north, apparently in opposition to the movement on the cay, as suggested by the alignment of the two spit areas. A net movement away from the cay was indicated on the western side. Under the southeasterly conditions that exist for a high proportion of the year the major movement of sediment is from the sanded reef flat to the south of the cay and around the western side, to be either deposited on the reef flat to the north of the cay or lost over the algal rim. On the eastern side the lagoon acts as a sediment sink. Similar patterns are recognizable at Wheeler cay, although the sediment movement appears far less organized and predictable. This is probably due to the small size of the reef, resulting in vastly different wave-refraction patterns from even small changes in wind direction. In contrast, on Three Isles no clear pattern of relationship exists between reef flat and most of the cay or between reef-flat sites. Only small amounts of reef-flat sediment movement and beach changes were noted on this cay, 70% of the shores being protected by massive beach rock.

At all three cays the amount of sediment being moved has been correlated with dynamic variables (see Hopley, 1978c, in press). The most important influences at both Wheeler and Bushy cays were wind speed and wind direction. At both sites winds deviating from the prevailing southeasterly direction could produce more response in sediment movement than could southeasterlies at similar wind speeds. At neither site were variables related to tidal heights or currents shown to be significant for sediment movement patterns.

Very poor relationships between all the dynamic variables and beach changes and sediment movement exist at Three Isles. This cay, protected behind mangroves and shingle ramparts and with a high reef flat, seems less affected by variations in "normal" weather conditions. Very local factors, such as variations in bioturbidity and discrete areas of sediment movement, appear to be more important for sediment dynamics on this sheltered reef flat.

Differences in dynamics of contrasting cay types are thus being demonstrated. These are summarized in Table 11.3, which compares long-term and short-term changes on the three cays. The rapidity of change on Wheeler is such as to preclude any vegetation gaining a foothold. In spite of wind strengths during the period of monitoring being lowest at Wheeler and highest at Three Isles, Wheeler is clearly seen as being far more volatile than its vegetated counterparts. At Bushy Island, the beach is approximately twice as responsive as that of Three Isles cay, but reef-flat movements are almost ten times as great. Quite clearly only abnormal cyclonic weather is likely to produce major cay changes at Three Isles. Bushy Island, however, shows sufficient mobility to respond to weather changes with periodicities measured over decades, while Wheeler responds to even daily shifts in wind and wave conditions. It is likely that changes of this magnitude also take place on other cays of similar types on the Great Barrier Reef.

DISTRIBUTION OF ISLANDS ON THE GREAT BARRIER REEF

Reef islands are far from evenly distributed in the Great Barrier Reef Province. They are most numerous at the northern and southern extremities of the Reef with a large central area lacking even unvegetated cays. Distribution of island types is seen in Figure 11.21. Areas for which ground surveys are not available have been mapped from aerial photography and for this reason unvegetated cays and sand, shingle, and mixed vegetated cays form single groups.

Table 11.3   Contrasting Beach Changes, Reef-Flat Sediment Movement and Cay Migration, Three Isles, Bushy Island, and Wheeler Cay

	Wheeler	Bushy	Three
Range of mean wind speeds (kn)	4–15	5–20	15–25
Mean daily beach change (cm)	17.43	2.74	1.51
Maximum mean daily beach change (cm)	24.95	3.76	1.98
Mean daily sediment trap recovery (g)	531.1	204.2	22.8
Maximum mean daily sediment, trap recovery (g)[a]	793.1	344.4	39.7
Recorded long term migration (m)	110	c 40 m	c 35 m
Period	1975–77	1936–64	1929–73

[a]This is the maximum mean recovery from all traps set. Individual traps have recorded up to 4063 g on a single day on Wheeler Reef.

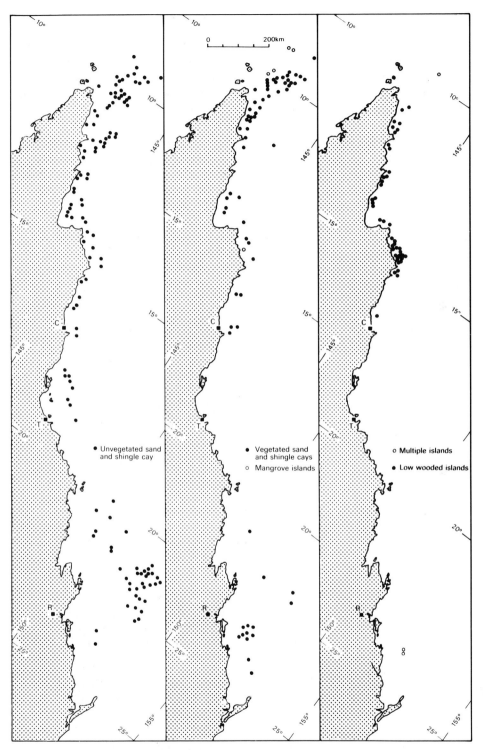

Figure 11.21 Distribution of (*a*) unvegetated cays, (*b*) vegetated sand and shingle cays and mangrove islands, and (*c*) low wooded islands and multiple islands.

Unvegetated cays are the most numerous. Many are small, less than 50 m in length, and very few have beach rock. Particular concentrations occur in the Swain Reefs, between 18° and 19°S and from Cairns northward, becoming most numerous in the approaches to the Torres Strait. They occur on all types of reefs including those in relatively exposed locations such as the southern Swain and on the outer ribbon reefs north of Lizard Island. However, location on the outer barrier appears to be determined by the small amount of protection given where the reef is oriented towards the north rather than southeast and on small reefs located just inside the main passages through the ribbons. There are no unvegetated cays between the northern Pompey Reefs and Wheeler Reef off Townsville, a distance of 315 km.

Vegetated islands, apart from mangrove cays, are not differentiated. They are also most numerous in the Torres Strait region where some are inhabited. They are common on inner reefs and the western ends of large midshelf reefs on the northern Great Barrier Reef north of Cairns. On the southern Great Barrier Reef, the Bunker–Capricorn Group form a distinctive set of well wooded islands. Two slightly vegetated cays are located in the Swain Reefs, and two well-vegetated cays on inner reefs, Bell Cay and Bushy Island. Between Bushy Island at 25°57′ S and Green Island at 16°46′ S near Cairns, a distance of 640 km, there are no vegetated cays on the Great Barrier Reef. Three vegetated cays are found on the outer barrier, Tydeman Cay, on an unnamed reef at 13°22′S, and Raine Island, all of which are provided with some degree of shelter to the southeast.

Only five mangrove islands occur, all except one being in the Torres Strait area. The one exception is Murdoch Island (14°37′ S), although Night Island, described by Steers (1938), is intermediate between a low wooded island and a mangrove island for, as Steers commented, there is a noticeable lack of shingle ridges on this island and only a very discontinuous lower platform. All these islands occur in sheltered areas with only low to moderate tidal ranges and are located where they may receive terrigenous sediments, especially those close to the New Guinea coastline.

Multiple islands are even more sparse. Apart from the two in the Bunker Group (Hoskyns and Fairfax) the only other example mapped is the Yorke Islands in Torres Strait (9°45′ S). Low wooded islands have a very distinctive distribution as previously noted by Steers (1929, 1937, 1938) and Fairbridge (1950, 1967). Forty-three have been mapped in Figure 11.21 all except Turtle-type Warrior Islet in Torres Strait (9°48′ S) being between 11°10′ S and 16°23′ S and occupying small high reefs of the inner shelf. Some of the islands mapped as solitary vegetated cays, such as East and West Hope, have characteristics of low wooded islands and have been named as such elsewhere. Some of the features of the fringing reefs of inner shelf high islands and of small Pandora Reef (Fig. 11.2) near Townsville are very similar to those of low wooded islands (see Chapter 12).

Distribution of islands shows some correlation with reef type; planar reefs have the greatest number of islands, but all reef types with reef flat have at least one example of an associated island. Cays are least associated with large reefs, probably because the wave refraction pattern does not produce the centripetal action required, but tends to spread sediment more evenly over the reef top. Spender (1930) considered that the distribution of low wooded islands, reefs with sand or shingle islands, and reefs without islands was the result of a difference in height of reef surfaces caused by tilting normal to the mainland coastline. Steers (1929, 1937), in contrast, argued for the distribution to be attributed to variation in wave energy, an argument that was supported by Stoddart (1965a). However, as shown in Chapter 8, there is a difference in height of reefs across the shelf. The central reef area from Cairns southward, where the main reef tract diverges from the coastline, contains evidence suggestive of more widespread submergence, a pattern that corresponds to a paucity of island development and a pattern to which other influential factors such as a predominance of more juvenile reefs and more recent reef-top ages may also be related. Younger, lower, reef flats have a greater cover of living coral giving the reef top a much more irregular surface over which much wave energy is lost (Chap. 4), creating conditions unsuited for sediment movement.

However, other factors contribute to the lack of islands on the central Great Barrier Reef. Stoddart and Steers (1977) stated that the greater the tidal range, the greater the submergence at high tide and the greater the effective exposure of the reef top. Reef islands are thus more easily formed in areas of low tidal range. It is significant that the cayless area of the Reef corresponds in general terms with the area of highest tides, with greater than 4 m range. The few islands such as Bushy in this area are situated on high reefs with large algal terraces, moating the main reef flat at almost mean sea level, thus negating the exposure effect of the high tidal range. This area also corresponds to the zone of maximum cyclone occurrence. While these storms undoubtedly play a part in the formation of some island features, particularly shingle islands and ramparts, the general evidence suggests that sand cays are severely eroded, if not removed, during a major cyclonic event. However, cyclonic incidence is not significantly less between Cairns and Princess Charlotte Bay although the height of associated storm surges is much lower. Cyclone frequency and high surges may be factors extending the area lacking cays northward from the zone of high tidal range. Cyclones may have other influences in island development. Notably all but one of the mangrove islands occurs in Torres Strait where there is a great increase in the density of cay distribution. At these lower latitudes cyclones are rarer and generally less intense. Reef blocks are rare on the northern reef. Similarly at the southern end of the reef tropical cyclones usually, though not always, are weakening. Thus, although there are shingle islands and most reef tops are high, as on the inner part of the northern reef, there are no low wooded islands. However a further factor may be the exposure of the reefs to open ocean swell. Windward margins have much higher energy conditions in "normal" weather and shingle deposits of cyclones are more evenly spread over the reef flat or concentrated into shingle cays. Island distribution is thus a product of the Holocene reef top history combined with current exposure conditions associated with both everyday weather and cyclonic storms.

DISCUSSION

The great variety and complexity of form of Great Barrier Reef cays results from the range of factors that affect island-building and that cannot be matched in any other single reef province. Variations in reef-top ages, morphology, and sea-level history combined with the differences in energy conditions and tidal ranges produce this diversity. Some authors (e.g., Umbgrove, 1928, p. 64) suggest that variations in reef island morphology are indicative of an evolutionary sequence. However, as Stoddart and Steers (1977) have pointed out, most of the changes observed in historical time are ecological rather than geomorphic. Even the catastrophic damage carried out during major storms (see, e.g., Stoddart, 1962b, 1963) may be part of the environment to which the morphology of reef islands is adapted and it is possible that, as Stoddart and Steers (1977, p. 93) noted, all the island types distinguished are equilibrium forms continually adjusting to the controlling processes. The sequence of events in island development has been especially controversial in relation to low wooded islands (Spender, 1930; Steers, 1930, 1937). The results of the 1973 Royal Society Expedition suggested that whether the sand cay forms before or after the ramparts is not a question to which there is a general answer (Stoddart et al., 1978c). Although in some situations the sand cay is the first part of the complex to form, as the ramparts will subsequently limit sediment supply to the leeward side of the reef as Steers (1929, p. 257) believed, in other examples it is the formation of the ramparts that may give sufficient stability and shelter to the reef top for the sand cay to accumulate. In yet other examples, it is likely that sand and shingle islands form contemporaneously.

Although an equilibrium form the reef island is dynamic and responds to changes in controlling factors such as climate, sea level, and reef-top morphology. In Indonesia, Verstappen (1954) recognized climatic changes from variations in island morphology between 1875 and 1950 that were in response to variations in the east and west monsoons. No such variations have been recognized in the Great Barrier Reef, but Kuchler (1978) suggested that changes in the location of the mobile spit on Green Island resulted from variations in cyclone incidence. Thom (1978) in particular has argued for variations in storminess on the east coast of Australia during the Holocene, but also noted that small variations in sea levels may have also played a part in sediment budgets of the last 6000 years. The accumulation of sediments on Great Barrier Reef cays has been episodic, radiometric dates suggesting that cays formed rapidly in leeward situations once the level of reef tops and sea level coincided at about 5000 yrs B.P. (McLean and Stoddart, 1978, Stoddart et al., 1978c). The existence of a high energy "window," as suggested by Neumann (1972), when outer reefs not quite at sea level may have given less protection to the inner shelf reefs on which the oldest islands are located, may have been an important factor at this early stage, although radiocarbon ages from the ribbon reefs (Hopley, 1977) indicate that the outer reefs did not lag behind the near-shore reefs on the northern Great Barrier Reef. However, the high energy "window" may have operated on the local scale with greater wave activity over individual reefs. Indications are that subsequent to this initial period of cay development, sediment supply diminished until a fall in sea level of about 1 m led to a new wave of sand and shingle being added to the cays as low terraces. The importance of negative movements of sea level in the formation of reef islands has been a major controversy in reef literature (Stoddart, 1969a, p. 472). Evidence from the Great Barrier Reef suggests that, while not mandatory for the accumulation of sediment masses, it is certainly a highly influential factor.

Changes in reef-top geometry are also important factors in long-term changes to reef islands. Widening of windward reef zones and heightening of rubble zones and algal ridges can greatly decrease the wave energy transmitted to the leeward reef flat. Of equal importance is the loss of wave energy due to friction over a rough coral bottom as shown by Dexter (1973), which suggests that the episodic nature of sediment accumulation in cays could be the result of changes in reef-top morphology. After the first phase of sediment accrual, there may be a paucity of sediments resulting not only from the form of the windward margins, but also from the great loss of wave energy over a reef flat with aligned or scattered coral heads. Only as the reef flat becomes smoother with infilling of the irregular reef-flat surface is there a decrease in the frictional loss of energy, and this together with the adequate supply of sediment now available on the sanded reef flat may lead to a second period of cay growth.

Interchange of sediments between the cay and its surrounding reef flat was shown to be important from the results at Bushy, Wheeler, and Three Isles cays. However, the effects of eutrophication and resultant expansion of sea-grass beds at Green Island, suggest that at a late stage of reef-flat development, when much of the reef top acquires a cover of sea grasses, this important interchange may cease and sediment lost from the cay will not be replaced. It is notable that most vegetated cays which Stoddart et al. (1978c) reported had decreased in size between 1926–36 and 1973 are located on reefs with extensive sea-grass beds (e.g., Low Isles, Michaelmas, Combe). If an evolutionary sequence does exist for reef islands, a degenerative phase of cay erosion may be the last stage of development. In the long term, reef islands are merely a temporary store of sediments in the total reef system, a store that may increase or decrease in size according to internal storage characteristics (cementation and vegetation), internal reef factors (changing morphology and reef top smoothness), or completely external factors over which the reef itself has no control (sea level and climatic changes).

12

Fringing Reefs and Associated Deposits

In 1977, Steers and Stoddart (1977) suggested that:

> Of the three main types, fringing reefs are the simplest, apparently the least in need of complex explanations, and also the least studied.

According to the Darwinian concept of reef development fringing reefs, that is, reefs directly attached to mainland or high island are the basic form, mainly characteristic of stationary or rising coasts and developing into barrier reefs on subsiding coastal foundations. Darwin also allowed for the growth of "second generation" fringing reefs on headlands during periods of stillstand. Thus the majority of fringing reefs have been regarded as young features. Indeed, Stoddart (1969c) has shown that they may be ephemeral and has reported largely dead fringing reefs smothered by red, clayey sediments around the eroding core of Kolombangara in the Solomon Islands. Umbgrove (1930) indicated the temporary nature of fringing reefs around Krakatoa subsequent to the 1883 explosion. Ladd (1977) also supported the idea that fringing reefs are young features, pointing out that drill holes in fringing reefs and exposures of emerged reef structures have indicated that most are thin and, in many instances, merely veneers over older nonreefal foundations. Recent work on Hanauma Reef, Oahu, Hawaii by Easton and Olsen (1976) illustrates what is regarded as the typical fringing reef structure, for this reef commenced to grow in a breached Pleistocene volcanic crater during the Holocene transgression about 7000 yrs B.P. Most of its vertical growth was between 5800 and 3500 yrs B.P. when average upward accretion rate was 3.3 mm/yr. Similarly Glynn and MacIntyre (1977) have shown that Panama reefs began to develop between 5600 and 4500 yrs B.P. on volcanic rocks and calcareous reef sediments, growing upwards at a mean rate of 7.5 mm/yr. However at other sites Lum and Stearns (1970) have described reef limestones 30 m in thickness in drill holes in the Waimanalo area of Oahu and Resig (1969) drilled through almost 300 m of reef limestone and lagoonal sediments near Pearl Harbor. Such deep sections, with presumed unconformities, suggest that many fringing reefs may not be the "simple" structure previously suggested. Although no major problems exist with the younger reefs, obviously these thicker reef sections have a more complex history. It is also questionable whether or not fringing reefs form the basic structures for barrier and atoll formation as suggested by Darwin, for as Vaughan (1916) pointed out,

> no evidence has yet been presented to show that any barrier reef began to form as a fringing reef on a sloping shore, and was converted into a barrier by submergence.

Such evidence is still lacking and is indicative of the generally small amount of research carried out on fringing reefs.

DISTRIBUTION OF FRINGING REEFS IN EASTERN AUSTRALIA

Fringing Reef Distribution at the Southern Limits of the Great Barrier Reef Province

Fringing reefs off the coast of eastern Australia have a far greater latitudinal spread than do the platform reefs of the Great Barrier Reef, although reefal structures do not extend as far south as do hermatypic corals (see Chap. 3), which at their southernmost extension are merely encrustations or isolated colonies on rock substrates. The corals of the Solitary Islands near Coffs Harbor (29°52'–30°14'S) in New South Wales (Veron, 1974) are close to the southern limit of reef structures. Here, 17 genera form platelike encrusting colonies that form a continuous structure only off the more sheltered northern shores of the islands.

Wider fringing reefs with significant reef flat development are found 630 km to the east on Lord Howe Island at 31°35'S (Fig. 12.1). These are considered to be the southernmost reefs in the world (Slater and Phipps, 1977). Coral growth is common on most rock surfaces around the island with 57 species of 33 genera being identified (Veron and Done, 1979). Soft corals, especially *Xenia* and *Sarcophyton*, are very common, and luxuriant growths of soft algae (*Padina*, *Caulerpa*, and *Chlorodesmis*) are reported. The widest reef is found on the western side of the island (Fig. 12.1) and contains a lagoon 1.5–2.5 m deep with occasional colonies of *Pocillopora damicornis* over a sandy bottom. Channels up to 7 m deep are cut into the lagoon and sparker profiles have indicated the presence of subsurface channels in bedrock beneath the lagoon floor (Slater and Phipps, 1977). The sediment over the lagoon, mainly reef skeletal fragments mixed with volcanic rocks, are 4.5 m thick except in channels where they exceed 25 m thickness. Three deep holes 8–10 m deep have the most luxuriant coral growth. Behind the reef front is a further zone of *Acropora* patch reefs. The reef front is formed of imbricated rubble that gives way seaward to a spur and groove system, the spurs 2–5 m high being riddled with caves and tunnels. Veron and Done (1979) have noted that the reef communities differ substantially from their tropical equivalents due to the growth-form deviations of dominant species. They suggest that existing coral communities are the result of a balance between periodic denudation by cold, subantarctic currents and recolonization by larvae from tropical currents, with low temperatures per se having little effect on coral growth, but affecting growth-form responses to light regimes. However, the morphology suggests that flourishing

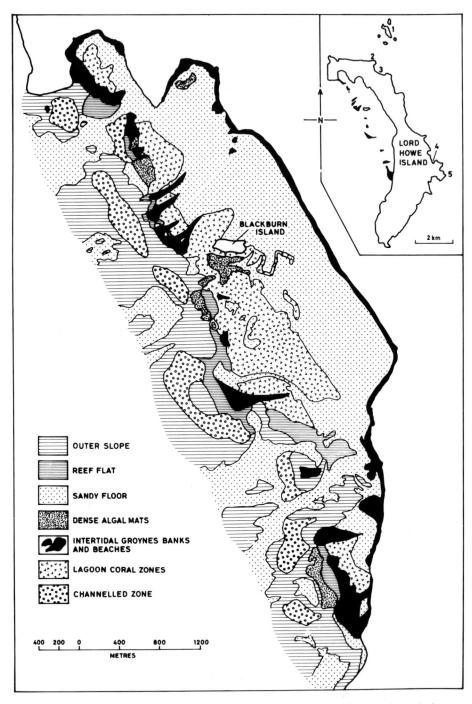

Figure 12.1 Fringing reef of Lord Howe Island, from Veron and Done (1979). (Reproduced by permission of the CSIRO Editorial and Publications Service.)

reefs existed in the past on Lord Howe Island. The present reefs appear to consist of only a thin veneer of Holocene growth over a severely eroded pre-Holocene reef foundation.

A parallel situation exists in Moreton Bay near Brisbane at 27°30′S, where small fringing reefs and reef patches exist around Peel, St. Helena, and Green Islands and fossil reefs elsewhere in the bay (Orme and Day, 1978). Moreton Bay is about 80 km long and 35 km wide and is sheltered from the open sea by the sand barriers of North Stradbroke, South Stradbroke, and Moreton Islands. The living reefs comprise 24 coral species representing 12 genera while the fossil reefs contain 36 species from 20 genera (Wells, 1955b). However the older reefs are of mid-Holocene not Pleistocene age. Uranium series dates from the Mud Island fossil reef were 4600 and 6000 yrs B.P. for *Acropora* sp. and 4100 yrs B.P. for a *Favia* sp. (Jones et al., 1977). A radiocarbon age of 3710 yrs B.P. was obtained for corals from the fossil Peel Island reef (Rubin and Alexandre, 1958). These older reefs and a younger beach rock dated at 2540 ± 85 yrs B.P. (Lovell, 1975) on adjacent St. Helena Island are all considered to be related to a sea level about 1 m higher than present (Jones et al., 1977). Although the surfaces of these reefs are mid-Holocene it is thought probable by Jones et al. (1977) that Pleistocene reef foundations exist.

Although hermatypic corals extend into southern Australian waters (see Chap. 3) the corals of the southernmost fringing reefs between 27° and 31°33′S appear to exist in a marginal situation. However, conditions appear to have been more favorable for coral growth in both mid-Holocene and late Pleistocene times and the bulk of the reef structure may have been built during these earlier periods. Indeed the southern limit of fringing reef development may have been much further south. Marshall and Thom (1976) have obtained uranium series dates from corals near Newcastle (32°50′S) of 143,000 and 142,000 yrs B.P. (*Goniopora lobata* and *Blasstomussa wellsi*), and of around 120,000 yrs from corals near Evans Head (29°07′S). This latter site includes *Acropora* sp., *Favites* sp., *Montipora* sp. and *Platygyra lamellina*. *Pocillopora damicornis* in growth position gave a date of 118,000 ± 9000 yrs B.P. A report (Thomson, 1905) of masses of coral and dead reef near the mouth of the Boyne River (24°S) may also represent a Pleistocene reef, and Cook and Mayo (1977, p. 25) report pre-Holocene reefs in Broad Sound, a recrystallized coral sample (*Favia* sp.) from which produced a minimal radiocarbon age of 30,700 ± 1200 yrs B.P.

Mainland Fringing Reefs

Although isolated living coral colonies, mainly Favids, occur attached to boulders and cliff bases around the prominent headlands of the Queensland mainland coast from Caloundra northward no true fringing reefs occur south of the Cape Conway region near Proserpine at 20°30′S. Distribution of reefs of the Whitsunday Passage area (Fig. 9.16) has been mapped by Stanley (1928). They continue northward, occupying both headland and bayhead positions, as far as Gloucester Passage, but then have no further development as far north as Kurrimine (17°46′S).

The Kurrimine fringing reef is, in many ways, an anomolous feature. The area has been described briefly by Bird and Hopley (1969). The reef is attached not to a hard rock coastline but to a multiple beach barrier system, the inner part of which is Pleistocene and contains illuvial ferruginous sand rock. Similar materials are found on the foreshore at Garners Beach to the south and it is clear that the Holocene and Pleistocene sand barriers overlie the reef, and in the past have overlain it even more extensively. Although the outer slope of this reef has a veneer of living coral there appears to be little doubt that the bulk of the reef structure is of Pleistocene age.

Small fringing reefs occur intermittently along the coastline of the Macalister Range north of Cairns (Bird, 1970b). However, northward from Yule Point to the mouth of the Mowbray River is an extensive fringing reef extending from a shoreline which is partly sandy beach, partly mangrove (Fig. 12.2). Bird (1971b) has shown that live corals are confined to the seaward margin of this reef where reef building is still in progress below neap tide level mainly by *Acropora* sp. The outer reef flat is dominated by coralline algae and the inner reef flat is blanketed by sediment, quartzose sand in the south but a soft, brown mud closer to the mouth of the Mowbray River. Only occasional living corals, mostly Alcyonarians and a few Favids occur on the inner reef flat, which is colonized on its inner side by mangroves (*Avicennia* and *Rhizophora* sp.). Fairbridge (1950) described an emerged reef on the inner side of this reef and this has been confirmed by Bird (1971b) who considers that 1.2 m of emergence is indicated. A radiocarbon date of 4130 ± 110 yrs B.P. was obtained for material from the reef suggesting a mid-Holocene age. However, Bird also showed that the reef was initiated not as a fringing reef, but as an offshore patch reef, subsequently joined to the mainland by rapid coastal progradation at the mouth of the Mowbray River.

Only north of 16°15′S at Cape Kimberly do mainland fringing reefs become more common and even here they are intermittently developed and far less continuous than suggested by Fairbridge (1950, 1967). They are rarely more than 250 m in width and, as indicated by Fairbridge are as much algal as coral reefs. There are many locations where Holocene sedimentation appears to have joined former patch reefs to the mainland in the same manner as described by Bird at Yule Point.

Fringing Reefs of the Continental Islands

Small fringing reefs commence just inside the Tropic of Capricorn in the Keppel Islands. Here, and in the Northumberland Group of islands to the north, they form only isolated reef patches attached to headlands or in bayhead locations without any significant reef-flat development. From 21°01′S northward, however, by far the greater number of high islands have fringing reefs. The sharpness of this boundary is remarkable, especially as the southernmost of the islands with well-developed fringing reefs, Penrith Island, has a reef flat 1300 m wide (Hopley, 1975). The majority of the Cumberland Islands have fringing reefs, some being very extensive. Carlisle and Brampton Island, for example are joined together by their fringing reefs (Fig. 12.3). Most extensive of all, however, are the fringing reefs of the Whitsunday Islands (Fig. 9.16), which extend up all the narrow islets of Hook and Whitsunday Islands, and which reach a maximum width of 700 m on Hayman Island.

Again it appears significant that at least some of the southernmost high-

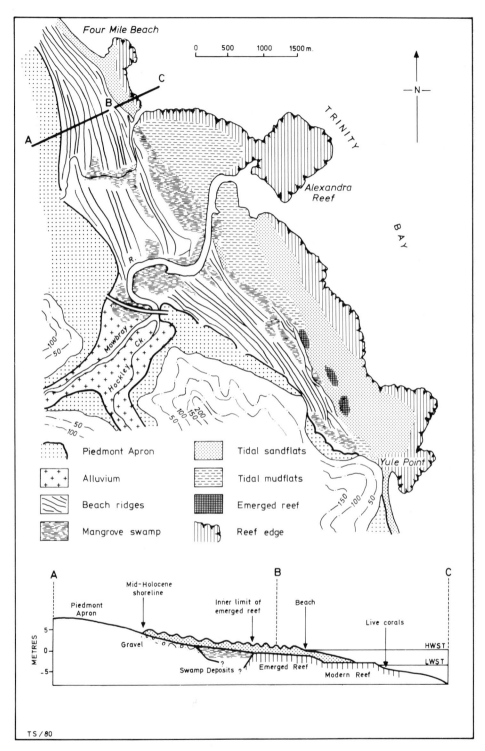

Figure 12.2 Yule Point fringing reef. (Redrawn from Bird, 1971b, by permission of the Institute of Australian Geographers.)

Figure 12.3 Carlisle and Brampton Islands, Cumberland Group. Extensive fringing reefs join these two islands. The lagoon on Carlisle Island is formed between 11 m high dunes on the southern side and a 6 m high boulder beach on the northern side in the foreground.

island fringing reefs have Pleistocene foundations. The most unequivocal evidence comes from Hayman Island where deep drilling and radiometric dating have clearly established a pre-Holocene reef at a depth of about 20 m. The fringing reef on Cockermouth Island is also largely Pleistocene. A wide reef flat extends around the eastern end of the island, incorporating a number of small islands (Fig. 12.4). The easternmost of these are bedrock but the three in the center of the flat are composed of dune calcarenite of Pleistocene age (Hopley, 1975) (Fig. 12.5). The reef flat appears to be a planed surface of the same material with minimal coral veneer, though with an intricate pattern of algal terraces. Solutional hollows with calcified soil infills are also found at this reef-flat level (c. MSL). The vertical extent of the calcarenite is unknown but it seems likely that it overlies Pleistocene reef. Even if the dune was deposited during lowered sea levels, as has been suggested for the calcarenites elsewhere in Australia (e.g. Fairbridge and Teichert, 1952) this does not detract from the fact that the Cockermouth reef basement is pre-Holocene. It is generally higher than most reef flats (above lowest neap tide level) and towards its southern edge has a series of algal-rimmed pools within which are small living corals. However, a drop of about 0.6 m occurs on the southern side onto a lower reef-flat area with deep pools and living coral cover, but also with an algal terrace about 50 m wide. This would appear to be a later addition to the reef flat and may represent Holocene outward growth.

Northward from the Whitsunday Passage the majority of high islands have significant fringing reef development. Only the largest with significant runoff

Figure 12.4 Reef flat of Cockermouth Island. The three islands of the reef flat are composed of Pleistocene dune calcarenite.

Figure 12.5 Etched Pleistocene dune calcarenite, reef-flat island Cockermouth Island. The upper beach may be a mid-Holocene erosional feature about 2 m above the present level of notching.

such as Gloucester Island or Hinchinbrook lack reefs, although some large islands such as Magnetic or Great Palm have good fringing reef development. Proximity to the mainland appears to be detrimental to reef development and some islands within 5 km of the mainland south of Cairns (such as the Family Group and Fitzroy Island) have poorly developed reefs. North of Cairns nearly all high islands have fringing reefs. Double Island 20 km north of Cairns for example has a fringing reef 1200 m wide and is only 1 km from the mainland. On the majority of these islands the reefs are narrowest on the windward side facing the prevailing southeasterlies and tend to be wider with more complete reef flat development on the northern and eastern sides. The windward reef front is steeply sloping, or even overhanging, whereas the leeward side is more gently sloping and may consist of a detrital slope.

The majority of fringing reefs have an area less than that of the high island to which they are attached. There are, however, many examples where the reef area many times exceeds that of the island. The rocky outcrop may be a very minor feature of the whole reef and obviously its influence in terms of sediment input and runoff is minimal. Most of these reefs are located at the northern end of the Great Barrier Reef, north of Cape Weymouth (12°37'S) but the southernmost, Redbill Reef (Fig. 9.7), is located at 20°57'S.

Several different rock types are represented by these islands, including trachite, volcanics, sandstone, and tertiary basalt. However, sediment yield to the adjacent reef is negligible. On Redbill Reef, even the beach sands banked against the outcrop have less than 1% noncarbonate content. On some of the larger islands bayhead beaches may contain larger proportions of terrigenous sediments. For example a small shingle beach of 2 cm diameter volcanic rock fragments occurs on the lee side of Bootie Island in the Cockburn Group, and bayhead beaches on Forbes Island contain 16% quartzose material. However, even within 10 m of the beach, sediments are entirely carbonate.

The small influence that these outcrops have on their adjacent reefs precludes their classification as fringing reefs but they do have some significance for the development of such reefs. They provide circumstantial evidence for suggesting that at least some of the reefs of the Great Barrier Reef have developed over rocky outcrops, that is, that they may have originated as fringing reefs. Pandora Reef 70 km north of Townsville, and only 16 km from the mainland, may represent the final stage (Fig. 10.13). This small reef with shingle cay and basset edges has a large number of boulders of up to 20 cm diameter of porphyritic granite similar to that on adjacent islands. There is no record of ships' ballast being left on this reef and the concentration is too great for the boulders to have floated onto the reef in the roots of trees. Concentration of the boulders into two areas of the reef, one on the western end, the other towards the northern side, suggests that bedrock may be buried at very shallow depth beneath the reef flat in these locations.

THE FOUNDATIONS AND STRUCTURE OF FRINGING REEFS

Easton and Olsen (1976) have suggested that the application of classic concepts of reef growth has led to an oversimplification of the circumstances under which fringing reefs grow. They suggest that this is not the mode of growth on gentle slopes and show that in Hanauma Reef in Hawaii coral growth commenced over a relatively wide band seaward of the shoreline, growing upwards to sea level and maintaining relative position as sea level changed. The horizon of the reef flat was thus maintained and in later stages of development the reef prograded seaward vigorously and landward less effectively. From this and other studies of fringing reefs (e.g. that of Glynn and McIntyre, 1977, in Panama) a number of important questions arise about the foundations and evolution of such reefs.

Circumstantial evidence presented in the early part of this chapter suggests that some fringing reefs are not primary structures but built over older Pleistocene foundations. By far the best evidence comes from Hayman Island (Fig. 12.6), where radiometric dating has confirmed the age structure of the reef (Hopley et al., 1978). The Holocene reef was established about 9500 years ago on the Pleistocene foundations at a depth of about 20 m, probably as a reef attached to the shoreline. However, the rapid rate of sea-level rise at this time almost certainly resulted in migration of the shoreline landward at a faster rate than the reef could develop. Age-depth isolines within the reef suggest that the reef grew upward most rapidly over its point of colonization, subsequently extending both seaward and landward to produce the modern reef flat. Most active coral growth, mainly *Acropora* sp., appears to have been near the top of the reef front at any particular time. In situ corals behind the reef front consist of both *Acropora* and more massive species (*Porites* sp. and Favids). The reef-front deposits are mainly sand and shingle and growth of the reef outward has been in the form of a detrital slope. Carbonate values are generally greater than 90% throughout the Holocene reef, indicating that terrigenous sediments have not made major contribution to the growth of the reef. Only in isolated lenses towards the rear of the reef do terrigenous contents exceed 30% (Smith, 1974). The rate of upward growth of the reef averaged 2.9 mm/yr from the time of reef initiation to formation of the present reef flat, but rates of 4 to 5 mm/yr occurred on the reef crest (see Chap. 8).

No other fringing reef in the Great Barrier Reef region has comparable detail. However, some have been drilled or jet-probed for civil-engineering works, mainly jetties, and the fringing reefs of Rattlesnake Island and Orpheus Island near Townsville have been drilled for scientific purposes by the author. Two types of fringing reef can be identified. The first appears analogous to the Hanauma Bay reef and is illustrated by the reefs at Orpheus Island (Fig. 12.7), Geoffrey Bay on Magnetic Island, and Coolgaree Bay, Great Palm Island, all bayhead reefs. At Magnetic Island, reef growth appears to have been isolated towards the outer edge of the reef flat over older Pleistocene reef or bedrock, with the intervening area, which now forms the bulk of the reef flat beneath a thin algal crust, infilled by a combination of terrigenous and biogenic sediments. The Coolgaree Bay reef is 280 m wide and forms a very thin veneer (18% coral, 82% sand and shingle) only 1.5–2.7 m thick over a weathered Pleistocene land surface that extends from the island. A similar situation exists at Orpheus Island although there is the indication of a pre-Holocene reef foundation here (Fig. 12.7).

The second type of reef is that which develops very commonly on the lee

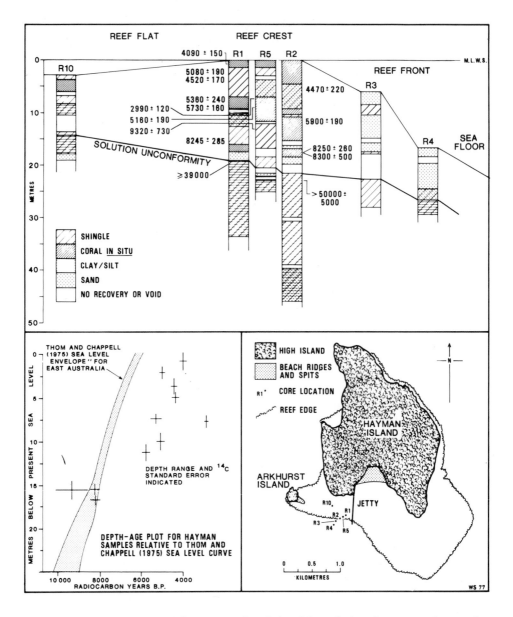

Figure 12.6 Hayman Island fringing reef and dated bore holes. (From Hopley et al., 1978.)

side of smaller high islands and that is surmounted by a subaerial spit of Holocene age (Hopley, 1971a). On Dunk Island (17°55′S) 7.3–8.2 m of mud, sand, and coral shingle overlies a compact clay surface of probable Pleistocene age. Similarly drilling through the mid-Holocene emerged reef on Rattlesnake Island (Chap. 6) indicated that coral formed a very thin veneer of no more than 1.5 m thickness overlying 10 m of mainly terrigenous sand, clay and some coral. Below 11.5 m is a mottled clay surface interpreted as the Holocene-Pleistocene

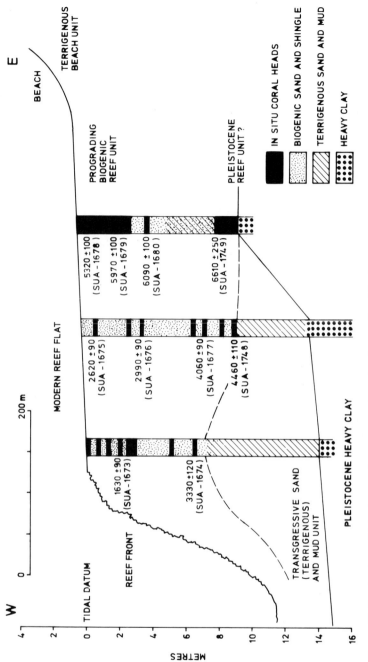

Figure 12.7 Section of fringing reef at Pioneer Bay. Orpheus Island (Palm Group) showing a relatively thin (5–7 m) reefal veneer developed during the last 6000 yrs over a transgressive mud and sand lens. This overlies a weathered Pleistocene surface.

boundary. Earliest coral growth just above this was dated at 7010 ± 180 yrs
B.P. (GaK-9292). The sequence suggests that this wide reef flat has developed
largely as a sand spit with only minor coral contribution until sea level had stabilized. The thin reefal veneer has been dated at between 6480 and 5380 yrs B.P.

The small amount of evidence available for fringing reefs of the Great Barrier Reef province suggests that many of these reefs have developed over pre-
Holocene foundations. However, in some cases it is also clear that the reef can
extend over unconsolidated sediments but initial reef growth may be on more
solid foundations. Early coral growth appears to take place landward of the
present shoreline, as suggested by the dated cores at Hanauma Bay, although
this may be simply a function of the location of the shoreline in response to the
lower sea level of the time. Subsequently, major coral growth is in the area of
initiation on the outer rim of the reef with the area between the reef rim and
the high island being infilled mainly by biogenic sediments from the reef front.
The dated cores from Hayman Island and elsewhere in the world, such as
Hawaii (Easton and Olsen, 1976), New Guinea (Chappell and Polach, 1976),
and Panama (Glynn and MacIntyre, 1977), suggest that the rate of upward
growth of fringing reefs may be higher than that of shelf reefs.

BIOLOGICAL, MORPHOLOGICAL, AND SEDIMENTOLOGICAL ZONATION ON FRINGING REEFS

Modifying influences on the zonation of fringing reefs are the input of sediment and runoff from adjacent mainland or high island. Fringing reefs generally rise from shallower depths compared to the reefs of the outer shelf and
thus the degree of variation found with depth in terms of biological and morphological zonation is lacking. In spite of these limitations there is no paucity
of variety in fringing reefs. Indeed, there is such a diversity of marine habitats
within these reefs that they contain the greatest diversity of benthic fauna anywhere within the Great Barrier Reef province (Veron and Pichon, 1976). Thus
of 81 coral species recorded from the Great Barrier Reef from the families
Thamnasteriidae, Astrocoeniidae, Pocilloporidae, Faviidae, and Trachyphylliidae, 79 have been recorded from fringing reefs and 74 from the fringing reefs
of the Palm Islands alone (Veron and Pichon, 1976; Veron et al., 1977).

Biological zonation of fringing reefs is far less striking than it is on outer
shelf reefs largely because of lower wave energy levels (Done and Pichon, in
press). Using a number of quantitative classification techniques, Done (1977)
has shown that the fringing reef at Iris Point, on Orpheus Island in the Palm
Group, has a basic, threefold ecological zonation, comprising reef flat, reef
crest, and reef-front communities. Unfortunately detailed zonation patterns
are not available, although there is considerable detail for reef-flat zonation
within the intertidal zone (e.g. Endean et al., 1956a,b; Slack-Smith, 1960). In
general the more open the reef is to the prevailing southeasterlies, the wider
the reef flat, and the smaller the outcrop, the more the reef-flat zonation resembles that of midshelf reefs of the Great Barrier Reef proper. Zonation on
narrower reefs or adjacent to large islands more closely resembles that of the
rocky shores of the adjacent mainland. In such locations abundant coral

growth is limited to reef margins, with only a few living microatolls (Favids or *Porites* sp.) in deeper pools. However soft alcyonarians may be much more abundant on these fringing reefs, especially where freshwater flushing or sediment influx has killed other organisms. Compared to zonation on the outer reefs, the inner continental islands show a clearer intertidal zonation than is possible on the outer reefs, where altitudes above MLWN are usually restricted to reef blocks and beach rock of cays.

The zonation within the intertidal zone of fringing reef flats varies in different parts of the Queensland coast (Table 12.1). Endean et al. (1956a,b) confirmed the presence of a zoogeographical boundary at about 25°S and considered it to be related to the diminution of wave energy within the Reef province.

The zones become more complex on the offshore islands, the variation from the typical mainland zonation of Table 12.1 depending on the distance from the mainland, the distance from the Great Barrier Reef, and the latitude (Endean et al., 1956a). In general low wave-energy island shores close to the mainland have zonations not markedly different from the mainland but with increasing exposure *Tetraclita rosea*, corals, zoanthids, and encrusting algae become more common, and *Tetraclita squamosa* becomes less common. With decreasing latitude the typical algal zone of the mainland, although well represented on islands south of 20°S not subjected to excessive wave action, is replaced by corals, zoanthids, and coralline algae; *Tetraclita rosea* is replaced by *T. vitiata* at about 19°S and the rock oyster *Crassostrea amasa* becomes much more abundant.

A further complicating factor is the nature of the evolution of these reef flats during the Holocene. The majority of fringing reef flats are relatively old with numerous radiocarbon dates in excess of 5000 yrs B.P. being recorded for reef-flat corals or reef top sediments (Fig. 12.8). Because of the variable nature of Holocene sea levels over this period, as discussed in Chapter 7, many fringing reef tops have had opportunity not only to attain maximum elevation with respect to modern sea level, but also incorporate areas of reef flat constructed during higher relative sea levels of the mid-Holocene. The example of Rattlesnake Island fringing reef near Townsville epitomizes the problem. The majority of this reef flat is covered in dead corals, some of which on the outer flat appear to be only recently killed (analogous to the Stone Island and Whitsunday Reefs killed by massive runoff in 1918 and described by Hedley, 1925e, and Rainford, 1925a). The zonation on the northwestern side of this reef is:

1 MHWS to 0.26 m above MSL; beach-rock outcrop with *Crassostrea amasa* and chitons.

2 0.26 m above MSL to MLWN: extending from beneath the beach rock, a zone of dead corals, many in microatoll form including Favids, *Porites* sp., and *Pocillopora verrucosa* with extensive algal cover.

3 MLWN to MLWS: an extensive field of *Acropora* sp., all dead. Algal cover is variable.

4 Below MLWS: a reef-edge zone consisting of soft corals (*Lithophyton, Sarcophyton*) sponges, and algae (*Caulerpa, Laurencia, Sargassum,* and *Padina*) with some living *Acropora*.

Table 12.1 Biological Zonations at Various Intertidal Locations in the Great Barrier Reef Province[a]

Approximate Level	South Queensland Mainland (Currumbin)	North Queensland Mainland (Etty Bay)	Central Queensland High Island Exposed (Bailey Island)	North Queensland High Island (Kent Island)
MHWS	*Nodilittorina pyrimidalis* (Upper littorinid zone) *Melaraphe unifasciata* (Lower littorinid zone) *Chthamalus antennatus* & *Melaraphe unifasciata* (Upper barnacle zone)	*Nodilittorina pyramidalis* (Upper littorinid zone) *Melaraphe melanacme* (Lower littorinid zone) *Chthamalus malayensis* (Upper barnacle zone)	*Nodilittorina pyramidalis* (Upper littorinid zone) *Melaraphe melanacme* (Lower littorinid zone)	*Nodilittorina pyramidalis* (Upper littorinid zone) *Melaraphe melanacme* (Lower littorinid zone)
MHWN	*Tetraclita rosea* (Lower barnacle zone)	*Crassostrea amasa* (Oyster zone)	*Crassostrea amasa* (Oyster zone)	*Chthamalus malayensis* (Barnacle zone)
MSL	*Galeolaria caespitosa* (Serpulid zone)	*Tetraclita squamosa* (Lower barnacle zone)	*Tetraclita rosea* (Barnacle zone)	*Crassostrea amasa* (Oyster zone)
MLWN	Algal-ascidian zone (*Pyura stolonifera*)	Algal zone	Zoanthid zone	*Acanthozostera gemmata* & *Patelloida saccharina* (Chiton zone) Lithothamnion zone
MLWS			Coral-lithothamnion zone	Zoanthids, corals, and *Lithophyton* sp.

[a] After Endean et al., (1956a,b).

370

Figure 12.8 Old eroded microatolls on the fringing reef of Middle Island near Bowen. The microatoll was dated at 5210 ± 115 yrs B.P. and a *Tridacna* valve in situ in a nearby microatoll at 5290 ± 120 yrs B.P.

The higher reef flat extending from beneath the beach rock is mid-Holocene, a head coral from this reef being dated at 5530 ± 130 yrs B.P. This is similar to ages for corals (5210 ± 115 yrs B.P.) and associated *Tridacna* sp. (5290 ± 120 yrs B.P.) from the inner reef flat at Middle Island near Bowen (Fig. 12.8) (Hopley, 1975). Clearly many of the fringing reef flats contain a modern biological zonation superimposed over a substrate containing a fossil zonation related to a higher Holocene sea level.

This situation is analogous to that of the inner shelf low wooded island reefs to the north of Cairns (Chap. 11). Indeed there are so many similarities between the fringing reefs and associated deposits of the high islands south of Cairns and the low wooded islands that a comparable Holocene history may be postulated. Morphological zonation is very similar, with reef margins rising from shallow depths to a reef crest frequently surmounted by shingle ridges like the rampart systems of the low wooded islands. Even cemented basset edges are found, indicating the former position of shingle ridges since removed by cyclone action. Basset edges are particularly well developed on Middle Island and Holbourne Island near Bowen (Hopley, 1975). Other common features are marginal reef blocks, rubbly reef flats, and the high elevation of the reef flats, the result not simply of a high sea level, but also of microatoll development within moated pools to elevations above the level of corals in open-water situations. Mangroves too are found on many of the high islands' reef flats while the cays and platform rocks have analogies in the sandy spits and raised beach rocks developed over the lee-side fringing reefs (Hopley, 1971a).

Sediments of fringing reefs also have a high degree of similarity to those of low wooded islands. In an analysis of sediments from fringing reefs on Magnetic Island and Havanna Island, A. S. Smith (1974, 1978) found that statistical grouping based on textural characteristics and proportion of carbonate closely correlated with morphological zonation. For the bayhead reefs in Geoffrey Bay and Nelly Bay, Magnetic Island, six sedimentary zones were defined (Table 12.2).

Sampling on other reef flats suggests that this pattern is typical of the majority of bayhead fringing reefs, the major variation being in the reef-margin unit that in more open situations is considerably coarser, and may consist of shingle, usually fragments of *Acropora*. On wider lee-side reefs and on headland fringing reefs the biogenic content is ubiquitously higher with terrigenous sediments very much limited to the upper beach facies. Amounts of terrigenous material are related to catchment areas and only the bayhead beaches on the larger islands such as Magnetic have significant drainage basins. On some reefs a further sedimentary unit may be identified, that belonging to the small areas of mangroves developed in sheltered locations. These sediments are highly variable, ranging from actively mobile medium sands such as on Orpheus Island where the mean sediment size in a *Rhyzophora stylosa* mangal ranges from 0.0 to 1.8 ϕ (A. P. Spenceley, personal communication) to silt-sized material in larger swamps.

SUBAERIAL DEPOSITS ON THE REEF PLATFORM

The fringing-reef platforms provide a foundation for the deposition of a variety of sediments above present tidal influence, particularly on the lee side (normally the northwest) of the high islands where they form spits over the wider parts of the reef flat (Hopley, 1968, 1971a, 1975). Beach-ridge sequences have also developed over the bayhead reefs, the ridges consisting of quartzose and biogenic sands similar to the modern beaches. In the high-carbonate environment of these deposits, cementation is common. The problems of interpretation of some of these cemented deposits has been discussed in Chapter 6, where it was argued that both higher Holocene sea levels and cyclone activity with storm surges were involved in the emplacement of sediments up to 8 m above MHWS.

Apart from the older dunes on larger islands such as Lizard and Hook, the majority of the deposits resting on the modern reef flats appear to be Holocene in age. Two exceptions are Cockermouth Island, discussed above, and Camp Island near Cape Upstart where a date of 20,200 ± 600 yrs B.P. suggests a Pleistocene age for a high beach-rock terrace at 4.4 m (Hopley, 1971a). Elsewhere, the oldest elements of the spit deposits are boulder beachers composed of local rocks up to 1.0 m in diameter. The spit on Curacoa Island (Fig. 12.9) in the Palm Group is typical (Hopley, 1968). Here the lee-side spit consists of a boulder embankment with a younger infill of coral shingle-beach ridges. The boulder beach is simple with a main crest rising to 5.2 m above MHWS and two lateral arms trailing to the south (Fig. 6.7). At its anchor point the boulders are 0.65 m in diameter but grade to 0.2 m at the distal end. Part of the original

Table 12.2 Mean Value and Standard Deviation of Sediment Variables, by Morphological Zone, Nelly Bay, and Geoffrey Bay Reefs[a]

| Morphological Zone | Mean Particle Size (ϕ) | Variable | | | Carbonate Content (Percent) |
		Sorting (ϕ)	Skewness	Kurtosis	
Nelly Bay					
Upper beach	1.1 ± 0.9	0.8 ± 0.2	−0.1 ± 0.6	0.5 ± 1.3	16.1 ± 10.6
Lower beach	2.8 ± 0.4	0.9 ± 0.5	−1.7 ± 1.0	5.6 ± 4.0	44.0 ± 11.1
Reef flat	−1.6 ± 1.0	2.7 ± 0.5	0.4 ± 1.5	1.3 ± 17.2[b]	81.4 ± 20.6[b]
Subaqueous delta	0.1 ± 1.0	1.4 ± 0.6	−0.1 ± 0.4	−0.4 ± 0.6	3.6 ± 2.7
Reef margin	1.2 ± 0.8	1.4 ± 0.5	−1.7 ± 1.1	4.2 ± 4.9	77.3 ± 28.1[b]
Forereef	−0.1 ± 0.3	1.1 ± 0.3	−0.1 ± 0.6	0.7 ± 1.9	44.7 ± 19.5
Geoffrey Bay					
Upper beach	0.2 ± 0.7	1.6 ± 0.3	0.1 ± 0.4	−0.7 ± 0.5	43.3 ± 12.1
Lower beach	2.5 ± 0.6	0.9 ± 0.3	−1.6 ± 1.0	6.4 ± 5.6	73.0 ± 7.1
Reef flat	−2.8 ± 2.0	2.0 ± 0.9	2.4 ± 3.5	18.7 ± 42.9[b]	81.9 ± 21.5[b]
Forereef	0.7 ± 1.1	1.3 ± 0.3	0.0 ± 1.3	1.3 ± 1.2	45.0 ± 19.7

[a]From Smith (1978).

[b]The distributions of values for reef-flat and reef-margin carbonate contents show strong negative skewness. Extreme leptokurtosis in some reef-flat samples leads to strong positive skewness of the distributions of kurtosis values.

Figure 12.9   The cuspate foreland of Curacoa Island, Palm Group. Radiometric dates of 5070 ± 110 yrs B.P. and 5250 ± 100 yrs B.P. have been obtained from the well-wooded boulder spit and 2620 ± 90 yrs B.P. from one of the rearmost coral shingle ridges.

spit has been truncated and cemented basal sections of the spit have been cemented to a height of 1.9 m above MHWS. Where the spit is eroded this conglomerate forms a level platform on which later coral shingle ridges rest. Coral cemented into the base of the ridge gave a radiocarbon age of 5070 ± 110 yrs B.P., while coral from near the crest gave a compatible date of 5250 ± 100 yrs B.P. (Hopley, 1968). This suggests that the boulder spit formed shortly after modern sea level was first achieved. Reef flat then developed between the spit and the high island and over this was deposited a series of coral shingle-beach ridges rising to a maximum of 4.4 m. Shell from one of the older ridges gave a radiocarbon date of 2620 ± 90 yrs B.P.

This pattern of initial deposition of terrigenous deposits with later influx of highly biogenic materials is typical of many of the island spits. The boulders are derived from the regolith of the hillslopes of the high islands developed during the last glacial low sea level and reworked by the sea when modern sea level was first achieved (c. 6000 yrs B.P.). With the stabilization of sea level new terrigenous materials were no longer available for supply to the spits but vigorous reef growth aided in some areas by a comparative fall in sea level provided ample biogenic material (Fig. 12.3).

It is mainly in these biogenic materials that the high cementation levels are found. Although some have a guano-derived phosphate cement and are identical to the cay sandstones found on many reef islands the majority of cements are carbonate, at least some of which is aragonitic. Arguments have already been put forward for the interpretation of these deposits as emerged beach rocks originally cemented in the intertidal zone. Their heights range from little more than a meter above MHWS to maximum of 4.9 m at Herald Island near Townsville (Fig. 6.8). Radiometric dates from these deposits generally range between 3000 and 5000 yrs B.P. their age and elevation fitting into the pattern of tectonic and isostatic adjustment discussed in Chapter 6. Holbourne Island near Bowen (Hopley, 1975) illustrates the nature and relationships of the deposits (Figs. 12.10 and 12.11). The granitic backbone of the island rises to 111 m, a low col occurring between the two major outcrops, which are continued to the southeast as a series of rocks that form the eastern boundary of the large fringing reef on the southern side of the island. It is over the northwestern part of this reef flat that a cuspate foreland of Quaternary deposits is formed. A smaller area of similar deposits infills the small bay on the northern side of Holbourne.

The oldest deposits are an earthy, partially silicified regolith. This is found in pockets over the entire higher part of the island but especially around the lower slopes where it passes beneath all other unconsolidated and cemented deposits. Along the rocky southern shores it has extensive outcrop and has been subject to cavernous weathering. On the major southern outcrop of Quaternary deposits, a black calcareous soil immediately overlies the cemented regolith. This is succeeded to seaward by a series of raised beach-rock terraces about 120 m wide. At the rear, the upper surface of cementation slopes upward from 2.5–2.7 m. There is then a clear step to a near horizontal surface with a cementation level ranging between 3.3 and 3.7 m. An even clearer unconformity is found to seaward where a lower terrace (2.1–2.3 m) occurs. The outer

Figure 12.10 Holbourne Island fringing reef flat from the east.

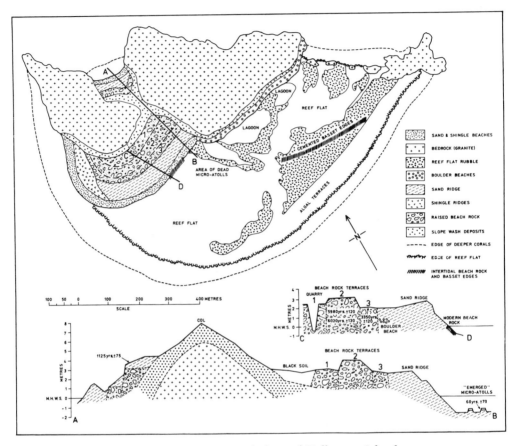

Figure 12.11   Geomorphology of Holbourne Island.

edge of this surface consists of broken beach-rock slabs similar to many modern outcrops. A wide, sandy beach ridge is found around the beach-rock terraces. A pit sunk 5 m away from the edge of the outer terrace to a depth of 1.5 m failed to reveal further cemented material. A granite boulder beach was found at this depth, apparently banked up against the beach rock. A series of *Acropora* shingle ridges is found on the northwestern side of the foreland. Modern beach rock outcrops along the southern beach.

Much of the finer fabric of the beach rock is phosphatized presumably by downward leaching of guano deposits (Saint-Smith, 1919). The oldest terrace has the highest phosphate content and was mined in the early part of the century. The resulting quarry shows that the material of the terrace is cemented down to a level very close to present MHWS. The bulk of the material is coralline throughout, mainly *Acropora* shingle. The bulk of the cement remains calcareous even where phosphatization has taken place. A coral sample and a shell (*Tridacna* sp.), weathered on the outside but with a solid core, from the southern wall of the quarry provided material for dating; the shell coming from a height approximately 2 m above the floor of the quarry, the coral from closer to the natural surface. The dates are compatible, the shell having a radiocarbon age of 6020 ± 130 yrs B.P., the coral 5980 ± 120 yrs B.P. A sample of uncontaminated coral (*Favia* sp.) was recovered from the outer terrace and its radiocarbon age of 3350 ± 95 yrs B.P. not only dates that terrace but indicates an age between 3500 and 6000 yrs B.P. for the highest level. The terraces apparently were emplaced and cemented during a transgressive, then regressive, phase, throughout which beach material continued to prograde. The infill sequence in the northern bay appears similar but telescoped into a smaller horizontal distance. Two beach rock terraces at 2.9 and 1.0 m occur. However, these are much broken, apparently by cyclone activity and storm ridges, probably emplaced by cyclonic seas, overlie the cemented deposits, and rise to 4.4 m. Shell (*Tridacna* sp.) from this overlying storm beach produced a radiocarbon date of 1125 ± 75 yrs B.P.

Other high islands, particularly those between Hinchinbrook Island and Cairns, and in the Whitsunday Passage area, show no signs of comparative emergence, either in the form of emerged corals or cemented deposits. However, the pattern of deposits is similar to that described above, with earliest deposits frequently terrigenous in origin, later ones mainly biogenic. Boulder beaches, sand ridges, and sand terraces rise to heights well above MHWS but without the corroborating evidence of cemented levels or corals in growth position, it seems most likely that they originated as cyclonic deposits.

FACTORS INFLUENCING THE MORPHOLOGY OF THE FRINGING REEFS AND RELATED DEPOSITS

From the number of radiocarbon dates obtained from fringing reef flats or their related deposits it is clear that in terms of their Holocene development, fringing reefs are relatively old or mature features. Reef-flat development appears to have taken place shortly after modern sea level was first achieved and ages in excess of 6000 yrs B.P. have been achieved for slightly emerged reef on the Flinders Islands (J. Chappell, personal communication, 1980). In Chapter 10 it was shown that such mature reef-flat development was related to a shallow pre-Holocene platform and the early attainment of modern sea level. Such factors led to the development of the low wooded island type of reef. In many ways the high island reefs south of Cairns are analogous to the low wooded islands of the northern Great Barrier Reef. Although some at least have Pleistocene reef foundations, the shallow platform upon which Holocene reef growth was first initiated about 6000 years ago may well have been the rocky shores of the islands themselves. Deeper Pleistocene reef foundations as, for example, at Hayman Island, are not inhibiting factors to fringing reef development as they are for the outer reefs of the Great Barrier Reef. In terms of their sea-level history, the high islands are also similar to the low wooded islands. Both are situated on the inner third of the continental shelf and thus have similar patterns of hydro-isostatic deformation as discussed in Chapter 6. Modern sea level was apparently attained very early, prior to 6000 yrs B.P. and in some areas sea levels comparatively higher than present have left a legacy of emerged features. There are examples of both low wooded islands and continental island fringing reefs with emerged in situ corals. High cemented platforms of the low wooded island are paralleled by emerged beach rock terraces on high islands such as Holbourne and Middle Island. Older terrace levels incorporated within the sand cays of the low wooded island have their counterpart in the sand terraces and older beach ridges of the continental islands.

Both reef types are affected by moating of tide levels behind shingle rampart systems, allowing the upward growth of reef flats in the form of microatolls to the maximum possible level. This also allows for a high degree of susceptibility to environmental change. Modifications to moat systems during cyclones can cause lowering of water levels and catastrophic mortality of reef top corals and other organisms. The type of changes described in Chapter 4 at Holbourne Island (Hopley and Isdale, 1977) are paralleled by the changes described by Moorhouse at Low Isles (Moorhouse, 1936). Such changes are the result of corals growing at the extreme end of their environmental tolerance levels. Not surprisingly therefore, these corals are particularly susceptible to environmental extremes. Both low wooded island reefs and fringing reefs, because of their inner-shelf location, suffer from the effects of siltation and fresh water from mainland sources. Fringing reefs are probably more prone to these factors as the high islands, especially the larger ones, provide catchment areas that may direct runoff and sediment onto the fringing reefs.

Although near-shore coral reefs have always suffered from silting and freshwater flushing, the impact of man on the hydrological cycle has probably intensified the problem. Clearing of coastal lands has led to more rapid runoff and greater sediment yield. Fairbridge and Teichert (1948, p. 87) and Endean (1976, p. 230) have noted the increased siltation on Low Isles as the result of clearing of the mainland for agriculture, observations that have recently been confirmed by Sir Maurice Yonge on a return to Low Isles in 1978. Similar problems of siltation can be seen on the majority of near-shore fringing reefs, particularly when the present situation is compared with the remarkable photography of Saville-Kent (1893). In some areas siltation has been blamed on particular activities. For example, the decline of fringing reef corals on Magnetic Island has been blamed on dredging by the Townsville Harbour Board (Brown, 1972; Endean, 1976) but clearance of mangroves around Cleveland Bay appears to be just as important a factor.

Mass mortality of shallow-water organisms as the result of drastic reductions in surface-water salinities following heavy rainfall is well documented from many parts of the world (e.g., Goodbody, 1961). On the Great Barrier Reef the widespread death of reef-flat corals has been reported from many areas. For example, as the result of a tropical cyclone in 1918 in the Bowen-Mackay area 1397 mm of rainfall fell at Mackay over a three-day period in January and 483 mm at Bowen. The widespread death of coral to depths of about 3 m has been described by Hedley (1925e) and Rainford (1925a), both of whom noted that the degree of recovery of the reef-flat corals some six years after the cyclone was small. Indeed, some 60 years later these same reef tops remain essentially devoid of living corals when compared to the photographs of Saville-Kent (1893). Siltation and soft algal colonization appear to be preventing any recovery. While these reefs have always been prone to freshwater influx during occasional cyclones, the present lack of recovery may well be the result of increased siltation and eutrophication of near-shore waters (as described, e.g., by Banner, 1974 in Hawaii), following increased clearing and settlements on the adjacent mainland.

Neither Hedley nor Rainford could provide figures to illustrate the degree of salinity change during these periods of high rainfall. However, more data is available for the reefs of Moreton Bay. Slack-Smith (1960) reported widespread mortality of corals, particularly the dominant *Favia speciosa* during the late 1950s as the result of excessive summer rainfall. Similar effects resulted from the record floods of the Brisbane River in 1974. Degenerated Cyclone Wanda, which crossed over southeast Queensland in late January 1974, deposited rainfall totals between 500 and 900 mm over the Brisbane metropolitan area in the 5-day-period 24–29 January. In the middle reaches of the Brisbane River totals exceeded 1300 mm for the same period (Bureau of Meteorology, 1974). Near the mouth of the Brisbane River, up to 1.5 m of sediments were deposited and generally 1–5 cm of silt were deposited over Moreton Bay where the mud content of sediments increased by about 10% (Stephenson et al., 1977). Salinities, normally about 32.5‰ were generally reduced to about 24‰ (in contrast to an average minimum of about 28‰). Even this figure is probably too high for surface waters, as Slack-Smith (1960) reported that in 1956, as the result of 281 mm of rainfall in four days, salinities as low as 13.27‰ were recorded. Similar downpours with resulting mortality of corals and related organisms and subsequent silting of the reef flat in the Mackay area in 1951 was described by Endean et al. (1956b, p. 138), where again the "blanket of silt" appeared to be the greatest deterrant to recolonization.

Factors of siltation and reduction in salinity are of great importance in controlling the distribution of fringing reefs off the eastern Australian coastline. Turbidity alone as the factor primarily responsible for the paucity of corals on the mainland was dismissed by Endean et al. (1956b) because the water at localities where coral was found was just as turbid as at other localities where coral was absent. They indicated that salinity was of much greater importance since the mainland areas where coral is found are well removed from the influence of large river systems. However, changes in distribution with increased runoff and associated increases in sedimentation may be taking place as the result of economic development of the Queensland coast, almost all of which has taken place in the last 100 years. Water temperature appears to be an influence only on the southernmost extremes of reef development. Limits of mainland (or sites in close proximity to the mainland), offshore island, and oceanic high-island reefs are Moreton Bay (27°27′S), Solitary Islands, Coffs Harbour (30°17′S), and Lord Howe Island (31°30′S) respectively, where lowest mean monthly air temperatures are 14.4°C, c. 13.0°C, and 15.6°C respectively. However, recorded absolute minima (Brisbane 2.3°C, Coffs Harbour c. 1.5°C, Lord Howe Island 7.2°C) indicate the probable control that influxes of cold water have on the mainland and at Moreton Bay in particular, where grass temperatures as low as −4.9°C have been recorded at Brisbane (Gentilli, 1971). These figures suggest that were suitable substrates available for reef growth, fringing reefs could be found at latitudes south of Lord Howe Island. However, from evidence presented in the early part of this chapter is seems likely that fringing reefs at their southern limits were more flourishing during mid-Holocene times, and during the last interglacial it is possible that they extended much further south than they do today.

13

Worldwide Geographical Variation of Factors Influencing Coral Reef Morphology

The worldwide distribution of coral reefs has been known in general since the map of Darwin, published in 1842, with increasing detail being provided by Joubin (1912), Schott (1935), Ladd (1950), Emery et al. (1954) and Wells (1957). They are found in all tropical seas but because of the nature of ocean currents tend to have widest distribution on the western sides of the oceans, where coral reefs may extend outside tropical latitudes (Fig. 13.1). Greatest restriction is found on the eastern sides of the world's oceans where upwelling and general oceanic circulation bringing waters from cooler, higher latitudes appears to place a limitation on coral growth, as first noted by Dana in 1843. Fairbridge (1950, 1967) suggested other factors involved in this asymmetric distribution of coral reefs, including aeration associated with onshore winds produced by the trade-wind pattern of mainland shores on the western sides of oceans as opposed to winds blowing offshore on the eastern sides. More important may be his observations on aspects of the dispersal of coral larvae that, as free-floating plankton, are influenced by general oceanic circulation. Although an equatorial counter current sets from the west, most reef waters are affected by a surface-water movement from the east which determines that potential reefal areas are washed increasingly towards the western sides of oceans by waters that have already passed through regions of coral.

Contrasting distribution patterns may thus be seen in the light of present ambient conditions. Nonetheless, as Goreau et al. (1979) have pointed out:

> The coral reefs of the Atlantic, the Caribbean and the Indo-Pacific do not differ fundamentally in their structural forms, their habitats and the interactions of their species, even though the organisms occupying specific ecological roles vary greatly between oceans and even between individual reefs.

Physical and chemical processes are determined by laws that have universal applicability. However, in spite of these uniformities of controls, great regional contrasts have been noted within even the single province of the Great Barrier Reef and the factors responsible for this geographical variation may be

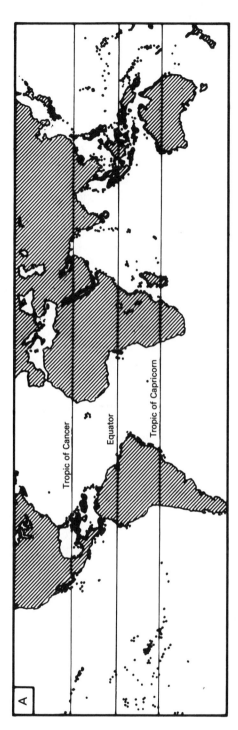

Warmer waters

Cooler waters

Figure 13.1 Distribution of coral reefs of the world and the influential pattern of ocean circulation. (After Emery et al., 1954 and others.)

expected to have an influence on reefs elsewhere. Use has been made already of studies from other reefal areas in aiding in the interpretation of the morphology of the Great Barrier Reef. A systemmatic approach to the factors that in previous chapters have been shown to be important in diversifying the reef forms off the Australian coastline and an examination of the geographical variation in coral reefs on a worldwide scale, may help to confirm some of the conclusions made about the evolution of the Great Barrier Reef.

Obvious contrasts exist between major types of reef forms such as open ocean atolls, shelf barrier reefs and high-island and mainland fringing reefs, but as highlighted by Purdy's arguments for the ubiquitous application of a karstic antecedent-platform hypothesis to reefs of all types, there may be closer affinities between contrasting reef types within a single region than there are between similar reef forms in geographically separated areas. Factors which have emerged from this review of the Great Barrier Reef have included underlying structure and its related bathymetric detail, biological variation (which might be expected to have even greater variation on a worldwide scale), late Quaternary environmental fluctuations, and regional differences in the present ambient environment.

STRUCTURAL VARIATIONS

Underlying structure and structural history of reef areas have been recognized as major determinants of reef form since Darwin (1838) proposed his theory of oceanwide subsidence and the challenges to such a theory by Semper (1880) and Guppy (1886) based on their observations on raised reefs in Palau and in the Solomons. These problems are no longer major issues in reef research since both major vertical and horizontal movements of the earth's crust are recognized and are basic to the concepts of plate tectonics and sea-floor spreading. Volcanic basements moving away from midoceanic ridges or hot spots will be subsiding, while close to plate boundaries along island arcs adjacent to subduction zones, rapid rates of uplift may be expected. Thus the problem of emerged atolls with substantial thickness of reefal limestone suggestive of subsidence (see Steers and Stoddart, 1977) can now be explained. Oceanic subsidence rates, which are probably within the range of 30–60 m/m.y (Ladd et al., 1970; Lalou et al., 1966; Chaveau et al., 1967) are greater than those for continental margins which are about 20 m/m.y. (Sheridan, 1974; Swift, 1974) but still well within the range possible for reef accretion.

Adey and Burke (1977) suggested contrasting models of reef evolution dependent on tectonic conditions. Based on the presumption of a worldwide lowering of sea level in late Tertiary times with the development of the Antarctic ice mass, they suggested that all reef areas would have become emerged. In areas of uplift or quasistability the older reef would have remained as subaerially exposed limestone with new fringing reefs added to the margins. These, in turn, may also have become exposed with further lowering of sea levels as glaciations became more widespread in Pliocene and Pleistocene times. During the Pleistocene, Adey and Burke suggest that shelf margins in emergent areas will adjust to a modal sea level of about − 25 m. Such areas are now characterized by emerged Tertiary and Pleistocene reefs (Fig. 13.2) and

Figure 13.2 Tectonically uplifted emerged reef terraces rising to 270 m on Misima Island, Louisiade Archipelago, Papua New Guinea.

Holocene reefs are limited to shallow bench bioherms at present depths of less than 6–10 m built on Pleistocene benches or other mound or edge features, and deeper bank barrier reefs as described by Adey and Burke (1976).

In contrast, on subsiding foundations the emergence of Tertiary reefs would have been temporary and, over a time determined by the rate of subsidence, the limestones would once more subside beneath the sea and acquire new reefal veneers. In most examples the period of exposure was probably sufficient for the development of karst features on a macroscale. Antecedent karst control of the morphology of the new reefal veneers might be expected at least initially, but would reduce in influence with time. During the Pleistocene the amount of subsidence occurring between each interglacial of c. 100,000 years could easily be rebuilt during the high sea-level period and reefs in subsiding areas have continued to build vertically over their older foundations.

Although there is need for revision of the time scale for glacio-eustatic sea-level variation around which the Adey and Burke model is developed, the long-term pattern of vertical movement will clearly have an effect on modern reef morphology as well as the thickness of reefal limestone or presence of emerged reefs. As the period of reef exposure during glacials has probably been insufficient to allow large-scale karst landforms to develop (see Chapter 7) karst control of modern reef morphology is very unlikely in areas of emergence or where subsidence rates have been such that Tertiary karst surfaces are now buried at depth in the reef column. Only very slow subsidence rates, resulting in the drowning of older karst late in the Quaternary period is likely to produce a karst-controlled reef morphology, including blue holes, as for example in the Pompey complex of the Great Barrier Reef.

Large horizontal movements are also implied in the now generally accepted ideas of plate tectonics, sea-floor spreading and continental drift. Only Stoddart (1976) has attempted to relate these movements specifically to the development of coral reefs. Based on the thickness and age of sediments (Winterer, 1973; Hammond et al., 1974), potassium-argon dating of oceanic island lavas (e.g., McDougall, 1964; Duncan and McDougall, 1974) and paleomagnetic evidence (e.g., Gromme and Vine, 1972), the Pacific plate has been shown to have had a generally northwestward movement at rates of between 6 and 15 cm/yr. Conservatively this could allow a reef to move through 1° latitude in a million years. Oldest reefs may be located furthest from the spreading oceanic ridges or isolated hot spots and/or on the slowest moving plates. In the Pacific the spreading zone is located on the eastern side of the ocean and, as Winterer (1973) has shown, age of oceanic crust generally increases towards the northwestern side of the ocean, where it may be in excess of 135 m.y. old. The reef columns of Pacific atolls and volcanic islands have developed on north-northwestward migrating foundations. As noted by Stoddart (1976), some, like Midway, are actively moving out of reef seas, while others such as Pitcairn at 24°S, a presently reefless island, are moving into reef seas at rates up to 11 cm/yr. Many older reefs may have disappeared into the subductive Benioff Zone.

Plate tectonics and sea-floor spreading also have implications for biogeographical aspects of coral reefs. Substantial spatial discontinuities exist, especially at subduction zones that Stoddart (1976) considered will be reflected in not only reef histories but biogeographic patterns. This has been noted for shallow marine organisms generally by Valentine (1971), who suggested that provincial boundaries formed by thermal barriers and by land and deep-sea barriers, are related to or controlled by plate-tectonic patterns. Similarly major oceanic dispersal routes are formed by island arcs and associated with subduction zones. Low species diversity with impoverished biotas is found in areas of new crust while areas of oceanic plate convergence support highly diverse biotas, not only as the result of plate collision but also because shallow platforms are much more abundant around convergent margins. It is notable that in the southeast Asian area, where the Pacific, Indo-Australian, and Asian Plates converge, coral reefs have the greatest species diversity in the world.

Even the fundamental land barrier of the isthmus of Panama, dividing the distinctive Caribbean and Indo-Pacific biotas, has been a product of late Tertiary uplift of Central America in the Miocene (Frost, 1972) although there have been suggestions of late Pleistocene connections across the isthmus based on the apparent reintroduction of *Pocillopora* to the Caribbean at the last interglacial (Geister, 1977). The result has been a reduction in Caribbean reef diversity in comparison to the Indo-Pacific region. Isolation of the Caribbean to the east is maintained by the structure of the Atlantic ocean, spreading longitudinally out from the mid-Atlantic ridge.

BIOLOGICAL VARIATION

The basic biological pattern is a decrease in diversity of corals and related species outwards from the southeast Asian area and the presence of a discrete area in the western Atlantic. This pattern applies not only to corals but to all broad groups of shallow, marine biota (Valentine, 1971).

A number of reasons have been forwarded for these patterns. As noted earlier, within the Pacific alone, Fairbridge (1950, 1967) considered that the set of tropical oceanic currents westward is important. However, the contrast between eastern and western sides of oceans is not particularly distinct in the Indian Ocean. More basic may be the meeting of Pacific, Indo-Australian, and Asian plates in this major area of subduction as suggested by Valentine (1971), and the greater latitudinal spread and lengths of suitable shelves and coastlines available in the southeast Asian archipelagoes and peninsulas when compared to the western Indian Ocean.

Adey and Burke (1977) similarly concluded that the paucity of species numbers in the Caribbean is also related to an order of magnitude difference in the available shallow coastal shore after isolation of the Caribbean from the Pacific. They suggested that the figure of 14 times as many species of corals in the Indo-Pacific is matched by the fact that coastline length where temperatures are above 24°C is approximately 14.5 times greater than in the tropical Atlantic. They dismissed the idea of a reduction in Caribbean reef diversity during the Quaternary due to greater cooling during glacial periods as has previously been hypothesized. Milliman (1973), for example, suggested that being adjacent to North America, Pleistocene temperature fluctuations throughout much of the Caribbean were more severe than in the tropical Pacific. As shown below, recent findings suggest that climatic deterioration in the Caribbean was minimal even at the glacial maximum 18,000 years ago, and was probably less than in most of the Indo-Pacific.

Nonetheless the lower species diversity of reef biota in the Caribbean is reflected in the biological zonation of reefs. The dominant shallow-water, reef-building genera (*Acropora*, *Millepora*, and *Porolithon*) are largely the same and occupy roughly the same morphologic and energy zones as in the Pacific (Adey and Burke, 1977) and zonation follows hydrodynamic gradients as suggested by Rosen (1971b, 1975), Pichon (1973, 1978) and Done and Pichon (in press). Species depletion, however, leads to the domination of zones by one or just a few corals, rather than complex associations as in the Indo-Pacific. Typically, under high energy conditions a Caribbean reef consists of:

1 A coral-head zone on the forereef slope with hemispherical and sometimes lamellar colonies, the most abundant corals being *Montastrea annularis*, *Siderastrea siderea*, *S. radians*, *Diploria strigosa*, and *D. labrynthiformis*.

2 An *Acropora cervicornis* zone, limited at its upper margin by wave activity, where it is sometimes associated with *Montastrea annularis*, *Siderastrea* sp., and *Diploria* sp.

3 An *Acropora palmata* zone in the higher energy, inner forereef area.

4 A reef crest dominated by the stinging coral *Millepora complanata* and sometimes capped by an algal ridge.

5 A back-reef zone of scattered coral heads and sea grasses. Dominant corals are *Montastrea annularis*, *Diploria labrynthiformis*, *Sidastrea siderea*, *Porites asteroides*, and *P. porites*.

Minor variations from this pattern occur at different locations in the Caribbean. However, it is notable that with a reduced species pool to call upon, and where there are sharp energy gradients zones dominated by single species occur, and the complex associations more typical of all zones on Indo-Pacific reefs are limited to zones of greater environmental uniformity such as the reef flat and the deeper forereef.

VARIATIONS IN PLEISTOCENE COOLING

Although the actual amount of relative lowering of sea level may have varied from place to place for hydro-isostatic and tectonic reasons, it can be safely concluded that all coral reefs were severely affected by the withdrawal of the sea during Pleistocene glacial phases. Conservatively estimated as 135 m of regression at the height of the last glacial 18,000 years ago, this fall in sea level would have led to the migration of living coral reefs to the edges of the continental shelves and the steep sides of midoceanic atolls. The effects have been described by Stoddart (1976, p. 5):

> If the area-diversity relations of MacArthur and Wilson (1967) hold for the marine environment, then we could hypothesize that such a reduction in area would result in massive local extinctions: instead of the sheltered, shallow lagoon, the reef flat and the reef edge, the main locus of Pleistocene reef growth would have been the present drop off and the upper seaward slope .... Many characteristic reef flat species must have undergone extreme environmental stress, with results at present unknown.

Stoddart (1976) further suggested that faunal discontinuities between modern and Pleistocene reefs, such as the presence of *Fungia* and *Acropora* on the Pleistocene reefs of Formosa and Hawaii, respectively, and their absence in the modern reefs of these areas, may result from these stresses.

On the Great Barrier Reef it has been suggested (see Chap. 7) that shelf depth may have had a great influence on the degree of continuity of reef growth during the last glacial period, shallow shelves such as on the northern Great Barrier Reef being too shallow even for interstadial growth. On a worldwide scale, many coral reefs presently grow on narrow shelves of no great depth, with steep drop-offs. Such situations are common around much of the Caribbean (e.g., Jamaica, see Goreau and Land, 1974) and reach their extreme in midoceanic atolls. In such areas the addition of fringing-reef terraces at higher interstadial sea level phases would be extremely unlikely. As these terraces have formed the basement from which multiple reef fronts grow, it is expected that only on deeper shelves periodically flooded since the last interglacial should such features be found. Data on double reef fronts is limited but where available certainly fits the hypothesis developed from the Great Barrier Reef. Guilcher (1976), extending the ideas of Davis (1928) reviewed the distribution and causes of double barrier systems. Although a number of his examples are large scale and consist of separate reefs, some, particularly in New Caledonia (see Chevalier, 1973a; Battistini et al., 1975, Fig. 5) are identical to the double reef fronts in Queensland. They are similarly surrounded by water depths of at least 50 m, sufficient to have allowed interstadial shelf flooding.

The effects of ocean cooling during the last glaciation were far less uniform than the effects of lowered sea levels, but generally appear to have been less drastic than envisaged by Daly (1948). The use of oxygen isotope stratigraphy and planktonic biota preserved in deep sea sediments have allowed the speculative reconstruction of sea surface temperatures (CLIMAP Project Members, 1976; Gates, 1976). The pattern (Fig. 13.3) suggests that the average global cooling was only 2.3°C and, because of the relatively stable positions and temperatures of the central gyres in the subtropical Atlantic, Pacific, and Indian Oceans, equatorward restriction of coral reef growth may have been minimal. In the Gulf of Mexico and the Caribbean surface temperature changes were possibly less than 2°C. In the Indian Ocean, except for cooler water in the eastern Arabian Sea, there was little change in sea-surface temperatures, probably insufficient to cause the cessation of coral growth. However, marked cooling did take place in the equatorial regions of the eastern and central Atlantic and Pacific Oceans. Increased upwelling along the Pacific equatorial divergence produced temperatures that were as much as 6°C cooler than today. These cool waters did not reach the western Pacific but could have had profound effect on coral growth in an area bounded by 10°S and the equator and 140°–170°W. This area contains few coral reefs (e.g., Malden and Starbuck Islands) but the Marquesas are peripheral to it. Mean water temperature in August is presently 26°C (Chevalier, 1973b) and although a 6°C temperature drop should not have been inhibitive to coral growth 18,000 years ago it is interesting to note that some coasts are almost entirely bare of reefs (Chevalier, 1973b) with only incipient fringing reefs on others (Davis, 1928). The area is poor in coral species (Crossland, 1927). Although Dana (1849) attributed these features to a too-rapid subsidence, Crossland (1927) suggested that periodic upwelling of cold waters was the cause. Davis (1928) believed that during glacial times the Marquesas were marginal for reef growth because of extensions of the cold Humboldt current. Latest data from CLIMAP indicate the accuracy of Davis's interpretation. In contrast, further south in the Society Islands, where winter water temperatures are only 0.5°C cooler than in the Marquesas, there was limited cooling in the Pleistocene and modern reefs are more luxuriant, with greater diversity of species. Coral growth may have even continued in the Austral Islands. At Rapa, August mean water temperatures are 20°C (Chevalier, 1973b) but no lowering from this level is suggested at 18,000 yrs B.P. by CLIMAP Project Members (1976).

Elsewhere, fringing reefs or near-shore reefs close to continental land masses with cooler than present runoff, may also have found difficulties surviving Pleistocene glacials. This may have been particularly true of the Florida reef tract where even today cooler-than-normal winter runoff can have drastic effects on the reefs.

VARIATIONS IN THE HOLOCENE TRANSGRESSION

The relationship between rates of sea-level rise and rates of reef accretion discussed in Chapter 8, gives particular significance to the recognition of regional variations in sea-level curves during the postglacial transgression due to hydro-

Figure 13.3 Ocean temperatures (°C) for Northern Summer (August) 18000 years ago and deviation from modern values (inset). (From CLIMAP, 1976, redrawn by permission of the American Association for Advancement of Science.

isostatic response (Fig. 8.5). Regional variation is produced by shelf subsidence under the weight of the transgressing seas (Bloom, 1967), compensatory downward movements of regions adjacent to glacio-isostatic rebound, and upward movements of continents generally (Walcott, 1972), with greatest variation occurring in ocean-margin hinge zones (Chappell, 1974a). The numerical model of Clark et al. (1978) predicts six contrasting sea-level zones, of which four are pertinent to the development of coral reefs (Fig. 13.4).

Area of Time Dependent Emergence (Zone III)

This zone is characterized by a sea-level curve that predicts modern sea level being achieved within the last 2000 years. Although Clark et al. (1978) considered its diagnostic feature to be a slight emergence shortly after modern sea level is achieved, the generally small amplitude (less than 0.5 m) and its timing (possibly prior to many reefs reaching up to the level of the sea surface) make it improbable that it will be recognized in modern reef sequences. The northern Caribbean is within this area, including the reef tracts of Florida, Cuba, Hispaniola, Jamaica, and the Bahamas. Sea-level curves from this region include those of Redfield (1967) for the southeastern United States generally and Neumann (1971) for Bermuda. They show modern sea level reached very recently from a postglacial rise that has generally slowed in the last 5000 years. Redfield (1967) suggested that modern sea level was first achieved about 500 years ago in Bermuda. No consistent reports of higher Holocene sea levels have been recorded from this area and it may be expected that reefs have continued to grow upwards throughout the Holocene.

Area of Oceanic Submergence (Zone IV)

Continued submergence is predicted for much of the northern Pacific, Indian Ocean, and Southern Caribbean. Notably Stoddart (1972b) has claimed that emerged beaches ring the margins but are absent from the central Indian Ocean. The sea-level curve of Montaggioni (1976) clearly shows a continuous but declining rate of sea-level rise on Reunion Island and probably on other islands of the Mascarenes (Montaggioni, 1979). Similarly in the north Pacific, Easton and Olson (1976) have shown a steady rise of sea level from around − 10 m over the last 6000 years and Bloom (1970) suggested a steady rise in sea level for the eastern Caroline Islands. Although departures from this pattern were predicted close to Zone V, areas of the Marshalls, Carolines, and Phoenix Islands have evidence of > 1 m emergence 3000–5000 yrs B.P.

Area of Oceanic Emergence (Zone V)

It is predicted that emergence of up to 1.5–2.0 m will have taken place in the last 5000 years in most of the southern Pacific and southern Indian Ocean. If vertical accretion of reefs was rapid enough to reach this higher sea level then emerged reefs and emerged intertidally cemented deposits can be expected. They should be particularly prominent on volcanic islands and around exposures of late Pleistocene emerged reef where suitable preexisting foundations would have allowed fringing reefs to grow to this higher level. Although Stearns (1961) claimed a Pacificwide eustatic 2 m terrace there are doubts about several of his examples. Nonetheless more recent work supports the

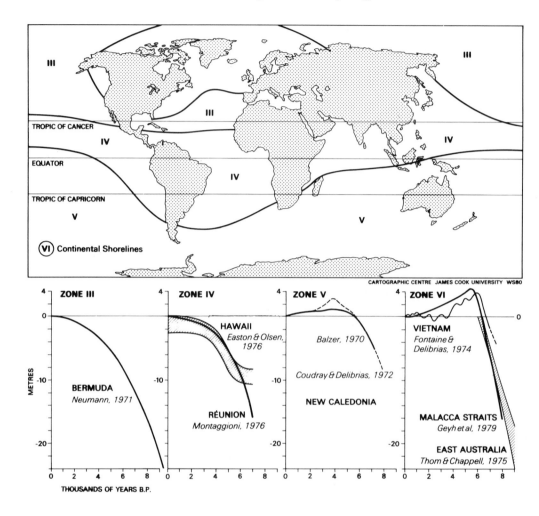

Figure 13.4 Holocene sea-level zones in reefal waters with representative examples of actual sea-level curves. Zone III, Bermuda (Neumann, 1971); Zone IV, Hawaii (Easton and Olsen, 1976); Zone V, New Caledonia (Baltzer, 1970); Zone VI, eastern Australia (Thom and Chappell, 1975). After Clark et al., 1978, by permission of the University of Washington.

concept of modern sea level being achieved at least 5000 yrs B.P. in these areas, with some localities showing evidence of minor emergence. Such a pattern has been demonstrated in French Polynesia by Lalou et al. (1966), Chevalier et al. (1968) and Labeyrie et al. (1969), although late Holocene tilting reported in Moorea by Chevalier (1977) indicates that neotectonic movements may complicate the regional pattern. Similarly Taylor and Bloom (1977) could not dismiss tectonic uplift in the formation of 2.2 m emerged features of mid-Holocene age in the Tonga Island arc. Schofield (1977a,b) indicated that in the Gilbert and Ellice Islands modern sea level was reached about 4000 yrs B.P. and achieved a maximum level of about 2.4 m 2760 yrs B.P. The best documented sea-level curve for this area, away from the major continents, is for New Caledonia. Baltzer (1970) showed modern sea level being achieved shortly after 6000 yrs B.P. and reached a level as much as 4 m above present, a pattern essentially supported by later work of Coudray and Delibrias (1972).

Continental Shorelines (Zone VI)

Because of the complexities imposed by the zone of continental to oceanic tilting, the hingeline over modern continental shelves is superimposed over the regional oceanic pattern on continental shorelines and, by implication, on shelf reefs. On the whole the pattern for any particular continental area is close to that for its adjacent oceanic region, except that locally continental uplift may result in an earlier achievement of modern sea level and sometimes higher-than-present sea levels. The curve of Thom and Chappell (1975) for eastern Australia, located adjacent to Zone V, is an excellent example, showing the very early attainment of modern sea level prior to 6000 yrs B.P. Similarly on continental coasts adjacent to Zone IV, Bartlett and Barghoorn (1973) and Macintyre and Glynn (1976) showed sea level approaching its present position in the last 2000 years in Panama, but raised shorelines occur around the margins of the Indian Ocean (Stoddart, 1972b, 1973b) and there are indications of higher sea levels following the achievement of modern sea level prior to 6000 yrs B.P. in Viet Nam (Fontaine and Delibrias, 1974) and the Malacca Straits (Geyh et al., 1979), although Holocene instability in the southeast Asian region has been clearly demonstrated (Tjia, et al., 1974, 1975). No reports of higher sea levels in the Holocene have been published recently for the northern Caribbean in Zone IV where the generally accepted sea-level curve is that of Scholl and Stuiver (1967), essentially the same as that predicted for the adjacent ocean.

Data from the Great Barrier Reef confirm that variations in the nature of the Holocene transgression took place both along and across the Queensland continental shelf. Such variation can be expected in other shelf reefs and points to a danger in extrapolating sea-level curves from even an adjacent region to explain the growth of coral reefs. More detailed work on sea levels, for example in the Caribbean, may indicate more variation than is presently suggested by the common use of Neumann's (1971) curve from Bermuda (e.g., by its application to St. Croix by Adey and Vassar, 1975; Adey and Burke, 1976; and Adey et al., 1977b; and to Panama by Macintyre and Glynn, 1976).

VARIATIONS IN THE PRESENT ENVIRONMENT

Geographical variation of many of the environmental factors that affect coral reefs has been reviewed by Davies (1972). He noted that the low latitudes are characterized by reduced wave energy, relatively consistent direction of wave approach in swell, and tradewind environments that may be responsible for the fundamental homogeneity of atoll shapes noted by Stoddart (1965b) although this suggests that the influential factors have operated for a period longer than just the Holocene. The distribution and strength of the tradewind belt has been well documented by Crowe (1949, 1950, 1951). It has a remarkable coincidence with the distribution of coral reefs (Fig. 13.5). Away from the equator southern hemisphere reefs are almost exclusively under the influences of the southeast trades, except for the Indian Ocean where the Indian monsoonal derivative of the trades produces a seasonal variation from a winter northeast trade to a summer southwest monsoon. Exceptions to the pattern are wedges of doldrums in equatorial latitudes off the west coasts of Africa and central America. Here, light variable winds of 4–6 kn occur throughout the year. Similarly, from the international date line to the east coast of Africa is another area of light variable winds, the width of which oscillates but is never less than 15° latitude.

The wind waves produced by the trades are superimposed over the larger, lower, but more energetic swell. Throughout tropical seas this is predominantly from the southwest, as most are generated in the temperate storm belt of the

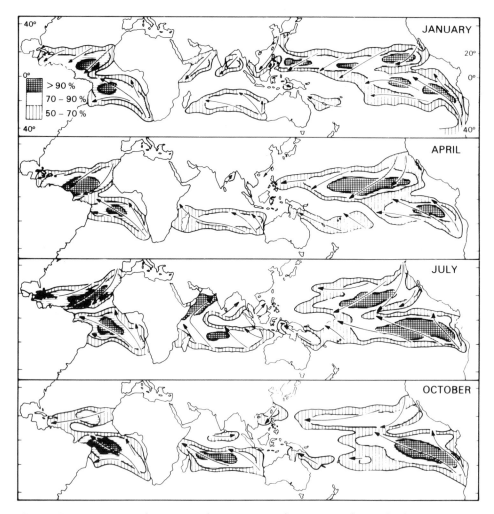

Figure 13.5 Percentage frequency of persistance of oceanic trade winds. (From Crowe, 1950, reproduced by permission of the Institute of British Geographers.)

southern hemisphere, and, as Davies (1972) has shown, waves produced by winds blowing from any direction between northwest and south all tend to take a general course from southwestward as they move from their area of origin along great-circle courses. The combination of swell and wind waves produces a number of distinctive wave-climate regions in coral reef areas:

1 In southern hemisphere oceans both wind waves and swell are predominantly from the south and distinctive windward and leeward margins can be expected on reefs. The most energetic tradewind area is in the southern Indian Ocean.

2 The western Atlantic is dominated by wind waves generated by the northeast trades, probably reinforced by swells from the northern temperate storm belt, as southern swells are excluded by the bulk of the South American continent (see, e. g., Adey et al., 1977c).

3 The northern Indian Ocean reefs may be similarly placed, except that the northeasterly influence is limited to winter and the southerly swells are reinforced by the southwesterly monsoon (see Stoddart, 1973b).

4 An equatorial region exists in the Indian Ocean, western Pacific, eastern Pacific, and Atlantic in which the southerly swell is probably dominant as winds here are light and variable but may show seasonal shifts in direction with migration of the Intertropical Convergence Zone.

This variation can be expected to produce differences in hard-line reef development and zonation on reefs around the world.

The equatorial region is also characterized by a low incidence of tropical cyclones because of insufficient Coriolis force at low latitudes. However, beyond about 10° north and south of the equator few coral reef areas are not affected by these storms. Stoddart (1971) has reviewed the relationships between cyclones and coral reefs and suggested that the only areas not affected are the reefs of the east African coast and Red Sea, the whole of the Maldive Islands, the equatorial region from Sumatra to the Solomon Islands and, in the Pacific, the atolls of the Gilberts, the Phoenix group, many of the Line Islands, the easternmost Tuamotus, the Hawaiin Islands, and northwestern Australia. However, all these areas have experienced major tropical disturbances in the last 100 years and northwestern Australia experiences severe storms regularly. Greatest frequency of storms is in the northwest Pacific (annual frequency about 21) closely followed by the southwest Pacific (20), with other regions generally being less than 8 cyclones per year (Davies, 1972, Fig. 21). The effects on reefs may not be of the same magnitude on oceanic atolls as compared to shelf reefs. It was shown that on the Great Barrier Reef many of the storm effects are related to the storm surge that builds up over the continental shelf. The steep drop-off around atolls and some midoceanic volcanic islands restricts the development of a major surge, although there are many records of atoll islands being submerged (see Wiens, 1962, Appendix C).

On oceanic atolls generally, any kind of sea-level fluctuation is minimal. Midoceanic tidal ranges are almost exclusively less than 2 m, often less then 1 m. Caribbean tidal ranges are also very small. Thus long-term episodic sea-level fluctuations that may approach 0.5 m in amplitude, when superimposed on a low tidal range, have far-reaching effects on reef-flat biota (Glynn, 1968; Fishelson, 1973; Yamaguchi, 1975). This is particularly important when tides are diurnal (as in the South China and Solomon Seas) or mixed with a strong diurnal component (Caribbean, northern Indian Ocean, and much of Indonesia) an effect that not only reduces the velocity of tidal currents even further, but also leads to long periods of exposure during the abnormal conditions. Macrotidal ranges of more than 3.0 m are found on midoceanic islands only in the Indian Ocean in the Comoros and the Aldabra group, an extreme that Stoddart (1973b) noted had no counterpart on atolls of other oceans. Large tidal ranges are more common in shelf reefal waters of the Arabian Sea (Gulf of Cambay, 8 m) Bay of Bengal, and Andaman Sea (Mergui Archipelago, 5 m) in the east Africa-Madagascar area, and in the Arafura and Timor Seas and adjacent waters of Indonesia. It can be expected that in these areas, as in the Great Barrier Reef, reef flats and their associated organisms will be more attuned to periodic exposure on low spring tides.

Effects of freshwater flushing and sedimentation on reefs have complex regional patterns that may vary over relatively short distances. Many reefs are situated in areas of neglible rainfall and these influences are minimal. Ladd (1977), for example, has suggested that one reason for the length, persistency, and health of the reefs along the shores of the Red Sea is the aridity of the climate. In contrast the slightly less arid coastline of Western Australia is relatively poor in reefs, a feature that Fairbridge (1967) attributed in part to the lack of an input of inorganic nutrients from continental runoff. The only midoceanic islands to have less than 500 mm annual rainfall are located along the equator in the east and central Pacific (Taylor, 1973). This area is characterized by upwelling of cool, nutrient-rich water of high productivity with significant modern guano deposition. Stoddart (1976) considered that at the glacial maximum these conditions could have extended further west and been responsible for the accumulation of the massive phosphate deposits of Ocean Island and Nauru, a concept that is given support by the ocean-temperature maps of CLIMAP Project Members (1976). The conditions on these dry oceanic atolls, with minimal runoff, small or ephemeral Ghyben-Herzberg lenses, and large phosphate accumulation can be contrasted with some of the reef areas adjacent to the continents. Climatic parameters, tectonically produced relief, and accidents of continental distribution result in some of the largest rivers in the world, with massive sediment loads, emptying into waters that are otherwise suitable for coral growth. High rates of sedimentation have limited reef development in the western Atlantic south of about 5°N (Milliman, 1973), coinciding with the front of the Amazon delta. Similar minimal growth, produced by massive freshwater plumes and sedimentation covering much of the potential substrate on which coral planulae could settle, is seen off the mouths of such rivers as the Niger and Congo in West Africa, and the Ganges, Irrawaddy, and Mekong in Asia.

However, temperature of the ocean is the main controlling parameter of reef distribution, and as previously noted the 20°C isotherm for the coolest month closely corresponds to the distribution of coral reefs. Because of the nature of oceanic circulation cooler waters on the eastern sides of oceans restrict reefs to within a 20° latitude belt but on the western perimeter of the Pacific and Indian

Oceans reefs can extend to greater than 30° north and south of the equator, and somewhat less than this in the Atlantic. Nonetheless, on any coral coast the development of reefs may be almost haphazard. As noted by Goreau et al., often there are no obvious environmental factors which can explain such differences in development. Instead:

> It seems rather that chance variations in the settlement of free swimming coral larvae and growth play a major role in determining the formation of reefs and that there simply has not been enough time for corals to occupy all favourable habitats. The role of chance in coral settlement is also reflected in the variability of major species that fill the same structural roles in any reef. . . . Hence in the creation of diversity in a coral reef historical variation is in many reefs just as significant as an approach to the ecological equilibrium where many specialized organisms co-exist.

Goreau et al., 1979, p. 118

If time is a factor, then the variation in the period at which sea level has been at its present position, varying from over 6000 years to less than 1000 years, may be even more important in producing the geographical variation in coral reefs.

DISCUSSION AND CONCLUSIONS

Within the literature comparisons have been made especially between the reefs of the Indo-Pacific and those of the Caribbean. Milliman (1973) and Glynn (1974) both showed that many of the traditional ideas of reefs of the Caribbean as pale images of their Indo-Pacific counterparts, are in error. More recently Adey and co-workers in a number of papers, summarized in Adey (1977, 1978a), have shown that many of the features of Caribbean reefs are as prolific as on Indo-Pacific reefs with growth potentials being equivalent. Nonetheless, the discussion of factors affecting reef development have shown some major contrasts. Biologically the Caribbean reefs are depauperate in species numbers of corals, coralline algae, and other biota but Adey (1977) suggested that this is the result mainly of the size of the region, compared to the Indo-Pacific, together with its tectonic history. The result is a clearer biological zonation on West Atlantic reefs even though generally lower energy conditions prevail. Presence or absence of particular organisms is reflected in the composition of reef sediments, for example Milliman (1974) suggested that Indo-Pacific reef flats are dominated by coralline algal fragments and benthonic foraminifera, whereas in the Caribbean coral and *Halimeda* fragments are more important. Another major contrast is the common occurrence of Alcyonarians and paucity of gorgonians on the Great Barrier Reef and the reverse pattern for these two organisms in the Caribbean.

Traditionally algal ridges have been considered rare or even absent from Caribbean reefs. However, recent studies from the Lesser Antilles in particular (Geister, 1975; Adey, 1975, 1978a; Adey and Burke, 1976; Adey et al., 1977c) have shown a widespread distribution of algal ridges, their abundance being related to the strength and constancy of the tradewinds. On the open Atlantic coasts a complete spectrum of algal ridge development is found where reefs are open to swell from the North Atlantic (Adey, 1977, 1978b). In many respects these features are better developed than on the Great Barrier Reef. In particular they have a thickness of up to 8 m, accumulated at rates of between 3 and 6 m per 1000 years during the late Holocene (Adey and Vassar, 1975). A major factor is the nature of the sea-level rise. On the Great Barrier Reef most reefs grow up to a sea level already stable at its modern position, or even falling slightly from a higher position, thus allowing only a thin veneer of encrusting corallines to develop. In contrast the Caribbean reefs appear to have caught up with the slowly rising sea level in mid-Holocene times and, where exposure conditions were suitable, developed an initial algal veneer that has continued to grow upward under the influences of the prolonged but declining rate of the Holocene transgression.

Growth rates of Caribbean reefs are generally higher than those on the Great Barrier Reef during the Holocene (Table 8.3). Although this may also be the result of the contrasting nature of the Holocene sea-level curves, Adey (1978a) considered that it is due to the generally moderate level of wave energy on most Caribbean reefs, favoring the growth of a porous, poorly cemented reef framework dominated by *Acropora cervicornis* or *A. palmata*.

The moderate level of wave energy and recent attainment of modern sea level, combined with low tidal range, are probably responsible for the poorer development of morphological zonation on Caribbean reefs. In many respects they are counterparts of the reefs of the outer shelf in the central region of the Great Barrier Reef, where subsidence has also resulted in the relatively late attainment of modern sea level and where reefs lack extensive algal pavement, rubble zones, and rampart systems and instead are capped by a continuous veneer of living corals. Similarly, although the Holocene sea-level history of southeast Asia is similar to that of the Great Barrier Reef, the archipelagic nature of this region and the location of a large proportion of it within the equatorial-doldrum belt provides shelter from oceanic swells and there is an absence of tropical cyclones from the core of the region. These factors militate against the development of a well-defined zonation, and descriptions of groove and spur systems and algal ridges are rare or absent from the literature dealing with the area between 10° north and south of the equator. Morton (1974) in the Solomons, for example, stated that there are no true algal rims even on exposed reefs. The most exposed reefs of this region apparently have a zonation similar to the inner shelf reefs of the Great Barrier Reef.

Stoddart (1972b, 1973b) has emphasized the influence of tropical cyclones on Indian Ocean reefs. No cyclones are experienced between 6°N and 5°S and the atolls of this area; notably, the Maldives and Chagos Groups display no shingle ridges or rubble banks and reef blocks are rare. Further, Stoddart (1972b) suggested that lack of high energy events may be responsible for the domination of more fragile branching corals on these reefs. In the Caribbean, rubble areas exist but extensive shingle ramparts are lacking even from many of the low wooded island forms of the Belize barrier reef, where the protection to the mangroves on many islands is given by sand, rather than shingle ridges (Stoddart, 1965a). This may reinforce the concept of a strong influence from a slight fall in sea level on the formation of these features on the Great Barrier Reef. Reef blocks are even more conspicuous by their absence or scarcity in the Caribbean. Reasons for this are probably twofold. Firstly, as noted on the Great Barrier Reef, most blocks are composed of a single massive coral colony and secondly, some at least are several thousand years old, thrown up onto a reef-flat surface that has remained basically unaltered since the mid–Holocene. In contrast, on Caribbean reefs massive coral colonies are rare in depths of the reef-front zone normally affected by hurricane waves, and *Acropora palmata*, which dominates this zone, is unlikely to remain intact as boulder-sized material when removed from the reef front. Moreover, the steady rise in sea level to its present position means that any blocks thrown up even 3000 years ago are likely to have been buried beneath the present reef surface. A much shorter period of time is available for their accumulation, probably not much more than 1000 years on most Caribbean reefs.

These examples of contrasting reef morphology from different parts of the world confirm the importance of the parameters described at the start of this chapter as being the major controls on reef development. Where similar structural histories exist giving a slow but steady subsidence then gross reef morphology may be similar to much of the Great Barrier Reef. Such conditions allow growth through addition of successive veneers of coral during interglacial high sea-level phases and exposure during low sea-level glacials. They lead to strong control of present morphology by antecedent-platform relief regardless of whether this relief is produced by growth or erosion. Where parallel Holocene environmental parameters exist then the mesoscale features of reef zonation are similar to those of the Great Barrier Reef. Of prime importance is the nature of the Holocene transgression but exposure conditions, incidence of tropical cyclones, protection by distance from the mainland from freshwater flushing, and at least a mesotidal range are all required to reproduce the features of the Great Barrier Reef. Maintenance of at least significant refuges for coral reefs during the last glacial cooling of ocean waters and location close to the boundaries of Pacific, Asian, and Indo-Australian tectonic plates are features that produce similarities in details of biota and in particular a highly diverse coral fauna. The multivariate nature of these controlling parameters means that even in the 617,000 km^2 of reefal waters (Smith, 1978) it is difficult to find an area where coral reefs are exactly the same as in the Great Barrier Reef of Australia.

This is emphasized even more by the fact that diversity itself is a basic characteristic of the Great Barrier Reef, and even where some parallels can be found elsewhere in the world, the similarity of morphology extends only to parts, not the whole, of the Great Barrier Reef. In size and latitudinal spread, no other reef system can match the Great Barrier Reef. Variations in all the controlling parameters occur, producing a diversity of morphology that cannot be approached by any other single region.

References

Adey, W. A., 1975. The algal ridges and coral reefs of St. Croix, their structure and Holocene development. *Atoll Res. Bull.*, **187**, 1–67.

Adey, W. H., 1977. Shallow water Holocene bioherms of the Caribbean Sea and West Indies. *Proc. Third Int. Coral Reef Symp.*, **2**, xxi–xxiv.

Adey, W. H., 1978a. Coral reef morphogenesis: a multidimensional model. *Science*, **202**, 831–837.

Adey, W. H., 1978b. Algal ridges of the Caribbean Sea and West Indies. *Phycologia*, **17**, 361–367.

Adey, W. H. and Burke, R., 1976. Holocene bioherms (algal ridges and bank barrier reefs) of the eastern Caribbean. *Geol. Soc. Amer. Bull.*, **87**, 95–109.

Adey, W. H. and Burke, R. B., 1977. Holocene bioherms of Lesser Antilles—geologic control of development. *Amer. Assoc. Petrol. Geol. Studies in Geol.*, **4**, 67–81.

Adey, W. H. and Macintyre, I. G., 1973. Crustose coralline algae: a re-evaluation in the geological sciences. *Geol. Soc. Amer. Bull.*, **84**, 883–904.

Adey, W. H. and McKibbin, D. L., 1970. Studies on the maerl species in the Ria de Vigo. *Bot. Marina*, **8**, 100–106.

Adey, W. H. and Vassar, J. M., 1975. Colonization, succession and growth rates of tropical crustose coralline algae (Rhodophyta, Cryptonemiales). *Phycologia*, **14**, 55–69.

Adey, W. H., Adey, P. J., Burke, R. and Kaufman, L., 1977a. The Holocene reef systems of eastern Martinique, French West Indies. *Atoll Res. Bull.*, **218**, 1–40.

Adey, W. H., Macintyre, I. G., Stuckenrath, R. and Dill, R. F., 1977b. Relict barrier reef system off St. Croix: its implications with respect to late Cenozoic coral reef development in the western Atlantic. *Proc. Third Int. Coral Reef Symp.*, **2**, 15–21.

Adey, W. H., Gladfelter, W., Ogden, J. and Dill, R., 1977c. Field guidebook to the reefs and reef communities of St. Croix, Virgin Islands. *Third Int. Coral Reef Symp. Field Guides*, 52 pp.

Agassiz, A., 1894. A reconnaissance of the Bahamas and the elevated reefs of Cuba in the steam yacht *Wild Duck*, January to April, 1893. *Bull. Mus. Comp. Zool. Harvard Coll.*, **26**, 1–203.

Agassiz, A., 1895. A visit to the Bermudas in March, 1894. *Bull. Mus. Comp. Zool. Harvard Coll.*, **26**, 205–281.

Agassiz, A., 1898. A visit to the Great Barrier Reef of Australia in the steamer *Croydon* during April and May, 1896. *Bull. Mus. Comp. Zool. Harvard Coll.*, **28**, 95–148.

Agassiz, A., 1899. The islands and coral reefs of Fiji. *Bull. Mus. Comp. Zool. Harvard Coll.*, **33**, 1–167.

Agassiz, L. J. R., 1837. *Système glaciaire ou recherches sur les glaciers... Pt. 1, Nouvelles études et expériences sur les glaciers actuals*, vol. 1, 598 pp.

Agassiz, L. J. R., 1840. *Études sur les glaciers*, Neuchâtel, 346 pp.

Ahr, W. M. and Stanton, R. J., 1973. The sedimentologic and paleo-ecologic significance of *Lithotrya*, a rock-boring barnacle. *J. Sed. Petrol.*, **43**, 20–23.

Alexandersson, T., 1972. Micritization of carbonate particles: processes of precipitation and dissolution in modern shallow-marine sediments. *Bull. Geol. Inst. Univ. Uppsala* N.S., **3**, 201–236.

Aller, R. C. and Dodge, R. E., 1974. Animal—sediment relations in a tropical lagoon—Discovery Bay, Jamaica. *J. Mar. Res.*, **32**, 209–232.

Andrews, E. C., 1900. The general geology of the Fiji Islands. *Bull. Mus. Comp. Zool. Harvard Coll.*, **38**, 1–50.

Andrews, E. C., 1900–04a. The geology of the New England plateau, Part 1, Physiography. *Recs. Geol. Surv. N. S. W.*, **7**, 140–216.

Andrews, E. C., 1900–1904b. An outline of the Tertiary history of New England. *Recs. Geol. Surv. N. S. W.*, **7**, 281–300.

Andrews, E. C., 1902. Preliminary note on the geology of the Queensland coast. *Proc. Linn. Soc. N. S. W.*, **27**, 146–185.

Andrews, E. C., 1903. Notes on the geography of the Blue Mountains and Sydney district. *Proc. Linn. Soc. N. S. W.*, **28**, 786–825.

Andrews, E. C., 1910. Geographical unity of eastern Australia in later and post-Tertiary time. *J. Proc. Roy. Soc. N. S. W.*, **44**, 420–480.

Andrews, E. C., 1922. Contributions to the hypothesis of coral reef formations. *J. Proc. Roy. Soc. N. S. W.*, **56**, 10–38.

Archibald, D. S. and Kenny, R., 1974. Hydrological Data from the Cleveland Bay Area. Unpubl. Rept. James Cook Univ. of N.Qld.

Asano, D., 1942. Coral reefs of the South Sea Islands. *Tok. Imp. Univ. Geol. and Palaeo. Inst. Rept.*, **39**, 1–19.

Atkins, W. R. G., 1926. The phosphate content of sea water in relation to the growth of algal plankton. *J. Biol. Assoc.*, **14**, 447–467.

Australian Institute of Marine Science, 1979. *Report for the Year 1978–1979*, 59 pp.

Australian Water Resources Council, 1971. *Stream Gauging Information Dec. 1969*, Dept. of Nat. Devel., Canberra, 169 pp.

Baas-Becking, L. G. M., 1951. Notes on some *Cyanophyceae* of the Pacific Region. *Proc. Kon. Ned. Akad. Wetensch.*, Ser. C, **54** (3), 213–225.

Backshall, D. G., Barnett, J., Davies, P. J., Duncan, D. C., Harvey, N., Hopley, D., Isdale, P., Jennings, J. N. and Moss, R., 1979. Drowned dolines—the blue holes of the Pompey Reefs, Great Barrier Reef. *B. M. R. J. Austr. Geol. and Geophys.*, **4**, 99–109.

Baines, G. B. K. and McLean, R. F., 1976. Resurveys of 1972 hurricane rampart on Funafuti atoll. *Search*, **7**, 36–37.

Baines, G. B. K., Beveridge, P. J. and Maragos, J. E., 1974. Storms and island building at Funafuti atoll, Ellice Islands. *Proc. Second Int. Coral Reef Symp.*, **2**, 485–496.

Baker, P. A. and Weber, J. N., 1975. Coral growth rate: variation with depth. *Earth Planet. Sci. Lett.*, **27**, 57–61.

Bakus, G. J., 1968. Sedimentation and benthic invertebrates of Fanning Island, Central Pacific. *Mar. Geol.*, **6**, 45–51.

Bakus, G. J., 1973. The biology and ecology of tropical Holothurians. In Jones, O. A. and Endean, R. (eds.) *Biology and Geology of Coral Reefs*, **II**, Biology I, 325–368.

Baltzer, F., 1970. Datation absolue de la transgression holocène sur la côte de Nouvelle—Calédonie sur des échantillons de tourbes à palétuviers. Interprétation neotéctonique. *C. R. Acad. Sci. Paris*, **271**, D, 2251–2254.

Banner, A. J., 1974. Kaneohe Bay, Hawaii: urban pollution and a coral reef ecosystem. *Proc. Second Int. Coral Reef Symp.*, **2**, 685–702.

Bardach, J. E., 1961. Transport of calcareous fragments by reef fishes. *Science*, **133**, 98–99.

Barnes, D. J., 1970. Coral skeletons: an explanation of their growth and structure. *Science*, **170**, 1305–1308.

Barnes, D. J., 1973. Growth in colonial scleractinians. *Bull. Mar. Sci.*, **23**, 280–298.

Barnes, D. J. and Taylor, D. L., 1973. In situ studies of calcification and photosynthetic carbon fixation in the coral *Montastrea annularis*. *Helg. wiss. Meeresunters*, **24**, 284–291.

Bartlett, A. S. and Barghoorn, E. S., 1973. Phytogeographic history of the isthmus of Panama during the past 12,000 years (a history of vegetation, climate and sea level change). In Graham, A. (ed.) *Vegetation and Vegetational History of Northern Latin America*, Elsevier, Amsterdam, 203-299.

Bateson, C., 1972. *Australian Shipwrecks, 1, 1622-1850*, Reed, A. H. and A. W., Sydney, 267 pp.

Bathurst, R. G. C., 1971. *Carbonate Sediments and their Diagenesis*, Devel. in Sedimentol., **12**, Elsevier, Amsterdam, 620 pp.

Battistini, R., 1963. L'age de l'encoche de corrosion marine flandrienne de 1-1.3 m de la Baie des Galions (extrême-sud de Madagascar). *C. R. Somm. Séance Soc. Geol. Fr.*, 1953, **16.**

Battistini, R. et al., 1975. Eléments de terminologie récifale indopacifique. *Téthys*, **7**, 1-111.

Bayer, F. M., 1956. Octocorallia. In Moore, R. C. (ed.) *Treatise on Invertebrate Paleonotology*, **F**, Coelenterata F166-F233.

Beach Protection Authority, 1978. Wave data recording programme, Cairns region. *Report*, W 01.1, 15 pp.

Beach Protection Authority, 1979. *Capricorn Coast Beaches*, 238 pp.

Beaglehole, J. C., 1962. *The Endeavour Journal of Joseph Banks 1768-1771*, Angus and Robertson, Sydney, 2 Vols.

Beechey, F. W., 1831. *Narrative of the Voyage of H. M. S. Blossom 1825-1829*, Henry Colburn and Richard Bentley, London, 2 vols., 742 pp.

Belcher, E., 1843. *Narrative of a Voyage Round the World, Performed in Her Majesty's Ship Sulphur, During the Years 1836-1842*, Henry Colburn, London, 2 vols.

Belperio, A. P., 1977. Burdekin River sediment load. Austr. Sedim. Group 1977 Meeting, Unpubl. paper.

Belt, T., 1874. An examination of the theories that have been proposed to account for the climate of the glacial period. *Quart. J. Sci.*, **11**, 421-464.

Benbow, D. D., 1980. The petroleum prospects of the Great Barrier Reef region. *A.P.E.A.J.*, **20**, 159-175.

Bender, M., Taylor, F. W. and Matthews, R. K., 1972. Helium—uranium dating of corals from middle Pleistocene Barbados reef tracts. *Quat. Res.*, **3**, 142-146.

Benjamin, G., 1970. Diving into the blue holes of the Bahamas. *Nat. Geogr. Mag.*, **138**, 347-363.

Bennett, I., 1971. *The Great Barrier Reef*, Lansdowne, Melbourne, 183 pp.

Bennett, I., 1973. Brief notes on the zonation and intertidal invertebrate fauna of Low Isles and Heron Island reefs. Unpubl. Field Notes for the 1973 Second International Coral Reef Symposium.

Berner, R. A., 1971a. Bacterial processes affecting the precipitation of calcium carbonate in sediments. In Bricker, O. R. (ed.) *Carbonate Cements*, 247-251.

Berner, R. A., 1971b. *Principles of Chemical Sedimentology*. McGraw Hill, New York, 240 pp.

Bird, E. C. F., 1965. The formation of coastal dunes in the humid tropics: some evidence from North Queensland. *Austr. J. Sci.*, **27**, 258-259.

Bird, E. C. F., 1970a. Coastal evolution in the Cairns district. *Austr. Geogr.*, **11**, 327-335.

Bird, E. C. F., 1970b. The steep coast of the Macalister Range, North Queensland, Australia. *J. Trop. Geog.*, **31**, 33-39.

Bird, E. C. F., 1971a. Holocene shore features at Trinity Bay, North Queensland. *Search*, **2**, 27-28.

Bird, E. C. F., 1971b. The fringing reefs near Yule Point, North Queensland. *Austr. Geog. Stud.*, **9**, 197-115.

Bird, E. C. F., 1973. Depositional evidence of fluvial sediment yield: an example from North Queensland. *Austr. Geogr.*, **12**, 250-253.

Bird, E. C. F. and Hopley, D., 1969. Geomorphological features on a humid tropical sector of the Australian coast. *Austr. Geog. Stud.*, **7**, 89-108.

Bloom, A. L., 1964. Peat accumulation and compaction in a Connecticut coastal marsh. *J. Sed. Petrol.*, **34**, 599-603.

Bloom, A. L., 1967. Pleistocene shorelines: a new test of isostasy. *Geol. Soc. Amer. Bull.*, **78**, 1477-1494.

Bloom, A. L., 1970. Paludal stratigraphy of Truk, Ponape and Kusaie, eastern Caroline Islands. *Geol. Soc. Amer. Bull.*, **81**, 1895-1904.

Bloom, A. L., 1971. Glacial eustatic and isostatic controls of sea level since the last glaciation. In Turekian, K. K. (ed.) *The Late Cenozoic Glacial Ages*, Yale Univ. Press, New Haven, 355–379.

Bloom, A. L., 1974. Geomorphology of reef complexes. In Laporte, L. F. (ed.) Reefs in Time and Space. *S.E.P.M. Spec. Publ.*, **18**, 1–8.

Bloom, A. L., Broeker, W. S., Chappell, J., Matthews, R. K. and Mesolella, K. J., 1974. Quaternary sea level fluctuations on a tectonic coast: new Th^{230}/U^{234} dates from New Guinea. *Quat. Res.*, **4**, 185–205.

Bögli, A., 1960. Kalklosung und Karrenbilding. *Zeits. f. Geomorph.*, *N.F.* Supp. B., **2**, 4–21.

Bögli, A., 1964. Mischungaskorrosion—ein Beitrag zur Verkastungsproblem. *Erdkunde*, **5**, 185–193.

Bonell, M., 1978. Aspects of the hydrology of the Townsville region. In Hopley, D. (ed.) Geographical Studies of the Townsville Area. *Dept. of Geog., James Cook Univ. of N.Qld. Monogr. Ser. Occ. Paper*, **2**, 18–27.

Bonham, K., 1965. Growth rate of giant clam *Tridacna gigas* at Bikini Atoll as revealed by radioautography. *Science*, **149**, 300–302.

Bonham, K. and Held, E. E., 1963. Ecological observations on the sea cucumbers *Holothuria atra* and *Holothuria leucospilata* at Rongelap Atoll. *Pac. Sci.*, **17**, 305–314.

Boschma, H., 1956. Milleporina and Stylasterina. In Moore, R. C. (ed.) *Treatise on Invertebrate Palaeontology: F*, Coelenterata, F90–F106.

Boucher, D. A., 1977. Submarine Diagenesis of the Corals of Bellairs Reef, Barbados. Unpubl. M.Sc. thesis, McGill Univ., Montreal.

Bowler, J. H., Hope, G. S., Jennings, J. N., Singh, G. and Walker, D., 1976. Late Quaternary climates in Australia and New Guinea. *Quat. Res.*, **6**, 359–394.

Braithwaite, C. J. R., 1973. Settling behaviour related to sieve analysis of skeletal sands. *Sedimentology*, **20**, 251–262.

Braithwaite, C. J. R., Taylor, J. D. and Kennedy, W. J., 1973. The evolution of an atoll: the depositional and erosional history of Aldabra. *Phil. Trans. Roy. Soc. London*, **B**, 266, 307–340.

Brandon, D. E., 1973. Waters of the Great Barrier Reef Province. In Jones, O. A. and Endean, R. (eds.) *Biology and Geology of Coral Reefs*, **1**, Geology I, 187–232.

Bretschneider, C. L., 1966. Shore Protection Planning and Design. *Coastal Eng. Res. Centre Tech. Rept.*, **4**.

Bricker, O. P. (ed.), 1971. *Carbonate Cements*, John Hopkins Univ. Stud. in Geol., **19**, 376 pp.

Broeker, W. S., Thurber, D. L., Goddard, J., Ku, T., Matthews, R. K. and Mesolella, K. J., 1968. Milankovitch hypothesis supported by precise dating of coral reefs and deep sea sediments. *Science*, **160**, 297–300.

Bromley, R. G., 1978. Bioerosion of Bermudan reefs. *Palaeogeog.*, **23**, 169–198.

Brown, T. W., 1972. Silt pollution—the destruction of Magnetic Island's coral fringing reefs. Unpubl. report, 62 pp.

Bryan, W. H., 1925. Earth movements in Queensland. *Proc. Roy. Soc. Qld.*, **37**, 3–82.

Buddemeier, R. W., 1974. Environmental controls over annual and lunar monthly cycles in hermatypic coral calcification. *Proc. Second Int. Coral Reef Symp.*, **2**, 259–267.

Buddemeier, R. W., 1978. Coral growth: retrospective analysis. In Stoddart, D. R. and Johannes, R. E. *Coral Reefs: Research Methods*, 551–571.

Buddemeier, R. W. and Holladay, G., 1977. Atoll hydrology: island groundwater characteristics and their relationship to diagenesis. *Proc. Third Int. Coral Reef Symp.*, **2**, 167–173.

Buddemeier, R. W. and Kinzie, R. A., 1975. The chronometric reliability of contemporary corals. In Rosenberg, G. D. and Runcorn, S. K. (eds.) *Growth Rhythms and the History of the Earth's Rotation*. Wiley, London, 135–147.

Buddemeier, R. W. and Kinzie, R. A., 1976. Coral growth. *Oceangr. Mar. Biol. Ann. Rev.*, **14**, 183–225.

Buddemeier, R. W., Maragos, J. E. and Knutson, D. W., 1974. Radiographic studies of reef coral exoskeletons: rates and patterns of coral growth. *J. Exp. Mar. Biol. and Ecol.*, **14**, 179–200.

Buddemeier, R. W., Smith, S. V. and Kinzie, R. A., 1975. Holocene windward reef-flat history, Enewetak Atoll. *Geol. Soc. Amer. Bull.*, **86**, 1581–1584.

Burdekin Project Committee, 1977. *Resources and Potential of the Burdekin River Basin, Queensland*, Australian Govt., Canberra, 193 pp.

Bureau of Meteorology, 1969. *Climatic Averages, Australia. Temperature Humidity, Rainfall*, 107 pp.

Bureau of Meteorology, 1974. Brisbane floods, January 1974. *Dept. of Sci. Bur. of Meteorol. Rept.*, 63 pp.

Bureau of Meteorology, 1975. *Climatic Atlas of Australia, Map Set 2, Global Radiation.*

Burgis, W. A., 1974. Cainozoic history of the Torilla Peninsula, Broad Sound, Queensland. *Bur. Min. Res. Geol. Geophys. Rept.*, **172**, 42 pp.

Burke, H. W., 1951. Contributions by the Japanese to the study of coral reefs. *U.S. Geol. Surv. Military Branch Memo.*, 43 pp.

Carey, S. W., 1970. Australia, New Guinea and Melanesia in the current revolution in concepts of the evolution of the earth. *Search*, **1**, 178–189.

Carriker, M. R., 1961. Comparative functional morphology of boring mechanisms in gastropods. *Amer. Zool.*, **1**, 263–266.

Carriker, M. R., 1969. Excavation of bore holes by the gastropod *Urosalpinx:* an analysis by light and scanning electron microscopy. *Amer. Zool.*, **9**, 917–933.

Carter, F., 1973. Brief summary—Great Barrier Reef expedition 1928–29. Notes prepared for Second International Coral Reef Symp. 1973, 2 pp.

Chappell, J., 1974a. Late Quaternary glacio- and hydro-isostasy on a layered earth. *Quat. Res.*, **4**, 429–440.

Chappell, J., 1974b. Geology of coral terraces, Huon Peninsula, New Guinea: a study of Quaternary tectonic movements and sea level changes. *Geol. Soc. Amer. Bull.*, **85**, 553–570.

Chappell, J. and Polach, H. A., 1976. Holocene sea level change and coral reef growth at Huon Peninsula, Papua New Guinea. *Geol. Soc. Amer. Bull.*, **87**, 235–240.

Chappell, J. and Veeh, H. H., 1978. Late Quaternary tectonic movements and sea level changes at Timor and Atauro Island. *Geol. Soc. Amer. Bull.*, **89**, 356–368.

Chappell, J., Broeker, W. S., Polach, H. A. and Thom, B. G., 1974. Problems of dating upper Pleistocene sea levels from coral reef areas. *Proc. Second Int. Coral Reef Symp.*, **2**, 563–571.

Chaput, E., 1917. Récherches sur les terrasses alluviales de la Loire et de ses principaux affluents. *Ann. Univ. Lyon, N.Sér.*, **1**, 1–303.

Chaput, E., 1927. Les principles phases de l'évolution de la vallée de la Seine. *Ann. Géog.*, **36**, 125–135.

Chave, K. E. and Schmalz, R. F., 1966. Carbonate—sea water interactions. *Geochem. et Cosmochem. Acta.*, **30**, 1037–1048.

Chave, K. E., Deffeyes, K. S., Weyl, P. K., Garrels, R. M. and Thompson, M. E., 1962. Observations on the solubility of skeletal carbonates in aqueous solutions. *Science*, **137**, 33–34.

Chave, K., Smith, S. V. and Roy, K. J., 1972. Carbonate production by coral reefs. *Mar. Geol.*, **12**, 123–140.

Chaveau, J. C., Deneufbourg, G. and Sarcia, J. A., 1967. Observations sur l'infrastructure de l'atoll de Mururoa (Archipel de Tuomotou, Pacifique Sud). *C.R. Acad. Sci. Paris*, 265–D, 1113–1116.

Chesher, R. H., 1969. Destruction of Pacific corals by the sea star *Acanthaster planci. Science*, **165**, 280–283.

Chevalier, J. P., 1973a. Coral reefs of New Caledonia. In Jones, O. A. and Endean, R. (eds.) *Biology and biology of Coral Reefs*, **1**, Geology 1, 143–167.

Chevalier, J. P., 1973b. Geomorphology and geology of coral reefs in French Polynesia. In Jones, O. A. and Endean, R. (eds.) *Biology and Geology of Coral Reefs*, **1**, Geology 1, 113–141.

Chevalier, J. P., 1977. Origin of the reef formations of Moorea Island (Archipelagoe of La Societe). *Proc. Third Int. Coral Reef Symp.*, **2**, 283–287.

Chevalier, J. P., Denizot, M., Mougin, J. L., Plessis, Y. and Salvat, B., 1968. Étude géomorphique et bionomique de l'atoll de Mururoa (Tuamotu). *Cahiers du Pacifique*, **13**, 3–143.

Chilingar, G. V., Bissell, H. J. and Wolf, K. H., 1967. Diagenesis of carbonate rocks. In Larsen, G. and Chilingar, G. V. (eds.) *Developments in Sedimentology*, **8**, 179–322.

Chorley, R. J., Beckinsale, R. P. and Dunn, A. J., 1973. *History of the Study of Landforms II: Life and Work of W. M. Davis*. Methuen, London, 874 pp.

Clack, W. J. and Mountjoy, E. W., 1977. Reef sediment transport and deposition off the east coast of Carriacou, W. I. *Proc. Third Int. Coral Reef Symp.*, **2**, 97–103.

Clapp, W. F. and Kenk, R., 1963. Marine borers, an annotated bibliography. *U.S. Office of Naval Res.*, 1136 pp.

Clarke, D. E., Paine, A. G. L. and Jensen, A. R., 1971. Geology of the Proserpine 1:250,000 Sheet Area, Queensland. *Bur. Min. Res. Geol. Geophys. Rept.*, **144**.

Clarke, J. A., Farrell, W. E. and Peltier, W. R., 1978. Global changes in post-glacial sea level: a numerical calculation. *Quat. Res.*, **9**, 265–287.

CLIMAP Project Members, 1976. The surface of the ice-age earth. *Science*, **191**, 1131–1137.

Cloud, P. E., 1954. Superficial aspects of modern organic reefs. *Amer. Assoc. Petrol. Geol. Bull.*, **36**, 2125–2149.

Cloud, P. E., 1959. Geology of Saipan, Mariana Islands, 4. Submarine topography and shoal water ecology. *U.S. Geol. Surv. Prof. Pap.*, **280-K**, 316–445.

Cloud, P. E., 1962. Environment of calcium carbonate deposition west of Andros Island, Bahamas. *U.S. Geol. Surv. Prof. Pap.*, **350**, 1–138.

Cloud, P. E., Schmidt, R. G. and Burke, H. W., 1956. Geology of Saipan, Mariana Islands. Part 1: General Geology. *U.S. Geol. Surv. Prof. Pap.*, **280-A**, 126 pp.

Cobb, W. R., 1969. Penetration of calcium carbonate substrates by the boring sponge *Cliona*. *Amer. Zool.*, **9**, 783–790.

Colquhoun, D. J., 1979. *World Shorelines Map: Pacific Indian Ocean Sector*. I.N.Q.U.A., Commission on Quaternary Shorelines.

Connell, J. H., 1973. Population ecology of reef building corals. In Jones, O. A. and Endean, R. (eds.) *Biology and Geology of Coral Reefs* **II**, Biology I, 205–246.

Conner, W. C., Kraft, R. H. and Harris, D. C., 1957. Empirical methods for forecasting the maximum storm tide due to hurricanes and other tropical storms. *Monthly Weather Rev.*, **85**, 113–116.

Connolly, J. R., 1969. Western Tasman sea floor. *N.Z. J. Geol. Geophys.*, **12**, 310–343.

Cook, P. J. and Mayo, W., 1977. Sedimentology and Holocene history of a tropical estuary (Broad Sound, Queensland). *Bur. Min. Res. Geol. Geophys. Bull.*, **170**, 206 pp.

Cook, P. J. and Polach, H. A., 1973. A chenier sequence at Broad Sound, Queensland and evidence against a Holocene high sea level. *Mar. Geol.*, **14**, 253–268.

Cook, P. J., Colwell, J. B., Firman, J. B., Lindsay, J. M., Schwebel, D. A. and van der Borch, C. C., 1977. The late Cainozoic sequence of south-east South Australia and Pleistocene sea level changes. *B.M.R. J. Austr. Geol. Geophys.*, **2**, 81–88.

Cotton, C. A., 1948. The present-day status of coral reef theories. *N.Z. Sci. Rev.*, **6**, (6), 111–113.

Couch, R. F., Fetzer, J. A., Goter, E. R., Ristvet, B. L., Tremba, E. L., Walter, D. R. and Wendland, V. P., 1975. Drilling operations on Eniwetok Atoll during project EXPOE. Rept. AFWL-TR-75-216, *Air Force Weapons Lab., Kirtland, AFB*, 270 pp.

Coudray, J. and Delibrais, G., 1972. Variations du niveau marin au-dessus de l'actuel en Nouveau—Calédonie depuis 6000 ans. *C.R. Acad. Sci. Paris*, **275**, D, 2623–2626.

Coventry, R. C., Hopley, D., Campbell, J. B., Douglas, J., Harvey, N., Kershaw, A. P., Oliver, J., Phipps, C. V. G., and Pye, K., 1980. The Quaternary of north-eastern Australia. In Henderson, R. A. and Stephenson, P. J. (eds.) *The Geology and Geophysics of North-east Australia*, 375–417.

Cribb, A. B., 1961. Some marine algae from Thursday Island and surrounding areas. *Univ. Qld. Publ. Dept. of Botany*, **4** (5), 51–59.

Cribb, A. B., 1966. The algae of Heron Island, Great Barrier Reef, Australia. *Univ. Qld. Pap., Gt. Barrier Reef. Comm. Heron Is. Res. Stn.*, **1** (1), 3–23.

Cribb, A. B., 1973. The algae of the Great Barrier Reef. In Jones, O. A. and Endean, R. (eds.) *Biology and Geology of Coral Reefs*, **II**, Biology, I, 47–75.

Cribb, A. B., 1975. Algal vegetation of Masthead Island. *Qld. Nat.*, **21**, 79–83.

Crossland, C., 1927. Marine ecology and coral formations in the Panama region, Galapagos and Marquesas Islands. *Trans. Roy. Soc. Edin.*, **55**, 531–554.

Crowe, P. R., 1949. The trade wind circulation of the world. *Trans. Inst. Brit. Geog.*, **15**, 37–56.

Crowe, P. R., 1950. The seasonal variation in the strength of the trades. *Trans. Inst. Brit. Geog.*, **16**, 23–47.

Crowe, P. R., 1951. Wind and weather in the equatorial zone. *Trans. Inst. Brit. Geog.*, **17**, 21–76.

Cuffey, R. J., 1972. The roles of bryozoans in modern coral reefs. *Geol. Rundsch.*, **61**, 542–550.

Cuffey, R. J., 1974. Delineation of bryozoan constructional roles in reefs from comparison of fossil bioherms and living reefs. *Proc. Second Int. Coral Reef Symp.*, **1**, 357–364.

Cuffey, R. J. and Fonda, S. S., 1977. Cryptic bryozoan species assemblages in modern coral reefs off Andros and Eleuthera, Bahamas. *Proc. Third Int. Coral Reef Symp.*, **1**, 81–86.

Curray, J. R., 1964. Transgressions and regressions. In Miller, R. L. (ed.) *Papers in Marine Geology—Shepard Commemorative Volume*, 175–203.

Curray, J. R. and Shepard, F. P., 1972. Some major problems of Holocene sea levels. *Amer. Quat. Assoc. Second Nat. Conf. Abstr.*, 16–18.

Dahl, A. L., 1974. The structure and dynamics of benthic algae in the coral reef ecosystem. *Proc. Second Int. Coral Reef Symp.*, **1**, 21–26.

Daly, R. A., 1910. Pleistocene glaciation and the coral reef problem. *Amer. J. Sci.*, Ser. 4, **30**, 297–308.

Daly, R. A., 1915. The Glacial-control theory of coral reefs. *Proc. Amer. Acad. the Arts and Sci.*, **51**, 155–251.

Daly, R. A., 1916. A new test of the subsidence theory of coral reefs. *Proc. Nat. Acad. Sci.*, **2**, 664–670.

Daly, R. A., 1917. Origin of the living coral reefs. *Scientia*, **22**, 188–199.

Daly, R. A., 1919. The coral reef zone during and after the Glacial period. *Amer. J. Sci.*, Ser. 4, **48**, 136–159.

Daly, R. A., 1920. Origin of beach rock. *Carnegie Inst. Wash. Yearbook* (1919), **18**, 192.

Daly, R. A., 1924. The geology of American Samoa. *Carnegie Inst. Wash. Pap. Geophys. Lab.*, **340**, 93–146.

Daly, R. A., 1925. Pleistocene changes of level. *Amer. J. Sci.*, Ser. 5, **10**, 281–313.

Daly, R. A., 1934. *The Changing World of the Ice Age*, Yale Univ. Press, New Haven, 271 pp.

Daly, R. A., 1948. Coral reefs—a review. *Amer. J. Sci.*, **246**, 193–207.

Dana, J. D., 1843. On the temperature limiting the distribution of corals. *Amer. J. Sci.*, **45**, 130–131.

Dana, J. D., 1849. *Geology U.S. Exploring Expedition*, Philadelphia, Pennsylvania.

Dana, J. D., 1863. *Manual of Geology*, Theodore Bliss and Co., Philadelphia, 798 pp.

Dana, J. D., 1872. *Corals and Coral Islands*, Dodd, Mead and Co., New York–London, 440 pp.

Dana, J. D., 1885. Origin of coral reefs and islands. *Amer. J. Sci.*, Ser. 3, **30**, 89–105, 169–191.

Dana, T. F., 1970. *Acanthaster:* a rarity in the past? *Science*, **169**, 894.

Darwin, C. R., 1838. On certain areas of elevation and subsidence in the Pacific and Indian Oceans, as deduced from the study of coral formations. *Proc. Geol. Soc. Lond.*, **2**, 552–554.

Darwin, C. R., 1842. *The Structure and Distribution of Coral Reefs*, Smith, Elder and Co., London, 214 pp.

Darwin, C. R., 1874. The Structure and Distribution of Coral Reefs, 2nd ed. rev., 1874.

David, T. E., 1911. Notes on some of the chief tectonic lines of Australia. *J. Proc. Roy. Soc. N.S.W.*, **45**, 4–60.

Davies, J. L., 1972. *Geographical Variation in Coastal Development*, Oliver and Boyd, Edinburgh, 204 pp.

Davies, J. L., 1977. The coast. In Jeans, D. N. (ed.) *Australia, A Geography*, 134–151.

Davies, P. J., 1974. Subsurface solution unconformities at Heron Island, Great Barrier Reef. *Proc. Second Int. Coral Reef Symp.*, **2**, 573–578.

Davies, P. J., 1975. Great Barrier Reef: Geological structure. *Habitat*, **3**, 3–8.

Davies, P. J., 1977. Modern reef growth—Great Barrier Reef. *Proc. Third Int. Coral Reef Symp.*, **2**, 325–330.

Davies, P. J., in press. Reef growth—a review. In Barnes, D. J. (ed.) *Growth, Maintenance and Change of Coral Reefs*, Austr. Inst. Mar. Sci., Townsville.

Davies, P. J. and Kinsey, D. W., 1973. Organic and inorganic factors in recent beach rock formation, Heron Island, Great Barrier Reef. *J. Sed. Petrol.*, **43**, 59–81.

Davies, P. J. and Kinsey, D. W., 1977. Holocene reef growth—One Tree Island, Great Barrier Reef. *Mar. Geol.* **24**, M1-M11.

Davies, P. J. and Marshall, J. F., 1979. Aspects of Holocene reef growth—substrate age and accretion rate. *Search*, **10**, 276–279.

Davies, P. J. and Marshall, J. F., 1980. A model of epicontinental reef growth. *Nature*, **287**, 37–38.

Davies, P. J. and Martin, K., 1976. Radial aragonite ooids, Lizard Island, Great Barrier Reef, Queensland, Australia. *Geology*, **4**, 120–122.

Davies, P. J., Radke, B. M. and Robinson, C. R., 1976. The evolution of One Tree Reef, southern Great Barrier Reef, Queensland. *B.M.R. J. Austr. Geol. Geophys.*, **1**, 231–240.

Davies, P. J., Marshall, J. F., Foulstone, D., Thom, B. G., Harvey, N., Short, A. D. and Martin, K., 1977a. Reef growth, southern Great Barrier Reef—preliminary results. *B.M.R. J. Austr. Geol. Geophys.*, **2**, 69–72.

Davies, P. J., Marshall, J. F., Thom, B. G., Harvey, N., Short, A. and Martin, K., 1977b. Reef development—Great Barrier Reef. *Proc. Third Int. Coral Reef Symp.*, **2**, 331–337.

Davies, P. J., Bubela, B. and Ferguson, J., 1978. The formation of ooids. *Sedimentology*, **25**, 703–730.

Davis, B., 1978. Tides. *Beach Conservation*, 33, Beach Protection Authority, Qld.

Davis, W. M., 1913. Dana's confirmation of Darwin's theory of coral reefs. *Amer. J. Sci.*, Ser. 4, **35**, 173–188.

Davis, W. M., 1917. The Great Barrier Reef of Australia. *Amer. J. Sci.*, Ser. 4, **44**, 339–350.

Davis, W. M., 1928. *The Coral Reef Problem.* Amer. Geog. Soc. Spec. Publ. **9**, 596 pp.

Deacon, E. L., 1979. The role of coral mucus in reducing the wind drag over coral reefs. *Bound-Layer Meteorol.*, **17**, 517–521.

Deboo, P. B., 1962. A preliminary petrographic study of beach rock. *Proc. Nat. Coast and Shallow Water Res. Conf.*, *1961*, 456–458.

De Keyser, F., Farden, R. S. H. and Cuttler, L. G., 1965. Ingham, Queensland. 1:250,000 Geological Series. *Bur. Min. Res. Geol. Geophys. Explan. Notes*, SE 155-10.

De Keyser, F. and Lucas, K. G., 1968. Geology of the Hodgkinson and Laura Basins, North Queensland. *Bur. Min. Res. Geol. Geophys. Bull.*, 84.

Delft Hydraulics Laboratory, 1970. Gold Coast, Queensland, Australia: Coastal erosion and related problems. *Report*, 257, 2 vols., 99 pp.

Denham, D., 1976. Earthquake hazard in Australia. *Bur. Min. Res. Geol. Geophys. Rec.* 1976/31.

Depéret, C., 1918–1922. Essai de coordination chronologique des temps quaternaires. *Comp. Rend.*, 116, 480, 636, 884: 118, 868; 120, 159; 121, 212; 124, 1502, 1594.

Dexter, P. E., 1973. A shallow water design wave procedure applicable to small cays and submerged reefs. *Engineering Dynam. of the Coastal Zone, First Austr. Conf. on Coast Eng. 1973*, 74–81.

Dexter, P. E. and Watson, K. B., 1976. A climatology of extreme wave heights in the Australian tropics. *Austr. Meteorol. Mag.*, **24**, 59–72.

Dill, R. F., 1977. The blue holes—geologically significant sink holes and caves off British Honduras and Andros, Bahama Islands. *Proc. Third Int. Coral Reef Symp.*, **2**, 238–242.

Di Salvo, L. H., 1969. Isolation of bacteria from the corallum of *Porites lobata* (Vaughan) and its possible significance. *Amer. Zool.*, **9**, 735–740.

Di Salvo, L. H., 1973. Microbial ecology. In Jones, O. A. and Endean, R. (eds.) *Biology and Geology of Coral Reefs*, **II**, Biology I, 1–15.

Dodge, R. E., 1978. The Natural Growth Records of Reef Building Corals. Unpubl. Ph.D. Thesis, Yale Univ., 237 pp.

Dodge, R. E., Aller, R. C. and Thomson, J., 1974. Coral growth related to resuspension of bottom sediments. *Nature*, **247**, 574–577.

Domm, S. B., 1971. The uninhabited cays of the Capricorn Group, Great Barrier Reef, Australia. *Atoll Res. Bull.*, **142**, 1–27.

Done, T. J., 1977. A comparison of units of cover in ecological classifications of coral communities. *Proc. Third Int. Coral Reef Symp.*, **1**, 9–13.

Done, T. J. and Pichon, M., in press. Zonation of corals. In Barnes, D. J. (ed.) *Growth, Maintenance and Change of Coral Reefs.* Austr. Inst. Mar. Sci., Townsville.

Doran, E., 1955. Landforms of the south-east Bahamas. *Univ. of Texas Publ.*, **5509**, 1–38.

Douglas, I., 1967a. Natural and man-made erosion in the humid tropics of Australia, Malaysia and Singapore. *Publ. Assoc. Int. Hydrol. Sci.*, **75**, 17–29.

Douglas, I., 1967b. Erosion of granite terrains under tropical rainforest in Australia, Malaysia and Singapore. *Publ. Assoc. Int. Hydrol. Sci.*, **75**, 30–39.

Douglas, I., 1968. The effects of precipitation chemistry and catchment area lithology on the quality of river water in selected catchments in eastern Australia. *Earth Sci. J.*, **2**, 126–144.

Douglas, I., 1969. The efficiency of humid tropical denudation system. *Trans. Inst. Brit. Geog.*, **46**, 1–16.

Douglas, I., 1973. Rates of denudation in selected small catchments in eastern Australia. *Univ. of Hull Occ. Papers in Geog.*, **21**, 127 pp.

Douglas, I., 1980. Geomorphic processes during the Quaternary. In Henderson, R. A. and Stephenson, P. J. (eds.) *The Geology and Geophysics of North-eastern Australia.* Geol. Soc. Austr., Qld. Divis., Brisbane, Ch. 21, 393–395.

Doyle, H. A., Everingham, I. B. and Sutton, D. J., 1968. Seismicity of the Australian continent. *J. Geol. Soc. Austr.*, **15**, 295–312.

Driscoll, E. M. and Hopley, D., 1967. Coastal development in a part of tropical Queensland, Australia. *J. Trop. Geog.*, **26**, 17–28.

Duerden, J. E., 1902. Boring algae as agents in the disintegration of corals. *Bull. Amer. Mus. Nat. Hist.*, **16**, 323–332.

Duncan, R. A. and McDougall, I., 1974. Migration of volcanism with time in the Marquesas Islands, French Polynesia. *Earth Planet. Sci. Lett.*, **21**, 414–420.

Dunn, G. E. and Miller, B. J., 1960. *Atlantic Hurricanes.* Louisiana State Univ., 326 pp.

Easton, A. K., 1970. *Tides of Australia.* Horace Lamb Cent. for Oceanog. Res., Flinders Univ., Res. Pap., **37**, 326 pp.

Easton, W. H. and Olson, E. A., 1976. Radiocarbon profile of Hanauma Reef, Oahu, Hawaii. *Geol. Soc. Amer. Bull.*, **87**, 711–719.

Ebanks, W. J., 1975. Holocene carbonate sedimentation and diagenesis, Ambergris Cay, Belize. In Wantland, K. F. and Pusey, W. C. (eds.) Belize Shelf—Carbonate Sediments, Clastic Sediments and Ecology. *Amer. Assoc. Petrol. Geol. Studies in Geol.*, **2**, 234–296.

Edgell, J. A., 1928a. Some remarks on coral formations. *Repts. Gt. Barrier Reef Comm.*, **2**, 52–56.

Edgell, J. A., 1928b. Changes at Masthead Island. *Repts. Gt. Barrier Reef Comm.*, **2**, 57.

Edmondson, C. H., 1929. Growth of Hawaian corals. *Bull. Bern. P. Bishop Mus.*, **58**, 1–38.

Edmondson, C. H., 1946. Behaviour of coral planulae under altered saline and thermal conditions. *Occ. Pap. Bern. P. Bishop Mus.*, **18**, 283–304.

Ek, C., 1969. L'effet de la loi de Henry sur la dissolution du CO_2 dans les eaux naturelles. In Stelcl, O. (ed.) *Problems in the Karst Denudation*, 53–55.

Emery, K. O., 1946. Marine solution basins. *J. Geol.*, **54**, 209–228.

Emery, K. O., 1962. Marine geology of Guam. *U.S. Geol. Surv. Prof. Pap.*, **403-B**, 76 pp.

Emery, K. O. and Cox, D. C., 1956. Beachrock in the Hawaiian Islands. *Pac. Sci.*, **10**, 382–402.

Emery, K. O., Tracey, J. I. and Ladd, H. S., 1954. Geology of Bikini and nearby atolls. *U.S. Geol. Surv. Prof. Pap.*, **260-A**, 1–265.

Endean, R., 1973. Population explosions of *Acanthaster planci* and associated destruction of hermatypic corals in the Indo-West Pacific region. In Jones, O. A. and Endean, R. (eds.) *Biology and Geology of Coral Reefs*, **II**, Biology I, 389–438.

Endean, R., 1974. *Acanthaster planci* on the Great Barrier Reef *Proc. Second. Int. Coral Reef Symp.*, **1**, 563–576.

Endean, R., 1976. Destruction and recovery of coral reef communities. In Jones, O. A. and Endean, R. (eds.) *Biology and Geology of Coral Reefs*, **II**, Biology II, 215–254.

Endean, R. and Chesher, R. H., 1973. Temporal and spatial distribution of *Acanthaster planci* population explosions in the Indo-West Pacific region. *Biol. Conserv.*, **5**, 87–95.

Endean, R., Stephenson, W. and Kenny, R., 1956a. The ecology and distribution of intertidal organisms on certain islands off the Queensland coast. *Austr. J. Mar. Freshw. Res.*, **7**, 317–342.

Endean, R., Kenny, R. and Stephenson, W., 1956b. The ecology and distribution of intertidal organisms on the rocky shores of the Queensland mainland. *Austr. J. Mar. Freshw. Res.*, **7**, 88–146.

Fairbanks, R. G. and Matthews, R. K., 1978. The marine oxygen isotope record in Pleistocene coral, Barbados, West Indies. *Quat. Res.*, **10**, 181–196.

Fairbridge, R. W., 1950. Recent and Pleistocene coral reefs of Australia. *J. Geol.*, **58**, 330–401.

Fairbridge, R. W., 1960. The changing level of the sea. *Sci. Amer.*, **202**, 70–79.

Fairbridge, R. W., 1961. Eustatic changes in sea level. *Phys. and Chem. Earth*, **4**, 99–185.

Fairbridge, R. W., 1962. World sea level and climatic changes. *Quaternaria*, **6**, 111–134.

Fairbridge, R. W., 1966. Mean sea level changes. In Fairbridge, R. W. (ed.) *Encyclopaedia of Oceanography*, 479–482.

Fairbridge, R. W., 1967. Coral reefs of the Australian region. In Jennings, J. N. and Mabbutt, J. A. (eds.) *Landform Studies from Australia and New Guinea*, A.N.U. press, Canberra, 386–417.

Fairbridge, R. W., 1968. Microatoll. In Fairbridge, R. W. (ed.) *Encyclopaedia of Geomorphology*, 701–705.

Fairbridge, R. W. and Teichert, C., 1947. The rampart system at Low Isles, 1928–1945. *Repts. Gt. Barrier Reef Comm.*, **6**, 1–16.

Fairbridge, R. W. and Teichert, C., 1948. The Low Isles of the Great Barrier Reef; a new analysis. *Geog. J.*, **111**, 67–88.

Fairbridge, R. W. and Teichert, C., 1952. Soil horizons and marine bands in the coastal limestone of Western Australia. *J. Proc. Roy. Soc. N.S.W.*, **86**, 68–87.

Field, R. M., 1920. Investigations regarding the calcium carbonate oozes at Tortugas and the beachrock at Loggerhead Key. *Carnegie Inst. Wash. Yearbook (1919)*, **18**, 197–198.

Fishelson, L., 1973. Ecological and biological phenomena influencing coral species composition on the reef tables at Eilat (Gulf of Aquaba, Red Sea). *Mar. Biol.*, **19**, 183–196.

Flinders, M., 1814. *A Voyage to Terra Australis*. G. and W. Nicol, London, 2 vols.

Flint, R. F., 1971. *Glacial and Quaternary Geology*. Wiley, New York, 892 pp.

Flint, D. E., Corwin, G., Dings, M. G., Fuller, W. P., MacNeil, F. S. and Saplis, R. A., 1953. Limestone walls of Okinawa. *Geol. Soc. Amer. Bull.*, **64**, 1247–1260.

Flood, P. G., 1974. Sand movements on Heron Island—a vegetated sand cay, Great Barrier Reef province, Australia. *Proc. Second Int. Coral Reef Symp.*, **2**, 387–394.

Flood, P. G., 1977a. The three southernmost reefs of the Great Barrier Reef Province—an illustration of the sequential/evolutionary nature of reef type development. In Day, R. W. (ed.) *Geol. Soc. Aust. Qld. Div. Field Conf. 1977*, 37–45.

Flood, P. G., 1977b. Coral cays of the Capricorn and Bunker Groups, Great Barrier Reef province, Australia. *Atoll Res. Bull.*, **195**, 1–7.

Flood, P. G. and Jell, J. S., 1977. The effect of cyclone *David* (January, 1976) on the sediment distribution patterns on Heron Reef, Great Barrier Reef, Australia. *Proc. Third Int. Coral Reef Symp.*, **2**, 119–125.

Flood, P. G. and Orme, G. R., 1977. A sedimentation model for platform reefs of the Great Barrier Reef, Australia. *Proc. Third Int. Coral Reef Symp.*, **2**, 111–117.

Flood, P. G. and Scoffin, T. P., 1978. Reefal sediments of the northern Great Barrier. *Phil. Trans. Roy. Soc. London*, A, **291**, 55–71.

Flood, P. G., Orme, G. R. and Scoffin, T. P., 1978. An analysis of the textural variability displayed by interreef sediments of the impure carbonate facies in the vicinity of the Howick Group. *Phil. Trans. Roy. Soc. London*, A, **291**, 73–83.

Flood, P. G., Harjanto, S. and Orme, G. R., 1979. Carbon—14 dates, Lady Elliot reef, Great Barrier Reef. *Qld. Govt. Min. J.*, Sept., 1979, 444–447.

Focke, J. W., 1978. Holocene development of coral fringing reefs, leeward off Curaçao and Bonaire (Netherlands Antilles). *Mar. Geol.*, **28**, M31–M41.

Folk, R. L., 1962. Sorting in some carbonate beaches of Mexico. *Trans. N.Y. Acad. Sci.*, **25** (2), 222–244.

Folk, R. L. and Robles, R., 1964. Carbonate sands of Isla Perez, Alacran Reef complex, Yucatan. *J. Geol.*, **72**, 255–292.

Folk, R. L., Roberts, H. H. and Moore, C. H., 1973. Black phytokarst from Hell. *Geol. Soc. Amer. Bull.*, **84**, 2351–2360.

Fontaine, H. and Delebrias, G., 1974. Nivaux marins pendant le Quaternaire au Viet-Nam. *Arch. Géol. du Viet-Nam*, **17**, 35–44.

Fosberg, F. R., 1954. Soils of the northern Marshall atolls, with special reference to the Jemo series. *Soil Sci.*, **78**, 99–107.

Fosberg, F. R., 1961a. Qualitative description of the coral reef ecosystem. *Atoll Res. Bull.*, **81**, 1–11.

Fosberg, F. R., 1961b. Description of Heron Island. *Atoll Res. Bull.*, **82**, 1–4.

Fosberg, F. R., 1975. Coral island vegetation. In Jones, O. A. and Endean, R. (eds.) *Biology and Geology of Coral Reefs*, **III**, Biology II, 255–277.

Fosberg, F. R. and Thorne, R. F., 1961. Vascular plants of Heron Island. *Atoll Res. Bull.*, **82**, 5–13.

Foster, D. R., 1974. Geomechanical Properties of Coral Rock. Unpubl. Hons. Thesis, Dept. Engin., James Cook Univ. of N. Qld., Townsville.

Frakes, L. A., 1978. Cenozoic climates: Antarctica and the southern ocean. In Pittock, A. B., Frakes, L. A., Jenssen, D., Peterson, J. A. and Zillman, J. W. (eds.) *Climatic Change and Variability, a Southern Perspective*, 53–69.

Frankel, E., 1968. Rate of formation of beachrock. *Earth Planet. Sci. Letters*, **4**, 439–440.

Frankel, E., 1974. Recent sedimentation in the Princess Charlotte Bay area, Great Barrier Reef province. *Proc. Second Int. Coral Reef Symp.*, **2**, 355–369.

Frankel, E., 1975. *Acanthaster* in the past: evidence from the Great Barrier Reef. *Crown of Thorns Starfish Seminar Proceedings, Brisbane*, 1974, 159–165.

Frankel, E., 1977. Previous *Acanthaster* aggregations in the Great Barrier Reef. *Proc. Third Int. Coral Reef Symp.*, **1**, 201–208.

Frankel, E., 1978. Evidence from the Great Barrier Reef of ancient *Acanthaster* aggregations. *Atoll Res. Bull.*, **220**, 75–93.

Friedman, G. M., 1968. Geology and geochemistry of reefs, carbonate sediments and waters, Gulf of Aquaba (Elat), Red Sea. *J. Sed. Petrol.*, **38**, 895–919.

Friedman, G. M., Amiel, A. J. and Schneidermann, N., 1974. Submarine cementation in reefs: example from the Red Sea. *J. Sed. Petrol.*, **44**, 818–825.

Fritsch, F. E., 1935. *The Structure and Reproduction of the Algae*. Camb. Univ. Press, 496 pp.

Frost, S. H., 1972. Evolution of Cenozoic Caribbean coral faunas, *Caribb. Geol. Cong. Trans.*, **6**, 461–464.

Frydl, P. and Stearns, C. W., 1978. Rate of bioerosion by parrot fish in Barbados reef environments. *J. Sed. Petrol.*, **48**, 1149–1158.

Futterer, D. K., 1974. Significance of the boring sponge *Cliona* for the origin of fine grained material of carbonate sediments. *J. Sed. Petrol.*, **44**, 79–84.

Galloway, R. W., 1970a. Coastal and shelf geomorphology and late Cenozoic sea levels. *J. Geol.*, **78**, 603–610.

Galloway, R. W., 1970b. Geology of the Mitchell-Normanby area. *C.S.I.R.O., Land Res. Ser.*, **26**, 45–52.

Galloway, R. W., 1972. Geology and geomorphology of the Shoalwater Bay area. *C.S.I.R.O. Tech. Memo. Div. Land Res.*, 72/10, 57–69.

Galloway, R. W. and Kemp, E. M., 1977. Late Cainozoic environments in Australia. *Bur. Min. Res. Geol. Geophys. Austr. Rec.*, 1977/40, 34 pp.

Gardiner, J. S., 1898a. The building of atolls. *Proc. Intern. Congress Zool.*, 119–124.

Gardiner, J. S., 1898b. The coral reefs of Funafuti, Rotuma and Fiji. *Proc. Cambridge Phil. Soc.*, **9**, 417–503.

Gardiner, J. S., 1902. The formation of the Maldives. *Geog. J.*, **19**, 277–286.

Gardiner, J. S., 1903. The origin of coral reefs as shown by the Maldives. *Amer. J. Sci.*, Ser. 4, **16**, 203–213.

Gardiner, J. S., 1903–1906. *The Fauna and Geography of the Maldive and Laccadive Archipelagoes.* Camb. Univ. Press, 2 vols., Vol. 1, 1903, Vol. 2, 1905–1906.

Gardiner, J. S., 1904. The formation of coral reefs. *Nature*, **69**, 371–373.

Garrett, R. N., 1975. A preliminary report of studies on Great Barrier Reef octocorallia. *Crown of Thorns Seminar Proceedings Brisbane, 1974*, 135–147.

Gates, W. L., 1976. Modeling the ice-age climate. *Science*, **191**, 1138–1144.

Gebelein, C. D., 1969. Distribution, morphology and accretion rate of recent subtidal algal stromatolites, Bermuda. *J. Sed. Petrol.*, **39**, 49–69.

Gebelein, C. D. and Hoffman, P., 1971. Algal origin of dolomite in interlaminated limestone—dolomite sedimentary rocks. In Bricker, O. P. (ed.) *Carbonate Cements*, 319–326.

Geikie, A., 1883. On the origin of coral reefs. *Nature*, **29**, 107–110, 124–128.

Geister, J., 1975. Riffbau und geolische entiwicklungs—geschichte der Insel San Andres. *Stuttg. Beit. z. Natur.*, Ser. B, **15**, 1–203.

Geister, J., 1977. Occurrence of *Pocillopora* in late Pleistocene coral reefs. *Mém. Bur. Rech. géol. min.*, **89**, 378–388.

Gentilli, J., 1971. *Climates of Australia and New Zealand.* World Survey of Climatology, 13, Elsevier, Amsterdam, 405 pp.

Geographic Section, Dept. of National Development, 1965b. Climate. *Fitzroy Region Resource Series*, 28 pp.

Geographic Section, Dept. of National Development, 1970. Climate. *Burdekin—Townsville Resource Series*, 19 pp.

Geyh, M. A., Kudras, H. R. and Streiff, H., 1979. Sea level changes during the late Pleistocene and Holocene in the Strait of Malacca. *Nature*, **278**, 441–443.

Gibbs, P. E., 1978. Macrofauna of the intertidal sand flats on low wooded islands, northern Great Barrier Reef. *Phil. Trans. Roy. Soc. London, B*, **284**, 81–97.

Gill, E. D. and Hopley, D., 1972. Holocene sea levels in eastern Australia—a discussion. *Mar. Geol.*, **12**, 223–233.

Gill, E. D. and Lang, J. G., 1977. Estimation of compaction in marine geological formations from engineering data commonly available. *Mar. Geol.*, **25**, M1–M4.

Gillham, M. E., 1963. Coral cay vegetation Heron Island, Great Barrier Reef. *Proc. Roy. Soc. Qld.*, **63**, 79–92.

Gilmour, D. A., 1977. Effect of rainforest logging and clearing on water yield and quality in a high rainfall zone of north-east Queensland. Nat. Comm. Hydrol., Instit. Engin. Austral. Hydrology Symposium 1977, *The Hydrology of Northern Australia*, 156–160.

Ginsburg, R. N., 1953. Beachrock in southern Florida. *J. Sed. Petrol.*, **23**, 89–92.

Ginsburg, R. N., 1956. Environmental relationships of grain size and constituent particles in some South Florida carbonate sediments. *Amer. Assoc. Petrol. Geol. Bull.*, **40**, 2384–2427.

Ginsburg, R. N. (ed.), 1972. South Florida carbonate sediments. *Sedimenta*, **11**, 72 pp.

Gleghorn, R. J., 1947. Cyclone damage on the Great Barrier Reef. *Repts. Gt. Barrier Reef Comm.*, **6**, 17–19.

Glynn, P. W., 1968. Mass mortalities of echinoids and other reef flat organisms coincident with midday low water exposures in Puerto Rico. *Mar. Biol.*, **1**, 226–243.

Glynn, P. W., 1974. Aspects of the ecology of coral reefs in the western Atlantic region. In Jones, O. A. and Endean, R. (eds.) *Biology and Geology of Coral Reefs*, **II**, Biology I, 271–324.

Glynn, P. and Macintyre, I. G., 1977. Growth rate and age of coral reefs on the Pacific coast of Panama. *Proc. Third Int. Coral Reef Symp. Miami*, **2**, 251–259.

Godfrey, J. S., 1973a. On the dynamics of the western boundary in Bryan and Cox's (1968) numerical model ocean. *Deep Sea Res.*, **20**, 1043–1058.

Godfrey, J. S., 1973b. Comparison of the East Australian Current with the western boundary flow in Bryan and Cox's (1968) numerical model ocean. *Deep Sea Res.*, **20**, 1059–1070.

Golubic, S., 1969. Distribution, taxonomy, and boring patterns of marine endolithic algae. *Amer. Zool.*, **9**, 747–751.

Goodbody, I., 1961. Mass mortality of tropical fauna after rains. *Ecology*, **42**, 150–155.

Goreau, T. F., 1959. The physiology of skeleton formation in corals I. A method for measuring the rate of calcium deposition by corals under different conditions. *Biol. Bull.*, **116**, 59–75.

Goreau, T. F., 1961a. Problems of growth and calcium deposition in reefs corals. *Endeavour*, **20**, 32–39.

Goreau, T. F., 1961b. On the relation of calcification to primary production in reef building organisms. In Lenhoff, H. M. and Loomis, W. F. (eds.) *The Biology of Hydra.*, 269–285.

Goreau, T. F. and Goreau, N. I., 1959. The physiology of skeleton formation in corals II. Calcium deposition by hermatypic corals under various conditions in the reef. *Biol. Bull.*, **117**, 239–250.

Goreau, T. F. and Goreau, N. I., 1960a. Distribution of labelled carbon in reef building corals with and without *Zooxanthellae. Science*, **131**, 668–669.

Goreau, T. F. and Goreau, N. I., 1960b. The physiology of skeleton formation in corals III. Calcification rate as a function of colony weight and total nitrogen content in the reef coral *Mancina arcolata* (Linnaeus). *Biol. Bull.*, **118**, 419–429.

Goreau, T. F. and Hartman, W. D., 1963. Boring sponges as controlling factors in the formation and maintenance of coral reefs. In Sognnaes, R. F. (ed.) Mechanisms of Hard Tissue Destruction. *Amer. Assoc. Adv. Sci. Publ.*, **75**, 23–54.

Goreau, T. F. and Hartman, W. D., 1966. Sponge: effect on the form of reef corals. *Science*, **151**, 343–344.

Goreau, T. F. and Land, L. S., 1974. Fore-reef morphology and depositional processes, north Jamaica. In Laporte, L. F. (ed.) Reefs in Time and Space, *S.E.P.M., Spec. Publ.*, **18**, 77–89.

Goreau, T. F. and Wells, J. W., 1967. The shallow water Scleractinia of Jamaica: revised list of species and their vertical distribution range. *Bull. Mar. Sci.*, **17**, 442–453.

Goreau, T. F., Goreau, N. I. and Goreau, T. J., 1979. Corals and coral reefs. *Sci. Amer.*, 110–120.

Goudie, A. S., 1973. *Duricrusts in Tropical and Subtropical Landscapes.* Clarendon Press, Oxford, 174 pp.

Grant, K. and Aitchison, G. D., 1970. The engineering significance of silcretes and ferricretes in Australia. *Eng. Geol.*, **4**, 93–120.

Graus, R. R. and Macintyre, I. G., 1976. Light control of growth form in colonial reef corals: computer simulation. *Science*, **193**, 895–897.

Grigg, H., 1972. The Taxonomy and Distribution of Pseudo dioptomus in the Townsville Region. Unpubl. M.Sc. Thesis, James Cook Univ. of N. Qld., Townsville.

Grigg, R. W. and Maragos, J., 1974. Recolonization of hermatypic corals on submerged lava flows in Hawaii. *Ecology*, **55**, 387–395.

Grommé, S. and Vine, F. J., 1972. Palaeomagnetism of Midway Atoll lavas and northward movement of the Pacific plate. *Earth Planet. Sci. Letters*, **17**, 159–168.

Grover, J. C., 1965. Seismological and vulcanological studies in the British Solomon Islands to 1961. *Br. Solomon Is. Geol. Rec.*, **2**, 183–188.

Guilcher, A., 1961. Le "beachrock" ou grès de plage. *Ann. Géog.*, **70**, 113–125.

Guilcher, A., 1969. Pleistocene and Holocene sea level changes. *Earth Sci. Rev.*, **5**, 69–97.

Guilcher, A., 1974. Coral reefs of the New Hebrides, Melanesia, with particular reference to open sea, not fringing reefs. *Proc. Second Int. Coral Reef Symp.*, **2**, 523–535.

Guilcher, A., 1976. Double and multiple barrier reefs in the world. *Stud. Soc. Sci. Torunensis*, **8**, C, 4–6, 85–99.

Guilcher, A. and Pont, P., 1957. Étude experimentale de la corrosion littorale des calcaires. *Bull. Assoc. Geogr. Franc.*, **265**, 48–62.

Guilcher, A., Berthois, L., Doumenge, F., Michel, A., Saint-Requier, A. and Arnold, R., 1969. Les récifs et lagons coralliens de Mopelia et de Bora-Bora (Îles de la Société). *Memo. Orstom.*, **38**, 1–103.

Guppy, H. B., 1885. Observations on the recent calcareous formations of the Solomons Group made during 1882–1884. *Nature*, **33**, 202–205.

Guppy, H. B., 1886. Notes on the characters and mode of formation of the coral reefs of the Solomon Islands. *Proc. Roy. Soc. Edinburgh*, **13**, 857–904.

Guppy, H. B., 1887. *The Solomon Islands. Their Geology, General features and Suitability for Colonization.* Swan, Sonnenschein, Lowry and Co., London, 152 pp.

Guppy, H. B., 1888. A recent criticism of the theory of subsidence as affecting coral reefs. *Scot. Geog. Mag.*, **4**, 121–137.

Guppy, H. B., 1889. The Cocos–Keeling Islands. *Scot. Geog. Mag.*, **5**, 281–297, 457–474, 569–588.

Guppy, H. B., 1890. The origin of coral reefs. *Proc. Vict. Inst.*, **23**, 51–68.

Haigler, S. A., 1969. The boring mechanism of *Polydora websteri* inhabiting *Crassostrea virginica*. *Amer. Zool.*, **9**, 821–828.

Hails, J. R., 1965. A critical review of sea level changes in eastern Australia since the last glacial. *Austr. Geog. Stud.*, **3**, 63–78.

Halley, R. B., Shinn, E. A., Hudson, J. H. and Lidz, B., 1977. Recent and relict topography of Boo Bee patch reef, Belize. *Proc. Third Int. Coral Reef Symp.*, **2**, 29–35.

Hammond, S. R., Theyer, F. and Sutton, G. H., 1974. Palaeo-magnetic evidence of northward movement of the Pacific Plate in deep sea cores from the central Pacific basin. *Earth Planet. Sci. Letters*, **22**, 22–28.

Hammer, W. H. and Jones, M. S., 1976. Distribution, burrowing and growth rates of the clam *Tridacna crocea* on interior reef flats. *Oecologia*, **24**, 207–227.

Hamon, B. V., 1958. Mean sea level variation on the coast of N.S.W. *Austr. Surveyor*, Sept., 188–199.

Hanor, J. S., 1978. Precipitation of beachrock cements: mixing of marine and meteoric waters versus CO_2 degassing. *J. Sed. Petrol.*, **48**, 489–501.

Harris, W. H., 1969. Coastal phreatic diagenetic environments, coral cap of Barbados, West Indies. *Geol. Soc. Amer. Abstracts for 1969*, **7**, 90–91.

Harris, W. H., 1971. Groundwater–Carbonate–Rock Chemical Interactions, Barbados, West Indies. Unpubl. Ph.D. thesis, Brown Univ., Providence, R.I., 348 pp.

Harris, W. H. and Matthews, R. K., 1968. Subaerial diagenesis of carbonate sediments: efficiency of the solution—reprecipitation process. *Science*, **160**, 77–79.

Harrison, R. S., 1974. Near-surface Diagenesis of Subaerially Exposed Pleistocene Carbonates, Barbados, West Indies. Unpubl. Ph.D. thesis, Brown Univ., Providence, R.I., 333 pp.

Harrison, R. S., 1975. Porosity in Pleistocene grainstones from Barbados: some preliminary observations. *Bull. Canad. Petrol. Geol.*, **23**, 383–392.

Harrison, R. S., 1977a. Caliche profiles: indicators of near-surface subaerial diagenesis, Barbados, West Indies. *Bull. Canad. Petrol. Geol.*, **25**, 123–173.

Harrison, R. S., 1977b. Subaerial versus submarine discontinuity surfaces in a Pleistocene reef complex, Barbados, W.I. *Proc. Third Int. Coral Reef Symp.*, **2**, 143–147.

Harrison, R. S. and Steinen, R. P., 1978. Subaerial crusts, caliche profiles and breccia horizons: Comparison of some Holocene and Mississippian exposure surfaces, Barbados and Kentucky. *Geol. Soc. Amer. Bull.*, **89**, 385–396.

Hartman, W. D. and Goreau, T. F., 1970. Jamaican coralline sponges: their morphology, ecology and fossil relations. *Symp. Zool. Soc. Lond.*, **25**, 205–243.

Harvey, N., 1977a. The identification of subsurface solution disconformities on the Great Barrier Reef, Australia between 14°S and 17°S, using shallow seismic refraction techniques. *Proc. Third Int. Coral Reef Symp.*, **2**, 45–51.

Harvey, N., 1977b. Application of shallow seismic refraction techniques to coastal geomorphology: a coral reef example. *Catena*, **4**, 333–339.

Harvey, N., 1978. Wheeler Reef: morphology and shallow reef structure. In Hopley, D. (ed.) Geographical Studies of the Townsville Area. *Dept. Geog. James Cook Univ. of N. Qld. Monogr. Ser. Occ. Pap.* **2**, 51–53.

Harvey, N., 1980. Seismic Investigations of a Pre-Holocene Substrate beneath Modern Reefs in the Great Barrier Reef Province. Unpubl. Ph.D. thesis, James Cook Univ. of N. Qld., 329 pp.

Harvey, N., Davies, P. J. and Marshall, J. F., 1978. Shallow reef structure: southern Great Barrier Reef. *Bur. Min. Res. Geol., Geophys. Rec.* 1978/96, 9 pp.

Harvey, N., Davies, P. J. and Marshall, J. F., 1979. Seismic refraction—a tool for studying coral reef growth. *B.M.R. J. Austr. Geol. and Geophys.*, **4**, 141–147.

Hays, J. D., Imbrie, J. and Shackleton, N. J., 1976. Variations in the earth's orbit: pacemaker of ice ages. *Science*, **194**, 1121–1132.

Heatwole, H., 1975. The ecology and biogeography of coral cays. In Jones, O. A. and Endean, R. (eds.) *Biology and Geology of Coral Reef*, **III**, Biology II, 369–387.

Hedley, C., 1925a. A raised beach at the North Barnard Islands. *Repts. Gt. Barrier Reef Comm.*, **1**, 61–62.

Hedley, C., 1925b. The Townsville plain. *Repts. Gt. Barrier Reef Comm.*, **1**, 63–65.

Hedley, C., 1925c. A disused river mouth at Cairns. *Repts. Gt. Barrier Reef. Comm.*, **1**, 69–72.

Hedley, C., 1925d. The Queensland earthquake of 1918. *Repts. Gt. Barrier Reef Comm.*, **1**, 151–156.

Hedley, C., 1925e. The natural destruction of a coral reef. *Repts. Gt. Barrier Reef Comm.*, **1**, 61–62.

Hedley, C., 1925f. An opacity meter. *Repts. Gt. Barrier Reef Comm.*, **1**, 67–68.

Hedley, C., 1925g. The surface temperature of Moreton Bay. *Repts. Gt. Barrier Reef Comm.*, **1**, 149–150.

Hedley, C., 1925h. Coral shingle as a beach formation. *Repts. Gt. Barrier Reef Comm.*, **1**, 66.

Hedley, C., 1925i. Report of the Scientific Director for 1924. *Repts. Gt. Barrier Reef Comm.*, **1**, 157–160.

Hedley, C. and Taylor, T. G., 1908. Coral reefs of the Great Barrier, Queensland: a study of their structure, life distribution, and relation to mainland physiography. *Rept. Australas. Ass. Adv. Sci.*, **11**, 397–413.

Hein, F. J. and Risk, M. J., 1975. Bioerosion of coral heads: inner patch reefs, Florida reef tract. *Bull. Mar. Sci.*, **25**, 133–138.

Henderson, D. A., 1931. Morinda Shoal. *Repts. Gt. Barrier Reef Comm.*, **3**, 46.

Henderson, R. A. and Stephenson, P. J. (eds.), 1980. *The Geology and Geophysics of North-eastern Australia*, Geol. Soc. Austr., 468 pp.

Hernandez-Avila, M. L., Roberts, H. H. and Rouse, L. J., 1977. Hurricane-generated waves and coastal boulder rampart formation. *Proc. Third Int. Coral Reef Symp.*, **2**, 71–85.

Hicks, B. B., Drinkrow, R. L., and Grauze, G., 1974. Drag and bulk transfer coefficients associated with a shallow water surface. *Bound. Layer Meteorol.*, **6**, 387–397.

Higgins, C. G., 1975. Theories of landscape development: a perspective. In Melhorn, W. N. and Flemal, R. C. (eds.) *Theories of Landform Development*, Proc. of Sixth Ann. Geomorphology Symposia Series State Univ., Binghampton, N.Y., 1–28.

Hill, D., 1974. An introduction to the Great Barrier Reef. *Proc. Second Int. Coral Reef Symp.*, **2**, 723–732.

Hillis-Collinvaux, L., 1974. Productivity of the coral reef alga Halimeda (Order Siphonales). *Proc. Second Int. Coral Reef Symp.*, **1**, 35–42.

Hillis-Collinvaux, L., 1977. *Halimeda* and *Tydemania*: distribution, diversity and productivity at Enewetak. *Proc. Third Int. Coral Reef Symp.*, **1**, 365–470.

Hoffmeister, J. E. and Ladd, H. S., 1935. The foundation of atolls. *J. Geol.*, **43**, 653–665.

Hoffmeister, J. E. and Ladd, H. S., 1944. The antecedent-platform theory. *J. Geol.*, **52**, 388–502.

Hoffmeister, J. E. and Ladd, H. S., 1945. Solution effects on elevated limestone terraces. *Geol. Soc. Amer. Bull.*, **56**, 809–818.

Holland, H. D., Kirsipu, T. V., Huebner, J. S. and Oxburgh, U. M., 1964. On some aspects of the chemical evolution of cave waters. *J. Geol.*, **72**, 36–67.

Hopley, D., 1968. Morphology of Curacoa Island spit, North Queensland. *Austr. J. Sci.*, **31**, 122–123.

Hopley, D., 1969. A coastal weathering sequence at Mount Douglas, North Queensland. *Rev. de Geomorph. Dynamique*, **19**, 9–14.

Hopley, D., 1970a. Geomorphology of the Budekin Delta, North Queensland. *Dept. of Geog. James Cook Univ. of N. Qld. Monograph Ser.*, **1**, 1-66.

Hopley, D., 1970b. Coastal Geomorphology in the Townsville Region. Unpubl. Ph.D. Thesis, James Cook Univ. of N. Qld., Townsville, 353 pp.

Hopley, D., 1971a. The origin and significance of North Queensland island spits. *Zeits. f. Geomorph. N.F.*, **15**, 371-389.

Hopley, D., 1971b. Sea level and environment changes in the late Pleistocene and Holocene in North Queensland, Australia. *Quaternaria*, **14**, 265-276.

Hopley, D., 1972. Coasts. In Dept. of Nat. Devel., *Burdekin-Townsville Region Resource Series: Landforms*, 21-24.

Hopley, D., 1973. Geomorphic evidence for climatic change in the late Quaternary of north-east Queensland, Australia. *J. Trop. Geog.*, **36**, 20-30.

Hopley, D., 1974a. Coastal changes produced by tropical cyclone *Althea* in Queensland, December, 1971. *Austr. Geogr.*, **12**, 445-456.

Hopley, D., 1974b. Investigations of sea level changes along the coast of the Great Barrier Reef. *Proc. Second Int. Coral Reef Symp.*, **2**, 551-562.

Hopley, D., 1974c. The cyclone *Althea* storm surge. *Austr. Geog. Stud.*, **12**, 90-106.

Hopley. D., 1975. Contrasting evidence for Holocene sea levels with special reference to the Bowen-Whitsunday area of Queensland. In Douglas, I., Hobbs, J. E. and Pigram, J. J. *Geographical Essays in Honour of Gilbert J. Butland*, Dept. of Geog., Univ. New England, Armidale, 51-84.

Hopley, D., 1977. The age of the outer ribbon reef surface, Great Barrier Reef, Australia: implications for hydro-isostatic models. *Proc. Third Int. Coral Reef Symp.*, **2**, 23-28.

Hopley, D., 1978a. The Great Barrier Reef in the Townsville region. In Hopley, D. (ed.) Geographical Studies of the Townsville Area. *Dept. of Geog., James Cook Univ. of N. Qld., Monograph Ser., Occ. Pap.* **2**, 45-50.

Hopley, D., 1978b. Sea level change on the Great Barrier Reef: an introduction. *Phil. Trans. Roy. Soc., London*, A, **291**, 159-166.

Hopley, D., 1978c. Wheeler Reef: cay mobility. In Hopley, D. (eds.) Geographical Studies of the Townsville area. *Dept. Geog. James Cook Univ. of N. Qld., Monogr. Ser., Occ. Pap.* **2**, 55-58.

Hopley, D., 1980. Mid-Holocene high sea levels along the coastal plain of the Great Barrier Reef province: a discussion. *Mar. Geol.*, **35**, 41-49.

Hopley, D., in press. Sediment movement around a coral cay, Great Barrier Reef, Australia. *Pacific Geol.*, **15**, 17-37.

Hopley, D. and Hamilton, D., 1973. Geomorphology of the high islands. In Manser, W. (ed.) New Guinea barrier reefs: preliminary results of the 1969 coral reef expedition to the Trobriand Islands and Louisiade archipelago, Papua-New Guinea. *Univ. Papua-New Guinea Geol. Dept. Occ. Pap.* **1**, 95-128.

Hopley, D. and Harvey, N., 1979. Regional variations in storm surge characteristics around the Australian coast: a preliminary investigation. In Heathcote, R. L. and Thom, B. G. (eds.) *Natural Hazards in Australia*, Aust. Acad. Sci., Canberra, 164-185.

Hopley, D. and Isdale, P., 1977. Coral micro-atolls, tropical cyclones and reef flat morphology: a North Queensland example. *Search*, **8**, 79-81.

Hopley, D. and Mackay, M. G., 1978. An investigation of morphological zonation of beachrock erosional features. *Earth Surface Proc.*, **3**, 363-377.

Hopley, D. and Murtha, G. G., 1975. The Quaternary deposits of the Townsville coastal plain. *Dept. of Geog., James Cook Univ. of N. Qld. Monograph Ser.*, **8**, 30 pp.

Hopley, D., McLean, R. F., Marshall and Smith, A. S., 1978. Holocene-Pleistocene boundary in a fringing reef: Hayman Island, North Queensland. *Search*, **9**, 323-325.

Hudson, J. H., 1977. Long-term bioerosion rates on a Florida reef: a new method. *Proc. Third Int. Coral Reef Symp.*, **2**, 491-497.

Hudson, J. H., Shinn, E. A., Halley, R. B. and Lidz, B., 1976. Sclerochronology: a tool for interpreting past environments. *Geology*, **4**, 361-364.

Hunter, I. G., 1977. Sediment production by *Diadema antillarum* on a Barbados fringing reef. *Proc. Third Int. Coral Reef Symp.*, **2**, 105-110.

Illing, L. V., 1954. Bahamian calcareous sands. *Amer. Assoc. Petrol. Geol. Bull.*, **38**, 1-95.

Ingleton, G. E., 1944. *Charting a Continent.* Angus and Robertson, Sydney, 145 pp.

Inman, D. L., 1949. Sorting of sediments in the light of fluid mechanics. *J. Sed. Petrol.*, **19**, 51-70.

Inman, D. L. and Nasu, N., 1956. Orbital velocity associated with wave action near the breaker zone. *B.E.B. Tech. Memo.*, **79.**

Isdale, P. J., 1977. Variations in growth rate of hermatypic corals in a uniform environment. *Proc. Third Int. Coral Reef Symp.*, **2**, 403-408.

Isdale, P. J., 1978. Wheeler Reef: coral growth rate studies. In Hopley, D. (ed.) Geological Studies of the Townsville Area. *Dept. of Geogr., James Cook Univ. of N. Qld. Mongr. Ser. Occ. Pap.* **2**, 54-55.

Isdale, P. J., in prep. Spatial Variation in Massive Coral Growth Rates on the Great Barrier Reef. Unpubl. Ph.D. Thesis, James Cook Univ. of N. Qld., Townsville.

Jack, R. L. and Etheridge, R., 1892. *The Geology and Palaeontology of Queensland and New Guinea.* Govt. Printer, Brisbane, 768 pp.

Jackson, J. B. C., Goreau, T. F. and Hartman, W. D., 1971. Recent brachiopod-coralline sponge communities and their palaeoecological significance, *Science*, **173**, 623-625.

Jacobson, G. and Hill, P. J., 1980. Hydrogeology of a raised coral atoll—Niue Island, South Pacific Ocean. *B.M.R. J. Austr. Geol. Geophys.* **5**, 271-278.

James N. P., 1972a. Holocene and Pleistocene calcareous crust (caliche) profiles: criteria for sub-aerial exposure. *J. Sed. Petrol.*, **42**, 817-836.

James, N. P., 1972b. Late Pleistocene Reef Limestones, Northern Barbados, W.I. Unpublished Ph.D. Thesis, McGill Univ., Montreal, 242 pp.

James, N. P., 1974. Diagenesis of scleractinian corals in the subaerial vadose environment. *J. Paleontol.*, **48**, 785-799.

James, N. P., Mountjoy, E. W. and Ohmura, A., 1971. An early Wisconsin reef terrace at Barbados, W.I., and its climatic implications. *Geol. Soc. Amer. Bull.*, **82**, 2011-2018.

James, N. P., Stearn, C. W. and Harrison, R. S., 1977. Field guidebook to modern and Pleistocene reef carbonates, Barbados, W.I. *Third Int. Coral Reef Symp. Field Guides*, 1-30.

Jardine, F., 1925a. The physiography of the Port Curtis district. *Repts. Gt. Barrier Reef Comm.*, **1**, 73-110.

Jardine, F., 1925b. The development and significance of benches in the littoral of eastern Australia. *Repts. Gt. Barrier Reef Comm.*, **1**, 111-130.

Jardine, F., 1925c. The drainage of the Atherton Tableland. *Repts. Gt. Barrier Reef Comm.*, **1**, 131-148.

Jardine, F., 1928a. The topography of the Townsville littoral. *Repts. Gt. Barrier Reef Comm.*, **2**, 70-87.

Jardine, F., 1928b. The Broadsound drainage in relation to the Fitzroy River. *Repts. Gt. Barrier Reef Comm.*, **2**, 88-92.

Jelesnianski, C. P., 1967. Numerical computations of storm surges with bottom stress. *Monthly Weather Rev.*, **95**, 740-756.

Jell, J. S., 1974. The microstructure of some scleractinian corals. *Proc. Second Int. Coral Reef Symp.*, **2**, 301-320.

Jell, J. S. and Flood, P. G., 1978. Guide to the geology of reefs of the Capricorn and Bunker Groups, Great Barrier Reef Province, with special reference to Heron Reef. *Pap., Dept. of Geol., Univ. of Qld.*, **8** (3), 85 pp.

Jell, J. S., Maxwell, W. G. H. and McKellar, R. G., 1965. The significance of the larger Foraminifera in the Heron Island reef sediments. *J. Paleontol.*, **39**, 273-279.

Jennings, J. N., 1965. Further discussion of factors affecting coastal dune formation in the tropics. *Austr. J. Sci.*, **28**, 166-167.

Jennings, J. N., 1969. Karst of the seasonally humid tropics in Australia. In Stelcl, O. (ed.) *Problems of the Karst Denudation*, 149-155.

Jennings, J. N., 1971. *Karst*, A.N.U., Canberra, 252 pp.

Jennings, J. N., 1972a. Some attributes of Torres Strait. In Walker, D. (ed.) Bridge and Barrier: the Natural and Cultural History of Torres Strait. *A.N.U. Res. Sch. Pacific Stud. Publ.* BG/3, 29–38.

Jennings, J. N., 1972b. The character of tropical humid karst. *Zeits. F. Geomorph.*, N.F., **16**, 336–341.

Jennings, J. N. and Bik, M. J., 1962. Karst morphology in Australian New Guinea. *Nature*, **194**, 1036–1038.

Jennings, J. N. and Sweeting, M. M., 1963. The Limestone Ranges of the Fitzroy Basin, Western Australia. *Bonn. Geogr. Abh.*, **32**, 1–60.

Jensen, A. R., Gregory, C. M. and Forbes, V. R., 1963. Regional geology of the Mackay 1:250,000 sheet area, Queensland. *Bur. Min. Res. Geol. Geophys. Rec.* 1963/71.

Johnson, J. H., 1961. *Limestone Building Algae and Algal Limestones.* Colorado School of Mines, Boulder, Colorado, 297 pp.

Jokiel, P. L., Coles, S. L., Guinther, E. B., Key, G. S., Smith, S. V. and Townsley, S. J., 1974. Effects of thermal loading on Hawaiian reef corals. *Final Rept. E.P.A. Proj. 18050 DDN.*

Jones, C. L., 1961. Petrography of some Recent Beachrock from the Caribbean. Unpubl. M.S. Thesis, Louisiana State Univ., Baton Rouge.

Jones, O. A., 1974. The Great Barrier Reef Committee 1922–1973. *Proc. Second Int. Coral Reef Symp.*, **2**, 733–740.

Jones, O. A. and Jones, J. B., 1956. Notes on the geology of some north Queensland islands. *Repts. Gt. Barrier Reef Comm.*, **6**, 31–54.

Jones, M., Hekel, H. and Searle, D. E., 1977, Late Quaternary sedimentation in Moreton Bay. In Orme, G. R. and Day, R. W. (eds.) *Handbook of Recent Geological Studies of Moreton Bay, Brisbane River and Stradbroke Island*, Austr. Sedimentol. Group, 1–10.

Jongsma, D., 1970. Eustatic sea level changes in the Arafura Sea. *Nature*, **228**, 150–151,

Jordan, G. F., 1954. Large sink holes in the Straits of Florida. *Amer. Assoc. Petrol. Geol. Bull.*, **38**, 1810–1817.

Joubin, L., 1912. Bancs et récifs de coreaux (madrépores). *Ann. Inst. Oceanog. (Paris)*, **4**, 1–7.

Judd, J. W., 1904. General report on the materials sent from Funafuti and the methods of dealing with them. In *The Atoll of Funafuti*, The Royal Society, London, 167–185.

Judd, J. W., 1910. Critical introduction. In Darwin, C. R., *Coral Reefs, Volcanic Islands, South American Geology*, World Library Edition, 3–10.

Jukes, J. B., 1847. *Narrative of the surveying voyage of H.M.S. Fly* commanded by Capt. F. P. Blackwood in Torres Strait, New Guinea and other islands of the Eastern Archipelago, during the years 1842–1846 together with an excursion into the interior of the eastern part of Java, London, T. and W. Boone, 2 vols.

Kawaguti, S., 1944. On the physiology of reef corals. VII. Zooxanthellae of the reef corals in *Gymnodinium* sp., Dinoflagellata; its culture *in vitro*. *Palao Trop. Biol. Stud.*, **2**, 675–679.

Kawaguti, S., 1953. Ammonium metabolism of the coral reefs. *Biol. J. Okayama Univ.*, **1**, 171–176.

Kaye, C. A., 1959. Shoreline features and Quaternary shoreline changes, Puerto Rico. *U.S. Geol. Surv. Prof. Pap.* 317-B, 49–140.

Kendall, C. G. St. C. and Skipworth, P. A. d'E., 1969. Geomorphology of a Recent shallow water carbonate province: Khor Al Bazam, Trucial Coast, South-west Persian Gulf. *Geol. Soc. Amer. Bull.*, **80**, 865–892.

Kenny, R., 1974. Inshore sea surface temperatures at Townsville. *Austr. J. Mar. Freshw. Res.*, **25**, 1–5.

Kershaw, A. P., 1970. A pollen diagram from Lake Euramoo northeast Queensland, Australia. *New Phytol.*, **69**, 785–805.

Kershaw, A. P., 1971. A pollen diagram from Quincan crater, northeast Queensland, Australia. *New Phytol.*, **70**, 669–681.

Kershaw, A. P., 1974. A long continuous pollen sequence from north-eastern Australia. *Nature*, **251**, 222–223.

Kershaw, A. P., 1975a. Late Quaternary vegetation and climate in north-eastern Australia. *Bull. Roy. Soc. N.Z.*, **13,** 181–187.

Kershaw, A. P., 1975b. Stratigraphy and pollen analysis of Bromfield Swamp, north-eastern Queensland, Australia. *New Phytol.*, **75,** 173–191.

Kershaw, A. P., 1976. A late Pleistocene and Holocene pollen diagram from Lynch's crater north-eastern Queensland, Australia. *New Phytol.*, **77,** 469–498.

Kershaw, A. P., 1978. Record of last interglacial-glacial cycle from north-eastern Queensland. *Nature*, **272,** 159–161.

Kershaw, A. P., 1980. Evidence for vegetation and climatic change in the Quaternary. In Henderson, R. A. and Stephenson, P. J. (eds.) *The Geology and Geophysics of North-eastern Australia.* Geol. Soc. Austr., Qld. Divis., Brisbane, Ch. 21, 398–402.

King, C. A. M., 1972. *Beaches and Coasts.* 2nd Ed., Arnold, London, 570 pp.

King, L. C., 1962. *Morphology of the Earth. A Study and Synthesis of World Scenery*, Oliver and Boyd, Edinburgh, 699 pp.

King, P. P., 1827. *Narrative of a survey of the intertropical and western coasts of Australia 1818–1822.* J. Murray, London, 2 vols.

Kinsey, D. W., 1972. Preliminary observations on community metabolism and primary productivity of the pseudo-atoll reef at One Tree Island, Great Barrier Reef. *Proc. Symp. Corals and Coral Reefs, Mar. Biol. Assoc. India*, 13–32.

Kinsey, D. W., 1977. Seasonality and zonation in coral reef productivity and calcification. *Proc. Third Int. Coral Reef Symp.*, **2,** 383–388.

Kinsey, D. W., 1978. Productivity and calcification estimates using slackwater periods and field enclosures. In Stoddart, D. R. and Johannes, R. E. (eds.) *Coral Reefs: Research Methods*, UNESCO, Paris, 439–468.

Kinsey, D. W., 1981. The absolute modal distribution of reef community metabolism and calcification. *Fourth Int. Coral Reef Symp. Manila, Abstracts*, 34.

Kinsey, D. W. and Davies, P. J., 1979a. Inorganic carbon turnover, calcification and growth in coral reefs. In Trudingar P. and Swaine, D. (eds.) *Biogeochemistry of Mineral Forming Elements*, 131–162.

Kinsey, D. W. and Davies, P. J., 1979b. Effects of elevated nitrogen and phosphorus on coral reef growth. *Linnol. Oceanogr.*, **24,** 935–940.

Kinsey, D. W. and Domm, A., 1974. Effects of fertilization on a coral reef environment—primary production studies. *Proc. Second Int. Coral Reef Symp.*, **1,** 49–66.

Kinsey, D. W. and Kinsey, B. E., 1967. Diurnal changes in oxygen content of the water over the coral reef platform at Heron Island. *Austr. J. Mar. and Freshw. Res.*, **18,** 23–34.

Kinsman, D. J. J., 1964. Reef coral tolerance of high temperatures and salinities. *Nature*, **202,** 1280–1282.

Kirkegaarde, A. G., Shaw, R. D. and Murray, C. G., 1970. Geology of the Rockhampton and Port Clinton 1:250,000 sheet areas. *Geol. Surv. Qld. Rept.*, **38.**

Kissling, D. L., 1977. Population structure characteristics for some Palaeozoic and modern corals. *Second Inter. Symp. on Corals and Fossil Coral Reefs Paris Bur. Rech. géol. et min.*, **89,** 457–506.

Knox, R. A., 1974. Reconnaissance of the Indian Ocean equatorial undercurrent near Addu Atoll. *Deep Sea Res.*, **21,** 123–129.

Knutson, D. W. and Buddemeier, R. W., 1973. Distribution of radionuclides in reef corals: opportunity for data retrieval and study of effects. In *Radioactive Contamination of the Marine Environment*, International Atomic Energy Agency, 735–746.

Knutson, D. W., Buddemeier, R. W. and Smith, S. V., 1972. Coral chronometers: seasonal growth bands in coral reefs. *Science*, **177,** 270–272.

Komar, P. D., 1976. *Beach Processes and Sedimentation.* Prentice-Hall, N.J., 429 pp.

Konishi, K., Schlanger, S. O. and Omura, A., 1970. Neotectonic rates in the Central Ryukyu Islands derived from Th^{230} coral ages. *Mar. Geol.*, **9,** 225–240.

Konishi, K., Omura, A. and Nakamichi, O., 1974. Radiometric coral ages and sea level records from the late Quaternary reef complexes of the Ryukyu Islands. *Proc. Second Int. Coral Reef Symp.*, **2**, 595–613.

Kornicker, L. S., 1958. Bahamian limestone coasts. *Gulf Coast Assoc. Geol. Soc. Trans.*, **8**, 167–170.

Kornicker, L. S. and Squires, D. F., 1962. Floating corals: a possible source of erroneous distribution data. *Limnol. Oceanogr.*, **7**, 447–452.

Krause, D. C., 1967. Bathymetry and geological structure of the northern Tasman Sea—Coral Sea—South Solomon Sea area of the south-west Pacific Ocean. *N.Z. Dept. Sci. Ind. Res. Bull.*, **183**, 1–50.

Ku, T. L., Kimmel, M. A., Easton, W. H. and O'Neil, T. J., 1974. Eustatic sea level 120,000 years ago on Oahu, Hawaii. *Science*, **183**, 959–961.

Kuchler, D. A., 1978. Coral Cay Shoreline Movements, Historical and Seasonal Patterns, Green Island, Great Barrier Reef, Australia. Unpubl. Hons. Thesis, Dept. of Geog., James Cook Univ. of N.Qld., Townsville, 163 pp.

Kuenen, P. H., 1933. Geology of coral reefs. *Snellius Exped. east. Part Neth.-E.-Indies*, **5** (2), 1–126.

Kuenen, P. H., 1947. Two problems of marine geology, atolls and canyons. *K. Ned. Akad. v. Wet. Amst.*, *Verh. afd. Nat.*, DI 43 (3), 69 pp.

Kukla, G. J., 1977. Pleistocene land-sea correlations I. Europe. *Earth Sci. Rev.*, **13**, 307–374.

Labeyrie, J., Lalou, C. and Delebrias, G., 1969. Études des transgressions marines sur l'atoll de Muroroa par la datation des différents niveaux de corail. *Cahiers du Pacifique*, **13**, 59–68.

Ladd, H. S., 1950. Recent reefs. *Amer. Assoc. Petrol. Geol. Bull.*, **34**, 203–214.

Ladd, H. S., 1961. Reef building. *Science*, **134**, 703–715.

Ladd, H. S., 1977. Types of coral reefs and their distribution. In Jones, O. A. and Endean, R. (eds.) *Geology and Biology of Coral Reefs*, **IV**, Geology II, 1–19.

Ladd, H. S. and Schlanger, S. O., 1960. Drilling operations on Eniwetok Atoll. *U.S. Geol. Surv. Prof. Pap.*, **206-Y**, 863–899.

Ladd, H. S., Ingerson, E., Townsend, R. C., Russell, M. and Stephenson, H. K., 1953. Drilling on Eniwetok Atoll, Marshall Islands. *Amer. Assoc. Petrol. Geol. Bull.*, **37**, 2257–2280.

Ladd, H. S., Tracey, J. I. and Gross, M. G., 1970. Deep drilling on Midway Atoll. *U.S. Geol. Surv. Prof. Pap.*, **680-A**, 1–22.

Lalou, C., Labeyrie, J. and Delebrias, G., 1966. Datations des calcaires coralliens de l'atoll de Muroroa (archipel des Tuamotu) de l'époque actuelle jusqu'à—500,000 ans. *C.R. Acad. Sci. Paris*, **263-D**, 1946–1949.

de Lamothe, L., 1911. Les anciennes lignes de rivages du Sahel d'Alger et d'une partie de la côte algerienne. *Mém. Soc. Géol. France*, **1**, (6), 1–288.

de Lamothe, L., 1918. Les anciennes nappes alluviales et lignes de rivages du bassin de la Somme et leurs rapports avec celles de la Méditerraneé occidentale. *Bull. Soc. Géol. France*, **18**, 3–58.

Land, L. S., 1970. Phreatic versus vadose meteoric diagenesis of limestones: evidence from a fossil water table. *Sedimentology*, **14**, 175–185.

Land, L. S., 1974. Growth rate of a West Indian (Jamaican) reef. *Proc. Second Int. Coral Reef Symp.*, **2**, 409–412.

Land, L. S. and Goreau, T. F., 1970. Submarine lithification of Jamaican reefs. *J. Sed. Petrol.*, **40**, 457–462.

Land, L. S., MacKenzie, F. T. and Gould, S. J., 1967. Pleistocene history of Bermuda. *Geol. Soc. Amer. Bull.*, **78**, 993–1006.

Lighty, R. G., 1977a. Relict shelf-edge Holocene coral reef: south-east coast of Florida. *Proc. Third Int. Coral Reef Symp.*, **2**, 215–221.

Lighty, R. G., 1977b. Submarine diagenesis in relict Holocene coral reef, south-east Florida—diagenetic control on porosity and stratigraphy. *Am. Ass. Petrol. Geol. Bull.*, **61**, 808.

Lighty, R. G., Macintyre, I. G. and Stuckenrath, R., 1978. Submerged early Holocene barrier reef south-east Florida shelf. *Nature*, **275**, 59–60.

Lighty, R. G., Macintyre, I. G. and Stuckenrath, R., 1979a. Holocene reef growth on the edge of the Florida shelf. *Nature*, **278**, 281–282.

Lighty, R. G., Macintyre, I. G. and Stuckenrath, R., 1979b. Shelf temperatures and reef growth on the south-east Florida coast: reply. *Nature*, **278**, 670.

LIMER, 1976. Metabolic processes of coral reef communities at Lizard Island, Queensland. *Search*, **7**, 463–468.

Littler, M. M., 1976. Calcification and its role among the macroalgae. *Micronesica*, **12**, 27–41.

Lloyd, A. R., 1968. Foraminifera from H.B.R. Wreck Island number 1 well and Heron Island bore, Queensland: their taxonomy and stratigraphic significance 1. Lituolacea and Miliolacea. *Bur. Min. Res. Geol. Geophys. Austr. Bull.*, **92**, 69–114.

Lloyd, A. R., 1973. Foraminifera of the Great Barrier Reef bores. In Jones, O. A. and Endean, R. (eds.) *Biology and Geology of Coral Reefs*, **I**, Geology I, 347–366.

Lloyd, A. R., 1977. The basement beneath the Queensland continental shelf. In Jones, O. A. and Endean, R. (eds.) *Biology and Geology of Coral Reefs*, **IV**, Geology II, 261–266.

Logan, A., 1977. Reef dwelling articulate brachiopods from Grand Cayman, B.W.I. *Proc. Third Int. Coral Reef Symp.*, **1**, 87–94.

Lourensz, R. S., 1977. *Tropical Cyclones in the Australian Region July 1969 to June 1975.* Bureau of Meteorology, Canberra, 111 pp.

Lovell, E. R., 1975. Evidence for a higher sea level in Moreton Bay, Queensland. *Mar. Geol.*, **18**, M87–M94.

Lowenstam, H. A., 1962. Magnetite in denticle capping in recent chitons. *Geol. Soc. Am. Bull.*, **73**, 435–438.

Lowenstam, H. A. and Epstein, S., 1957. On the origin of sedimentary aragonite needles of the Great Bahama Bank. *J. Geol.*, **65**, 364–375.

Ludington, C. A., 1979. Tidal modifications and associated circulation in a platform reef lagoon. *Aust. J. Mar. Freshw. Res.*, **30**, 425–430.

Lum, D. and Stearns, H. T., 1970. Pleistocene stratigraphy and eustatic history based on cores at Waimanolo, Oahu, Hawaii. *Geol. Soc. Am. Bull.*, **81**, 1–16.

Lyell, C., 1832. *Principles of Geology*, **2**, J. Murray, London, 330 pp.

Lyell, C., 1839. *Nouveaux Eléments de Geologie*. Pitois–Levrault, Paris, 648 pp.

Ma, T. Y. H., 1959. Effect of water temperature in growth rate of reef corals. *Oceanogr. Sin., Spec. Vol.* **I**, 1–116.

MacArthur, R. H. and Wilson, E. O., 1967. *The Theory of Island Biogeography.* Princeton Univ. Press, Princeton, 203 pp.

Macdonald, H. V., 1978. Design waves and design water levels, field data collection. In *Design for Tropical Cyclones*, Vol. 2, Dept. of Civil and Systems Engineering, James Cook University of North Queensland, 6 pp.

McDougall, I., 1964. Potassium-argon ages from lavas of the Hawaiian Islands. *Geol. Soc. Amer. Bull.*, **75**, 107–128.

MacGeachy, J. K., 1977. Factors controlling sponge boring in Barbados reef corals. *Proc. Third Int. Coral Reef Symp.*, **2**, 477–483.

MacGillivray, T., 1852. *Narrative of a Voyage of H.M.S. Rattlesnake, 1846–1850*, T. and W. Boone, London, 2 vols.

MacGillivray, W. D. K. and Rodway, F. A., 1931. Plants on islands of the Bunker and Capricorn Groups. *Repts. Gt. Barrier Reef Comm.*, **3**, 58–63.

Macintyre, I. G., 1972. Submerged reefs of the eastern Caribbean. *Amer. Assoc. Petrol. Geol. Bull.*, **56**, 720–738.

Macintyre, I. G., 1977. Distribution of submarine cements in a modern Caribbean fringing reef, Galeta Point, Panama. *J. Sed. Petrol.*, **47**, 503–516.

Macintyre, I. G. and Glynn, P., 1976. Evolution of modern Caribbean fringing reef, Galeta Point, Panama. *Amer. Assoc. Petrol. Geol. Bull.*, **60**, 1054–1072.

Macintyre, I. G. and Pilkey, O. H., 1969. Tropical reef corals: tolerance to low temperatures on the North Carolina continental shelf. *Science*, **166**, 374–375.

Macintyre, I. G. and Smith, S. V., 1974. X-radiographic studies of skeletal development in coral colonies. *Proc. Second Int. Coral Reef Symp.*, **2**, 277–287.

Macintyre, I. G., Burke, R. B. and Stuckenrath, R., 1977. Thickest recorded Holocene reef section, Isla Pérez core hole, Alacran Reef, Mexico, *Geology*, **5**, 749–754.

McKee, E. D., 1959. Storm sediments on a Pacific atoll. *J. Sed. Petrol.*, **29**, 354–364.

McLaren, C., 1842. The glacial theory of Professor Agassiz of Neuchàtel. *Amer. J. Sci.*, **42**, 346–365.

McLean, R. F., 1967a. Measurements of beachrock erosion by some tropical marine gastropods. *Bull. Mar. Sci.*, **17**, 551–561.

McLean, R. F., 1967b. Erosion burrows in beachrock by the tropical sea urchin *Echinometra lucunter*, *Can. J. Zool.*, **45**, 586–588.

McLean, R. F., 1972. Nomenclature for rock-destroying organisms. *Nature*, **240**, 490.

McLean, R. F., 1974. Geologic significance of bioerosion of beachrock. *Proc. Second Int. Coral Reef Symp.*, **2**, 401–408.

McLean, R. F. and Stoddart, D. R., 1978. Reef island sediments of the northern Great Barrier Reef. *Phil. Trans. Roy. Soc. London*, A, **291**, 101–117.

McLean, R. F., Stoddart, D. R., Hopley, D. and Polach, H., 1978. Sea level change in the Holocene on the northern Great Barrier Reef. *Phil. Trans. Roy. Soc. London*, A, **291**, 167–186.

MacNeil, F. S., 1954. The shape of atolls: an inheritance from subaerial erosion forms. *Amer. J. Sci.*, **252**, 402–427.

Maiklem, W. R., 1968a. The Capricorn reef complex, Great Barrier Reef, Australia. *J. Sed. Petrol.*, **37**, 1023–1030.

Maiklem, W. R., 1968b. Some hydraulic properties of bioclastic carbonate grains. *Sedimentology*, **10**, 101–109.

Malone, E. J., Olgers, F. and Kirkegaarde, A. G., 1969. The geology of the Duaringa and St. Lawrence 1:250,000 sheet areas. *Bur. Min. Res. Geol. Geophys. Rept.*, 121.

Mannheim, F. T., 1967. Evidence for submarine discharge of water on the Atlantic continental slope of the Southern United States and suggestions for future search. *Trans. N.Y. Acad. Sci.*, **29**, 839–853.

Manton, S. M., 1935. Ecological surveys of coral reefs. *Sci. Repts. Gt. Barrier Reef Exped.*, **3**, 274–312.

Maragos, J. E., 1972. A Study of the Ecology of Hawaiian Reef Corals. Unpubl. Ph.D. Thesis, Univ. of Hawaii, Honolulu.

Maragos, J. E., Baines, G. B. K. and Beveridge, P. J., 1973. Tropical cyclone creates a new land formation on Funafuti atoll. *Science*, **181**, 1161–1164.

Marks, E. O., 1925. Some doubts in Queensland physiography. *Proc. Roy. Soc. Qld.*, **36**, 3–18.

Marsh, J. A., 1976. Energetic role of algae in reef ecosystems. *Micronesica*, **12**, 13–21.

Marshall, J. F., 1971. Phosphatic sediments on the eastern Australian continental slope. *Bur. Min. Res. Austr. Rec.*, 1971/59.

Marshall, J. F., 1977. Marine geology of the Capricorn Channel area. *Bur. Min. Res. Geol. Geophys. Austr. Bull.*, **163**, 81 pp.

Marshall, J. F. and Davies, P. J., 1975. High magnesium calcite ooids from the Great Barrier Reef. *J. Sed. Petrol.*, **45**, 285–291.

Marshall, J. F. and Thom, B. G., 1976. The sea level in the last interglacial. *Nature*, **263**, 120–121.

Marshall, P., 1931. Coral reefs—rough water and calm water types. *Repts. Gt. Barrier Reef Comm.*, **3**, 64–72.

Marshall, P., Richards, H. C. and Walkom, A. B., 1925. Recent emergence at Holbourne Island, Great Barrier Reef. *Repts. Gt. Barrier Reef Comm.*, **1**, 29–34.

Marszalek, D. S., Babashoff, G., Noel, M. R. and Worley, D. R., 1977. Reef distribution in southern Florida. *Proc. Third Int. Coral Reef Symp.*, **2**, 224–229.

Mather, P. and Talbot, F. H., 1975. Research facilities on the Great Barrier Reef. *Search*, **6**, 335–338.

Matthews, R. K., 1968. Carbonate diagenesis: equilibration of sedimentary mineralogy to the sub-aerial environment, coral cap of Barbados, West Indies. *J. Sed. Petrol.*, **38**, 1110–1119.

Matthews, R. K., 1971. Diagenetic environments of possible importance to the explanation of cementation fabric in subaerially exposed carbonate sediments. In Bricker, O. P. (ed.) *Carbonate Cements*, 127–132.

Matthews, R. K., 1973. Relative elevation of late Pleistocene high sea level stands: Barbados uplift rates and their implications. *Quat. Res.*, **3**, 147–153.

Matthews, R. K., 1974. A process approach to diagenesis of reefs and reef associated limestones. In Laporte, L. F. (ed.) Reefs in Time and Space, *S.E.P.M. Spec. Publ.*, **18**, 234–256.

Maung Maung Aye, 1976. Variation in Drainage Basin Morphometry in North Queensland. Unpubl. M.A. Thesis, James Cook Univ. of N.Qld., Townsville, 282 pp.

Maxwell, W. G. H., 1962. Lithification of carbonate sediments, in the Heron Island Reef, Great Barrier Reef. *J. Geol. Soc. Austr.*, **8**, 217–238.

Maxwell, W. G. H., 1968. *Atlas of the Great Barrier Reef*, Elsevier, Amsterdam, 258 pp.

Maxwell, W. G. H., 1969. Radiocarbon ages of sediment: Great Barrier Reef. *Sed. Geol.*, **3**, 331–333.

Maxwell, W. G. H., 1970. Deltaic patterns in reefs. *Deep Sea Res.*, **17**, 1005–1018.

Maxwell, W. G. H., 1973a. Geomorphology of eastern Queensland in relation to the Great Barrier Reef. In Jones, O. A. and Endean, R. (eds.) *Biology and Geology of Coral Reefs*, **I**, Geology I, 233–272.

Maxwell, W. G. H., 1973b. Sediments of the Great Barrier Reef Province. In Jones, O. A. and Endean, R. (eds.) *Biology and Geology of Coral Reefs*, **I**, Geology I, 299–346.

Maxwell, W. G. H., 1976. Review of Reefs in Time and Space. Laporte, L. F. (ed.) S.E.P.M. Spec. Publ. 18, *Mar. Geol.*, **20**, 77–84.

Maxwell, W. G. H. and Swinchatt, J. P., 1970. Great Barrier Reef: regional variation in a terrigenous carbonate province. *Geol. Soc. Amer. Bull.*, **81**, 691–724.

Maxwell, W. G. H., Day, R. W. and Fleming, P. J. G., 1961. Carbonate sedimentation on the Heron Island reef, Great Barrier Reef. *J. Sed. Petrol.*, **31**, 215–230.

Maxwell, W. G. H., Jell, J. S. and McKellar, R. G., 1964. Differentiation of carbonate sediments on the Heron Island Reef. *J. Sed. Petrol.*, **34**, 294–308.

May, V., 1951. The marine algae of Brampton Island, Great Barrier Reef, off Mackay, Queensland. *Proc. Linn. Soc. N.S.W.*, **76**, 88–104.

Mayer, A. G., 1915. The lower temperatures at which reef corals lose their ability to capture food. *Carnegie Inst. Wash. Yearbook*, **14**, 212.

Mayer, A. G., 1924. Causes which produce stable conditions in the depth of the floors of Pacific fringing reef flats. *Carneg. Inst. Wash. Pap. Dept. Mar. Biol.*, **19**, 27–36.

Mesolella, K. J., 1967. Zonation of uplifted Pleistocene coral reefs on Barbados, West Indies. *Science*, **156**, 638–640.

Mesolella, K. J., 1968. The Uplifted Reefs of Barbados: Physical Stratigraphy, Facies Relationships and Absolute Chronology. Unpubl. Ph.D. Thesis, Brown Univ., Providence, R.I., 417 pp.

Mesolella, K. J., Matthews, P. K., Broeker, W. S. and Thurber, D. L., 1969. The astronomical theory of climatic change: Barbados data. *J. Geol.*, **77**, 250–274.

Mesollela, K. J., Sealy, H. A. and Matthews, R. K., 1970. Facies geometries within Pleistocene reefs on Barbados, West Indies. *Amer. Assoc. Petrol. Geol. Bull.*, **54**, 1890–1917.

Miller, J. A. and Macintyre, I. G., 1977. Field guidebook to the reefs of Belize. *Third Int. Coral Reef Symp. Field Guides*, 36 pp.

Milliman, J. D., 1973. Caribbean coral reefs. In Jones, O. A. and Endean, R. (eds.) *Biology and Geology of Coral Reefs*, **I**, Geology I, 1–50.

Milliman, J. D., 1974. *Marine Carbonates*, Recent Sedimentary Carbonates, 1. Springer-Verlag, Berlin, 375 pp.

Milliman, J. D. and Emery, K. O., 1968. Sea levels during the past 35,000 years. *Science*, **162,** 1121–1123.

Mitterer, R. M., 1971. Influence of natural organic matter on $CaCO_3$ precipitation. In Bricker, O. P. (ed.) *Carbonate Cements*, 252–258.

Mitterer, R. M., 1972. Biogeochemistry of aragonite mud and oolites. *Geochim. et Cosmochem. Acta.*, **36,** 1407–1422.

Montaggioni, L., 1976. Holocene submergence on Réunion Island (Indian Ocean). *Ann. S. Afr. Mus.*, **71,** 69–75.

Montaggioni, L. F., 1979. Le problème de l'absence de hauts stationnements marins d'âge holocène dans l'archipel des Mascareignes, Océan Indien occidental. *C. R. Acad. Sci. Paris*, 288-D, 1591–1594.

Moore, C. H. and Shedd, W. W., 1977. Effective rates of sponge bioerosion as a function of carbonate production. *Proc. Third Int. Coral Reef Symp.*, **2,** 499–505.

Moore, W. S. and Krishnaswami, S., 1974. Correlation of X-radiography revealed by banding in corals with radiometric growth rates. *Proc. Second Int. Coral Reef Symp.*, **2,** 269–276.

Moore, W. S. and Somayajulu, B. L. K., 1974. Age determinations of fossil corals using ^{230}Th/^{234}Th and ^{230}Th/^{227}Th. *J. Geophys. Res.*, **79,** 5065–5068.

Moorhouse, F. W., 1933. The recently-formed natural breastwork on Low Isles. *Repts. Gt. Barrier Reef Comm.*, **4,** 1, 35–36.

Moorhouse, F. W., 1936. The cyclone of 1934 and its effects on Low Isles, with special observations on *Porites*, *Repts. Gt. Barrier Reef Comm.*, **4,** 37–44.

Morgan, G. A., 1973. Sea state statistics for the Australian region. In *Report of Seminar on the Measurement and Application of Sea State Data*. Bureau of Meteorology, June, 1973, 9 pp., 182 figs.

Morita, R. Y., 1976. Anaerobic microbial calcite formation: Great Barrier Reef studies. *Abstr. Joint Oceanographic Assembly, Edinburgh 1976 FAO*, Rome, 117.

Mörner, N. A., 1971a. The position of the ocean level during the interstadial at about 30,000 B.P. A discussion from climatologic—glaciologic point of view. *Can. J. Earth Sci.*, **8,** 132–143.

Mörner, N. A., 1971b. Eustatic changes during the last 20,000 years and a method of separating the isostatic and eustatic factors in an uplifted area. *Palaeogeog. Palaeoclimatol. Paleoecol.*, **9,** 153–181.

Mörner, N. A., 1971c. The Holocene eustatic sea level problem. *Geol. Mijnb.*, **50,** 699–702.

Mörner, N. A., 1972. Isostasy, eustasy and crustal sensitivity. *Tellus*, **24,** 586–592.

Mörner, N. A., 1976. Eustasy and geoid changes. *J. Geol.*, **84,** 123–151.

Mörner, N. A., 1978. Faulting, fracturing and seismicity as functions of glacio-isostasy in Fennoscandia. *Geology*, **6,** 41–45.

Morton, J., 1974. The coral reefs of the British Solomon Islands: a comparative study of their composition and ecology. *Proc. Second Int. Coral Reef Symp.*, **2,** 31–53.

Motoda, S., 1939. Submarine illumination, silt content and quantity of food plankton of reef corals in Iwayama Bay, Palao. *Palao Trop. Biol. Stud.*, **1,** 637–650.

Muller, P. H., 1974. Sediment production and population biology of the benthic foraminifer *Amphistegina madagascariensis*. *Limnol. Oceanogr.*, **19,** 802–809.

Multer, H. G. and Hoffmeister, J. E., 1968. Subaerial laminated crusts of the Florida Keys. *Geol. Soc. Amer. Bull.*, **79,** 183–192.

Munk, W. H. and Sargent, M. C., 1948. Adjustment of Bikini Atoll to ocean waves. *Amer. Geophys. Union Trans.*, **29,** 855–860.

Munk, W. H. and Sargent, M. S., 1954. Adjustment of Bikini Atoll to ocean waves. *U.S. Geol. Surv. Prof. Paper*, **260-C,** 275–280.

Murray, C. G., 1975a. Port Clinton, Queensland. 1:250,000 Geological Series. *Bur. Min. Res. Geol. Geophys. Explan. Notes*, SF/56-9.

Murray, C. G., 1975b. Rockhampton, Queensland. 1:250,000 Geological Series. *Bur. Min. Res. Geol. Geophys. Explan. Notes*, SF/56-13.

Murray, J., 1880. On the structure and origin of coral reefs and islands. *Proc. Roy. Soc. Edinburgh*, **10,** 505–518.

Murray, J., 1887–1889. Structure, origin and distribution of coral reefs and islands. *Proc. Roy. Inst.*, **12**, 251–262.

Murray, J., 1889a. Coral reefs. *Nature*, **40**, 222.

Murray, J., 1889b. Structure, origin and distribution of coral reefs and islands. *Nature*, **39**, 424–428.

Murray, S. P., Roberts, H. H., Conlon, D. M. and Rudder, G. M., 1977. Nearshore current fields around coral islands: control of sediment accumulation and reef growth. *Proc. Third Int. Coral Reef Symp.*, **2**, 53–59.

Muscatine, L., 1973. Nutrition of corals. In Jones, O. A. and Endean, R. (eds.) *Biology and Geology of Coral Reefs*, **II**, Biology I, 77–115.

Muscatine, L. and Cernichiari, E., 1969. Assimilation of photosynthetic products of zooxanthellae by a reef coral. *Biol. Bull.*, **137**, 506–523.

Mutter, J. C., 1975. A structural analysis of the Gulf of Papua and north-west Coral Sea region. *Bur. Min. Res. Geophys. Rept.*, **179**.

Nelson, A. W., 1980. Preliminary results of a shallow marine seismic survey—Thursday Island to Townsville. *Geol. Surv. Qld. Rec. 1980/6*, 4 pp.

Nelson, C. S. and Rodgers, K. A., 1969. Algal stabilization of Holocene conglomerates by micritic high-magnesium calcite, southern New Caledonia. *N.Z. J. Mar. Freshw. Res.*, **3**, 395–408.

Nelson, R. C., 1975. Tropical cyclone storm surges in Australia 1880 to 1970. *Proc. Second Austr. Conf. on Coastal and Ocean Eng.*, 193–199.

Nesteroff, W. D., 1954. Sur la formation des grès de plage ou "beach-rock" en Mer Rouge. *C.R. Acad. Sci. Paris*, **238**, 2547–2548.

Nesteroff, W. D., 1959. Age de derniers mouvements du grabeu de la mer Rouge detérminé par la méthode du C^{14} appliquée aux récifs fossiles. *Bull. Soc. Géol. France*, **7**, 415–418.

Neumann, A. C., 1966. Observations on coastal erosion in Bermuda and measurements of the boring rate of the sponge *Cliona lampa*. *Limnol. Oceanog.*, **11**, 92–108.

Neumann, A. C., 1971. Quaternary sea level data from Bermuda. *Quaternaria*, **14**, 41–43.

Neumann, A. C., 1972. Quaternary sea level history of Bermuda and the Bahamas. *Amer. Quat. Assoc. Second Nat. Conf. Abstr.*, 41–44.

Neumann, A. C., Gebelein, C. D. and Scoffin, T. P., 1970. Composition, structure and erodability of subtidal mats, Abaco, Bahamas. *J. Sed. Petrol.*, **40**, 274–297.

Newell, N. D., 1956. Geological reconnaissance of the Raroia (Kon Tiki) Atoll, Tuamotu Archipelago. *Bull. Amer. Mus. Natl. Hist.*, **109**, 315–372.

Newell, N. D., 1961. Recent terraces of tropical limestone shores. *Zeits f. Geomorph. N.F. Suppl. Bd.* **3**, 87–106.

Newell, N. D. and Rigby, J. K., 1957. Geological studies on the Great Bahama Bank. In Regional Aspects of Carbonate Deposition, *S.E.P.M. Spec. Publ.*, **5**, 15–79.

Newell, N. D., Rigby, J. K., Whiteman, A. J. and Bradley, J. S., 1951. Shoal-water geology and environments, eastern Andros Island, Bahamas. *Bull. Amer. Mus. Nat. Hist.*, **97**, 1–30.

Newman, W. A., 1970. *Acanthaster*: a distaster? *Science*, **167**, 1274.

Nickerson, J. W., 1971. Storm surge fore-casting. *NAVYWEARSCHFAC, Tech. Rept.*, 10–71, 44 pp.

Nix, H. A. and Kalma, J. D., 1972. Climate as a dominant control in the biogeography of northern Australia and New Guinea. In Walker, D. (ed.) *Bridge and Barrier: the Natural and Cultural History of Torres Strait*, A.N.U. Canberra, 61–91.

Northrop, J. I., 1890. Notes on geology of Bahamas. *Trans. N.Y. Acad. Sci.*, **10**, 4–22.

Noshkin, V. E., Wong, K. M., Eagle, R. J. and Gatrousis, C., 1975. Transuranics and other radionuclides in Bikini lagoon: concentration data retrieved from aged coral sections. *Limnol. Oceanogr.*, **20**, 729–742.

Odum, H. T. and Odum, E. P., 1955. Trophic structure and productivity of a windward coral reef community on Eniwetak Atoll. *Ecol. Monogr.*, **25**, 291–320.

Oliver, J., 1973. Tropical cyclone: Australian weather example 1. *Austr. Geogr.*, **12**, 257–263.

Oliver, J., 1978a. The climatic environment of north and central Queensland. In Murray, R. M. and Entwistle, K. W. (eds.) *Beef Cattle Production in the Tropics*, Dept. of Trop. Vet. Sci., James Cook Univ. of N. Qld., 1–11.

Oliver, J., 1978b. The climatic environment of the Townsville area. In Hopley, D. (ed.) Geographical Studies of the Townsville Area. *Dept. of Geography, James Cook Univ. of N. Qld., Monograph Series, Occ. Papers,* **2,** 3–17.

Oliver, J., 1980. Considerations affecting palaeoclimatic models of north-eastern Australia. In Henderson, R. A. and Stephenson, P. J. (eds.) *The Geology and Geophysics of North-eastern Australia,* Geol. Soc. Austr. Qld. Divis., Brisbane, Chap. 21, 395–398.

Ollier, C. D., 1975. Coral island geomorphology—the Trobriand Islands. *Zeits. f. Geomorph. N.F.,* **19,** 164–190.

Ollier, C. D., 1977. Early landform evolution. In Jeans, D. N. (ed.) *Australia, a Geography,* 85–98.

Ollier, C. D., 1978. Tectonics and geomorphology of the Eastern Highlands. In Davies, J. L. and Williams, M. A. J. (eds.) *Landform Evolution in Australasia,* A.N.U. Canberra, 5–47.

Orme, G. R., 1977a. Aspects of sedimentation in the coral reef environment. In Jones, O. A. and Endean, R. (eds.) *Biology and Geology of Coral Reefs,* **IV,** Geology II, 129–182.

Orme, G. R. and Day, R. W., (eds.), 1978. Handbook of recent geological studies of Moreton Bay, Brisbane River and Stradbroke Island. *Pap. Dept. Geol. Univ. of Qld.,* **8** (2), 104 pp.

Orme, G. R. and Flood, P. G., 1977. The geological history of the Great Barrier Reef: a re-appraisal of some aspects in the light of new evidence. *Proc. Third Int. Coral Reef Symp.,* **2,** 37–43.

Orme, G. R., Flood, P. G. and Ewart, A. E., 1974. An investigation of the sediments and physiography of Lady Musgrave reef—a preliminary account. *Proc. Second Int. Coral Reef Symp.,* **2,** 371–386.

Orme, G. R., Webb, J. P., Kelland, N. C. and Sargent, G. E. G., 1978a. Aspects of the geological history and structure of the northern Great Barrier Reef. *Phil. Trans. Roy. Soc. London, A,* **291,** 23–35.

Orme, G. R., Flood, P. G. and Sargent, G. E. G., 1978b. Sedimentation trends in the lee of outer (ribbon) reefs, Northern Region of the Great Barrier Reef Province. *Phil. Trans. Roy. Soc. London, A,* **291,** 85–99.

Orr, A. P., 1933. Physical and chemical conditions in the sea in the neighbourhood of the Great Barrier Reef. *Sci. Repts. Gt. Barrier Reef Exped. 1928–29, Brit. Mus. (Nat. Hist.),* **2,** 37–98.

Orr, A. P. and Moorhouse, F. W., 1933. Variations in some physical and chemical conditions on and near Low Isles reef. *Sci. Repts. Gt. Barrier Reef Exped. 1928–29, Brit. Mus. (Nat. Hist.),* **2,** 87–98.

Otter, G. W., 1932. Rock-burrowing echinoids. *Biol. Rev.,* **7,** 89–107.

Otter, G. W., 1937. Rock-destroying organisms in relation to coral reefs. *Sci. Repts. Gt. Barrier Reef Exped. 1928–29, Brit. Mus. (Nat. Hist.),* **1,** 323–352.

Paine, A. G. L., 1972. Proserpine, Queensland, 1:250,000 Geological Series. *Bur. Min. Res. Geol. Geophys. Explan.* Notes, SF/55-4.

Paine, R. T. and Vadas, R. L., 1969. Calorific values of benthic marine algae and their postulated relationships to invertebrate food preferences. *Mar. Biol.,* **4,** 79–86.

Paine, A. G. L., Gregory, C. M. and Clarke, D. E., 1966. Geology of the Ayr, 1:250,000 sheet area, Queensland. *Bur. Min. Res. Geol. Geophys. Austr. Rec.,* 1966/68.

Palmieri, V., 1971. Tertiary subsurface biostratigraphy of the Capricorn basin. *Geol. Surv. Qld. Rept.,* **52,** 1–18.

Paradice, W. E. J., 1925. The pinnacle- or mushroom-shaped coral growths in connection with the reefs of the outer barrier. *Repts. Gt. Barrier Reef Comm.,* **1,** 52–59.

Pearson, R. G., 1974. Recolonization by hermatypic corals of reefs damaged by *Acanthaster. Proc. Second Int. Coral Reef Symp.,* **2,** 207–215.

Pearson, R. G., 1975. Coral reefs, unpredictable climatic factors and *Acanthaster. Crown of Thorns Starfish Seminar Proceedings Brisbane 1974,* 131–134.

Pedley, L. and Isbell, R. F., 1971. Plant communities of Cape York Peninsula. *Proc. Roy. Soc. Qld.,* **82,** 51–74.

Penck, A., 1894. *Morphologie der Erdoberfläche.* J. Engelhorn, Stuttgart, 2 vols.

Penck, A., 1896. Das grosse australische Wallriffe. *Vorträge Verein z. Verbr. Naturw. Kenntnisse in Wien,* **36,** No. 13.

de Peysonnel, A., 1727. Sur de corail. *Histoire de l'Académie royale des sciences,* 37–39.

Phillips, A. W., 1970. The use of the Woodhead sea bed drifter. *Brit. Geomorph. Res. Gr. Tech. Bull.,* **4,** 29 pp.

Phipps, C. V. G., 1970. Dating of eustatic events from cores taken in the Gulf of Carpentaria and samples from the New South Wales continental shelf. *Austr. J. Sci.,* **32,** 329–330.

Pichon, M., 1973. Recherches sur les peuplements á dominance d'Anthezoaires dans les récifs coralliens de Tuléar (Madagascar). *A.O. Centre Nat. Res. Sci. Paris,* 9255.

Pichon, M., 1974. Dynamics of benthic communities in the coral reefs of Tuléar (Madagascar): succession and transformation of the biotopes through reef tract evolution. *Proc. Second Int. Coral Reef Symp.,* **2,** 55–68.

Pichon, M., 1978. Récherches sur les peuplements á dominance d'Anthezoaires dans les recifs coralliens de Tuléar (Madagascar). *Atoll Res. Bull.,* **222,** 1–444.

Pickard, G. L., 1977. The Great Barrier Reef. In Pickard, G. L., Donguy, J. R., Henin, C. and Rougerie, F. A Review of the Physical Oceanography of the Great Barrier Reef and Western Coral Sea. *Aust. Inst. Mar. Sci. Monogr. Series,* **2,** 1–59.

Pickard, G. L., Donguy, J. R., Henin, C. and Rougerie, F., 1977. The Western Coral Sea. In Pickard, G. L., Donguy, J. R., Henin, C. and Rougerie, F. A Review of the Physical Oceanography of the Great Barrier Reef and Western Coral Sea. *Austr. Inst. Mar. Sci. Monogr. Series,* **2,** 61–127.

Pingitore, N. E., 1970. Diagenesis and porosity modification in *Acropora palmata,* Pleistocene of Barbados, West Indies. *J. Sed. Petrol.,* **40,** 712–722.

Pittman, E. D., 1974. Porosity and permeability changes during diagenesis of Pleistocene corals, Barbados, West Indies. *Geol. Soc. Amer. Bull.,* **85,** 1811–1820.

Polach, H. A., McLean, R. F., Caldwell, J. R. and Thom, B. G., 1978. Radiocarbon ages from the northern Great Barrier Reef. *Phil. Trans. Roy. Soc. London, A,* **291,** 139–158.

Pomponi, S., 1977. Etching cells of boring sponges: an ultrastructural analysis. *Proc. Third Int. Coral Reef Symp.,* **2,** 485–490.

Price, I. R., 1975. The development of algae on the skeletons of reef-building corals. *Crown of Thorns Starfish Seminar Proc., Brisbane, Sept. 1974,* 181–191.

Price, I. R., Larkum, A. W. D. and Bailey, A., 1976. Check list of marine benthic plants collected in the Lizard Island area. *Austr. J. Plant Physiol.,* **3,** 3–8.

Proctor, V. W., 1968. Long distance dispersal of seeds in digestive tracts of birds. *Science,* **160,** 321–322.

Purdy, E. G., 1974a. Reef configurations, cause and effect. In Laporte, L. F. (ed.) Reefs in Time and Space, *S.E.P.M., Spec. Publ.,* **18,** 9–76.

Purdy, E. G., 1974b. Karst-determined facies patterns in British Honduras: Holocene carbonate sedimentation model. *Amer. Assoc. Petrol. Geol. Bull.,* **58,** 825–855.

Puri, H. S. and Collier, A., 1967. Role of micro-organisms in formation of limestones. *Gulf Coast Geol., Soc. Trans.,* **17,** 355–367.

Quoy, J. R. and Gaimard, J. P., 1825. Mémoire sur l'accroissement des polypes lithophytes considéré géologiquement. *Annls. Sci. Nat.,* **6,** 373–390.

Rainford, E. H., 1925a. Destruction of the Whitsunday Group fringing reefs. *Austr. Mus. Mag.,* **2,** 175–177.

Rainford, E. H., 1925b. Letter to the Great Barrier Reef Committee. *Repts. Gt. Barrier Reef Comm.,* **1,** 161.

Randall, J. E., 1972. Chemical pollution in the sea and the crown of thorns starfish (*Acanthaster planci*). *Biotropica,* **4,** 132–144.

Ranson, G., 1955. La consolidation des sédiments calcaires dans les régions tropicales. *C. R. Acad. Sci. Paris,* **240,** 640–642.

Rattray, A., 1869. Notes on the geology of the Cape York Peninsula. *Geol. Soc. London Quart. J.,* **25,** 297–305.

Redfield, A. C., 1967. Post-glacial changes in sea level in the western North Atlantic Ocean. *Science*, **157**, 687–692.

Reid, J. H., 1946. Underground water supplies, Fitzroy River valley, Rockhampton district. *Qld. Govt. Min. J.*, **47**, 366–369.

Rein, J. J., 1870. Beiträge zur physikalischen Geographie der Bermuda-Inseln. *Bericht. Senckenb. Naturf. Gesell. Frankfurt a.M.*, 140–158.

Rein, J. J., 1881. Die Bermudas-Inseln und ihre Korallenriffe, nebst einem Nachtrage gegen die Darwińsche Senkungstheorie, Verhandl. *Deutschen Geograph.*, **1**, 19–46.

Resig, J. M., 1969. Palaeontological investigations of deep borings on the Ewa Plain, Oahu, Hawaii. *Hawaii Inst. Geophys.*, HIG-69-2, 1–99.

Revelle, R. and Emery, K. O., 1957. Chemical erosion of beachrock and exposed reef rock. *U.S. Geol. Surv. Prof. Pap.*, **260-T**, 699–709.

Rice, M. K., 1969. Possible boring structures of sipunculids. *Amer. Zool.*, **9**, 803–812.

Richards, H. C., 1923. The Great Barrier Reef of Australia. *Proc. Second Pan-Pac. Sci. Congr., Australia 1923*, **2**, 1104–1119.

Richards, H. C. and Hedley, C., 1925. A geological reconnaissance in North Queensland. *Repts. Gt. Barrier Reef Comm.*, **1**, 1–28.

Richards, H. S. and Hill, D., 1942. Great Barrier Reef bores, 1926 and 1937. Descriptions, analyses and interpretations. *Repts. Gt. Barrier Reef Comm.*, **5**, 1–122.

Rigby, J. K. and Roberts, H. H., 1976. Grand Cayman Island: geology, sediments and marine communities. *Brigham Young Univ. Geol. Stud. Spec. Publ.*, **4**, 17–26.

Risk, M. J. and MacGeachy, 1978. Aspects of bioerosion of modern Caribbean reefs. *Rev. Biol. Trop.*, 26 (Suppl.), 85–105.

Ristvet, B. L., Couch, R. F., Fetzer, J. A., Goter, E. R., Tremba, E. L., Walter, D. R. and Wendland, V. P., 1974. A Quaternary diagenetic history of Eniwetak Atoll. *Geol. Soc. Amer. Abstracts*, 715–716.

Ristvet, B. L., Couch, R. F., Fetzer, J. A., Goter, E. R., Tremba, E. L., Walter, D. R. and Woodland, V. P., 1975. General geology of Eniwetak Atoll. *Rept. AFWL-TR-75-xxx, Airforce Weapons Lab. Kirtland AFB.*

Roberts, H. H., 1974. Variability of reefs with regard to changes in wave power around an island. *Proc. Second Int. Coral Reef Symp.*, **2**, 497–512.

Roberts, H. H., Murray, S. P. and Suhayda, J. N., 1975. Physical processes in a fringing reef system. *J. Mar. Res.*, **23**, 233–260.

Roberts, H. H., Murray, S. P. and Suhayda, J. N., 1977. Physical processes on a fore-reef shelf environment. *Proc. Third Int. Coral Reef Symp.*, **2**, 507–515.

Rooney, W. S. and Perkins, R. D., 1972. Distribution and geologic significance of microboring organisms within sediments of the Arlington Reef complex, Australia. *Geol. Soc. Am. Bull.*, **83**, 1139–1150.

Roques, H., 1964. Contribution á l'étude statique et cinétique des systèmes gaz carbonique-eau-carbonate. *Ann. Spéléol.*, **19**, 255–484.

Roques, H., 1969. A review of present day problems in the physical chemistry of carbonates in solution. *Trans. Cave Res. Gp. Gt. Brit.*, **11**, 139–164.

Rosen, B. R., 1971a. Principle features of reef coral ecology in shallow water environments, Mahé Seychelles. In Stoddart, D. R. and Yonge, C. M. (eds.) Regional Variation in Indian Ocean Coral Reefs. *Symp. Zool. Soc. Lond.*, **28**, 163–184.

Rosen, B. R., 1971b. The distribution of reef coral genera in the Indian Ocean. In Stoddart, D. R. and Yonge, C. M. (eds.) Regional Variation in Indian Ocean Coral Reefs, *Symp. Zool. Soc. Lond.*, **28**, 263–299.

Rosen, B. R., 1975. The distribution of reef corals. *Rept. Underwater Assoc.* (n.s.), **1**, 1–16.

Ross, C. A., 1972. Biology and ecology of *Marginopora vertebralis* (Foraminiferida), Great Barrier Reef. *J. Protozool.*, **19**, 181–192.

Ross, J. R. P., 1974. Reef associated Ectoprocta from central region, Great Barrier Reef. *Proc. Second Int. Coral Reef Symp.*, **1**, 349–352.

Rubin, M. and Alexandre, C., 1958. Geological survey radiocarbon dates IV. *Science*, **127,** 1476–1487.

Runnels, D. D., 1969. Diagenesis, chemical sediments and the mixing of natural waters. *J. Sed. Petrol.*, **39,** 1188–1201.

Russell, R. J., 1959. Caribbean beachrock observations. *Zeits. f. Geomorph.*, *N.F.*, **3,** 227–236.

Russell, R. J., 1962. Origin of beachrock. *Zeits. f. Geomorph.*, *N.F.*, **6,** 1–16.

Russell, R. J., 1963. Beachrock. *J. Trop. Geog.*, **17,** 24–27.

Russell, R. J., 1967. *River Plains and Sea Coasts.* Univ. California Press, Berkeley and Los Angeles, 173 pp.

Russell, R. J. and MacIntyre, W. G., 1965. Southern hemisphere beachrock. *Geog. Rev.*, **55,** 17–45.

Rutzler, K. and Macintyre, I. G., 1978. Siliceous sponge spicules in coral reef sediments. *Mar. Biol.*, **49,** 147–159.

Ryland, J. S., 1974. Bryozoa of the Great Barrier Reef Province. *Proc. Second Int. Coral Reef Symp.*, **1,** 341–348.

Sachet, M-H., 1962. Geography and land ecology of Clipperton Island. *Atoll Res. Bull.*, **86,** 115 pp.

Sachet, M-H., 1974. State of knowledge of coral reefs as ecosystems. *Atoll Res. Bull.*, **172,** 121–169.

Saenger, P., 1979. Records of subtidal algae from the Swains Reef complex, Great Barrier Reef, Queensland. *Proc. Roy. Soc. Qld.*, **90,** 51–55.

Saint-Smith, E. C., 1919. Rock phosphate deposits on Holbourne Island near Bowen. *Qld. Govt. Min. J.*, **20,** 122.

Salvat, B., Richard, G., Poli, G., Chevalier, J. P. and Bagnis, R., 1977. Geomorphology and biology of Taiaro atoll, Tuamotu Archipelago. *Proc. Third Int. Coral Reef Symp.*, **2,** 289–295.

Sargent, M. C. and Austin, T. S., 1954. Biologic economy of coral reefs. *U.S. Geol. Surv. Prof. Pap.*, **260-E,** 293–300.

Saville-Kent, W., 1893. *The Great Barrier Reef of Australia: Its Products and Potentialities.* Allan, London, 387 pp.

Savin, S. M., 1977. The history of the earth's surface temperature during the past 100 million years. *Ann. Rev. Earth Planet. Sci.*, **5,** 319–355.

Schlanger, S. O., 1963. Subsurface geology of Eniwetok Atoll. *U.S. Geol. Surv. Prof. Pap.*, **260-BB,** 991–1066.

Schmalz, R. F., 1967. Kinetics and diagenesis of carbonate sediments. *J. Sed. Petrol.*, **39,** 1188–1201.

Schmalz, R. F., 1971. Formation of beachrock at Eniwetok Atoll. In Bricker, O. P. (ed.) *Carbonate Cements*, 17–24.

Schmalz, R. F. and Swanson, F. S., 1969. Diurnal variations in the carbonate saturation of seawater. *J. Sed. Petrol.*, **39,** 255–267.

Schofield, J. C., 1977a. Late Holocene sea-level, Gilbert and Ellice Islands, west central Pacific Ocean. *N. Z. J. Geol. Geophys.*, **20,** 503–529.

Schofield, J. C., 1977b. Effect of late Holocene sea-level fall on atoll development. *N. Z. J. Geol. Geophys.*, **20,** 531–536.

Scholl, D. W. and Stuiver, M., 1967. Recent submergence of southern Florida: a comparison with adjacent coasts and other eustatic data. *Geol. Soc. Amer. Bull.*, **78,** 437–454.

Schopf, T. J. M., 1974. Ectoprocts as associates of coral reefs: St. Croix, U.S. Virgin Islands. *Proc. Second Int. Coral Reef Symp.*, **1,** 353–356.

Schott, G., 1935. *Geographie des Indischen und Stillen Ozeans.* C. Boysen, Hamburg.

Schubert, C., 1977. Pleistocene marine terraces of La Blanquila Island, Venezuela, and their diagenesis. *Proc. Third Int. Coral Reef Symp.*, **2,** 149–154.

Schuhmacher, H., 1977. Ability in fungiid corals to overcome sedimentation. *Proc. Third Int. Coral Reef Symp.*, **1,** 503–509.

Schumm, S. A., 1965. Quaternary palaeohydrology. In Wright, H. E. and Frey, D. G. (eds.) *The Quaternary of the United States.* Princeton Univ. Press, Princeton, N. J., 789–794.

Scoffin, T. P., 1970. The trapping and binding of subtidal carbonate sediments by marine vegetation in Bimini Lagoon, Bahamas. *J. Sed. Petrol.*, **40**, 249–273.

Scoffin, T. P., 1977. Sea-level features on reefs in the northern province of the Great Barrier Reef. *Proc. Third Int. Coral Reef Symp.*, **2**, 319–324.

Scoffin, T. P. and Garrett, P., 1974. Processes in the formation and preservation of internal structures in Bermuda patch reefs. *Proc. Second Int. Coral Reef Symp.*, **2**, 429–448.

Scoffin, T. P. and McLean, R. F., 1978. Exposed limestones of the northern province of the Great Barrier Reef. *Phil. Trans. Roy. Soc. London, A*, **291**, 119–138.

Scoffin, T. P. and Stoddart, D. R., 1978. The nature and significance of micro atolls. *Phil. Trans. Roy. Soc. London, B*, **284**, 99–122.

Scoffin, T. P., Stoddart, D. R., McLean, R. F. and Flood, P. G., 1978. Recent development of reefs in the Northern Province of the Great Barrier Reef. *Phil. Trans. Roy. Soc. London, B*, **284**, 129–139.

Scoffin, T. P., Stearn, C. W., Boucher, D., Frydal, P., Hawkins, C. M., Hunter, I. G. and Mac-Geachy, J. K., 1980. Calcium carbonate budget of a fringing reef on the west coast of Barbados II Erosion, sediments and internal structure. *Bull. Mar. Sci.*, **302**, 475–508.

Searle, D. E. and Harvey, N., in press. Seismic investigations of late Quaternary reefal and inter-reefal sediments of the Great Barrier Reef province. In Barnes, D. J. (ed.) *Growth, Maintenance and Change of Coral Reefs.* Austr. Inst. Mar. Sci., Townsville.

Searle, D. E., Davies, P. J., Hekel, H., Kennard, J., Marshall, J. F. and Thom, B. G., 1978. Preliminary results of a continuous seismic profiling survey in the Capricorn Group, Southern Great Barrier Reef. *Geol. Surv. Qld. Rec.* 1978/46.

Searle, D. E., Harvey, N. and Hopley, D., 1980. Preliminary results of continuous seismic profiling on the Great Barrier Reef province between 16°10'S and 19°20'S. *Geol. Surv. Qld. Rec.* 1980/23, 32 pp.

Semper, C., 1863. Reisebericht (Palau-Inseln). *Zeits. f. Wiss. Zool.*, **13**, 558–570.

Semper, C., 1873. *Die Palau-Inseln im Stillen Ocean.* Leipzig.

Semper, C., 1880. *Die natürliche Existenzbedingungen der Thiere.* Leipzig (Eng. transl. 1881, *The Natural Conditions of Existence as they Affect Animal Life,* Kegan, Paul, Trench, Trubner and Co., London, 472 pp.

Shackleton, N. J., 1978. Some results of the CLIMAP project. In Pittock, A. B., Frakes, L. A., Jenssen, D., Peterson, J. A. and Zillman, J. W. (eds.) *Climatic Change and Variability, a Southern Perspective,* 69–76.

Shackleton, N. J. and Opdyke, N. D., 1973. Oxygen isotope and palaeo-magnetic stratigraphy of Equatorial Pacific core V28-238: oxygen isotope temperatures and ice volumes in a 10^5 year and 10^6 year scale. *Quat. Res.*, **3**, 39–55.

Shepard, F. P., 1964. Sea level changes in the past 6,000 years: possible archaeological significance. *Science*, **143**, 574–576.

Shepard, F. P. and Wanless, H. R., 1971. *Our Changing Coastlines.* McGraw-Hill, New York, 579 pp.

Sheridan, R., 1974. Atlantic continental margin of North America. In Burke, C. A. and Drake, C. L. (eds.) *The Geology of Continental Margins,* N.Y., Springer-Verlag, 391–407.

Shinn, E., 1963. Spur and groove formation on the Florida reef tract. *J. Sed. Petrol.*, **33**, 291–303.

Shinn, E. A., 1969. Submarine lithification of Holocene carbonate sediments in the Persian Gulf. *Sedimentology*, **12**, 109–144.

Shinn, E. A., Hudson, J. H., Halley, R. B. and Lidz, B., 1977. Topographic control and accumulation rate of some Holocene coral reefs: South Florida and Dry Tortugas. *Proc. Third Int. Coral Reef Symp.*, **2**, 1–7.

Silvester, R. and Mitchell, H. L., 1977. Storm surges around Australian coastlines. *Proc. Third Aust. Conf. Coastal and Ocean Eng.*, 49–57.

Sissons, J. B., 1972. Dislocations and non-uniform uplift of raised shorelines in the western part of the Forth valley. *Trans. Inst. Brit. Geog.*, **55**, 145–160.

Skinner, A. F., Gillies, C. C. and Milton, L. E., 1972. An Erosion Survey of the Upper Nogoa River Catchement. *Div. of Land Utilization, Dept. of Prim. Ind. Tech. Bull.*, **6**.

Slack-Smith, R. J., 1960. An investigation of coral deaths at Peel Island, Moreton Bay, in early 1956. *Univ. Qld., Dept. Zool. Pap.*, **1** (7), 211–222.

Slater, R. A. and Phipps, C. V. G., 1977. A preliminary report on the coral reefs of Lord Howe Island and Elizabeth Reef. *Proc. Third Int. Coral Reef Symp.*, **2**, 313–318.

Smart, J. and Senior, B. R., 1980. Jurassic-Cretaceous basins of north-eastern Australia. In Henderson, R. A. and Stephenson, P. J. (eds.) *The Geology and Geophysics of North-eastern Australia*, 315–328.

Smart, J., Powell, B. S. and Gibson, D. L., 1974. Auger drilling, northern Cape York Peninsula, 1973. *Bur. Min. Res. Geol. Geophys. Rec.*, 1974/75.

Smith, A. S., 1974. Classification and Distribution of Sediments on some North Queensland Fringing Reefs. Unpubl. M.A. Thesis, Dept. of Geog., James Cook Univ. of N. Qld., Townsville.

Smith, A. S., 1978. Magnetic Island and its fringing reefs. In Hopley, D. (ed.) Geographical Studies of the Townsville Area. *Dept. of Geog., James Cook Univ. of N. Qld. Monogr. Ser. Occ. Pap.*, **2**, 59–64.

Smith, D. F., 1977. Primary productivities of two foraminifera—zooxanthellae symbionts. *Proc. Third Int. Coral Reef Symp.*, **1**, 593–598.

Smith, D. I. and Atkinson, T. C., 1976. Processes, landforms and climate in limestone regions. In Derbyshire, E. (ed.) *Geomorphology and Climate*, Wiley, London, 367–409.

Smith, J. F. and Albritton, C. C., 1941. Solution effects on limestone as a function of slope. *Geol. Soc. Amer. Bull.*, **52**, 61–78.

Smith, P. T., 1972. Geomechanical Properties of Coral Rock. Unpubl. B. Eng. Thesis, James Cook Univ. of N. Qld.

Smith, S. V., 1977. Kaneohe Bay: a preliminary report on the responses of a coral reef/estuary ecosystem to relaxation of sewage stress. *Proc. Third Int. Coral Reef Symp.*, **2**, 577–583.

Smith, S. V., 1978. Coral-reef area and the contributions of reefs to processes and resources of the World's oceans. *Nature*, **273**, 225–226.

Smith, S. V. and Harrison, J. T., 1977. Calcium carbonate production of the "Mare Incognitum" of the upper windward reef slope at Enewetak atoll. *Science*, **197**, 556–559.

Smith, S. V. and Kinsey, D. W., 1976. Calcium carbonate production, coral reef growth, and sea level change. *Science*, **194**, 937–939.

Smith, S. V. and Kinsey, D. W., 1978. Calcification organic carbon metabolism as indicated by carbon dioxide. In Stoddart, D. R. and Johannes, R. E. (eds.) *Coral Reefs: Research Methods*, UNESCO, 469–484.

Smith, S. V. and Marsh, J. A., 1973. Organic carbon production on the windward reef flat of Eniwetok Atoll. *Limnol. and Oceanog.*, **18**, 953–961.

Smith, S. V., Jokiel, P. L. and Key, G. S., 1978. Biogeochemical budgets in coral reef systems. *Atoll Res. Bull.*, **220**, 1–11.

Sneh, A. and Friedman, G. M., 1980. Spur and groove patterns on the reefs of the northern gulfs of the Red Sea. *J. Sed. Petrol.*, **50**, 981–986.

Sorokin, Y. I., 1973. Microbiological aspects of the productivity of coral reefs. In Jones, O. A. and Endean, R. (eds.) *Biology and Geology of Coral Reefs*, **II**, Biology I, 17–45.

Sorokin, Y. I., 1974. Bacteria as a component of the coral reef community. *Proc. Second Int. Coral Reef Symp.*, **1**, 3–10.

Soule, J. D. and Soule, D. F., 1974. The bryozoan-coral interface on coral and coral reefs. *Proc. Second Int. Coral Reef Symp.*, **1**, 335–340.

Sournia, A., 1976. Primary production of sands in the lagoon of an atoll and the role of foraminifera symbionts. *Mar. Biol.*, **37**, 29–32.

Spenceley, A. P., 1976. Unvegetated saline tidal flats in North Queensland. *J. Trop. Geog.*, **42**, 78–85.

Spenceley, A. P., 1977. The role of pneumatophores in sedimentary processes. *Marine Geol.*, **24**, M31–M37.

Spencer-Davis, P., 1977. Carbon budgets and vertical zonation of Atlantic reef corals. *Proc. Third Int. Coral Reef Symp.*, **1**, 391–396.

Spender, M. A., 1930. Island reefs of the Queensland coast. *Geog. J.*, **76**, 194–214, 273–297.

Spillane, K. T. and Dexter, P. E., 1976. Design waves and wind in the Australian tropics. *Austr. Meteorol. Mag.*, **24** (2), 37–58.

Stanley, G. A. V., 1928. The physiography of the Bowen district and of the northern isles of the Cumberland Group. *Repts. Gt. Barrier Reef Comm.*, **2**, 1–51.

Stark, K. P., 1978. Storm surges and sea characteristics associated with tropical cyclones. In *Design for Tropical Cyclones*, **1**, Dept. of Civil and Systems Engineering, James Cook Univ. of N. Qld.

Stark, L. M., Almodovar, L. and Krauss, R. W., 1969. Factors affecting the rate of calcification in *Halimeda opuntia* (L.) Lamouroux and *Halimeda discoidea* Decaisne. *J. Phycol.*, **5**, 305–312.

Stearn, C. W. and Scoffin, T. P., 1977. Carbonate budget of a fringing reef, Barbados. *Proc. Third Int. Coral Reef Symp.*, **2**, 471–476.

Stearn, C. W., Scoffin, T. P. and Martindale, W., 1977. Calcium carbonate budget of a fringing reef on the west coast of Barbados, Pt 1—zonation and productivity. *Bull. Mar. Sci.*, **27**, 479–510.

Stearns, H. T., 1946. An integration of coral reef hypotheses. *Amer. J. Sci.*, **244**, 245–262.

Stearns, H. T., 1961. Eustatic shorelines on Pacific Islands. In Russell, R. J. (ed.) Pacific Island Terraces: Eustatic? *Zeits. f. Geomorph. Supp. Bd.*, **3**, 3–16.

Steers, J. A., 1929. The Queensland coast and the Great Barrier Reef. *Geog. J.*, **74**, 232–257, 341–370.

Steers, J. A., 1937. The coral islands and associated features of the Great Barrier Reefs. *Geog. J.*, **89**, 1–28, 119–146.

Steers, J. A., 1938. Detailed notes on the islands surveyed and examined by the geographical expedition to the Great Barrier Reef in 1936. *Repts. Gt. Barrier Reef Comm.*, **4**, Pt. 3, 51–96.

Steers, J. A., 1945. Coral reefs and air photography. *Geog. J.*, **106**, 232–235.

Steers, J. A. and Stoddart, D. R., 1977. The origin of fringing reefs, barrier reefs and atolls. In Jones, O. A. and Endean, R. (eds.) *Geology and Biology of Coral Reefs*, **IV**, Geology II, 21–57.

Steinen, R. P., 1974. Phreatic and vadose diagenetic modification of Pleistocene limestone: petrographic observations from the subsurface of Barbados, West Indies. *Amer. Assoc. Petrol. Geol. Bull.*, **58**, 1008–1024.

Steinen, R. P., Harrison, R. S. and Matthews, R. K., 1973. Eustatic low stand of sea level between 105,000 and 125,000 B.P.: evidence from the subsurface of Barbados, West Indies. *Geol. Soc. Amer. Bull.*, **84**, 63–70.

Stephenson, P. J., 1970. The Townsville-Charters Towers area: physiography. *1970 Field Conf. Townsville-Charters Towers Guidebook*, Geol. Soc. Austr., Qld. Div., 51 pp.

Stephenson, P. J. and Griffin, T. J., 1976. Some long basaltic lava flows in north Queensland. In Johnson, W. R. (ed.) *Volcanism in Australasia*, 41–51.

Stephenson, P. J., Griffin, T. J. and Sutherland, P. L., 1980. Cainozoic volcanism in northeastern Australia. In Henderson, R. A. and Stephenson, P. J. (eds.) *The Geology and Geophysics of Northeastern Australia*, Geol. Soc. Austr., Qld. Div., Brisbane, Chap. 20, 349–374.

Stephenson, T. A., Tandy, G. and Spender, M. A., 1931. The structure and ecology of Low Islands and other reefs. *Sci. Repts. Gt. Barrier Reef Exped. 1928-29, Brit. Mus. (Nat. Hist.)*, **3** (2), 17–112.

Stephenson, W., 1961. Experimental studies of the ecology of intertidal environments at Heron Island II. The effects of substratum. *Austr. J. Mar. Freshw. Res.*, **12**, 164–176.

Stephenson, W. and Searles, R. B., 1960. Experimental studies on the ecology of intertidal environments at Heron Island I. Exclusion of fish from beachrock. *Austr. J. Mar. Freshw. Res.*, **11**, 241–267.

Stephenson, W., Endean, R. and Bennett, I., 1958. An ecological survey of the marine fauna of Low Isles, Queensland. *Austr. J. Mar. Freshw. Res.*, **9**, 261–318.

Stephenson, W., Cook, S. D. and Raphael, Y. I., 1977. The effect of a major flood on the macrobenthos of Bramble Bay, Queensland. *Mem. Qld. Mus.*, **18**, (1), 95–119.

Stewart, J., 1973. Rainfall Trends in North Queensland. *Dept. of Geog., James Cook Univ. of N.Qld., Monogr. Ser.*, **4**, 197 pp.

Stocker, G. C., 1971. The age of charcoal from jungle fowl nests and vegetation change on Melville Island. *Search*, **2**, 28–30.

Stockman, K. W., Ginsburg, R. N. and Shinn, E. A., 1967. The production of lime mud by algae in South Florida. *J. Sed. Petrol.*, **37**, 633–648.

Stoddart, D. R., 1962a. Three Caribbean atolls: Turneffe Islands, Lighthouse Reef and Glover's Reef, British Honduras. *Atoll Res. Bull.*, **87**, 151 pp.

Stoddart, D. R., 1962b. Catastrophic storm effects on the British Honduras reefs and cays. *Nature*, **196**, 512–515.

Stoddart, D. R., 1963. Effects of hurricane Hattie on the British Honduras reefs and cays, October 30–31, 1961. *Atoll Res. Bull.*, **95**, 1–142.

Stoddart, D. R., 1964. Storm conditions and vegetation in equilibrium of reef islands. *Proc. Ninth Conf. Coast. Eng.*, 893–906.

Stoddart, D. R., 1965a. British Honduras cays and the Low Wooded Island problem. *Trans. Inst. Brit. Geog.*, **36**, 131–147.

Stoddart, D. R., 1965b. The shape of atolls. *Mar. Geol.*, **3**, 369–383.

Stoddart, D. R., 1965c. Re-survey of hurricane effects on the British Honduras reefs and cays. *Nature*, **207**, 589–592.

Stoddart, D. R., 1966. Darwin's impact on geography. *Ann. Assoc. Amer. Geog.*, **56**, 683–698.

Stoddart, D. R., 1969a. Ecology and morphology of Recent coral reefs. *Biol. Rev.*, **44**, 433–498.

Stoddart, D. R., 1969b. Post-hurricane changes on the British Honduras reefs and cays: re-survey of 1965. *Atoll Res. Bull.*, **131**, 1–25.

Stoddart, D. R., 1969c. Geomorphology of the Solomon Islands coral reefs. *Phil. Trans. Roy. Soc., London, B.*, **255**, 355–382.

Stoddart, D. R., 1971. Coral reefs and islands and catastrophic storms. In Steers, J. A. (ed.) *Applied Coastal Geomorphology*, 155–197.

Stoddart, D. R., 1972a. Catastrophic damage to coral reef communities by earthquake. *Nature*, **239**, 51–52.

Stoddart, D. R., 1972b. Regional variation in Indian Ocean coral reefs. *Proc. Symp. on Corals and Coral Reefs, Mar. Biol. Assoc. India*, 155–174.

Stoddart, D. R., 1973a. Coral reefs: the last two million years. *Geog.*, **58**, 313–323.

Stoddart, D. R., 1973b. Coral reefs of the Indian Ocean. In Jones, O. A. and Endean, R. (eds.) *Biology and Geology of Coral Reefs*, **I**, Geology I, 51–92.

Stoddart, D. R., 1974. Post-hurricane changes on the British Honduras reefs: re-survey of 1972. *Proc. Second Int. Coral Reef Symp.*, **2**, 473–483.

Stoddart, D. R., 1976. Continuity and crisis in the reef community. *Micronesica*, **12**, 1–9.

Stoddart, D. R., 1980. Mangroves as successional stages, inner reefs of the northern Great Barrier Reef. *J. Biogeog.*, **7**, 269–284.

Stoddart, D. R. and Cann, J. R., 1965. Nature and origin of beach rock. *J. Sed. Petrol.*, **35**, 243–247.

Stoddart, D. R. and Johannes, R. E. (eds.) 1978. *Coral Reefs: Research Methods*, UNESCO, Paris, 581 pp.

Stoddart, D. R. and Scoffin, T. P., 1979. Microatolls: review of form, origin and terminology. *Atoll Res. Bull.*, **224**, 1–17.

Stoddart, D. R. and Steers, J. A., 1977. The nature and origin of coral reef islands. In Jones, O. A. and Endean, R. (eds.) *Biology and Geology of Coral Reefs*, **IV**, Geology II, 59–105.

Stoddart, D. R., Taylor, J. D., Fosberg, F. R. and Farrow, J. E., 1971. The geomorphology of Aldabra Atoll. *Phil. Trans. Roy. Soc. London, B*, **260**, 31–65.

Stoddart, D. R., McLean, R. F. and Hopley, D., 1978a. Geomorphology of reef islands, northern Great Barrier Reef. *Phil. Trans. Roy. Soc. London, B*, **284**, 39–61.

Stoddart, D. R., McLean, R. F., Scoffin, T. P., Thom, B. G. and Hopley, D., 1978b. Evolution of reefs and islands, northern Great Barrier Reef: synthesis and interpretation. *Phil. Trans. Roy. Soc. London, B*, **284**, 149–159.

Stoddart, D. R., McLean, R. F., Scoffin, T. P. and Gibbs, P. E., 1978c. Forty-five years of change on low wooded islands, Great Barrier Reef. *Phil. Trans. Roy. Soc. London, B*, **284,** 63–80.

Stoddart, D. R. et al, in press. Natural history of Raine Island, Great Barrier Reef. *Atoll Res. Bull.*

Storr, J. F., 1964. Ecology and oceanography of the coral reef tract, Abaco Islands, Bahamas. *Geol. Soc. Amer. Spec. Pap.*, **79,** 1–98.

Story, R., 1970. Vegetation of the Mitchell-Normanby area. *C.S.I.R.O. Land Res. Ser.*, **26,** 75–88.

Straughan, D., 1967. Some Serpulidae (Annelida: Polychaeta) from Heron Island, Queensland. *Univ. Qld., Gt. Barrier Reef Comm., Heron Is. Res. Stat. Pap.*, **1,** 27–45.

Suess, E., 1888. *Das Antlitz der Erde*. Tempsky, Vienna.

Suess, E., 1969. Interaction of organic compounds with calcium carbonate. I Associated phenomena and geochemical implications. *Geochem. et Cosmochem. Acta*, **34,** 157–168.

Sugden, W., 1972. The Great Barrier Reef. In Dept. of Nat. Devel. *Burdekin-Townsville Resource Ser., Landforms.* Appendix, **1,** 25–27.

Suhayda, J. N. and Roberts, H. H., 1977. Wave action and sediment transport on fringing reefs. *Proc. Third Int. Coral Reef Symp.*, **2,** 65–70.

Supko, P. R., Marszalek, D. and Bock, W., 1970. Sedimentary environments and carbonate rocks of Bimini, Bahamas. *Fourth Ann. Field Trip Miami Geol. Soc.*, 1–30.

Sweeting, M. M., 1972. *Karst Landforms*, MacMillan, London, 362 pp.

Swift, D., 1974. Continental shelf sedimentation. In Burke, C. A. and Drake, C. L. (eds.) *The Geology of Continental Margins*, Springer-Verlag, New York, 117–135.

Szabo, B. J., 1979. Uranium-series age of coral reef growth on Rottnest Island, Western Australia. *Mar. Geol.*, **29,** M11–M15.

Szabo, B. J., Ward, W. C., Weidie, A. E. and Brady, M. J., 1978. Age and magnitude of the late Pleistocene sea-level rise on the eastern Yucatan Peninsula. *Geology*, **6,** 713–715.

Taft, W. H. and Harbaugh, J. W., 1964. Modern carbonate sediments of southern Florida, Florida and Espiritu Santo Island, Baja, California: a comparison of their mineralogy and chemistry. *Stanford Univ. Publ. Geol. Sci.*, **8,** (2), 133 pp.

Tait, R. J., 1972. Wave set-up on coral reefs. *J. Geophys. Res.*, **77,** 2207–2211.

Tanner, J. J., 1969. The ancestral Great Barrier Reef in the Gulf of Papua. *E.C.A.F.E., Conf., Canberra*, 1969, 1–5.

Tayama, R., 1952. Coral reefs of the South Seas. *Bull. Hydrogr. Dept. Tokyo*, **11,** 1–292.

Taylor, D. L., 1977. Microbiology of coral reefs. *Proc. Third Int. Coral Reef Symp.*, **1,** xxiii–xxiv.

Taylor, J. C. M. and Illing, L. V., 1971. Development of Recent cemented layers within intertidal sand flats, Qatar, Persian Gulf. In Bricker, O. P. (ed.) *Carbonate Cements*, 27–31.

Taylor, T., 1924. Movement of sand cays. *Qld. Geog. J.*, **39,** 38–39.

Taylor, T. G., 1911. Physiography of eastern Australia. *Bull. Comm. Bur. Meteorol.*, **8,** 1–17.

Taylor, F. W., 1974. The Uplifted Reef Tracts of Barbados, West Indies. Detailed Mapping and Radiometric Dating of Selected Areas. Unpubl. M.S. Thesis, Brown Univ., Providence, R.I., 235 pp.

Taylor, F. W. and Bloom, A. L., 1977. Coral reefs on tectonic blocks, Tonga island arc. *Proc. Third Int. Coral Reef Symp.*, **2,** 275–281.

Taylor, J. D., 1971. Reef associated molluscan assemblages in the Western Indian Ocean. In Stoddart, D. R. and Yonge, C. M. (eds.) *Regional Variation in Indian Ocean Coral Reefs, Proc. Symp. Zool. Soc. London*, **28,** 501–534.

Taylor, L. and Falvey, D., 1977. The Queensland Plateau and Coral Sea Basin: stratigraphy, structure and tectonics. *A.P.E.A.*, **17,** 13–29.

Taylor, R. C., 1973. An atlas of Pacific islands rainfall. *Hawaii Inst. Geophys. Data Rept.*, **25.**

Tebbutt, G. E., 1975. Paleoecology and diagenesis of Pleistocene limestone on Ambergris cay, Belize. In Wantland, K. F. and Pusey, W. C. (eds.) Belize Shelf—Carbonate Sediments, Clastic Sediments, and Ecology. *Amer. Assoc. Petrol. Geol. Studies in Geol.*, **2,** 297–331.

Teichert, C. and Fairbridge, R. W., 1950. Photo interpretation of coral reefs. *Photogramm. Eng.*, **16,** 744–755.

Thom, B. G., 1973. The dilemma of high interstadial sea levels during the last glaciation. *Prog. in Geog.*, **5,** 170–246.

Thom, B. G., 1978. Coastal sand deposition in Southeast Australia during the Holocene. In Davies, J. L. and Williams, M. A. J. (eds.) *Landform Evolution in Australasia*, 197–214.

Thom, B. G. and Chappell, J., 1975. Holocene sea levels relative to Australia. *Search*, **6**, 90–93.

Thom, B. G. and Chappell, J., 1978. Holocene sea level change: an interpretation. *Phil. Trans. Roy. Soc. London, A*, **291**, 187–194.

Thom, B. G., Hails, J. R. and Martin, A. R. H., 1969. Radiocarbon evidence against higher post-glacial sea levels in eastern Australia. *Mar. Geol.*, **7**, 161–168.

Thom, B. G., Hails, J. R., Martin, A. R. H. and Phipps, C. V. G., 1972. Post-glacial sea levels in eastern Australia—a reply. *Mar. Geol.*, **12**, 233–242.

Thom, B. G., Orme, G. R. and Polach, H. A., 1978. Drilling investigation of Bewick and Stapleton Islands. *Phil. Trans. Roy. Soc., London, A*, **291**, 37–54.

Thomassin, B. A. and Ganelon, P., 1977. Molluscan, assemblages on the boulder tracts of Tuléar coral reefs (Madagascar). *Proc. Third Int. Coral Reef Symp.*, **1**, 247–252.

Thomson, J. and Walton, A., 1972. Redetermination of chronology of Aldabra Atoll by $^{230}U/^{234}U$ dating. *Nature*, **240**, 145–146.

Thomson, W. C., 1905. Upheavals and depressions in the Pacific and on the Australian coast. *Qld. Geog. J.*, **20**, 1–8.

Thrailkill, J. V., 1968. Chemical and hydrological factors in the excavation of limestone caves. *Geol. Soc. Amer. Bull.*, **79**, 19–45.

Thurber, D. L., Broeker, W. S., Blanchard, R. L. and Potratz, H. A., 1965. Uranium-series ages of Pacific atoll coral. *Science*, **149**, 55–58.

Tjia, H. D., Fujii, S., Kigoshi, K. and Sugimura, A., 1974. Late Quaternary uplift in eastern Indonesia. *Tectonophysics*, **23**, 427–433.

Tjia, H. D., Fujii, S., Kigoshi, K. and Sugimura, A., 1975. Additional dates on raised shorelines in Malaysia and Indonesia. *Sains Malaysiana*, **4**, 69–84.

Tomlinson, J. T., 1969. Shell-burrowing barnacles. *Amer. Zool.*, **9**, 837–840.

Towe, K. M. and Cifelli, R., 1967. Wall ultra-structure in calcareous foraminifera: crystallographic aspects and a model for calcification. *J. Paleontol.*, **41**, 742–762.

Tracey, J. I. and Ladd, H. S., 1974. Quaternary history of Eniwetok and Bikini atolls, Marshall Islands. *Proc. Second Int. Coral Reef Symp.*, **2**, 537–550.

Tracey, J. I., Ladd, H. S. and Hoffmeister, J. E., 1948. Reefs of Bikini, Marshall Islands. *Geol. Soc. Amer. Bull.*, **59**, 861–878.

Tracey, J. I., Schlanger, S. O., Stark, J. T., Doan, D. B. and May, H. G., 1964. General geology of Guam. *U.S. Geol. Surv. Prof. Pap.*, **403-A**, 1–104.

Tricart, J., 1968. Notes géomorphologique sur la karstification en Barbade (Antilles). *Mém. Docums. Cent. Docum. cartogr. geogr.*, **4**, 329–334.

Trudgill, S. T., 1976a. The marine erosion of limestones on Aldabra Atoll, Indian Ocean. *Zeits. f. Geomorph., Suppl. Bd.*, **26**, 164–200.

Trudgill, S. T., 1976b. The subaerial and subsoil erosion of limestones on Aldabra Atoll, Indian Ocean. *Zeits. f. Geomorph., Suppl. Bd.*, **26**, 201–210.

Trudgill, S. T., 1979. Surface lowering and landform evolution on Aldabra. *Phil. Trans. Roy. Soc. London, B*, **286**, 35–45.

Tyerman, D. and Bennet, G., 1832. *Journal of Voyages and Travels in the South Sea Islands*. Boston, 3 vols.

Umbgrove, J. H. F., 1928. De Korallriffen in de Baai van Batavia. *Wet. Med. Dienst. v.d. Mijn. in Ned.-Indic.*, **7**, 68 pp.

Umbgrove, J. H. F., 1929. De Koraffriffen der Duizend-Eilanden (Java See). *Wet. Med. Dienst. v.d. Mijn. in Ned.-Indic.*, **12**, 47 pp.

Umbgrove, J. H. F., 1930. The end of Sluiter's coral reef at Krakatoa. *Leidse Geol. Meded.*, **3**, 261–264.

Umbgrove, J. H. F., 1947. Coral reefs of the East Indies. *Geol. Soc. Amer. Bull.*, **58**, 729–778.

Upham, W., 1878. Changes in the relative heights of land and sea during the glacial and Champlain periods. In Hitchcock, C. H., *Geology of New Hampshire*, **3** (3) 329–333.

Valentine, J. W., 1971. Plate tectonics and shallow marine diversity and endemism, an actualistic model. *Syst. Zool.*, **20**, 253–264.

Van Andel, T. H. and Veevers, J. J., 1967. Morphology and sediments of the Timor Sea. *Bur. Min. Res. Geol. Geophys. Bull.*, **83**, 173 pp.

Van Andel, T. H., Heath, G. R., Moore, T. C. and McGeary, D. F. R., 1967. Late Quaternary history, climate and oceanography of the Timor Sea, northwestern Australia. *Amer. J. Sci.*, **265**, 737–758.

Vaughan, T. W., 1914a. Geologic history of the Florida coral-reef tract. *Geol. Soc. Amer. Bull.*, **25**, 41–42.

Vaughan, T. W., 1914b. The platforms of barrier coral reefs. *Bull. Amer. Geog. Soc.*, **46**, 426–429.

Vaughan, T. W., 1916. Results of investigation of ecology of the Floridian and Bahaman shoal-water corals. *Proc. Nat. Acad. Sci.*, **2**, 95–100.

Vaughan, T. W., 1919. Corals and the formation of coral reefs. *Smithsonian Inst. Ann. Rept.* for 1917, 189–276.

Vaughan, T. W., 1923. Coral reefs and submerged platforms. *Proc. Second Pan. Pacific Sci. Congr., Australia*, **2**, 1128–1131.

Vaughan, T. W. and Wells, J. W., 1943. Revision of the suborders, families and genera of the Scleractinia. *Geol. Soc. Amer. Spec. Pap.*, **44**, 1–363.

Veeh, H. H., 1966. Th^{230}/U^{238} and U^{234}/U^{238} ages of Pleistocene high sea level stand. *J. Geophys. Res.*, **71**, 3379–3386.

Veeh, H. H. and Green, D. C., 1977. Radiometric geochronology of coral reefs. In Jones, O. A. and Endean, R. (eds.) *Biology and Geology of Coral Reefs*, **IV**, Geology II, 183–200.

Veeh, H. H. and Veevers, J. J., 1970. Sea level at − 175 m off the Great Barrier Reef 13,600 to 17,000 years ago. *Nature*, **226**, 536–537.

Veevers, J. J. and McElhinny, M. W., 1976. The separation of Australia from other continents. *Earth Sci. Rev.*, **12**, 139–159.

Veron, J. E. N., 1974. Southern geographic limits to the distribution of Great Barrier Reef hermatypic corals. *Proc. Second Int. Coral Reef Symp.*, **1**, 465–473.

Veron, J. E. N., 1978a. Deltaic and dissected reefs of the far Northern Region. *Phil. Trans. Roy. Soc. London, B*, **284**, 23–37.

Veron, J. E. N., 1978b. Evolution of the far northern barrier reefs. *Phil. Trans. Roy. Soc. London, B*, **284**, 123–127.

Veron, J. E. N. and Done, T. J., 1979. Corals and coral communities of Lord Howe Island. *Austr. J. Mar. Freshw. Res.*, **30**, 203–236.

Veron, J. E. N. and Hudson, R. C. L., 1978. Ribbon reefs of the Northern Region. *Phil. Trans. Roy. Soc. London, B*, **284**, 3–21.

Veron, J. E. N. and Pichon, M., 1976. Scleractinia of Eastern Australia I Thamnasteriidae, Astrocoeniidae, Pocilloporidae. *Austr. Inst. Mar. Sci. Monogr. Ser.*, **1**, 86 pp.

Veron, J. E. N., Pichon, M. and Wijsman-Best, M., 1977. Scleractinia of Eastern Australia, II, Families Faviidae, Trachyphylliidae. *Austr. Inst. Mar. Sci., Monogr. Ser.*, **3**, 233 pp.

Verstappen, H. Th., 1954. The influence of climatic changes on the formation of coral islands. *Amer. J. Sci.*, **252**, 428–435.

Verstappen, H. Th., 1960. On the geomorphology of raised coral reefs and its tectonic significance. *Zeits. f. Geomorph., N.F.*, **4**, 1–28.

Verstappen, H. Th., 1964. Karst morphology of the Star Mountains (central New Guinea) and its relation to lithology and climate. *Zeits. f. Geomorph., N.F.*, **8**, 40–49.

Verstappen, H. Th., 1968. Coral reefs—wind and current growth control. In Fairbridge, R. W. (ed.) *Encyclopaedia of Geomorphology*, 197–202.

Vittor, B. A. and Johnson, P. G., 1977. Polychaete abundance, diversity and trophic role in coral reef communities at Grand Bahama Island and the Florida Middle Ground. *Proc. Third Int. Coral Reef Symp.*, **1**, 163–168.

Von Arx, W. S., 1948. The circulation systems of Bikini and Rongelap lagoons. *Trans. Amer. Geophys. Union.*, **29**, 861–870.

Von Arx, W. S., 1954. Circulation systems of Bikini and Rongelap lagoons. *U.S. Geol. Surv. Prof. Pap.*, 260-B, 265–273.

Von Chamisso, A., 1821. *Reise um die Welt mit der Romanzoffischen Entdeckungs—Expedition.*

Wainwright, S. A., 1969. Stress and design in bivalved mollusc shell. *Nature*, **224**, 777–779.

Walcott, R. I., 1972. Past sea levels, eustasy and deformation of the earth. *Quat. Res.*, **2**, 1–14.

Walker, D., 1978. Quaternary climates of the Australian region. In Pittock, A. B., Frakes, L. A., Jenssen, D., Peterson, J. A. and Zillman, J. W. (eds.) *Climatic Change and Variability, a Southern Perspective*, 82–97.

Wall, J. R. D. and Wilford, G. E., 1966. Two small-scale solution features of limestone outcrops in Sarawak, Malaysia. *Zeits. f. Geomorph., N.F.*, **10**, 90–94.

Wallace, C. C., 1975. Distribution patterns of the coral genus *Acropora* on the reef slope: a preliminary report. *Crown of Thorns Starfish Seminar Proc. Brisbane 1974*, 81–107.

Wallace, C. C., 1978. The coral genus *Acropora* (Scleractinia: Astrocoeniina: Acroporidae) in the central and southern Great Barrier Reef province. *Mem. Qld. Mus.*, **18**, 273–319.

Wallace, C. C. and Lovell, E. R., 1977. Topography and coral distribution of Bushy and Redbill Islands and surrounding reef, Great Barrier Reef, Queensland. *Atoll Res. Bull.*, **194**, 1–27.

Walsh, D. E., Reid, R. O. and Bader, R. G., 1962. Wave refraction and wave energy on Cayo Arenas, Campeche Bank. *Texas A and M Res. Found. Proj.*, **286** (A), 1–62.

Wantland, K. F. and Pusey, W. C. (eds.) 1975. Belize Shelf-Carbonate Sediments, Clastic Sediments and Ecology. *Amer. Assoc. Petrol. Geol., Stud. in Geol.*, **2**, 599 pp.

Ward, P. and Risk, M. J., 1977. Boring pattern of the sponge *Cliona vermifera* in the coral *Montastrea annularis*. *J. Paleontol.*, **51**, 520–526.

Ward, P. E., Hoffard, S. H. and Davis, D. A., 1965. Hydrology of Guam. *U.S. Geol. Surv. Prof. Pap.*, **403-H**, 1–28.

Ward, W. C., 1970. Diagenesis of Quaternary Eolianites of NE Quintana Roo, Mexico. Unpubl. Ph.D. Thesis, Rice Univ., Houston, Texas, 243 pp.

Webster, P. J. and Streten, N. A., 1978. Late Quaternary ice age climates of tropical Australasia: interpretations and reconstructions. *Quat. Res.*, **10**, 279–309.

Weber, J. N., Deines, P., White, E. W. and Weber, P. H., 1975. Seasonal high and low density bands in reef coral skeletons. *Nature*, **255**, 697–698.

Wellman, H. W. and Wilson, A. T., 1965. Salt weathering, a neglected geological erosive agent in coastal and arid environments. *Nature*, **205**, 1097–1098.

Wellman, P., 1974. Potassium-argon ages on the Cainozoic volcanic rocks of eastern Victoria, Australia. *J. Geol. Soc. Austr.*, **21**, 359–375.

Wellman, P. and McDougall, J., 1974. Potassium-argon ages on the Cainozoic volcanic rocks of N.S.W. *J. Geol. Soc. Austr.*, **21**, 247–272.

Wells, J. W., 1955a. A survey of the distribution of coral genera in the Great Barrier Reef region. *Repts. Gt. Barrier Reef Comm.*, **6**, 2, 21–29.

Wells, J. W., 1955b. Recent and subfossil corals of Moreton Bay, Queensland. *Pap., Dept. Geol. Univ. Qld.*, **4**, 10, 1–23.

Wells, J. W., 1956. Scleractinia. In Moore, R. C. (ed.) *Treatise on Invertebrate Palaeontology*, F Coelenterata. F328–F440.

Wells, J. W., 1957. Coral reefs. In Hedgpeth, J. (ed.) Treatise on Marine Ecology. *Geol. Soc. Amer. Mem.*, **67**, 609–631.

Wells, J. W., 1963. Coral growth and geochronology. *Nature*, **197**, 948–950.

Wells, J. W., 1969. The formation of dissepiments in Zoantharian corals. In Campbell, K. S. W. (ed.) *Stratigraphy and Paleontology: Essays in Honour of Dorothy Hill*. 17–26.

Wharton, W. J. L., 1890. Coral reefs, fossil and recent. *Nature*, **42**, 172.

Wharton, W. J. L., 1897. Foundations of coral atolls. *Nature*, **55**, 390–393.

Whitehead, D. R. and Jones, C. E., 1969. Small islands and the equilibrium theory of insular biogeography. *Evolution*, **23**, 171–179.

Whittingham, H., 1958. The Bathurst Bay hurricane and associated storm surge. *Austr. Meteorol. Mag.*, **23**, 14–36.

Wiens, H., 1962. *Atoll Environment and Ecology.* Yale Univ. Press, New Haven, 532 pp.

Wilford, G. E. and Wall, J. R. D., 1965. Karst topography in Sarawak. *J. Trop. Geog.*, **21**, 44–70.

Williams, P. W., 1971. Illustrating morphometric analysis of karst with examples from New Guinea. *Zeits. f. Geomorph.*, *N.F.*, **15**, 40–61.

Williams, P. W., 1972. Morphometric analysis of polygonal karst in New Guinea. *Geol. Soc. Amer. Bull.*, **83**, 761–796.

Williams, P. W., 1978. Interpretations of Australasian karsts. In Davies, J. L. and Williams, M. A. J. (eds.) *Landform Evolution in Australasia*, A.N.U. Canberra, 259–286.

Winland, H. D., 1969. Stability of calcium carbonate polymorphs in warm shallow sea water. *J. Sed. Petrol.*, **39**, 1579–1587.

Winland, H. D., 1971. Diagenesis of Carbonate Grains in Marine and Meteoric Waters. Unpubl. Ph.D. Thesis, Brown Univ., Providence, R.I., 320 pp.

Winterer, E. L., 1970. Submarine valley systems around the Coral Sea basin (Australia). *Mar. Geol.*, **8**, 229–224.

Winterer, E. L., 1973. Sedimentary facies and plate tectonics of equatorial Pacific. *Amer. Assoc. Petrol. Geol. Bull.*, **57**, 265–282.

Wood, A., 1949. The structure of the wall of the test in the foraminifera, its value in classification. *Quart. J. Geol. Soc. London*, **104**, 229–252.

Wood-Jones, F., 1910. *Coral and Atolls*, L. Reeve, London, 392 pp.

Wyatt, D. H. and Webb, A. W., 1970. Potassium-argon ages of some northern Queensland basalts and an interpretation of late Cainozoic history. *J. Geol. Soc. Austr.*, **17**, 39–51.

Yabe, H., 1942. Problems of the coral reefs. *Toh. Imp. Univ. Geol. and Palaeo. Inst. Rept.*, **39**, 1–6.

Yamaguchi, M., 1975. Sea level fluctuations and mass mortalities of reef animals in Guam, Mariana Islands. *Micronesica*, **11**, 227–243.

Yonge, C. M., 1930. Studies on the physiology of corals I. Feeding mechanisms and food. *Sci. Repts. Gt. Barrier Reef Exped. Brit. Mus. (Nat. Hist.)*, **1**, 13–57.

Yonge, C. M., 1931a. The Great Barrier Reef expedition, 1929. *Repts. Gt. Barrier Reef Comm.*, **3** (1), 1–25.

Yonge, C. M., 1931b. Studies on the physiology of corals III. Assimilation and excretion. *Sci. Repts. Gt. Barrier Reef Exped. Brit. Mus. (Nat. Hist.)*, **1**, 83–92.

Yonge, C. M., 1944. Experimental analysis of the association between invertebrates and unicellular algae. *Biol. Rev.*, **19**, 68–80.

Yonge, C. M., 1963a. Rock-boring organisms. In Sognnaes, R. F. (ed.) Mechanisms of Hard Tissue Destruction. *Amer. Assoc. Adv. Sci. Publ.*, **75**, 1–24.

Yonge, C. M., 1963b. Animals that bore through rock. *New Sci.*, **328**, 368–372.

Yonge, C. M., 1968. Living corals. *Proc. Roy. Soc. London, B*, **169**, 329–344.

Yonge, C. M. and Nicholls, A. G., 1931a. Studies on the physiology of corals IV. The structure, distribution and physiology of the zooxanthellae. *Sci. Repts. Gt. Barrier Reef Exped., Brit. Mus. (Nat. Hist.)*, **1**, 135–176.

Yonge, C. M. and Nicholls, A. G., 1931b. Studies on the physiology of corals V. The effect of starvation in light and in darkness on the relation between corals and zooxanthellae. *Sci. Rept. Gt. Barrier Reef Exped., Brit. Mus. (Nat. Hist.)*, **1**, 177–211.

Zankl, H. and Multer, H. G., 1977. Origin of some internal fabrics in Holocene reef rocks, St. Croix, U.S. Virgin Islands. *Proc. Third. Int. Coral Reef Symp.*, **2**, 127–134.

Zankl, H. and Schroeder, J. H., 1972. Interaction of genetic processes in Holocene reefs off North Eleuthera Island, Bahamas. *Geol. Rund.*, **61**, 520–541.

Geographical Index

Subject Index

Systematic Index